Effective Teaching Methods
Research-Based Practice

SIXTH EDITION

Gary D. Borich
The University of Texas at Austin

PEARSON

Merrill
Prentice Hall

Upper Saddle River, New Jersey
Columbus, Ohio

Library of Congress Cataloging-in-Publication Data

Borich, Gary D.
  Effective teaching methods: research-based practice/Gary D. Borich.—6th ed.
    p. cm.
  Includes bibliographical references and index.
  ISBN 0-13-171496-1 (pbk.)
  1. Effective teaching—United States. 2. Lesson planning—United States. 1. Title.
  LB1025.3.B67 2007 371.102—dc22   2006002094

Vice President and Executive Publisher: Jeffery W. Johnston
Executive Editor: Debra A. Stollenwerk
Assistant Development Editor: Elisa Rogers
Senior Editorial Assistant: Mary Morrill
Production Editor: Kris Roach
Production Coordination and Text Design: Thistle Hill Publishing Services, LLC
Photo Coordinator: Monica Merkel
Design Coordinator: Diane C. Lorenzo
Cover Designer: Jill McDonald
Cover Image: Corbis
Production Manager: Susan W. Hannahs
Director of Marketing: David Gesell
Senior Marketing Manager: Darcy Betts Prybella
Marketing Coordinator: Brian Mounts

This book was set in Garamond by Carlisle Publishing Services. It was printed and bound by Courier/Kendallville, Inc. The cover was printed by Phoenix Color Corp.

The Interstate New Teacher Assessment and Support Consortium (INTASC) standards were developed by the Council of Chief State School Officers and member states. Copies may be downloaded from the Council's website at *http://www.ccsso.org*.

Council of Chief State School Officers. (1992). Model standards for beginning teacher licensing, assessment, and development: A resource for state dialogue. Washington, DC: Author. *http://www.ccsso.org/content/pdfs/corestrd.pdf*.

Photo Credits: Scott Cunningham/Merrill, pp. 1, 12, 26, 51, 79, 168, 196, 207, 221, 244, 281, 301, 391, 403; Anthony Magnacca/Merrill, pp. 23, 83, 133, 141, 233, 285, 317, 319; KS Studios/Merrill, p. 41; Barbara Schwartz/Merrill, pp. 61, 95, 421; Anne Vega/Merrill, pp. 65, 377; David Mager/Pearson Learning Photo Studio, pp. 111, 257; Tom Watson/Merrill, pp. 158, 343, 370; Silver Burdett Ginn, p. 176; Laima Druskis/PH College, p. 192; Valerie Schultz/Merrill, p. 335; Lynn Saville, p. 349; Larry Hamill/Merrill, p. 399.

Pearson Education Ltd.
Pearson Education Singapore Pte. Ltd.
Pearson Education Canada, Ltd.
Pearson Education—Japan

Pearson Education Australia Pty. Limited
Pearson Education North Asia Ltd.
Pearson Educación de Mexico, S.A. de C.V.
Pearson Education Malaysia Pte. Ltd.

10 9 8 7 6 5 4 3 2
ISBN: 0-13-171496-1

Preface

Communication technologies, teacher performance standards, standardized testing, curriculum reform, multicultural classrooms, and new teacher certification requirements are but a few of the factors changing the face of American schools. This book has been written to help you prepare to meet these challenges and to discover the opportunities for professional growth and advancement they provide.

Goals of This Edition

The sixth edition of *Effective Teaching Methods* has four simple goals. The first is to present effective teaching practices derived from nearly four decades of classroom research. In this research, different teaching practices were systematically studied for their effectiveness on learners. The results have made it possible to replace many age-old anecdotal suggestions for "good" teaching with modern-day research-based teaching practices that are empirically related to positive outcomes in learners. Describing these teaching practices and how to use them to become an effective teacher is a major focus of this book.

Second, this text describes these effective teaching practices in a friendly, conversational manner. The language of classrooms is informal, and there is no reason why a book about teachers in classrooms should not use the same language. Therefore, this book talks straight, avoiding complicated prescriptions, rambling discussions, or pseudo-scholarly language. The intent is to get the point across quickly and in a user-friendly style.

The third goal of this book is to be practical. Positive prescriptions for your classroom teaching show you how to engage students in the learning process, manage your classroom, and increase student achievement. This book not only tells you what to do to obtain these results, it also shows you how to obtain them with extensive examples from classroom videos, written classroom dialogues, and case studies.

The final goal of this book is to be realistic. Some of the literature on effective teaching has been theoretical and speculative. However, this book describes what real teachers do in real classrooms to be effective and which teaching practices have or have not been found to be effective. Nothing in this book is pie-in-the-sky theorizing about effective teaching, because most of what is presented results directly from years of research and observation of effective teaching practices in real classrooms.

These, then, are this book's four goals: to provide research-based effective teaching practices, presented in a conversational style, that are practical and realistic.

New to This Edition

Users of earlier editions of this book will notice that each chapter has been revised. The rapid pace of change and new research occurring in nearly every aspect of teaching have resulted in a sixth edition that considerably updates and extends earlier editions and provides an extensive complement of new features to get beginning teachers confident and up to speed on their very first day of classroom observation and practice teaching.

See instructional strategies implemented in the classroom. The sixth edition contains a new **Video Windows DVD** of classroom footage that illustrates how the chapters' key strategies and methods can be implemented in real classroom situations. In each chapter, the **Video Windows** feature introduces each clip, links it to chapter content, and asks readers to consider relevant questions and issues while viewing. Students can respond to these questions online through the Companion Website at *www.prenhall.com/borich*.

Learn how to apply instructional strategies. The new **In Practice** feature shows how the concepts discussed in each chapter can work in the real world of the classroom. These practical teaching tips, strategies, and techniques can help new teachers extend their textbook knowledge to their very first lesson plans, showing them tangible approaches to putting theory into practice. These include how to apply constructivist principles and use the concepts of multiple intelligences, interdisciplinary teaching, democratic approaches to learning, mastery learning, project-based learning, performance assessment, and new collaborative techniques.

Practice research-based instructional strategies. Three complementary new sets of activities at the ends of chapters provide "hands-on" opportunities to engage your students in decision making and problem solving as they would be carried out in a real classroom.

- **Field Experience Activities** are designed to get the beginning teacher to make decisions and solve practical classroom problems related to the content within each chapter, with regard to lesson planning, classroom management, cultural diversity, and project-based learning.
- **Digital Portfolio Activities** guide the learner in creating a professional portfolio of accomplishments with entries related to the content of each chapter. This portfolio will be a vehicle with which you can put your best foot forward to future instructors in your teacher preparation program, cooperating or supervisory teachers during your student teaching, professional colleagues, and, most importantly, future employers. The portfolio will chronicle and present evidence of your very best accomplishments in this course.
- **Classroom Observation Activities** can be completed either from classroom videos provided with this text or from classroom videos available from your teacher preparation program. You may also have opportunities from time to time to visit classrooms as part of other courses in your teacher preparation program. These observation activities will give you the skills and confidence you will need to complete the observation requirements required in your teacher preparation curriculum.

Together all three sets of activities provide a menu of opportunities from which students can advance the skills learned in each chapter.

Also revised for this edition are the **Case History and Praxis Test Preparation** questions at the end of each chapter to help you prepare for the *Praxis II®: Principles of Learning and Teaching* exam and other exams that may be required at the end of your teacher preparation program. Following the objectives, format, and content of the *Praxis II®: Principles of Learning and Teaching* exam, these case studies and practice assessment questions provide an updated and in-depth targeted rehearsal that will help prepare you for the test-taking skills and pedagogical knowledge that may be expected of you on exit exams from your teacher preparation program and for certification and licensing.

Also new to this edition is an updated and expanded treatment of standardized tests. Probably no other development in education during the last decade has generated more controversy than the use of standardized tests for making "high-stakes" decisions involving grade promotion, the selection of students for advanced academic programs, and high school graduation. Equally problematic is the amount of classroom time that you may have to de-vote to preparing your students for standardized tests. In chapter 12 you will find out what's right and what's wrong about standardized tests, their proper use and their abuse, and how you can help your students perform better on them.

Special Features

Other special features of this sixth edition include:

- A beginning chapter on the characteristics of an effective teacher and what an effective teacher does in the classroom (chapter 1). This chapter also acquaints you with the NBPTS and INTASC standards that will be important for your certification and licensing.
- A chapter on understanding how individual differences and learner diversity—prior achievement, learning style, culture and language, and home and family life—affect student learning needs and classroom management (chapter 2). This chapter will introduce you to the real nature and challenges of today's multicultural classrooms and the teaching of English-language learners, immigrant populations, and at-risk learners.
- A revised and expanded chapter on instructional goals and objectives that shows you how to assess the extent to which you are achieving thinking and problem-solving behaviors in your classroom (chapter 3). This chapter expands the traditional taxonomies of cognitive and affective behavior to include the important higher-order objectives of metacognition, problem solving, decision making, critical thinking, and valuing.
- A revised chapter on unit and lesson planning that will improve your skills in linking subject matter content to teaching methods and student outcomes in a continuous process of lesson planning. This chapter also shows you how to compose thematic and interdisciplinary lessons to promote higher-order thought processes and problem-solving behavior in your learners (chapter 4).
- Two chapters on classroom management, including how to build a cohesive classroom of learners who work in harmony (chapter 5) and anticipatory management (chapter 6), which tells you how an "ounce of prevention" is worth a "pound of cure." Both chapters have now been placed closer to the beginning of the text to provide a complement of techniques and strategies that can quickly change your beginning days in the classroom from a concern for your own survival to the impact you are having on your learners.
- Two chapters on teaching strategies that explain how to use direct instructional methods (such as explaining, presenting, drill and practice, and recitation—chapter 7) and indirect instructional methods (such as group discussion, concept-learning inquiry and problem-solving activities—chapter 8). These chapters will provide you with an interchangeable menu of instructional activities that can be mixed and matched to the needs of your learners and goals of your lesson.
- A chapter on teacher questioning that shows you how to raise questions at different levels of cognitive complexity and how to use probes and follow-up questions to promote higher-order thinking and problem-solving behavior (chapter 9). This chapter will help you prepare your learners not only to engage in higher-order thought processes with the questions you ask but will also teach your students to ask higher-order questions of you.
- A chapter on self-directed learning and how to use metacognitive techniques, teacher mediation, and the social dialogue of the classroom to help learners control,

regulate, and take responsibility for their own learning (chapter 10). This chapter will help you unleash your learners' intuitive and imaginative capacities to learn on their own, with you as a resource, leaving them with a sense of ownership in what they have explored and discovered.

- A chapter on cooperative learning and the collaborative process for productively organizing and managing group and team activities that promote communication skills, self-esteem, and problem solving (chapter 11). This chapter will introduce you and your students to the enthusiasm, motivation, and creativity that can result from learners working together on real-world projects and performances and how to teach your students the collaborative skills they will need.
- A chapter on the assessment of student achievement and interpreting student progress using teacher-made objective tests, essays, performance assessments, and portfolios (chapter 12). This chapter will not only help you assess your learners' day-to-day understanding, but will help you bridge the gap between your learners' daily performance and their standardized test results. It will also show you how you can bring the real world of adult products and performances through the development of portfolios, into your classroom to add yet another measure of your students' achievements.
- A glossary of key terms and definitions.

For the Student

There are also features created specifically with you, the student, in mind:

- Classroom application questions at the beginning of each chapter that focus you on the key aspects of each chapter.
- An In Practice feature that places a major theme of each chapter into the real world of the classroom with practical tips, strategies, and techniques that can enhance a teacher's very first lesson plans.
- End-of-chapter summaries that restate key concepts in an easy-to-follow outline format.
- End-of-chapter questions for discussion and practice, and keyed answers in appendix B.
- End-of-chapter case studies and practice multiple-choice and constructed response questions aligned with the *Praxis II®: Principles of Teaching and Learning* exam used by many teacher education programs, professional associations, and states for teacher certification and licensing. This feature also provides examples of good and poor student answers to constructed response questions on the Praxis and the professional scoring guide used to grade it (appendix D).
- A self-report survey instrument for measuring concerns about yourself, concerns about the teaching task, and concerns about your impact on students, which can inform you of your growth and development in the teaching profession over time (chapter 1 and appendix A).
- New procedures for organizing unit and lesson plans that let you graphically visualize the relationship between lessons and units (chapter 4).
- A Higher-Order Thinking and Problem-Solving Checklist to help you achieve a thinking curriculum in your classroom that encourages your students to learn to problem-solve, make decisions, and think critically (chapters 3, 10, 12, and appendix C).

COMPANION WEBSITE

A Virtual Learning Environment

The Companion Website for this text can be found at *www.prenhall.com/borich*. Technology is a continually growing and changing aspect of our field that is creating a need for content and resources, and the Companion Website is a customized, fully integrated technology resource that provides the professor and student with a variety of meaningful resources for each chapter. The Companion Website provides an online learning environment that includes more assessment items keyed to each chapter for additional practice, observation instruments for viewing classroom videos and in actual classrooms, and a format for corresponding with your instructor about assigned activities that support and build upon the focus of the text.

Online for the Professor

- New to this edition are PowerPoint presentations supporting the content in every chapter, for professors to use in their classes. The PowerPoints can be downloaded from the Companion Website at *www.prenhall.com/borich*.
- An Instructor's Manual with media guide and test bank can be downloaded from the Prentice Hall Instructor's Resource Center at *http://vig.prenhall.com/catalog*.
- A Test Generator is also available for download from the Instructor's Resource Center.

Online for the Student

Each chapter of the Companion Website offers a variety of features for students:

- *Chapter Objectives*. This list of key concepts outlines the organization and focus of each chapter.
- *Chapter Overview*. A concise summary of the chapter recaps major topics and concepts presented in the text.
- *Self-Quiz: More Assessment Options*. Multiple-choice and true/false questions for each chapter, complete with automatic grading and feedback, allow students to assess their understanding of chapter concepts and topics.
- *Praxis Prep*. Students can review the chapter case study, submit answers to case short-answer and discrete multiple-choice questions, and answer additional multiple-choice questions about the case. The chapter cases and questions provide preparation for the Praxis II exam in addition to testing chapter-related content knowledge and building students' critical thinking skills.
- *Classroom Observation*. Forms, charts, and other tools to aid students in recording the classroom observations they make in the Classroom Observation Activities in each chapter.
- *Video Windows*. Students can complete the chapter feature activities and submit their answers online (chapters 1, 2, 4, 5, 6, 7, 8, 9, 10, 11, 12).
- *Web Destinations*. Annotated links to relevant education resources enable students to perform research and learn more about teaching as a profession.

Additional Resources

There is a companion volume to this text called *Observation Skills for Effective Teaching, Fourth Edition* (Borich, 2003, also from Merrill/Prentice Hall. Fifth edition to be released in 2008). This companion volume and workbook is intended to be used either in a preteaching observation experience or as an applications resource to the present volume. *Observation Skills for Effective Teaching* provides extensive examples, entertaining and instructional classroom dialogues, and practical observation and recording instruments keyed to and coordinated with the effective teaching methods presented in this text. Together, these texts provide a sequence of learning for the preservice and beginning teacher.

Acknowledgments

Many individuals contributed to the preparation of this book. Not the least are the many professionals whose studies of classroom life have contributed to the effective teachers described in this text.

I also wish to acknowledge those teachers who over the years have shared their insights about the teaching process with me. Among these have been teachers in the Austin, Texas, Independent School District, especially William B. Travis High School and Travis Heights Elementary School, who provided the opportunity to observe many of the effective teaching methods described herein. For their helpful reviews and contributions to the manuscript, I extend my gratitude to my good friends and colleagues Marty Tombari and Tom Kubiszyn, and also to those who reviewed the text: Barrie A. Brancato, Clarion University of Pennsylvania; Thomas R. Dobbins, Clemson University; Andrew P. Johnson, Minnesota State University, Mankato; and Catherine Kearney, San Joaquin County Office of Education.

GDB
Austin, Texas

About the Author

*G*ary Borich grew up on the south side of Chicago, where he attended Mendel High School, and later taught in the public school system of Niles, Illinois. He received his doctoral degree from Indiana University, where he was director of evaluation at the Institute for Child Study. Dr. Borich is professor and a Kellogg Endowed Fellow in the College of Education at the University of Texas at Austin and a past member of the Board of Examiners of the National Council for the Accreditation of Teacher Education.

Dr. Borich's other books include *Observation Skills for Effective Teaching, Fourth Edition; Educational Assessment for the Elementary and Middle School Classroom, Second Edition* (with M. Tombari); *Clearly Outstanding: Making Each Day Count in Your Classroom; Becoming a Teacher: An Inquiring Dialogue for the Beginning Teacher; Educational Psychology: A Contemporary Approach, Second Edition* (with M. Tombari); *Educational Testing and Measurement, Eighth Edition* (with T. Kubiszyn); and *The Appraisal of Teaching: Concepts and Process.*

Dr. Borich lives in Austin, Texas, with his wife, Kathy, and his two children, Brandy and Damon. His interests include training and riding Arabian horses.

Teacher Preparation Classroom

TEACHER PREP

MERRILL
PRENTICE HALL

See a demo at
www.prenhall.com/teacherprep/demo

Your Class. Their Careers. Our Future. Will your students be prepared?

We invite you to explore our new, innovative and engaging website and all that it has to offer you, your course, and tomorrow's educators! Organized around the major courses pre-service teachers take, the Teacher Preparation site provides media, student/teacher artifacts, strategies, research articles, and other resources to equip your students with the quality tools needed to excel in their courses and prepare them for their first classroom.

This ultimate on-line education resource is available at no cost, when packaged with a Merrill text, and will provide you and your students access to:

Online Video Library. More than 150 video clips—each tied to a course topic and framed by learning goals and Praxis-type questions—capture real teachers and students working in real classrooms, as well as in-depth interviews with both students and educators.

Student and Teacher Artifacts. More than 200 student and teacher classroom artifacts—each tied to a course topic and framed by learning goals and application questions—provide a wealth of materials and experiences to help make your study to become a professional teacher more concrete and hands-on.

Research Articles. Over 500 articles from ASCD's renowned journal *Educational Leadership*. The site also includes Research Navigator, a searchable database of additional educational journals.

Teaching Strategies. Over 500 strategies and lesson plans for you to use when you become a practicing professional.

Licensure and Career Tools. Resources devoted to helping you pass your licensure exam; learn standards, law, and public policies; plan a teaching portfolio; and succeed in your first year of teaching.

How to ORDER *Teacher Prep* for you and your students:

For students to receive a *Teacher Prep* Access Code with this text, instructors **must** provide a special value pack ISBN number on their textbook order form. To receive this special ISBN, please email **Merrill.marketing@pearsoned.com** and provide the following information:

- Name and Affiliation
- Author/Title/Edition of Merrill text

Upon ordering *Teacher Prep* for their students, instructors will be given a lifetime *Teacher Prep Access* Code.

Brief Contents

Contents

CHAPTER 2

Understanding Your Students   41

CHAPTER 3

Goals and Objectives   79

CHAPTER 4

Unit and Lesson Planning   111

CHAPTER 5

Classroom Management I: Establishing the Learning Climate   158

CHAPTER 6

Classroom Management II: Promoting Student Engagement 192

CHAPTER 7

Teaching Strategies for Direct Instruction   221

CHAPTER 8

Teaching Strategies for Indirect Instruction   257

CHAPTER 10

Self-Directed Learning 335

CHAPTER 11

Cooperative Learning and the Collaborative Process 370

CHAPTER 12

Assessing Learners   399

Note: Every effort has been made to provide accurate and current Internet information in this book. However, the Internet and information posted on it are constantly changing, so it is inevitable that some of the Internet addresses listed in this textbook will change.

Chapter 1

The Effective Teacher

This chapter will help you answer the following questions and meet the following Interstate New Teacher Assessment and Support Consortium (INTASC) principles for effective teaching:

1. What is an effective teacher?
2. How can I become an effective teacher?
3. Are there different definitions of effective teaching?
4. What are some of the teaching practices used by effective teachers?
5. How will I know if I am an effective teacher?

INTASC 1: The teacher understands the central concepts, tools of inquiry, and structures of the discipline(s) he or she teaches and can create learning experiences that make these aspects of subject matter meaningful for students.

INTASC 3: The teacher understands how students differ in their approaches to learning and creates instructional opportunities that are adapted to diverse learners.

INTASC 4: The teacher understands and uses a variety of instructional strategies to encourage students' development of critical thinking, problem solving, and performance skills.

How easily or quickly could you answer the question: What is an effective teacher? This question has been asked by every teacher, young or old. It is a deceptively simple question, for it has many different answers. Teaching is a complex and difficult task that demands extraordinary abilities. Despite decades of experience and research, one of the most important questions in education today is: What is an effective teacher?

This chapter offers no pat definitions of an effective teacher. Instead, the goal is to introduce you to practices used by effective teachers that are related to positive outcomes in learners. These effective teaching practices do not tell the whole story of what an effective teacher is, but they do form an important foundation to help you become an effective teacher and profit from the chapters ahead. Subsequent chapters blend these practices with other activities, such as lesson planning, problem-based learning, questioning strategies, classroom management, and learner assessment, and the attitudes and dispositions you will need to build a warm and nurturing relationship with your students. These topics will give you a rich and comprehensive picture of an effective teacher and, most importantly, help you become one.

WHAT IS AN EFFECTIVE TEACHER?

The Role-Model Definition

If you had grown up a century ago, you would have been able to answer "What is an effective teacher?" very simply: A good teacher was a good person—a role model who met the community ideal for a good citizen, good parent, and good employee. At that time, teachers were judged primarily on their goodness as people and only secondarily on their behavior in the classroom. They were expected to be honest, hardworking, generous, friendly, and considerate, and to demonstrate these qualities in their classrooms by being organized, disciplined, insightful, and committed. Practically speaking, this meant that to be effective, all a beginning teacher needed was King Solmon's wisdom, Sigmund Freud's insight, Albert Einstein's knowledge, and Florence Nightingale's dedication!

It soon became evident that this definition of an ideal teacher lacked clear, objective standards of performance that could be consistently applied and that could be used to train future teachers.

The Psychological Characteristics Definition

This early definition of an effective teacher soon gave way to another, which attempted to identify the psychological characteristics of a good teacher that included a teacher's personality, attitude, experience, aptitude, and past achievement. Table 1.1 lists some of these

Table 1.1 Commonly studied teacher characteristics.

Personality	Attitude	Experience	Aptitude/Achievement
Permissiveness	Motivation to teach	Years of teaching experience	National Teachers Exam
Dogmatism	Attitude toward children	Experience in subject taught	Graduate Record Exam
Authoritarianism			
Achievement-motivation	Attitude toward teaching	Experience in grade level taught	Scholastic Aptitude Test
Introversion-extroversion	Attitude toward authority	Workshops attended	1. verbal 2. quantitative
Abstractness-concreteness	Vocational interest	Graduate courses taken	Special ability tests, (e.g., reasoning ability, logical ability, verbal fluency)
Directness-indirectness	Attitude toward self (self-concept)	Degrees held	Grade-point average
Locus of control	Attitude toward subject taught	Professional papers written	1. overall 2. in major subject
Anxiety 1. general 2. teaching			Professional recommendations
			Student evaluations of teaching effectiveness
			Student teaching evaluations

psychological characteristics. Because they have a certain intuitive appeal, it is worth noting why they have not been useful criteria for defining a good teacher.

Personality. Over the years, only a few personality measures have been developed that relate specifically to teaching. Because most personality measures have been designed to record behavior in clinical settings, much of what they measure has been of little help in identifying the positive behaviors that may be needed to be an effective teacher. Consequently, the usefulness of many personality tests in predicting a teacher's classroom behavior must be inferred from their more general success in the field of mental health. Although certain interpersonal, emotional, and coping behaviors are believed to be required for effective teaching (Levis, 1987; National Mental Health Information Center, 2005), personality tests have provided few insights into the positive social behaviors that may be needed for effective teaching. As any experienced teacher will tell you, however, much of your success in teaching will depend upon your skills in building a cohesive learning culture in your classroom for which your attitude toward and relationship with your learners provide an essential foundation.

Attitude. Attitude assessments may be either global (for example, attitude toward the educational system and the teaching profession) or specific (for example, attitude toward a particular teaching task, type of learner, or curriculum). But most attempts to measure teacher attitude have failed to forecast what a teacher who has a particular attitude actually does differently in the classroom, and more importantly, how that teacher relates to individual learners. Research has shown little correspondence between a teacher's attitude toward the tools of learning (for example, curriculum, instructional technology, and teaching methods) and his or her interactions in the classroom that motivate students to learn (Jackson, 1968; Walberg, 1986).

Therefore, the use of attitude data for measuring teacher effectiveness has had to rest on the assumption that attitudes are related to activities that are one or more steps removed from the actual teaching process, such as more organized lesson plans or better subject-matter preparation (Clark & Peterson, 1986; Kagan & Tippins, 1992). However, measuring a teacher's attitude as an index of effective teaching would always be less credible than observing actual classroom practices that involve the relationship of teacher with learners.

Experience.   You probably, at one time or another, provided biographical data about yourself when applying for a job. You may have found that a listing of your general qualifications, such as years of experience, credits earned, or degrees granted, defined your experience so broadly as not to be very predictive of what you could do on that specific job. Such descriptions typically do not describe experience relevant to performing the day-to-day tasks required in a specific context, such as classroom, grade level, or subject matter. A teacher's experience with a specific grade level, curriculum, and type of learner, if available, has been more predictive of actual classroom performance than general biographical information, which may represent only a small portion of a teacher's qualifications for a particular teaching assignment (Goldhaber & Anthony, 2003).

Aptitude and Achievement.   Like general experience, most aptitude and achievement data do not accurately predict classroom performance. Regardless of the fact that these measures often are used to predict student performance, a teacher's recorded school achievement seldom has correlated strongly with classroom performance—and here is why.

As an example of recorded achievement, consider a teacher's college GPA. Achieving good grades might indicate enthusiasm for teaching and a promise of good classroom performance. But standards set by training institutions require teachers to meet minimum levels of competence for certification. This usually results in small variations in grades among beginning teachers that are not very predictive of actual practice in the classroom. Licensure and exit tests that examine teachers over specific teaching behaviors and curriculum-specific knowledge, such as the ***Praxis***™[1] *Series of Professional Assessments for Beginning Teachers* (*www.ets.org/praxis*), tend to be better predictors of classroom performance than measures of general achievement or aptitude (see Figure 1.1). For this reason, example case histories, constructed-response and multiple-choice questions for the *Praxis II®: Principles of Learning and Teaching Assessments* are provided at the end of each chapter in this text.

To summarize, using general information about a teacher's personality, attitude, experience, achievement, and aptitude to define a good teacher represented early attempts to predict a teacher's classroom behavior objectively. But these characteristics often were too remote from the teacher's day-to-day work in the classroom to contribute meaningfully to a definition of an effective teacher. Most notably, these definitions excluded the most important measure of all for determining good teaching: the interaction of teacher with learner and the performance of the students being taught.

---

[1] Boldfaced terms appear in the Glossary at the end of this text.

A New Direction

In the last three decades, a revolution has occurred in the definitions of good teaching. We have seen that defining good teachers by community ideals proved unrealistic. We also have seen how teachers' psychological characteristics proved to be poorly related to what teachers

The Praxis™ Series: Professional Assessments for Beginning Teachers is a set of validated assessments that provide information to colleges, state education agencies, and school districts for graduation, licensing, and hiring decisions. In addition, colleges and universities may use the basic academic skills component of the Praxis Series to qualify individuals for entry into teacher education programs.

The three areas of assessment in the Praxis Series are:

1. For entering a teacher training program: *Praxis I: Academic Skills Assessments*
2. For licensure into the teaching profession: *Praxis II: Subject and Pedagogy Assessments*
3. For the first year of teaching: *Praxis III: Classroom Performance Assessments*

The *Praxis II: Subject and Pedagogy* test contains two types of assessments:

The Praxis II: Principles of Learning and Teaching
The Praxis II: Multiple Subjects Assessments

The Praxis II®: Principles of Learning and Teaching Assessments are designed to assess pedagogical knowledge at the end of your undergraduate teacher preparation program in such areas as educational psychology, human growth and development, classroom management, instructional design and delivery techniques, and evaluation and assessment. The assessments are divided into Early Childhood, grades K–6, grades 5–9 and grades 7–12 to reflect areas of certification. Students at the end of their teacher preparation program usually take one of the three tests, which are of 2 hours duration. Each assessment includes four case histories each followed by short-answer questions related to the case history scored on a scale of 0 to 2 by two or more raters using question-specific scoring guides and model answers. This section is followed by 24 multiple-choice questions in two sections of 12 items each that assess the student's general knowledge in the following areas, some of which may require the reading and analysis of passages pertaining to pedagogical content:

Students as Learners

Student development and the learning process
Students as diverse learners
Student motivation and the learning environment

Instructional Strategies

Instructional strategies
Planning instruction
Assessment strategies

Communication Techniques

Basic, effective verbal and nonverbal communication techniques
Effect of cultural and gender differences on classroom communications
Types of communications and interactions that can stimulate discussion in different ways for particular purposes

(continued on next page)

Figure 1.1 About the Praxis.

Profession and Community
    The reflective practitioner
    The larger community

The Praxis II: Multiple Subjects Assessments include specialty area tests in over 100 subject areas in grades K–12 designed to assess content knowledge at the end of your teacher preparation program in the areas for which you are being trained and licensed to teach. The number and content of the tests taken are indicated by the subject areas and/or grade levels for which you wish to receive certification. Although formats vary among tests, most of the tests are from 1 to 2 hours in duration and include a combination of short-answer essay questions based on a specific teaching situation or passage and/or multiple-choice questions. Some typical content tests are: Early Childhood Education; Biology; Physics; Business Education; General Science, English Language, Literature and Composition; Physical Education; Social Studies; and Art. See www.ets.org.

Figure 1.1   *Continued*

actually do in the classroom. This directed researchers to study the impact of specific teacher activities on the specific cognitive and affective behaviors of their students. The term *good teaching* changed to *effective teaching*, and the research focus shifted from exclusively studying teachers to include their effects on students. These new ways of studying classroom behavior have made the student and teacher–student relationship in the classroom the focus of modern definitions of effective teaching.

Linking Teacher Behavior with Student Performance.   During the 1970s and 1980s, researchers developed new methods for studying the classroom interaction patterns of teachers and students. Their goal was to discover which patterns of teacher behavior promote desirable student performance. But before unveiling the findings of this research and their implications for effective teaching, let's see how this research was performed.

The Research Process.   To collect data on the classroom interaction patterns of teachers and students, researchers often used instruments like those shown in Figures 1.2 to 1.4. These particular instruments, devised by Good and Brophy (2003) for their research on effective teaching, record patterns of student–teacher interaction. Using the response form in Figure 1.3, an observer codes both student responses to questions and the teacher's reaction and feedback. For example, in the tenth interchange recorded on this form, a male student fails to answer a question (coded 0), is criticized by the teacher for not answering (- -), and then is given the answer by the teacher (Gives Ans.). Numbers for the interchanges are assigned as they occur, allowing the pattern of question-answer-feedback to be recorded over an entire class period across many classrooms.

In Figure 1.4, the observer codes the student performance being praised by the teacher (perseverance, progress, success, good thinking, etc.). Individual students are identified by assigning each a unique number. This form records not only the praise behavior of the teacher in relation to individual student behavior but also the overall pattern or sequence of action. For example, student 8 is praised three times in a row for "perseverance or effort."

With instruments such as these, a rich and varied picture of classroom activity could be captured over the course of a research study and related to various measures of school achievement. Obviously, a single observation of a single class would produce too little data

Symbol Label		Definition
Student Sex		
M	Male	The student answering the question is male.
F	Female	The student answering the question is female.
Student Response		
+	Right	The teacher accepts the student's response as correct or satisfactory.
±	Part right	The teacher considers the student's response to be only partially correct or to be correct but incomplete.
−	Wrong	The teacher considers the student's response to be incorrect.
0	No answer	The student makes no response or says he doesn't know (code student's answer here if teacher gives feedback reaction before he is able to respond).
Teacher Feedback Reaction		
++	Praise	Teacher praises student either in words ("fine," "good," "wonderful," "good thinking") or by expressing verbal affirmation in a notably warm, joyous, or excited manner.
+	Affirm	Teacher simply affirms that the student's response is correct (nods, repeats answer, says "Yes," "OK," etc.).
0	No reaction	Teacher makes no response whatever to student's response—he or she simply goes on to something else.
−	Negate	Teacher simply indicates that the student's response is incorrect (shakes head, says "No," "That's not right," "Hm-mm," etc.).
− −	Criticize	Teacher criticizes student, either in words ("You should know better than that," "That doesn't make any sense—you better pay close attention," etc.) or by expressing verbal negation in a frustrated, angry, or disgusted manner.
Gives Ans.	Teacher gives answer	Teacher provides the correct answer for the student.
Ask Other	Teacher asks another student	Teacher redirects the question, asking a different student to try to answer it.
Other Calls	Another student calls out answer	Another student calls out the correct answer, and the teacher acknowledges that it is correct.
Repeat	Repeats question	Teacher repeats the original question, either in its entirety or with a prompt ("Well?" "Do you know?" "What's the answer?").
Clue	Rephrase or clue	Teacher makes original question easier for student to answer by rephrasing it or by giving a clue.
New Ques.	New question	Teacher asks a new question (i.e., a question that calls for a different answer than the original question called for).

Figure 1.2 Coding categories for question-answer-feedback sequences.

Source: From Thomas L. Good and Jere E. Brophy, *Looking in Classrooms,* 5/e. Published by Allyn and Bacon, Boston, MA. Copyright © 1991 by Pearson Education. Reprinted by permission of the publisher.

to reveal a consistent pattern of interaction. However, multiple observation extending across different teachers, schools, and school districts could reveal consistent patterns of teacher–student interactions. These patterns of classroom behavior then were related to student outcomes, such as classroom tests, student projects, oral performances, portfolio assessments, and standardized tests, to determine their effects on student performance.

Stu. No.	Sex M	Sex F		Student Response +	±	−	0		Teacher Feedback Reaction ++	+	0	−	−−	Gives Ans.	Ask Other	Other Calls	Repeat	Clue	New Ques.
1	-	√		√	-	-	-		-	√	-	-	-	—	—	—	—	—	—
2	√	-		√	-	-	-		-	√	-	-	-	—	—	—	—	—	—
3	√	-		-	-	-	√		-	-	-	-	-	—	—	—	—	√	—
4	√	-		√	-	-	-		√	-	-	-	-	—	—	—	—	—	—
5	√	-		√	-	-	-		-	√	-	-	-	—	—	—	—	—	—
6	-	√		-	-	√	-		-	-	-	-	√	—	—	—	—	—	√
7	√	-		√	-	-	-		√	-	-	-	-	—	—	—	—	—	—
8	√	-		√	-	-	-		-	-	√	-	-	—	—	—	—	—	—
9	√	-		√	-	-	-		-	-	√	-	-	—	—	—	—	—	—
10	√	-		-	-	-	√		-	-	-	-	√	√	—	—	—	—	—
11	-	-		-	-	-	-		-	-	-	-	-	—	—	—	—	—	—
12	-	-		-	-	-	-		-	-	-	-	-	—	—	—	—	—	—
13	-	-		-	-	-	-		-	-	-	-	-	—	—	—	—	—	—
14	-	-		-	-	-	-		-	-	-	-	-	—	—	—	—	—	—
15	-	-		-	-	-	-		-	-	-	-	-	—	—	—	—	—	—
-	-	-		-	-	-	-		-	-	-	-	-	—	—	—	—	—	—
-	-	-		-	-	-	-		-	-	-	-	-	—	—	—	—	—	—
-	-	-		-	-	-	-		-	-	-	-	-	—	—	—	—	—	—
-	-	-		-	-	-	-		-	-	-	-	-	—	—	—	—	—	—

Figure 1.3 Coding response form.

Source: From Thomas L. Good and Jere E. Brophy, *Looking in Classroms*, 5/e. Published by Allyn and Bacon, Boston, MA. Copyright © 1991 by Pearson Education. Reprinted by permission of the publisher.

It was in this manner that patterns of effective teaching began to emerge in studies conducted by different researchers. As in all research, some studies provided contradictory results or found no relationships among certain types of classroom interactions and student outcomes. But many studies found patterns of interaction that consistently produced desirable student outcomes in the form of higher test scores, increased problem solving, and improved learning skills.

Now that you know how the research was conducted, let's look at a preview of the teaching strategies and methods that researchers generally agree contribute to effective teaching and that will be addressed in the following chapters.

USE: Whenever the teacher praises an individual student
PURPOSE: To see what behaviors the teacher reinforces through praises, and to see how the teacher's praise is distributed among the students.

Behavior Categories	Student Number	Codes
1. Perseverance or effort; worked long or hard	14	1. 3
2. Progress (relative to the past) toward achievement	23	2. 34
3. Success (right answer, high score) achievement	6	3. 3
4. Good thinking, good suggestions, good guess, or nice try	18	4. 3
5. Imagination, creativity, originality	8	5. 1
6. Neatness, careful work	8	6. 1
7. Good or compliant behavior, follows rules, pays attention	8	7. 1
8. Thoughtfulness, courtesy, offering to share, prosocial behavior		8.
9. Other (specify)		9.
		10.
		11.

NOTES:

All answers occurred during social studies discussion

Was particularly concerned about #8, a low-achieving male.

Figure 1.4 Coding form for measuring individual praise.

Source: From Thomas L. Good and Jere E. Brophy, *Looking in Classrooms*, 5/e. Published by Allyn and Bacon, Boston, MA. Copyright © 1991 by Pearson Education. Reprinted by permission of the publisher.

KEY BEHAVIORS CONTRIBUTING TO EFFECTIVE TEACHING

From this research approximately 10 teacher behaviors have shown promising relationships to desirable student performance, primarily as measured by classroom assessments and standardized tests. Five of these behaviors have been consistently supported by research studies over the past three decades (Brophy, 2002; Brophy & Good, 1986; Cantrell, 1998/1999; Dunkin & Biddle, 1974; Marzano, Pickering & Pollock, 2001; Rosenshine, 1971; Saunders, 2005; Taylor, Pearson, Clark, & Walpole, 1999; Teddlie & Stringfield, 1993; Walberg, 1986). Another five have had some support and appear logically related to effective teaching. The first five we call **key behaviors,** because they are considered essential for effective teaching. The second five we call **helping behaviors** that can be used in combinations to implement the key behaviors. These are the five key behaviors essential for effective teaching:

1. Lesson clarity
2. Instructional variety
3. Teacher task orientation

4. Engagement in the learning process
5. Student success rate

Let's take a closer look at each of these.

Lesson Clarity

Lesson clarity refers to how clear a teacher's presentation is to the class as indicated in the following examples:

More Effective Teachers
- Make their points clear to learners who may be at different levels of understanding.
- Explain concepts in ways that help students follow along in a logical step-by-step order.
- Have an oral delivery that is direct, audible to all students, and free of distracting mannerisms.

Less Effective Teachers
- Use vague, ambiguous, or indefinite language: "might probably be," "tends to suggest," "could possibly happen."
- Use overly complicated sentences, such as, "There are many important reasons for the start of World War II but some are more important than others, so let's start with those that are thought to be important but really aren't."
- Give directions that often result in student requests for clarification.

One result from research on lesson clarity is that teachers vary considerably on this behavior. Not all teachers are able to communicate clearly and directly to their students without wandering, speaking above students' levels of comprehension, or using speech patterns that impair their presentation's clarity (Brown & Wragg, 1993; Cruickshank & Metcalf, 1994; Wilen, 1991).

If you teach with a high degree of clarity, you will spend less time going over material. Your questions will be answered correctly the first time, allowing more time for instruction. Clarity is a complex behavior because it is related to many others, such as your organization of the content, lesson familiarity, and delivery strategies (whether you use a discussion, recitation, question-and-answer, or small-group format). Nevertheless, research shows that both the cognitive clarity and oral clarity of presentations vary substantially among teachers. This in turn produces differences in student performance on cognitive tests of achievement (Marx & Walsh, 1988). Table 1.2 summarizes some of the indicators of lesson clarity and teaching strategies you will learn about in this text, especially in chapters 7 (direct instruction), 8 (indirect instruction), and 9 (questioning strategies).

Instructional Variety

Instructional variety refers to your variability or flexibility of delivery during the presentation of a lesson (Brophy, 2002; Brophy & Good, 1986; Rohrkemper & Corno, 1988). One of the most effective ways of creating variety during instruction is to ask questions. As you will learn in chapter 9, many different types of questions can be integrated into the pacing and sequencing of a lesson to create meaningful variation (Chuska, 2003; Wilen, 1991). Therefore, the effective teacher needs to know the art of asking questions and how to discriminate among different question formats—fact questions, process questions,

Table 1.2 Indicators for clarity.

Being Clear (An effective teacher . . .)	Examples of Teaching Strategies
1. Informs learners of the lesson objective (e.g., describes what behaviors will be tested or required on future assignments as a result of the lesson).	Prepare a behavioral objective for the lesson at the desired level of complexity (e.g., knowledge, comprehension, etc.). Indicate to the learners at the start of the lesson in what ways the behavior will be used in the future.
2. Provides learners with an advance organizer (e.g., places lesson in perspective of past and/or future lessons).	Consult or prepare a unit plan to determine what task-relevant prior learning is required for this lesson and what task-relevant prior learning this lesson represents for future lessons. Begin the lesson by informing the learner that the content to be taught is part of this larger context.
3. Checks for task-relevant prior learning at beginning of the lesson (e.g., determines level of understanding of prerequisite facts or concepts and reteaches, if necessary).	Ask questions of students at the beginning of a lesson or check assignments regularly to determine if task-relevant prior knowledge has been acquired.
4. Gives directives slowly and distinctly (e.g., repeats directives when needed or divides them into smaller pieces).	Organize procedures for lengthy assignments in step-by-step order and give as handout as well as orally.
5. Knows ability levels and teaches at or slightly above learners' current level or understanding (e.g., knows learner's attention spans).	Determine ability level from standardized tests, previous assignments, and interests and retarget instruction accordingly.
6. Uses examples, illustrations, and demonstrations to explain and clarify (e.g., uses visuals to help interpret and reinforce main points).	Restate main points in at least one modality other than the one in which they were initially taught (e.g., visual vs. auditory).
7. Provides review or summary at end of each lesson.	Use key abstractions, repetition, or symbols to help students efficiently store and later recall content.

convergent questions, and divergent questions. These question types are introduced in chapter 9 and expanded on in chapter 10.

Another aspect of variety in teaching is perhaps the most obvious: the use of learning materials, equipment, displays, and space in your classroom. The physical texture and visual variety of your classroom can contribute to instructional variety. This, in turn, influences student achievement on end-of-unit tests, performance assessments, and student engagement in the learning process (Walqui, 2000a). For example, some studies found the amount of disruptive behavior to be less in classrooms that had more varied activities and materials (Emmer, Evertson, & Worsham, 2006; Evertson, Emmer, & Worsham, 2006). Others have shown variety to be related to student attention (Borich, 2004; Lysakowski & Walberg, 1981).

Some ways to incorporate variety into your teaching are presented in chapter 7 (direct instruction), chapter 8 (indirect instruction), and chapter 11 (cooperative learning and the collaborative process). Table 1.3 summarizes some of the indicators of instructional variety and teaching strategies covered in these chapters.

Table 1.3 Indicators for variety.

Using Variety (An effective teacher . . .)	Examples of Teaching Strategies
1. Uses attention-gaining devices (e.g., begins with a challenging question, visual, or example).	Begin lesson with an activity in a modality that is different from last lesson or activity (e.g., change from listening to seeing).
2. Shows enthusiasm and animation through variation in eye contact, voice, and gestures (e.g., changes pitch and volume, moves about during transitions to new activity).	Change position at regular intervals (e.g., every 10 minutes). Change speed or volume to indicate that a change in content or activity has occurred.
3. Varies modes of presentation (e.g., presents, asks questions, then provides for independent practice [daily]).	Preestablish an order of daily activities that rotates cycles of seeing, listening, and doing.
4. Uses a mix of rewards and reinforcers (e.g., extra credit, verbal praise, independent study, etc. [weekly, monthly]).	Establish lists of rewards and expressions of verbal praise and choose among them randomly. Provide reasons for praise along with the expression of praise.
5. Incorporates student ideas or participation in some aspects of the instruction (e.g., uses indirect instruction or divergent questioning [weekly, monthly]).	Occasionally plan instruction in which student opinions are used to begin the lesson (e.g., "What would you do if . . .".
6. Varies types of questions (e.g., divergent, convergent, [weekly] and probes (e.g., to clarify, to solicit, to redirect [daily]).	Match questions to the behavior and complexity of the lesson objective. Vary complexity of lesson objectives in accord with the unit plan.

An important key behavior for effective teaching is the variability or flexibility of delivery during the presentation of a lesson.

Table 1.4 Learning time and student achievement: Example from second-grade reading.

Reading Score at First Testing (October)		Student Engaged Time in Reading with High Success Rate		Estimated Reading Score, Second Testing (December)	
Raw Score (out of 100)	*Percentile*	*Total Time Over 5 Weeks (Minutes)*	*Average Daily Time (Minutes)*	*Raw Score (out of 100)*	*Percentile*
36	50	100	4	37	39
36	50	573	23	43	50
36	50	1300	52	52	66

Note: An average of 25 school days occurred between the first and the second testing.

Source: From *Teaching and Learning in the Elementary School: A Summary of the Beginning Teacher Evaluation Study,* Beginning Teacher Evaluation Study Report VII-I, by Charles W. Fisher et al., 1978. San Francisco: Far West Laboratory for Research and Development.

Teacher Task Orientation

Teacher task orientation is a key behavior that refers to how much classroom time the teacher devotes to the task of teaching an academic subject. The more time allocated to the task of teaching a specific topic, the greater the opportunity students have to learn.

For example, Table 1.4 shows the results achieved in a second-grade reading class when the teacher's task orientation—or time teaching an academic subject—was increased over a 5-week period. Increasing the time devoted to this instructional objective from 4 minutes to 52 minutes a day, over an average of only 25 school days, yielded an increase of 27 percentile points (from 39 to 66) on a standardized achievement test. The researchers who recorded these data indicated that, although such large increases in instructional time might appear unusual, they actually were achieved by teachers in these elementary school classrooms.

Some task-related questions a teacher must answer are: (1) How much time do I spend planning for teaching and getting my students ready to learn? (2) How much time do I spend presenting, asking questions, and encouraging students to inquire or think independently? (3) How much time do I spend assessing my learners' performance?

These questions pertain to how much material is presented, learned, and assessed, as opposed to how much time is delegated to procedural matters (for example, taking attendance, distributing handouts, collecting homework, checking for materials). All teachers need to prepare their students to learn and want them to enjoy learning. However, most researchers agree that student performance has been higher in classrooms with teachers who spent the maximum amount of time available teaching subject-specific content as opposed to devoting large amounts of time to the process and materials needed to acquire that content. It follows that classrooms in which teacher–student interactions focus more on subject matter content that allows students the maximum opportunity to learn and to practice what was taught are more likely to have higher rates of achievement. But these classrooms also are those in which the relationship between teacher and learner provides the energy to motivate and challenge the learner to reach increasingly higher levels of understanding (Berliner & Biddle, 1995; Brophy, 2002; Porter, 1993).

These topics are covered in chapter 3, which prepares you to set goals and prepare objectives, and chapter 4, which prepares you to execute them in your classroom with unit and

Table 1.5   Indicators for teacher task orientation.

Being Task Oriented (An effective teacher . . .)	Examples of Teaching Strategies
1. Develops unit and lesson plans that reflect the most relevant features of the curriculum guide or adopted text (e.g., each unit and lesson objective can be referenced back to curriculum guide or text).	Key each lesson to a unit plan, the curriculum guide, and the text to test its relevance. Confer with other teachers concerning the most relevant portions of the text and curriculum guide.
2. Handles administrative and clerical interruptions efficiently (e.g., visitors, announcements, collection of money, dispensing of materials and supplies) by anticipating and preorganizing some tasks and deferring others to noninstructional time.	Establish a 5- to 10-minute restriction on how much time per every hour of instruction you will devote to noninstructional tasks. Defer all other tasks to before or after the lesson.
3. Stops or prevents misbehavior with a minimum of class disruption (e.g., has preestablished academic and work rules to "protect" intrusions into instructional time).	Establish rules for the most common misbehaviors and post them conspicuously. Identify only the offender and offense during instructional time, deferring consequence to later.
4. Selects the most appropriate instructional model for the objectives being taught (e.g., primarily uses direct instruction for knowledge and comprehension objectives and indirect instruction for inquiry and problem-solving objectives).	Using your unit plan, curriculum guide, or adopted text, divide the content to be taught into (1) facts, rules, and action sequences, and (2) concepts, patterns, and abstractions. Generally, plan to use direct instruction for the former content and indirect instruction for the latter.
5. Builds to unit outcomes with clearly definable events (e.g., weekly and monthly review, feedback, and testing sessions).	Establish a schedule in which major classroom activities begin and end with clearly visible events (e.g., minor and major tests, and review and feedback sessions).

lesson plans. Table 1.5 summarizes some of the indicators of a teacher's task orientation and the effective teaching strategies that are covered in these chapters.

Engagement in the Learning Process

Student engagement in the learning process—or **engaged learning time**—is a key behavior that refers to the amount of time students devote to learning in your classroom. Student engagement is related to but different from a teacher's task orientation. We learned in the previous section that a teacher's task orientation should provide students the greatest possible opportunity to learn and to practice the material to be assessed.

Distinct from your task orientation—or amount of time you devote to teaching a topic—is the time your students are actively engaged in learning the material being taught. This has been called their *engagement rate*, or the percentage of time devoted to learning when your students are actually on task, engaged with the instructional materials, and benefiting from the activities being presented. Even though a teacher may be task oriented, providing maximum content coverage, the students may be disengaged. This means they are not actively thinking about, working with, or using what is being presented (Borich & Tombari, 1997; Marx & Walsh, 1988; Savage, 1991; Weinstein & Mignano, 1996).

Such disengagement can involve an emotional or mental detachment from the lesson that may or may not be obvious. When students jump out of their seats, talk, read a magazine, or leave for the restroom, they obviously are not engaged in instruction. Students also can be disengaged in far more subtle ways, such as looking attentive while their thoughts are many miles away. An unpleasant fact of life is that a quarter of a class may be off task at any one time, distracted for personal reasons that are often amplified by an impending lunch period, a Friday afternoon, or the day before a holiday. Correcting this type of disengagement may be much more difficult, requiring changes in the structure of the task itself and the cognitive demands placed on the learner (Baum, Viens, & Slatin, 2005; N. Bennett & Desforges, 1988; Brophy, 1996; Doyle, 1983). Strategies for composing tasks and activities that elicit the active participation of your learners are presented in chapters 7 through 11.

Several authors (Evertson, 1995; Kuh, Kinzie, Schuh, & Whitt, 2005; Meichenbaum & Biemiller, 1998; Tauber, 1990) have contributed useful suggestions for increasing learning time and, more importantly, student engagement during learning. Their work, updated by Emmer et al. (2006), has provided the following suggestions for teachers to promote student engagement:

1. Set rules that let pupils attend to their personal needs and work routines without obtaining your permission each time.
2. Move around the room to monitor pupils' seatwork and to communicate your awareness of student progress.
3. Ensure that independent assignments are interesting, worthwhile, and easy enough to be completed by each pupil without your direction.
4. Minimize time-consuming activities such as giving directions and organizing the class for instruction by writing the daily schedule on the board. This will ensure that pupils know where to go and what to do.
5. Make abundant use of resources and activities that are at, or slightly above, a student's current level of understanding.
6. Avoid timing errors. Act promptly to prevent misbehaviors from occurring or increasing in severity so they do not influence others in the class.

These teaching practices have also been found to be beneficial for small groups and independent seatwork (L. Anderson, Stevens, Prawat, & Nickerson, 1988). These and other more specific ways of increasing your students' engagement rate are explored in chapters 10 and 11, which cover strategies for self-directed learning and cooperative and collaborative learning. Table 1.6 summarizes some of the indicators of student engagement and effective teaching strategies covered in these chapters.

Student Success Rate

Our final key effective teaching behavior is student success rate. **Student success rate** refers to the rate at which your students understand and correctly complete exercises and assignments.

A crucial aspect of the previously cited research on task orientation and student engagement has been the level of difficulty of the material being presented. In these studies, level of difficulty was measured by the rate at which students understood and correctly answered questions on tests, exercises, and assignments. Three levels of difficulty are as follows:

- *High success:* The student understands the subject matter taught and makes only occasional careless errors.

Table 1.6 Indicators for engaging students in the learning process.

Engaging Students Effectively in the Learning Process (An effective teacher...)	Examples of Teaching Strategies
1. Elicits the desired behavior immediately after the instructional stimuli (e.g., provides exercise or workbook problems with which the desired behavior can be practiced).	Schedule practice exercises or questions to immediately follow each set of instructional stimuli.
2. Provides opportunities for feedback in a nonevaluative atmosphere (e.g., asks students to respond as a group or covertly the first time through).	Require covert responding or nonevaluative (e.g., group) feedback at the start of a guided practice session.
3. Uses inidiviual and group activities (e.g., performance contracts, CD-ROMs, games and simulations, and learning centers as motivational aids) when needed.	Have individualized instructional materials available (e.g., remedial exercises or texts) for those who may need them.
4. Uses meaningful verbal praise to get and keep students actively participating in the learning process.	Maintain a warm and nurturing atmosphere by providing verbal praise and encouragement that is meaningful (e.g., explain why the answer was correct). Praise partially correct answers, with qualification.
5. Monitors seatwork and frequently checks progress during independent practice.	Limit contact with individual students during seatwork to about 30 seconds each, providing instructionally relevant answers. Circulate among entire class.

- *Moderate success:* The student has partial understanding but makes some substantive errors.
- *Low success:* The student has little or no understanding of the subject matter.

Not surprisingly, Berliner (1979), Good and Brophy (2003), Karweit and Slavin (1981), and Marzano, Pickering, and Pollock (2001), found that student engagement, that is, the time the learner is actively engaged with, thinking about, and working with the content being taught, was closely related to student success rate, as shown in Figure 1.5. Instruction that produces a moderate-to-high success rate results in increased performance, because more content is covered at the learner's current level of understanding. This result was initially found for expository or didactic forms of instruction with which learners are taught basic academic skills most easily learned through practice and repetition (Rosenshine, 1986). But more recent research has extended these findings to thinking skills instruction (Beyer, 1995) and project-based learning (Blumenfeld et al., 1991; Costa & Kallick, 2000b). Research has also shown that instruction promoting low error rates (high success) can contribute to increased levels of student self-esteem and to positive attitudes toward the subject matter and the school (Slavin, 1991b) that provide the motivation to move toward higher levels of achievement.

The average student in a typical classroom spends about half of the time working on tasks that provide the opportunity for high success. But researchers have found that students who spend more than the average time in high-success activities have higher achievement, better retention, and more positive attitudes toward school. These findings have led to the suggestion that students should spend about 60% to 70% of their time on tasks that allow almost complete understanding of the material being taught with only occasional errors (Rosenshine, 1986).

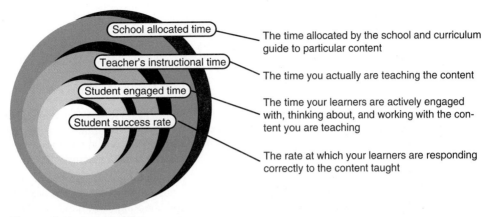

Levels of time labels:

School allocated time — The time allocated by the school and curriculum guide to particular content

Teacher's instructional time — The time you actually are teaching the content

Student engaged time — The time your learners are actively engaged with, thinking about, and working with the content you are teaching

Student success rate — The rate at which your learners are responding correctly to the content taught

Figure 1.5 Levels of time.

Moderate-to-high success rates can produce mastery of lesson content. But they also provide the foundation for your students to apply what they have learned and to reason, problem-solve, and think critically and independently about the content (Duffy & Roehler, 1989; Meichenbaum & Biemiller, 1998; Rohrkemper & Corno, 1988). Many teachers devote insufficient time to this stage of learning, which is particularly crucial for attaining the goals of problem solving and critical thinking. A key activity for the effective teacher is organizing and planning instruction that yields moderate-to-high success rates but then challenges learners to go beyond the information given to construct their own understandings and meanings from lesson content. We will learn more about this approach to learning, called constructivism (Fosnot, 2005; Richardson, 1997), in this chapter and chapters 8 and 10. Table 1.7 summarizes some of the indicators of student success and the teaching strategies covered in these chapters.

Summary of Five Key Behaviors

All five key behaviors—lesson clarity, instructional variety, teacher task orientation, student engagement, and success rate—are essential for effective teaching. Classroom researchers are studying other effective teaching behaviors and attaining a more thorough understanding of those already described. However, for the first time, research has provided a basis for better definitions of effective teaching and for training teachers. These five behaviors are the skeleton of the effective teacher, and the remainder of this text constructs the heart, mind, and body of the effective teacher.

You learned earlier there can be no simple answer to the question, What is an effective teacher? Many activities must be orchestrated into patterns of behavior for your teaching to be effective. The identification of only five behaviors makes teaching appear deceptively simple. However, as the following section reveals, your success in implementing these five key behaviors in the classroom will be assisted by many other helping behaviors.

SOME HELPING BEHAVIORS RELATED TO EFFECTIVE TEACHING

To fill out our picture of an effective teacher, you also need to adopt other behaviors to help you implement the five key behaviors in your classroom. These behaviors can be thought of as helping behaviors for performing the five key behaviors.

Research findings for helping behaviors, although promising, are not as strong and consistent as those that identified the five key behaviors. The research has not identified

Table 1.7 Indicators for student success.

Moderate-to-High Rates of Success (An effective teacher...)	Examples of Teaching Strategies
1. Establishes unit and lesson content that reflects prior learning (e.g., planning lesson sequences that consider task-relevant prior information).	Create a top-down unit plan in which all the lesson outcomes at the bottom of the hierarchy needed to achieve unit outcomes at the top of the hierarchy are identified. Arrange lessons in an order most logical to achieving unit outcomes.
2. Administers correctives immediately after initial response (e.g., shows model of correct answer and how to attain it after first crude response is given).	Provide for guided practice prior to independent practice, and provide means of self-checking (e.g., handout with correct answers) at intervals of practice.
3. Divides instructional stimuli into small chunks (e.g., establishes bite-size lessons that can be easily digested by learners at their current level of functioning).	Plan interdisciplinary thematic units to emphasize relationships and connections that are easily remembered.
4. Plans transitions to new material in easy to grasp steps (e.g., changes instructional stimuli according to a preestablished thematic pattern so that each new lesson is seen as an extension of previous lessons).	Extend unit-plan hierarchy downward to more specific lessons that are tied together above with a single unit theme and outcome.
5. Varies the pace at which stimuli are presented and continually builds toward a climax or key event.	Use review, feedback, and testing sessions to form intervals of increasing and decreasing intensity and expectation.

explicitly how these behaviors should be used. This is why helping behaviors need to be employed in the context of other behaviors to be effective, making them catalysts rather than agents unto themselves (Marzano, Pickering & Pollock, 2001; Saunders, 2005). Among these helping behaviors are the following:

1. Using student ideas and contributions
2. Structuring
3. Questioning
4. Probing
5. Teacher affect (developing the teacher–learner relationship)

Using Student Ideas and Contributions

Using student ideas and contributions is a behavior that includes acknowledging, modifying, applying, comparing, and summarizing student responses to promote the goals of a lesson and to encourage student participation. Note how any one of these activities (Flanders, 1970) could be used in achieving one or more of the five key behaviors:

- *Acknowledging:* Taking a student's correct response and repeating it to the class (to increase lesson clarity).
- *Modifying:* Using a student's idea by rephrasing it or conceptualizing it in your words or another student's words (to create instructional variety).
- *Applying:* Using a student's idea to teach an inference or take the next step in a logical analysis of a problem (to increase success rate).

- *Comparing:* Taking a student's idea and drawing a relationship between it and ideas expressed earlier by the student or another student (to encourage engagement in the learning process).
- *Summarizing:* Using what was said by an student or a group of students as a recapitulation or review of concepts taught (to enhance task orientation).

More recently, the use of student ideas and contributions has been extended to reasoning, problem solving, and independent thinking. This has been achieved through **teacher-mediated dialogue** that helps learners restructure what is being learned using their own ideas, experiences, and thought patterns. Teacher-mediated dialogue asks the learner not just to respond with a correct answer, but to internalize the meaning of what was learned by elaborating, extending, and commenting on it using the learner's own unique thoughts. In this manner, learners are encouraged to communicate the processes by which they are learning, thereby helping them to construct their own meanings and understandings of the content (Fosnot, 2005; Phillips, 2000; Richardson, 1997). We will present strategies for constructivist teaching and teacher-mediated dialogue in chapters 8 and 10.

Use of student ideas and contributions also can increase a student's engagement in the learning process. Thus it has become a frequently used catalyst for helping achieve that key behavior (Emmer et al., 2006). Consider this brief instructional dialogue that uses student ideas to promote engagement:

◆ ◆ ◆

Teacher: Tom, what is the formula for the Pythagorean theorem?
Tom: $c^2 = a^2 + b^2$.

◆ ◆ ◆

At this point the teacher simply could have said "Good!" and gone on to the next question. Instead, this teacher continues:

◆ ◆ ◆

Teacher: Let's show that on the board. Here is a triangle; now let's do exactly as Tom said. He said that squaring the altitude, which is *a*, and adding it to the square of the base, which is *b*, should give us the square of the hypotenuse, which is *c*. Carl, would you like to come up and show us how you would find the length of *c*, using the formula Tom just gave us?
Carl: Well, if *a* were equal to 3 and *b* equal to 4, the way I would solve this problem would be to add the squares of both of them together and then find the square root—that would be *c*.
Teacher: So, we square the 3, square the 4, add them together, and take the square root. This gives us 5, the length of the hypotenuse.

◆ ◆ ◆

Which of the five ways of using student ideas are in this dialogue? First, by putting Tom's response graphically on the blackboard, this teacher applied Tom's answer by taking it to the next step, constructing a proof. Second, by repeating orally what Tom said, the teacher acknowledged to the entire class the value of Tom's contribution. And third, by having another student prove the correctness of Tom's response, a summary of the concept was provided. All this was accomplished from Tom's simple (and only) utterance: $c^2 = a^2 + b^2$.

Research indicates that student ideas and contributions, especially when used in the context of the naturally occuring dialogue of the classroom, are more strongly and consistently related to student engagement than simply approving a student's answer with "Good!" (Brophy, 1981; Good & Brophy, 2003). The standard phrases we use to acknowledge and reward students ("correct," "good," "right") are so overused that they may not always convey the reward intended.

Although the use of student ideas looks simple, it takes skill and planning. Even when your response is unplanned, you should be prepared to seize opportunities to incorporate student ideas and contributions into your lesson.

Structuring

Teacher comments made for the purpose of organizing what is to come, or summarizing what has gone before, are called *structuring*. Used before an instructional activity or question, structuring serves as instructional scaffolding that assists learners in bridging the gap between what they are capable of doing on their own and what they are capable of doing with help from the teacher, thereby aiding their understanding and use of the material to be taught. Used at the conclusion of an instructional activity or question, structuring reinforces learned content and places it in proper relation to other content already taught. Both forms of structuring are related to student achievement and are effective catalysts for performing the five key behaviors (Meichenbaum & Biemiller, 1998; Rogoff, 1990; Rosenshine & Meister, 1992).

Typically, before- and after-structuring takes the following form:

◆   ◆   ◆

Teacher: (At beginning of lesson) OK, now that we have studied how the pipefish change their color and movements to blend in with their surroundings, we will study how the pipefish gathers its food. Most important, we will learn how the pipefish grow and provide the means for other fish, like the kind we eat for food, to flourish deep below the ocean's surface.

Teacher: (At end of lesson) So, we have discovered that the pipefish protects itself by changing colors to blend in with plants on the ocean's floor and by swaying back and forth to fool its enemies. We might conclude from this that the pipefish evade rather than capture their natural enemies and feed close to the ocean's floor where they can't be noticed. Can you think of when this clever strategy might not work, making the pipefish prey to other fish deep below the ocean's surface? (Adapted from Palincsar & Brown, 1989)

◆   ◆   ◆

This sequence illustrates some of the many ways you can use structuring. One way is to *signal* that a shift in direction or content is about to occur. A clear signal alerts students to the impending change. Without such a signal, students may confuse new content with old, missing the differences. Signals such as "Now that we have studied how the pipefish change their color and movements . . . we will learn . . ." help students switch gears and provide a perspective that makes new content more meaningful.

Another type of structuring uses *emphasis*. Can you find a point of emphasis in the previous dialogue? By using the phrase "most important," this teacher alerts students to the knowledge and understanding expected at the conclusion of this activity. This structuring helps the student to organize what is to follow, called an *advance organizer*.

In this instance, the students are clued to consider the factors that extend beyond the color and movement of the pipefish to include how they grow and provide the means for other fish to flourish. This makes the teacher's final question more meaningful ("Can you think of when this clever stategy might not work, making the pipefish prey to other fish deep below the ocean's surface?"). The students have been clued that such a question might be raised and that generalizations beyond the concepts discussed will be expected. Phrases such as

Now this is important.
We will return to this point later.
Remember this.

are called *verbal markers*. They can emphasize your most important points.

In addition to verbal markers and advance organizers, the effective teacher organizes a lesson into an activity structure. An *activity structure* is a set of related tasks that differ in cognitive complexity and that to some degree may be placed under the control of the learner. Activity structures (Marx & Walsh, 1988; Meichenbaum & Biemiller 1998; Rogoff, 1990) can be built in many ways (e.g., cooperatively, competitively, independently) to vary the demands they make on the learner and to give tempo and momentum to a lesson. For the effective teacher, they are an important means for engaging students in the learning process and moving them from simple recall of facts to the higher response levels that require reasoning, critical thinking, and problem-solving behavior.

The Art of Questioning

Questioning is another important helping behavior. Few other topics have been researched as much as the teacher's use of questions (Dantonio & Beisenherz, 2000; Falk & Blumenreich, 2005; Power & Hubbard, 1999). One of the most important outcomes of research on questioning has been the distinction between content questions and process questions.

Content Questions. Teachers pose content questions to have the student deal directly with the content taught. An example is when a teacher asks a question to see if students can recall and understand specific material. The correct answer is known well in advance by the teacher. It also has been conveyed directly in class, in the text, or both. Few, if any, interpretations or alternative meanings of the question are possible.

Researchers have used various terms to describe content questions, such as the following:

Types of Content Questions
- *Direct:* The question requires no interpretation or alternative meanings.
  Example: "What is the meaning of the word *ancient* in the story just read?"
- *Lower-Order:* The question requires the recall only of readily available facts, as opposed to generalizations and inferences.
  Example: "What was the mechanical breakthrough that gave the cotton gin superiority over all previous machines of its type?"
- *Convergent:* Different data sources lead to the same answer.
  Example: "What is one of the chemical elements in the air we breathe?"
- *Closed:* The question has no possible alternative answers or interpretations.
  Example: "What is the function of a CPU in a computer?"
- *Fact:* The question requires the recall only of discrete pieces of well-accepted knowledge.
  Example: "What is the result of the number 47 divided by 6?"

Some estimates have suggested that up to 80% of the questions teachers ask refer directly to specific content and have readily discernible and unambiguous correct answers (Gall, 1984; Gall & Gall, 1990; Risner et al., 1992). Perhaps even more important is the fact that approximately the same percentage of teacher-made test items (and behavioral objectives) are written at the level of recall, knowledge, or fact (Borich & Tombari, 1997, 2004). Therefore, test items, behavioral objectives, and most instruction seem to emphasize readily known facts as they are presented in curriculum guides, workbooks, and texts, leaving much less time for encouraging higher-order thinking, such as problem solving, decision making, and valuing.

The art of questioning will become one of your most important skills as a teacher. The variety you convey to your students will be determined in large measure by your flexible use of questions. Questions are rarely ends in themselves but rather a means of engaging students in the learning process by getting them to act on, work through, or think about the material presented.

Process Questions.   From the previous discussion, you can see why not all questions can be content questions. There are different purposes for which questions can be asked, with the intent of encouraging different mental processes. To problem-solve, to guide, to arouse curiosity, to encourage creativity, to analyze, to synthesize, and to judge also are goals of instruction that should be reflected in your questioning strategies. For these goals, content is not an end itself but a means of achieving higher-order goals.

Researchers have used various terms to describe process questions, such as the following:

Types of Process Questions

- *Indirect:* The question has various possible interpretations and alternative meanings.
  Example: "What are some of the ways you have used the word *ancient?*"
- *Higher-Order:* The question requires more complex mental processes than simple recall of facts (e.g., making generalizations and inferences).
  Example: "What were the effects of the invention of the cotton gin on attitudes in the North?"
- *Divergent:* Different data sources will lead to different correct answers.
  Example: "From what we know about the many forms of pollution today, what would be one of the first things we have to do to clean the air we breathe?"
- *Open:* A single correct answer is not expected or even possible.
  Example: "How have recent advances in computer technology influenced your life?"
- *Concept:* The question requires the processes of abstraction, generalization, and inference.
  Example: "Using examples of your own choosing, can you tell us some of the ways division and subtraction are similar?"

Can you see the difference between this set of process questions and the list of content questions that preceded it? Notice that the process questions encourage more thinking and problem solving by requiring the learner to use personal sources of knowledge to actively construct her or his own interpretations and meanings rather than acquiring understanding by giving back knowledge already organized in the form in which it was told. As we saw earlier, this view of teaching and learning represents a movement in education called *constructivism*. **Constructivist teaching strategies** emphasize the learner's direct experience and the dialogue of the classroom as instructional tools while de-emphasizing lecturing and telling (Fosnot, 2005; Phillips, 2000; Richardson, 1997). See In Practice: Focus on Constructivism.

Process questions and the use of probes, our next helping behavior, are important aids in constructivist thinking and action in the classroom. We will have more to say about the role of direct experience and the use of constructivist strategies in the classroom in the chapters ahead, especially chapters 8 and 10.

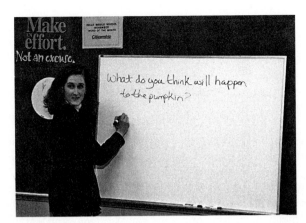

Constructivist teaching strategies emphasize the learner's direct experience and the dialogue of the classroom as instructional tools.

IN PRACTICE

Focus on Constructivism

Constructivism is a philosophy of learning that explains how people come to understand or to know. In the late 1980s and early 1990s, many psychologists began to turn their attention to a constructivist view of learning, which assumes that learning is an active process in which learners internally construct knowledge from interpretations of their interactions with their physical and social environment. This view does not necessarily deny the existence of an objective reality but does recognize the limitations it places on what people can know, since knowledge always stands in relation to the context from it was derived and the experiences of the observer who must make sense of it. Therefore, constructivists believe that much of what we know are interpretations influenced by context and prior experiences. Conceptual growth from a constructivist perspective results from sharing of multiple perspectives and from refining our interpretations in response to other perspectives.

Constructivists focus on engaging learners in richly textured contexts, reflective of the natural environment. In such an environment, learners have opportunities to negotiate meanings and collaborate with each other. As a result, learners have exposure to multiple perspectives and have opportunities to actively construct, refine, and take ownership of what they see and the meanings they derive from it. The knowledge constructed from this context is complex, personal, and insightful, which more easily allows learners to transfer it beyond textbook and classroom. By being able to construct meaning for themselves, students take ownership of their learning while teachers serve as facilitators that help students grow. Teachers are no longer the information transmitters; instead, they provide guidance and scaffolding with which students can discover knowledge for themselves. In constructivist learning environments, teachers promote a learning climate and context that extends students' experiences and interests, thus providing students with the opportunity to see multiple perspectives and develop their own understandings.

Savery and Duffy (1995) identify three essential attributes of constructivism:

1. Cognitive conflict or confusion is the stimulus for learning and influences the reorganization and nature of what is learned. According to Dewey (1938), it is the problem that leads to and is the organizer for learning, and according to Piaget (1977), it is the need for accommodation when the current experience cannot be assimilated into the existing schema.
2. Knowledge evolves through negotiation and evaluation of the viability of individual understandings, primarily because shared language and knowledge contributes a great deal to how reality is actively constructed for each individual. Other individuals are a primary mechanism for testing the understanding. Collaborative groups are important because learners can test their own understanding and examine the understanding of others as a mechanism for enriching, interweaving, and expanding the understanding of particular issues or phenomena. Other people are the greatest source of alternative views.
3. Understanding comes from one's interactions with the environment. Cognition is not only within the individual, but also comes from perceptions and experiences that are distributed across the entire context in which the learner is situated.

By examining the perspectives of constructivism, we can recognize that learning is an ongoing and active process, and inquiry an appropriate vehicle for facilitating the cognitively based, constructivist approach to learning. In an inquiry-based learning environment, students are engaged in a hands-on subject-related question, problem, or investigation, during which they observe, question, and gather information to test their understanding in an ongoing and active process (Llewellyn, 2002).

Probing

Another helping behavior is *probing*, which refers to teacher statements that encourage students to elaborate on an answer, either their own or another student's. Probing may take the form of a general question or can include other expressions that *elicit* clarification of an answer, *solicit* additional information about a response, or *redirect* a student's response in a more fruitful direction. Probing often is used to shift a discussion to some higher thought level.

Generally, student achievement is highest when the eliciting, soliciting, and (if necessary) redirecting occur in cycles. This systematically leads the discussion to a higher level of complexity, as when interrelationships, generalizations, and problem solutions are being sought (J. Dillon, 1995). In this manner, you may begin a lesson with a simple fact question; then, by eliciting clarification of student responses, soliciting new information, or redirecting an answer, you can move to a higher level of questioning.

A typical cycle might occur in the following manner:

◆　◆　◆

Teacher:	Bobby, what is a scientific experiment?
Bobby:	Well, it's when you test something.
Teacher:	But what do you test? (elicit)
Bobby:	Mmm, Something you believe in and want to find out if it's really true.

Teacher:	What do you mean by that? (solicit)
Mary:	He means you make a prediction.
Teacher:	What's another word for *prediction*? (redirect)
Tom:	Hypothesis. You make a hypothesis, then go into the laboratory to see if it comes true.

◆ ◆ ◆

Can you find the teacher's soliciting, eliciting, and redirecting behaviors in the remainder of the dialogue?

◆ ◆ ◆

Teacher:	OK. So a scientist makes a prediction or hypothesis and follows up with an experiment to see if it can be made to come true. Then what?
Billy:	That's the end!
Teacher:	(No comment for 10 seconds; then . . .) Is the laboratory like the real world?
David:	The scientist tries to make it like the real world, but it's much smaller, like the greenhouse pictured in our book.
Teacher:	So what must the scientist do with the findings from the experiment, if they are to be useful? (No one answers, so the teacher continues.) If something important happens in my experiment, wouldn't I argue that what happened could also happen in the real world?
Bobby:	You mean, if it's true in a specific situation, it will also be true in a more general situation?
Betty Jo:	That's making a generalization.
Teacher:	Good. So we see that a scientific investigation usually ends with a generalization. Let's summarize. What three things does a scientific investigation require?
Class:	A prediction, an experiment, and a generallization.
Teacher:	Good work, class.

◆ ◆ ◆

Notice that all of the ingredients in this teacher's lesson were provided by the clsss. The concepts of hypothesis, experiment, and generalization were never defined for the class. The students defined these concepts for themselves with only an occasional "OK" or "Good" to let them know they were on track. The teacher's role was limited to eliciting clarification, soliciting additional information, and redirecting. The purpose of this cycle of eliciting, soliciting, and redirecting is to promote inquiry or independent discovery of the content of the lesson. Generally, retention of material learned has been greater from inquiry teaching than from formal lecturing methods (Paul, 1990).

Teacher Affect

Anyone who has ever been in a classroom where the teacher's presentation was lifeless, static, and without vocal variety can appreciate the commonsense value of the affective side of teaching. However, unlike the behaviors discussed previously, affect cannot be captured in transcripts of teaching or by classroom interaction instruments. Consequently, narrowly focused research instruments often miss a teacher's affective nature, which emerges from a more holistic view of the classroom. This affective nature is the foundation on which you can build a warm and nurturing relationship with your learners.

What the instruments miss, the students see clearly. Students are good perceivers of the emotions and intentions underlying a teacher's actions, and they often respond accordingly.

A teacher who is excited about the subject being taught and shows it by facial expression, voice inflection, gesture, and movement, communicating respect and caring for the learner, is more likely to hold the attention of students and motivate them to higher levels of achievement than one who does not exhibit this behavior.

Students take their cues from these affective signs and lower or heighten their engagement with the lesson accordingly. Enthusiasm is an important aspect of a teacher's affect. Enthusiasm

is the teacher's vigor, power, involvement, excitement, and interest during a classroom presentation and willingness to share this emotion with learners, who will want to respond in kind. We know from experience that enthusiasm is contagious. It can be displayed to your students in many ways, the most common being vocal inflection, gesture, eye contact, and animation, but most importantly, how you coordinate these signs to communicate that you care about and respect the experiences, knowledge, and understandings your students bring to the classroom. A teacher's enthusiasm was found to be related to student achievement (Bettencourt, Gillett, Gall, & Hull, 1983; Cabello & Terrell, 1994). And, as noted

Effective teachers provide a warm and encouraging classroom climate by letting students know help is available.

earlier, it is believed to be important in promoting student engagement in the learning process and achievement (Kuh, Kinzie, Smith, & Whitt, 2005).

Obviously, no one can maintain a heightened state of enthusiasm for very long without becoming exhausted emotionally. Nor is this what is meant by enthusiasm. A proper level of enthusiasm is far more subtle, and perhaps that is why it has been so difficult to research. A proper level of enthusiasm involves a delicate balance of vocal inflection, gesturing, eye contact, and movement. In combination, these behaviors send to students a unified signal of vigor, involvement, and interest that conveys the message that you care. Timing and the ability to incorporate these behaviors into a consistent pattern make possible an unspoken behavioral dialogue with students that is every bit as important as your spoken words.

 *Video Window*

Using Student Ideas and Contributions

In this video you will see Rebecca teaching a lesson on gardening to her kindergarten class. Her lesson goal is to use an experience shared by most of her learners to teach vocabulary and spelling. We see how easily she accomplishes this by using the ideas and contributions of her learners, one of the five helping behaviors, to shape her lesson. As the lesson develops, see if you can find instances of the other four helping behaviors—structuring, questioning, probing, and teacher affect—and describe them. Do you believe the combination of all five behaviors working together helped Rebecca execute a successful lesson?

 To answer these questions online, go to the Video Windows *module for this chapter on the Companion Website at www.prenhall.com/borich.*

TEACHING EFFECTIVELY WITH DIVERSE LEARNERS AND CONTENT

Researchers have uncovered behaviors of special importance to specific types of students and content. Two areas of findings having the most consistent results are these:

1. Teaching behaviors that affect learners of lower and higher socioeconomic status
2. Teaching behaviors that affect the teaching of reading and mathematics

How Does Effective Teaching Differ with Learners Who Have Different Socioeconomic Levels, Culture, and Ethnicity?

The phrase **socioeconomic status (SES)** can mean many different things, but generally it is an approximate index of one's income and education level. For the classroom researcher, the SES of students is determined directly by the income and education of their parents or indirectly by the nature of the school the student attends. For example, a school in which a high percentage of students qualify for a nationally sponsored free or reduced price lunch program due to the income level of their parents may be considered a lower SES school.

Some schools are in impoverished areas where the overall income and education levels of the community are low, whereas other schools are located in more affluent communities. Many schools in impoverished areas qualify for special financial assistance from the federal government, based on the median income of their students' parents. These schools are called "Title 1" schools in which the majority of students come from lower-SES homes and may be disadvantaged, "at risk" of school failure, limited English proficient, and/or of a cultural or ethnic minority. In our nation's 25 largest cities, SES is strongly tied to one's culture or ethnicity.

Because lower-SES and higher-SES students and the conditions (e.g., access to fewer books and a computer in the home) to which they are tied are likely to exist for some time, classroom researchers have determined what teacher practices promote the most achievement in these different settings. Researchers such as Dilworth and Brown (2001), Bowers and Flinders (1991), Good and Brophy (2003), Hill (1989), Kennedy (1991) and McNary, Glasgow, and Hicks (2005) provide suggestions for teaching these two student populations. Some important teaching behaviors to emphasize for these two groups are summarized in Table 1.8.

Notice in the table that, although each behavior is applicable to both lower and higher SES students, teacher affect is particularly important in lower-SES classrooms. Also, notice that some of these teaching behaviors received little or no mention in our preceding discussions, because those discussions applied to students generally. Four of the behaviors shown for lower-SES classrooms (student responses, content organization, classroom instruction, and individualization) can be seen as special ways of creating student engagement at high rates of success for these learners. This presents a particular challenge when teaching lower-SES students who may be at risk of school failure.

Also, frequently correcting wrong answers in the absence of support or encouragement could be construed more often as a personal criticism by lower-SES, who may already have a poor self-concept, than higher-SES students. Therefore, feedback that could be construed as personal criticism would need to be provided in a consistently supportive and encouraging context (Cabello & Terrell, 1994).

Because much of the research on SES has been conducted in elementary classrooms, it is as yet uncertain to what extent the teaching practices in Table 1.8 apply to the secondary classroom. However, many of the learning characteristics of higher-SES and lower-SES students appear to be similar across school grades. Therefore, your success as a teacher in a predominantly lower-SES or higher-SES classroom will depend on your ability to vary the extent to which you emphasize the behaviors in Table 1.8.

Table 1.8 Important teaching behaviors for lower-SES and higher-SES students.

Helping Lower SES Populations Achieve Success	
Teacher Affect	Provide a warm and encouraging classroom climate by consistently letting students know help is available.
Student Responses	Encourage an initial response before moving to the next student.
Content Organization	Present material with opportunity to practice what has been learned immediately afterward.
	Show how related pieces of information fit together and are to be applied before each new segment of instruction begins.
Classroom Instruction	Emphasize applications before teaching patterns and abstractions. Present most concrete learnings first.
	Monitor each student's progress at regular intervals. Use progress charts to help record learner improvement.
	Help students who need help immediately. Use peer and cross-age tutors, if necessary.
	Maintain structure and flow between activities to maintain momentum. Organize and plan transitions in advance.
Individualization	Supplement standard curriculum with specialized materials to meet the needs of individual students.
	Emphasize the importance of the personal experiences of students to promote interest and attention.

Helping Higher SES Populations Achieve Success	
Correcting	Check right answers by requiring extended oral or written reasoning.
Thinking and Decision Making	Supplement curriculum with individualized material, some of which is slightly above students' current level of attainment.
	Assign homework and/or extended projects that require original sources of information obtained outside the classroom.
Classroom Interaction	Encourage student-to-student and student-to-teacher interactions in which learners take responsibility for evaluating their own learning.
Verbal Activities	Consistently engage students in verbal questions and answers that go beyond text and workbook content.

Source: Based on information from Bowers and Flinders (1991); Good and Brophy (2003); Hill (1989); Irvine and York (2001); Kennedy (1991); Knapp and Woolverton (2001); Levine and Lezotte (2001).

How Does Effective Teaching Differ Across Content Areas?

Another set of findings pertains to the different teaching behaviors that distinguish reading and language arts from basic mathematics instruction (Ball, Lubienski, & Mewborn, 2001; Barr, 2001; Brophy & Evertson, 1976; Good & Grouws, 1987; Reynolds, 1989). Although not all teachers will teach either reading or mathematics, this set of findings may be generalized to some extent to other types of content that are similar in form and structure.

Table 1.9 Important teaching behaviors for reading and mathematics instruction.

Findings for Reading Instruction	
Instructional Activity	Devote sufficient time during reading instruction to discussing, explaining, and questioning to stimulate cognitive processes and promote learner responding.
Interactive Technique	Use cues and questions that require every student to attempt a response during reading instruction.
Questions	Pose thought-provoking questions during reading instruction that require the student to predict, question, summarize, and clarify what has been read.

Findings for Basic Mathematics Instruction	
Instructional Materials	Use application- and experience-oriented activities and media during mathematics instruction to foster task persistence.
Instructional Content	Maximize coverage of instructional applications during mathematics instruction through the use of activity sheets, handouts, and problem sets at graduated levels of difficulty.
Instructional Organization	Initially, emphasize full-class or larger group instruction during mathematics instruction. Gradually, transition to less guided and independent work, when it does not interfere with on-task behavior and learner persistence.

Source: Based on information from Carpenter, Dossey, and Koehler (2004); English (2002); Grouws (1992); Kilpatrick, Martin, and Schifter (2003); National Council of Teachers of English (1996).

For example, social studies, history, and language instruction all have high reading content and share some of the same problem-solving features as reading. General science, biology, physics, and chemistry are similar to the science of mathematics in that concepts, principles, and laws play a prominent role. Also, visual forms and symbolic expressions are at least as important in understanding science subjects as is the written word. Therefore, some cautious generalizations may be made about the teaching practices important for reading and basic mathematics instruction and for subjects similar to each.

Some important findings are summarized in Table 1.9. Notice the two different approaches implied by the practices listed. For basic mathematics instruction, at first a formal, direct approach appears to be most effective. This approach includes maintaining structure through close adherence to texts, workbooks, and application-oriented activities. It also maximizes instructional coverage by minimizing unstructured work that could diminish engaged learning time. In contrast, reading instruction allows for a more interactive and indirect approach, using more classroom discussions and experience-oriented questions and answers.

These approaches, however, are not mutually exclusive. What the research shows is that, at first, a more direct approach during basic mathematics instruction tends to result in greater student progress than would, say, the exclusive use of an inquiry approach. For reading, the reverse appears to be true: At first, an exploratory, interactive approach that encourages the use of classroom dialogue and student ideas tends to result in greater student progress over time.

These different approaches represent degrees of emphasis and not exclusive practices. Clearly, teaching the basics of mathematics will at times require an inquiry approach, just as reading sometimes requires a presentation or telling approach. More important than either of these approaches or the practices in Table 1.8 and 1.9 that represent them is the ability of the teacher to be flexible. From these research studies the message is clear: There are not only effective and ineffective ways to teach, but the effectiveness of any method will likely depend on the content being taught and the learners to whom it is being taught. The effective teacher is sensitive when a change from one emphasis to another is necessary, regardless of the content or learner being taught.

THE COMPLEXITY OF TEACHING

At this point, you might think an effective teacher simply is one who has mastered all of the key behaviors and helping behaviors. But teaching involves more than a knowledge of how to perform individual behaviors. Much like an artist who blends color and texture into a painting to produce a coherent impression, so must the effective teacher blend individual behaviors into teaching practices that promote student achievement. Teaching practices are larger than individual teaching behaviors that blend key and helping behaviors in different degrees. This requires the orchestration and integration of the key and helping behaviors into meaningful patterns and rhythms that can achieve the goals of instruction within your classroom.

The truly effective teacher, then, knows how to execute individual behaviors with a larger purpose in mind. This larger purpose requires placing behaviors in sequences and patterns that accumulate to create an effect greater than can be achieved by any single behavior or small set of them. This is why teaching involves a sense of timing and pacing that cannot be conveyed by any list of behaviors. The interrelationships among these behaviors, giving each its proper emphasis in the context of your classroom, are important to the effective teacher. And it is the combination of curriculum, learning objectives, instructional materials, and learners that provides the context for the proper blend.

PROFESSIONAL TEACHING STANDARDS

The effective teaching methods described in this book draw on more than 30 years of research on effective teaching and on national and state standards for the teaching profession that have been closely aligned with current views of how and what students and teachers should learn.

For decades, American teaching reflected a direct instruction model. Teachers were expected to present or "transmit" knowledge to students—who were expected to receive, store, and return that knowledge upon request (Weiss & Weiss, 1998). Many researchers and educators have challenged this view, suggesting that learners do not simply "receive" knowledge; rather, they actively construct knowledge through interacting with the social, cultural, and linguistic context in which an experience occurs (Fosnot, 2005; Phillips, 2000; Richardson, 1997). Effective teachers function as able facilitators, coaches, and guides for students' knowledge-building processes.

Reflecting this more interactive view of teaching, the National Board for Professional Teaching Standards (NBPTS) was formed in 1987 with three major outcomes:

1. To establish high and rigorous standards for what effective teachers should know and be able to do;
2. To develop and operate a national, voluntary system to assess and certify teachers who meet these standards;
3. To advance related education reforms for the purpose of improving student learning in American schools.

Governed by a board of 63 directors, the majority of whom are classroom teachers, the NBPTS (2001) listed five propositions essential to accomplished teaching:

1. Teachers are committed to students and their learning;
2. Teachers know the subjects they teach and how to teach those subjects to students;
3. Teachers are responsible for managing and mentoring student learning;
4. Teachers think systematically about their practice and learn from experience;
5. Teachers are members of learning communities.*

During the same year (1987), the Interstate New Teacher Assessment and Support Consortium (INTASC) was formed to create "board-compatible" standards that could be reviewed by professional organizations and state agencies as a basis for licensing beginning teachers. The **INTASC standards** (Miller, 1992) are written as 10 principles, which are then further explicated in terms of teacher knowledge, dispositions, and performances—in other words, what a beginning teacher should know and be able to do.

Because you will probably work with the INTASC standards during your professional development program (and perhaps with the NBPTS standards for advanced certification later in your career), this text discusses research-based practices used by effective teachers to achieve the INTASC and NBPTS standards. At the end of each chapter are test preparation exercises aligned with these standards to help you prepare for the *Praxis II:® Principles of Learning and Teaching* examination. These end-of-chapter case histories and self-assessments provide a targeted rehearsal preparing you for the level of pedagogical knowledge that may be expected of you at the end of your teacher preparation program and for teacher certification and licensing.

Here are the 10 INTASC standards written as principles, which can be accessed with the full document at *www.ccsso.org/intascst.html*. We identify these standards and the chapters and appendices in this text that will provide you with the effective teaching methods for attaining them.

1. *Principle 1:* The teacher understands the central concepts, tools of inquiry, and structures of the discipline(s) he or she teaches and can create learning experiences that make these aspects of subject matter meaningful for students (chapters 1, 3, 4).

2. *Principle 2:* The teacher understands how children learn and develop, and can provide learning opportunities that support their intellectual, social and personal development (chapters 2, 3, 4, 11).

3. *Principle 3:* The teacher understands how students differ in their approaches to learning and creates instructional opportunities that are adapted to diverse learners (chapters 7, 8, 10, 11).

4. *Principle 4:* The teacher understands and uses a variety of instructional strategies to encourage students' development of critical thinking, problem solving, and performance skills (chapters 8, 9, 10, 11, 12, appendix B).

5. *Principle 5:* The teacher uses an understanding of individual and group motivation and behavior to create a learning environment that encourages positive social interaction, active engagement in learning, and self-motivation (chapters 2, 10, 11).

6. *Principle 6:* The teacher uses knowledge of effective verbal, nonverbal, and media communication techniques to foster active inquiry, collaboration, and supportive interaction in the classroom (chapters 7, 8, 9, 10).

---

* Reprinted with permission from the National Board for Professional Teaching Standards, What Teachers Should Know and Be Able to Do, *www.nbpts.org*. All rights reserved.

7. *Principle 7:* The teacher plans instruction based upon knowledge of subject matter, students, the community, and curriculum goals (chapters 2, 3, 4).

8. *Principle 8:* The teacher understands and uses formal and informal assessment strategies to evaluate and ensure the continuous intellectual, social and physical development of the learner (chapter 12).

9. *Principle 9:* The teacher is a reflective practitioner who continually evaluates the effects of his or her choices and actions on others (students, parents, and other professionals in the learning community) and who actively seeks out opportunities to grow professionally (chapters 1, 4, 5, 6, 12, appendix A).

10. *Principle 10:* The teacher fosters relationships with school colleagues, parents, and agencies in the larger community to support students' learning and well-being (chapters 2, 5).

These principles require the ability to integrate knowledge of subject-matter content, students, and the community in order to relate classroom objectives to the lives of learners. They also require the application of research-based principles of effective teaching that not only define what teachers need to know but also how to apply what they know in culturally rich and diverse classrooms. This book devotes chapter content to each of these dimensions of effective teaching. Within each chapter you will find teaching methods, examples, research, a test preparation scenario, and a Companion Website to help you better integrate and implement these key principles of teaching in your classroom.

YOUR TRANSITION TO THE REAL WORLD OF TEACHING

An important question for you as a prospective teacher is what type of knowledge and experiences will be needed to pass successfully into the real world of teaching. The chapters ahead convey the types of knowledge you will need to move quickly up the hierarchy of knowledge and experiences that make an effective teacher. But before learning about the tools and techniques that will help you progress up this hierarchy, you will want to reflect on your own concerns about teaching at this point in your career. Appendix A contains the *Teacher Concerns Checklist*, a 45-item self-report instrument for assessing the stages of concern with which teachers, like yourself, most strongly identify at different periods in their careers. Using the *Teacher Concerns Checklist*, rank your own level of teaching concerns and with the instructions provided, express the concerns with which you identify most closely. Then return to this chapter and read further to learn more about this interesting facet of your growth and development as a teacher.

Stop now and complete the Teacher Concerns Checklist in appendix A.

Now that you have ranked your most important teaching concerns, let's see what it means for your teaching. Your transition to the real world of teaching will usher in the first stage of teacher development, sometimes called the *survival stage* (Borich, 1993; Borich & Tombari, 1997; Burden, 1986; Fuller, 1969; Ryan, 1992). The distinguishing feature of this first stage of teaching is that your **teaching concerns** and plans will focus on your own well-being more than on the teaching task or your learners. Bullough (1989) has described this stage as "the fight for one's professional life" (p. 16). During it, your concerns typically are focused on the following:

- Will my learners like me?
- Will they listen to what I say?
- What will parents and other teachers think of me?
- Will I do well when I'm being observed?

Typically, during this time, behavior management concerns become a major focus of your planning efforts. For most teachers, survival—or *self*—concerns begin to diminish rapidly during the first months of teaching, but there is no precise time when they end. What signals their end is the transition to a new set of concerns and planning priorities. This new set of priorities focuses on how best to deliver instruction. Various labels have been used to describe this second stage, such as the mastery stage of teaching (Ryan, 1992), consolidation and exploration (Burden, 1986), and trial and error (Sacks & Harrington, 1982). Fuller (1969) described this stage as one marked by concerns about the teaching *task*.

At this stage you are beginning to feel confident you can manage the day-to-day routines of the classroom and deal with a variety of behavior problems. You are at the point where you now can plan your lessons without an exclusive focus on managing your classroom. Your planning turns instead toward improving your teaching skills and achieving greater mastery over the content you are teaching.

Typically, your concerns during this stage are with the following:

* Where can I find individualized instructional materials?
* Will I have enough time to cover the content?
* Where can I get ideas for an interdisciplinary thematic unit?
* What is the best way to teach writing skills?

The third and highest level of teacher planning is characterized by concerns that have less to do with management and lesson delivery and more with the impact of your teaching on learners. This stage of planning is sometimes referred to as the *impact stage*. At this stage you will naturally view learners as individuals and will be concerned that each of your students fulfills her or his potential to learn. At this time, your principal concerns may include the following:

* How can I increase my learners' feelings of accomplishment?
* How do I meet my learners' social and emotional needs?
* What is the best way to challenge my unmotivated learners?
* What skills do they need to best prepare them for the next grade?

Fuller (1969) speculated that concerns for *self, task,* and *impact* are the natural stages that most teachers pass through, representing a developmental growth pattern extending over months and even years of a teacher's career. Although some teachers may pass through these stages more quickly than others and at different levels of intensity, Fuller suggested that almost all teachers can be expected to move from one to another, with the most effective and experienced teachers expressing student-centered (impact) concerns at a high level of commitment.

Fuller's concerns theory has several other interesting implications. A teacher might return to an earlier stage of concern—move from a concern for students back to a concern for task as a result of having to teach a new grade or subject, or move from a concern for task back to a concern for self as a result of having to teach different and unfamiliar students. The second time spent in a stage might be expected to be shorter than the first. Finally, the three stages of concern need not be exclusive of one another. A teacher could have concerns predominantly in one area while still having concerns at lesser levels of intensity in the other stages. Record your scores on the *Teacher Concerns Checklist* that you have just taken and compare them with your scores at the end of this course to find out in what direction your concerns may have changed.

FOR FURTHER INFORMATION

During the past decade, there have been a number of national and state efforts, such as those by the National Council of Teachers of Mathematics (NCTM), the International Reading Association (IRA), and others, which have sought to define the knowledge and performance for students or teachers in particular subject areas. The Mid-continent Regional Educational Laboratory (McREL) has created a large database that synthesizes many of these efforts. You can visit their Web site at *www.mcrel.org* to learn more about standards.

SUMMING UP

This chapter introduced you to definitions of effective teaching and key behaviors that help achieve it. Its key terms and main points were:

What Is an Effective Teacher?

1. Early definitions of effective teaching focused primarily on a teacher's goodness as a person and only secondarily on his or her behavior in the classroom.
2. The psychological characteristics of a teacher—personality, attitude, experience, achievement, and aptitude—do not relate strongly to the teacher's behavior in the classroom.

A New Direction

3. Most modern definitions of effective teaching identify patterns of teacher–student interaction in the classroom that influence the cognitive and affective performance of students.
4. Classroom interaction analysis is a research methodology in which the verbal interaction patterns of teachers and students are systematically observed, recorded, and related to student performance.

Key Behaviors Contributing to Effective Teaching

5. Five key behaviors for effective teaching and some indicators pertaining to them are the following:
   - Lesson clarity: logical, step-by-step order; clear and audible delivery free of distracting mannerisms.
   - Instructional variety: variability in instructional materials, questioning, types of feedback, and teaching strategies.
   - Task orientation: achievement (content) orientation as opposed to process orientation, maximum content coverage, and time devoted to instruction.
   - Student engagement: limiting opportunities for distraction and getting students to work on, think through, and inquire about the content.

   - Success rate: 60% to 70% of time spent on tasks that afford moderate-to-high levels of success, especially during expository or didactic instruction.

Some Helping Behaviors Related to Effective Teaching

6. Five helping behaviors for effective teaching and some indicators pertaining to them are the following:
   - Using student ideas and contributions: Using student responses to foster the goals of the lesson and getting students to elaborate on and extend learned content using their own ideas, experiences, and thought patterns.
   - Structuring: Providing advance organizers and cognitive or mental strategies at the beginning of a lesson and creating activity structures with varied demands.
   - Questioning: Using both content (direct) and process (indirect) questions to convey facts and to encourage inquiry and problem solving.
   - Probing: Eliciting clarification, soliciting additional information, and redirecting when needed.
   - Teacher affect: Exhibiting vigor, involvement, excitement, and interest during classroom presentations through vocal inflection, gesturing, eye contact, and animation, communicating a warm and nurturing relationship to the learner.

Teaching Effectively with Diverse Learners and Content

7. The key behaviors, such as lesson clarity, instructional variety, and teacher's task orientation appear to be consistently effective across all or most teaching contexts.
8. The helping behaviors, such as use of student ideas and contributions, structuring, and questioning, can be thought of as helping behaviors for performing the five key behaviors. These behaviors may be applied differently in helping lower and higher SES

students achieve success and across areas of instruction, such as the teaching of reading and the teaching of mathematics.

The Complexity of Teaching

9. Effective teaching involves the orchestration and integration of key and helping behaviors into meaningful patterns to create effective teaching practices.

Professional Teaching Standards

10. Governed by a board of directors, the majority of whom are classroom teachers, the National Board for Professional Teaching Standards (NBPTS) proposed five propositions essential to effective teaching.

11. The Interstate New Teacher Assessment and Support Consortium (INTASC) standards are written as 10 principles, which are then further explicated in terms of teacher knowledge, dispositions, and performances—in other words, what a beginning teacher should know and be able to do.

Your Transition to the Real World of Teaching

12. Fuller (1969) postulated three stages of concerns through which teachers pass on the way to becoming a professional: concern for self, concern for the teaching task, and concern for their impact on learners.

KEY TERMS

Constructivist teaching strategies, 22
Engaged learning time, 14
Helping behaviors, 9
Instructional variety, 10
INTASC standards, 31
Key behaviors, 9
Lesson clarity, 10

Praxis, 4
Socioeconomic status (SES), 27
Student success rate, 15
Teaching concerns, 32
Teacher-mediated dialogue, 19
Teacher task orientation, 13

DISCUSSION AND PRACTICE QUESTIONS

Questions marked with an asterisk are answered in appendix B. See also the Companion Website for this text at *www.prenhall.com/borich* for more assessment options.

*1. In the following list, place the number 1 beside those indicators that most likely would appear in early definitions of effective teaching, based on the characteristics of a "good" person. Place the number 2 beside those indicators that most likely would appear in later definitions of effective teaching, based on the psychological characteristics of teachers. Place a check beside those indicators most likely to appear in modern definitions of effective teaching, based on the interaction patterns of teachers and students.

_____ Is always on time for work
_____ Is intelligent
_____ Stays after class to help students
_____ Works well with those in authority
_____ Has plenty of experience at his or her grade level
_____ Varies higher-level with lower-level questions
_____ Likes his or her job

_____ Uses attention-getting devices to engage students in the learning task
_____ Is open to criticism
_____ Shows vitality when presenting
_____ Has worked with difficult students before
_____ Always allows students to experience moderate-to-high levels of success
_____ Matches the class content closely with the curriculum guide

2. In your opinion, which of the following helping behaviors on the right would be most helpful in implementing the key behaviors on the left? More than a single helping behavior may be used for a given key behavior. Compare your results with those of another and discuss the reasons for any differences.

Lesson clarity _____
Instructional variety _____
Task orientation _____
Engagement in the
learning task _____
Success rate _____

1. Student ideas
2. Structuring
3. Questioning
4. Probing
5. Enthusiasm

3. Identify two teaching effectiveness behaviors you would emphasize if you were teaching fifth-grade mathematics. Identify two you would emphasize when teaching fifth-grade reading. Justify your choices from the summary reserach tables in this chapter.

4. Indicate your perceived strengths in exhibiting the five key and five helping behaviors, using the following technique. First, notice the number assigned to each of the key behaviors.

   1 lesson clarity

   2 instructional variety

   3 teacher task orientation

   4 student engagement in the learning process

   5 student success rate

   Now, for each of the following rows of numbers listed, circle the number representing the key behavior in which you perceive yourself to have the greater strength.

1 versus 2	2 versus 4
1 versus 3	2 versus 5
1 versus 4	3 versus 4
1 versus 5	3 versus 5
2 versus 3	4 versus 5

   Count up how many times you circled a 1, how many times you circled a 2, a 3, and so on, and place the frequencies on the following lines.

_____	1
_____	2
_____	3
_____	4
_____	5

   Your perceived greatest strength is the key behavior having the highest frequency. Your perceived least strength is the key behavior with the lowest frequency.

5. Repeat the paired comparison technique in the same manner for the five helping behaviors.

   1 use of student ideas

   2 structuring

   3 questioning

   4 probing

   5 enthusiasm

1 versus 2	2 versus 4
1 versus 3	2 versus 5
1 versus 4	3 versus 4
1 versus 5	3 versus 5
2 versus 3	4 versus 5

_____	1
_____	2
_____	3
_____	4
_____	5

FIELD EXPERIENCE ACTIVITIES

1. Recall a particularly good teacher you had during your high school years—and a particularly poor one. Try to form a mental image of each one. Now rate each of them on the five key behaviors in the following list. Use 1 to indicate strength in that behavior, 2 to indicate average performance, and 3 to indicate weakness in that behavior. Are the behavioral profiles of the two teachers different? How?

Behavior	Teacher X (good)	Teacher Y (poor)
Lesson clarity	_____	_____
Instructional variety	_____	_____
Task orientation	_____	_____
Engagement in the learning process	_____	_____
Success rate	_____	_____

2. Now do the same for the five helping behaviors, using the same two teachers. Is the pattern the same? What differences in ratings, if any, do you find across key and helping behaviors for the same teacher? How would you account for any differences that occurred?

DIGITAL PORTFOLIO ACTIVITIES

The following digital portfolio activities relate to INTASC principle 9:

What is a digital portfolio? A digital portfolio contains the same materials that would be placed in a traditional portfolio, except that they are captured, organized, saved, and presented in a digital format. There are many advantages to being able to save and present important information relevant to your professional development in a digital format. First, a digital portfolio of your professional development can contain all the entries you might want to show a prospective employer in a fraction of the space that an accordion file, file box or even binder would consume. Second, it can provide immediate access to exactly what you need at the time you need it to respond to a specific request for information without your having to clumsily rummage through reams of information. And, third, it can place audio, video, graphics, as well as text at your fingertips in seconds. Accessibility, ease of duplication, minimal storage space, and portability make a digital portfolio the most advanced and efficient means of saving and displaying your professional accomplishments. Each chapter of this text will suggest what you should consider placing in your digital portfolio to present your professional skills and experiences and start you toward your first teaching job.

How do I start a digital portfolio? Your digital portfolio can be started using your personal computer and commonly available software, such as Microsoft PowerPoint. However, several commercially available software applications for a professional portfolio can make the task even easier. Here are some identified by Bullock and Hawk (2005), some of which can also be used for the student portfolios that will be discussed in chapter 12.

Scholastic Electronic Portfolio (Scholastic, Inc., 1995) (Macintosh only). This is one of the more flexible and powerful programs available that allows you to create a variety of portfolio designs, including text, sound, slide shows, video, and launch views.

The Portfolio Assessment Toolkit (Forest Technologies) (Macintosh and Windows). This multimedia electronic portfolio program includes three customizable portfolios at the primary, intermediate, and secondary levels for students as well as teachers.

The Portfolio Builder for PowerPoint (Visions-Technology in Education) (Macintosh and Windows). This is a companion product for PowerPoint that can be used by teachers as well as students. It provides elementary, middle school, and secondary templates for constructing a portfolio.

The Teacher's Portfolio (Aurbach & Associates) (Macintosh). Includes the features of other software but, in addition, customized features for the new teacher, including places for self-reflection, domains based on INTASC standards, and a place for teachers to display their personal information, professional goals, educational philosophy, experience, competencies, and academic record.

Now here are some suggestions for your first portfolio entries that relate to INTASC principle 9:

1. This activity is designed to give you experience in creating a 2-minute video in which you state your philosophy of teaching—often required for your first job interview. This will give you the opportunity of having an introduction to yourself on your laptop to show the person interviewing you, rather than having to speak unrehearsed at what might be a stressful moment. You will need an inexpensive Web camera that will come with appropriate software. You may want to write out your 2-minute talk and use it as a guide to what you will say extemporaneously. Your objective is to look natural and relaxed, to speak clearly, and look directly into the camera. View your first trial and repeat the process as necessary until you give a confident picture of yourself. If you do not have the oppurtunity to use a Web cam, place your written statement in a binder, box file, or accordion file. Place this product in a folder on your computer labeled *Teaching Philosophy.*

2. Complete the *Teacher Concerns Checklist* in appendix A, if you have not already done so. Set up and date a new computer folder with the name *Teacher Concerns* and place it in a file with your scores for concerns for Self, concerns for Task, and concerns for Impact. As your professional experience grows retake the *Teacher Concerns Checklist* (for example, at the end of this course and occasionally thereafter) and place your new scores for these dimensions side by side with your previous scores. Over time, note how your scores shift from self concerns to concerns for the teaching task and finally to concerns about your impact on students.

CLASSROOM OBSERVATION ACTIVITIES

The following classroom observation activities relate to INTASC principles 5, 6, and 8:

1. To gain a sense of the pace of student–teacher interactions in a classroom, arrange to observe in a classroom where there is likely to be some teacher–student dialogue (questions and answers, discussion, or oral checking and feedback). You will find a format for recording your observations in the *Classroom Observation* module for this chapter on the Companion Website at *www.prenhall.com/borich*. This activity may also be completed by viewing an available video of a classroom lesson that may be available from your instructor or selected from among the *Video Windows* lesson excerpts that accompany this text.

   A. Be prepared to divide your observation time into three equal parts (for example, three 20-minute segments). During the first 20 minutes, count the number of teacher-to-student and student-to-teacher interchanges that occur, and record their occurrence with a tally in the appropriate box provided for this activity in the chapter 1 *Classroom Observation* module on the Companion Website. A teacher question addressed to a student would count as one tally, and a student response back to the teacher would count as another.

   B. During the next 20-minute segment of your observation, continue observing teacher–student interaction, but this time record the number of student-to-teacher and teacher-to-student exchanges that pertain to (a) lesson content, (b) procedural matters (directions and clerical tasks), and (c) discipline or classroom management (restating rules, giving warnings, or assigning punishment). Use the record in the *Classroom Observation* folder on the Companion Website to tally the number of teacher–student exchanges in each of these areas during this part of your observation.

   C. During the last 20 minutes of your observation, continue observing teacher–student interactions. This time, record your tallies according to whether the exchange is brief (lasting approximately 5 seconds or less) or extended (lasting more than 5 seconds), using the boxes provided. Include the complete exchange as a single tally. That is, record the teacher-to-student statement and the student response to the teacher (if applicable) as a single unit.

   After your observations, state three general conclusions about the pace of activity in this classroom supported by the data you have collected in each of the three boxes. Begin building your digital portfolio by placing your tallies from each of the three boxes along with your general conclusion into a folder labeled *Classroom Observations* for your digital portfolio.

2. Reflecting on the classroom you have just observed, complete the *General Observation Form* provided in the *Classroom Observation* module for this chapter on the Companion Website. This observation instrument will ask you to rate your classroom according to its lesson clarity (clear/unclear), instructional variety (varied/static), teacher's task orientation (focused/unfocused), student engagement in the learning process (involved/uninvolved), and student success (high/low). How typical do you feel your ratings are of this teacher's lessons throughout the year? Why or why not? Place a copy of the completed rating scale in the *Classroom Observation* folder of your digital portfolio.

CHAPTER CASE HISTORY AND PRAXIS TEST PREPARATION

The following is a case history and test preparation exercise intended to help you prepare for the *Praxis II:*® *Principles of Learning and Teaching* exam that may be required by your teacher preparation program and your state for certification and licensing. You will find similar case histories and Praxis test preparation exercises at the end of each chapter. Following the objectives and content of the *Praxis II*®: *Principles of Learning and Teaching* exam and the INTASC and NBPTS standards, these practice exercises include an in-depth case history representing key concepts in the chapter, followed by a short-answer question requiring analysis of the case history and discrete multiple-choice questions pertaining to Praxis test content. (See Figure 1.1 for the composition of the *Praxis II*®.) When you have completed the test preparation exercises, you will find in appendix D example student responses to the short-answer question, a scoring rubic to help you follow the reasoning behind the score given to each short-answer response, and the correct answers and explanations for each multiple-choice question. Although not intended as a comprehensive assessment of chapter content, these questions provide a targeted rehearsal preparing you for the level of pedagogical knowledge and question formats that will be expected of you on the *Praxis II* exam and other exams that may be required at the end of your teacher preparation program. See the Companion Website for additional chapter 1 test items pertaining to Praxis content.

DIRECTIONS: The following case history pertains to chapter 1 content. After reading the case history, answer the short-answer question that follows and consult appendix D to find different levels of scored student responses and the rubric used to determine the quality of each response. You also have the opportunity to submit your responses online to receive feedback by visiting the *Case History* module for this chapter on the Companion Website, where you will also find additional questions pertaining to Praxis test content.

Case History

Mrs. Travis teaches seventh-grade English to a class of 29 students. In this class, there is a balance of boys and girls from low to high performing. Several students are mainstreamed, a few are limited English speaking, and several are designated gifted. The majority perform at the average level. This case focuses in particular on the following students.

Brady is a mainstreamed special education student new to the district. Her official classification is emotionally disturbed, but some of her standardized test scores, particularly reading comprehension and vocabulary, put her near the gifted category. Her assigned seat is in the rear corner of the class, and she seems to enjoy the detachment it offers. Much of the time she is reading a novel; her current choice is Kafka's *Metamorphosis.*

Dalia is an honor roll student whose high motivation and study habits rather than her test scores underlie her achievement. She is always the first to class and begins on the daily warm-up even before the bell rings. Dalia is painstaking about her writing and anxious to get everything right. Often she stays after class or school to ask additional questions about an upcoming assignment. She is intent on becoming the first of her family to go to college.

Jim, an average student, is tall and outgoing and very excited that he has made the school football team. He has a good sense of humor and often jokes with fellow classmates. Although he has good attendance and is never late for class, his study habits are not very good. Sometimes he forgets his book or brings the wrong notebook, which he often uses as an excuse to "take the day off." And, when he is on task, he often talks without raising his hand or interrupts other students in a burst of enthusiasm.

During the first several minutes of class, Mrs. Travis takes the roll while the class completes its usual warm-up, writing down the quote of the day, looking up synonyms for key underlined words, and finally paraphrasing it. They also copy the daily lesson and homework assignment from the front board. A few students who have been absent go to the class calendar on the bulletin board to catch up on makeup assignments.

Mrs. Travis asks Jim to read the quote: "The roots of education are bitter, but the fruit is sweet. Aristotle."

He reads from the board rather than his notebook, which he has "forgotten" today. Since he has not written down a synonym, she waits for him to look one up for the word "roots" in the thesaurus. Jim takes his time, but finally says, "base."

"That's a good choice," Mrs. Travis tells him. While she calls on others, she quietly slips him a blank page and suggests he write down the warm-up now so he can transfer it to his notebook at home. She remains standing next to his desk as she asks for more synonyms from the class. Reluctantly he begins to write.

Throughout the discussion of the quotation, Brady has been reading her novel. When Mrs. Travis asks her to read her paraphrasing of the quote, she replies without hesitation: "The underlying foundation of learning can be difficult or harsh, but the rewards are immense and joyous." She is about to go back to her book, but Mrs. Travis probes.

"Can you give some examples of those 'bitter roots,' Brady?"

"Well, having to do lesson warm-ups, for example, keeping a notebook, or putting up with someone who can hardly read." She stares at Jim.

Mrs. Travis admits that schoolwork can be difficult. "Those are some examples, Brady. Now, tell us about some of the sweet fruit?"

There is no reply. After about 10 seconds, Mrs. Travis probes, "Is reading a Kafka book sweet fruit?"

A shrug is her response. "Well, if you like *The Metamorphosis,* I'd recommend you read *The Judgment* next." Brady looks up from her reading and stares at Mrs. Travis, a look of surprise stamped on her face. Then she writes down the title on her hand.

After a discussion the class gives several examples of "the bitter roots of education" they'd rather do without. The examples of the sweet fruits are a little more difficult to elicit, so Mrs. Travis changes gear.

"Well, maybe now you don't see too much sweet fruit because you are in the midst of it, but what about when you graduate from high school or college? What rewards will your education provide?"

"I want to be first in my family to go to college," Dalia says.

"I'm going to get a football scholarship," adds Jim. Several others mention the cars they plan to buy when they finish their education. Just as the shared enthusiasm is on the edge of getting too noisy, Mrs. Travis directs them to a 10-minute writing assignment on today's lesson: The Rewards of Education.

For the next 10 minutes, they write while Mrs. Travis walks around the room to monitor their progress and make suggestions. Even Brady lays aside the novel she has been reading.

Short-Answer Question

This section presents a sample Praxis short-answer question. In appendix D you will find sample responses along with the standards used in scoring these responses.

DIRECTIONS: The following question requires you to write a short answer. Base your answer on your knowledge of principles of learning and teaching from chapter 1. Be sure to answer all parts of the question.

Discrete Multiple-Choice Questions

DIRECTIONS: Each of the multiple-choice questions that follow is based on Praxis-related pedagogical knowledge in chapter 1. Select the answer that is best for each question and compare your results with those in appendix D. See also the Companion Website for this text at *www.prenhall.com/ borich* for more assessment options.

1. Research findings suggest that one of the ways effective teachers can increase learning time and, more importantly, student engagement during learning is which of the following?
   a. Maintain a quiet classroom where students can concentrate and work undisturbed.
   b. Provide tangible rewards for work well done, such as free reading time, passes to the library, or extra credit.
   c. Ensure that assignments are interesting, worthwhile, and easy enough to be completed by each learner at his or her current level of understanding.
   d. Demonstrate a commitment to group discussion and cooperative learning.
2. Ms. Jones is a veteran teacher who takes pride in her job. She is a strict disciplinarian and never has any problems with classroom management. She volunteers in the community, gives generously to charitable causes, and is the last one to leave the school. Which description best characterizes her and takes into account recent research on effective teaching practices?
   a. Ms. Jones aspires to a prototype of the teacher as a good role model and ideal citizen. She may or may not be effective in the classroom.

1. Discuss some positive and some negative aspects of Mrs. Travis's strategy for dealing with Brady's off-task behavior during the warm-up and the follow-up discussion. In your discussion, comment on Mrs. Travis's response to Brady's reading a novel during class as well as her reaction to Brady's negative comments about a fellow classmate.

   b. Ms. Jones probably will not be an effective teacher in the long run, because she spreads herself too thin with all her volunteering and that will deplete the high level of energy she needs for teaching.
   c. Ms. Jones is the ideal teacher who is all too rare. As a good citizen she is a role model and inspiration to her students.
   d. Ms. Jones may or may not be a good teacher. Without seeing her transcripts we have no idea of her ability to teach at her grade or in her subject area.
3. Which of the following situations is least likely to promote achievement among students of lower socioeconomic status?
   a. Warm classroom climate
   b. Frequent correction of wrong answers
   c. Peer and cross-age tutors
   d. Material presented in small pieces
4. Which of the following best represents an example of a verbal marker?
   a. "Homework will be assigned for this lesson."
   b. "Now this will be important."
   c. "Look at the table of contents."
   d. "Turn to page 57."
5. A convergent question requires:
   a. No interpretation
   b. Only recall
   c. One right answer
   d. The use of different data sources that point to the same answer

Chapter 2

Understanding Your Students

This chapter will help you answer the following questions and meet the following INTASC principles for effective teaching:

1. What is a reflective teacher?
2. How can I adapt my instruction to the needs and abilities of my learners?
3. What are some of the ways I can use peer group membership to foster the goals of my instruction?
4. How can I help learners acquire a positive self-concept?
5. What are some ways I can promote family–school partnerships in my classroom?

INTASC 2: The teacher understands how children learn and develop and can provide learning opportunities that support their intellectual, social, and personal development.

INTASC 3: The teacher understands how students differ in their approaches to learning and creates instructional opportunities that are adapted to diverse learners.

INTASC 5: The teacher uses an understanding of individual and group motivation and behavior to create a learning environment that encourages positive social interaction, active engagement in learning, and self-motivation.

INTASC 9: The teacher is a reflective practitioner who continually evaluates the effects of his or her choices and actions on others (students, parents, and other professionals in the learning community) and who actively seeks out opportunities to grow professionally.

Chapter 1 explained that teaching is not simply the transmission of knowledge from teacher to learner but rather is the interaction of teacher with learner. This chapter discusses the decisions you must make about whom you will teach. In subsequent chapters, we consider the decisions you must make about what and how you will teach.

Not so long ago, students were viewed as empty vessels into which the teacher poured the contents of the day's lesson. Teachers perceived their task to be the skilled transmission of appropriate grade-level content as it appeared in texts, curriculum guides, workbooks, and the academic disciplines.

Contradictions arose from such a simplistic definition of teaching and learning. For example, this definition could not explain why some students get poor grades and others good ones even when the teacher is skilled at transmitting the contents of the day's lesson. Nor could it explain why some students want to learn, whereas others do not even want to come to school; why some students do extra work and others do little at all; or why some students are actively engaged in the learning process while others are not.

*These are just some of the individual differences that exist in every classroom that can influence the outcome of your teaching, regardless of how adept you may be at transmitting the content of the day's lesson. Adapting your teaching to individual differences will require you to make many decisions about your learners that cannot be reduced to simple formulas or rules. It will require that you become a **reflective teacher**, which means you take the time to ask tough questions about the success of your teaching efforts and the individual differences among your learners.*

Reflective teachers are thoughtful and self-critical about their teaching. That is, they take the time necessary to adapt their lessons to their learners' needs, prior histories, and experiences, and to analyze and critique the success of their lessons afterward.

To help adapt subject matter content to the world of their learners, reflective teachers use their learners' prior experiences and what they already know as instructional tools. By de-emphasizing lecturing and telling, reflective teachers encourage their learners to use their own experiences to actively construct understandings that make sense to them and for which they can take ownership. In other words, reflective teachers bridge the gap between teaching and learning by actively engaging students in building lesson content and encouraging them to gradually accept greater responsibility for their own learning. In the chapters ahead, we have more to say about how you can become a reflective teacher who adapts subject matter to the individual differences of learners and who uses student experiences and the dialogue of the classroom to actively engage students in the learning process. In this chapter we will provide some important facts about the psychology of your learners that will help you understand and appreciate their individual differences.

WHY PAY ATTENTION TO INDIVIDUAL DIFFERENCES?

Any observer in any classroom quickly notices that schoolchildren vary in their experiences, socioeconomic status (SES), culture and ethnicity, language, and learning style. Differences in experiences, SES, culture/ethnicity, language, and learning style influence what students learn (Banks & Banks, 2001; Banks, 1997; Dunn & Griggs, 1995). Of what consequence is such an obvious observation? After all, you must teach all the students assigned to you, regardless of their differences.

Two of the reasons for being aware of individual differences among your learners are these:

1. By recognizing individual differences, you can help your learners to use their own experiences and learning histories to derive meaning and understanding from what you are teaching. With that knowledge, you will be better able to adapt your instructional methods to the learning needs of your students.

2. When counseling students and talking with parents about the achievement and performance of your learners, you will be able to convey some of the reasons for their behavior. Understanding your students' individual differences can provide important information to parents, counselors, and other teachers when they wonder why Jared is not learning, why Anita learns without studying, or why Angela doesn't want to learn.

Researchers have discovered that different instructional methods, when matched to the individual strengths of learners, can significantly improve their achievement (Cronbach & Snow, 1981; Mayer, 1998, 2002). For example, student-centered discussions improve the achievement of highly anxious students by providing a more informal, nurturing climate, whereas teacher-centered lectures increase the achievement of low-anxiety students by allowing for a more efficient and faster pace. And the linguistic approach to the teaching of reading results in higher vocabulary achievement for students high in auditory ability and who learn best by hearing, whereas the whole-word approach is more effective for students low in auditory ability and who learn best by seeing. Researchers have found that achievement can be increased when the instructional method favors the learners' natural modalities for learning (Cushner, McClelland, & Safford, 1992; Darling-Hammond & Bransford, 2005; Messick, 1995).

Adaptive Teaching

The general approach to achieving a common instructional goal with learners whose individual differences, such as prior achievement, aptitude, or learning styles, differ is called **adaptive teaching**. Adaptive teaching techniques apply different instructional strategies to different groups of learners so the natural diversity prevailing in the classroom does not prevent any learner from achieving success. Two approaches to adaptive teaching have been reported to be effective (Corno & Snow, 1986). They are the remediation approach and the compensatory approach.

The Remediation Approach. The **remediation approach** provides the learner with the prerequisite knowledge, skill, or behavior needed to benefit from the planned instruction. For example, you might attempt to lower the anxiety of highly anxious students with a student-centered discussion before an important presentation, so the presentation could equally benefit all students. Or you might teach listening skills to students low in auditory ability before using a linguistic approach to reading so both groups could profit equally from the linguistic approach.

The remediation approach to adaptive teaching will be successful to the extent that the desired prerequisite information, skill, or behavior can be taught within a reasonable period of time. When this is not possible or represents an inefficient use of classroom time, the compensatory approach to adaptive teaching can be taken.

The Compensatory Approach.   Using the **compensatory approach**, teachers choose an instructional method to compensate for the lack of information, skills, or ability known to exist among learners by altering the content presentation to circumvent a weakness and promote a strength. This is accomplished by using alternate modalities (e.g., pictures vs. words) or by supplementing content with additional learning resources (instructional games and simulations) and activities (group discussions or experience-oriented activities). This may involve modifying the instructional technique to focus on known strengths. Techniques include the visual representation of content, using more flexible instructional presentations (films, pictures, illustrations), shifting to alternate instructional formats (self-paced texts, simulations, experience-oriented workbooks), or using performance-based assessment procedures that might require students to respond orally or assemble a portfolio of experiences, ideas, and products pertaining to a topic. For example, students who are slower to develop their reading comprehension and lack a technical math vocabulary might be taught a geometry unit supplemented with visual handouts. Portraying each theorem and axiom graphically emphasizes the visual modality.

Benefits of Adaptive Teaching.   Notice that adaptive teaching goes beyond the simpler process of ability grouping, in which learners are divided into groups and then presented approximately the same material at different rates. Some research suggests that differences in academic performance between high and low achievers may actually increase with the use of ability grouping by creating a loss of self-esteem and motivation for the low group (Slavin, 1991a).

Adaptive teaching, in contrast, works to achieve success with all students, regardless of their individual differences. It does so either by remediation (building up the knowledge, skills, or abilities required to profit from the planned instruction) or by compensation (emphasizing instructional methods/materials that rely on learner abilities that may be more highly developed). Therefore, adaptive teaching requires an understanding of your students' learning strengths and experience with regard to specific lesson content and the alternative instructional methods that can maximize their strongest receptive modalities (e.g., visual vs. auditory; discussion vs. presentation; student experience–driven vs. text driven).

The chapters ahead provide a menu of such strategies from which to choose. Some of the most promising instructional alternatives in adaptive teaching include the following:

- Cooperative grouping versus whole-class instruction
- Inquiry versus expository presentation
- Rule-example versus example-rule ordering
- Teacher-centered versus student-centered presentation
- Direct versus indirect instruction
- Examples from experience versus examples from text
- Group phonics versus individualized phonics instruction
- Individual responses versus choral responses
- Subvocal responses versus vocal responses

- Self-directed learning versus whole-group instruction
- Computer-driven text versus teacher presentation

Each of these teaching methods has been found more effective for some types of learners than for others. The research literature and curriculum texts in your teaching area offer many examples of specific content areas in which a particular instructional method—in association with a particular student characteristic—has enhanced student performance. However, your classroom experience will suggest many other ways in which you can alter your teaching to fit the individual needs of your learners. By knowing your students and by having knowledge of a variety of instructional methods, you can adapt your instruction to the learning needs of your students.

THE EFFECTS OF GENERAL INTELLIGENCE ON LEARNING

One thing everyone remembers about elementary school is how some students seemed to learn so easily while others had to work so hard. In high school the range of student ability seemed even greater. In a practical sense, we associate the terms *smart, bright, ability to solve problems, learn quickly,* and *figure things out* with intelligence. Both in the classroom and in life, it seems that some have more abilities than others. This observation often has been a source of anxiety, concern, and jealousy among learners. Perhaps because the topic of intelligence can so easily elicit emotions like these, it is one of the most talked about and one of the least understood aspects of student behavior.

One of the greatest misunderstandings that some teachers, parents, and learners have about intelligence is that it is a single, unified dimension. Such a belief is often expressed by the use of word pairs such as *slow/fast* and *bright/dull* when referring to different kinds of learners. Unfortunately, these phrases indicate that a student is either fast or slow, either bright or dull; in fact, each of us, regardless of our intelligence, may be all of these at one time or another. On a particular task of a certain nature, you may appear to be slow, but given another task requiring different abilities, you may be fast. How do such vast differences occur within a single individual?

Everyone knows from personal experience in school, hobbies, sports, and interpersonal relationships that degree of intelligence depends on the circumstances and conditions under which the intelligence is exhibited. Observations such as these have led researchers to study and identify more than one kind of intelligence. This relatively new way of looking at intelligence has led to a better understanding of classic contradictions like why Carlos is good in vocabulary but not in spelling, why Angela is good in social studies but poor at reading maps, or why Tamara is good at analyzing the reasons behind historical events but not at memorizing the names and dates that go along with them. Each of these seemingly contradictory behaviors can be explained by the special abilities required by each task. These specific abilities, in which we all differ, are the most useful aspects of intelligence for understanding the learning needs of your students.

Before turning to these specific abilities, you should be aware of some controversial issues about the use of general intelligence when discussing intelligence with parents, teachers, and school administrators. These issues often strongly divide individuals into two camps, known as the environmentalist position and the hereditarian position.

The Environmentalist Position

The **environmentalist position** criticizes the use of general IQ tests in the schools in the belief that they are culturally biased. Environmentalists believe that differences in IQ scores among groups such as African Americans, Hispanics, and Anglos can be attributed largely to social class or environmental differences. Environmentalists reason that some groups of students, particularly minorities, may come from impoverished home environments in which the verbal skills generally required to do well on intelligence tests are not practiced as much as in the general population. Therefore, a significant part of minority-student scores on any IQ test represents the environment in which they grew up and not their true intelligence.

Environmentalists conclude and some research suggests that the effect of home and even the classroom environment can be as important as heredity in contributing to one's IQ (Bloom, 1981; Doll, Zucker, & Brehm, 2004; Sternberg & Grigorenko, 2001; Weinberg, 1989). This group believes intelligence tests are biased in favor of the white middle class, who, it is believed, are able to provide their children with more intense patterns of verbal interaction, greater reinforcement for learning, more learning resources, and better physical health during the critical preschool years when cognitive growth is fastest.

The Hereditarian Position

The **hereditarian position** concludes that heredity rather than environment is the major factor determining intelligence. Hereditarians base their beliefs on the research and writings of Herrnstein and Murray (1994) and Jensen (1969, 1998). They believe that not all children have the same potential for developing the same mental abilities. They contend that efforts such as compensatory education programs to make up for environmental disadvantages in the early elementary grades through remediation have limited success because the origin of the difference is mostly genetic and not environmental.

General Versus Specific Intelligence

Common sense tells us there is some truth in both arguments. However, despite how parents, other teachers, and even your own students may feel, these positions are highly dependent on the notion of *general* intelligence. The arguments become less relevant in the context of specific abilities. General intelligence only moderately predicts school grades, whereas specific abilities tend to predict not only school grades but also the more important real-life performances that school grades are supposed to represent (Borich & Tombari, 2004). For example, tests of general intelligence cannot predict success as a salesperson, factory worker, carpenter, computer programmer, or teacher, because they measure few of the specific abilities required for success in these occupations.

If we think of school learning as a pie and IQ as a piece of it, we can ask this question: How large a piece of the classroom learning pie is taken up by IQ? Another way of asking this same question is: What percentage of school learning can be attributed to IQ and what percentage to other factors? Knapczyk and Rodes (2001) and Scarr (1981) indicate that many factors, in addition to IQ, contribute to your learners' success: their motivation, health, social skills, quality of teaching, prior knowledge, emotional well-being, and family support, to name only some. Scarr classifies these factors under the term **social competence**. What percentage of school learning can be assigned to IQ and what percentage to all the other factors, Scarr's social competence? The answer, illustrated in Figure 2.1, is that only about 25% can be attributed to IQ; about 75% must be assigned to social competence. So knowing your learners' specific strengths and altering your instructional goals and activities accordingly will contribute far more to your effective teaching than will categorizing your students' performances in ways that indicate only their general intelligence.

Figure 2.1   Factors contributing to school learning

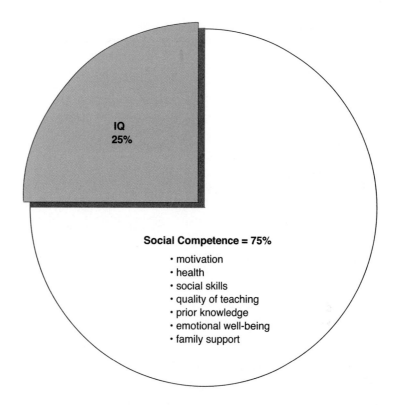

IQ
25%

Social Competence = 75%
- motivation
- health
- social skills
- quality of teaching
- prior knowledge
- emotional well-being
- family support

THE EFFECTS OF SPECIFIC ABILITIES ON LEARNING

Specific definitions of intelligence and the behaviors they represent commonly are called *aptitudes*. As a teacher, you are unlikely to measure aptitudes in your classroom, but you need to know of their influence on the performance of your students. Your students may already have been aptitude-tested in a district-wide testing program, or you can ask the school counselor or psychologist to measure a specific aptitude to find the source of a specific learning problem. Your acquaintance with the division of general intelligence into specific aptitudes will help you see how a learner's abilities in specific areas can directly affect the degree of learning that takes place.

Multiple Intelligences

The work of L. L. Thurstone (1947) was among the first to advocate the use of specific as opposed to general measures of intelligence. Instead of reinforcing the idea of a single IQ score, Thurstone's theory of intelligence led to the development of seven different IQs—verbal comprehension, general reasoning, memory, use of numbers, psychomotor speed, spatial relations, and word fluency—each measured by a separate test. For example, some learning activities require a high degree of memory, such as memorizing long lists of words in preparation for a spelling bee or a vocabulary test. Likewise, spatial relations, use of numbers, and general reasoning ability are essential for high levels of performance in mathematics. The concept of separate intelligences had the advantage that instructional methods could be adapted to learners' strengths, compensating for less well developed abilities or used to strengthen them.

Such distinctions in aptitude also were more useful than general intelligence in explaining to parents why Alexis got excellent scores on math tests that emphasize number problems (12 + 2 − 1 =) but poor scores on math tests that emphasize word problems (If Bob rows 4 mph against a current flowing 2 mph, how long will it take him to row

Table 2.1 Gardner's multiple intelligences.

Dimension	Example	Things They Are Good At
Linguistic intelligence: Sensitivity to the meaning and order of words and the varied uses of language	Poet, journalist	Creative writing, humor/jokes, storytelling
Logical-mathematical intelligence: The ability to handle long chains of reasoning and to recognize patterns and order in the world	Scientist, mathematician	Outlining, graphic organizers, calculation
Musical intelligence: Sensitivity to pitch, melody, and tone	Composer, violinist	Rhythmic patterns, vocal sounds/tones, music performance
Spatial intelligence: The ability to perceive the visual world accurately, and to recreate, transform, or modify aspects of the world based on one's perceptions	Sculptor, navigator	Active imagination, patterns/designs, pictures
Bodily-kinesthetic intelligence: A fine-tuned ability to use the body and to handle objects	Dancer, athlete	Folk/creative dance, physical gestures, sports/games
Interpersonal intelligence: The ability to notice and make distinctions among others	Therapist, salesperson	Intuiting others' feelings, person-to-person communication, collaboration skills
Intrapersonal intelligence: Access to one's own "feeling life"	Self-aware individual	Silent reflection, thinking strategies, inventing
Naturalist intelligence: Observing, understanding, and organizing patterns in the natural environment	Molecular biologist, rock climber	Sensing, observing, nurturing

Source: Adapted from Campbell et al. (1996), Gardner and Hatch (1989), and Lazear (1992).

16 miles?). Such apparent contradictions become more understandable in the light of specific abilities.

Thurstone's (1947) dimensions were among the earliest, but other, more recent components of intelligence have been proposed. For example, Gardner (1999) and Gardner and Hatch (1989) describe eight different intelligences based on skills found in a modern technological society. The eight abilities identified by Gardner and the things individuals who possess high levels of these abilities would be good at are identified in Table 2.1. To these may be added a ninth intelligence, called "existential intelligence," exemplified by a philosopher, theologian, or systems analyst who would be good at solving problems that are not tied to any single discipline or way of thinking (Gardner, 2004). Gardner reasons that alternative forms of learning could tap into still other dimensions of intelligence that in the traditional classroom may go unnoticed or underutilized.

Campbell, Campbell, and Dickinson (1996) and Lazear (1992) have developed instructional materials and modules to teach some of these abilities. The materials and methods developed by Campbell et al. and Lazear derive from the observation that many individuals who are successful in life do not score high in traditional indicators of ability, such as verbal or mathematical reasoning. Gardner (2000, 2004) suggests that these individuals, to be successful, used other abilities, such as those in Table 2.1, to minimize their weaknesses in some areas and emphasize their strengths in others. His theory may have particular relevance for teaching at-risk learners, some of whom may not learn from school in the traditional class-room setting using the traditional curriculum.

Some practical classroom applications of Gardner's theory of multiple intelligences might include the following. See also In Practice: Focus on Multiple Intelligences in the Classroom.

1. Allowing students to take differentiated paths to achieve common goals.
2. Allowing students to display their best, not just average, performance.
3. Providing alternative ways of assessing a student's achievements and talents.
4. Providing opportunities to add to the student's self-identity beyond the traditional logical/linguistic aptitudes demanded by the majority of schoolwork.

IN PRACTICE

Focus on Multiple Intelligences in the Classroom

Adapted from Multiple Intelligences in the Classroom *by Bruce Campbell. Copyright (c) 1991, 2000 by Context Institute.*

Here is how one teacher organized his classroom for multiple intelligences.

To implement Gardner's theory in an educational setting, I organized my third-grade classroom in Marysville, Washington, into seven learning centers, each dedicated to one of the seven intelligences. The students spend approximately two thirds of each school day moving through the centers—15 to 20 minutes at each center. Curriculum is thematic, and the centers provide seven different ways for the students to learn the subject matter.

Each day begins with a brief lecture and discussion explaining one aspect of the current theme. For example, during a unit on outer space, the morning's lecture might focus on spiral galaxies. In a unit about the arts of Africa, one lecture might describe the Adinkra textile patterns of Ghana. After the morning lecture, a timer is set and students in groups of three or four start work at their centers, eventually rotating through all seven.

What Kinds of Learning Activities Take Place at Each Center?

All students learn each day's lesson in seven ways. They build models, dance, make collaborative decisions, create songs, solve deductive reasoning problems, read, write, and illustrate all in one school day. Some more specific examples of activities at each center follow:

- In the **Personal Work Center** (Intrapersonal Intelligence), students explore the present area of study through research, reflection, or individual projects.
- In the **Working Together Center** (Interpersonal Intelligence), they develop cooperative learning skills as they solve problems, answer questions, create learning games, brainstorm ideas, and discuss that day's topic collaboratively.
- In the **Music Center** (Musical Intelligence), students compose and sing songs about the subject matter, make their own instruments, and learn in rhythmical ways.
- In the **Art Center** (Spatial Intelligence), they explore a subject area using diverse art media, manipulatives, puzzles, charts, and pictures.
- In the **Building Center** (Kinesthetic Intelligence), they build models, dramatize events, and dance, all in ways that relate to the content of that day's subject matter.
- In the **Reading Center** (Verbal/Linguistic Intelligence), students read, write, and learn in many traditional modes. They analyze and organize information in written form.
- In the **Math & Science Center** (Logical/Mathematical Intelligence), they work with math games, manipulatives, mathematical concepts, science experiments, deductive reasoning, and problem solving.

Following their work at the centers, a few minutes are set aside for groups and individual students to share their work from the centers. Much of the remainder of the day is spent with students working on independent projects, either individually or in small groups where they apply the diverse skills developed at the centers. The daily work at the seven centers profoundly influences their ability to make informative, entertaining, multimodal presentations of their studies. Additionally, it is common for parents to comment on how much more expressive their children have become at home.

What Were the Results?

An action research project was conducted in my classroom to assess the effects of this multimodal learning format. The research data revealed the following:

1. *The students develop increased responsibility, self-direction, and independence over the course of the year.* Although no attempt was made to compare this group of students with those in other third-grade classes, the self-direction and motivation of these students was apparent to numerous classroom visitors. The students became skilled at developing their own projects, gathering the necessary resources and materials, and making well-planned presentations of all kinds.

2. *Discipline problems were significantly reduced.* Students previously identified as having serious behavior problems showed rapid improvement during the first six weeks of school. By mid-year, they were making important contributions to their groups. And by year's end, they had assumed positive leadership roles that had not formerly been evident.

3. *All students developed and applied new skills.* In the fall, most students described only one center as their "favorite" and as the one where they felt confident. (The distribution among the seven centers was relatively even.) By mid-year, most identified three to four favorite centers. By year's end, every student identified at least six centers that were favorites and at which they felt skilled. Moreover, they were all making multimodal presentations of independent projects including songs, skits, visuals, poems, games, surveys, puzzles, and group participation activities.

4. *Cooperative learning skills improved in all students.* Since so much of the center work was collaborative, students became highly skilled at listening, helping each other, sharing leadership in different activities, accommodating group changes, and introducing new classmates to the program. They learned not only to respect each other, but also to appreciate and call upon the unique gifts and abilities of their classmates.

5. *Academic achievement improved.* Standardized test scores were above state and national averages in all areas. Retention was high on a classroom year-end test of all areas studied during the year. Methods for recalling information were predominantly musical, visual and kinesthetic, indicating the influence of working through the different intelligences. Students who had previously been unsuccessful in school became high achievers in new areas.

In summary, many students said they enjoyed school for the first time. And as the school year progressed, new skills emerged: Some students discovered musical, artistic, literary, mathematical, and other new-found capacities and abilities. Others became skilled leaders. In addition, self-confidence and motivation increased significantly. Finally, students developed responsibility, self-reliance, and independence as they took an active role in shaping their own learning experiences.

Related Link: www.context.org/ICLIB/IC27/Campbell.htm

Content area specialists have identified still other specific forms of intelligence nestled within those suggested by Gardner. For example, content specialists in reading have identified no fewer than nine verbal comprehension factors, which indicate the ability to do the following:

- Know word meanings
- See contextual meaning
- See organization
- Follow thought patterns
- Find specifics
- Express ideas
- Draw inferences
- Identify literary devices
- Determine a writer's purpose

In other words, a learner's general performance in reading may be affected by any one or a combination of these specific abilities. This and similar lists point up an interesting and sometimes controversial aspect of intelligence: Once abilities such as draw inferences, follow thought patterns, and find contextual meaning are defined, is it possible to teach these so-called components of intelligence?

Hereditarians say that intelligence is not teachable, but it seems logical that, with proper instruction, a learner could be taught to draw inferences, follow thought patterns, and find contextual meaning. As general components of intelligence, such as those defined by Gardner, become divided into smaller and more specific aptitudes, the general concept of intelligence has become demystified. At least some elements of intelligence depend on achievement in certain areas that can be influenced by instruction. Therefore, another advantage of the multidimensional approach to intelligence is that some specific abilities once thought to be unalterable can be taught.

Sternberg's Definition of Intelligence

Another recent conception of intelligence comes from Sternberg (1995, 2003) and Sternberg and Grigorenko (2001). Sternberg's work has been important in forming new definitions of intelligence that allow for intellectual traits, previously believed to be inherited and unalterable, to be improved through instruction. Further, Sternberg suggests not only that intelligence can be taught but also that the classroom is the logical place to teach it.

One important part of Sternberg's definition of intelligence is that intelligence is the ability to learn and to think using previously discovered patterns and relationships to solve new problems in unfamiliar contexts. By experiencing many novel tasks and conditions early in life, we discover the patterns

Some aspects of the age-old concept of intelligence, once thought to be unalterable, now may be taught in the classroom.

and relationships that tell us how to solve new problems with which we may be totally unfamiliar (perhaps related to Gardner's "existential intelligence"). In other words, the greater our experience in facing unique and novel conditions, the more we grow and can adapt to the changing conditions around us. Sternberg suggests that confronting novel tasks and situations and learning to deal with them is one of the most important instructional goals in learning intelligent behavior. This part of intelligence is governed by how well one learns to adapt to the environment (change his or her way of doing things to fit the world), to select from the environment (avoid unfamiliar things and choose familiar and comfortable ones), and to shape the environment (change it to fit a personal way of doing things). Therefore, perhaps the most important aspect of Sternberg's definition of intelligence is that intelligence results as much from how people learn to cope with the world around them as it results from the internal mental processes with which they are born (e.g., memory, symbol manipulation, mental speed).

This notion of coping is expressed by 20 characteristics that Sternberg (1994, 1995) suggests often impede intelligent behavior:

- Lack of motivation
- Lack of impulse control
- Lack of perseverance
- Using the wrong abilities
- Inability to translate thought into action
- Lack of a product orientation
- Inability to complete tasks and to follow through
- Failure to initiate
- Fear of failure
- Procrastination
- Misattribution of blame
- Excessive self-pity
- Excessive dependency
- Wallowing in personal difficulties
- Distractibility and lack of concentration
- Spreading oneself too thin
- Inability to delay gratification
- Inability or unwillingness to see the forest for the trees
- Lack of balance between critical thinking and creative thinking
- Too little or too much self-confidence

According to Sternberg and Grigorenko (2001), many aspects of intelligence, such as those, can and should be taught and the classroom is the logical place to convey the attitudes and behaviors that can help learners avoid these impediments to intelligent behavior.

THE EFFECTS OF PRIOR ACHIEVEMENT ON LEARNING

The effectiveness of your instruction will depend, in part, on the task-relevant prior knowledge and skill your learners bring to a lesson. *Task relevant* means those facts, skills, and understandings that must have been taught in order for subsequent learning to occur. The prior knowledge of your learners is important not only for planning lessons at your learners' current level of understanding but also for knowing why desired lesson outcomes may have been partially attained by some learners and not at all by others.

Task-relevant facts, skills, and understandings come in various shapes and sizes. In each content area, they are part of the logical progression of ideas with which a lesson is

Figure 2.2 Organization of content indicating a logical progression for a unit on government

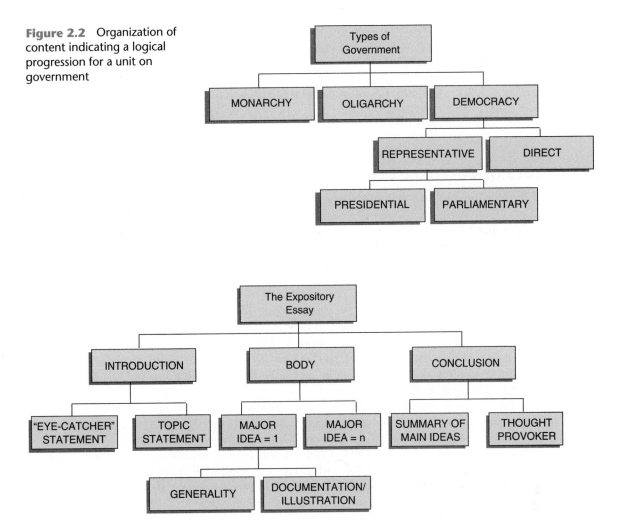

Figure 2.3 Organization of content indicating a logical progression for a unit on writing skills

conveyed. For example, various ways of reasoning may be used to present the contents of a lesson, for example, from general to detailed, simple to complex, abstract to concrete, or conceptual to procedural. These logical progressions are called **learning structures** that identify what needs to be known by the learner at each previous step before new learning can take place (e.g., concepts must come before procedures, and simple facts must come before concepts). Task-relevant knowledge, skills, and understandings are indicated by the learning structure. And it is on this task-relevant knowledge, skill, and understanding that the final outcomes of a lesson or unit depend. This point is illustrated in Figure 2.2 for a high school unit on government and Figure 2.3 for an elementary school unit on writing skills.

Notice that in Figure 2.2, the concepts of presidential and parliamentary would have to be learned before the concept of a representative democracy could be understood. And the concepts of monarchy, oligarchy, and democracy would have to be learned before attaining an understanding of types of government. These task-relevant prior understandings provide a structure for learning that allows larger concepts, principles, and generalizations to be learned at the end of a lesson or unit. Notice that a breakdown in the flow of learning at almost any level would prevent learning from taking place at any subsequent level. Failure to attain concepts at higher levels in the unit plan may not indicate a lack of learner ability but a failure to have adequately attained task-relevant prior understandings. Variation in your students' task-relevant facts, knowledge, and understandings can have a significant effect on their future learning. Classroom tests and diagnostic profiles from standardized achievement tests can help indicate the task-relevant achievement that may be needed before your unit and lesson plans can be successful. But the careful inclusion of task-relevant knowledge, skills, and understandings in previous lessons will be your best guide to successful lesson planning.

THE EFFECTS OF CULTURAL DIFFERENCES ON LEARNING

Although the physical school setting has remained largely unchanged over the past 75 years, the major participants—the students—have not. The typical classroom of today contains a more diverse group of learners than at any time in our history. Today, a large number of public school students represent non-European cultures and speak a variety of languages. For millions of students, English is not the native language. This diversity reflects not only the culture that children bring to school, but also the language, learning, and motivational skills that accompany them (Bruner, 1996; Olneck, 2001). It is no longer accurate to say that we are a nation and an educational system with minorities; rather, we are a nation and an educational system of minorities. Currently, nonwhite students make up over 40% of all students in America (Sable & Hoffman, 2005). And non-Anglo students currently make up the majority of learners in our 27 largest school districts. Add to this medley of cultures in our schools an increasingly diverse assortment of family patterns and lifestyles (Sable & Hoffman, 2005).

The result of this cultural, familial, linguistic, and socioeconomic diversity is an ever-increasing range of individual differences in the classroom. This diversity must be matched by the diversity in how teachers plan for it. For example, the research of Bowers and Flinders (1991); Cheng (1996, 1998); Cheng, Chen, Tsubo, Sekandari, and Alfafara-Killacky (1997); Griggs and Dunn (1995); and Tharp and Gallimore (1989) present convincing arguments that different cultures react differently to the nonverbal and verbal classroom management techniques of proximity control, eye contact, warnings, and classroom arrangement. Research suggests that students from Hispanic and Asian cultures respond more positively to a quiet, private correction, as opposed to a public display such as listing their name on the board (Adeed & Smith in Banks, 1997; Cheng, 1998; Lockwood & Secada, 1999; Saito, 1999; Walqui, 2000a). Furthermore, these authors cite numerous examples of how teachers from one culture interpret behaviors of children differently than teachers from another culture (for example, with respect to the degree of unsolicited talk and movement that is accepted in the classroom). This has been called **reciprocal distancing** (Larson & Irvine, 1999).

In one form of reciprocal distancing, teachers and students (both consciously and unconsciously) use language to include or exclude various individuals from the group. For example, in an exchange between a Caucasian teacher and her African American students about Martin Luther King, students use the pronoun "we" to clearly position themselves as members of a group that excluded the teacher. And the teacher, in kind, chooses a response that distances her from the class. Here are two examples of the effects of the reciprocal distancing on learners:

◆   ◆   ◆

[An African American boy takes a picture of Martin Luther King out of his desk to color.]

Teacher:	Let's not look at that now! That's after lunch.
Student:	I like him. I just want to look at him.
Teacher:	Well, that's nice. Put him away. We'll do Martin Luther King after lunch.

[An African American boy across the room calls out, "*We* call him Dr. King."]

Teacher: He's not a real doctor like you go to for a cold or sore throat. . . . (Larson & Irvine, 1999, p. 395)

◆   ◆   ◆

To capitalize on the positive aspects of group membership and encourage a sense of inclusion rather than distancing, many teachers implement discussion sessions, student teams, small groups, and the sharing of instructional materials to create opportunities for positive social interaction among their students. These various forms of cooperative learning provide alternatives to the traditional lecture/presentation format that can heighten motivation and the excitement of learning (Jacobs, Power & Loh, 2002; Johnson & Johnson, 1996).

Along with this diversity comes a need to be aware of potential biases related to diversity. For example, gender-, racial-, and ethnic-specific clothing, dialect, and mannerisms can lead us to expect and look for one type of behavior more than another or to place stereotypic interpretations on classroom behavior to which gender, race, and ethnicity have no relationship (Santos & Reese, 1999). These researchers remind us that some of the teaching techniques you will study and use in your classroom will be culturally sensitive.

Miller (2000); Antón-Oldenburg (2000); Diller (1999); and Santos and Reese (1999) suggest a number of ways teachers can develop the ability to interact smoothly and effectively with members of various cultures—or, in other words, achieve "intercultural competence" (Lustig & Koester, 1998). Walqui (2000a) notes that one of the most important is that teachers and students work together to construct a culture that values the strengths of all participants and respects their interests, abilities, languages, and dialects. Another is the important role of cooperative grouping where culturally different learners must act together to accomplish group goals. In the chapters to follow we will discuss the important role of cooperative grouping as a tool for developing intercultural competence as well as many other techniques for teaching in culturally diverse classrooms.

Socioeconomic and Cultural Diversity

Researchers have studied the relationship among social class, culture/ethnicity, and school achievement (Banks & Banks, 2001; Mansnerus, 1992; Sleeter & Grant, 1991). Their studies generally conclude that most differences in educational achievement occurring among racial and ethnic groups can be accounted for by social class, *even after the lower socioeconomic status (SES) of minority groups is considered* (Gamoran, 1992; Levine & Havinghurst, 1984). In other words, if you know the SES of a group of students, you can pretty much predict their achievement with some accuracy. Information about their racial and ethnic group does little to improve the prediction.

It is now appropriate to ask, "What is it about SES that creates differences in the classroom?" and "What can I as a teacher do to lessen these differences?" Obviously, if SES plays such an important role in student achievement, it must stand for something more specific than income and the educational level of parents. Research has provided a number of more meaningful characteristics of the home and family lives of higher-and lower-SES families. These characteristics—which are the indirect results of income and education—are thought to influence the achievement of schoolchildren.

The U.S. Bureau of the Census (2002) estimated that as many as 35 million Americans may be living in poverty, including 20% of all children. One characteristic that seems to distinguish children of those who do and do not live in poverty is that the latter are more likely to acquire knowledge of the world outside their home and neighborhood at an earlier age.

Through greater access to books, magazines, social networks, cultural events, and others who have these learning resources, middle- and upper-class students develop their reading and speaking abilities more rapidly. This, in combination with parental teaching (which tends to use the formal or elaborated language that trains the child to think independently of the specific communication context), may give students in the middle and upper classes an advantage at the start of school. This contrasts with children who come from lower-class homes, which may emphasize obedience and conformity more than independent thinking and may emphasize rote learning (memorization, recall of facts, etc.) more than independent, self-directed learning (Christenson, Rounds, & Franklin, 1992).

Contributing to these differences is the fact that 70% of working-age mothers of disadvantaged students must work. In the last 30 years, the composition of the family has undergone a dramatic change. The traditional family unit is no longer the rule, but the exception. In 1965, more than 60% of American families were traditional: a working father and a mother who kept the house and took care of the children. Only 10% of today's families represent the traditional family of past generations. Today's family is more likely to be a dual-career family, a single-parent family, a stepfamily, or a family that has moved an average of 14 times. All of these conditions affect the fabric of the family and the development of the school-age learners within it.

By some estimates, the majority of children now being born will live in a household where there is no adult 10 to 12 hours a day. Less time for parents to become involved in their child's education, more distracting lifestyles, and greater job and occupational stress can be expected to contribute to the growing numbers of disadvantaged learners. Some time ago H. Levin (1986) estimated that the educationally disadvantaged comprise more than one third of all school-age children. Today, this proportion is even larger (U.S. Census Bureau, 2002). These learners are less likely to be immunized, more likely to be in poorer health, less ready to enter school, and more likely to experience academic failure and to drop out.

Language and Cultural Diversity

Minami and Ovando (2001), Valencia (1997), and Delgado-Gaitan (1992) point to the important role of language in accounting for achievement difficulties of minority and immigrant learners. Many teachers are now responsible for teaching children with limited or no English-language capacity in classrooms that include students who may speak many different languages. For example, more than 100 languages are spoken in the school systems of New York City, Chicago, and Los Angeles, Spanish being the language most frequently spoken by new immigrants (McDonnell & Hill, 1993). These researchers point out that if language is used by a cultural group differently at home than in the classroom, members of that subculture are at a disadvantage. Children whose language at home corresponds to that expected in the classroom more easily transfer their prior experiences to the classroom in ways that facilitates their academic progress. Learners who speak another language in the home than at school often experience difficulties transferring what they already know to classroom tasks and are often misunderstood.

Some have accounted for the differences between cultural minorities and mainstream learners by pointing out what minority learners lack in order to do well in school, the most prominent being proficiency in English and the Standard American English dialect prominent among Anglo Americans and the middle and upper social economic classes. Using genetically or culturally inspired factors to explain these differences, such as aptitude and language, has come to be called the **cultural deficit model** (Herrnstein & Murray, 1994; Jensen, 1969, 1998). The cultural deficit model has been strongly criticized for providing what is missing in the child, not what must be provided to the child for school performance to improve.

Although the cultural deficit model has influenced instructional practice (for example, with the practice of tracking), it has come to be replaced with another way of thinking about diversity, called the **cultural difference model**, which itself is undergoing some reformulation. Rather than focus on a learner's "deficits," the cultural difference model focuses on solutions that require more culturally sensitive links to and responses from the school and educational system that can improve the performance of students who are socially, economically, and linguistically different from the mainstream. In other words, the school's role is not to eliminate or diminish a child's use of his or her home language or dialect or culturally ingrained learning style but to compensate for it by providing a rich and natural instructional environment that circumvents the effects these contextual factors may have on learning and uses them as a valued vehicle in which to transmit learning.

More recently the cultural difference model has been revised and built upon by Ogbu, (1995a, 1995b, 2003). Ogbu's research suggests that while one's cultural history may cause him or her to respond differently to school, it is the individual's **cultural frame** of reference acquired from experience that is the lens through which one interprets and responds to life's events. It is these cultural frames, not just one's cultural status, that can sometimes provide a better explanation of why children respond to school differently. For example, when the cultural frame about schooling acquired from home is positive, differences between home and school are easily overcome. But when the cultural frame is negative, these differences are harder to overcome. And cultural frames may not only derive from home and one's cultural history, because some frames are shared by learners independent of culture or minority status. What is popular, places to hang out, participation in athletics, and readiness to read may all be shared by the same individuals who do not have a common cultural history or home life, making the individual's acquired frame of reference an important addition to the cultural difference model for explaining school performance among learners.

Here are some suggestions for teachers that derive from these models that can lessen the relationship between culture and school achievement:

- Provide more opportunities for learners to experience indirect and self-directed models of instruction to which they can bring their own background and experiences to the classroom.
- Maintain high expectations for all learners, regardless of diversity. The overall learning environment should be leveled up, not scaled down.
- Include parents in the planning and implementing of important changes in curriculum, instructional techniques, and assessment aimed at eliminating the differences in performance among learners.
- Form groups heterogeneously that include culturally as well as linguistically diverse students.
- Learn and experiment with instructional techniques suitable for diverse learners, such as cooperative learning, peer tutoring, and within-class heterogeneous grouping.

The Teacher's Role in Improving Achievement Among Culturally and Language-Diverse Learners

The classroom is the logical place to begin the process of reducing some of the achievement differences that have been noted between lower-and middle/upper-SES and language-diverse students. Disadvantaged and language-diverse learners have an important characteristic in common. Both have difficulty in expressing their past experience and knowledge in a format that is expected by the teacher and used by other learners, which can produce a classroom of many silent learners. Many formal interventions are trying to reduce these effects, from preschools to federally funded compensatory education programs. However, these interventions and programs are not likely to eliminate achievement differences among various groups of students who have highly divergent home and family lifestyles.

This leaves the teacher to plan for these differences as a daily fact of classroom life. The general tendencies are clear: The home and family backgrounds of lower- and higher-SES and English-language learners differentially prepare them for school. For the classroom teacher, the task becomes one of planning instruction around these differences in ways that reduce them as much as possible.

There are several ways you can reduce these achievement differences in your classroom. One of these is your willingness to incorporate a variety of learning aids (such as computer instructional software, audiovisuals, learning centers, and exploratory materials) into your lessons. This variety of materials encourages your learners to use their own experiences, past learnings, and preferred learning modalities in which to construct and demonstrate what they have learned. Lesson variety can be an important resource for those who may benefit from alternative ways of learning.

Another way in which to reduce achievement differences is to have high expectations for all your students and to reward them for their accomplishments. Sufficiently high expectations and rewards for learning outside the classroom may not be equally available to all of your learners; thus your support and encouragement for learners to bring their personal experiences and culture into the classroom is important. Your role in providing high expectations, support, and encouragement could be instrumental in bridging some of the differences in achievement among your learners.

Finally, as an effective teacher in a diverse classroom, you will need to provide learners the opportunity to express their own sense of what they know and to build connections or relationships among the ideas and facts being taught using their own experiences. Encourage learners to construct their own meanings and express their understandings in a form that is most comfortable to them, linguistically and culturally. This has two important effects in helping you attain the instructional goals of your classroom: It promotes student engagement and interest in school while showing them that someone thinks they have something worthwhile to say.

Other ways you can reduce the differences among learners in your classroom include the following:

1. Organizing learning and instruction around important ideas that your students already know something about
2. Acknowledging the importance of your students' prior learning by having them compare what they know with what you are teaching
3. Challenging the adequacy of your students' prior knowledge by designing lessons that create the opportunity for your students to resolve conflict and construct new meanings for themselves
4. Providing some tasks that make students confront ambiguity and uncertainty by exploring problems that have multiple solutions in authentic, real-world contexts
5. Teaching students how to find their own approaches or systems for achieving educational goals, for which they can take ownership
6. Teaching students that knowledge construction is a collaborative effort rather than a solitary search of knowledge or an exclusively teacher-controlled activity

7. Monitoring and assessing a student's knowledge acquisition frequently and providing feedback during the lesson

It is evident that teachers will increasingly need to implement suggestions such as these as they face greater diversity in race, culture, language, and social class and in a larger number of combinations than ever before.

THE EFFECTS OF PERSONALITY AND LEARNING STYLE

Preceding sections discussed the potential influence on learning of students' general intelligence, specific aptitude, prior achievement, and culture. In this section we add your students' personalities and learning styles to this equation.

When words such as *trustworthy, creative, independent, anxious, cheerful, authoritarian,* or *aggressive* are used to describe a student, they refer to an aspect of that student's personality. Personality is the integration of one's traits, motives, beliefs, and abilities, including emotional responses, character, and even values.

Some parts of personalities lie dormant until stimulated into action by some event. This is the reason teachers often are dismayed to hear, for example, that an aggressive child in fifth-period social studies is shy and cooperative in someone else's seventh-period mathematics. It also is the reason that some students and teachers may never quite see eye to eye. Although such personality conflicts are rare, they can be harmful to classroom rapport if left to smolder beneath the surface. Let's look at some crises of the school years to better understand the role of personality in the classroom.

Erikson's Crises of the School Years

Some psychologists believe that different personality traits dominate at certain periods of our lives. For example, Erikson (1968), who developed a theory on how we form our personalities, hypothesized eight different stages of personality growth between infancy and old age that he called *crises.* Three of these stages, shown in Figure 2.4, occur during the school years:

1. The crisis of accomplishment versus inferiority
2. The crisis of identity versus role confusion
3. The crisis of intimacy versus isolation

During the first crisis, of accomplishment versus inferiority, the learner seeks ways of producing products or accomplishments that are respected by others. In this manner the child creates a feeling of worth to dispel feelings of inferiority or inadequacy that result from competing in a world where adults appear confident and competent. At first, such accomplishments may take the easiest course—being good at sports, being good in school, or being helpful at home. For the teacher this is a particularly challenging time, because student engagement at high rates of success is needed to keep some feelings of worth focused in the classroom. Seeing that every student has some successful experiences in the classroom can be an important vehicle for helping students through this crisis.

Erikson's second crisis during the school years is precipitated by the student's need to understand oneself—to find his or her identity, "the real me." One's gender, race, ethnicity, religion, and physical attractiveness can play important roles in producing—or failing to produce—a consistent and acceptable self-image. This is a process of accepting oneself as one truly is, apart from illusions, made-up images, and exaggerations.

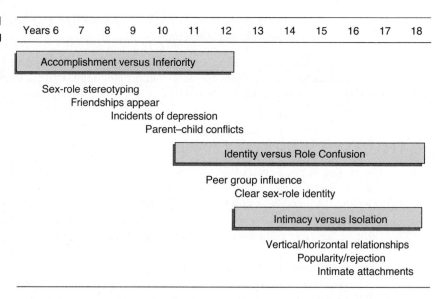

Figure 2.4 Personal and social development during Erikson's three crises during the school years

Social psychologists believe that, in the process of finding and accepting oneself during this crisis, the individual must experience *recognition*, a sense of *control* over her or his environment, and *achievement*. Being a member of a group intensifies these needs. Social psychologists, such as Patricia and Richard Schmuck (2001), urge teachers to recognize that groups help provide opportunities for recognition, control, and achievement and to use this heightened motivation to achieve academic goals. And they caution that classrooms failing to satisfy these three basic needs may contain large numbers of learners who feel rejected, listless, and powerless, creating motivational and conduct problems within the classroom.

Erikson's third crisis during the school years is that of giving up part of one's identity to develop close and intimate relationships with others. Learning how to get along with teachers, parents, and classmates is one of the key developmental tasks learners must master to successfully resolve this crisis. Successful relationships with parents and teachers, referred to as **vertical relationships** (Hartup, 1989), meet a learner's needs for safety, security, and protection. Successful relationships with peers, referred to as **horizontal relationships**, are of equal developmental significance for learners. They meet learners' needs for belonging and allow them to acquire and practice important social skills. Providing opportunities for learners to develop healthy relationships when they enter school helps them develop skills important in getting along with others, helping others, and establishing intimacy. The failure to experience healthy horizontal relationships and learn friendship-building attitudes and skills can have undesirable consequences. This failure often results in *social rejection*.

Research suggests that rejected children are more likely to be aggressive and disruptive in school (Hartup, 1989), experience intense feelings of loneliness (Cassidy & Asher, 1992), and suffer emotional disturbances in adolescence and adulthood (T.J. Dishon, Patterson, Stoolmiller, & Skinner, 1991). Nevertheless, researchers have shown that learners can be taught some of the social skills necessary to gain acceptance by peers. More importantly, by helping your learners construct their own well-functioning horizontal relationships, they will acquire friendship-building attitudes and skills that can have desirable consequences in your classroom.

To help meet your learners' needs during these three crises during the school years, teachers can actively engage learners in ways that let them express themselves

Successful relationships with peers, referred to as horizontal relationships, meet learners' needs for belonging and allow them to acquire and practice important social skills. These friendship patterns often are created through peer groups that exhibit strong commitments of loyalty, protection, and mutual benefit.

and their uniqueness. Here are some example activities that provide learners opportunities for recognition, control, and achievement during these critical school years:

- Art (e.g., drawing, sketching, and painting)
- Autobiographical recollections (e.g., of a major event growing up)
- Oral histories of personal experiences (e.g., of a vacation)
- Cooperative activities (e.g., team or group projects)
- Demonstrations and exhibits (e.g., use of poster boards)
- Discussions of a completed classroom activity (e.g., debriefing)
- Drama/improvisation (e.g., reenactments of personal or historical events)
- Acting/role playing (e.g., making believe you're someone else)
- Portfolios (e.g., accumulating drafts that show change or growth)
- Projects (e.g., solving a school, community, or national problem)
- Storytelling (e.g., reading aloud or in a group)

Learning Style

An aspect of personality that will influence your learners' achievement is their **learning style**, representing the classroom conditions under which someone prefers to learn. Although there are a number of learning styles, the one most studied has been identified as field dependence and field independence.

Field Dependence Versus Field Independence

Much has been written about how some learners are more global than analytic in how they approach learning (Irvine & York, 2001). Some researchers use the terms *holistic/visual* to describe global learners and *verbal/analytic* to describe the opposite style or orientation

(Tharp & Gallimore, 1989). Still others prefer the term *field sensitive* to refer to the holistic/visual learning style and the term *field insensitive* to refer to the verbal/analytic learning style. To what are these researchers referring?

Basically, these terms have come to refer to how people view the world. People who are **field dependent** see the world in terms of large, connected patterns. Looking at a volcano, for example, a field-dependent person would notice its overall shape and its major colors and topographical features. A **field-independent** person, in contrast, would tend to notice the specific parts of a scene. Thus she might notice more the individual trees, the different rocks, the size of the caldera, where the caldera sits in relation to the rest of the structure, topographical features showing the extent of lava flow, and so on.

Franklin (1992) and Tharp (1989) believe that field dependence and independence are stable traits of individuals affecting different aspects of their lives, especially their approach to learning. Table 2.2 summarizes some of the characteristics associated with both types of learners. These researchers agree that the different personality characteristics or traits of field-dependent and field-independent learners suggest that at least some learners think about and process information differently during classroom learning activities. Those authors suggest that each group would benefit from different instructional strategies, as suggested in Table 2.3.

Learning Style and Culture. Educators have become interested in the relationship between learning style and culture. The work of several researchers has suggested that Native Americans, Hispanic Americans, and African Americans are more field-dependent than Anglo Americans and Asian Americans (Bennett, 1990; Cushner et al., 1992; Garcia, 1991; Hilliard, 1992; Tharp, 1989). These researchers advocate that teachers who work with these groups of learners use more field-dependent teaching styles.

What evidence have these studies found that suggests minority groups have different learning styles than Anglo Americans? Although the evidence is sometimes inconsistent, in general, some evidence suggests that minority learners are more visual/holistic or field dependent in their approach to learning than verbal/analytic or field independent. Shade

Table 2.2 Field-dependent and field-independent learner characteristics.

Field-Dependent (Field-Sensitive) Learners	Field-Independent Learners
1. Perceives global aspects of concepts and materials	1. Focuses on details of curriculum material
2. Personalizes curriculum—relates concepts to personal experience	2. Focuses on facts and principles
3. Seeks guidance and demonstrations from teacher	3. Rarely seeks physical contact with teacher
4. Seeks rewards that strengthen relationship with teacher	4. Formal interactions with teacher are restricted to tasks at hand—seeks nonsocial rewards
5. Prefers to work with others and is sensitive to their feelings and opinions	5. Prefers to work alone
6. Likes to cooperate	6. Likes to compete
7. Prefers organization provided by teacher	7. Can organize information by himself or herself

Table 2.3 Instructional strategies for field-dependent and field-independent learners.

Field-Dependent (Field-Sensitive) Learners	Field-Independent Learners
1. Display physical and verbal experiences of approval or warmth.	1. Be direct in interactions with learners; show content expertise.
2. Motivate by use of social and tangible rewards.	2. Motivate by use of nonsocial rewards such as grades.
3. Use cooperative learning strategies.	3. Use more mastery learning and errorless teaching strategies.
4. Use corrective feedback often.	4. Use corrective feedback only when necessary.
5. Allow interaction during learning.	5. Emphasize independent projects.
6. Structure lessons, projects, homework, etc.	6. Allow learners to develop their own structure.
7. Assume role of presenter, demonstrator, checker, reinforcer, grader, materials designer.	7. Assume role of consultant, listener, negotiator, facilitator.

(1982) presented evidence suggesting that African American learners have a learning style emphasizing field-dependent or person-oriented classroom activities (cooperative learning and activities that focus on people and what they do, rather than on things or objects). Other researchers (Irvine & York, 2001) concluded that Mexican Americans are more field dependent as a group than Anglo Americans. Some of these authors explain the higher relative performance of this group on measures of field dependence by pointing out that the child-rearing practices of this group stress strong family ties and respect and obedience to elders. These experiences, the authors conclude, lead to a more field-dependent learning style.

Cultural Differences in Learning Styles: Some Cautions.   Is there sufficient justification to advocate field-dependent teaching styles in classrooms with significant numbers of minority learners? Should teachers make greater use of instructional practices that emphasize cooperative learning, person and movement/action-oriented activities, visual/holistic learning, and so on, when teaching significant numbers of African, Hispanic, or Native American learners? Before implementing culturally responsive teaching without qualification, keep in mind the following cautions:

   1. *Beware of perpetuating stereotypes.* Grant (1991) cautions that cultural information such as that described previously may be used to "perpetuate ideas from the cultural deficit hypothesis that encourages teachers to believe that these students have deficits and negative differences and, therefore, are not as capable of learning as white students" (p. 245). Others (Valencia, 1997; Weisner, Gallimore, & Jordan, 1988) suggest that cultural explanations of differential achievement of minority groups often result in global and stereotypical descriptions of how minority cultures behave that exceed available evidence. Kendall (1983) argues that it is one thing to be aware of the potential effect of culture-specific learning and learning styles on classroom achievement but another to expect a child of a particular group to behave and to learn in a particular way.

   2. *Note within-group differences.* Almost all studies of the learning style preferences of different minority groups have shown that differences within the cultural groups studied were as great as the differences between the cultural groups (Cushner et al., 1992; Tharp, 1989). In other words, Native Americans, Hispanic Americans, African Americans, and Anglo Americans vary considerably on tests of field dependence and independence.

Some Anglo Americans will be field dependent in their pattern of scores, and some Native Americans will be field independent. On the average, the groups may differ. But around these averages are ranges of considerable magnitude. Thus using a field-dependent teaching style, even in a monocultural classroom, may fail to match the preferred learning style of at least some learners.

3. *Culturally responsive teaching may be more difficult in multicultural classrooms.* Culturally responsive teaching appears to be most efficient and practical in monocultural classrooms. In classrooms that are multicultural, it may be difficult to match the different learning styles of different groups of children representing several different cultures.

4. *Culturally responsive concerns may take the focus away from "expert practice."* Educators such as Lindsley (1992) argue that, before assuming that differences in achievement are due to characteristics within the learner (for example, learning style), factors external to the learner, such as ineffective teaching practices, should be ruled out. Also, the quality of instruction provided to minority learners should be equivalent to that provided to Anglo Americans. Majority- and minority-group learners should experience similar schooling in terms of resources, quality of teachers, expectations, expert practice in instruction, testing, and motivation techniques before teachers embrace specialized techniques specifically adapted to minorities. Although some evidence indicates that African American and Native American children improve in reading and math with culturally responsive teaching techniques (Franklin, 1992; Tharp, 1989), studies fail to indicate that expert instruction using traditional instructional methods could not have achieved the same or similar results.

THE EFFECTS OF THE PEER GROUP ON LEARNING

As a teacher you will quickly notice that one of the most powerful influences on a student's behavior is the peer group. Often considered as the source of a hidden curriculum, the peer group can influence and even teach students how to behave in class, study for tests, and converse with teachers and school administrators, and it can contribute to the success or failure of performance in school in many other ways. From the play group in elementary school to the teenage clique in high school, a student learns from peers how to behave in ways that are acceptable to the group and will establish status in the eyes of others.

The power of the peer group in influencing student behavior comes from the voluntary submission of one's will to some larger cause. Teachers and parents must sometimes beg, plead, cajole, and reward to exact appropriate behavior from their students, sons, and daughters. But peer groups need not engage in any of these behaviors to obtain a high level of conformity to often unstated principles of behavior. Trendy school fashions, new slang words, places to hang out, acceptable social mates, and respected forms of out-of-school activities are communicated and learned to perfection without lesson plans, texts, or even direct verbalization. Instead, these and other behaviors are transmitted by "salient others" and received by those who anxiously wish to maintain membership in or gain acceptance to a particular peer group.

Friendship patterns often are created through peer groups and sometimes are adhered to with strong commitments of loyalty, protection, and mutual benefit. These commitments can create individual peer cultures or even gangs within a school. Such cultures can rival the academic commitments made in the classroom and frequently supersede them in importance.

Studying for a test or completing homework frequently may be sacrificed for the benefit of the peer group. Peer groups can form on the basis of many different individual differences, such as intelligence, achievement, personality, home life, physical appearance, and personal and social interests. But they commonly result from complex combinations of these factors that are not always discernible to outsiders and sometimes not even to those within the peer group (Hartup, 1989; Schmuck & Schmuck, 2001).

The importance of peer group characteristics in the classroom lies in the extent to which they can be used to promote behaviors that enhance a member's engagement in the learning process. Here are several approaches for constructively using peer relationships to foster classroom goals:

1. *Stress group work in which members are from different peer groups.* When forming work or cooperative groups, be sure group members represent different backgrounds and interests, which can bring different skills and talents to an assignment. When different types of individuals are assigned to work cooperatively, group behavior tends to follow a middle ground, discouraging extreme or disruptive behavior.

2. *Conduct a group discussion of class norms, describing what class members should and should not do to be socially acceptable.* Tell group members what you expect of them, and give some examples of what they might expect of others. Glasser (1998a) suggests discussing with students ideas on how the class might be run, problems that may interfere with the group's performance, and needed rules and routines.

3. *Build group cohesiveness by promoting the attractiveness of each student to one another.* Provide opportunities for your students to know one another through one or more of the following: Construct a bulletin board around the theme of friendships; have students write a brief biography about themselves for all to read; publish a class directory that includes names, hobbies, jobs, and career aspirations; and have students bring something they have made or really care about (a toy, tool, model, etc.).

4. *Assign older or more mature students who are more likely to be respected as role models to interact with and help younger students in a peer tutoring situation.* Many schools

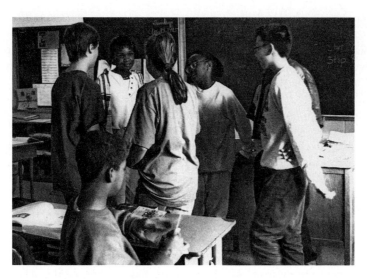

An important way to positively influence peer groups in your classroom is to conduct group discussions of class norms, describing what class members should and should not do to be socially acceptable, what you expect of them, and what they should expect of each other.

have a formal peer tutoring program called *cross-age tutoring,* in which tutors may be chosen from higher grades to help younger students who may be at risk or discouraged learners. Research has shown that tutoring has been most successful when tutors have been trained and given explicit instruction on how to tutor.

THE EFFECTS OF HOME LIFE AND SOCIAL CONTEXT ON LEARNING

Closely connected with the influence of the peer group on learning is the social context in which your learners live, play, and work. Among the most prominent sources of influence in this context will be your learners' family and its relationship to the school.

In 1993, the National Governors Conference for educational reform set forth a formidable agenda for educators. Their agenda, updated and approved by Congress (*Goals 2000: Reforming Education to Improve Student Achievement,* 1998), established the following national goals for education and set out clear and rigorous standards for what every child should know and be able to do:

1. All children in America will start school ready to learn.
2. The high school graduation rate will increase to at least 90%.
3. American students will leave grades 4, 8, and 12 having demonstrated competency over challenging subject matter in the sciences and humanities.
4. The nation's teachers will have access to programs for professional development.
5. American students will be the best in the world in mathematics and science achievement.
6. Every adult American will be literate and will possess the knowledge and skills to compete in a global economy and exercise the rights and responsibilities of citizenship.
7. Every school in America will be free of drugs and violence and will offer a disciplined environment conducive to learning.
8. Every school will promote parental involvement and participation to promote the social, emotional, and academic growth of children.

(See related strategies on the Web at *www.ed.gov/legislation/GOALS2000/TheAct/* and at *www.ed.gov/pubs/G2KReforming/index.html.*)

A theme throughout the commentaries on the governors' agenda was the realization that schools would have to develop genuine partnerships with parents to achieve these goals. A singular focus on just teachers, parents, or administrators as the agents of reform would not produce the hoped-for results. Only the active participation of parents, community groups, and educators in partnership with one another to create a "learning culture" would bring about the desired objectives (Lambert, 1991).

When parents and teachers become partners, not only can student achievement increase, but also parents can learn about you and your school. Research confirms that coordination and collaboration between home and school improve learner achievement, attitude toward school, classroom conduct, and parent and teacher morale (Cochran & Dean, 1991). As INTASC Principle 10 states, establishing genuine partnerships with the parents and guardians of your learners is as essential a teacher practice as those that involve building a cohesive classroom climate, establishing a well-managed work environment, developing goals and objectives, conducting effective instruction, and assessing student performance. The practice of parent involvement requires that throughout the school year you develop and strengthen "linking mechanisms" for parent participation and collaboration.

Family–school linking mechanisms are opportunities for school and family involvement and may involve parent–teacher conferences, home visits, participation of teachers in community events, newsletters, phone calls, personal notes, volunteering as classroom aides, and the use of home-based curriculum materials. These efforts require more than just a handout sent home to parents at the beginning of the school year, an obligatory presentation during back-to-school night, or an occasional note home. The opportunities to develop and nurture linking mechanisms will be the culmination of your efforts to build a successful classroom workplace.

To assist in this process, Bronfenbrenner (1989, 2005) has urged us to view the family–school partnership from a **systems-ecological perspective**. Bronfenbrenner looks at the learner as a naturalist looks at nature—as an ecosystem. In the learner's ecosystem, the major systems include the family, school, and peer group.

One way to picture the learner's ecosystem is as a series of concentric circles, as shown in Figure 2.5. Each of these circles and their connections has a special term. The most central layer is called the *microsystem*. It includes all those settings where the child lives or spends significant portions of his or her time: the family, school, classroom, day care setting, playground, and job setting if the child is old enough. Bronfenbrenner (1989) refers to these settings as *subsystems*.

Each subsystem can be viewed within itself as a system. The school system is made up of subsystems that include teachers, administrators, support personnel, school board members, and learners. The family system includes a marital, parental, sibling, and often a grandparental subsystem. The peer system includes social friendships, academic friendships, and sports or hobby friendships.

The next layer of the system includes those subsystems the child does not directly experience but that affect the child because of the influence they exert on the microsystem. This layer is called the *exosystem*. It may include the parents' workplace, their friends, the PTA, the school board, and so on.

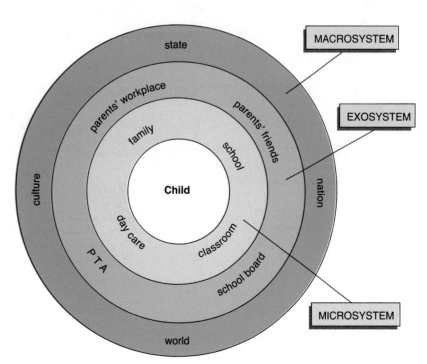

Figure 2.5 The child from a systems-ecological perspective

Finally, both microsystems and exosystems exist in a larger setting called the *macro-system.* This system refers to the larger culture or society in which the micro- and exosystems function. Figure 2.6 indicates some of the relationships among these systems.

A systems-ecological perspective urges us to view a learner's behavior, not as a product of that individual alone, but as a product of the learner and the demands and forces operating within the systems of which the learner is a member. Family experiences and the culture of the family system influence school behavior and performance, which, in turn, affect the family system. School adjustment problems, which may be influenced by problems within the family, may, in turn, exacerbate conditions within the family system itself. For example, the parent who never signs and returns a note from the teacher may not be an uninterested and uninvolved parent—as might be assumed. Dynamics within the family system (e.g., other siblings who demand extensive care, adjustment to a new child, or work schedule) may explain the parents' apparent lack of involvement in their child's education.

Thus when trying to understand the behavior of parents, teachers, and learners, the systems-ecological perspective recommends that we first ask ourselves, "What forces within the family–school environment impel the person to act this way?" When the goal is to promote the academic and social development of the learner, the systems-ecological perspective focuses our most immediate concern on the family–school partnership.

Here are some guidelines for understanding and promoting family–school partnerships in your classroom:

1. *View the family from a systems-ecological perspective.* Avoid viewing the behavior of your learners or their mothers or fathers as simply products of individual psychological forces. Instead, recognize that the family system is made up of several subsystems, including

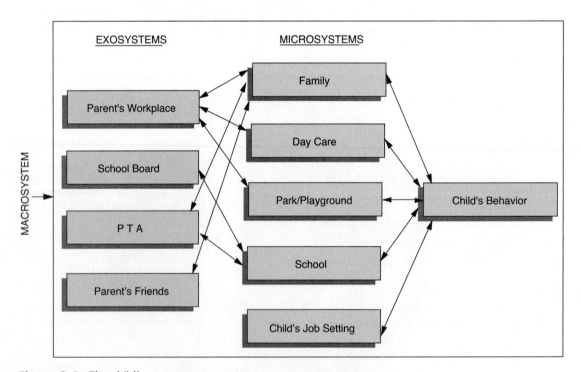

Figure 2.6   The child's ecosystem.

Source: From *The Developing Child,* 6th edition, by Helen Bee. Copyright © 1992 by Allyn and Bacon, Boston, MA. Adapted by permission of the publisher.

the marital subsystem, parental subsystem, the sibling subsystem, and extrafamily or exosystems such as grandparents and employers. Changes in one subsystem inevitably bring about changes in another. Asking parents to take greater responsibility for getting their child to bed earlier at night can result in an argument at home between husband and wife, punishment of the child, teasing by siblings, and concern and criticism by in-laws. Likewise, demands by school staff that parents do something at home to make the child complete homework inevitably reverberate throughout the entire family system. These effects may be so great as to preclude any change in parental behavior.

2. *Acknowledge changes in the American family.* Most families have two working parents. Research on teacher beliefs regarding families in which both parents work shows that teachers believe working parents are less involved with their children's education (Coontz, Parson, & Raley, 1998; Linney & Vernberg, 1983). However, a study conducted by Medrich, Roizen, Rubin, and Burkley (1982) concludes that working and nonworking mothers spend the same amount of time in child-related activities. Furthermore, their data show that children of working mothers are just as involved in extracurricular activities as are the children of nonworking mothers.

Single-parent families make up about 25% of the families of schoolchildren. Yet many teachers view this family pattern as an abnormality (Carlson, 1992). Joyce Epstein, a researcher at the Johns Hopkins Center for Research on Elementary and Middle Schools, reports that teachers have lower expectations for the achievement of children from single-parent families despite the fact that no data support this (Epstein, 1987). Some researchers suggest that the requirements in single-parent families for organization, schedules, routines, and division of responsibilities better prepare children to accept such structure in schools (Aaron, 2001; Linney & Vernberg, 1983).

3. *View parent participation from an empowerment model rather than a deficit model.* Delgado-Gaitan (1991) and Valencia (1997) propose that we view parent participation as a process that involves giving parents both the power and the knowledge to deal with the school system. Typically, deficit model explanations have been offered for reasons why culturally different parents have not become involved with schools. These perspectives sometimes have portrayed parents as passive, incompetent, or unskilled. They propose that parents are unable to become involved in their children's education because they work long hours away from the home or are simply not interested. But Delgado-Gaitan (1992) points out, when examined closely, research has shown that Hispanic families who speak a different language and have a different culture from that of the school do indeed care about their children and possess the capacity to advocate for them. This holds true for African Americans, Hispanic Americans, Native Americans, and other cultural and linguistic groups as well. The question is not can they become genuine partners with the school but how to empower them to do so.

4. *Recognize the unique needs of mothers and fathers when planning opportunities to involve parents.* Turnbull and Turnbull (1986) urge teachers to promote nonsexist views of parenting and parent involvement. They stress that teachers recognize the importance of mothers and fathers when designing home–school linkages. Encourage visiting opportunities for both parents and develop flexible schedules to accommodate the working schedules of both parents. Send information about the children and schooling to both parents. Seek to promote teaching skills in fathers as well as mothers. Finally, give consideration to the father's interests and needs when suggesting ways for parents to work with their children at home.

5. *Appreciate that parents are just like you—they experience periodic emotional, family, and economic problems.* Many parents may have personal, family, work, health, or other problems that remain hidden. Make a special effort to provide the benefit of the doubt, particularly when parents fail to respond in a timely manner to your requests. Carlson (1992)

Video Window

Incorporating the Home Experiences of Culturally Diverse Students into the Classroom

In this video you will see teachers, some of whom have come from culturally diverse homes, speak of the importance of tapping into a student's home experiences as a valuable source of instructional content. You will hear them speak passionately about the importance of teachers believing the parents of culturally diverse students do care about their child's education and that much of the knowledge they have is relevant to your classroom. As you watch this video, look for information that can help you answer the following questions:

- What does the phrase "funds of knowledge" mean?
- What are some ways of using funds of knowledge in your classroom to help you connect with the culturally and linguistically diverse learner?
- What are some of the informal ways in which families communicate knowledge to their children that could be important to your classroom?

 To answer these questions online, go to the Video Windows *module for this chapter on the Companion Website at www.prenhall.com/borich.*

documents the overwhelming economic as well as divorce, custody, and career problems of single parents. Their failure to monitor their child's homework, or attendance, or tardiness to class may be due less to a lack of interest than to attempts to cope with day-to-day problems. When parents do not live up to your expectations, avoid trying to assign personal blame.

6. *Understand the variety of school–family linkages and respect family preferences for different degrees of school participation.* As you are planning for parent involvement early in the school year, consider and evaluate the full range of ways in which parents can participate. These activities can be placed on a continuum anchored on one end by activities that involve parents as receivers of information (parent–teacher conference, notes home, classroom newsletter) and on the other end by activities that involve parents as active educational decision makers (school and classroom advisory councils, site-based management teams, teacher aids, tutoring).

Developing partnerships with the parents of your learners should be as much a focus of your planning for a new school year as your classroom rules, routines, instructional goals, and objectives. As the research suggests, your learners' achievement of academic goals, their adherence to rules and routines, and their attitudes and expectations about school can be enhanced by having parents as partners.

CULTURAL, LINGUISTIC, AND SES BIASES IN THE CLASSROOM

Much of what has been said about individual differences suggests that planning to eliminate bias in classroom teaching can be one of the most significant aspects of becoming an effective teacher. Pintrich and Schunk (2002) remind us that the way in which you interact with your students in the classroom can have a considerable influence on their motivation and attitudes toward school. Consciously or unconsciously, everyone has biases of one kind or another. When applied in ways that affect only our own behavior and not that of others, we use the word *preference*. Biases, on the other hand, are not harmless. They can injure the personal growth and well-being of others and, if left unchecked, can significantly affect the growth and development of learners. Let's look at some of the ways you might show bias.

Many examples of teacher biases have been catalogued. For example, Good and Brophy (2003) summarize how teachers sometimes respond unequally to high and low achievers by more frequently criticizing the wrong answers of low achievers, communicating low expectations, and thereby accepting, and unintentionally encouraging, a low level of performance among some students. Other researchers have documented how some teachers respond differently to students from various cultures and linguistic backgrounds than to those from their own background (Anderson, 1996; Compton-Lilly, 2000; DeLeon, 1996; Lockwood & Secada, 1999; Schwartz, 1998). These researchers identify the following areas in which some teachers have responded differently toward low achievers and/or culturally and linguistically different learners:

- Wait longer for the student to answer.
- Give the answer after the student's slightest hesitation.
- Praise marginal or inaccurate answers.
- Criticize more frequently than other students for having the wrong answer.
- Praise less when the right answer is given.
- Do not give feedback as to why an answer is incorrect.
- Pay attention to (e.g., smile at) and call on low achievers less.
- Seat them further from the teacher.
- Allow the student to give up more easily.

Generally, these findings confirm that teachers usually do not allow more response opportunities and more teacher contact for culturally different or low-achieving learners who may need them.

Other types of bias have been known to affect whom a teacher calls on. For example, Gage and Berliner (1998) identified several biased ways in which teachers called on their students and then analyzed the extent to which experienced teachers actually exhibited these biases in their classrooms. Their biases included calling on students disproportionately in these ways:

- Nonminority group members versus minority group members
- Seated in front half of class versus seated in back half of class
- Nicer-looking students versus average-looking students
- More-able students versus less-able students

Gage and Berliner calculated the number of student–teacher interactions that would be expected by chance for these classifications, and then from observation they determined the actual number of interactions that occurred. Somewhat surprisingly, their results indicate that every teacher showed some bias in these categories. In other words, every teacher favored at least one student classification over another by naming, calling on, requiring information from, and otherwise interacting with those in some classification disproportionately to those not in that classification.

Bias in the way a teacher interacts with students is undesirable in any form, but it is particularly distasteful when it pertains to students who are among a cultural, ethnic, or linguistic minority. Our nation and our educational system are based on respect for individual differences of all types. This means that our classrooms become one of the most important showplaces of our democratic values. It is disturbing that researchers report frequent ethnic bias or cultural insensitivity during student–teacher interactions in mixed ethnic classrooms. Studies (D.Dillon, 1989; Tharp & Gallimore, 1989) have pointed out that many actions of teachers diminish the classroom participation of minority students and/or build resentment because the teachers' actions are culturally incongruent.

Stipek (2002), Gage and Berliner (1998), and Bowers and Flinders (1991) contribute the following suggestions for eliminating bias and increasing cultural sensitivity in the classroom: Each suggestion promotes the equitable distribution of power in the classroom by calling on all students— volunteers as well as nonvolunteers—to increase achievement as well as motivation.

1. Plan to spread your interactions as evenly as possible across student categories by deciding in advance which students to call on. Because the many classifications of potential bias are cumbersome to deal with, choose one or two bias categories you know or suspect you are most vulnerable to.

2. If you plan on giving special assignments only to some of your students, choose the students randomly. Place all of your students' names in a jar, and have one student draw the names of individuals needed for the special assignment. This protects you from inadvertently choosing the same students repeatedly and conveying the impression that you have favorites.

3. Try consciously to pair opposites in what you believe to be a potential area of bias for you; for example, pair minority with nonminority, more able with less able, easy to work with and difficult to work with, and so on. In this manner, when you are interacting with one member of the pair, you will be reminded to interact with the other. Frequently change one member of the pair so your pairing does not become obvious to the class.

4. When you discover a bias, plan a code to remind you of the bias and then embed it within your class notes, text, or lesson plan at appropriate intervals. For example, should you discover you systematically favor more able learners over less able learners, place a code on the margins of your exercise to remind you to choose a less able learner for the next response.

Instead of being pulled along unconsciously by the stream of rapidly paced events in the classroom, you can be an active decision maker who influences the quality of events in your classroom by continually questioning and monitoring your interaction patterns with culturally and linguistically different learners.

FINAL WORD

There is no question that your students' individual differences in intelligence, achievement, personality, culture, peer group, and social context can dramatically affect your teaching methods and classroom achievement. So why place such diverse students in the same classroom? Would it not be more efficient to segregate students by intelligence and achievement level, personality type, degree of disadvantageness, or even according to the most advantageous peer group? The results of such grouping might be quite astounding, if it were tried.

It is difficult to imagine life in such a segregated environment, for we live, work, and play in a world that is complex and diverse. However, our forefathers seriously considered this very question. Their answer is in the first 10 amendments to the U.S. Constitution, known as the Bill of Rights, and in the Declaration of Independence, which gives every citizen the unqualified right to "life, liberty, and the pursuit of happiness." This constitutional guarantee specifically precludes any attempt to advance a single group at the expense of any other group. It even precludes segregating groups when "separate but equal" treatment is accorded them, because even the labeling of groups as different implies inequality, regardless of the motives for forming them.

These are important constitutional implications for the American classroom. They promote an environment that not only tolerates differences among individuals but also celebrates diversity in human potential. In a world complicated by such social and technological problems as pollution, disease, illiteracy, and congestion, we need divergent viewpoints, different abilities, and diverse values to address these problems. No single set of skills, attitudes, temperaments, personalities, or abilities can provide all that is needed to solve our problems. Your willingness to be flexible in your teaching can harness the diversity needed to solve these problems by adapting instruction to the strengths of your learners, by using different instructional approaches in teaching students of differing ethnic and racial backgrounds, and by promoting the family–school partnership. Above all, your teaching must emphasize the importance of all students working cooperatively with each other. In the chapters ahead, we explore many ways of accomplishing these important goals.

SUMMING UP

This chapter introduced you to the diversity of students found in classrooms and how this diversity must be acknowledged in your teaching methods. Its key terms and main points were:

Why Pay Attention to Individual Differences?

1. Early conceptions of teaching viewed students as empty vessels into which the teacher poured the content of the day's lesson. These conceptions failed to consider the effect of individual differences on learning.

2. A knowledge of the individual differences among learners is important (1) to adapt instructional methods to individual learning needs, and (2) to understand and place in perspective the reasons behind the school performance of individual learners.

The Effects of General Intelligence on Learning

3. One misunderstanding that some teachers and parents have about intelligence, or IQ, is that it is a single, unified dimension.

4. Specific aptitudes are more predictive of success in school and specific occupations than is general intelligence.

5. Knowing your learners' specific strengths and weaknesses and altering instructional goals and methods accordingly will contribute to greater learning than will categorizing and teaching your students according to their general intelligence.

The Effects of Prior Achievement on Learning

6. Task-relevant prior learning represents the facts, skills, and understandings that must be taught if subsequent learning is to occur. Mastery of task-relevant prior learning often is required for subsequent learning to take place.

The Effects of Cultural Differences on Learning

7. An important characteristic that distinguishes lower-class children from middle-class and upper-class children is that the latter more rapidly acquire knowledge of the world outside their homes and neighborhoods.

Language and Cultural Diversity

8. The cultural deficit model emphasizes what is missing in the child using genetically or culturally inspired factors, such as aptitude and language, to explain differences among culturally diverse and mainstream students. Rather than focus on a learner's "deficits," the cultural difference model focuses on solutions that require more culturally sensitive links to and responses from the school and educational system that can improve the performance of students who are socially, economically, and linguistically different from the mainstream.

The Effects of Personality and Learning Style

9. Erikson's (1968) three crises during the school years are (1) accomplishment versus inferiority, (2) identity versus confusion, and (3) intimacy versus isolation.

10. Learning style refers to the classroom or environmental conditions under which someone prefers to learn. One of the most frequently studied learning styles is field independence/dependence.

11. Research has shown that some learners to be field sensitive—or holistic/visual learners—whereas others tend to be less field sensitive—or verbal/analytic learners.

12. Before implementing instructional strategies to match students' learning styles, be cautions not to

perpetuate stereotypes and ignore within-group differences.

The Effects of the Peer Group on Learning

13. Peer groups are an influential source of learner behavior both in and out of the classroom. Group work, group norms, group cohesiveness, and cross-age tutoring are means of using peer group influence to foster instructional goals of the classroom.

The Effects of Home Life and Social Context on Learning

14. Closely connected with the influence of peer group on learning is the social context in which your learners live, play, and work. Among the most prominent sources of influence in this

context will be your learners' family and their relationship to the school.

Cultural, Linguistic, and SES Biases in the Classroom

15. Almost every teacher shows some type of bias in interacting with students. Bias may be avoided by
    * Consciously spreading interactions across categories of students toward whom you have identified bias
    * Randomly selecting students for special assignments
    * Covertly pairing students who are opposite in your category of bias and then interacting with both members of the pair
    * Coding class notes to remind yourself to call on students toward whom you may be biased

KEY TERMS

Adaptive teaching, 43
Compensatory approach, 44
Cultural deficit model, 56
Cultural difference model, 57
Cultural frame, 57
Environmentalist position, 45
Family–school linking mechanisms, 67
Field dependent, 62
Field independent, 62
Hereditarian position, 46

Horizontal relationships, 60
Learning structures, 53
Learning style, 61
Reciprocal distancing, 54
Reflective teacher, 42
Remediation approach, 43
Social competence, 46
Systems-ecological perspective, 67
Vertical relationships, 60

DISCUSSION AND PRACTICE QUESTIONS

Questions marked with an asterisk are answered in appendix B. See also the Companion Website for this text at *www.prenhall.com/borich* for more assessment options.

*1. In what two ways might you use knowledge of the individual differences in your classroom to become a more effective teacher?
*2. Describe the environmentalist and hereditarian positions concerning the use of general IQ tests in schools. Devise a counterargument you could use in responding to an argument from an extremist in each camp.
*3. Explain the role that social competence is believed to play in school learning. If behaviors solely related to SES could be eliminated, how might differences in the tested IQ among subgroups of learners change?

*4. Identify some aptitudes or factors that are likely to be more predictive than general IQ of success in selected school subjects and occupations.
5. Give an example of some task-relevant prior knowledge that might be required before each of the following instructional objectives could be taught successfully.

   a. Adding two-digit numbers
   b. Reading latitude and longitude from a map
   c. Writing a four-sentence paragraph
   d. Seeing an amoeba under a microscope
   e. Correctly pronouncing a new two-syllable word
   f. Understanding how the executive branch of government works
   g. Playing 10 minutes of basketball without committing a foul

h. Responding correctly to a fire alarm
i. Solving the equation $c^2 = a^2 + b^2$
j. Punctuating two independent clauses

6. Using specific examples in the life of a child that you have known, explain what is meant by a systems-ecological perspective.

*7. Gage and Berliner (1998) identify a number of ways in which your interactions with students can be biased. Name four, and then add one of your own not mentioned by Gage and Berliner. Why do you think the one you added is important? Can you think of an experience that you saw or encountered that made you add it to your list?

*8. Identify four procedures for reducing or eliminating the biases you may have when interacting with your students. Which would be the easiest to implement, and which would be the most difficult?

FIELD EXPERIENCE ACTIVITIES

1. Using a school subject you will teach, identify a lesson topic in which a learner's aptitude would not be expected to predict his or her score on a classroom test on that topic. How would you explain this to a parent? What teaching strategies might account for this result?

2. In thinking back to some of your observations in schools, what might be some teaching practices that could be used to shrink differences in achievement due to SES?

3. Think of two learners at the grades you will teach who have different learning style preferences. What different types of products would each likely submit to you for their portfolio assessment as evidence of their learning?

*4. Identify two methods for dealing with a disruptive peer group in your classroom. How might they be applied in a heterogeneous classroom?

5. Imagine a typical child you will have in your classroom and explain in your own words what is meant by the family–school partnership. What are some things you can do to promote this partnership in your classroom?

DIGITAL PORTFOLIO ACTIVITIES

These digital portfolio activities relate to INTASC principles 2 and 3.

1. In this chapter you read that:

Studies generally conclude that most differences in educational achievement occurring among racial and ethnic groups can be accounted for by social class. . . . In other words, if you know the SES of a group of students, you can pretty much predict their achievement with some accuracy. Information about their racial and ethnic group does little to improve the prediction.

Given the preceding statement, outline a plan that indicates what you would do at your grade to improve the achievement of minority learners in your classroom. Cite some of the suggestions provided in this chapter, add some of your own, and place your response in your digital portfolio in a folder labeled *Teaching the Culturally Diverse.*

2 Prepare a brief outline of a lesson plan that shows that you know the difference between planning instruction from the perspective of the *cultural deficit model* as opposed to the *cultural difference model* and its recent extensions and revisions. Be sure to indicate what specifically you would do differently in your classroom to reach diverse learners with the cultural difference model that you would not do with the cultural deficit model. Place your response in your digital portfolio in the *Teaching the Culturally Diverse* folder. Both these entries will show others that you are aware of key issues in teaching the culturally diverse learner.

CLASSROOM OBSERVATION ACTIVITIES

The following classroom observation activities relate to INTASC principles 3 and 9.

1. You learned in this chapter that in teaching culturally diverse learners you must provide learning activities that are targeted to or that can span different student backgrounds, interests, and learning styles. Too much diversity in a classroom can make teaching difficult, because students may share little in terms of language, culture, and related expectations. On the other hand, too little diversity may encourage teachers to believe students are more alike than they are and thus overlook individual needs. For example, a teacher may plan a single lesson for a class of English-language learners, assuming they are more alike than different. However, this teacher's lesson may overlook a number of important differences among students, including students' varying levels of proficiency in their native language, students' past experiences with English, and the motivation of each student to learn English.

 For this activity go to the *Classroom Observation* module for this chapter on the Companion Website at *www.prenhall.com/borich.* There you will find an observation instrument titled "Sign System with Items from Soar and Soar" that is divided into 17 teacher behaviors labeled "verbal control" and another 10 teacher behaviors labeled "physical control." Rearrange the 27 items into two new columns—one column including behaviors that you believe would be detrimental to teaching culturally diverse learners and a second column including items that could aid in teaching culturally diverse learners. Copy both the original observation instrument and your new rearranged instrument into your digital portfolio in the folder *Teaching the Culturally Diverse.* Keep both instruments as a reminder of what behaviors to emphasize in a culturally diverse classroom.

2. It is a good idea to examine your own background from a cultural, ethnic, and economic point of view. Your experiences and expectations play an important role not only in what you notice about the culture, ethnicity, and economic status of others, but also in how you value what you see. Observing in a classroom without prior examination of your personal beliefs will be less productive than if you have taken some time to consider your own background and culture, and how these may affect what you see and interpret during your observation. It may not be possible or necessary for an observer to leave his or her worldview behind entirely. However, periodic examination of our own cultural background helps us become aware of the powerful interaction between ourselves and how we observe and interpret the behavior of others.

Describe the culture (e.g., U.S./Western), ethnicity (e.g., Hispanic), and social and economic status (e.g., upper middle class,) with which you most closely identify. Indicate how your personal beliefs arising from this description might not only affect what you value in your students, but also what you might see or not see in your classroom. Place this description in the *Teaching the Culturally Diverse* folder of your digital portfolio as a reminder when you begin teaching of how much your own cultural background may limit what you see and how you interpret what you see.

CHAPTER CASE HISTORY AND PRAXIS TEST PREPARATION

DIRECTIONS: The following case history pertains to chapter 2 content. After reading the case history, answer the short-answer question that follows and consult appendix D to find different levels of scored student responses and the rubric used to determine the quality of each response. You also have the opportunity to submit your responses online to receive feedback by visiting the *Case History* module for this chapter on the Companion Website, where you will also find additional questions pertaining to Praxis test content.

Case History

Anna Ramirez is a seventh grader who lives with her family of five siblings and their parents in a modest house about a mile from the middle school she attends. She looks up to her two older brothers, one who is a strong athlete in high school and the other who plays the trumpet in the band. Her older sister, who dropped out of school two years ago at age 16, now has a 2-year-old child. Anna helps take care of him on weekends and sometimes school nights. She also helps with her two younger sisters, aged 7 and 9, and answers their questions about their schoolwork.

She is very patient with her nephew and her younger sisters and creative in finding ways to keep them busy. She plays and even roughhouses with them, letting them ride her like a horse or put her on a leash as a pet dog. She likes to draw and often has all of them coloring or painting around the kitchen table. The walls in her part of a shared bedroom are decorated with sketches she has made of her favorite singers. Her brother has nicknamed her "Leonardo" because she is always drawing something.

She also enjoys helping her mother and aunts prepare elaborate meals for special family dinners. While they chop and mince the fresh vegetables and herbs, they banter back and forth and tease each other. It is a very happy kitchen and Anna feels safe and secure in its hub.

But it is a very different Anna who enters Mrs. Dodge's math classroom. She picks up her folder with a frown and goes to her assigned seat in the back of the room. Instead of doing the daily warm-up problem on the board, Anna draws in her notebook. When it is time to discuss the answer, she stares at her desk. Mrs. Dodge calls on one of several eager students who raise their hands and sends him to the board to show his work. When he is finished, she tells him he has done a good job. Meanwhile Anna has copied down the problem and its answer from the board. When Mrs. Dodge asks if there are any questions, she says nothing, although she does not understand the problem.

Next, Mrs. Dodge has Juan, a straight A student, read the chapter section introducing the concept of percent and how it relates to fractions and decimals. She stops him occasionally to ask a question.

"If you were converting $\frac{1}{2}$ to a percentage, what would it be?"

Miguel is one of several in the front of the class who raises his hand and Mrs. Dodge calls on him. "Fifty percent," he responds.

"That's very good, Miguel. You see, it is just like money, just like the change from a dollar. Fifty cents is $\frac{1}{2}$ a dollar, just as 50 percent also stands for $\frac{1}{2}$."

She notices that Anna is drawing on the back of her notebook and walks over to her. Mrs. Dodge picks it up and smiles sarcastically. "Oh, I thought you were graphing our work, but it only seems that you were drawing again."

The rest of the class laughs and Anna turns red. "Anna, what is 50 percent of 200?"

Anna looks down for a second or two and is about to reply when Mrs. Dodge turns to Edgar, who is waving his hand. He gives the correct answer.

The last part of the period is labeled Cooperative Learning in large bold letters on the board. Mrs. Dodge allows the students to join small self-selected groups to work on the homework assignment. Cooperative learning is not often used by Mrs. Dodge and even goes against her grain, because she sees it as cheating. However, many of the inservice presentations stress cooperative learning, and Mrs. Dodge knows she will not get a good evaluation if she doesn't show it in her lesson plans.

The good math students sit together in a group, although they really work separately. However, they always manage to finish before the bell rings. In many of the groups, there is interaction, but it is mainly about things other than math. Anna works with a few others she has known since early elementary school, but they seldom are able to help one another. She finishes only a few problems and even then she is not sure they are correct.

The bell rings and Anna leaves the room. There is new vigor in her step and confidence in her stride. The next class is art.

Short-Answer Question

This section presents a sample Praxis short-answer question. In appendix D you will find sample responses along with the standards used in scoring these responses.

DIRECTIONS: The following question requires you to write a short answer. Base your answer on your knowledge of principles of learning and teaching from chapter 2. Be sure to answer all parts of the question.

1. Given what we know about Anna's behavior at home, it seems that she would be an ideal candidate for cooperative learning. Why was this activity, as instituted by Mrs. Dodge, not particularly successful with either Anna or the rest of the class? Using your knowledge of research on teaching practices, explain how Mrs. Dodge could adapt the cooperative learning activity to be more successful.

Discrete Multiple-Choice Questions

DIRECTIONS: Each of the multiple-choice questions that follow is based on Praxis-related pedagogical knowledge in chapter 2. Select the answer that is best for each question and compare your results with those in appendix D. See also the Companion Website for this text at *www.prenhall.com/borich* for more assessment options.

1. All of the following methods are instructional adapatations for dealing with culturally diverse learning populations. These teaching practices derive from both the cultural deficit model and the cultural difference model. Which method best corresponds with the cultural deficit model?
    a. Intensive English instruction
    b. High expectations for all learners
    c. Indirect and self-directed models of instruction
    d. Cooperative learning and peer tutoring

2. Researchers continue to study the role of the family in relation to school achievement. Which of the following statements best represents recent research findings regarding this issue?
    a. Apathy and working long hours away from the home are the chief reasons for the lack of parent involvement in the achievement of culturally different students.
    b. Children of working mothers are just as involved in extracurricular activities than are the children of nonworking mothers.
    c. Teachers have unrealistic expectations for the achievement of children from single-parent families.
    d. As trained professionals, teachers and administrators are best suited to make decisions regarding curriculum and instruction. The involvement of parents should focus on the emotional, social, and disciplinary problems of the learner.

3. Current research on cultural, linguistic, and SES biases in classroom interaction suggests which of the following would be most appropriate:
    a. Give special assignments to minority students to make them feel included.
    b. Pair a minority with a nonminority to remind you that when you are interacting with one member of the pair, interact with the other, frequently changing one member of the pair.
    c. Wait longer for a minority student to respond than for other students.
    d. Call on low achievers more frequently than high achievers and then high achievers more than low achievers in a back and forth cycle.

4. Which of the following behaviors would be consistent with a field-dependent learner?
    a. Relates concepts to personal experience
    b. Tends to organize information by him or herself
    c. Focuses on facts and principles
    d. Likes to compete

5. When viewing the family–school partnership from a systems-ecological perspective, which of the following would *not* be considered relevant sources of information for understanding the behavior of the learner?
    a. Parent's workplace
    b. Learner's extended family
    c. Park and playground
    d. INTASC principles

Chapter

3

Goals and Objectives

*This chapter will help you answer the following questions and meet the following
INTASC principles for effective teaching:*

1. Where do instructional goals come from?
2. What are some important educational goals for the next decade?
3. Why do I need behavioral objectives?
4. What are the steps in writing a behavioral objective?
5. What types of cognitive, affective, and psychomotor behaviors will I want to teach in my classroom?
6. How can I help my learners achieve higher-order thinking behaviors, such as problem solving, decision making, critical thinking, and valuing?

INTASC 1: The teacher understands the central concepts, tools of inquiry, and structures of the discipline(s) he or she teaches and can create learning experiences that make these aspects of subject matter meaningful for students.

INTASC 2: The teacher understands how children learn and develop and can provide learning opportunities that support their intellectual, social, and personal development.

INTASC 7: The teacher plans instruction based upon knowledge of subject matter, students, the community, and curriculum goals.

Chapters 1 and 2 introduced some important teaching behaviors expected of you and some individual differences among your students you can expect to see in your classroom. This chapter and the next show you how to plan and organize who, what, and how you will teach in ways that reach all of your students, whatever their differences may be. First, let's consider the distinction among standards, goals, and objectives and how they can help you reach all of your students.

STANDARDS, GOALS, AND OBJECTIVES

The words *standards, goals,* and *objectives* often are used interchangeably without recognizing their different, but related, meanings. **Standards** are general expressions of our values that give us a sense of direction. They are written broadly enough to be acceptable to large numbers of individuals, such as teachers, school administrators, parents, and American taxpayers. In Chapter 1 we saw two sets of standards: one setting forth essential requirements for the advanced certification of teachers (National Board for Professional Teaching Standards, NBPTS) and another setting forth the expected knowledge, dispositions, and performances for the beginning teacher (Interstate New Teacher Assessment and Support Consortium standards, INTASC). These two sets of standards represent the values of large numbers of professionals and, therefore, direction for the training, support, and assessment of teachers.

Goals are derived from standards to more specifically identify what must be accomplished and who must do what in order for the standards to be met. Goals express standards from the teacher's, learner's, or school's point of view and identify what teachers must teach, students must learn, and schools must do. They also can energize and motivate teachers, students, and schools to become actively engaged in and committed to meeting the standards. When you hear a state legislator, school superintendent, or your principal remark that schools need to "increase the time they devote to teaching elementary school science," "improve the problem-solving and decision-making skills of high school graduates," or "better integrate technology and Web-based learning into the classroom," they are setting goals for you to meet.

Although standards and goals can answer the question "Why am I teaching this?" they are not a satisfactory response to what or how you will teach on any given day. Standards and goals provide little direction as to what strategies to use in the classroom to achieve them or when or if they are met. A satisfactory answer to these questions requires that you prepare unit and lesson **objectives,** which convey to your learners the specific behaviors to be

Table 3.1 The differences among standards, goals, and objectives.

Standards	Goals	Objectives
Express our values that give us a sense of direction	Identify what will be learned—energize and motivate	Convey the specific behavior to be attained, the conditions under which the behavior must be demonstrated, and the proficiency at which the behavior must be performed.
Examples:	**Examples:**	**Examples:**
1. Every citizen should be prepared to work in a technological world. 2. Every adult should be functionally literate. 3. Every American should be able to vote as an informed citizen in a democracy.	1. Students should understand the use of the computer at home and at work. 2. Students should be able to read and write well enough to become gainfully employed. 3. Students should know how to choose a candidate and vote in an election.	1. Students will, using their own choice of a word-processing application, produce an edited two-page manuscript free of errors in 15 minutes or less. 2. Students will, at the end of the 12th grade, be able to write a 500-word essay with no more than two grammatical and punctuation errors. 3. Students will, at the end of an eighth-grade unit on government, participate in a mock election by choosing a candidate and giving reasons for their choice.

attained, the conditions under which the behavior must be demonstrated, and the proficiency level at which the behaviors are to be performed. The examples in Table 3.1 show the distinctions among standards, goals, and objectives.

Several approaches have been formulated to help you prepare educational objectives. One approach comes from the work of Tyler (1974).

Tyler's Goal Development Approach

The idea of an educational objective can be traced to the early part of the 20th century, when Tyler (1934) first conceived of the need for goal-directed statements for teachers. He observed that teachers were concerned far more with the content of instruction (what to teach) than with what the student should be able to do with that content (i.e., whether it could be used in some meaningful context).

Tyler's approach to generating educational objectives has had a major influence on curriculum development. Tyler believed that as society becomes more complex, there are more things for people to learn. But the time to learn this ever-expanding amount of knowledge and skills may actually decrease in a technologically complex society. Consequently, educators must make informed choices about which goals are worth teaching.

Figure 3.1 Tyler's considerations in goal selection.

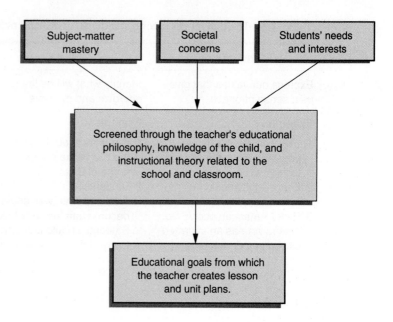

Tyler identified five factors to consider when establishing priorities for what students should learn. First, goals must include

1. The subject matter we know enough about to teach (subject-matter mastery)
2. Societal concerns, which represent what is valued in both the society at large and the local community
3. Student needs and interests and the abilities and knowledge they bring to school. Then, these goals must be refined to match
4. Your school's educational philosophy and your community's priorities, and
5. What instructional theory and research tells us can be taught

Goals are important because they tell your learners, their parents, and the community why you are teaching the lessons you have planned, which then energizes and motivates them to become actively engaged in the learning process. Educational goals

- Provide direction for your unit and lesson planning.
- Communicate the importance of your instruction to parents and to the community.
- Energize your learners to higher levels of commitment and engagement in the learning process.

Tyler's approach to establishing educational goals is illustrated in Figure 3.1.

SOCIETAL GOALS FOR EDUCATION

In the past decade, several important developments have highlighted concerns about academic goals and how we measure them. In addition to the National Education Goals for the first decade of the new millennium, which we saw in chapter 2, professional groups and associations have also become involved in establishing educational goals. Several of these groups and associations have reviewed comprehensive studies of the state of education in American elementary and secondary schools in an effort to set criteria by which to judge the adequacy of what students learn in their subject-matter fields. Their reports include *Knowing What Students Know,* by the National Research Council (2001); *Assessment Standards for School Mathematics,* by the National Council of Teachers of Mathematics (2000); *Benchmarks for Science Literacy,* by the American Association for the Advancement of Sciences (1996); *Expectations of Excellence: Curriculum Standards for Social Studies,* by the National Council for the Social Studies (2002); *National Science Education Standards,* by the National Research Council (1996); and *Standards for the English Language Arts,* by the National Council of Teachers of English (1996). Each of these reports has set forth new frameworks for curricula in its subject area and is continually being updated.

These new standards suggest that instruction at all levels of schooling has been predominantly focused on memorization, drill, and workbook exercises. These reports call for a commitment to developing a **thinking curriculum,** one that focuses on teaching learners how to think critically, reason, and problem-solve in authentic, real-world contexts (Borich & Hao, 2007). They advocate that American schools adopt such a thinking curriculum and a performance-based examination system that would adequately measure complex cognitive skills (Borich, 2007; Borich & Tombari, 2004; Loucks-Horsley et al., 1990; Mitchell, 1992; Parker, 1991; Resnick & Resnick, 1991; Tombari & Borich, 1999).

These new curriculum frameworks were stimulated in part by a disenchantment with the quality of public school education voiced by many segments of our society, including parents, taxpayers, legislators, business and military leaders, and some teacher groups. This disenchantment was not limited to matters of curriculum. It extended to the quality of teaching and teacher education (Council for Basic Education, 1996), leading in some cases to recommendations for teacher competency testing and new requirements for teacher certification. For example, the *Praxis II Elementary Education Curriculum, Instruction and Assessment Test* to be completed after completion of a bachelor's degree program in elementary/middle school education was designed for just this purpose. Test questions cover the breadth of material a new teacher needs to know and assess knowledge of both principles and processes of teaching. Some questions assess basic understanding of curriculum planning, instructional design, and assessment of student learning. But many other questions pose particular problems that teachers routinely face in the classroom, and, most importantly, many are based on authentic real-world examples of student work in the context of the subject matters most commonly taught in the elementary and middle school (see Praxis test 10011 at *www.ets.org/praxis*).

You will become familiar with Praxis II test questions on the principles of teaching and learning at each level of certification (K–6, grades 5–9, and grades 7–12) in this and the following chapters. When you study these practice

An important recommendation for curriculum reform in the next decade is that learners should be better trained to work independently and to attain more high-level thinking, conceptual, and problem-solving skills.

questions and the skills and performances they require, keep in mind that many have come from reports representing a broad consensus among professional groups and associations (for example, the consortium and associations representing INTASC and NBPTS) that have expressed what our schools need to do to strengthen teaching and learning in the classroom. For example, several of the reports cited agreed that our schools needed to strengthen curricula in math, science, English, foreign languages, and social studies. Also, technology was represented by a call for higher levels of computer literacy, both as separate courses and as a tool integrated into the core disciplines. The reports also called for renewed effort in teaching higher-order thinking skills, including the teaching of concepts, problem solving, and creativity (as opposed to rote memorization and parroting of facts, lists, names, and dates divorced from a more authentic problem-solving context).

Not surprisingly, all the reports recommended increasing both grading standards and the number of required core courses (as opposed to elective courses), especially at the secondary level. This recommendation went hand in hand with the suggestion that colleges raise their admission requirements by requiring more course work in core subjects, especially math, science, and foreign languages. Most of the reports recommended increasing school hours and homework time. For example, one report suggested a minimum 7-hour school day (some schools have fewer than 6 hours) and a 200-day school year (many have a 180-day year). Time spent on noninstructional activities was to be reduced accordingly, as would administrative interruptions.

By taking a broad view of our educational establishment, these reports recommended the following goals:

- Students should be trained to live and function in a technological world.
- Students should possess minimum competencies in reading, writing, and mathematics.
- Students should possess higher-order thinking, conceptual, and problem-solving skills.
- Students should be required to enroll in all the core subjects each school year, to the extent of their abilities.
- Students should be trained to work independently and to complete assignments without direct supervision.
- Students should improve school attendance and stay in school longer each day and year.
- Students should be given more activities that provide practice in problem solving and decision making and that require critical thinking and making value judgments.

The basis for setting these goals was the perception that our schools may have lost sight of their role in teaching students how to think. Traditionally, this was accomplished through the core curriculum (English, math, science, foreign languages, and social studies). However, with fewer advanced offerings in these areas and with additional time being spent in remedial and elective courses, the time devoted to teaching children how to think may have been insufficient. These reports suggested that schools should reverse this trend by requiring students to study both the core and more advanced content areas. Such instruction would require complex thinking skills in authentic problem-solving contexts, homework, higher assessment and grading standards, and performance assessments of what students can actually do with what was learned. Mastering thinking skills, such as problem solving, decision making, and learning to make value judgments, was considered important because they are required in advanced grades, in the world of work, and to gain admittance to advanced education and training opportunities.

Figure 3.2 The funneling of standards into instructional objectives.

Source: From *Educational Testing and Measurement: Classroom Application and Practice*, 8th edition, by Tom Kubiszyn and Gary Borich. Copyright © 2007 by Addison-Wesley Longman. Reprinted by permission.

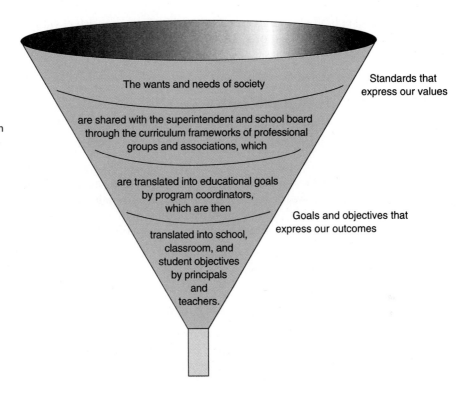

Figure 3.2 illustrates the translation of standards into objectives as a funneling or narrowing of focus in which goals, guided by our standards, are gradually translated through subject matter curricula into specific objectives for instruction.

The Purpose of Objectives

Objectives have two practical purposes. The first is to move goals toward classroom accomplishments by identifying the specific classroom strategies by which the goals can be achieved. The second is to express teaching strategies in a format that allows you to measure their effects on learners. A written statement that achieves these two purposes is called a **behavioral objective.**

What Does *Behavioral* Mean?

When the word *behavioral* precedes the word *objective*, learning is being defined as a change in observable behavior. Therefore, the writing of behavioral objectives requires that the behavior being addressed be observable and measurable (with a test, observational checklist, student work sample, etc.). Activities occurring in the seclusion of your learners' minds are not observable and thus cannot be the focus of a behavioral objective. Unobserved activities, such as creating mental images or rehearsing a response subvocally, can precede learning, but they cannot constitute evidence that learning has occurred, because they cannot be directly observed.

Further, the behavior of your learners must be observable over a period of time during which specific content, teaching strategies, and instructional materials have been presented.

This limits a behavioral objective to a time frame consistent with the logical divisions in school curricula, such as lessons, chapters, units, and grading periods. Feedback from behavioral objectives provides data for monitoring the consequence of your instructional strategies.

AN OVERVIEW OF BEHAVIORAL OBJECTIVES

The goal of this chapter is to show you how to prepare behavioral objectives for your classroom as painlessly as possible. Simply put, writing behavioral objectives involves three steps:

1. Identifying a specific goal that has an observable learning outcome
2. Stating the conditions under which a learning outcome can be expected to occur (e.g., with what materials, texts, and facilities and in what period of time)
3. Specifying the criterion level, that is, the degree of learning that can be expected from your instruction under the specified conditions

Before considering the actual written form of behavioral objectives, let's look at these three steps in more detail.

Specifying the Learning Outcomes

The first step in writing a behavioral objective is to identify an observable **learning outcome.** For an objective to be behavioral, it must be observable and measurable, so you can determine whether the behavior is present, partially present, or absent (Gronlund, 2003; Mager, 1997). The key to identifying an observable outcome is your choice of words to describe it.

Word choice in writing behavioral objectives is important because the same word may have different meanings, depending on who is reading or hearing it. The endless puns heard in our culture are humorous illustrations of this: Does "well-rounded person" mean broadly educated or well fed? Words can express a concept not only accurately or inaccurately but also specifically or vaguely. It is vague usage that gives us the most trouble in writing behavioral objectives.

In a behavioral objective, learning outcomes must be expressed directly, concretely, and observably, unlike the way behaviors usually are described in the popular press, television, and even some textbooks. If you took these everyday sources as a guide for writing the behavioral expressions needed in the classroom, you would quickly find that they could not be easily observed and probably could not be measured, either. For example, we often hear these expressions as desirable goals:

Mentally healthy citizens

Well-rounded individuals

Self-actualized schoolchildren

Informed adults

Literate populace

But, what do mentally *healthy, well-rounded, self-actualized, informed,* and *literate* actually mean? If you asked a large number of individuals to define these terms, you would receive quite an assortment of responses. These diverse responses would have widely divergent implications for how to achieve each desired behavior and for observing its attainment. The reason, of course, is that the words are vague and open to many interpretations. Imagine the confusion such vagueness could cause in your classroom if your objective for the first grading period were simply "to inform the class about the content" or "to make them higher achievers." Johnny's parents would have one interpretation of *informed,* but

Betty's parents might have quite another. Let's hope they both don't show up on parent–teacher night! Also, you might mean one thing by *higher achiever*, but your principal might mean another.

The point is that vague behavioral language quickly becomes a problem for those who are held accountable for bringing about the behavior in question. You can avoid this problem by writing behavioral objectives in precise language that makes their measurement specific and noncontroversial.

One way to make your behavioral objectives specific and noncontroversial is to choose behavioral expressions from a list of action verbs that have widely accepted meanings. These action verbs also allow easy identification of the operations necessary for displaying the behavior. For example, instead of expecting students to be informed or literate in a subject, expect them to

Differentiate between . . .
Identify the results of . . .
Solve a problem in . . .
Compare and contrast . . .

These action verbs describe what being *informed* or *literate* mean by stating specific, observable behaviors that the learner must perform. Although we have not yet indicated how well the learner must be able to perform these behaviors, we are now closer to the type of evidence that can be used to determine whether these objectives have been achieved.

Although a behavioral objective should include an action verb that specifies a learning outcome, not all action verbs are suitable for specifying learning outcomes. Some are better suited to specifying **learning activities.** Unfortunately, learning outcomes often are confused with learning activities. For example, which of the following examples represent learning outcomes and which represent learning activities?

1. The student will identify pictures of words that sound alike.
2. The student will demonstrate an appreciation of poetry.
3. The student will subtract one-digit numbers.
4. The student will show a knowledge of punctuation.
5. The student will practice the multiplication tables.
6. The student will sing "The Star-Spangled Banner."

In the first four objectives, the action words *identify, demonstrate, subtract,* and *show* all point to outcomes—end products of an instructional lesson or unit. However, the action word in the fifth example, *practice,* is only a learning activity; it is not an end in itself and only can work toward a learning outcome. The sixth objective is more ambiguous. Is *sing* an outcome or an activity? It is hard to say without more information. If the goal is to have a stage-frightened student sing in public, then it is a learning outcome. However, if singing is only practice for a later performance, it is a learning activity. Learning activities are important but only in relation to the specific learning outcomes, or end products, they are attempting to achieve. Without a learning outcome clearly in mind, there would be no way to determine the value of a learning activity for promoting desirable student outcomes.

The following examples differentiate between verbs used for learning outcomes and verbs used for learning activities:

Learning Outcomes (Ends)	Learning Activities (Means)
identify	study
recall	watch
list	listen
write	read

Behavioral objectives must include the end product, because you will use this end product in choosing your instructional procedures and evaluating whether you have achieved the desired result (Gronlund, 2003; Kubiszyn & Borich, 2007).

Identifying the Conditions

The second step in writing a behavioral objective is to identify the specific **learning conditions** under which learning will occur. If the observable learning outcome can be achieved only through use of particular materials, equipment, tools, or other resources, state these conditions in the objective. Here are some examples of objectives that state conditions:

- Create a candy store price list and use pretend money to make several purchases. Show how to add the value of different coins and how to determine and give proper change.
- Using the map of strategic resources handed out in class, identify the economic conditions in the South resulting from the Civil War.
- In the first chapter of *Charlotte's Web* we meet Fern. Circle all the words that correctly describe her: (Persuasive, Lazy, Fair-minded, Emotional, Hardhearted)
- Using an electronic calculator, solve problems involving the addition of two-digit signed numbers.
- Using pictures of fourteenth- to eighteenth-century Gothic and Baroque European cathedrals, compare and contrast the styles of architecture.

If the conditions are obvious, they need not be specified. For example, it is not necessary to specify "Using a writing instrument and paper, write a short story." However, when conditions can focus learning in specific ways, eliminating some areas of study and including others, the statement of conditions can be critical to attaining the objective, and you should include it. For example, imagine a student will be tested on the behavior indicated in the first objective in the preceding list but without the condition indicated: "Create a candy store price list and use pretend money to make several purchases. . . ." Adding the value of different coins and making change without reference to concrete examples would likely produce a more general, less structured response. If students are told the conditions, they can focus their studying on the precise behavior called for (e.g., relating different coins to the price of real purchases as opposed to memorizing the value of different coins).

Note also that without a statement of conditions to focus your instruction, your students may assume different conditions than you intend. For example, in our third example, in the absence of concrete examples, some students might prepare by memorizing the definitions of the words *persuasive, lazy, fair-minded, emotional,* and *hardhearted* instead of learning what characteristics of a person, such as Fern, would need to be present for each adjective to apply. And because objectives form the basis for tests, your tests might be more fair to some students than others, depending on the assumptions they make in the absence of stated conditions.

Notice in the other preceding examples that learning can take on different meanings, depending on whether students study and practice with or without the use of a map, electronic calculator, or pictures of fourteenth- to eighteenth-century cathedrals. Teaching and learning become more structured and resources more organized when you state conditions as part of your objectives. And, as we have seen, objectives that specify conditions of learning lead to tests that are fairer.

Conditional statements within a behavioral objective can be singular or multiple. It is possible, and sometimes necessary, to have two or even three conditional statements in an objective to focus the learning. Although too many conditions attached to an objective can narrow learning to irrelevant details, multiple conditions often are important adjuncts to improving the clarity of the behavior desired and the organization and preparation of instructional resources. Here are examples of multiple conditions, indicated by italics:

- In the first chapter of *Charlotte's Web* we meet Fern. Circle all the words *from the list* that correctly describe her: (Persuasive, Lazy, Fair-minded, Emotional, Hardhearted)
- Using a centigrade *thermometer*, measure the temperature of 2 liters of *water* at a depth of 25 centimeters.
- Using a *compass, ruler*, and *protractor*, draw three conic sections of different sizes and three triangles of different types.
- Using 4 grams of *sodium carbonate* and 4 grams of *sodium bicarbonate*, indicate their different reactions in H_2O.
- *Using the list of foods provided*, fill in the blanks in the food pyramid to represent a healthy, well-balanced diet.
- *Within 15 minutes* and using the *reference books* provided, write the formulas for wattage, voltage, amperage, and resistance.
- Using a *computer* with word processing capability, correct the spelling and punctuation errors on a *two-page manuscript in 20 minutes or less.*

It is important not to add so many conditions that learning is reduced to trivial detail. It is also important to choose conditions that are realistic—that represent authentic, real-life circumstances your learners are likely to find in as well as out of the classroom. The idea behind stating conditions, especially multiple conditions, is not to complicate the behavior but rather to make it more natural and close to the conditions under which the behavior will have to be performed in the real world and in subsequent instruction. Always check the conditions specified to see if they match those under which the behavior is most likely to be needed in subsequent instruction and outside the classroom.

Stating Criterion Levels

The third step in writing a behavioral objective is to state the level of performance required to meet the objective. Specifying the outcome and conditions reveals the procedures necessary for the behavior to be observed. However, one important element is missing. How much of the behavior is required for you to consider the objective to be attained? This element of objective writing is the **criterion level.** It is the degree of performance desired or the level of proficiency that will satisfy you that the objective has been met.

Setting criterion levels is one of the most misunderstood aspects of objective writing. At the root of this misunderstanding is failure to recognize that criterion or proficiency levels are value judgments as to what performance level is required for adequately performing the behavior in some later setting. The mistaken assumption is often made that a single correct level of proficiency exists and that once established it must forever remain in its original form. At first, criterion levels should be taken as educated guesses. They should indicate the approximate degree of proficiency needed to adequately perform the behavior in another instructional setting, in the next grade, or in the real world. Also, criterion levels should be adjusted periodically up or down to conform with how well your students are able to perform the behavior.

Often, criterion levels are set to establish a benchmark for testing whether an objective has been met, without recognizing that this level may not be relevant to subsequent learning tasks, instructional settings, or students. To avoid this, always consider criterion levels to be adjustable and dependent on your evaluation of how well students can adequately use the behavior at subsequent times and in contexts beyond your classroom.

Criterion levels come in many sizes and shapes. For example, they can be stated in the following ways:

Number of items correct on a test
Number of consecutive items correct (or consecutive errorless performances)
Essential features included (as in an essay question or paper)
Completion within a prescribed time limit (where speed of performance is important)
Completion with a certain degree of accuracy

Consider the objective "Using a short story by John Steinbeck and another by Mark Twain, differentiate between their writing styles." Is a criterion stated? Remember, a criterion level establishes the degree of behavior required for the objective to be met. How would the teacher know if a student's written response to this objective has demonstrated the minimum acceptable level of differentiation? With only the information given, it would be difficult and arbitrary. Now, let's add a criterion to this objective:

• Using short stories by John Steinbeck and Mark Twain, differentiate their writing styles by selecting four passages from each author that illustrate differences in their writing styles.

Now there is a basis for evaluating the objective. This particular criterion level requires considerable skill in applying learned information in different contexts and allows for flexibility in the range of responses that are acceptable. This type of objective is sometimes called an **expressive objective** (Eisner, 1969, 1998) because it allows for a variety of correct responses or for students to express themselves in a variety of ways for which there is no single correct answer. The amount of expressiveness in a response allowed by an objective is always a matter of degree. In other words, objectives can have more—or less—rigid criterion levels.

Consider another example:

• Using an electronic calculator, the student will solve problems involving the addition of two-digit signed numbers.

Is there a stated criterion level for this objective? No. There is no unambiguous basis for deciding whether Angela met the objective and Bobby did not. Now, let's add a criterion level:

• Using an electronic calculator, the student will correctly solve 8 of 10 problems involving the addition of two-digit signed numbers.

This objective now precisely identifies the minimum proficiency that must be observed to conclude the desired behavior has been attained. Unlike the first version of this objective, little flexibility is allowed in the required response. Notice that far less expression is possible in answering a question about mathematics than about literature; the former is more highly structured and more rigid in terms of possible responses. Notice also that this more structured approach to an acceptable response fits well with the nature of this particular objective; the less structured approach fits well with the literature example.

Both of these objectives illustrate that the expressiveness of an objective is established by how you set an acceptable criterion. Also, the level of expressiveness that fits best often is a function of the objective itself—how many correct answers are possible. As a teacher, you control

1. Learning outcomes
2. Conditions
3. Criterion levels
   a. Proficiency level
   b. Level of expressiveness

Here are some of the earlier objectives with criterion levels added in brackets (or italicized where a criterion already was included):

- In the first chapter of *Charlotte's Web* we meet Fern. Circle [all] the words from the list that correctly describe her: (Persuasive, Lazy, Fair-minded, Emotional, Hardhearted).
- Using a centigrade thermometer, measure the temperature of 2 liters of water at a depth of 25 centimeters [to within 1 degree accuracy].
- Using a compass, ruler, and protractor, draw *three* conic sections of *different sizes* and three triangles of *different types*.
- Using 4 grams of sodium carbonate and 4 grams of sodium bicarbonate, indicate their different reactions with H_2O [by testing the alkalinity of the H_2O and reporting results in parts per million (PPM)].
- Using the list of foods provided, fill in the blanks in the food pyramid to represent a healthy, well-balanced diet, [placing every food correctly].
- Within 15 minutes and using the reference books provided, find [and write correctly] the formulas for wattage, voltage, amperage, and resistance.
- Using a computer with word processing capability, correct the spelling and punctuation errors for a two-page manuscript in *20 minutes* [with 100% accuracy].

These examples illustrate well-written behavioral objectives.

You have seen how to specify learning outcomes, state conditions for learning, and establish criterion levels. These are the three most important ingredients of well-written behavioral objectives. But there is one more point to know about preparing objectives: Keep them simple.

Keeping Objectives Simple

Teachers often make the mistake of being too complex in measuring learning outcomes. As a result, they resort to indirect methods of measurement. If you want to know whether Johnny can write his name, ask him to write his name—but not while blindfolded! Resist the temptation to be tricky. Consider these examples:

- The student will show his or her ability to recall characters of the book *Tom Sawyer* by painting a picture of each.
- Discriminate between a telephone and television by drawing an electrical diagram of each.
- Demonstrate that you understand how to use an encyclopedia index by listing the page on which a given subject can be found in the *Encyclopaedia Britannica*.

In the first example, painting a picture surely would allow you to determine whether the students can recall the characters in *Tom Sawyer*, but is there an easier (and less time-consuming) way to measure recall? How about asking the students simply to list the characters? If the objective is to determine recall, listing is sufficient. For the second example, how about presenting students with two illustrations, one of a telephone, the other of a television, and simply ask them to tell (verbally or in writing) which is which?

The third example is on target. The task required is a simple and efficient way of measuring whether someone can use an encyclopedia index.

In this chapter you will begin writing objectives on your own. Be sure to include these three essential components in every objective you write: (1) observable learning outcome, (2) conditions, and (3) criterion level.

THE COGNITIVE, AFFECTIVE, AND PSYCHOMOTOR DOMAINS

You might have noticed that some of the example objectives shown earlier in this chapter have illustrated very different types of behavior. For example, compare the behaviors called for in these objectives:

- Using short stories by John Steinbeck and Mark Twain, differentiate their writing styles by selecting four passages from each author that illustrate differences in their writing styles.
- Using a centigrade thermometer, measure the temperature of 2 liters of water at a depth of 25 centimeters to within 1 degree accuracy.

Common sense tells us that the behaviors called for require different patterns of preparation and study to attain. In the former objective, study and practice would focus on analyzing their writing styles and noting the differences in actual examples of their writing. Contrast this complicated process with how one might study to acquire the behavior in the second objective. Here the study and practice might consist simply of learning to accurately perceive distances between the markings on a centigrade scale. Such practice might be limited to training one's eyes to count spaces between the gradations and then assigning the appropriate number to represent temperature in degrees centigrade.

Note also the difference in study and preparation time required to achieve these two different objectives: The second could be learned in minutes, but the other might take hours, days, or even weeks. These different objectives represent only two examples of the variety of learning outcomes possible in your classroom.

Objectives can require vastly different levels not only of cognitive complexity but of affective and psychomotor complexity as well. The following section introduces behaviors at different levels of complexity for which behavioral objectives can be prepared. For convenience, these are organized into the following behaviors:

- **Cognitive** (development of intellectual abilities and skills)
- **Affective** (development of attitudes, beliefs, and values)
- **Psychomotor** (coordination of physical movements and performance)

The Cognitive Domain

Bloom, Englehart, Hill, Furst, and Krathwohl (1984) devised a method for categorizing objectives according to cognitive complexity. They delineate six levels of cognitive complexity, ranging from the knowledge level (least complex) to the evaluation level (most complex). As illustrated in Figure 3.3, Bloom et al. describe the levels as hierarchical; the higher-level objectives include, and are dependent on, lower-level cognitive skills. Thus objectives at the evaluation level require more complex mental operations—higher cognitive skills—than objectives at the knowledge level.

Also, notice that higher-level objectives are more authentic than lower-level objectives. Let's consider what *authenticity* means.

So far in this chapter, you have seen a variety of skills and behaviors that children learn in school. Some of these require learners to acquire information by memorizing, for example, vocabulary, multiplication tables, dates of historical events, or the names of important persons. In addition, you saw some example objectives in which students had to acquire concepts, rules, and generalizations that allowed them to understand what they read, to analyze, and to compare and contrast. These types of learning outcomes represent what is called **declarative** or **factual knowledge,** which contains the *facts, concepts, rules*, and *generalizations* pertaining to a specific area or topic. They include, for example, knowledge

Figure 3.3 Taxonomy of educational objectives: Cognitive domain (Bloom et al., 1984).

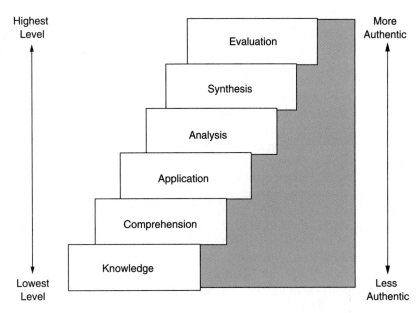

of technical vocabulary, the names of major natural resources, periods of geological time, the Pythagorean theorem, or the theory of evolution.

Other skills and behaviors involve learning *action sequences* or *procedures* to follow when, for example, using drawing materials, performing mathematical computations, operating a calculator, or practicing handwriting. These types of outcomes represent what is called **procedural knowledge.** Procedural knowledge is knowledge of how to do things. If you know the names of the parts of a shoe, for example, lace, eyelet, tongue, and knot, you have declarative knowledge. If you know how to use this knowledge to actually tie your shoe, you have procedural knowledge.

Still other skills and behaviors require learners to think about their own thinking to determine when it is and is not leading to a desirable outcome; for example, becoming *aware* of the procedure one is using to tie one's shoe, *monitoring* the effectiveness of that procedure, and making a conscious *commitment* to use that procedure again. This type of behavior represents what is called **metacognitive knowledge**—or thinking about your thinking to become aware of your own level of knowledge.

Some of these skills are best assessed with paper and pencil tests. But skills requiring independent judgment, critical thinking, and decision making are best assessed with performance assessments. **Performance assessments** measure a skill or behavior directly, as it is used in the world outside your classroom.

Classroom assessment of learning, particularly beyond the early elementary grades, has been almost exclusively based on paper and pencil tests, which indicate rather than directly measure what children have learned. For example, you may measure an understanding of the scientific method, not by having learners plan, conduct, and evaluate an experiment (a direct assessment), but by asking them to list the steps in conducting an experiment, write about the difference between an hypothesis and a theory, or choose the correct definition of a control group from a list of choices (all indirect assessment). Or you may measure children's understanding of money, not by observing them buy food, pay for it, and get the correct change (direct assessment), but by asking them to recall how many pennies there are in a dollar or to write down how much change they would get back from a $10 bill if they paid $6.75 for a T-shirt (indirect assessment).

Indirect assessment of achievement and learning has obvious advantages, not the least of which is efficiency. It would be very time consuming to directly and, therefore, authentically measure all learning that goes on in a classroom. But indirect assessment raises a problem: How do you know your test is telling you if your learners can apply the skills and behaviors you are teaching? **Authentic tests** ask learners to display their skills and behaviors in the way that they would be displayed outside the classroom—in the real world. Authentic tests measure directly the skills and behaviors teachers and learners really care about. In other words, they ask the learners to do what was modeled, coached, and practiced during instruction as it would be done outside the classroom. If learners saw you demonstrate how to focus a microscope, were coached to do this, and practiced doing it, then an authentic assessment would ask them to focus a microscope rather than label the parts of the microscope on a diagram. If, however, your learners only needed to know the parts of a microscope so they could read a story about the invention of the microscope—not use one—asking them to label the parts could be an authentic assessment.

Objectives requiring higher-level cognitive, affective, and psychomotor skills—those that most closely represent the thinking curriculum introduced earlier in this chapter—represent more **authentic behaviors** because they identify the types of performances required of your learners in the world in which they must live, work, and play.

Now let's look at how each behavior in the cognitive domain varies according to cognitive skill and authenticity. These behaviors are described with examples of action verbs that represent them.

Knowledge. Objectives at the knowledge level require your students to remember or recall information such as facts, terminology, problem-solving strategies, and rules. Some action verbs that describe learning outcomes at the knowledge level are

define	list	recall
describe	match	recite
identify	name	select
label	outline	state

Examples of knowledge objectives that use these verbs:

- The student will recall the four major food groups, without error, by Friday.
- From memory, the student will match U.S. generals with their most famous battles, with 80% accuracy.

Comprehension. Objectives at the comprehension level require some degree of understanding. Students are expected to be able to change the form of a communication; translate; restate what has been read; see connections or relationships among parts of a communication (interpretation); or draw conclusions or see consequences from information (inference). Here are some action verbs that describe learning outcomes at the comprehension level:

convert	estimate	infer
defend	explain	paraphrase
discriminate	extend	predict
distinguish	generalize	summarize

Examples of comprehension objectives that use these verbs:

- By the end of the six-week grading period, the student will summarize the main events of a story in grammatically correct English.
- The student will discriminate between the realists and the naturalists, citing examples from the readings.

Objectives requiring higher-level cognitive, affective, and psychomotor skills are more authentic behaviors because they are more likely to represent the types of performances required of your learners in the world in which they must live, work, and play.

Application. Objectives written at the application level require the student to use previously acquired information in a setting other than the one in which it was learned. Application objectives differ from comprehension objectives in that application requires the presentation of a problem in a different and often applied context. Thus the student can rely on neither the content nor the context in which the original learning occurred to solve the problem. Here are some action verbs that describe learning outcomes at the application level:

change	modify	relate
compute	operate	solve
demonstrate	organize	transfer
develop	prepare	use

Examples of application objectives that use these or similar verbs:

- On Monday, the student will demonstrate for the class an application to real life of the law of conservation of energy.
- Given single-digit fractions not covered in class, the student will multiply them on paper with 85% accuracy.

Analysis. Objectives written at the analysis level require the student to identify logical errors (e.g., point out a contradiction or an erroneous inference) or to differentiate among facts, opinions, assumptions, hypotheses, and conclusions. At the analysis level, students are expected to draw relationships among ideas and to compare and contrast. Here are some action verbs that describe learning outcomes at the analysis level:

break down	distinguish	point out
deduce	illustrate	relate
diagram	infer	separate out
differentiate	outline	subdivide

Examples of analysis objectives that use these verbs:

- Given a presidential speech, the student will be able to point out the positions that attack an individual rather than that individual's program.
- Given absurd statements (e.g., A man had flu twice. The first time it killed him. The second time he got well quickly.), the student will be able to point out the contradiction.

Synthesis. Objectives written at the synthesis level require the student to produce something unique or original. At the synthesis level, students are expected to solve some unfamiliar problem in a unique way or to combine parts to form a unique or novel solution. Here are some action verbs that describe learning outcomes at the synthesis level:

categorize	create	formulate
compile	design	predict
compose	devise	produce

Examples of synthesis objectives that use these or similar verbs are:

- Given a short story, the student will write a different but plausible ending.
- Given a problem to be solved, the student will design on paper a scientific experiment to address the problem.

Evaluation. Objectives written at the evaluation level require the student to form judgments and make decisions about the value of methods, ideas, people, or products that have a specific purpose. Students are expected to state the bases for their judgments (e.g., the external criteria or principles they drew on to reach their conclusions). Here are some action verbs that describe learning outcomes at the evaluation level:

appraise	criticize	justify
compare	defend	support
contrast	judge	validate

Examples of evaluation objectives that use these verbs are:

- Given a previously unread paragraph, the student will judge its value according to the five criteria discussed in class.
- Given a description of a country's economic system, the student will defend it, basing arguments on principles of democracy.

Anderson and Krathwohl (2001) have prepared an updated version of Bloom et. al's taxonomy of educational objectives from a cognitive learning perspective that helps teachers not only identify and assess the outcomes they desire but the thinking processes their students must use to achieve those outcomes. Their edited volume explores curricula from three perspectives—the cognitive learning perspective, the teaching perspective, and the assessment perspective—providing a useful framework for writing objectives that connect all three perspectives. Figure 3.4 illustrates their extensions to the original taxonomy that emphasize the distinctions among factual (declarative), conceptual, procedural, and metacognitive knowledge when writing objectives and selecting a teaching strategy that can most effectively achieve those objectives. See In Practice: Focus on the New Field of Cognitive Science.

The Affective Domain

Another method of categorizing objectives was devised by Krathwohl, Bloom, and Masia (1999). This taxonomy delineates five levels of affective behavior ranging from the receiving level to the characterization level (see Figure 3.5). As in the cognitive domain, these levels

The Knowledge Dimension	The Cognitive Process Dimension					
	1. Remember	2. Understand	3. Apply	4. Analyze	5. Evaluate	6. Create
A. Factual knowledge: The basic facts that must be known within a discipline.						
B. Conceptual knowledge: The interrelationships that function together to form a concept.						
C. Procedural knowledge: How to apply skills, algorithms, techniques, and methods.						
D. Metacognitive knowledge: Awareness and knowledge of one's own thinking.						

Figure 3.4 A taxonomy for learning, teaching, and assessing.

Source: Adapted from Anderson, L. & Krathwohl, D. (Eds.). (2001). *Taxonomy for learning, teaching, and assessing: A revision of Bloom's taxonomy of educational objectives.* New York, NY: Longman.

are presumed to be hierarchical—higher-level objectives are assumed to include and be dependent on lower-level affective skills. As one moves up the hierarchy, more involvement, commitment, and reliance on oneself occurs, as opposed to having one's feelings, attitudes, and values dictated by others.

The following sections contain examples of action verbs indicating each level of the affective domain.

Receiving.   Objectives at the receiving level require the student to be aware of, or to passively attend to, certain phenomena and stimuli. At this level students are expected simply to listen or be attentive. Here are some action verbs that describe outcomes at the receiving level:

attend	discern	look
be aware	hear	notice
control	listen	share

Examples of receiving objectives that use these verbs are:

- The student will be able to notice a change from small-group discussion to large-group lecture by following the lead of others in the class.
- The student will be able to listen to all of a Mozart concerto without leaving his or her seat.

IN PRACTICE

Focus on the New Field of Cognitive Science

In this chapter you studied two taxonomies of objectives in the cognitive domain: one by Bloom et al., first published in 1956, and another, more recent, by Anderson and Krathwohl (2001). The development of these taxonomies represents a gradual shift from a behavioral model, which emphasizes how to arrange the learning environment to bring about desired outcomes (for example, through rewards and disincentives), to a cognitive model that places more emphasis on how the brain functions during problem solving, decision making, creativity, and critical thinking and the cognitive strategies that promote these outcomes. Although both taxonomies consider the acquisition of knowledge to be important, Anderson and Krathwohl have extended Bloom et al.'s taxonomy to include the cognitive and metacognitive strategies that can help learners improve their thinking and more efficiently achieve higher order outcomes. Much of what we know about the content of thinking and assessment today we owe to advances in the cognitive science of learning.

The Behavioral Model

B. F. Skinner is considered the "grandfather of behaviorism." He generated much of the experimental data that form the basis of behavioral learning theory. He and other behavioral theorists were concerned mainly with observable indications of learning and what those observations could imply for teaching. They concentrated on observable "cause and effect" relationships. Skinner and others viewed the teacher's job as modifying the behavior of students by setting up situations to reinforce students when they exhibit desired responses. Behaviorists viewed learning as a sequence of stimulus and response actions in the learner. They reasoned that teachers could link together responses involving lower-level skills and create a learning "chain" to teach higher-level skills. The teacher would determine all of the skills needed to lead up to the desired behavior and make sure students learned them all in a step-by-step manner (Roblyer, Edwards, & Havriluk, 1997, p. 59).

The Cognitive Model

Many educational psychologists, however, found the behavioral approach unsatisfying. In the areas of problem solving and learning strategies they became more concerned with what was unobservable—what was going on inside the brain. These theories are based on the work of educational philosopher John Dewey and educational psychologists Lev Vygotsky, Jean Piaget, and Jerome Bruner. They proposed that children actively construct knowledge and this construction of knowledge happens in a social context. Vygotsky proposed that all learning takes place in the "zone of proximal development." This "zone" is the difference between what a child can do alone and what he or she can do with assistance. By building on the child's experiences and providing moderately challenging tasks teachers can provide the "intellectual scaffolding" to help children learn and progress through the different stages of development. Whereas the behavioral approach to learning emphasizes how to establish a learning environment to produce more correct answers than incorrect ones, the cognitive approach emphasizes that good thinking results from studying the cognitive processes and outcomes that underlie right and wrong answers. Cognitive psychologists believe that learners, even at the earliest grade levels, have some knowledge about nearly every topic they study (Tombari & Borich, 1999, p. 7).

Closely connected to the cognitive approach are the methods of constructivism. These methods emphasize students' ability to solve real-life, practical problems. Students typically work in cooperative groups rather than individually; they tend to focus on projects that require solutions to problems rather than on instructional sequences that require learning certain content skills. The job of the teacher in constructivist models is to arrange for required resources and act as a guide to students while they set their own goals and "teach themselves" (Roblyer, Edwards, & Havriluk, 1997, p. 70).

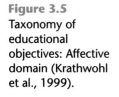

Figure 3.5
Taxonomy of educational objectives: Affective domain (Krathwohl et al., 1999).

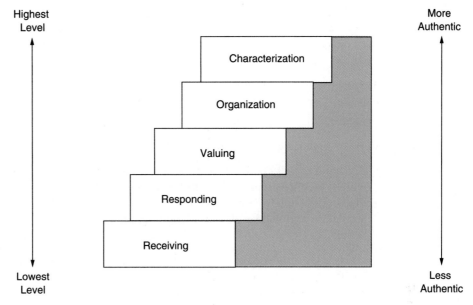

Responding.   Objectives at the responding level require the student to comply with given expectations by attending or reacting to certain stimuli. Students are expected to obey, participate, or respond willingly when asked or directed to do something. Here are some action verbs that describe outcomes at the responding level:

applaud	follow	play
comply	obey	practice
discuss	participate	volunteer

Examples of responding objectives that use these verbs are:

- The student will follow the directions given in the book without argument when asked to do so.
- The student will practice a musical instrument when asked to do so.

Valuing.   Objectives at the valuing level require the student to display behavior consistent with a single belief or attitude in situations where he or she is neither forced nor asked to comply. Students are expected to demonstrate a preference or display a high degree of certainty and conviction. Here are some action verbs that describe outcomes at the valuing level:

act	debate	help
argue	display	organize
convince	express	prefer

Some examples of valuing objectives that use these verbs are:

- The student will express an opinion about nuclear disarmament whenever national events raise the issue.
- The student will display an opinion about the elimination of pornography when discussing this social issue.

Organization.   Objectives at the organization level require a commitment to a set of values. This level of the affective domain involves (1) forming a reason why one values certain things and not others, and (2) making appropriate choices between things that are and are not valued. Students are expected to organize their likes and preferences into a value system and then decide which ones will be dominant. Here are some action verbs that describe outcomes at the organization level:

abstract	decide	select
balance	define	systematize
compare	formulate	theorize

Examples of organization objectives that use these verbs are:

- The student will be able to compare alternatives to the death penalty and decide which ones are compatible with his or her beliefs.
- The student will be able to formulate the reasons why she or he supports civil rights legislation and will be able to identify legislation that does not support her or his beliefs.

Characterization.   Objectives at the characterization level require that all behavior displayed by the student be consistent with his or her values. At this level the student not only has acquired the behaviors at all previous levels but also has integrated his or her values into a system representing a complete and pervasive philosophy that does not allow expressions that are out of character with these values. Evaluations of this level of behavior involve the extent to which the student has developed a consistent philosophy of life (e.g., exhibits respect for the worth and dignity of human beings in all situations). Here are some action verbs that describe outcomes at this level:

avoid	internalize	resist
display	manage	resolve
exhibit	require	revise

Some example objectives are:

- The student will exhibit a helping and caring attitude toward students with disabilities by assisting with their mobility both in and out of classrooms.
- The student will display a scientific attitude by stating and then testing hypotheses whenever the choice of alternatives is unclear.

The Psychomotor Domain

A third method of categorizing objectives has been devised by Harrow (1972) and by Moore (1992). Harrow's taxonomy delineates five levels of psychomotor behavior ranging from the imitation level (least complex and least authentic) to the naturalization level (most complex and most authentic). Figure 3.6 illustrates the hierarchical arrangement of the psychomotor domain. These behaviors place primary emphasis on neuromuscular skills involving various degrees of physical dexterity. As behaviors in the taxonomy move from least to most complex and authentic, behavior changes from gross to fine motor skills.

Each of the levels—imitation, manipulation, precision, articulation, and naturalization—has different characteristics as described in the following sections with example verbs that represent them.

Imitation.   Objectives at the imitation level require that the learner be exposed to an observable action and then overtly imitate it, such as when an instructor demonstrates the use of a microscope by placing a slide on the specimen tray. Performance at this level usually lacks neuromuscular coordination (e.g., the slide may hit the side of the tray or be improperly

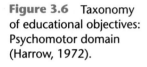

Figure 3.6 Taxonomy of educational objectives: Psychomotor domain (Harrow, 1972).

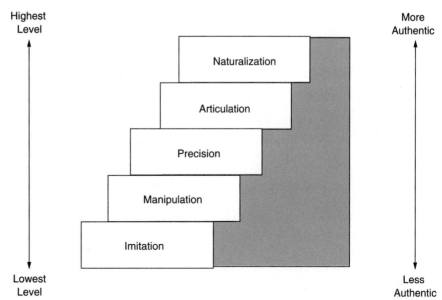

aligned beneath the lens). Thus the behavior generally is crude and imperfect. At this level students are expected to observe and be able to repeat (although imperfectly) the action being visually demonstrated. Here are some action verbs that describe outcomes at this level:

align	grasp	repeat
balance	hold	rest (on)
follow	place	step (here)

Examples of imitation objectives that use these or similar verbs are:

- After being shown a safe method for heating a beaker of water to boiling temperature, the student will be able to repeat the action.
- After being shown a freehand drawing of a triangle, the student will be able to reproduce the drawing.

Manipulation.   Objectives at the manipulation level require the student to perform selected actions from written or verbal directions without the aid of a visual model or direct observation, as in the previous (imitation) level. Students are expected to complete the action from reading or listening to instructions, although the behavior still may be performed crudely and without neuromuscular coordination. Useful expressions to describe outcomes at the manipulation level are the same as at the imitation level, using the same action verbs, except they are performed from spoken or written instructions.

Here are examples of some manipulation objectives:

- Based on the picture provided in the textbook, type a salutation to a prospective employer using the format shown.
- With the instructions on the handout in front of you, practice focusing your microscope until you can see the outline of the specimen.

Precision.   Objectives at the precision level require the student to perform an action independent of either a visual model or a written set of directions. Proficiency in reproducing the action at this level reaches a higher level of refinement. Accuracy, proportion, balance, and exactness in performance accompany the action. Students are expected to reproduce the action with control and to reduce errors to a minimum. Expressions that describe outcomes at this level include performing the behavior

accurately	independently	with control
without error	proficiently	with balance

Some examples of precision objectives are:

- The student will be able to place the specimen accurately on the microscope tray and use the high-power focus with proficiency as determined by the correct identification of three out of four easily recognizable objects.
- The student will be able to balance a light pen sufficiently to place it against the computer screen to identify misspelled words.

Articulation.   Objectives at the articulation level require the student to display coordination of a series of related acts by establishing the appropriate sequence and performing the acts accurately, with control as well as with speed and timing. Expressions that describe outcomes at this level include performing the behaviors with

confidence	integration	speed
coordination	proportion	stability
harmony	smoothness	timing

Examples of articulation objectives are:

- Students will be able to write all the letters of the alphabet, displaying the appropriate proportion between uppercase and lowercase, in 10 minutes.
- Students will be able to complete 10 simple arithmetic problems accurately on a handheld electronic calculator quickly and smoothly within 90 seconds.

Naturalization.   Objectives at the naturalization level require a high level of proficiency in the skill or performance being taught. At this level the behavior is performed with the least expenditure of energy and becomes routine, automatic, and spontaneous. Students are expected to repeat the behavior naturally and effortlessly time and again. Here are some expressions that describe this level of behavior:

automatically	professionally	with ease
effortlessly	routinely	with perfection
naturally	spontaneously	with poise

Some examples of naturalization objectives are:

- At the end of the semester, students will be able to write routinely all the letters of the alphabet and all the numbers up to 100 each time requested.
- After the first grading period, students will be able to automatically draw correct isosceles, equilateral, and right triangles, without the aid of a template, for each homework assignment that requires this task.

SOME MISUNDERSTANDINGS ABOUT BEHAVIORAL OBJECTIVES

Before beginning to write objectives, you should be aware of several misconceptions about the cognitive, affective, and psychomotor domains. Following are some cautions to be mindful of when using behavioral objectives, each stated in the form of a question a parent or teacher may ask.

Are Some Behaviors More Desirable Than Others?

One misconception that often results from study of the cognitive, affective, and psychomotor domains is that simple behaviors, like the recall of facts and dates, are less desirable than more complex behaviors requiring the cognitive operations of analysis, synthesis, and decision making. However, the simple-to-complex ordering of behaviors within the cognitive, affective, and psychomotor domains does not imply desirability, because many lower-order behaviors must be learned before higher-order behaviors can be attempted.

Some teachers pride themselves on preparing objectives almost exclusively at the highest levels of cognitive complexity. But objectives at a lower order of complexity often represent the knowledge base from which students achieve more complex behaviors. When task-relevant prior knowledge or skills necessary for acquiring more complex behaviors have not been taught, students may demonstrate high error rates and less active engagement in the learning process at the higher levels of behavioral complexity (Alexander, 1996).

One of the most important uses of the taxonomies of behavior we have studied is to provide a menu of behaviors at different levels of complexity. As with any good diet, variety and proper proportion are the keys to good results.

What Is an Authentic Behavior?

Another misconception involves the meaning of the word *authentic*, which means relevant to the real world. If a learner needed to list the names of the presidents in the real world—for example, on a job, at home, in a training program—that behavior could be measured authentically by asking the learner to repeat the names of the presidents, perhaps in the order in which they held office. Your measurement of this objective would be authentic because you are asking that the behavior be displayed in your classroom exactly as it would be performed outside. However, few occupations, courses, or programs of study will require your learners to recite the names of the presidents.

Knowledge (cognitive domain), receiving (affective domain), and imitation (psychomotor domain) are seldom sufficient in the world outside the classroom. Although they often are necessary in acquiring more complex behaviors, they seldom take on importance by themselves. Behaviors representing higher cognitive skills often do take on importance outside the classroom exactly as they are taught. Evaluation (cognitive domain), characterization (affective domain), and naturalization (psychomotor domain) are examples of such behaviors. Deciding which candidate to vote for, assuming the responsibility of an informed citizen, and being able to read and complete a voting ballot are all authentic behaviors because they are necessary performances in daily life. Therefore, higher cognitive skills often are more authentic than lower cognitive skills because they represent more integrated behaviors necessary for living, working, and performing in the world outside your classroom. This is one of the best reasons for a "thinking curriculum" that teaches higher cognitive skills in your classroom. To help you with this, you will find in appendix C the *Higher-Order Thinking and Problem-Solving Checklist* (Borich & Tombari, 2004) to help you select and prioritize some of the authentic behaviors you may want to teach and assess. Borich and Tombari (2004) provide lesson contexts and objectives across the K–12 grades that illustrate higher-order thinking and problem-solving behaviors you can teach in your classroom. Write behavioral objectives for some of these behaviors and you will be teaching a thinking curriculum.

Are Less Complex Behaviors Easier to Teach?

Another misconception is that behaviors of less complexity are easier to teach than behaviors of greater complexity. This is an appealing argument because intuition tells us that this should be so. After all, complexity—especially cognitive complexity—often has been associated with greater difficulty, greater amounts of study time, and more extensive instructional resources.

Although simpler behaviors may be easier to teach some of the time, it can be just the opposite. For example, consider the elaborate visual materials and mnemonic system that might be needed to recall a portion of the periodic table of chemical elements, as opposed to the simple demonstration that may be required to teach its application. In this case, the so-called less complex behavior requires greater time and instructional resources. Also, whether a behavior is easier or more difficult to teach always will depend on the learning needs of your students. Keep in mind, then, that ease with which a behavior can be taught is not necessarily synonymous with the level of the behavior in the taxonomy. These designations refer to the mental—or cognitive—operations required of the student and not the preparation required of the teacher to assure that your learners have attained the desired outcome.

Are Cognitive, Affective, and Psychomotor Behaviors Mutually Exclusive?

Categorizing behaviors into separate cognitive, affective, and psychomotor domains does not mean that behaviors listed in one domain are not needed for attaining those listed in other domains (Anderson & Krathwohl, 2001). For example, it is not possible to think without having some feeling about what we are thinking or to feel something without thinking, so the affective and cognitive domains are intertwined. Also, much thinking involves physical movements and bodily performances that require psychomotor skills and abilities. For example, conducting a laboratory experiment requires not only thinking about what you are doing but pouring from one test tube to another, safely igniting a Bunsen burner, or adjusting a microscope correctly. Similarly, legible handwriting requires neuromuscular coordination, timing, and control while you are thinking about what is being written.

Although it is convenient for an objective to contain behavior from only one of the three domains at a time, keep in mind that one or more behaviors from the other domains also may be required. This is one of the best reasons for preparing objectives in all three domains: It is evidence of your awareness of the close and necessary relationship among cognitive, affective, and psychomotor behaviors.

THE CULTURAL ROOTS OF OBJECTIVES

Finally, be prepared to have the source of your objectives questioned by parents, community members, and students. Some typical teacher responses to an inquiring parent question about the source of a lesson or unit objective may include "from the textbook . . . curriculum guide . . . or department policies."

These answers are technically correct but miss the fundamental point, which is that objectives have roots much deeper than any single text, curriculum guide, or set of policies. These roots lie in the educational values we espouse as a nation. Although parents, students, and other teachers may argue with the text used, the curriculum guide followed, or the department policies adopted, it is quite another matter to take exception to the values we share as a nation and that were created by many different interest groups over years of thoughtful deliberation, such as the INTASC and NBPTS standards presented in chapter 1.

Texts, curricula, and policies are interpretations of these values shared at the broadest national level and translated into practice through standards, goals, and objectives. Texts, curriculum guides, and school district policies can no more create objectives than they can create values. Goals and their objectives, as we have seen earlier in this chapter, are carefully created to reflect our values from sources such as curriculum reform committees, state and national legislative mandates, and the professional associations to which you belong. This is why you must have a knowledge of these ultimate sources from which your objectives have been derived, or else you may continually be caught in the position of justifying a particular text, curriculum, or policy to parents, students, and peers—some of whom will always disagree with you. Reference to any one text, curriculum, or policy cannot prove that your students should appreciate art or know how to solve an equation. But our values, as indicated by curriculum reform committees, state and national mandates, and professional associations, can provide appropriate and adequate justification for your intended learning outcomes. Your attention to these values as reported by professional papers and reports, curriculum committees, and national teacher groups is as important to your teaching as the objectives you write.

SUMMING UP

This chapter introduced you to instructional objectives. Its key terms and main points were:

Standards, Goals, and Objectives

1. Standards are expressions of societal values that provide a sense of direction broad enough to be accepted by large numbers of individuals.
2. Goals identify what will be learned from your instruction and energize and motivate you and your learners to achieve practical end products.
3. Objectives have two purposes: (1) to tie standards to specific classroom strategies that will achieve those standards, and (2) to express teaching strategies in a format that allows you to measure their effects on your learners.
4. When the word *behavioral* precedes the word *objective*, the learning is being defined as a change in observable behavior that can be measured within a specified period of time.

Tyler's Goal Development Approach

5. The need for behavioral objectives stems from a natural preoccupation with concerns for self and task, sometimes to the exclusion of concerns for the impact on students.

An Overview of Behavioral Objectives

6. Simply put, behavioral objectives do the following:
   - Focus instruction on a specific goal whose outcomes can be observed.
   - Identify the conditions under which learning can be expected to occur.
   - Specify the level or amount of behavior that can be expected from the instruction under the conditions specified.
7. Action verbs help operationalize the learning outcome expected from an objective and identify exactly what the learner must do to achieve the outcome.
8. The outcome specified in a behavioral objective should be expressed as an end (e.g., to identify,

recall, list) and not as a means (e.g., to study, watch, listen).
9. If the observable learning outcome is to take place with particular materials, equipment, tools, or other resources, these conditions must be stated explicitly in the objective.

Identifying the Conditions

10. Conditional statements within a behavioral objective can be singular (one condition) or multiple (more than one condition).
11. Conditions should match those under which the behavior will be performed in the real world.

Stating Criterion Levels

12. A proficiency level is the minimum degree of performance that will satisfy you that the objective has been met.
13. Proficiency levels represent value judgments, or educated guesses, as to what level of performance will be required for adequately performing the behavior in some later setting beyond your classroom.
14. The expressiveness of an objective refers to the amount of flexibility allowed in a response. Less expressive objectives may call for only a single right answer, whereas more expressive objectives allow for less structured and more flexible responses. The expressiveness allowed is always a matter of degree.

The Cognitive, Affective, and Psychomotor Domains

15. "Complexity" of a behavior in the cognitive, affective, or psychomotor domain pertains to the operations required of the student to produce the behavior, not to the complexity of the teaching activities required.
16. Behaviors in the cognitive domain, from least to most complex, are knowledge, comprehension, application, analysis, synthesis, and evaluation.

17. Behaviors in the affective domain, from least to most complex, are receiving, responding, valuing, organization, and characterization.
18. Behaviors in the psychomotor domain, from least to most complex, are imitation, manipulation, precision, articulation, and naturalization.

The Cultural Roots of Objectives

19. Behavioral objectives have their roots in the educational values we espouse as a nation. Texts, curricula, and department and school policies are interpretations of these values shared at the broadest national level and translated into practice through behavioral objectives.

Some Misunderstandings About Behavioral Objectives

20. Four important cautions in using the taxonomies of behavioral objectives are as follows:
   - No behavior specified is necessarily more or less desirable than any other.
   - Higher cognitive skills often are more authentic than lower cognitive skills.
   - Less complex behaviors are not necessarily easier to teach, less time consuming, or dependent on fewer resources than are more complex behaviors.
   - Behavior in one domain may require achievement of one or more behaviors in other domains.

KEY TERMS

Affective domain, 92
Authentic behaviors, 94
Authentic tests, 94
Behavioral objective, 85
Cognitive domain, 92
Criterion level, 89
Declarative (factual) knowledge, 92
Expressive objective, 90
Goals, 80
Learning activities, 87

Learning conditions, 88
Learning outcome, 86
Metacognitive knowledge, 93
Objectives, 80
Performance assessments, 93
Procedural knowledge, 93
Psychomotor domain, 92
Standards, 80
Thinking curriculum, 83

DISCUSSION AND PRACTICE QUESTIONS

 Questions marked with an asterisk are answered in appendix B. See also the Companion Website for this text at *www.prenhall.com/borich* for more assessment options.

1. Select one of the 10 INTASC principles identified in chapter 1 and translate it into one or more objectives for your teacher preparation program. Make sure your objective is responsive to the principle from which it was derived.
*2. Identify the two general purposes for preparing behavioral objectives. If you could choose only one of these purposes, which would be more important to you? Why?
*3. Explain what three things the word *behavioral* implies when it appears before the word *objectives.*
*4. Identify the three components of a well-written behavioral objective, and give one example of each component.
*5. Historically, why did the concept of behavioral objectives emerge?
*6. Why are action verbs necessary in translating goals such as mentally healthy citizens, well-rounded

individuals, and self-actualized schoolchildren into learning outcomes?
*7. Distinguish learning outcomes (ends) from learning activities (means) by placing an O or A beside the following expressions:

   Working on a car radio
   Adding signed numbers correctly
   Practicing the violin
   Playing basketball
   Using a microscope
   Identifying an amoeba
   Naming the seven parts of speech
   Punctuating an essay correctly

*8. Define a condition in a behavioral objective. Give three examples.
*9. How can the specification of conditions help students study and prepare for tests?
*10. In trying to decide what condition(s) to include in a behavioral objective, what single most important consideration should guide your selection?
*11. What is the definition of *criterion level* in a behavioral objective? Give three examples.

*12. The following Group A contains objectives. Group B contains levels of cognitive behavior. Match the levels in group B with the most appropriate objective in group A. Group B levels can be used more than once.

Group A: Objectives

_____ 1. Given a two-page essay, the student can distinguish the assumptions basic to the author's position.

_____ 2. The student will correctly spell the word *mountain*.

_____ 3. The student will convert the following English passage into Spanish.

_____ 4. The student will compose new pieces of prose and poetry according to the classification system emphasized in class.

_____ 5. Given a sinking passenger ship with 19 of its 20 lifeboats destroyed, the captain will decide, based on his perceptions of their potential worth to society, who is to be placed on the last lifeboat.

Group B: Levels

a. knowledge
b. comprehension
c. application
d. analysis
e. synthesis
f. evaluation

FIELD EXPERIENCE ACTIVITIES

1. Based on your experience in classrooms, provide examples of two behavioral objectives that differ in the degree of expressiveness they allow.

2. Using a topic you are likely to teach, write an objective for each of the knowledge, comprehension, application, analysis, synthesis, and evaluation levels of the taxonomy of cognitive objectives. Select verbs for each level from the lists provided in the chapter. Have each of your objectives cover the same subject.

3. Exchange the objectives you have just written with a classmate. Have the classmate check each objective for (1) an observable behavior, (2) any special conditions under which the behavior must be displayed, and (3) a performance level considered sufficient to demonstrate mastery. Revise your objectives if necessary.

4. A parent calls to tell you that, after a long talk with her son, she disapproves of the objectives you have written for health education—particularly those referring to the anatomy of the human body—but that you have taken almost verbatim from the teachers' guide to the adopted textbook. Compose a written response to this parent that shows your understanding of where objectives come from.

DIGITAL PORTFOLIO ACTIVITIES

These digital portfolio activities relate to INTASC principles 7 and 8.

1. On your very first teaching assignment or job interview you may be asked to provide evidence of your ability to write behavioral objectives properly. The objectives you've written for the preceding Field Practice Activities 1 and 2 provide examples of your proficiency in writing objectives that represent (1) different degrees of expressiveness, following Eisner's view of objectives and (2) the knowledge, comprehension, application, analysis, synthesis, and evaluation outcomes, following Bloom et al.'s view of behavioral objectives. Place these objectives in your digital portfolio in a folder titled *Behavioral Objectives*.

2. To complete your knowledge of the various approaches to objectives, write one objective each for a topic you are likely to teach that represent the categories of procedural knowledge and metacognitive knowledge suggested by Anderson and Krathwohl. Place these also in your *Behavioral Objectives* digital portfolio folder.

CLASSROOM OBSERVATION ACTIVITIES

The following classroom observation activities relate to INTASC principles 7 and 8.

1. For this activity go to the *Classroom Observation* module for this chapter on the Companion Website at *www.prenhall.com/borich*. There you will find an observation instrument titled *Format for Recording Information Pertaining to Behavioral Objectives*. From a video of an actual classroom lesson or visit to a classroom, record in the first part of the instrument whether the learners were informed of the objective, and if not, why not. This is important because not every lesson will require informing learners of the objective (for example, when the lesson is a continuation of a series of related lessons for which the objective is already well known to learners, or when the lesson is devoted entirely to a review, in which case many different objectives may be touched on but not taught directly). After recording this information, indicate whether the objective(s) stated is (are) cognitive, affective, psychomotor, or some combination thereof. If possible, indicate the highest level of performance expected of the learner by selecting the expected outcome that comes closest to the action verbs listed on the instrument. Place your record in the *Classroom Observation* folder of your digital portfolio as documentation of your understanding of behavioral objectives and observation skills.

2. Return to the *Classroom Observation* module on the Companion Website for this chapter. You will find a second instrument titled *Form for Recording the Relationship Between Levels of Behavioral Complexity and Teaching Strategies*. This instrument illustrates a method of recording the relationship among behavioral outcomes at different levels of complexity and the instructional strategies most commonly used to teach them. The behavioral outcomes listed across the top are divided into two types: lower order and higher order. The phrase *lower order* is used to describe knowledge, comprehension, and application outcomes; the phrase *higher order* is used to describe outcomes at the analysis, synthesis, and evaluation levels. The teaching functions listed on the left side of the instrument are divided into direct teaching strategies representing the lecture/presentational approach in which the teacher is the primary provider of information and into indirect teaching strategies representing the concept learning, inquiry, and problem-solving approaches to instruction.

Observe a video of a classroom lesson and place a checkmark in the appropriate box each time there is a change in teaching strategy or behavioral outcome. At the end of your observation, checkmarks should appear in the upper left quadrant (lower order/direct) and lower right quadrant (higher order/indirect), because direct instruction strategies tend to be more efficient for teaching outcomes at the lower levels of behavioral complexity, and indirect instruction strategies tend to be more efficient for teaching outcomes at the higher levels of behavioral complexity. Place your recording form in the *Classroom Observation* folder of your digital portfolio as evidence of your observational skills.

CHAPTER CASE HISTORY AND PRAXIS TEST PREPARATION

DIRECTIONS: The following case history pertains to chapter 3 content. After reading the case history, answer the short-answer question that follows and consult appendix D where you will find different levels of scored student responses and the rubric used to determine the quality of each response. You also have the opportunity to submit your responses online to receive feedback by visiting the *Case History* module for this chapter on the Companion Website, where you will also find additional questions pertaining to Praxis test content.

Case History

Max is a prospective teacher in the last year of his program. Today he will be observing two science classes at a middle school.

Mr. Goldthorp's Science Classroom

Mr. Goldthorp's students are working quietly at their desks. They are in the midst of a two-week field investigation unit devoted to identifying leaves. The directions for the unit are written on the handout Mr. Goldthorp has shared with Max.

Using the specimens available to them during school nature walks as well as those close to home, the students will collect, identify, and label the leaves of 10 trees native to their area. Work is expected to be neat and accurate and completed in 10 school days.

Several students leave their desks to consult the reference table, where books are available with colored pictures and detailed sketches of trees and leaves. Sometimes students help each other to decide among possible choices. Mr. Goldthorp encourages this informal cooperation and steps in with questions to guide them when needed.

Another table has a laminating machine. Aurora's eyes sparkle as she watches her dusty red oak leaf emerge encased in shining plastic.

Some take their turns with the calligraphy pens available for labeling; others wait to use the computer to do the labeling.

Four or five students make themselves comfortable on the carpet and pillow-lined library corner where they leaf through an assortment of poetry books in hopes of finding "just the right poem" about nature to express their feelings about trees. If they recite one in front of the class, they can get up to 10 points extra credit.

Mr. Gonzales's Science Classroom

Across the hall, Max sees that Mr. Gonzales is also working on a unit concerned with nature. Over the past few days his class has been discussing the deer problem that has made the local news. Recently a woman was seriously injured when her car ran into a deer. One of the students in class knew the injured woman and brought the topic up during a class discussion about ecology. The passion the class generated was so intense that Mr. Gonzales has abandoned his usual field investigation of local stream water purity and allowed them to pursue their interest in the deer problem.

Today, during Max's observation, they are debating some of the proposals brought up in the newspaper and on the radio. Mr. Gonzales is at the board writing down the ideas. Next to each idea is a column labeled "Positives" and another labeled "Negatives." The class is discussing a plan that would make it illegal for residents to feed deer. Susan is animated in her disapproval of such a law.

"Our country is founded on freedom and property rights. You should be able to feed deer on your own property without having to ask anybody's permission." Mr. Gonzales puts "Ignores freedom and property rights" under the negative column.

"It's because people treat them like pets that causes the accidents," Carmen blurts out before she remembers to raise her hand. She is the girl who knows the injured woman.

After noting her idea in the positive column, under "Safety concerns," Mr. Gonzales hands out the following assignment.

Using our class discussion, as well as ideas proposed in the newspaper, write a proposal for dealing with the deer problem. You may combine the ideas we have read or talked about or come up with your own unique solution. Your proposal should be 300 to 400 words in length and be supported by sound reasons based on common sense and scientific principles. The final copy will be due in three days.

Short-Answer Question

This section presents a sample Praxis short-answer question. In appendix D you will find sample responses along with the standards used in scoring these responses.

DIRECTIONS: The following question requires you to write a short answer. Base your answer on your knowledge of principles of learning and teaching from chapter 3. Be sure to answer all parts of the question.

1. Some critics might contend that Mr. Goldthorp's unit on leaf collection and identification was too time consuming. These same skills could just as easily be taught in much less time by "telling" students about the topic and having them consult reference texts. Using your knowledge of research and curriculum standards, give at least three reasons to justify the longer unit.

Discrete Multiple-Choice Questions

DIRECTIONS: Each of the multiple-choice questions that follow is based on Praxis-related pedagogical knowledge in chapter 3. Select the answer that is best in each case and compare your results with those in appendix D. See also the Companion Website for this text at *www.prenhall.com/borich* for more assessment options.

1. A behavioral objective must include a specific goal that has an observable learning outcome, a set of conditions under which the learning can be expected to occur, and a specific criterion level of performance required to meet the objective. Which of the following adequately meets all these goals?
   a. Using a thesaurus, look up synonyms for the underlined words in the paragraph.
   b. Using the headlines in today's newspaper, list five examples of alliteration with 100% accuracy.
   c. Study the chapter of our text that deals with the Civil War until you have memorized all the important names and dates.
   d. Read the chapter on cell division and answer the study questions.

2. Action verbs, such as *deduce, differentiate, subdivide,* or *break down,* describe learning outcomes at which cognitive level?
   a. Synthesis
   b. Application
   c. Comprehension
   d. Analysis

3. A high school government class is discussing the recent legislative changes in blood/alcohol levels constituting driving while intoxicated. Susan is a strong proponent of the higher standard. "We must do whatever is necessary to end drunk driving deaths," she argues. Which level of the affective domain does Susan demonstrate?
   a. Characterization
   b. Organization
   c. Valuing
   d. Responding

4. Indicate with an "O" or an "A" which of the following are learning outcomes and which learning activities.

   _____ The student will practice playing the violin one hour a day.

   _____ The student will know the dates of the Civil War.

   _____ The student will locate the five largest cities in the U.S. on a map.

   _____ The student will demonstrate her knowledge of typing.

5. Which of the following lists of verbs consistently reflects the cognitive, affective, *or* psychomotor domain?
   a. to define, to solve, to share
   b. to participate, to organize, to balance
   c. to attend, to notice, to explain
   d. to list, to diagram, to predict

Chapter 4

Unit and Lesson Planning

This chapter will help you answer the following questions and meet the following INTASC principles for effective teaching:

1. How do I use a curriculum guide to plan a lesson?
2. How do I make a unit plan?
3. What is in an effective lesson plan?
4. How can I prepare lessons at or slightly above my learners' current level of understanding?
5. How can my lessons provide for student diversity?

INTASC 1: The teacher understands the central concepts, tools of inquiry, and structures of the discipline(s) he or she teaches and can create learning experiences that make these aspects of subject matter meaningful for students.

INTASC 2: The teacher understands how children learn and develop, and can provide learning opportunities that support their intellectual, social, and personal development.

INTASC 7: The teacher plans instruction based upon knowledge of subject matter, students, the community, and curriculum goals.

INTASC 9: The teacher is a reflective practitioner who continually evaluates the effects of his or her choices and actions on others (students, parents, and other professionals in the learning community) and who actively seeks out opportunities to grow professionally.

*Y*ou *are now ready to consider planning and its relationship to the decisions you will make in the classroom. Planning is the systematic process of deciding what and how your students should learn. Teachers make one such decision on average every 2 minutes they are teaching, according to an estimate by Clark and Peterson (1986). However, these thinking "on your feet" decisions are only part of the decision-making process. Teachers also make many other decisions about the form and content of their instruction, such as how much presenting, questioning, and discussing to do; how much material to cover in the allotted time; and how in-depth to make their instruction. In chapter 3 you saw the importance of goals and objectives in the planning process. Now let's consider three other factors in the planning process: knowledge of the learner, knowledge of your subject matter, and knowledge of teaching methods.*

TEACHER AS DECISION MAKER

Knowledge of Instructional Goals and Objectives

Chapter 3 noted that, before you can prepare a lesson, you must decide on your instructional goals and objectives. These planning decisions are crucial for developing effective lesson plans, because they give structure to lesson planning and, as we saw in chapter 3, tie it to important sources of societal values and professional standards. In this chapter, we present unit and lesson plans as tools for tying these values and standards to your classroom.

Knowledge of the Learner

A review of research on planning by Clark and Peterson (1986) found that teachers reported spending more of their time (an average of 43%) planning instruction around the characteristics of their learners than around any other area of consideration (for example, assessment, classroom management, or the curriculum). Recall from chapter 2 that some of the characteristics of your learners that will influence your instruction are their specific abilities, prior knowledge, learning styles, and home and family life. These are the windows through which you will "see" the special needs of your learners and begin to plan for them.

Planning with respect to your learners begins by consciously noting their unique abilities and experiences that can provide you the opportunity to select content, materials, objectives, and methods that match their current level of understanding and meet their special learning needs. This knowledge will be instrumental in helping you organize, select, sequence, and allocate time to various topics of instruction.

Knowledge of Subject Matter

A second aspect of planning is knowledge of your academic discipline and grade level. As a student, you have spent much time and effort becoming knowledgeable in the subjects you will teach. You have observed and absorbed valuable information about how textbook authors, your instructors, and subject-matter specialists organize concepts in your teaching area. This information includes how parts of a subject relate to the whole, how content is prioritized, how transitions are made between topics, and which themes are major and which minor. Consciously reflecting on this content organization as presented by subject-matter specialists, texts, and curriculum guides when preparing your lessons will make learning for your students easier, more orderly, and more conducive to retention and later use. Deriving your content organization from these sources also can be instrumental in helping you select, sequence, and allocate time for what you will teach.

Knowledge of Teaching Methods

A third input to the planning process is your knowledge of teaching methods. With this knowledge comes an awareness of different teaching strategies with which you can implement the key and helping behaviors introduced in chapter 1. Also included under teaching methods are your decisions about:

- Appropriate pacing or tempo (the speed at which you introduce new material)
- Mode of presentation (direct presentation vs. group discussion)
- Class arrangement (small groups, full class, independent study)
- Classroom management (raise hand, speak out)

Your decisions about pacing, mode of presentation, class arrangement, and classroom management should work together to form a well-thought-out plan from which you teach individual lesson objectives.

Summary of Inputs to Planning

To recap, the four primary inputs to the planning process are the following:

1. Knowledge of goals and objectives
2. Knowledge of learner characteristics
3. Knowledge of subject matter
4. Knowledge of teaching methods

Shulman (1992) identifies four specific sources from which you may obtain knowledge about goals and objectives, learners, subject matter, and teaching methods: (1) practical experiences, such as viewing classroom video, observing in classrooms, and student teaching; (2) reading case studies about what more successful and less successful teachers have done; (3) reading the professional literature about important ideas, conceptual systems, and paradigms for thinking about teaching; and (4) reading empirical studies about what the research says about your subject and how to teach it. Each of these is a valuable source for extending and updating your knowledge of learners, content, and teaching methods. The chapters ahead present key findings for effective teaching from each of these four areas.

Figure 4.1 Inputs to the planning process.

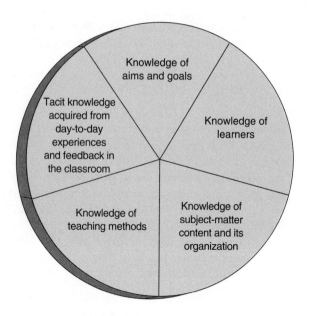

REFLECTIVE PRACTICE AND TACIT KNOWLEDGE

As a beginning teacher, you probably regard your content and method knowledge as hard won during four long years of professional training. To be sure, it is—but you have only just begun. Your knowledge in content and methods will change with the interaction of your formal university training and your actual classroom experience.

This change will result in what is called **reflective practice** fueled by your tacit, or personal, knowledge gained from your day-to-day experience (Canning, 1991; Gill, 2000; Polanyi, 1958). **Tacit knowledge** represents your reflection on what works in your classroom, discovered over time and through personal experience. Through everyday experiences, such as observation of other teachers, your experience with learners, lesson planning, and testing and grading, you will be accumulating tacit knowledge and reflecting on new ways of doing things that can guide your actions as effectively as knowledge from texts and formal training. This knowledge, if you take the time to reflect upon it, can add to the quality of your planning and decision making by bringing variety and flexibility to your lessons, leading to revisions and refinements that can improve your unit and lesson planning. Tacit knowledge can make your planning less rigid and repetitious and over time add fresh insights to your personal teaching style. Thus we add this fifth input to the planning process, shown in Figure 4.1.

UNIT AND LESSON PLANS

The important process of unit and lesson planning begins with implementing the five planning inputs (Figure 4.1). This stage of the planning process takes a **system perspective,** meaning your lessons will be part of a larger system of interrelated learning, called a *unit*.

The word *system* brings to mind phrases like *school system, mental health system,* and *legal system.* Schools, mental health services, and criminal justice agencies are supposed to work as systems. This means their component parts are to interrelate and build toward some unified concept. For example, in a school system, discrete facts, skills, and understandings learned at the completion of sixth grade not only are important in themselves but also are important for successfully completing seventh grade. Seventh grade outcomes, in turn, are important for completing eighth grade, and so on through the educational system until the high school graduate has accumulated many of the facts, skills, and understandings necessary for adult living.

The true strength of a system, however, is that the whole is greater than the sum of its parts. Can a unit of instruction comprising individual lessons ever add up to anything more than the sum of the individual lessons? This sounds like getting something for nothing, a concept that does not ring true. But if the system of individual lessons really can produce outcomes in learners that are greater than the sum of the outcomes of the individual lessons, then there must be a missing ingredient we have not mentioned.

That missing ingredient is the relationship among the individual lessons. This relationship must allow the outcome of one lesson to build on the outcomes of preceding lessons. Knowledge, skills, and understanding evolve gradually through the joint contribution of many lessons arranged to build toward more and more complex outcomes. It is this invisible but all-important relationship among the parts of an instructional unit that allows the unit outcomes to be greater than the sum of the lesson outcomes.

Of considerable importance is the relationship of your district's curriculum guide to your unit and lesson plans. Units generally extend over an instructional time period of approximately 1 to 4 weeks. They usually correspond to well-defined topics or themes in the curriculum guide. Lessons, however, are considerably shorter, spanning a single class period or occasionally two or three periods. Because lessons are relatively short, they are harder to associate with a particular segment of a curriculum guide. This means you can expect unit content to be fairly well structured and defined but lesson content—what you do on any given day—to be much less detailed in a curriculum guide.

This is as it should be, because the arrangement of day-to-day content in the classroom must be flexible to meet individual student needs, your instructional preferences, and special priorities and initiatives in your school and community. So, although the overall picture at the unit level may be clear from the district's curriculum guide, at the lesson level, you must apply considerable independent thought, organization, and judgment. Figure 4.2 indicates the flow of teaching content from the state level to the classroom, illustrating the stages through which a curriculum framework is translated into unit and lesson plans.

MAKING PLANNING DECISIONS

Unit planning begins with an understanding of your goals, your students' learning needs, the content you will teach, and the teaching methods available to you. Let's take a closer look at several types of decisions you will make pertaining to these inputs to the lesson planning process.

Goals

Curriculum guides at the grade, department, and school district level clearly specify what content must be covered in what period of time. But they may be far less clear about the specific outcomes that students are expected to acquire. For example, an excerpt from a curriculum guide for English language instruction might take this form:

1. Writing concepts and skills. The student shall be expected to learn
   a. The composing process
   b. Descriptive, narrative, and expository paragraphs
   c. Multiple paragraph compositions
   d. Persuasive discourse
   e. Meanings and uses of colloquialism, slang, idiom, and jargon

Figure 4.2 Flow of teaching content from the state level to the classroom level.

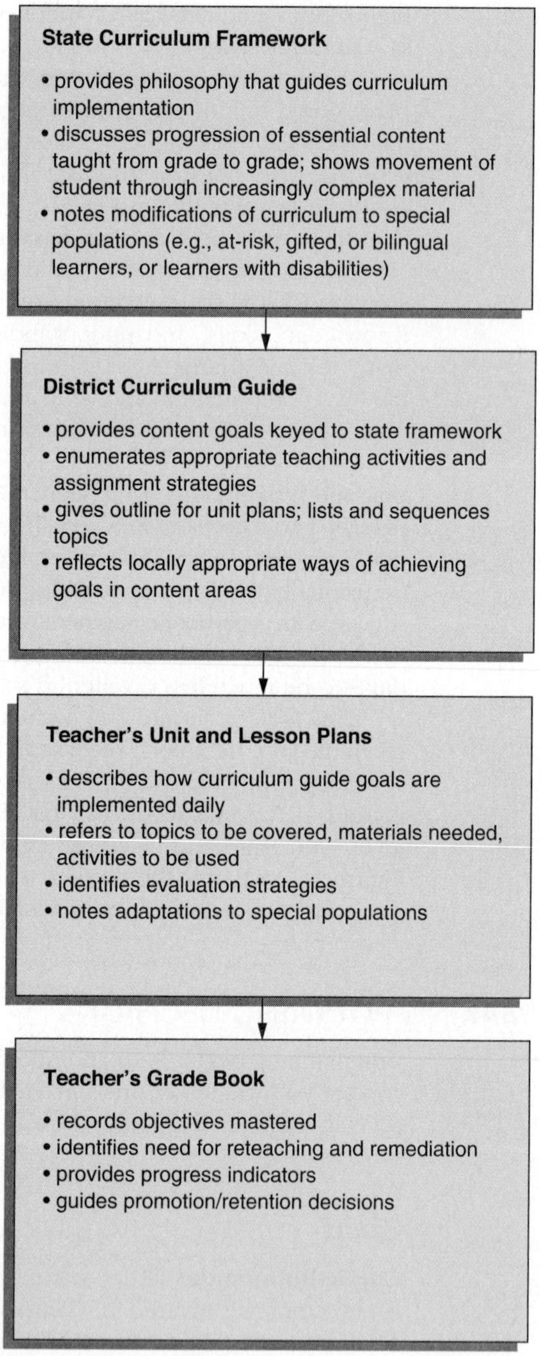

State Curriculum Framework

- provides philosophy that guides curriculum implementation
- discusses progression of essential content taught from grade to grade; shows movement of student through increasingly complex material
- notes modifications of curriculum to special populations (e.g., at-risk, gifted, or bilingual learners, or learners with disabilities)

District Curriculum Guide

- provides content goals keyed to state framework
- enumerates appropriate teaching activities and assignment strategies
- gives outline for unit plans; lists and sequences topics
- reflects locally appropriate ways of achieving goals in content areas

Teacher's Unit and Lesson Plans

- describes how curriculum guide goals are implemented daily
- refers to topics to be covered, materials needed, activities to be used
- identifies evaluation strategies
- notes adaptations to special populations

Teacher's Grade Book

- records objectives mastered
- identifies need for reteaching and remediation
- provides progress indicators
- guides promotion/retention decisions

Or, for a life science curriculum:

2. Life science. The student shall be expected to learn
   a. Skills in acquiring data through the senses
   b. Classification skills in ordering and sequencing data
   c. Oral and written communication of data in appropriate form

      d. Concepts and skills of measurement using relationships and standards

      e. Drawing logical inferences, predicting outcomes, and forming generalized statements

And, for a geography curriculum:

   3. Geography. The student shall be expected to be able to

      a. Use cardinal and intermediate directions to locate places such as the Amazon River, Himalayan Mountains, and Washington, D.C. on maps and globes

      b. Use a scale to determine the distance between places on maps and globes

      c. Identify and use the compass rose, grid, and symbols to locate places on maps and globes

      d. Draw maps of places and regions that contain map elements including a title, compass rose, legend, scale, and grid system

Notice in these excerpts the specificity at which the content is identified (e.g., the composing process; skills in acquiring data through the senses; and use of cardinal and intermediate directions). In contrast, note the lack of clarity concerning the level of learning outcome to which the instruction should be directed. This is typical of many curriculum guides. Recalling the taxonomy of behavior in the cognitive domain in chapter 3, you could ask the following questions:

- For which of these content areas will the simple recall of facts be sufficient?
- For which areas will comprehension of those facts be required?
- For which areas will application be expected of what the student comprehends?
- For which areas will higher-level outcomes be desired, involving analysis, synthesis, and decision-making skills?

One of the most important decisions you will make with your curriculum guide will be to select the level of learning outcome(s) for which an instructional unit or lesson will be prepared. The flexibility afforded by most curriculum guides in selecting the learning outcome to which instruction can be directed is both purposeful and advantageous for you. For the curriculum guide to be adapted to the realities of your classroom, a wide latitude of expected outcomes must be possible. These will depend on the unique characteristics and individual differences among your students, the time you can devote to a specific topic, and the overall learning outcomes desired at the unit level.

Learners

As we have seen, curriculum guides allow you the flexibility to adapt your instruction to the individual learning needs of your students. Chapter 2 presented several categories of individual differences that will be characteristic of students in your classroom. These included differences in ability, prior achievement, individual and cultural differences, learning style, peer group, and home and family life. These factors can reflect entire classrooms as well as individuals. Other categories of learners—such as at-risk, bilingual, gifted, and learners with disabilities—may add even greater diversity to your classroom. They may create the need for task-related subgroups that require individual attention or time-limited groups of higher and lower performing learners, alternatives that will be addressed in the chapters to come.

Content

Perhaps foremost in the mind of beginning teachers is the content to be taught. Your content decisions appear easy inasmuch as textbooks, workbooks, and curriculum guides may have been selected before your first day in the classroom. Indeed, as you saw in the excerpts from the curriculum guides, content often is designated in great detail. Textbooks and workbooks carry this detail one step further by offering activities and exercises that further define and expand the content in the curriculum guide. From this perspective it may appear as if all of the content has been handed to you, if not on a silver platter, then surely in readily accessible and highly organized tests, workbooks, and curriculum materials.

Although some teachers might wish this were true, most quickly realize that as many decisions must be made about content—what to teach—as about learning needs and outcomes. You will quickly come to realize that adopted texts, workbooks, and even detailed curriculum guides identify the content to be taught but do not select, organize, and sequence that content according to the needs of your learners. And increasingly, school districts, textbook publishers, and software companies are providing alternative texts, software, and workbooks from which teachers can choose to better target specific populations of learners. Effective teachers know they must select from this content for some learning outcomes and learners and add to this content for other learning outcomes and learners to actively engage them in the learning process at or slightly above their current level of understanding.

Organization

Establishing relationships between your lessons is one of the most important planning decisions you will make. How your lessons interrelate can even determine if and how well your learners achieve higher-level outcomes in the cognitive, affective, and psychomotor domains. And this decision, in turn, will determine how well your unit and lesson plans reflect a thinking curriculum.

The higher levels of behavior can rarely if ever be achieved in a single lesson. Thus lessons must be placed within a unit, or system of lessons, in which individual lessons build on previously taught outcomes to achieve higher-order outcomes at the end of a unit. This is why your structuring of lesson content is so important to unit planning: Without it, outcomes at the unit's end may be no different from the outcomes achieved at the completion of each single lesson. Unlike miscellaneous items stored in the attic or the glove compartment of your car, units should have a coherent, unified theme that rises above the cognitive, affective, and psychomotor outcomes of any single lesson.

For example, the reason you might organize a particular series of lessons (e.g., on acid rain, new technologies, and conservation legislation) might be to show how several content areas can be brought together with a single theme for the purpose of solving a problem, thinking critically, or forming an independent judgment. In this case, the unit goal and needs of your learners will have played an important role in selecting this particular organization. Thus your decisions about unit structure will depend on the match between the level of learning outcomes you choose and your students' current level of understanding of the content you are teaching.

Now let's put your knowledge of goals, learners, content, and organization to work in preparing unit and lesion plans.

DISCIPLINARY AND INTERDISCIPLINARY UNIT PLANNING

The following two sections introduce unit plans and how to communicate them in a clear and orderly manner. The first approach to unit planning will show you how to plan and to teach knowledge and understanding within a discipline—or vertically. **Vertical unit planning** is a method of developing units within a discipline in which the content to be taught is arranged hierarchically or in steps (e.g., from least to most complex, or from concrete to abstract) and presented in an order that ensures that all task-relevant prior knowledge required for subsequent lessons has been taught in previous lessons.

Following our discussion of disciplinary unit planning, we present a second means of communicating knowledge and understanding to your learners, called *interdisciplinary unit planning*, which involves a technique called *lateral planning*. **Lateral unit planning** can be used for planning units that integrate bodies of knowledge across disciplines or content areas to convey relationships, patterns, and abstractions that run across disciplines and bind different aspects of our world together in some systematic way. Lateral unit plans move across the established boundaries of content areas to elicit problem solving, critical thinking, cooperative activity, and independent thought and action that emphasizes the whole is greater than the sum of its parts. As you will see, both vertical and lateral unit planning are valuable tools for acquiring the skills of an effective teacher and meeting the unique needs of your learners.

Disciplinary (Vertical) Unit Plans

An old Chinese proverb states, "A picture is worth a thousand words." This chapter applies this age-old idea to unit planning by showing how you can develop a unit plan by creating a visual blueprint of your unit. This section shows you how to use a written and graphic format to express a unit plan within a discipline, subject matter, or content area.

Of course a visual device cannot substitute for a written description or outline of what you plan to teach, but it is an effective means of organizing your thinking. Scientists, administrators, engineers, and business executives long have known the value of visuals in the form of flowcharts, organization charts, blueprints, diagrams, and mindmaps (Buzan, 1994; Kenny, 2004; Mintzes, Wandersee, & Novak, 2000) to convey the essence of a concept, if not the details. From the beginning, teachers have used this basic method, too. Pictures not only communicate the results of planning but are useful during that process to organize and revise a unit plan and to see the big picture—or final outcome—you are working hard to achieve.

Although teaching parallels many other fields by using visual devices in planning, in many ways teaching is a unique profession. Unlike business, education's product does not roll off an assembly line, and education does not build its product with the mathematical laws and physical materials used by the scientist and engineer. Consequently, your visual blueprints differ from those of others, but at the same time reflect the qualities that have made pictures so important to planning in these other professions. You already have been introduced to two of these qualities: the concept of *hierarchy*, which shows the relationship of parts to the whole (lessons to unit), and the concept of *task-relevant prior knowledge*, which shows the necessity for a certain lesson sequence (Walberg, 1991, p. 38). In vertical unit planning, both concepts are put to work in creating a visual picture of a unit; such a picture can both stimulate and organize your thoughts and communicate the results to others in an easy-to-follow graphic format.

Two simple rules are used in drawing a picture of a vertically planned unit. The first is to diagram how the unit goal is divided into specific lessons. The second is to show the sequence of these lessons and how their outcomes build on one another to achieve the unit goal. Let's look at these two rules.

Visualizing Specific Teaching Activities.

Our first rule simply uses boxes to visualize areas of content—or instructional goals—at various levels of generality. In other words, any goal at the unit level can be broken into its component parts at the lesson level. Those component parts represent everything that is important for attaining the goal. This idea is illustrated in Figure 4.3.

Notice that Figure 4.3 has three levels. For now, focus on the top and bottom levels. The top shows the unit goal, which is derived from the curriculum guide and adopted textbook, which in turn are based on societal, state, and locally stated goals. The bottom row shows content expressed at a level specific enough to prepare individual lessons.

Figure 4.3 Example of a hierarchy of reading content at different levels of specificity.

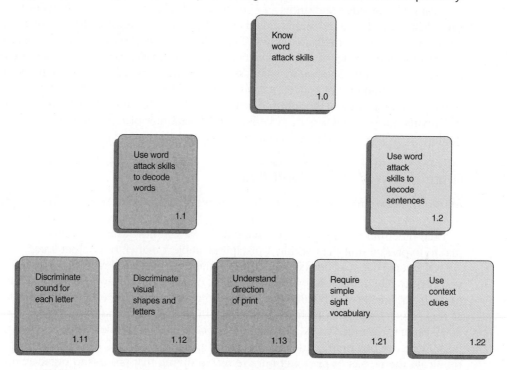

This unit plan ends with bite-sized chunks that together exhaust the content specified at the higher levels. Just as in the story of Goldilocks and the three bears, the bottom of the unit plan hierarchy must end with the portion of content being served up as not too big and not too small—but just right for individual lesson planning. How can you know whether you have achieved the right size and balance for a single lesson?

The second level of Figure 4.3 is a logical means of getting from the general unit goal to specific lesson content. It is an intermediate thinking process that produces the lower level of just-right-sized pieces. How many intermediate levels should you have? There is no magic number; this depends on how broadly the initial goal is stated and the number of steps needed to produce content in just the right amounts for individual lesson plans. Experience and judgment are the best guides, although logical divisions within the curriculum guide and text are helpful, too.

In some cases, the route from unit to lesson content can be very direct (two levels); in other instances, several levels may have to be worked through before arriving at lesson-sized chunks. If you have trouble getting sufficiently specific for lesson-sized content, you may need to revise the unit goal by dividing it into two or more subgoals and beginning a new hierarchy from each subgoal. This was done in Figure 4.3, where the unit planner had to create two units of instruction (1.1 and 1.2) from the same goal (1.0). Notice that this is done in the same way you create an outline. This process of building a content hierarchy will guide you in making the important distinction between unit and lesson content and can prevent false starts in lesson planning.

Visualizing the Sequence of Activities. The second rule shows the sequence of lessons and how lesson outcomes build on one another to achieve a unit goal. This second rule, illustrated in Figure 4.4, shows the order of the individual lessons, when order is important. Notice that in Figure 4.4, we chose the first box from the second level (1.1) of the hierarchy in Figure 4.3 as our unit goal. The procedure is to indicate the intended unit outcome with

Figure 4.4 A unit plan showing a sequence of lessons.

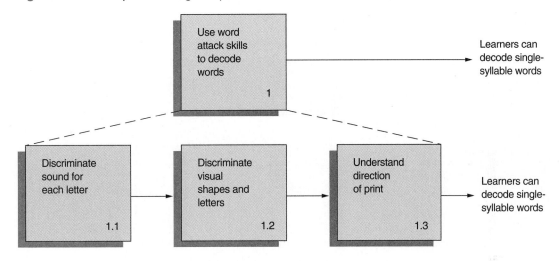

Figure 4.5 A unit plan without lesson sequence (Lessons 1.1, 1.2, and 1.3 can occur in any order).

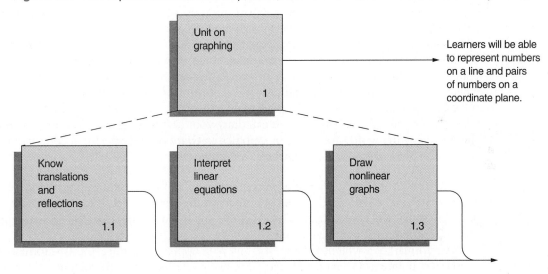

an arrow extending from the right of this top box, as shown in Figure 4.4. The outcome of all the lessons derived from it, taken together, should be the same as this unit outcome. This will always be true, whether or not the sequence of your lessons is important. In some instances, this sequence may be unimportant (Figure 4.5); for others, a partial sequence may be appropriate (Figure 4.6).

This second rule recognizes how previous lessons can modify or constrain the outcomes of subsequent lessons. It encourages you to build on previously taught learning to provide increasingly more authentic and higher-order thinking outcomes at the unit level. This will be important if your unit plan is to promote a thinking curriculum. If lesson outcomes are unrelated, it is unlikely your unit outcome will be at any higher a level of cognitive, affective, or psychomotor complexity than your individual lesson outcomes. As an effective teacher, you should plan the interrelationships among lessons in a way that encourages higher-order thinking to emerge at the unit level. (You may want to consult again the taxonomies of behavioral outcomes in chapter 3 and the *Checklist of Higher-Order Thinking and Problem Solving* in appendix C.)

Figure 4.6 A unit plan with partial lesson sequence (Lesson 1.1 must precede Lesson 1.2).

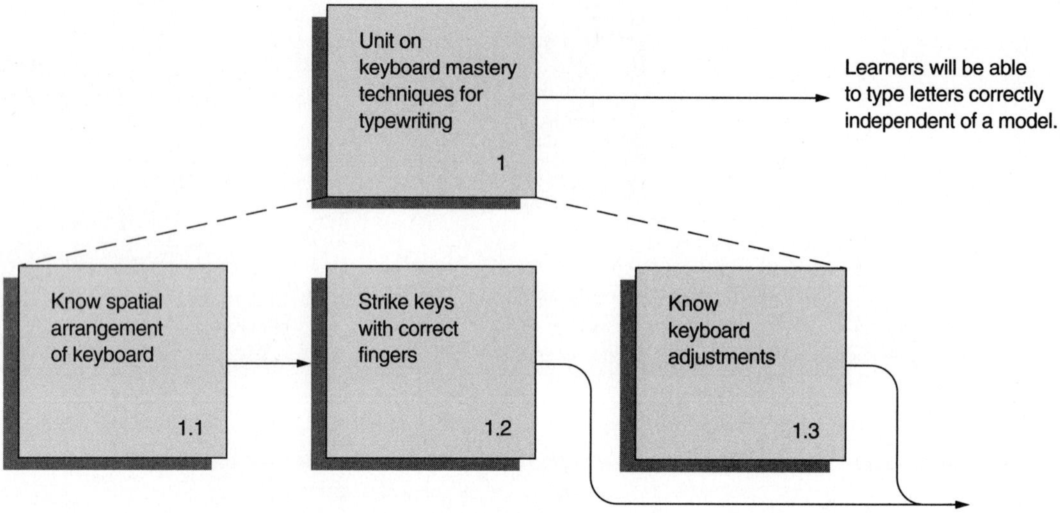

Picturing your unit plan visually has several advantages. Seeing a lesson in context with other lessons that share the same purpose focuses your attention on the importance of knowledge and understandings that must be taught prior to your lesson for it to be a success. Recall that if learners have inadequately acquired (or not acquired at all) prerequisite knowledge and skills relevant to your lesson, some or most of your learners will not attain your lesson objective. One purpose of seeing lessons within a unit plan is to determine whether you have provided all the task-relevant prior knowledge required by each lesson. Because unit plans precede lesson plans, you can easily add overlooked lessons and objectives prerequisite to later lessons. You can draw your unit plans graphically, as shown in this chapter, using the word processing or graphics software on your personal computer or from *Inspiration Software* at *www.inspiration.com/home.cfm.*

The Written Unit Plan. Planning units graphically will be helpful in organizing, sequencing, and arriving at bite-sized pieces of content at the lesson level. But you will also need a description that will communicate details of the unit to others and that you can place in your digital portfolio for use at a later time.

One format for a written version of a unit plan appears in Figure 4.7. This format divides a written plan into its (1) main purpose, (2) behavioral objectives, (3) content, (4) procedures and activities, (5) instructional aids and resources, and (6) evaluation methods. To this written plan, attach your visual blueprint to indicate at a glance the organization, sequence, and sizing of the unit and to provide an introduction and overview of the written details. Together, they will give you a powerful tool for communicating your unit plans.

Finally, notice that in Figure 4.7 both objectives and individual learners progress from the lower levels of cognitive and psychomotor behavioral complexity (comprehension, application, imitation) to the higher levels (analysis, synthesis, precision). This illustrates how early lessons in a unit can be used as building blocks to attain higher levels of authenticity, helping to achieve a thinking curriculum (Borich, 2007; Kagan & Tippins, 1992).

Interdisciplinary (Lateral) Unit Plans

Results of recent research indicate that a unit in which many content areas are integrated can lead to high levels of thinking and meaningful learning, if the instructional techniques used

Figure 4.7 Example of a unit plan.

Grade: 10

Unit Topic: Pizza with Yeast Dough Crust

Course/Subject: Contemporary Home Economics

Approximate Time Required: One week

1. Main Purpose of the Unit: The purpose of this unit is to acquaint the students with the principles of making yeast dough by making pizza. The historical background, nutritional value, and variations of pizza will also be covered.
2. Behavioral Objectives
    The student will be able to:
    A. Describe the functions of each of the ingredients in yeast dough. (Cognitive-knowledge)
    B. Explain the steps in preparing yeast dough. (Cognitive-comprehension)
    C. Make a yeast dough for a pizza crust. (Cognitive-application and psychomotor imitation)
    D. State briefly the history of pizza. (Cognitive-knowledge)
    E. Match the ingredients in pizza to the food groups they represent. (Cognitive-knowledge)
    F. Classify and give examples of different types of pizza. (Cognitive-analysis)
    G. Create and bake a pizza of their choice. (Cognitive-synthesis and psychomotor-precision)
3. Content Outline
    A. Essential ingredients in yeast dough
        (1) Flour
        (2) Yeast
        (3) Liquid
        (4) Sugar
        (5) Salt
    B. Non-essential ingredients
        (1) Fats
        (2) Eggs
        (3) Other, such as fruit and nuts
    C. Preparing yeast dough
        (1) Mixing
        (2) Kneading
        (3) Rising (fermenting)
        (4) Punching down
        (5) Shaping
        (6) Baking

    D. History of pizza
        (1) First pizza was from Naples.
        (2) *Pizza* is an Italian word meaning pie.
        (3) Originally eaten by the poor, pizza was also enjoyed by royalty.
        (4) Italian immigrants brought pizza to the United States in the late 1800s.
    E. Types of pizza
        (1) Neapolitan
        (2) Sicilian
        (3) Pizza Rustica
        (4) Pizza de Polenta
    F. Nutritional value of pizza
        (1) Nutritious meal or snack
        (2) Can contain all four food groups
        (3) One serving of cheese pizza contains:
            (a) Protein
            (b) Vitamins
            (c) Minerals
    G. Making a pizza
        (1) Prepare dough
        (2) Roll out dough
        (3) Transfer to pan
        (4) Spread sauce
        (5) Top as desired
        (6) Bake
4. Procedures and Activities
    A. Informal lecture
    B. Discussion
    C. Demonstration of mixing and kneading dough
    D. Filmstrip on pizza
    E. Education game (Pizzeria): Each time a student answers correctly a question about yeast dough or pizza, he gets a part of a paper pizza. The first to collect a complete pizza wins.
    F. Cooking lab
5. Instructional Aids or Resources
    A. Text: Guide to Modern Meals (Webster, McGraw-Hill, 1970)
    B. Filmstrip: Pizza, Pizza 10 minutes
    C. Pizza, Pizza booklets by Chef Boyardee
    D. Educational game (Pizzeria)
    E. Bake-it-easy Yeast Book by Fleischmann's Yeast
    F. Poster (showing different kinds of pizza from Pizza Hut)
6. Evaluation
    A. Unit test
    B. Lab performance

Source: From *Curriculum Planning: A Ten-Step Process,* by W. Zenger and S. Zenger, 1982. Palo Alto, CA: R and E Research Associates. Copyright ©1982 by R and E Research Associates.

involve students in interactive learning and higher-order thinking (National Research Council, 2001; Richmond & Striley, 1994; Roblyer, 2005; Shavelson & Baxter, 1992).

An **interdisciplinary unit** is a laterally planned unit of study in which topics are integrated to provide a focus on a specific theme (Martin, 1995; Martinello & Cook, 1994; Roberts, 2003). This approach to learning helps students visualize connections. The principal aim of interdisciplinary instruction is to present learners with an opportunity to discover relationships and patterns that go beyond a specific discipline and that bind together different aspects of our world in some systematic way (McDonald & Czerniak, 1994). For example, interdisciplinary units often represent themes that can be related to several different subject-matter areas at the same time, such as to English or reading, science, social studies, and the expressive arts. Effective interdisciplinary units also often require learners to conduct investigations that require the cooperation of other learners and the independent use of reference materials.

Interdisciplinary units provide opportunities for classroom dialogue in which learners are expected to reason critically, ask questions, make predictions, and, with the aid of the teacher, evaluate the appropriateness of their own responses. Recent trends in interdisciplinary thematic teaching can help teachers achieve these goals, but only if the themes that organize the unit are chosen carefully and in ways that help students understand content connections and relationships to their own lives (Ritter, 1999).

For example, Roberts and Kellough (2003) describe one teacher who planned an interdisciplinary unit for her middle school students by having them read a story about a young boy who travels through time and journeys to a fantasy planet. As the boy struggles to adapt to his new culture, he experiences isolation, loneliness, domination, and imprisonment. To relate this story to several different disciplines based on their reading, the teacher planned a unit in which the following relationships were drawn between and within disciplines:

- *Related to English.* The students discussed changes in the novel's setting, the development of the plot, and the author's use of the literary device of foreshadowing.
- *Related to expressive arts.* The students made a model of the planet and a floor plan of some of the buildings, and they designed a robot that was described in the story. They also staged a dramatic reenactment of a scene in the novel.
- *Related to science.* Some students studied the flora and fauna on the planet and compared it to the plants and animals of their own state; others attempted to identify the chemical composition of the environment on the planet and identify a probable location for it in our solar system.
- *Related to social studies.* The students engaged in a map study of the planet, developed a government for the fantasy planet, compared the segregation practiced in the story with segregation elsewhere, compared the freedoms of the inhabitants on the planet with the freedoms in our own Bill of Rights, and discussed issues of prejudice and class structure.
- *Related to additional research.* The students studied popular research on dreams and experiments about the sleep of humans, which played a predominant role in the story.

Notice how the relationships and patterns across subject areas in this unit did not just happen. This teacher developed her unit from a carefully constructed list of interrelated themes that she could select from and add to when determining the areas of the curriculum to be taught. To prepare her unit plan, this teacher developed a list of possible themes, like those shown in Table 4.1. These thematic concepts, topics, and categories were mapped onto existing subject matter in her and other teachers' classrooms and brought to life through the interdisciplinary thematic unit.

Table 4.1 Theme development for interdisciplinary units.

Concepts	Topics	Categories
freedom	individual	autobiographies
cooperation	society	dreams
challenge	community	fantasies
conflict	relationships	tall tales
discovery	global concerns	experiences
culture	war	firsthand accounts
change	partnerships	
perseverance		

Interdisciplinary units can help you achieve the following objectives:

1. Emphasize that the process of learning is sometimes best pursued as an interconnected whole rather than as a series of specific subjects.
2. Encourage students to work cooperatively in partnerships and small groups that focus on the social values of learning.
3. Teach students to be independent problem solvers and thinkers.
4. Assist students to develop their own individual interests and learning styles.
5. Help students find out what they need to know and what they need to learn rather than always expecting the teacher to give it to them.

A key component of **thematic units** is the varied structure of the instructional strategies used. For example, you can give your students a variety of activities and materials in several related content areas along with some challenging questions to facilitate collaboration and to create a desire to learn more about a topic. Or have students work independently at times, but also collaborate in groups to read, pose and investigate problems, and complete projects from the perspective of two or three different content areas. One group investigates a problem from one content area while another group takes a different perspective. In this way, students interact and learn from each other. Your role is that of a facilitator or moderator of learning.

The Spectrum of Integrated Curricula.   Roberts and Kellough (2003) identify four ways you can implement **integrated thematic teaching** in your classroom, representing different degrees of involvement (Parkay & Hass, 2000):

Level 1.   At this level, you would use a thematic approach to relate content and material from various content areas during the same day. For example, the theme "Natural Disasters Cause Social Effects" could originate from the topics of weather normally taught within a science or geography lesson and the topic of community taught within a social studies lesson. You would convey the theme of this interdisciplinary lesson to learners at the beginning of the unit in the form of a question, such as "What necessary functions in a community are often disrupted after a natural disaster?" Encourage students to suggest adding other content and questions.

Level 2.   The next level of implementation requires you to consult with other teachers and agree on a common theme. Each teacher who decides to participate in the interdisciplinary unit teaches to that theme in his or her own classroom. In this manner students learn from a teacher in one classroom something that is related to what they are learning in another classroom. In the early elementary grades, a single teacher can perform this same function by referring back, say, during reading instruction to a related concept in social studies, math, or science. Display on the bulletin board a list of themes developed beforehand based on interconnections among subject areas to remind both you and your learners to identify and discuss the connections, and then have students create the connections with examples of their work.

Level 3. At the third level, you and your students work together to form a list of common themes across subject areas. For example, in the later elementary and high school grades, you might give an assignment to search the table of contents of your text and those of other teachers for the topic of a thematic unit you might teach in your classroom. If other teachers agree on the theme developed, they, too, can be encouraged to mutually reinforce the connections identified in their classrooms, thereby providing momentum across disciplines for your thematic unit. This level of implementation is an effective way to initiate a team approach to your interdisciplinary teaching.

Level 4. At the fourth level, your students develop on their own a list of common themes or problems across disciplines. Your charge to students is to arrive at one or more themes in which a traditional subject, discipline, or content area would be inadequate for addressing a theme or resolving a problem. In other words, you instruct your students to find current, contemporary dilemmas, moral issues, and problems that defy solution in the context of any one or a small number of traditionally defined subject areas. Students may therefore be challenged to raise such thorny problems as "How can we know when someone has really died?" requiring the simultaneous consideration of the latest advances in the fields of medicine, religion, and philosophy, or "How can we rid our planet of life-threatening pollution?" possibly requiring your class to consider knowledge from general science, physics, and chemistry and from social studies, government, and the law. At this level, your students are playing the role of independent and socially responsible thinkers, and you are playing the role of resource, guiding their thoughts and refocusing them when necessary in increasingly productive avenues for elaborating relationships, patterns, and abstractions for adult living.

Visualizing Your Interdisciplinary Unit.   Because interdisciplinary units emphasize lateral knowledge, their graphic portrayal is different from disciplinary units, which emphasize vertical knowledge. The graphic technique you use for expressing lateral knowledge should allow for content to be woven in and out of lessons as the opportunity arises, without a predetermined sequence. Hence a more free-form, or web type, visual format is required, sometimes called a *concept map* or *thinking map* (Buzan, 1994; Hyerle, 1995–1996; Novak, 2001). This type of format shows how content is nestled within other content, how different subject areas share a common theme, how a single theme is threaded through different content areas, or how one field of study is immersed in another. Thus all important themes and issues in an interdisciplinary plan are shown simultaneously in association with one another (see *www.inspiration.com/home.cfm* for software that can help you develop and visually display interdisciplinary units and lessons). The rules for creating these types of graphic outlines or webs are as follows:

- Identify the single most essential theme or idea.
- Place this theme or idea in the center of your web.
- Use arrows or lines going outward from the main idea to show relationships with other, subordinate issues, topics, or content, which can become the topics of individual lessons.
- Label the arrows and all key concepts with code words or phrases to describe the relationships you have expressed.

Figures 4.8 and 4.9 provide examples of thematic webs for expressing an interdisciplinary thematic unit. See In Practice: Focus on Interdisciplinary Lesson Planning.

Figure 4.8 Visual representation of the interdisciplinary unit theme "Adventures of Lewis and Clark."

Source: From *The Classroom of the 21st Century, by* S. Kovalik, 1994. Federal Way, WA: Books for Educators. Copyright © 1994 by S. Kovalik. Reprinted with permission.

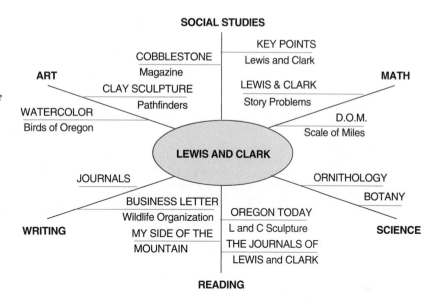

SOCIAL STUDIES

ART

MATH

WRITING

SCIENCE

KEY POINTS
Lewis and Clark

COBBLESTONE
Magazine

LEWIS & CLARK
Story Problems

CLAY SCULPTURE
Pathfinders

D.O.M.
Scale of Miles

WATERCOLOR
Birds of Oregon

LEWIS AND CLARK

JOURNALS

ORNITHOLOGY

BOTANY

BUSINESS LETTER
Wildlife Organization

OREGON TODAY
L and C Sculpture

MY SIDE OF THE
MOUNTAIN

THE JOURNALS OF
LEWIS and CLARK

READING

Figure 4.9 Visual representation of the interdisciplinary unit theme "Dimensions of Time."

Source: From *Kid's Eye View of Science: A Teacher's Handbook for Teaching Science That Matters,* S. Kovalik, 2002.

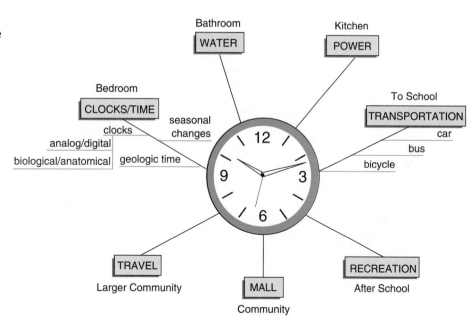

Bathroom
WATER

Kitchen
POWER

Bedroom
CLOCKS/TIME

seasonal
changes

To School
TRANSPORTATION

clocks

car

analog/digital

bus

biological/anatomical | geologic time

bicycle

12

9   3

6

TRAVEL

RECREATION

Larger Community

MALL

After School

Community

WHAT MAKES IT TICK?

FUNCTION / SYSTEMS

The Written Unit Plan. The written format for an interdisciplinary unit plan is the same as that for a disciplinary unit. Recall that a written unit is divided into its (1) main purpose, (2) behavioral objectives, (3) content, (4) procedures and activities, (5) instructional aids and resources, and (6) evaluation methods. An example of a written interdisciplinary plan appears in Figure 4.10. To this written plan attach the visual outline or web of your theme and its interrelationships.

Figure 4.10 Example of an interdisciplinary thematic unit.

Grade: 5

Unit Topic: Gold Rush

Course/Subject: Interdisciplinary

Approximate Time Required: One month

1. **Main Purpose of the Unit**
   The purpose of this unit is to acquaint the students with the excitement, the hardships and the challenges of the nineteenth-century gold rush.

2. **Behavioral Objectives**
   The student will be able to:
   A. *History/Social Science*—Give reasons why people came to California in the 1840s.
   B. *History/Social Science*—Describe the three routes the pioneers took to California.
   C. *History/Social Science*—Compare life in the United States in the 1840s to life in the United States now.
   D. *History/Social Science*—List supplies brought by the pioneers on the trip West.
   E. *Language Arts*—Write a journal entry to describe some of the hardships associated with the trip West.
   F. *Science*—Research and write a report on how gold is mined.
   G. *Math*—Weigh gold nuggets (painted rocks) and calculate their monetary value.
   H. *Art*—Design a prairie quilt pattern using fabric scraps.

3. **Content Outline**
   A. Reasons people came to California in the 1840s
      1. Gold
      2. Job opportunities
      3. Weather
   B. Supplies for the trip
      1. Tools
      2. Personal supplies
      3. Food
      4. Household items
   C. Life on the trip West
      1. Weather conditions
      2. Roles of men, women, children
      3. Hazards of the trail
   D. Life in California after arrival
      1. Inflated prices
      2. Staking a claim
      3. Striking it rich
      4. A typical day in the life of a miner

4. **Procedures and Activities**
   A. Read aloud
   B. Small-group reading
   C. Independent reading
   D. Discussion
   F. Journal entries
   G. Measurement
   H. Cooking
   I. Singing

5. **Instructional Aids and Resources**
   A. Literature selections
      1. *Patty Reed's Doll*
      2. *By the Great Horn Spoon*
      3. *If You Traveled West in a Covered Wagon*
      4. *Children of the Wild West*
      5. *Joshua's Westward Journal*
      6. *The Way West, Journal of a Pioneer Woman*
      7. *The Little House Cookbook*
   B. Items indicative of the period (if obtainable)
      1. Cast-iron skillet
      2. Bonnet or leather hat
      3. Old tools

6. **Assessment/Evaluation**
   Develop a rubric to grade these.
   A. Essay—Choose one route that the pioneers took to get to California and describe the journey.
   B. Gold Rush Game Board—Design a board game detailing the trip to California. The winner arrives in California and strikes it rich!

Source: Written by Cynthia Kiel, teacher, Glendora, California.

IN PRACTICE

Focus on Interdisciplinary Lesson Planning

Adapted from Carla Mathison and Cheryl Mason, Planning Interdisciplinary Curriculum: A Systematic and Cooperative Approach, *San Diego State University.*

> *In his literature class, Mr. Cline gives students the dates of the birth and death of a famous author, and asks them to figure out how old the author was when she died. Silence falls over the class as students scratch their heads in frustration. One student exclaims, "It's hard to do math in English class!"*

How often do we find our students reluctant or unable to recognize and use knowledge they already posses to help them solve new problems or understand new, related concepts? This phenomenon can be directly tied to the ways in which students initially learn information. In an educational era when tremendous emphasis is placed upon specialized knowledge, the segregated clustering of subject area instruction often prevents students from identifying important interconnections among the subjects they study.

The challenge for teachers is to find a healthy and meaningful balance between curricular breadth and depth. The long history of research on the ways in which students learn provides a strong rationale for the value of interdisciplinary instruction. Research in cognitive science strongly supports this view. The work of Ausubel (1968), Neisser (1976), and others in the 1980s and 1990s led to our current notion of schematic structures in the brain. These schematic structures, composed of hundreds, sometimes thousands of interconnected bits of information, serve as a framework for our knowledge. The goodness of our schematic structures is highly dependent upon the way in which we initially process information presented to us. Ausubel referred to these associations as "cognitive hooks." Instruction that provides students with links to connect otherwise discrete bits of knowledge enhances their ability to recognize and apply prior knowledge to new, related learning situations.

Obstacles to Interdisciplinary Lesson Planning

Although the development of integrated learning experiences is important, teachers often find it difficult to plan such experiences for students. Although a current emphasis on a whole language orientation in the elementary curriculum assists us as we help students understand relationships among reading, writing, and oral language, most school curricula retain a nonintegrated approach to subject matter instruction. Textbooks and teachers' guides rarely emphasize relationships between the subject area of major concentration and other disciplines. As a result, teachers have neither the information nor the time needed to realistically include interdisciplinary experiences in curricular planning.

Although we cannot always change the existing middle and high school curricular materials rapidly or directly, we can employ a planning process that will allow us to periodically incorporate cross-disciplinary ideas and activities into our repertoire of instructional strategies.

Guidelines for Planning

Each of us has particular subject matter expertise, and we have also accumulated knowledge and developed interests in other areas. Additionally, we have access to colleagues whose subject matter concentrations differ from our own. Using these resources, we can conceptualize and construct instructional lessons that help students understand important and interesting relationships between the disciplines. The following guidelines can help us as we develop interdisciplinary lessons.

1. *Formulate a goal statement that indicates the principle(s) or concept(s) to be understood at the completion of the lesson.* What are the primary pieces of information or concepts that you want students to understand? Often, interdisciplinary lessons do not concentrate on the mastery of specific skills. By their very nature, these lessons usually focus on the application of skills and

knowledge to novel situations. For this reason, goals of interdisciplinary lessons will usually involve helping students understand how the skills and knowledge they possess can be combined to accomplish a task, discover a solution, or explain a situation.

2. *Select the primary content base that will serve as the catalyst for instruction.* Often, the content base will be determined by the text. There are times, however, when your goal necessitates the use of other, ancillary materials. In either case, determine the primary vehicle that will drive the instruction (e.g., a work of art or literature, a scientific or mathematical principle, an event or era in history, etc.).

3. *Identify events, discoveries, and writings within other disciplines that relate to the primary content base in a meaningful way.* Through talking with colleagues and brainstorming on your own, consider information in other disciplines that seems to relate to the primary content. At this point, you may find it helpful to look at the table of contents in the textbooks you will be using. However, don't discount your own expertise, the films or plays you've seen, the books or magazine articles you've read, and your life experience.

4. *Determine the key points of intersection between the disciplines that correspond to the established terminal goal of instruction.* As you investigate each cross-discipline idea in more depth, keep your terminal goal well in mind. Often we become so enthralled in the idea itself that we lose sight of our major instructional intent. This is intellectually enjoyable, but it is a time-consuming luxury that few of us can afford. Some ideas will probably need to be discarded, either because they are too complex or because they do not fully address the goal. Other ideas may be so compelling and enlightening that you may want to revise the terminal goal to reflect new insights you have gained.

5. *Formulate instructional objectives.* Most interdisciplinary lessons will not focus on the mastery of specific skills. Nevertheless, it is important to determine what you expect your students to be able to do when they have completed the lesson. As in other instructional planning, objectives serve as the springboard for the development of the instructional strategies and activities you will use.

6. *Identify the necessary prerequisite knowledge that students must possess in each discipline area you will address.* Interdisciplinary instruction can fall apart if students lack knowledge of key principles or concepts within each discipline. Carefully consider the prerequisite skills students must have before they can successfully accomplish the objectives you have set forth. Sometimes, missing skills or pieces of information can be taught rather quickly. However, when this is not the case, it will be necessary to revise the interdisciplinary content.

7. *Formulate instructional strategies that will compel students to use their knowledge in one discipline to better understand and appreciate another.* Students are not used to activating their knowledge in one discipline while studying another. For this reason, it is important to develop activities that require this transfer in a purposeful way. Depending upon the content and timeframe of instruction, you may want to use concept mapping, in-class debates, group projects, and/or a variety of discovery techniques to accomplish your goal. The critical component of interdisciplinary lessons, as in most instruction, is active and invested participation.

Giving our students opportunities to explore interconnections among the subject areas they are studying has many advantages. Interdisciplinary instruction adds meaning and relevancy to learning as students discover fascinating and compelling relationships between disciplines.

MAKING LESSON PLANS

Up to this point, we have emphasized the importance of choosing unit outcomes at a higher level of thinking (for example, application, analysis, synthesis, decision making) more than lesson outcomes to achieve a thinking curriculum. If you plan lessons without a higher-level unit outcome in mind, your students' attention will fall exclusively on each individual lesson without noticing the relationship among lessons. This relationship may appear deceptively unimportant until it becomes apparent that your lessons seem to pull students first in one direction (e.g., knowledge acquisition) and then abruptly in another (e.g., problem solving), without instruction to guide them in the transition. The result of such isolated lesson outcomes may well be confusion, anxiety, and distrust on the part of your students, regardless of how well you prepare each individual lesson and how effective they are in accomplishing their stated—but isolated—outcomes. Because outcomes at higher levels rarely can be attained within the time frame of a single lesson, they must be achieved in the context of unit plans.

Before you actually write a lesson plan, two preliminary considerations are necessary for your unit plan to flow smoothly: (1) determining where to start, and (2) providing for learner diversity.

Determining Where to Start

Perhaps most perplexing to new teachers is deciding the level of learning at which a lesson should begin, for example, knowledge or comprehension or application. Do you always begin by teaching facts (instilling knowledge), or can you begin with activities at the application level or even at the synthesis and decision-making levels? Both alternatives are possible, but each makes different assumptions about the prior task-relevant knowledge of your students and the interrelationship among your lessons.

Beginning a lesson or a sequence of lessons at the knowledge level (e.g., list, recall, recite, etc.) assumes that the topic you will be teaching is mostly new material. Such a lesson usually occurs at the beginning of a sequence that will progressively build this knowledge into more authentic behavior—perhaps ending at the application, synthesis, or evaluation (decision-making) level. When no task-relevant prior knowledge is required, the starting point for a lesson often is at the knowledge or comprehension level. When some task-relevant prior knowledge has been taught, lessons can begin at higher levels of thinking. Notice from the list of objectives in Figure 4.7 that each lesson having an outcome at a higher level is preceded by a lesson at some lower level. The complexity with which a lesson can start depends on the learning outcome of the lessons that preceded it.

As we have seen, unit plans should attempt to teach a range of outcomes that begin at a lower level and end at a higher level. Some units might begin at the application level and end at a higher level, if a previous unit has provided the task-relevant prior knowledge and understandings required. It also is possible to progress from one level of a learning outcome to another within a single lesson. This may be increasingly difficult when lessons start at higher levels, but it is possible and often desirable to move from knowledge to comprehension and on to application activities within a single lesson. This is illustrated in the flow of behaviors for the following third-grade social studies lesson:

Unit Title: Local, State, and National Geography

Lesson Title: Local Geography

Behaviors

- Student will know geographical location of community relative to state and nation (knowledge).
- Student will be able to describe physical features of community (comprehension).
- Student will be able to locate community on map and globe (application).
- Student will be able to discuss how the community is similar to and different from other communities (analysis).

In this lesson a comprehensive list of outcomes is required in a relatively brief time (a single lesson) by using objects already known to the students (their own community, map, globe) and by dovetailing one outcome into another so each new activity is a continuation of the preceding one. When the teacher plans a transition across learning levels within a single lesson, the necessary question before each new level is, "Have I provided all the required task-relevant prior knowledge?" If your answer is "Yes," your lesson will be directed at the students' current level of understanding, and they will have the maximum opportunity to attain the unit objective.

Providing for Learner Diversity with Alternative Methods and New Technologies

A second consideration before writing a lesson plan is the extent to which the lesson provides for student diversity or individual differences. Thus far, we have considered all the students within a class to be identical, sharing the same behavioral characteristics and task-relevant prior knowledge. But diversity is the rule in any classroom.

Regardless of where you position the entry level of a lesson, some students will be above it and other students will be below it. Much of the work of unit and lesson planning is playing a game of averages in which you attempt to provide most of the instruction at the current level of understanding of most of the learners. Unless an entire unit of study is individualized (as is the case with some computerized curricula), most instruction must be directed at the "average" learner in your classroom while attempting to meet the needs of special learners.

However, some instructional methods and **tutorial and communication technologies** can help you meet the needs of special learners. These methods and technologies share the following characteristics:

- Allow rapid movement within and across content, depending on the learners' success at any given time.
- Allow students the flexibility to proceed at their own pace and level of difficulty.
- Provide students immediate feedback on the accuracy of their responses.
- Gradually shift the responsibility for learning from teacher to student.

Before you begin your lesson plan, decide on the extent to which methods and technologies for individualizing instruction are needed by the diversity of learning needs in your classroom. The following methods describe some of your options for meeting the special needs of your learners. Be sure to include them in your lesson plans when they can contribute to the goals of your lesson.

Task-Ability Grouping. You can group your class for a specified period of time by the skills required to learn the material you are presenting. For example, higher performing readers can read ahead and work independently on advanced exercises while you direct your lesson to the average and lower performing readers. You can divide lesson plans, objectives, activities, materials, and tests into two or more appropriate parts when learners exhibit noticeable strengths and weaknesses that cannot be bridged in a single lesson. The intent is to group learners homogeneously by learning skills relevant to a specific task or lesson for a limited amount of time, after which you should regroup when new tasks place different demands on your learners.

Learning Centers. Students tend to learn better when solving real-life problems. As a result, many schools are working to reorganize curriculum to support real-world problem solving and application (Baden & Mayor, 2004; Boyer, 1993). One way to promote real-

Learning centers containing media, supplemental resources, demonstration materials, and exercises can help individualize a lesson for those who may lack the prerequisite knowledge or skills required at the beginning of the lesson. The use of learning centers should be indicated in the lesson plan whenever applicable.

world problem solving and help individual learners apply what they have learned is through the use of a learning—or activity—center. Learning centers can individualize a lesson by providing resources for review and practice for those who may lack task-relevant prior knowledge or skills. When a learning center can contain media, supplemental resources, and/or practice exercises directly related to applying your lesson content, include it as an integral part of your lesson plan. The more hands-on activity your learning center elicits from your learners, the more effective it will be in helping you achieve your lesson and unit goals.

Review and Follow-Up Materials.   Some of your lessons will need to stimulate the recall of task-relevant prior knowledge. An oral summary, together with a supplementary handout on which individual learners may look up the required information, can bring some students up to the required level while not boring others. The key to this procedure is to carefully prepare a summary and review sheet covering critically needed prerequisite knowledge for the day's lesson—important names, dates, concepts, themes, and formulas, This lets you limit your review to the essentials and requires the least amount of time.

Tutoring.   During **peer tutoring,** one student teaches another at the same grade and age level. During **cross-age tutoring,** the tutor may be one or more years and grade levels above the learner receiving the instruction. Cross-age tutoring, generally, has been more effective than peer tutoring, owing to the fact that older students are more likely to be familiar with the material and are more likely to be respected as role models. Tutoring has been most successful as an adjunct to regular instruction, usually in the form of providing greater amounts of instructional practice than could be provided in a whole-class or group setting.

Interactive Instructional CD-ROMs.   Instructional CD-ROMs can provide computer-generated activities that students work through at their own level and at their own pace. CD-ROMs can also hold different sound tracks, for example, one in English and another in

Spanish. These instructional CDs typically break skills down into small subskills, such as those that might be identified in a learning hierarchy through which students work in small steps. Questions and prompts actively engage learners in formulating responses and give them immediate knowledge of whether they are correct, providing **interactive individualized practice activities.**

Interactive CD-ROMs are now available from publishers and commercial vendors for many different grade levels and content areas to give students practice, assess understanding, and provide remediation. They can quickly assess the accuracy of student responses to practice activities and change the sequence and difficulty of the activities to correspond with the learners' current level of understanding. In this manner, practice can be tailored to individual learners, depending on how well they respond at a certain level of difficulty. Students can spend more time on a particular topic or skill, or the program can return to an earlier sequence of instruction to review or reteach prerequisite learning. CD-ROMs also have the capability of providing color pictures, simulated motion, charts, and diagrams that can motivate learners and enhance the authenticity of the practice experience. As with other individualized learning methods, instructional CD-ROMs have been found most effective when providing practice opportunities for content that has already been taught.

Online and Desktop Simulations and Games.   Students who need an alternative or supplementary means of attaining your classroom objectives can use instructional simulations and games, either cooperatively or independently. Lessons may begin with whole-class instruction and, depending on interests and abilities, some students can be directed to instructional simulations and games to receive hands-on experiences that may remediate or enrich skills taught during full-class instruction (for example, for simulations across grade levels, see Aldrich, 2005; Grabe & Grabe, 1996; K. Jones, 1995). Textbook publishers are increasingly providing computer simulations and practice-based instruction that teach performance skills relevant to your curriculum. Some of these curriculum supplements also can be used by learners in cooperative groups.

A number of instructional simulations and games have been developed to teach and assess problem-solving behavior from K to 12. Among the most successful have been the *AmericaQuest* program with its technology-based *MashpeeQuest* performance task and a middle-school science curriculum called *ThinkerTools.* (Their Web sites may be found at *quest.classroom.com* and *thinkertools.soe.berkeley.edu.*)

MashpeeQuest is an example of an online performance task used as a tool to assess problem-solving behavior within the context of an instructional program (*AmericaQuest*) that teaches learners the reasoning and problem-solving skills used by professional historians and archaeologists. The *MashpeeQuest* performance task is designed to assess the following problem-solving skills taught by the *AmericaQuest* program:

- Ability to synthesize disparate ideas through reasoning in a problem-solving context
- Ability to offer reasoned arguments rather than brief guesses
- Ability to formulate creative, well-founded theories for unsolved questions in science and history

The online performance task, described by Mislevy, Steinberg, Almond, Haertel, and Penuel (2000) and the National Research Council (2001), is as follows:

During instruction, students participate via the Internet in an expedition with archaeologists and historians who are uncovering clues about the fate of a Native American tribe, the Anasazi, who are believed to have abandoned their magnificent cliff dwellings in large numbers between 1200 and 1300. To collect observations of students' acquisition of the targeted skills, the MashpeeQuest assessment task engages students in deciding a court case involving recognition of another tribe, the Mashpee Wampanoags, who some believe disappeared just as the Anasazi did. A band of people claiming Wampanoag ancestry has been trying for some years to gain recognition from the federal government as a tribe that still exists. Students are asked to investigate the evidence, select Websites that provide evidence to support their claim, and justify their choices based on the evidence. They are also asked to identify one place to go to find evidence that does not support their claim and to address how their theory of what happened to the Mashpee is still justified. (National Research Council, 2001, p. 268)

One of the goals of the *AmericaQuest* program is to assist students in learning persuasive arguments for problem-solving supported by evidence from the program's Web site and their own research. Since the problem-solving skills and data that serve as evidence are embedded in the Web site, some of the assessments of student performance are made automatically by counting the number of sources used and the time spent examining each source. Other assessments involving the organization of evidence and its oral presentation are made by the teacher using a structured format provided by the program. The *MashpeeQuest* problem-solving task is a good example of the role technology can play in assessment and in presenting an authentic learning task. Similar problem-solving tasks can be teacher prepared in the Internet-connected classroom.

ThinkerTools is another example of a program that harnesses the computer for teaching and assessment—this time to promote metacognitive skills with which students assess their own and others' work (White & Frederiksen, 1998, 2000). *ThinkerTools* is a middle-school science curriculum that teaches students how to formulate and test competing theories with experiments simulated on the computer. Software enables each learner to simulate experiments to accurately measure distances, times, and velocities, and to compare findings and reach a consensus about the best explanation for different naturally occurring phenomena. As with the *MashpeeQuest* problem-solving task, the computer provides feedback to the student.

Most importantly, *ThinkerTools* focuses on development of the metacognitive skills needed to create and revise scientific explanations from evidence. The curriculum encourages students to reflect on their own procedures and choices in order to evaluate their research using established scientific criteria, such as reasoning, problem solving and collaborative skills. The *ThinkerTools* program has been found to be effective in improving students inquiry and problem-solving skills and in reducing the performance gap between low and high achievers in urban classrooms (White & Frederiksen, 2000).

Fiber Optics/Telecommunications. Fiber optics/telecommunications technology, also known as the Internet, offers the most opportunities to stimulate the senses through multimedia, making the learning environment more fluid and personalized. Often referred to as the **living curriculum,** the combination of laser technology and telecommunications has many of the same features of CD-ROMs with the added advantage that the subject matter being studied no longer must reside on a single disk inside a PC. Students may acquire information flexibly and instantaneously from communication superhighways, which can give the individual learner rapid access to human and textual resources across schools, geographical locations, and the world.

With the aid of a computer, learners create their own living curriculum with which to practice and apply the content learned. By selecting information networks and pathways and conducting searches that increasingly bring authentic detail and professional expertise, responsibility for retaining and applying content passes gradually from the teacher to learners and to the world outside the classroom, encouraging cooperative ventures with other students, professionals, and resources. Once established, these information pathways provide students with many opportunities, among which are the following:

- Search beyond their local libraries; for example, browse through holdings on early flight in the Library of Congress, visually tour a space station circling in space, or ask questions of a curator at the Air and Space Museum via electronic mail.
- Become more specialized and focused on current issues; for example, query a database being compiled by the *New York Times* on a fast-breaking story, scan a recent index of *Scientific American* for the latest advances on gene splicing, or communicate via electronic mail with a researcher stationed in Antarctica.
- Cooperate with other learners at a distance to create class newspapers; for example, team up with students in another school, state, or nation to share news of mutual interest on acid rain, deforestation, or the global economy.
- Work with cross-age mentors outside their own school; for example, to explore connections between academic work and job opportunities or to see how principles and concepts are used at more advanced levels, such as in subsequent courses, in the workplace, or in different community contexts.

These methods and communication technologies are only some of the ways your lesson plans can provide for diverse learning needs among your students. To be effective, technology should be integrated across the curriculum (Roblyer, 2005). Table 4.2 suggests some technology applications in reading/language arts, math, science, and social studies

Table 4.2 Integrating technology into different content areas.

Content Area	Application
Reading/language arts	• Software programs to develop basic reading skills
	• Word processing to teach writing skills
	• Internet search engines to develop basic research skills
Math	• Tutorial and drill-and practice software to develop math facts
	• Graphing calculations to illustrate abstract or hard to visualize relationships
	• Software to illustrate and explore geometry concepts
Science	• Simulations to illustrate complex relationships
	• Data-gathering instruments to conduct experiments in and out of the lab
	• Internet links to access information and communicate with other scientists
Social Studies	• Simulations to explore distant places and times
	• Online archives to access many years of social science research
	• Spreadsheets and databases to organize information

Video Window

Computers in the Classroom

In this video, you will find Sue teaching a lesson on graphing and math to her second-grade learners. Her students are positioned in small groups at six computer stations. Each group is given different graphing and data recording problems to solve and then left to work independently to find the solution to their problem with the use of their computers. You will see how Sue monitors and guides her students through their assignment during which she fulfills the important functions of feedback and reinforcement. As you watch Sue's lesson, see if her lesson contained any of the following four criteria for the effective use of tutorial and computer technology. Describe one instance of any that you find. How well do you believe Sue implemented these criteria?

- Students are allowed to rapidly move within and across content.
- Student can proceed at their own pace.
- Students receive immediate feedback as to the accuracy of their responses.
- The responsibility for learning is gradually shifted from teacher to student.

 To answer these questions online, go to the Video Windows *module for this chapter on the* Companion Website at www.prenhall.com/borich.

EVENTS OF INSTRUCTION

After you have determined where to start the lesson and how to provide for diverse learning needs, you are ready to begin planning your lesson. At this time, you will specify the key events that occur during the lesson—and for which you are responsible. By placing the responsibility on you for providing these events, we distinguish between teaching and learning. *Learning* refers to the internal events that go on inside your learners' heads. *Teaching* is the sum of the instructional activities you provide to influence what goes on in your learners' heads.

The sequence of steps you follow in lesson planning assumes that the instructional events you plan will influence learning. It is not unusual for teaching to be unrelated to learning, as when teachers teach and students listen, but nothing sinks in. The process of getting instructional events to sink in is one of planning instruction that fosters a close relationship between the external events of instruction and the internal events of learning, actively engaging your learners in the learning process.

You can achieve this tightly knit relationship between teaching and learning by considering seven instructional events suggested by R. Gagné and Briggs (2005). These steps include the most relevant parts of other models of lesson preparation. For example, Hunter (1982) proposed a sequence of events, called the *Mastery Learning Program*, which are similar to and overlap those of Gagné and Briggs, as shown in Figure 4.11. Although not all of the events in either model are applicable to every lesson, they provide a basis—or menu— from which you can formulate many different lesson plans. Let's consider the types of instructional activity that each event entails, as described by Gagné and Briggs (2005), and how you can actively engage your learners in the learning process with them. The terminology of Hunter (1982) appears in parentheses.

Figure 4.11 Two related perspectives on events of instruction.

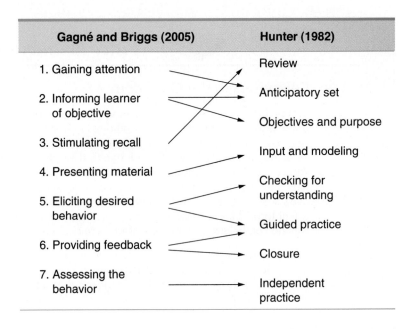

Gagné and Briggs (2005)	Hunter (1982)
1. Gaining attention	Review
2. Informing learner of objective	Anticipatory set
3. Stimulating recall	Objectives and purpose
4. Presenting material	Input and modeling
5. Eliciting desired behavior	Checking for understanding
6. Providing feedback	Guided practice
7. Assessing the behavior	Closure
	Independent practice

1. Gaining Attention (Anticipatory Set)

Without your students' attention, little of your lesson will be heard, let alone actively engage your students in the learning process. Thus each lesson plan begins with an instructional event to engage student interest, curiosity, and attention. In some classes this will mean raising your students' attention from almost complete disengagement to where their vision and hearing are receptive. In other classes this may mean raising their attention from an already receptive mode to a higher level of curiosity, interest, and attention. The intensity of your attention-gaining event will depend on the starting point of your learners. A fifth-period class that meets after lunch may require a more dramatic attention-getting event than will an eager first-period class. You will need to find the right event for gaining your students' attention.

One of the most common attention-gaining devices is to arouse curiosity. Often this can be accomplished by asking questions:

- Have you ever wondered how we got the word *horsepower?* Who would like to guess? (from a lesson on energy)
- Can anyone think of a popular automobile with the name of a Greek god? (from an introductory lesson on mythology)
- Have you ever wondered how some creatures can live both in the water and on land? (from a lesson on amphibious animals)

These questions, called *openers*, are designed not to have any single correct answer or even to accurately reflect the fine details of what is to follow. Instead they amuse, stimulate, or even bewilder students so that they become receptive to the content and questions that follow. Following are other thought-provoking openers:

- Why do some scientists think that traveling to the planets will make the space traveler younger? (from a lesson in general science or physics)
- Why do we have the word i-t-s and another word i-t-apostrophe-s? (from a lesson in punctuation)

- Why is the dollar worth more today in Mexico than in Switzerland? (from a lesson in social studies)
- Why do you think some eloquent lawyers become disliked by the juries they speak to? (from a lesson in public speaking)

Another useful technique for gaining students' attention is to present the following:

An apparent *contradiction*:

- Why do you think the Greek empire collapsed when it was at its strongest?

Or a seeming *inconsistency* in real life:

- Why do some lower forms of animal life live longer than human beings?

Or something that at first appears to be *illogical*:

- Why must something go backward every time something else goes forward?

For example, introducing a lesson in signed numbers by informing your learners that the multiplication of two negative numbers always results in a positive product may puzzle them, but it can arouse their curiosity about how two negatives could result in something positive. You could continue by explaining the number line and mathematical rules behind this apparent contradiction.

Diagrams, pictures, illustrations, scale models, and films are other attention-getting aids. Use these devices to appeal to your learners' sense of vision while your oral presentation appeals to their sense of hearing. Graphics or visuals are particularly effective openers with students who are known to be more oriented and responsive to visual than auditory presentations. A visual opener can include samples of materials for the day's lesson so students can touch them before the lesson begins. A visual opener also can show equipment you will use during the lesson (e.g., scales, meters, pictures and models).

2. Informing Learners of the Objective (Anticipatory Set, Objectives, and Purpose)

Just because your learners have been turned on with some attention-getting device does not mean they will be tuned to the wavelength at which you present the lesson. Now you need to tell them the channel on which your lesson is being transmitted. The most effective way to focus your learners' receptivity is to inform them of the behavioral outcome they will be expected to attain by the end of the lesson. You can do this by telling them early in the lesson or unit how they will be examined or expected to show competence. For example, such expectations might be expressed in the following ways:

- Remember the four definitions of *power* that will be presented (science).
- Be able to express ownership orally in a sentence to the class (language arts).
- Identify correctly a mystery specimen of lower animal life using the microscope (life science).
- State your true feelings about laws dealing with the death penalty (social studies).

Such statements allow learners to know when they have attained the expected level of behavior and to become selective in how to use and remember the lesson information. If your students know they will be expected to recall four definitions of power at the end of your lesson on energy, then they know to focus their search, retrieval, and retention processes during the lesson on the definitions or categories of power you present.

Informing learners of your objective helps them organize their thinking in advance of the lesson by providing mental hooks on which to hang the key points. This activates the learning process and focuses your learners on obtaining the required behavioral outcome.

The key to the success of this instructional event is to communicate your objective clearly. Therefore, choose your words with your learners' vocabulary and language level in mind and record what you tell them as a reminder in this second part of your lesson plan. The best way to communicate your objective is to provide examples of tasks that you expect your students to be able to perform after the lesson. This translates the action verb associated with a learning outcome into some ways this behavior might be measured on tests, in class discussions, and in question-and-answer sessions.

For example, at the beginning of a unit on lower forms of animal life, you might write on the blackboard the following examples of expected outcomes, and then check off the ones that most apply at the start of each day's lesson:

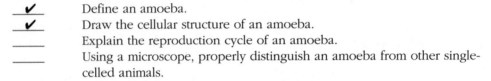

✔	Define an amoeba.
✔	Draw the cellular structure of an amoeba.
____	Explain the reproduction cycle of an amoeba.
____	Using a microscope, properly distinguish an amoeba from other single-celled animals.

Notice that these lesson outcomes range from recounting a fact to making decisions and judgments in a real biological environment. Without knowing in advance at which of these levels they are expected to perform, your learners will have no way of selecting and focusing their attention on those parts of the instruction leading to the desired behavior. This is not to say they should ignore other aspects of the presentation, but students can now see the other aspects as tools or means for gaining the highest level outcome required and not as ends in themselves.

3. Stimulating Recall of Prerequisite Learning (Review)

Before you can proceed with the new lesson content, one final preliminary instructional event is needed. Because learning cannot occur in a vacuum, the necessary task-relevant prior information must be retrieved and made ready for use. This calls for some method of reviewing, summarizing, restating, or otherwise stimulating the key concepts acquired in previous lessons. This information is instrumental for achieving the level of outcome intended in the present lesson.

For example, if your goal is to have learners use a microscope to properly distinguish an amoeba from other single-celled animals, it is clear that some previously acquired facts, concepts, and skills are relevant to this new task. Definitions of single-celled animals, unique characteristics of an amoeba that make it distinguishable from other one-celled animals, and skill in using the microscope are among the task-relevant prior knowledge that will influence your learners' attainment of this outcome.

Helping students retrieve earlier information requires condensing the key aspects into brief, easily understood form. It is not possible to summarize all of this information in a few minutes. So you need to use thought-provoking and stimulating techniques to focus learners on sizable amounts of prior learning. Questions like these can help your students recall the most significant and memorable parts of earlier lessons:

- Do you remember why Joshua couldn't see the amoeba in the microscope? (it was on low magnification instead of high)

Before the actual presentation of new content begins, the necessary task-relevant prior information must be retrieved and made ready for use. This can be accomplished by reviewing, summarizing, and restating, stimulating into action the key concepts acquired in previous lessons.

- Do you remember Natasha's humorous attempt to relate the reproduction cycle of an amoeba to that of human beings? (she had equated cell division with waking up one morning to find a new baby in the family)
- Do you remember the three-color picture Rico drew of the cellular structure of an amoeba? (everyone had commented on how lifelike the picture was)

These questions help students retrieve task-relevant prior learning—not by summarizing that learning, but by tapping into a single mental image that recalls that learning. Once the image has been retrieved, students can turn it on and off at will to search for details that may be nestled within it, achieving still greater recall. Describing how to stimulate the recall of prerequisite learning, then, is our third entry in your lesson plan.

4. Presenting the Stimulus Material (Input, Modeling)

Presenting the stimulus material will be the heart of your lesson plan. At first glance, this component may seem to require little explanation, but several important considerations for completing it often go unnoticed. These pertain to the authenticity, selectivity, and variety of your lesson presentation. Let's look closely at each of these.

Authenticity. To teach a behavior that is authentic, your lesson must present content in a way in which it will be used by your learners on assessments, in subsequent grades, and in the world outside your classroom. If your goal is to teach learners to *use* a microscope to identify single-celled animals, then teaching them to *label* the parts of a microscope would not be authentic. Although naming the parts may be a prerequisite skill and an important objective of an earlier lesson, it would not be sufficient to attaining the desired goal of this lesson. In other words, how you use a behavior in daily life must always be how you teach a behavior for it to be authentic. Reading in the context of a story would also be an example of an authentic behavior, because the learner is being provided the opportunity to derive meaning from text, as would be expected in the real world.

You can make the behaviors you teach more authentic by changing the irrelevant aspects—or context—of what you are teaching as often as possible and in as many different ways as possible. This prevents learning a response under only one condition but not under others that may be encountered in subsequent lessons, grades, and courses. Following are examples of changing the irrelevant aspects of a learning stimulus:

- In math, show both stacked format and line format.
- Introduce learners to examples of proper punctuation by using popular magazines and newspapers as well as the text and workbook (English or a foreign language).
- Show how the laws of electricity apply to lightning during a thunderstorm as well as to electrical circuitry in the laboratory (science).
- Relate rules of social behavior found among humans to those often found among animals (social studies).
- Compare the central processing unit in a computer to the executive processes in the human brain (computer science).
- Show how the reasons for a particular war also can be applied to other conflicts hundreds of years earlier (history).

In each of these examples, the lesson designer is applying key lesson ideas in different contexts. As a result, learners are more likely (1) to focus on correct mathematical operations and not the format of the problem, (2) to notice improper punctuation when it appears in a popular publication, (3) to understand the universality of physical laws governing electricity, (4) to not think that social behavior is a uniquely human phenomenon, (5) to not confuse the wonders of data processing with the hardware and equipment that only sometimes are needed to perform it, and (6) to understand that some reasons for conflict, war, and hostility are general as well as specific.

Selectivity.   A second consideration during this stage of lesson preparation is emphasizing the content most important to your lesson. Not everything in a chapter, workbook, film, presentation, or on the chalkboard will be of equal importance to the day's objective. Consequently, highlighting key aspects of the text and workbook at the beginning of the lesson will help students selectively review and retain the main points of your lesson. For example, focusing your learners' attention on the "six concepts on the bottom of page 50" or the "tables and figures at the end of chapter 3" can help your learners place the day's lesson in the context of their curriculum and provide an anchor for future reference.

You will also want to highlight content during your lesson. Examples of such highlighting include verbally emphasizing the importance of certain events; telling students what to look for in a video (even stopping it to reinforce an idea); emphasizing key words on the chalkboard with underlining, circling, or color; and using verbal markers ("This is important"; "Notice the relevance of this"; "You'll need this information later"). These and other methods for selectively emphasizing key parts of your lesson will be taken up in later chapters, but remember to consider them at this stage of your lesson plan.

Variety.   A key behavior of the effective teacher is instructional variety. Gaining students' attention at the start of the lesson is one thing, but keeping their attention is quite another. Variety in the modalities of instruction (for example, visual, oral, tactile) and instructional activity (large-group lecture, question and answer, small-group discussion) stimulates student thinking and interest. Shifting from visually dominated instruction to orally dominated instruction (or using both simultaneously) and breaking a lesson into several instructional activities (for example, explanation followed by question and answer) are important.

Planning changes in modality and instructional activities presents the lesson in varied contexts, giving learners the opportunity to grasp material in several different ways, according to their individual learning styles. Such changes also give students the opportunity to see previously learned material used in different ways. This reinforces learned material better than simply restating it in the same mode and form. It also encourages learners to extend or expand material according to the new mode or procedure being used. For example, material learned from a presentation may be pushed to its limit in a question-and-answer period when the learner answers a question and finds out that previous understandings were partly incorrect due to the limited context in which they were learned. Quite apart from the well-known fact that instructional variety helps keep students attentive and actively engaged in the learning process, it also offers them a more memorable and conscious learning experience. Be sure to consider these and other methods of adding instructional variety to your lesson during this stage of your lesson plan.

5. Eliciting the Desired Behavior (Checking for Understanding, Guided Practice)

After presenting the content of the lesson, provide your learners an opportunity to show whether they have acquired the knowledge or understanding expected. Learning cannot occur effectively in a passive environment—one that lacks activities to engage the learner in the learning process at moderate-to-high rates of success. Active engagement in the learning process at an appropriate level of difficulty must be a goal of every lesson, because without it little or no learning occurs.

Such engagement can be accomplished in many ways. It may even occur spontaneously as a result of getting your students' attention, informing them of the objectives, stimulating the recall of prerequisite learning, and presenting the content—but don't count on it! Active engagement, especially at an appropriate level of difficulty, is a slippery concept. If left to chance, it rarely occurs to the extent required for significant learning. Although all of the instructional events presented thus far are required to actively engage your learners, they cannot guarantee engagement. Therefore, a fifth instructional event is needed; when added to a lesson plan it encourages and guides learners through a process that can be expected to exhibit the outcome intended.

This fifth event—eliciting the desired behavior—differs from the four preceding ones in that it seeks the individual's covert and personal engagement in the learning process. Each learner must be placed in a position of grappling in a trial-and-error fashion with summarizing, paraphrasing, applying, or solving a problem involving the lesson content. It is not important that a response be produced accurately at this stage, as long as the activity provided stimulates the learner to attempt a response. This activity encourages the learner to organize a response that meets the learning outcome stated when the student was informed of the objective.

The primary ways of staging this instructional event include workbooks, handouts, textbook study questions, verbal and written exercises, and oral questions that have students apply what was learned, if only in the privacy of their minds. The idea is to pose a classroom activity that encourages students to use the material in a nonevaluative atmosphere, as close in time as possible to presentation of new material. Sometimes such activities can be inserted throughout the lesson at the end of each new chunk of information, which also adds variety. In other instances, these activities occur near the end of the presentation of content.

Either way, the eliciting activity is brief, nonevaluative, and focused exclusively on posing a condition for which the learner must organize a response (e.g., from a question, problem, or exercise). This response may be written, oral, or subvocal (students respond in their own minds). Eliciting activities can be as simple as your posing a question anywhere in a lesson, or as complex as a problem exercise completed in a workbook at lesson's end. The main attribute is that these activities be nonevaluative, to encourage a response unhampered by the anxiety and conservative response patterns that generally occur during testing situations. Rosenshine and Stevens (1986) suggest additional ways of eliciting the desired behavior:

- Prepare a large number of oral questions beforehand.
- Ask many brief questions on main points, on supplementary points, and on the process being taught. (Have students create their own questions.)
- Call on students whose hands are not raised in addition to those who volunteer.
- Ask students to summarize a rule or process in their own words.
- Have all students write their answers (on paper or the chalkboard) while you circulate.
- Have all students write their answers and check them with a neighbor (this is frequently used with older students).
- At the end of a presentation/discussion (especially with older students), write the main points on the chalkboard, and then have the class meet in groups to summarize the main points to each other.

6. Providing Feedback (Guided Practice, Closure)

The sixth instructional event is closely connected in time to the fifth event (eliciting the desired behavior). Eliciting the desired behavior promotes learning to the extent that learners come to understand the correctness of their responses. The response itself must be an individual attempt to recall, summarize, paraphrase, apply, or problem-solve, but the feedback that immediately follows can be directed to the entire class. For example, you can anonymously report to the class an individual's correct answer or hold up several students' answers for comparison.

However, an eliciting activity's main attribute is that it is nonevaluative. At this stage of the learning process, it is important to respond to a wrong answer encouragingly, to maintain the nonevaluative flavor of the eliciting activity. Responses such as "That's a good try," "That's not quite what I'm looking for this time," or "Keep thinking" can switch the focus to more useful responses without penalizing students for responding.

Ways of confirming a correct response are to read aloud the correct answers from a workbook, or to provide a handout with the correct answers, or to provide a copy of the exercise with correct answers penciled in. You could use a transparency to pose the eliciting activity and then record volunteered answers. If students are working silently at their seats, you can walk about the room, using a simple nod and smile to indicate the correctness of an individual performance or to encourage the revision of a wrong response. This part of the lesson plan should include the means by which feedback will be given learners about their responses. These and additional ways of providing feedback to individual students, small groups, and the entire class are summarized in Table 4.3.

Table 4.3 Some methods of providing feedback.

Individual Students	Small Groups	Class
Nod while walking past	Sit with group and discuss answers	Place answers on a transparency
Point to correct answer in workbook or text	Have one group critique another group's answers	Provide answers on a handout
Show student the answer key	Give each group the answer key when finished	Read answers aloud
Place a check alongside incorrect answers	Assign one group member the task of checking the answers of other group members	Place answers on the chalkboard
Have students grade each others' papers by using the text, or assign references as a guide		Have selected students read their answers aloud
		Have students grade each others' papers as you give answers

7. Assessing the Behavior (Independent Practice)

This final instructional event specifies the way in which you will evaluate the degree to which the learner has acquired the desired behavior. As we have seen, eliciting activities can be immediate or delayed (an oral question or a report or essay) and evaluative or nonevaluative. The fifth event described an immediate and nonevaluative eliciting activity. But for this instructional event on your lesson plan you will identify a delayed eliciting activity that is primarily evaluative.

Evaluative eliciting activities such as tests, research papers, graded homework, classroom performances, and student portfolios can be disadvantageous at earlier stages of learning because they can limit risk-taking—or exploratory—behavior and their feedback lacks immediacy. Both of these factors can be counterproductive to learning when the instructional goal is to get learners to respond for the first time. But they are instrumental for evaluating the degree to which the learner has attained the desired behavior. Some of the ways for completing this final, graded event include:

Tests and quizzes	Oral presentations
Homework exercises	Extended essays
In-class workbook assignments	Research papers
Performance evaluations	Independent practice
Lab assignments	Portfolios

EXAMPLE LESSON PLANS

We are now ready to place our seven instructional events into a brief but effective lesson plan. To be both practical and effective, lesson plans must be short and yet provide all the ingredients needed to deliver the lesson. Following are some example plans on various subjects and grade levels that show how easy lesson planning can be when the task is organized by these seven instructional events. Let's review each of them with some examples.

EXAMPLE LESSON PLAN: *Reading Skills*

Unit Title: Reading: Word Attack Skills (Vertically Planned Unit)

Lesson Title: Sound Discrimination, Letters of the Alphabet—Lesson 2.1

The preceding titles indicate the general content of the lesson and its placement in a unit on word attack skills. The lesson identifier, 2.1, indicates this lesson is the first one in Unit 2. It would appear on the graphic unit plan, as indicated in Figure 4.12.

Next appears a description of how you will use each of the seven instructional events to deliver this lesson to students. To this is added some elaboration that further defines each of the events.

1 **Gaining attention**   Play an audiotape of a voice articulating the sounds.
This instructional event gains student attention and focuses learners on what is to be presented. Whatever device or procedure you use should not only gain their attention but also motivate their continued concentration well into the lesson. Keep in mind that students, especially young ones, have trouble picking up subtle transitions in classroom activities. Often their attention is steadfastly on what has immediately preceded the lesson, and they are reluctant to change focus unless something new, interesting, or exciting is on the horizon.

Figure 4.12 The relationship of lessons, units, and a course or domain.

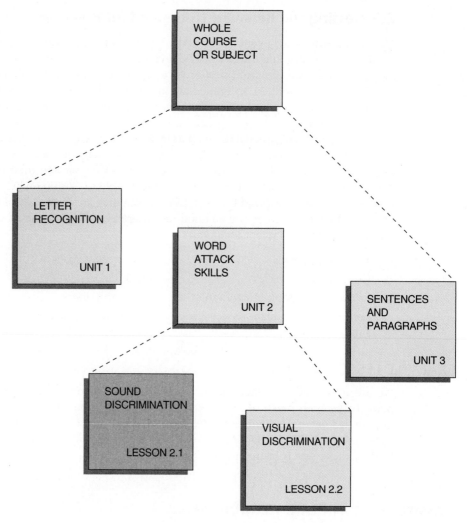

Visual or auditory stimuli often are effective as attention getters, because their ability to penetrate the senses exceeds that of more neutral stimuli like written words, verbal expressions, or pronouncements. Changing sensory modalities from listening to looking (or vice versa) often provides the incentive necessary to more selectively perceive and receive the message about to be communicated.

2 **Informing the learner of the objective** When the tape is finished, indicate that at the end of the lesson students will be expected to repeat the vowel sounds out loud, independently of the tape.

This instructional event translates the behavioral objective for the lesson into a form that is meaningful to students. In this example, information is being transferred from one modality (listening) to another (speaking), indicating that the objective for this lesson is written at the comprehension level of the cognitive domain, requiring a change in modalities. Your attention-getting device should be chosen to lead into the objective for the lesson. Simply clapping one's hands to gain attention, followed by the objective, would not be as effective as having the objective actually contained within the attention-getting procedure.

In this example, the audiotape was directly related to the lesson's content, allowing these two instructional events to work together to produce a unified theme, enhancing the learners' attention. Other simple but effective attention getters that could be made to reflect the lesson objective are a picture or chart, a question on the chalkboard, or a demonstration derived directly from lesson content.

3 **Stimulating recall of prerequisite learning**   Show how each vowel sound is produced by the correct positioning of the mouth and lips.

Identifying and successfully communicating task-relevant prior knowledge to students is critical to attaining the lesson objective. Unless you paraphrase, summarize, or otherwise review this information, at least some students will be unable to comprehend the information being conveyed. Among the most frequent reasons that learners are unable to attain lesson outcomes is that they lack the needed skills and understandings of previously taught lessons necessary for subsequent learning to occur.

Prerequisite content must be recalled or stimulated into action for it to play a meaningful role in acquiring new learning. Most lessons require some previous facts, understandings, or skills, and these should be recalled and identified at this step of the lesson plan. You can achieve this by touching on the high points of this prior learning.

4 **Presenting the stimulus material**   Say each vowel sound, and then have the class repeat it twice, pointing to a chart of the position of the mouth and lips during the articulation of each vowel sound. I will do the most commonly used vowels first.

You may feel this is the heart of the lesson. You are partly right, except that there are six other hearts, each of which could entail as much effort in planning and instructional time as this event does. Beginning teachers tend to pack their lessons almost entirely with new stimulus material. They devote far less effort to gaining attention, to informing the learner of the objective, to recalling prerequisite learning, and to other instructional nonevaluative and evaluative events that must follow the presentation of new material.

The presentation of new material is indispensable in any new lesson, but it need not always encompass most (or even a large portion) of the lesson. The result of devoting a large portion of the lesson to new material, exclusive of the other instructional events, is that the lesson is likely to present content in pieces too big for learners to grasp. This often results in having to reteach content during subsequent lessons and ultimately less content coverage at the end of a unit. The next three instructional events will make clear that this new content must itself be a stimulus for something more to come.

5 **Eliciting the desired behavior**   Have students silently practice forming correct mouth and lip positions for each vowel sound, following the pictures in their workbooks.

For this instructional event, the learner is given guidance in how to perform the behavior and an opportunity to practice it—two activities that must go hand in hand if learning is to occur. Eliciting the desired behavior for the first time without providing an opportunity to practice could diminish the effect of this instructional event. The stimulus material described in the previous event should be presented in a form that affords the learner the opportunity to use the behavior in a nonthreatening, nonevaluative environment. Grading or performance evaluations, therefore, should not be part of the performance being elicited in this instructional event, where spontaneity, freedom to make mistakes, and an opportunity for immediate feedback are the goals.

6 **Providing feedback**   Randomly choose students to recite the vowel sounds; correct their errors to demonstrate to the class the desired sound.

Feedback should be given immediately after the eliciting activity. As short a time as possible between performance and feedback is one of the most essential elements of learning: the closer the correspondence between a performance and feedback, the more quickly learning will occur.

Your feedback can be part of the eliciting activity, or it can be a separate activity. In the previous instructional event, feedback was not provided and learners had no way of knowing the correctness of their behavior (mouth and lip movements). Pictures in the text guided their behavior, but because students could not see themselves performing the movements, they could not tell if they performed accurately. In this case, feedback would have to follow the eliciting activity, making this instructional event essential for learning. The previous eliciting activity, however, might have included feedback if, for example, students were asked to recite aloud the vowel sounds and the teacher provided group feedback on the accuracy of their utterances. The correspondence of an eliciting activity and feedback is a matter of degree, but these two events should take place as closely in time as possible.

7 **Assessing the behavior**   The lesson objective will be assessed as part of the unit test on word attack skills and from exercises completed on pages 17 and 18 in the workbook.

Few lesson objectives are assessed by individual lesson tests. Amounts of content larger than that contained in a single lesson usually are necessary to make tests efficient and practical. However, it is important to indicate which unit or subunit tests cover the lesson content and what additional means, other than formal tests (e.g., classroom performances, projects, and portfolios), you will use to grade student responses. The information from this assessment will provide important feedback about your students' readiness for new stimulus material and possible reasons for poor performance in later lessons for which the current material is prerequisite.

EXAMPLE LESSON PLAN: *Literature and U.S. History*

Unit Title: Gold Rush (Laterally Planned Unit)

Lesson Title: Westward Journals

Subject Areas: History/Social Science, Language Arts, Art (Written by Cynthia Kiel)

The preceding titles indicate the general content of the lesson and the unit of which it is a part. This lesson appears on an interdisciplinary unit plan as a lesson in reading or literature titled "Westward Journals," as shown in Figure 4.13.

1 **Gaining attention**   Display items or pictures of items that pioneers may have brought with them on their trip West. These will include a diary, bonnet, old tools, the Bible, and cast-iron skillet.

2 **Informing the learner of the objective**   Students will be expected to choose one of the routes to California and write a diary entry from the 1840s detailing a day on the trip. Students may be creative in their presentation of this product, choosing to design a diary, journal, or perhaps write their entry on a ship or wagon made of construction paper.

3 **Stimulating recall of prerequisite learning**   As a class, students will brainstorm on a large chart the main events learned about the trip West.

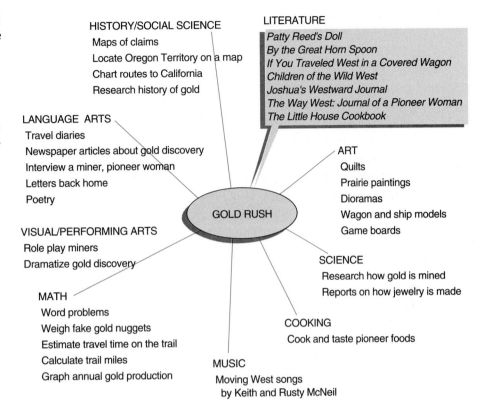

Figure 4.13 Visual representation of the interdisciplinary unit theme "Gold Rush," which includes the lesson "Westward Journals."

(Developed by Cynthia Kiel, teacher, Glendora, California.)

HISTORY/SOCIAL SCIENCE
Maps of claims
Locate Oregon Territory on a map
Chart routes to California
Research history of gold

LITERATURE
Patty Reed's Doll
By the Great Horn Spoon
If You Traveled West in a Covered Wagon
Children of the Wild West
Joshua's Westward Journal
The Way West: Journal of a Pioneer Woman
The Little House Cookbook

LANGUAGE ARTS
Travel diaries
Newspaper articles about gold discovery
Interview a miner, pioneer woman
Letters back home
Poetry

VISUAL/PERFORMING ARTS
Role play miners
Dramatize gold discovery

GOLD RUSH

ART
Quilts
Prairie paintings
Dioramas
Wagon and ship models
Game boards

SCIENCE
Research how gold is mined
Reports on how jewelry is made

MATH
Word problems
Weigh fake gold nuggets
Estimate travel time on the trail
Calculate trail miles
Graph annual gold production

COOKING
Cook and taste pioneer foods

MUSIC
Moving West songs
by Keith and Rusty McNeil

4 **Presenting the stimulus material** Students read excerpts from *The Way West, Journal of a Pioneer Woman*, by Amelia Stewart Knight, and *Joshua's Westward Journal*, by Joan Anderson. I will lead a discussion of how each author details and summarizes events on the journey.

5 **Eliciting the desired behavior** Students are to pretend they are children in a wagon train or aboard a ship on the trip West in the 1840s. I will tell them to write journal or diary entries about their experiences. I will provide a variety of writing paper and construction paper and invite creativity in designing their journal.

6 **Providing feedback** While the students are writing, ask individuals to share an excerpt from their entries. Point out how the students are including items listed on the brainstorming chart made at the beginning of the lesson.

7 **Assessing the behavior** Design a rubric describing various degrees of proficiency to grade the journal entries. Criteria may include adherence to factual events in 1840, descriptive language, and creativity.

Table 4.4 presents the approximate amount of time during a 50-minute class period that you might devote to each instructional event. Some periods will differ considerably from these amounts of time, such as when the entire lesson is devoted to a review or when recall of prior learning and assessing behavior is not relevant to the day's lesson. Keep in mind that experience, familiarity with content, and common sense always are your best guides for the percentage of time to devote to each instructional event.

Table 4.4 Approximate distribution of instructional time across instructional events for a hypothetical 50-minute lesson.

Instructional Event	Ranges in Minutes	Ranges in Percentages of Time
Gaining attention	1–5	2–10
Informing learners of the objective	1–3	2–6
Stimulating recall of prerequisite learning	5–10	10–20
Presenting the stimulus material	10–20	20–40
Eliciting the desired behavior	10–20	20–40
Providing feedback	5–10	10–20
Assessing behavior	0–10	0–20

From Table 4.4 it is apparent that when you emphasize one instructional event, another must be deemphasized; trade-offs always occur. Although every teacher would like to have more (sometimes less) time than allotted for an instructional period, decisions must be made that fit a lesson into the available time. Table 4.4 indicates some of the ways this might be done when planning a typical lesson.

The following lesson plans illustrate the seven instructional events in other content areas and grade levels.

EXAMPLE LESSON PLAN: *United States History*

Unit Title: United States History (Early Beginning Through Reconstruction)

Lesson Title: Causes of the Civil War—Lesson 2.3

1 **Gaining attention**   Show the following list of wars on a transparency:

French and Indian War, 1754–1769
Revolutionary War, 1775–1781
Civil War, 1861–1865
World War I, 1914–1918
World War II, 1941–1945
Korean War, 1950–1953
Vietnam War, 1965–1975

2 **Informing the learner of the objective**   Learners will be expected to know the causes of the Civil War and to show that those causes also can apply to at least one of the other wars listed on the transparency.

3 **Stimulating recall of prerequisite learning**   I will briefly review the causes of both the French and Indian War and the Revolutionary War as covered in Lessons 2.1 and 2.2.

4 Presenting the stimulus material   (a) I will summarize major events leading to the Civil War: rise of sectionalism, labor-intensive economy, and lack of diversification. (b) Identify significant individuals during the Civil War and their roles: Lincoln, Lee, Davis, and Grant. (c) Describe four general causes of war and explain which are most relevant to the Civil War: economic (to profit), political (to control), social (to influence), and military (to protect).

5 Eliciting the desired behavior   I will ask the class to identify which of the four causes is most relevant to the major events leading up to the Civil War.

6 Providing feedback   I will ask for student answers and indicate the plausibility of the volunteered responses.

7 Assessing the behavior   I will assign as homework a one-page essay assessing the relative importance of the four causes for one of the wars listed on the transparency.

EXAMPLE LESSON PLAN: *Language Arts*

Unit Title: Writing Concepts and Skills

Lesson Title: Descriptive, Narrative, and Expository Paragraphs—Lesson 1.3

1 Gaining attention   I will read examples of short descriptive, narrative, and expository paragraphs from Sunday's newspaper.

2 Informing the learner of the objective   Students will be able to discriminate among descriptive, narrative, and expository paragraphs from a list of written examples in the popular press.

3 Stimulating recall of prerequisite learning   I will review the meanings of the words description, narration, and exposition as they are used in everyday language.

4 Presenting the stimulus material   Using a headline from Sunday's newspaper, I will give examples of how this story could be reported by description, narration, and exposition.

5 Eliciting the desired behavior   I will take another front-page story from Sunday's newspaper, and ask students to write a paragraph relating the story in descriptive, narrative, or expository form, whichever they prefer.

6 Providing feedback   I will call on individuals to read their paragraphs, checking each against the type of paragraph he or she intended to write.

7 Assessing the behavior   I will provide multiple-choice examples of each form of writing on the unit test. Have students revise their paragraphs as needed and turn it in as homework the following day.

EXAMPLE LESSON PLAN: *Mathematics*

Unit Title: Consumer Mathematics

Lesson Title: Operations and Properties of Ratio, Proportion, and Percentage—Lesson 3.3

1 **Gaining attention** I will display so all can see: (a) can of diet soft drink, (b) 1-pound package of spaghetti, (c) box of breakfast cereal.

2 **Informing the learner of the objective** Learners will be expected to know how to determine ratios, proportions, and percentages from the information on labels of popular food products.

3 **Stimulating recall of prerequisite learning** I will review the definitions of ratio, proportion, and percentage from the math workbook.

4 **Presenting the stimulus material** I will place the information from the soft drink label on a transparency and ask students to identify the percentage of sodium.

5 **Eliciting the desired behavior** I will write on the board the list of ingredients given on the cereal box; ask students to determine (1) the percentage of daily allowance of protein, (2) the proportion of daily allowance of vitamin A, and (3) the ratio of protein to carbohydrates.

6 **Providing feedback** Using the information on the board, I will point to the correct answer for behaviors 1 and 2, and show how to find the appropriate numerator and denominator for behavior 3 (in step 5) from the ingredients on the label.

7 **Assessing the behavior** I will provide on the weekly quiz five problems covering ratios (two problems), proportions (two problems), and percentages (one problem) using labels from other consumer products.

EXAMPLE LESSON PLAN: *Science*

Unit Title: Manipulative Laboratory Skills

Lesson Title: Use of the Microscope—Lesson 1.1

1 **Gaining attention** I will show the first 5 minutes of a video about making a lens.

2 **Informing the learner of the objective** Learners will be expected to be able to focus correctly a specimen of one-celled animal life, using both high and low magnification.

3 **Stimulating recall of prerequisite learning** I will review procedures for selecting a slide from the one-celled specimen collection and mounting it on the specimen tray of the microscope.

4 **Presenting the stimulus material** Using a student in front of the class as a demonstrator, I will help position his or her posture and hands on the microscope. I will gently bend body and hands until the correct posture results. I will demonstrate the position of the eyes and show clockwise and counterclockwise rotation of low and then high magnification adjustment.

5   **Eliciting the desired behavior**   I will have each student obtain a specimen slide, mount it on a microscope, and focus on low magnification. I will randomly check microscopes, correcting slide, positions, and focus as needed with student observing, and repeat step 5 for high magnification.

6   **Providing feedback**   I will provide feedback in the context of the eliciting activity (step 5) to increase immediacy of the feedback. Also I will refer students to the text for examples of focused and unfocused specimens.

7   **Assessing the behavior**   At the completion of the unit, I will assess students during a practical lab exam requiring the correct mounting and identification of three unknown specimens using the microscope.

SUMMING UP

This chapter introduced you to unit and lesson planning. Its key terms and main points were:

Teacher as Decision Maker

1. Four primary inputs to the planning process are knowledge of instructional goals, knowledge of learner needs, knowledge of subject matter content, and knowledge of teaching methods.
2. Four sources from which you can obtain information about the four inputs to planning are (1) practical experiences, such as observing in classrooms; (2) reading case studies about what more successful and less successful teachers have done; (3) reading the professional literature about important ideas, conceptual systems, and paradigms for thinking about teaching; and (4) reading empirical studies about what the research says about your subject and how to teach it.
3. Another input to the planning process is "tacit knowledge" representing what works, discovered over time and through experience.

Unit and Lesson Plans

4. A unit of instruction may be thought of as a system; individual lessons within the unit are its component parts.
5. The concept of hierarchy tells us the relationship of parts to the whole (in this case, lessons to units), and the concept of task-relevant prior knowledge tells us what must come before what in a sequence of events (lesson sequence).

Disciplinary and Interdisciplinary Unit Planning

6. Units can be planned vertically, emphasizing hierarchy of lesson content and task-relevant prior knowledge within a discipline, or laterally, emphasizing themes that integrate bodies of knowledge across disciplines to convey relationships and patterns that bind different aspects of our world together.
7. In vertical planning, boxes illustrate areas of content, or instructional goals, at various levels of generality. Lines and arrows indicate sequences among lessons and how outcomes of lessons build on one another to achieve a unit goal.
8. Three activities of vertical unit planning are:
   - Classifying unit outcomes at a higher level in the taxonomies of behavior than lesson outcomes
   - Planning the instructional sequence so the outcomes of previously taught lessons are instrumental in achieving the outcomes of subsequent lessons
   - Rearranging or adding lesson content where necessary to provide task-relevant prior knowledge where needed
9. In lateral—or interdisciplinary—planning, a central theme is identified, and lines or arrows are connected to it to indicate subordinate ideas for lesson content.
10. Three activities of lateral—or disciplinary—planning are:
   - Identifying an interdisciplinary theme

- Integrating bodies of knowledge across disciplines
- Identifying relationships and patterns that bind different aspects of our world together

Making Lesson Plans

11. Before starting the preparation of a lesson plan, you should identify the learning outcome desired for the lesson (e.g., knowledge, application, evaluation, etc.) and what provisions for student diversity needs to be included in the lesson plan (e.g., time-limited ability grouping, peer tutoring, learning centers, specialized handouts, cooperative grouping).

Events of Instruction

12. Learning refers to internal events in the heads of learners that result from external teaching events you provide. Hence, the words *teaching* and *learning* refer to two different but related sets of activities.
13. The following external events can be specified in a lesson plan:
    - Gaining attention
    - Informing the learner of the objective
    - Stimulating recall of prerequisite learning
    - Presenting the stimulus material
    - Eliciting the desired behavior
    - Providing feedback
    - Assessing the behavior
14. Gaining attention involves gaining your students' interest in what you will present and getting them to switch to the appropriate modality for the coming lesson.
15. Informing learners of the objective involves informing them of the learning outcome expected at the end of the lesson.
16. Stimulating recall of prerequisite learning is reviewing task-relevant prior information required by the lesson.
17. Presenting the stimulus material is delivering the desired content using procedures that stimulate thought processing and maintain interest.
18. Eliciting the desired behavior encourages the learner to attempt a response that displays the desired learning outcome.
19. Providing feedback tells the learner the accuracy of her or his elicited response in a nonthreatening, nonevaluative atmosphere.
20. Assessing the behavior evaluates the learner's performance with tests, homework, and extended assignments.

KEY TERMS

Cross-age tutoring, 133
Curriculum guides, 115
Integrated thematic teaching, 125
Interactive individualized practice activities, 134
Interdisciplinary unit, 124
Lateral unit planning, 119
Living curriculum, 135

Peer tutoring, 133
Reflective practice, 114
System perspective, 114
Tacit knowledge, 114
Thematic units, 125
Tutorial and communication technologies, 132
Vertical unit planning, 118

DISCUSSION AND PRACTICE QUESTIONS

Questions marked with an asterisk are answered in appendix B. See also the Companion Website for this text at *www.prenhall.com/borich* for more assessment options.

*1. Identify the five inputs to the planning process from which the preparation of lesson plans proceeds. When would you consult each input in the design of a lesson or unit plan?

*2. How can a unit outcome be more than the sum of its individual lesson outcomes? Can you give an example using content for a specific unit in your subject matter area?

*3. Explain in your own words how the concepts of hierarchy and task-relevant prior knowledge are used in unit planning.

*4. Name the levels of behavior in each of the three domains (cognitive, affective, and psychomotor) that generally would be most suitable for a unit outcome.

*5. How are the boxes further down on a vertical unit plan different from the boxes higher up? Use the example you provided in question 4 to illustrate your answer.

*6. Explain how a graphic unit plan for a vertical unit is different from a graphic unit plan for a lateral unit. In your own words, why must there be a difference?

7. In your own words, how would you explain to another the distinction between teaching and learning? What examples might you use to

illustrate the difference with respect to a learner in your classroom?

*8. Identify the instructional event for which the key behavior of *instructional variety* would be most important.

*9. Identify the instructional event for which the key behavior of *student success* would be most important.

*10. Identify the instructional event for which the key behavior of *student engagement in the learning process* would be most important.

*11. Indicate how the instructional events of (1) providing feedback and (2) assessing behavior differ according to (a) the evaluative nature of the feedback provided and (b) the immediacy with which the feedback is given.

FIELD EXPERIENCE ACTIVITIES

*1. How are the concepts of hierarchy and task-relevant prior learning related? Can you provide an example of a unit plan in which your knowledge of the hierarchy in which content is organized would help you determine task-relevant prior learning?

2. Vertically plan a three-lesson unit within a discipline in which the sequence of lessons is critical to achieving the outcome. Then laterally plan a three-lesson interdisciplinary unit in which lesson sequence is unimportant. Be sure lesson outcomes for each unit reflect the unit outcome. In both cases follow the graphic format shown in this chapter using either the standard MS Word or Inspiration (*www.inspiration.com/home.cfm*) software.

*3. Identify some ways of providing for student diversity in the context of a lesson plan of your choice. Which do you believe will be most effective at your grade level or content area?

*4. Name the seven events of instruction that can be described in a lesson plan. Give an example of how you would implement each event for a lesson of your own choosing.

5. Following the form of the examples provided in this chapter, prepare a lesson plan for a topic in your major teaching area. Include the approximate number of minutes you expect to devote to each event out of a 50-minute class period.

DIGITAL PORTFOLIO ACTIVITIES

The following digital portfolio activities relate to INTASC principles 4, 7, and 9.

Place your unit and lesson plans for Field Experience Activity 2 and 5 into your digital portfolio in a folder titled *Lesson and Unit Plans*. These will provide examples of your skill at planning disciplinary and interdisciplinary units and lessons. Add other examples of your lesson and unit plans that also represent your best planning as they become available.

CLASSROOM OBSERVATION ACTIVITY

The following classroom observation activity relates to INTASC principles 7 and 9.

The teacher's interpretation of the curriculum guide will depend on the unique characteristics of the students, their learning needs, the time that can be devoted to a specific topic, and the overall knowledge, skills, and understandings you want your learners to acquire at the end of a unit. Your knowledge of instructional goals and standards at the state and school-district level can help ensure that the choice of content at the classroom level results in lesson plans that are closely related to your curriculum guide and adopted text. A close relationship among standards at the state level (as expressed by laws and policies), goals at the school-district level (as expressed by the curriculum guide), and objectives at the classroom level (as identified by the teacher and curriculum) is necessary for maintaining a teacher's task orientation, which provides the maximum time possible for student learning.

For this activity go to the *Classroom Observation* module for this chapter on the Companion Website at *www.prenhall.com/borich,* where you will find an observation instrument titled *Format for Studying the Relationship Between Unit/Lesson Plans and Curriculum Guide/Text.* Identify a lesson you would like to teach. In the first part of the instrument, you will indicate the chapter and/or workbook subheadings and pages pertaining to your lesson objective(s) and check off the instructional activities you will use to teach this lesson. Then, comment on the degree to which your lesson objective(s) correspond with your lesson activities and to the text or workbook. Place this recording form in your digital portfolio folder labeled *Lesson and Unit Planning* as further evidence of your lesson and unit planning skills.

CHAPTER CASE HISTORY AND PRAXIS TEST PREPARATION

DIRECTIONS: The following case history pertains to chapter 4 content. After reading the case history, answer the short-answer question that follows and consult appendix D to find different levels of scored student responses and the rubric used to determine the quality of each response. You also have the opportunity to submit your responses online to receive feedback by visiting the *Case History* module for this chapter on the Companion Website, where you will also find additional questions pertaining to Praxis test content.

Case History

A Latin student, Sean, is wearing a toga showing his calves and sandaled feet. Short strips of leather dangle from his hand as he trots about Mr. Cody's tenth-grade English classroom, where he was invited to show how the Romans dressed and acted for the Feast of the Lupercal. He playfully laughs and slaps his classmates on the back as though at a party.

"That's what the Feast of the Lupercal was all about," he says. "The young Roman men ran races carrying strips of goat hide, which they considered symbols of fertility. The racecourse was lined with women who wished to have children; they stood alongside the road, hoping to be touched by the leather."

A few students ask Sean for more about the Lupercal Feast and he tells them about some of the athletic games and competitions not mentioned in their current unit, Shakespeare's *Julius Caesar*. It is time for him to return to his Latin class, and Mr. Cody fields some of the remaining questions.

"So Caesar wanted his wife to stand in Antony's way so she could have a baby?" Lupe asks.

Instead of answering, Mr. Cody asks another question. "If that were true, Lupe, why would it be significant? What might that tell us about Caesar's ambitions?"

"That he wanted a family. Being emperor wasn't enough to make him happy." Tiffany looks up from the *Glamour* magazine inserted between the pages of her text.

"No," Lupe smiles. "It means he wanted an heir. That he wasn't content to be emperor just for life. He wanted to start his own—how do you call it—dynasty, I think."

"Exactly right, Lupe. Now, you can see why some of those senators had a right to be worried." Mr. Cody adjusts his reading glasses and opens his book. "Now let's get back to that section we talked about yesterday, the part about the 'falling sickness.'" He pauses while students open their books to the designated page.

"Angelique, just what is the falling sickness?" Mr. Cody waits for a reply and then reminds her to look at the footnote.

After a few flustered attempts at pronunciation, she responds with "epilepsy."

"We were talking about that yesterday, about how the senators made such a mockery of Caesar's physical weaknesses behind his back, and some of you felt that was very mean spirited of them. Now those of you taking a history class volunteered to bring up this issue with your teachers, and I suggested that the rest might ask an older relative about it."

"My grandpa says that Franklin Roosevelt had polio, but that he never appeared out in public in his wheelchair."

Nathan volunteers, "Well, it's not really being mean, Mr. Cody. I mean, our president is the commander in chief. He has to be ready to lead us into war; he has to be healthy." Tim looks up from his text.

"He doesn't have to lead the troops himself, though. I mean, wheelchair or not, FDR led us to victory in World War II." Wanda has the last word as Mr. Cody puts up his hand to quell further discussion.

"Let's take the next twenty minutes to put our thoughts into words. To what extent do we, like the Romans of Julius Caesar's time, expect our leaders to be physically vigorous? What is your personal opinion on the subject? Support it with reasons."

Short-Answer Question

This section presents a sample Praxis short-answer question. In appendix D you will find sample responses along with the standards used in scoring these responses.

DIRECTIONS: The following question requires you to write a short answer. Base your answer on your knowledge of principles of learning and teaching from chapter 4. Be sure to answer all parts of the question.

1. Gagné and Briggs subdivide lessons into seven events of instruction. The heart of the lesson is step 4, presenting the stimulus material, and should include authenticity, selectivity, and variety. Demonstrate and explain the ways in which Mr. Cody met these three requirements as he presented the stimulus material for this lesson.

Discrete Multiple-Choice Questions

DIRECTIONS: Each of the multiple-choice questions that follow is based on Praxis-related pedagogical knowledge in chapter 4. Select the answer that is best in each case and compare your results with those in appendix D. See also the Companion Website for this text at *www.prenhall.com/borich* for more assessment options.

1. What works, as discovered over time and through personal experience, is called
   a. Empirical study
   b. Tacit knowledge
   c. Case history
   d. System perspective

2. The terms *tempo, mode, arrangement,* and *management* pertain to which aspect of the planning process?
   a. Teaching methods
   b. Learner characteristics
   c. Subject matter
   d. Goals and objectives

3. A type of planning that presents learners with an opportunity to discover relationships and patterns that cut across subject matter is called
   a. Disciplinary planning
   b. Vertical planning
   c. Thematic planning
   d. Unit planning

4. Which of the following represent events of instruction that, when appropriate, should be described in a lesson plan?
   a. Planning
   b. Gaining attention
   c. Providing feedback
   d. Assessing the behavior

5. Which of the following could be considered ways of assessing student behavior at the end of a lesson or unit?
   a. Tests and quizzes
   b. In-class workbook assignments
   c. Portfolio submission
   d. Lab assignment

Chapter 5

Classroom
Management I
Establishing the Learning Climate

This chapter will help you answer the following questions and meet the following INTASC principles for effective teaching:

1. What can I do during the first weeks of school to build a classroom climate of trust and cohesiveness?
2. What can I teach my learners to help them discuss and resolve group conflicts on their own?
3. How do I get my class to develop group norms?
4. What types of classroom rules will I need?
5. How might I use the social organization of my classroom to bridge cultural gaps?

INTASC 2: The teacher understands how children learn and develop and can provide learning opportunities that support their intellectual, social, and personal development.

INTASC 5: The teacher uses an understanding of individual and group motivation and behavior to create a learning environment that encourages positive social interaction, active engagement in learning, and self-motivation.

INTASC 9: The teacher is a reflective practitioner who continually evaluates the effects of his or her choices and actions on others (students, parents, and other professionals in the learning community) and who actively seeks out opportunities to grow professionally.

INTASC 10: The teacher fosters relationships with school colleagues, parents, and agencies in the larger community to support students' learning and well-being.

F or most teachers, confronting some sort of classroom management problem is a daily occurrence. These problems may include simple infractions of school or classroom rules, or they may involve more serious events, including disrespect, cheating, obscene words and gestures, and open displays of hostility.

The management of your classroom must begin with developing trusting relationships with your students. Without mutual feelings of trust and respect, you will be unable to assume the role of an instructional leader in your classroom. To accomplish this, we discuss how you can

1. *Design an orderly workplace that promotes your academic goals.*
2. *Develop rules for the workplace that create group norms that students respect and follow.*
3. *Change in the face of unproductive rules, routines, and procedures.*
4. *Maintain a workplace that fosters feelings of belonging and group solidarity.*
5. *Know how to seek help from other school professionals and from parents.*

EARNING TRUST AND BECOMING A LEADER THE OLD-FASHIONED WAY

According to social psychologists (French & Raven, 1959; Raven, 1974), to establish yourself as an effective leader, you have to gain your students' trust and respect the old-fashioned way: You have to earn it. But how? French and Raven provide a way of looking at how you earn respect by asking the question, "How do you achieve social power?" They identify five types of **social power** or leadership a teacher can strive for: expert power, referent power, legitimate power, reward power, and coercive power.

Expert Power

Certain individuals become leaders because others perceive them as experts. Successful teachers have **expert power.** Their students see them as competent to explain or do certain things and as knowledgeable about particular topics. Such influence is earned, rather than conferred by virtue of having a particular title. Teachers with expert power explain things well, show enthusiasm and excitement about what they teach, and appear confident and self-assured before their classes.

New teachers often find it difficult to establish leadership through expert power. Even though they are knowledgeable and competent in their field, uncertainty and inexperience in front of a group may make them appear less so. Students are attuned to body language suggesting lack of confidence and indecision and may test the competence and challenge the authority of teachers who appear not to be in command of their subject.

Referent Power

Students often accept as leaders teachers they like and respect. They view such teachers as trustworthy, fair, and concerned about them (Glasser, 1998b; Goodlad, 2004). The term **referent power** describes leadership earned in this way. Ask any group of junior high or high school students about why they like particular teachers, and invariably they describe the teachers they like as "fair," "caring," and "someone you can talk to." Without referent power, even teachers with expert power may have their authority challenged or ignored.

One often hears teachers say they would rather be respected than liked, as if these two consequences were mutually exclusive. Research by Soar and Soar (1983) and Letts (1999) suggests that teachers can be both respected and liked: Teachers who were both respected and liked were associated with greater student satisfaction and higher achievement. Glasser (1998a) emphasizes that students' needs for belonging in a classroom will more likely be met by a teacher who is perceived as both warm and competent.

Legitimate Power

Some roles carry with them influence and authority by their very nature. Police officers, presidents, and judges exert social power and leadership by their very titles. Influence in such cases may be conferred by the role itself rather than depend on the nature of the person assuming the role. Savage (1999) refers to this type of power as **legitimate power,** and, unlike expert and referent power, it may not be earned. Teachers possess a certain degree of legitimate power. Our society expects students to give teachers their attention, respect them, and follow their requests. Most families also stress the importance of listening to the teacher. Every new teacher begins her or his first day of class with legitimate power.

Legitimate power, therefore, gives the new teacher some breathing room during the first few weeks of school. Most students will initially obey and accept the authority of new teachers by virtue of their position of authority. However, building classroom leadership solely through legitimate power may be like building a house on a foundation of sand. Teachers should use their legitimate power to establish referent and expert power.

Reward Power

Individuals in positions of authority are able to exercise **reward power** in relation to the people they lead. These rewards can take the form of privileges, approval, or more tangible compensation, such as money. To the extent that students desire the rewards conferred by teachers, teachers can exert a degree of leadership and authority. There are, however, few rewards available to teachers and a great number of rewards available to students without the aid of a teacher. Students who do not care much about good grades or teacher approval are difficult to lead solely by exerting reward power, because students can attain outside of school much of what is reinforcing to them. In such cases some teachers resort to using tangible reinforcers such as access to desired activities, objects, and even food. In this chapter, you will learn that reward power can be an effective tool in the classroom but cannot substitute for referent and expert power.

Coercive Power

Through state and local government, teachers are allowed to act *in loco parentis,* that is, in place of the parent. Consequently, within limits, schools can punish students who defy the authority or leadership of the teacher by such techniques as suspension or expulsion, denial of privileges, or removal from the classroom. Teachers who rely on such techniques to maintain social power in their classroom are using coercive power. The use of **coercive power** may stop misbehavior for a time, but this will sometimes be at the cost of developing trust and meeting student needs. Overreliance on coercive power has the danger of increasing attitudes that may lead to antagonism and disengagement from the learning process.

Using Power

Although each of the preceding sources of power, when properly used, is a legitimate tool for managing the classroom, teachers, especially new teachers, should work quickly to achieve expert and referent power. You can achieve expert power by keeping up-to-date with developments in your teaching field, completing in-service and graduate programs, attending seminars and workshops, and completing career ladder and mentoring activities provided by your school district. From your very first day in the classroom, you can exhibit referent power by giving your students a sense of belonging and acceptance.

STAGES OF GROUP DEVELOPMENT

Social psychologists, such as Schmuck and Schmuck (2001) and Johnson and Johnson (1996, 1998), believe the sources of social power you acquire are important for guiding your learners through the process of group development. They believe every successful group passes through a series of **stages of group development** during which it has certain tasks to accomplish and concerns to resolve. The way the group accomplishes these tasks and resolves these concerns determines the extent to which you can effectively and efficiently manage the group and accomplish the goals of your classroom. Mauer (1985) describes these stages:

> Stage 1, *forming*: Resolving concerns about acceptance and responsibilities
>
> Stage 2, *storming*: Resolving concerns about shared influence
>
> Stage 3, *norming*: Resolving concerns about how work gets done
>
> Stage 4, *performing*: Resolving concerns about freedom, control, and self-regulation

Stage 1: Forming

When learners come together at the start of the school year, they usually are concerned about two issues: (1) finding their place in the social structure, and (2) finding out what they are expected to do. This raises concerns about inclusion, or group membership.

During the first several days of class, learners (and teachers) naturally ask, "How will I fit in?" "Who will accept or reject me?" "What do I have to do to be respected?" At this time, a phenomenon called *testing* takes place (Froyen, 1993). Learners engage in specific actions to see what kind of reaction they get from teachers and peers. At this stage of group formation, learners are curious about one another. They want to know where other class members live, who their friends are, what they like to do, and where they like to go. As students learn more about one another, they begin to see how and with whom they fit in. Putnam (1997) urges teachers to engage in activities during the first few weeks of school to help learners trust one another and feel like members of a group.

Table 5.1 Important questions about group development.

Stage 1: Forming	Stage 2: Storming	Stage 3: Norming	Stage 4: Performing
1. Are there activities for everyone to get to know about one another?	1. Are conflicts openly recognized and discussed?	1. Is there a process for resolving conflict?	1. Can this group evaluate its own effectiveness?
2. Has everyone had a chance to be heard?	2. Can the group assess its own functioning?	2. Can the group set goals?	2. Can the group and individuals solve their own problems?
3. Do learners interact with a variety of classmates?	3. Are new and different ideas listened to and evaluated?	3. Can learners express what is expected of them?	3. Does the group have opportunities to work independently and express themselves through a medium of their own choosing?
4. Do learners and teachers listen to one another?	4. Are the skills of all members being used?	4. Is there mutual respect between teacher and learners?	4. Can individuals evaluate themselves and set goals for personal improvement?
5. Have concerns and/or fears regarding academic and behavioral expectations been addressed?	5. Do all learners have an opportunity to share leadership and responsibility?	5. What happens to learners who fail to respect norms?	5. Is the group prepared to disband?

Source: From Richard A. Schmuck and Patricia A. Schmuck, *Group Processes in the Classroom*, 6th edition. Copyright © 1992 Wm. C. Brown Communications, Inc., Dubuque, Iowa. Reproduced with permission of The McGraw-Hill Companies.

Social psychologists caution teachers of a tendency during the first stage of classroom group development to concentrate almost exclusively on concerns about work and rules to the exclusion of concerns about inclusion. They warn that learners who have unresolved fears about acceptance by their teacher and where they fit in the peer group will find it difficult to concentrate on academic work without first developing trust and feeling like valued members of a group (Schmuck & Schmuck, 2001).

Table 5.1 lists questions you can ask yourself to assess group development during the forming stage.

Stage 2: Storming

The goal of the forming stage of group development is to help learners feel secure and perceive themselves as members of a classroom group. Healthy group life at this stage occurs if learners have accepted the teacher as their leader, made some initial commitment to follow rules and procedures, and agreed to respect other members of the class.

During the storming stage of group development, they begin to test the limits of these commitments. This limit testing may take the form of amiable challenges to academic expectations (homework, classwork, tests, etc.) and rules in order to establish under what conditions they do and do not apply. Learners may question seating arrangements, homework responsibilities, seatwork routines, and so on. Social psychologists refer to these amiable challenges to teacher authority and leadership as examples of **distancing behavior.** They occur in any group where a leader initially establishes authority by virtue of his or her position rather than through competence or credibility. This distancing behavior represents reservations learners have at this stage of group development about the commitments they made during the forming stage to class expectations and group participation.

A second type of amiable limit testing, which often accompanies distancing behavior, is called **centering.** Centering occurs when learners question how they will personally benefit from being a group member. Their behavior can be described with the question, "What's in it for me?" The questions they ask and assertions they make reflect a preoccupation with fairness. They are quick to notice favoritism toward individual members of the group.

These distancing and centering conflicts arising between teachers and learners and among learners are a natural part of group development. Social psychologists caution teachers about overreacting at this stage. During these types of conflicts, you will need to monitor compliance with rules and procedures but be willing to reconsider those that may not be working.

Buehl (2001), Glasser (1998b), and Putnam (1997) urge teachers to have class discussions centering around group conflict resolution. They recommend that teachers instruct their learners on how to problem-solve using the following guide:

1. *Agree there is a problem.* The teacher gets all members of the class to agree there is a problem and that they will work together to solve it.
2. *State the conflict.* The teacher states concisely what the conflict is and assures all learners that they will have the opportunity to state their perspective.
3. *Identify and select responses.* Teachers and learners brainstorm and record solutions to the problem. They assess the short- and long-term consequences of the solutions and discard those that have negative consequences.
4. *Create a solution.* The class discusses and records a solution that all basically agree will resolve the conflict.
5. *Design and implement a plan.* The class discusses and works out the details of when, where, and how to resolve the conflict.
6. *Assess the success of the plan.* The students identify information they can gather to determine the success of the plan. The teacher identifies checkpoints to evaluate how the class is doing. When the conflict is resolved, the whole class discusses the value of the problem-solving process.

Table 5.1 lists questions you can ask yourself to assess group development during the storming stage.

Stage 3: Norming

The security learners develop at the forming stage provides them with a safe foundation to challenge teacher authority during the storming stage. Skilled leadership during the storming stage assures learners that they will be listened to, treated fairly, and allowed to share power and influence. This assurance leads them during the norming stage to accept both academic expectations, procedures, and rules for the group and the roles and functions of the various group members.

Norms are shared expectations among group members regarding how they should think, feel, and behave. Social psychologists view norms as the principal regulators of group behavior (Schmuck & Schmuck, 2001; Zimbardo, 1992). Norms may take the form of either written or unwritten rules that all or most of the group voluntarily agree to follow.

A classroom group has norms when learners, for the most part, agree on what is and is not socially acceptable classroom behavior.

Norms play an important role in governing behavior in the classroom. But their role differs from that of rules and procedures. Norms are more personally meaningful than rules, as seen in the following examples:

It's OK to be seen talking to the teacher.

Learners in this class should help one another.

We're all responsible for our own learning.

We shouldn't gloat when one of our classmates gives the wrong answer.

We need to respect the privacy of others.

The most important thing for this class is learning.

Social psychologists believe that positive norms serve several important functions in the classroom (Putnam & Burke, 1998; Schmuck & Schmuck, 2001).

- Norms orient group members to which social interactions are and are not appropriate and then regulate these interactions. When norms are present, learners can anticipate the ways others will behave in the classroom and also how they are expected to behave.
- Norms create group identification and group cohesiveness (Zimbardo, 1992). Social psychologists believe the process of group formation begins when its members agree to adhere to the norms of the group. This process begins during the forming stage of group development and ends during the norming stage.
- Norms promote academic achievement and positive relationships among class members. Academic and social goals are more likely to be achieved in classrooms with consistent norms. For example, peer group norms represent one of the most important influences on school performance (Schmuck & Schmuck, 2001).

Group norms, whether in support of a teacher's goals or opposed to them, begin to develop on the first day of school during the forming stage of group development. Social psychologists have identified two basic processes by which norms develop: **diffusion** and **crystallization.** Diffusion takes place as learners first enter a group or class. They bring with them expectations acquired from experiences in other classes, from other group memberships, and from experiences growing up. As learners talk and mingle with each other during breaks and recess, they communicate with one another. Their various expectations for academic and social behavior are diffused and spread throughout the entire class. Eventually, as learners engage in a variety of activities together, their expectations begin to converge and crystallize into a shared perspective of classroom life.

You should do all you can to influence the development of norms that support your classroom goals. It is important that you know how to positively influence the development of class norms and to identify and alter existing ones. Here are some suggestions for developing, identifying, and altering group norms:

- Explain to the class the concept of a group norm. Draw up a list of norms with the class and, over time, add and delete norms that either help or impede the work of the group.
- Conduct discussions of class norms and encourage learners to talk among themselves about them. Glasser (1998b) suggests discussing with students ideas on how the class might be run, problems that may interfere with the group's performance, and needed rules and routines.

- Appoint or elect a class council to make recommendations for improving class climate and productivity. Have the group assess whether the norms are working.
- Provide a model of the respect, consistency, and responsibility for learning that you want your learners to exhibit.

Healthy group development at the norming stage is characterized by group behavior primarily focused on academic achievement.

Stage 4: Performing

By the time the group has reached the fourth developmental stage, learners feel at ease with one another, know the rules and their roles, accept group norms, and are familiar with the routine of the classroom. The principal concern for the group at this stage is establishing its independence.

Just as the storming stage of development was characterized by a testing of limits, the performing stage is characterized by learners wanting to show they can do some things independently of the teacher. Social psychologists urge teachers to encourage the desire for independence at this stage by focusing less on classroom control and more on teaching the group how to set priorities, budget its time, and self-regulate.

The performing stage ends when the school year or semester ends. Thus this stage represents a time of transition. Assuming all four stages of development have been successfully completed, learners will have developed relationships with one another and with their teacher through which they may manage themselves with the guidance and direction of the teacher. For this transition to occur successfully, however, you will need to establish a classroom climate in which group development can flourish through all four stages. See In Practice: Focus on a Democratic Approach to Classroom Management.

IN PRACTICE

Focus on a Democratic Approach to Classroom Management

Adapted from an article by Cara Bafile, EducationWorld.com (2002). Used with permission.

Patterned after family meetings in her own home, teacher Donna Styles's format for class meetings enables her students to share their thoughts and solve classroom issues on their own. In Styles's model, students take turns acting as a discussion leader, while the teacher promotes a respectful atmosphere and participates as a group member. Encouraged by the students' positive response to her approach, Styles decided to share her expertise with other teachers.

A teacher for more than thirty years, Styles is a veteran educator who has taught students in kindergarten through seventh grade, in both regular and multi-aged settings. She has worked as a regular classroom teacher, in English and French immersion classes, and as a thinking skills/enrichment resource teacher. She currently teaches grades five and six at Len Wood Elementary School in Armstrong, British Columbia (Canada). Styles's practical and effective approach to classroom management did not develop from her extensive teaching experience, however, but from her hands-on experience as a parent! She explains:

My husband and I had successfully used family meetings in our own family for years. We saw the positive effects of including our children in family decision-making. We saw firsthand how much more responsible our kids acted on an everyday basis, how much more an integral part of our family unit they felt, and how elevated their self-esteem became when their views were heard and considered. I realized the possible application in the classroom setting.

In her view, family-style class meetings can play a critical role in the development of students' emotional, social, moral, and intellectual development. Styles suggests that class meetings also can promote personal growth, leadership, organizational and public-speaking skills, thinking skills and cognitive gains, problem-solving skills, and interpersonal skills—creating a community of learners.

An Idea Worth Sharing

"Class meetings are most successful in classrooms that have a warm, caring, supportive environment—classrooms in which students feel comfortable to learn, feel safe to share their ideas, and feel free to ask questions and take risks," explains Styles. "Students in those kinds of classrooms are supportive of one another, work together cooperatively, encourage one another, assume responsibility for their own learning and behavior, and are allowed to make decisions."

Styles outlines several key components that make class meetings unique and effective:

Students sit on chairs in a circle.
Meetings are held every week.
A set format is followed.
Students lead the meetings.
Both problems and suggestions are discussed.
Students encourage and compliment one another.

Styles maintains that incorporating class meetings is a reasonable task if teachers prepare students for meetings in about two to three lessons during the first weeks of school. She proposes that lessons involve the teaching and practice of encouragement, creative problem solving, and circle formation. After several trial meetings, with the teacher leading and modeling the process, students become meeting leaders, with each student taking a turn as discussion leader during the school year.

Conducting Class Meetings

"Class meetings help make good classrooms even better," says Styles. "The true power of meetings lies in their ability to empower students, to motivate them to learn, and to help them discover their personal best. When both students and teachers are able to voice opinions and thoughts in a quiet, respectful atmosphere, mutual respect and understanding develops. The students realize that it is *their* classroom as much as the teacher's, and they take ownership and pride in that."

In a typical class meeting desks are moved to the perimeter of the room and students take their designated places in a circle of chairs. The meeting leader opens the meeting. Old business is discussed and new business is dealt with. "Thank you's" and compliments are offered and the meeting is closed.

If a student wants an issue raised at a meeting, he or she places a slip of paper inside a box provided in the classroom. The papers, which include the name of the student and the date, constitute the new business of the next meeting. Typically, three types of issues are put in the box: a problem involving one or more people, a problem or issue affecting the whole class, or a suggestion for a class activity.

During class meetings, the teacher

- Acts as a coach—providing guidance to the leader, when necessary.
- Fulfills the role of secretary.
- Performs as a group member—offering information only when needed, and making comments only when necessary to keep the tone positive and helpful.

The student leader

- Keeps the meeting running smoothly.
- Opens and closes the meeting.
- Follows the order of steps for conducting the meeting.
- Follows steps for solving problems.

- Follows steps for discussing suggestions.
- Makes eye contact with each person speaking.
- Participates like any other member.
- Keeps discussions on topic.
- Lets students know if they are out of order.
- Asks questions, clarifies, or restates problems or ideas.
- Summarizes.
- Speaks loudly and clearly.

Accountability Made Simple

Styles has found that, with classroom meetings, discipline becomes a minor issue. Problems are discussed in meetings and students themselves determine the consequences for misbehavior. Students become highly accountable for their actions in the classroom, she observes, when their peers are taking note of their behavior and discussing poor behavior in class meetings.

"When students choose solutions to problems, they have a stake in seeing that the consequences are followed," Styles states. "Problems in the classroom are no longer just the teacher's problems to solve—they become the class's problems. Practice with the process each week enables students to become excellent problem solvers, coming up with fair and effective methods of helping classmates improve and change behaviors that interfere with others or with their learning."

Suggestions put into the box give students an opportunity to work on committees and to plan and orchestrate many interesting and fun activities during the year. This generates excitement and energy in the classroom, helping students to "buy into" coming to school and to feel a sense of belonging to the group. "As a teacher, I think there is no other tool that has such a long list of benefits. Conducting weekly class meetings with this format easily makes it one of the most powerful tools a classroom teacher can use. And it's so simple." Styles reports that—without exception—students love class meetings, and that the approach is conducive to the inclusion of students with special needs.

Styles's book, *Class Meetings: Building Leadership, Problem-Solving and Decision-Making Skills in the Respectful Classroom,* is available from Pembroke Publishing.

Related Links:

For more about class meetings: *www.sd83.bc.ca/classmtg/classindex.html*

For more about what kids say about class meetings: *www.sd83.bc.ca/classmtg/quotes.html*

ESTABLISHING AN EFFECTIVE CLASSROOM CLIMATE

Classroom climate is the atmosphere or mood in which interactions between you and your students take place. Your classroom climate is created by the manner and degree to which you exercise authority, show warmth and support, encourage competitiveness or cooperation, and allow for independent judgment and choice. The climate of your classroom is your choice, just as your instructional methods are.

This section introduces two related aspects of an effective classroom climate: the **social environment,** meaning the interaction patterns you promote in the classroom, and the **organizational environment,** meaning your physical or visual arrangement of the classroom. Both are your choice, and you can alter them to create just the right climate.

The Social Environment

The social environment of your classroom can vary from *authoritarian,* in which you are the primary provider of information, opinions, and instruction, to *laissez-faire,* in which your students become the primary providers of information, opinions, and instruction. Between these extremes lies the middle ground in which you and your students share responsibilities: Students are given freedom of choice and judgment under your direction. Many variations are possible.

For example, a group discussion might be a colossal failure in a rigid authoritarian climate, because the climate clues students that their opinions are less important than yours, that teacher talk and not student talk should take up most of the instructional time, and that the freedom to express oneself spontaneously is your right but not theirs. In a more open atmosphere, this same attempt at discussion might well be a smashing success, because the classroom climate provides all the ingredients of a good discussion—freedom to express one's opinion, high degree of student talk, and spontaneity.

The social atmosphere you create, whether authoritarian, laissez-faire, or somewhere between, is determined by how you see yourself: Are you a commander in chief who carefully controls and hones student behavior by organizing and providing all the learning stimuli? Or are you a translator or summarizer of the ideas provided by students? Or are you an equal partner with students in creating ideas and problem solutions? Consider the effects of each climate and how you can create it.

The effective teacher not only uses a variety of teaching strategies but also creates a variety of classroom climates. However, your ability to create a certain climate is as important as your ability to change the climate when the objectives and situation demand. Although early research in social psychology tried to identify the type of climate most conducive to individual behavior (Lippitt & Gold, 1959), the results suggest that different climates have both their advantages and disadvantages, depending on the intended goal.

Because goals change from lesson to lesson and week to week, so too must your classroom climate that supports the goals. When the goals change but your classroom climate does not, the stage is set for off-task, disruptive, and even antagonistic behavior among your students.

Competitive, Cooperative, or Individualistic.   We have already examined several ways you can vary your authority, and that of your students, in accordance with your objectives. These variations correspond not only with how much you relinquish your authority and therefore your control of the learning process, but also how competitive, cooperative, or

One aspect of an effective learning climate is the physical or visual arrangement of the classroom. This arrangement is a matter of choice that can be altered to create just the right climate for your learning objectives.

Table 5.2 Three types of classroom climate.

Social Climate	Example of Activity	Authority Vested in Students	Authority Vested in Teacher
Competitive: Students compete for right answers among themselves or with a standard established by the teacher. The teacher is the sole judge of the appropriateness of a response.	Drill and practice	None	To organize the instruction, present the stimulus material, and evaluate correctness of responses
Cooperative: Students engage in dialogue that is monitored by the teacher. The teacher systematically intervenes in the discussion to sharpen ideas and move the discussion to a higher level.	Small- and large-group discussion	To present opinions, to provide ideas, and to speak and discuss freely and spontaneously	To stimulate the discussion, arbitrate differences, organize and summarize student contributions
Individualistic: Students complete assignments monitored by the teacher. Students are encouraged to complete the assignment with the answers they think are best. Emphasis is on getting through and testing one's self.	Independent seatwork	To complete the assignment with the best possible responses	To assign the work and see that orderly progress is made toward its completion

individualistic you wish the interactions among members of your class to be. These three conditions are illustrated in Table 5.2. You can see in the table that, as you shift classroom climate from competitive to cooperative to individualistic, you relinquish control over the learning process until, in the individualistic mode, students have almost sole responsibility for judging their own work.

Applying the Three Climates.   In addition to encouraging the proper climate for a given instructional activity, you must decide whether each climate can be applied to the full class, to groups, and to individuals with equal effectiveness. For example, as shown in Figure 5.1, it is not necessary to conduct all group discussions in a cooperative climate.

Although some cells in Figure 5.1 may be more popular than others, various arrangements of students and climates are possible, depending on your instructional goals. Your job is to ensure that the degree of authority you impose matches your instructional goal (for example, the expression of student opinion you allow, the amount of time you devote to student talk, and the spontaneity with which you want your students to respond).

Figure 5.1 Targets for three types of classroom climates.

	Competitive	Cooperative	Individualistic
Full Class	Students compete with other students by having the correct answer when it's their turn.	Students are allowed to call out hints or clues when a student is having difficulty finding the right answer.	The entire class recites answers in unison.
Groups	Subgroups compete against each other as opposing teams.	Subgroups work on different but related aspects of a topic, combining their results into a final report to the class.	Each subgroup completes its own assigned topic, which is independent of the topics assigned the other subgroups. No shared report is given to the class.
Individual	Individuals compete with each other by having to respond to the same question. The quickest, most accurate response "wins."	Pairs of individuals cooperate by exchanging papers, sharing responses, or correcting each other's errors.	Individuals complete seatwork on their own without direct teacher involvement.

The Organizational Environment

In addition to arranging the social climate of your classroom, you also must arrange the physical climate. It goes without saying that a classroom should be attractive, well lighted, comfortable, and colorful. But, aside from a colorful bulletin board and neatness, you may have very little influence over the external features of your classroom. It is not unusual for teachers to bring essential items at the beginning of the year, such as a clock, bookcase, file cabinet, rug, or pillows for younger learners, to establish the climate of their classroom.

What may be more important than these items, however, is the way the internal features of your classroom (desks, chairs, tables) are arranged. Students quickly get used to and accept the external features of a classroom, good or bad. But the internal arrangement of the classroom will affect your students every day of the school year.

In the upper grades, the most flexible furniture arrangement places your desk at the front of the room and aligns the student desks or tables toward you. Although it may seem strange to associate this traditional format with flexibility, it can be the most flexible when you use it to create competitive, cooperative, and individualistic environments interchangeably. This, plus the difficulty of rearranging classroom furniture every time a change in social climate is desired, makes the traditional classroom arrangement in the upper grades almost as popular today as it was 50 years ago.

There are times, however, when you will want to change the arrangement to encourage a more cooperative, interactive, and group-sharing climate. Such a classroom arrangement has many variations that depend on the external features of the classroom and available furniture. One example is shown in Figure 5.2.

This change represents your deliberate attempt to get learners together. The barriers to interpersonal sharing and communication that sometimes result from the rigid alignment of desks can be avoided by a more informal, but still systematic, furniture arrangement. Because this arrangement communicates to learners that interpersonal communication and sharing are permitted, increased interpersonal communication and sharing will undoubtedly occur, whether you desire it or not.

Figure 5.2 A classroom arrangement emphasizing positive relations and learning to cooperate.

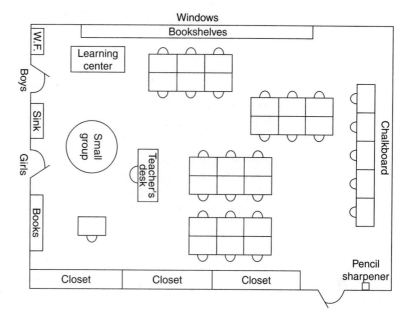

Figure 5.3 A compromise classroom arrangement allowing independent, group, and cooperative learning.

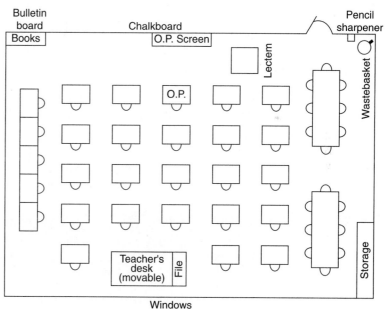

By grouping four or five student desks or tables together, you expect more expression of student opinion, increased student talk, and greater spontaneity in student responses. This emphasizes the important notion that the social climate created by your words and deeds always should match the organizational climate created by the physical arrangement of your classroom.

Of course, changing the internal arrangement of a classroom from time to time for the sake of variety is refreshing. You might compromise by maintaining the basic nature of the formal classroom but, space permitting, setting aside one or two less formal areas (for example, a learning center, group discussion table or pillow, and reading center) for times when instructional goals call for independent work or interpersonal communication and sharing. In the early grades these are almost always a part of the classroom arrangement—and its climate. A version of this arrangement is shown in Figure 5.3.

Establishing Rules and Procedures

Establishing **rules and procedures** to prevent classroom discipline problems will be one of your most important classroom management activities (Emmer et al., 2006, Evertson, 1995; Evertson et al., 2006; Evertson & Harris, 1992). These rules and procedures, which you should formulate before the first school day, are your commitment to applying the ounce of prevention to avoid having to provide a pound of cure.

Teachers need different types of rules and procedures for effectively managing a classroom; these fall into four basic categories:

- Rules related to academic work
- Rules related to classroom conduct
- Rules that must be communicated your first teaching day
- Rules that can be communicated later, at an appropriate opportunity

The top half of Figure 5.4 identifies some rules that may be needed during the very first days of school, either because students will ask about them or because events are likely to arise requiring their use. Notice that these rules are divided into seven conduct rules and seven work rules. For the elementary grades, it is best that you present them orally, *and* provide a handout, *and* post them for later reference by the students. In the lower grades, learners can forget oral messages quickly—or choose to ignore them if there is no physical representation of the rule as a constant reminder. In the later elementary grades and middle school, your recital of the rules while students copy them into their notebooks may be sufficient. For high school students, simply hearing the rules may be sufficient, as long as they are posted for later reference.

Not all "first-day" rules are equally important, and other rules may have to be added as special circumstances require. But rules about responding and speaking out, making up work, determining grades, and violation of rules are among the most important. It is in these

Figure 5.4
Classroom rules related to conduct and work.

	Rules related to classroom conduct	Rules related to academic work
Rules that need to be communicated first day	1. Where to sit 2. How seats are assigned 3. What to do before the bell rings 4. Responding, speaking out 5. Leaving at the bell 6. Drinks, food, and gum 7. Washroom and drinking privileges	8. Materials required for class 9. Homework completion 10. Makeup work 11. Incomplete work 12. Missed quizzes and examinations 13. Determining grades 14. Violation of due dates
Rules that can be communicated later	15. Tardiness/absences 16. Coming up to desk 17. When a visitor comes to the door 18. Leaving the classroom 19. Consequences of rule violation	20. Notebook completion 21. Obtaining help 22. Note taking 23. Sharing work with others 24. Use of learning center and/or reference works 25. Communication during group work 26. Neatness 27. Lab safety

Figure 5.5 Issues to be decided for some classroom rules.

Responding, speaking out
- Must hands be raised?
- Are other forms of acknowledgment acceptable (e.g., head nod)?
- What will happen if a student speaks when others are speaking?
- What will you do about shouting or using a loud voice?

Makeup work
- Will makeup work be allowed?
- Will there be penalties for not completing it?
- Will it be graded?
- Whose responsibility is it to know the work is missing?

Getting out of seat
- When is out-of-seat movement permissible?
- When can a student come to the teacher's desk?
- When can reference books or learning centers be visited?
- What if a student visits another?

Communicating during group work
- Can a student leave an assigned seat?
- How loudly should a student speak?
- Who determines who can talk next?
- Will there be a group leader?

Determining grades
- What percentage will quizzes and tests contribute to the total grade?
- What percentage will class participation count?
- When will notification be given of failing performance?
- How much will homework count?

Violation of due dates
- What happens when repeated violations occur?
- Where can a student learn the due dates if absent?
- What penalties are there for copying another person's assignment?
- Will makeup work be required when a due date is missed?

Early completion of in-class assignments
- Can work for other classes or subjects be done?
- Can a newspaper or magazine be read?
- Can the next exercise or assignment be worked on?
- Can students rest their heads on their desks?

Rule violation
- Will names be written on the board?
- Will extra work penalties be assigned?
- Will you have after-class detention?
- When will a disciplinary referral be made?

areas that confusion often occurs beginning with the very first day. Figure 5.5 shows some of the issues you will want to consider pertaining to these four rule areas.

A few moments of thought before these issues are raised in class can avoid embarrassing pauses and an uncertain response when a student asks a question. You will want to identify issues to be decided for the remaining rule areas in Figure 5.4.

The bottom half of Figure 5.4 identifies areas for which rules can be communicated as the situation arises. Some are specific to a particular situation (for example, safety during a lab experiment, notebook completion, obtaining help) and are best presented in the context to which they apply. They will be more meaningful and more easily remembered when a circumstance or event applies to the rule and thus aids in its retention. Even though you may not communicate these rules on the first day of school, they usually are required so soon afterward that you will want to compose a procedure for them before your first class day.

Here are several general suggestions for creating classroom rules:

- Specify only necessary rules. There are four reasons to have rules, and each should reflect at least one of these purposes:

  Enhance work engagement and minimize disruption

  Promote safety and security

  Prevent disturbance to others or other classroom activities

  Promote acceptable standards of courtesy and interpersonal relations

- Make your rules consistent with the classroom climate you wish to promote. As a beginning teacher, now is the time to recognize your values and preferences for managing your classroom. Articulate your personal philosophy of classroom management and have your class rules reflect it. For example, do you want your classroom climate to emphasize independent judgment, spontaneity, and risk taking, or do you want it to emphasize teacher-initiated exchanges, formal classroom rules, and teacher-solicited responses?

- Don't establish rules you cannot enforce. A rule that says "No talking" or "No getting out of your seat" may be difficult to enforce when your personal philosophy continually encourages spontaneity, problem solving, and group work. Unfairness and inconsistency may result in applying rules you do not fully believe in.

- State your rules at a general enough level to include a range of specific behaviors. The rule "Respect other people's property and person" covers a variety of problems, such as borrowing without permission, throwing objects, and so on. Similarly, the rule "Follow teacher requests" allows you to put an end to a variety of off-task, disruptive behaviors that no list of rules could anticipate or cover comprehensively. However, be careful not to state a rule so generally that the specific problems to which it pertains remain unclear to your learners. For example, a rule stating simply, "Show respect" or "Obey the teacher" may be sufficiently vague to be ignored by most of your learners and unenforceable by you. If you follow this suggestion and the preceding one, you should have prepared about four to six classroom rules for your very first day.

Unless you clearly communicate your rules and apply them consistently, all your work in making them will be meaningless. Consistency is a key reason why some rules are effective while others are not. Rules that are not enforced or not applied consistently over time result in a loss of prestige and respect for the person who has created the rules and has the responsibility for enforcing them.

Following are the most frequently occurring reasons why a particular rule is not applied consistently (Emmer et al., 2006; Evertson et al., 2006):

1. The rule is not workable or appropriate. It does not fit a particular classroom context or is not reasonable, given the nature of the individuals to whom it applies.
2. The teacher fails to monitor students closely, and consequently, some individuals violating the rule are caught while others are not.
3. The teacher does not feel strongly enough about the rule to be persistent about its enforcement and thus makes many exceptions to the rule.

Keep in mind that minor deviations to a rule may not be worth your effort to respond when (1) it would provide an untimely interruption to your lesson, or (2) it is only momentary and not likely to recur. However, when problems in applying a rule persist over time, either increase your vigilance or adjust the rule to allow more flexibility in your response (for example, coming up to the desk without permission for help may be acceptable, but coming up just to talk may not).

PROBLEM AREAS IN CLASSROOM MANAGEMENT

A primary purpose of effective classroom management is to keep learners actively engaged in the learning process. Active engagement means getting learners to work with and act on the material presented, as evidenced by carefully attending to the material, progressing through seatwork at a steady pace, participating in class discussions, and being attentive when called on. This section describes four events that are particularly crucial for keeping students actively engaged in the learning process: monitoring students, making transitions, giving assignments, and bringing closure to lessons. Following are some effective classroom management practices in each of these areas.

Monitoring Students

Monitoring is the process of observing, mentally recording, and, when necessary, redirecting or correcting students' behaviors. Monitoring occurs when you look for active, alert eyes during discussion sessions; faces down and directed at the book or assignment during seatwork; raised hands during a question-and-answer period; and, in general, signs that indicate that learners are participating in what is going on. These signs of engagement (or their absence) indicate when you need to change the pace of your delivery, the difficulty of the material, or even the activity itself.

Kounin (1970) used the word *with-it-ness* to refer to a teacher's ability to keep track of many different signs of engagement at the same time. Kounin observed that one of the most important distinctions between effective and ineffective classroom managers is the degree to which they exhibit with-it-ness. Effective classroom managers who exhibited with-it-ness were aware of what was happening in all parts of the classroom and were able to see different things happening in different parts of the room at the same time. Furthermore, these effective classroom managers were able to communicate this awareness to their students.

There are several simple ways to increase your with-it-ness and the extent of your students' active engagement in the learning process. One way is to increase your physical presence through eye contact. If your eye contact is limited to only a portion of the classroom, you effectively lose with-it-ness for the rest of the classroom. It is surprising to note that a great many beginning teachers consistently do the following:

Talk only to the middle-front rows.

Talk with their backs to the class when writing on the chalkboard.

Talk while looking toward the windows or ceiling.

Talk while not being able to see all students because other students are blocking their view.

In each of these instances, you see only a portion of the classroom, and the students know you see only a portion of the classroom. Your eye contact that covers all portions of the classroom is one of the most important ingredients in conveying a sense of with-it-ness.

A second ingredient for improving with-it-ness is learning to monitor more than one activity at a time. Here the key not only is to change your eye contact to different parts of the room but also to change your focus of attention. For example, progress on assigned seatwork might be the focus of your observations when scanning students in the front of the class, but potential behavior problems might be your focus when scanning students in the back of the class.

Switch back and forth from conduct-related observations to work-related observations at the same time you change eye contact. However, a great impediment to such switching is a tendency to focus exclusively on one student who is having either conduct- or work-related problems. Once other students realize you are preoccupied with one of their peers, problems with other students in other parts of the classroom may be inevitable.

Making Transitions

Another problem area is transitions. It is difficult to keep students' attention during a transition from one instructional activity to another. Moving the entire class from one activity to another in a timely and orderly manner can be a major undertaking. Problems in making these transitions often occur for two reasons: (1) learners are not ready to perform the next activity (or may not even know what it is), and (2) learners have unclear expectations about appropriate behavior during the transition.

One approach to moving the entire class from one activity to another in a timely and orderly manner is to communicate clearly the actual divisions in time between activities.

When students are uncertain or unaware of what is coming next, they naturally become anxious about their ability to perform and to make the transition. This is the time when transitions can get noisy, with some students feeling more comfortable clinging to the previous activity than changing to the next. The beginning of the school year is a time of noisy transitions as students fumble to find the proper materials (or guess which ones are needed) and to find out what is expected of them next. They will not rush headlong into a new activity, for fear they will not like it or will be unable to do well.

In this sense, transitions are as much psychological barriers as they are actual divisions between activities. Students must adjust their psychology for the next activity, just as they must adjust their books and papers. You can help in their adjustment by telling them the daily routine you expect of them. This routine becomes second nature after a few weeks, but it deserves special attention during the first days of school. This is the time for you to describe these daily activities and the order in which they will occur (for example, 10 minutes of presentation, 15 minutes of questions and discussion, 15 minutes of seatwork, and 10 minutes of checking and correcting).

Figure 5.6 provides some suggestions for addressing the problems that occur during transitions.

Giving Assignments

Another crucial time for effective classroom management is when you are giving or explaining assignments. This can be a particularly troublesome time because it often means assigning work that at least some students will not be eager to complete. Grunts and groans are common student expressions of distaste for homework or other assignments that must be completed outside of the regular school day. At times like these, outbursts of misbehavior are most likely to occur.

Evertson and Emmer (1982) found that one difference between effective and ineffective classroom managers was the manner in which they gave assignments, particularly homework. The difference was attributed to several simple procedures that were commonplace among experienced teachers but not among inexperienced teachers.

One procedure was to attach assignments directly to the end of an in-class activity. By doing so, the teacher avoided an awkward pause and even the need for a transition, because the assignment was seen as a logical extension of what already was taking place.

Figure 5.6 Addressing problems that occur during transitions.

Problems	Solutions
Students talk loudly at the beginning of transitions.	It is difficult to *allow* a small amount of talking and *obtain* a small amount. So establish a no-talking rule during transitions.
Students socialize during the transition, delaying the start of the next activity.	Allow no more time than is necessary between activities (e.g., to close books, gather up materials, select new materials).
Students complete assignments before the scheduled time for an activity to end.	Make assignments according to the time to be filled, not the exercises to be completed. Always assign more than enough exercises to fill the allotted time.
Students continue to work on the preceding activity after a change.	Give 5-minute and 2-minute warnings before the end of any activity and use verbal markers such as "Shortly we will end this work," and "Let's finish this up so that we can begin . . ." Create definite beginning and end points to each activity, such as "OK, that's the end of this activity; now we will start . . ." or "Put your papers away and turn to . . ."
Some students lag behind others in completing the previous activity.	Don't wait for stragglers. Begin new activities on time. When a natural break occurs, visit privately with students still working on previous tasks to tell them that they must stop and change. Be sure to note the reason they have not finished (e.g., material too hard, lack of motivation, off-task behavior).
You delay the beginning of the activity to find something (file cabinet keys, materials, roster, references, etc.).	Be prepared—pure and simple! Always have the materials you need in front of you at the start of the activity.

By contrast, imagine how you might feel being given an assignment under these conditions:

◆   ◆   ◆

Teacher A: I guess I'll have to assign some homework now, so do problems 1 through 10 on page 61.

Teacher B: For homework, do the problems under Exercise A and Exercise B—and be sure all of them are finished by tomorrow.

Teacher C: We're out of time, so you'll have to finish these problems on your own.

◆   ◆   ◆

In each of these assignments, there is a subtle implication that the homework may not really be needed or is being given mechanically or as some sort of punishment. Why this homework is being assigned may be a complete mystery to most students, because none of the teachers mentioned either the in-class activities to which the homework presumably relates or the benefits that may accrue from the assignment. Students appreciate knowing why an assignment is made before they are expected to do it.

Now consider these assignments again, this time with some explanations added:

◆　◆　◆

Teacher A: Today we have talked a lot about the origins of the Civil War and some of the economic unrest that preceded it. But some other types of unrest also were responsible for the Civil War. These will be important for understanding the real causes behind this war. Questions 1 through 5 on page 61 will help you understand some of these other causes.

Teacher B: We have all had a chance now to try our skill at forming possessives. As most of you have found out, it's harder than it looks. So let's try Exercises A and B for tonight, which should give you just the right amount of practice in forming possessives.

Teacher C: Well, it looks like time has run out before we could complete all the problems. The next set of problems we will study requires a lot of what we have learned today. So let's complete the rest of these tonight, to see if you've got the concept. This should ensure everyone gets a good grade on the test.

◆　◆　◆

Keep in mind that effective classroom managers give assignments that immediately follow the lesson or activities to which they relate, explain which in-class lessons the assignment relates to, and avoid any unnecessary negative connotations (e.g., "finish them all," "be sure

Table 5.3　Some motivators and their appropriate use.

Motivator	Use Phrases such as . . .	Motivator	Use Phrases such as . . .
Using praise and encouragement	You've got it. Good work. Good try. That was quick.	Accepting diversity	That's not the answer I expected, but I can see your point. That's not how I see it, but I can understand how others might see it differently.
Providing explanations	The reason this is so important is . . . We are doing this assignment because . . . This will be difficult, but it fits in with . . . Experience has shown that without these facts the next unit will be very difficult.	Emphasizing reinforcement and reward	This is not something I'm familiar with. Where did you get that idea? That is not a word I've heard before. Tell us what it means. All homework completed means five extra points. If you get a C or better on all the tests, I'll drop the lowest grade.
Offering to help	Should you need help, I'll be here. Ask if you need help. I'll be walking around; catch me if you have a problem. Don't be afraid to ask a question if you're having trouble.		Those who complete all the exercises on time can go to the learning center. If you have a C average, you get to choose any topic for your term paper.

they are correct," "complete it on time"), which may make your assignment sound more like a punishment than an instructional activity.

It is also important to convey assignments in a manner that motivates your students to complete them. Table 5.3 summarizes five different ways in which you can convey assignments positively and motivate your learners to continue engaging in the activity at a high level of involvement.

Finally, it is always a good idea to display prior assignments somewhere in your classroom so students who have missed an assignment can conveniently look it up without requiring your time to remember or find an old assignment. A simple 2′ by 3′ sheet of poster board, divided into days of the month and covered with plastic to write on, can be a convenient and reusable way of communicating past assignments on a monthly basis.

Bringing Closure

Another time for effective classroom management is when you are bringing a lesson to its end. This is a time when students sense the impending end of the period and begin in advance of your close to disengage themselves from the lesson. It is a time when noise levels increase and students begin to fidget with books, papers, and personal belongings in anticipation of the next class or activity.

Closing comments also should serve a double purpose—not only ending the lesson but also keeping students actively engaged in the lesson until its very end by reviewing, summarizing, or highlighting its most important points. Closure, therefore, is more than simply calling attention to the end of a lesson. It means keeping the momentum of a lesson going by reorganizing what has gone before into a unified body of knowledge that can help students remember the lesson and place it into perspective. Following are ways you can keep your learners actively engaged at the end of your lessons and help them retain what you have taught.

Combining or Consolidating Key Points.   One way of accomplishing closure is by combining or consolidating key points into a single overall conclusion. Consider the following:

◆　◆　◆

Teacher:　Today we have studied the economic systems of capitalism, socialism, and communism. We have found each of these to be similar in that some of the same goods and services are owned by the government. We have, however, found them different with respect to the degree to which various goods and services are owned by the government: The least number of goods and services are owned by a government under capitalism, and the most goods and services are owned by a government under communism.

◆　◆　◆

This teacher is drawing together and highlighting the single most important conclusion from the day's lesson. The teacher is doing so by expressing the highest level generalization or conclusion from the lesson without reference to any of the details that were necessary to arrive at it. This teacher consolidated many different bits and pieces by going to the broadest, most sweeping conclusion that could be made, capturing the essence of all that went before.

Summarizing or Reviewing Key Content.   Another procedure for bringing closure to a lesson is by summarizing or reviewing key content. The teacher reviews the most important content to be sure everyone understands it. Obviously, not all of the content can be repeated in this manner, so some selecting is in order, as illustrated by the following:

◆   ◆   ◆

Teacher: Before we end, let's look at our two rules once again. Rule 1: Use the possessive form whenever an *of* phrase can be substituted for a noun. Rule 2: If the word for which we are denoting ownership already ends in an *s,* place the apostrophe after, *not* before, the *s.* Remember, both these rules use the apostrophe.

◆   ◆   ◆

Now the teacher is consolidating by summarizing, or touching on, each of the key features of the lesson. The teacher's review is rapid and to the point, providing students with an opportunity to fill in any gaps about the main features of the lesson.

Providing a Structure.   Still another method for closing consists of providing learners with a structure so they can remember key facts and ideas without an actual review of them. With this procedure, the teacher reorganizes facts and ideas into a framework for easy recall, as indicated in this example:

◆   ◆   ◆

Teacher: Today we studied forming and punctuating possessives. Recall that we used two rules: one for forming possessives wherever an *of* phrase can be substituted for a noun and another for forming possessives for words ending in *s.* From now on, let's call these rules the *of rule* and the *s rule,* keeping in mind that both rules use the apostrophe.

◆   ◆   ◆

By giving students a framework for remembering the rules (the *of rule* and *s rule*), the teacher organizes the content and indicates how it should be stored and remembered. The key to this procedure is giving a code or symbol system so students can more easily store lesson content and recall it for later use.

Notice that in each of the previous dialogues, the teacher accomplished closure by looking back at the lesson and reinforcing its key components. In the first instance, the teacher accomplished this by restating the highest level generalization that could be made; in the second, by summarizing the content at the level at which it was taught; and in the third, by helping students remember the important categories of information by providing codes or symbols. Each of these closings has the potential of keeping your learners engaged when the main part of your lesson has ended. Endings to good lessons are like endings to good stories: They keep you engaged and in suspense and leave you with a sense that you have understood the story and can remember it long afterward.

LEARNER DIVERSITY AND CLASSROOM MANAGEMENT

A number of authors have studied the effects of various styles of classroom management and the engagement of their learners. For example, researchers (Cheng, 1996; Cheng et al., 1997; Griggs & Dunn, 1995) found connections between different cultures and the nonverbal and verbal behavioral management techniques of proximity control, eye contact, warnings, and classroom rules. For example, the greater the spatial distance between teacher and student, the more some students became passive listeners and engaged in off-task behavior. As the teacher moved closer to students, communication tended to become more interactive, with more students following the wishes of the teacher. Standing closer to individual students promoted compliance to classroom rules, because students were drawn into nonverbal forms of communication, such as eye contact and changes in voice and body movement, that send a message of involvement.

Bowers and Flinders (1991) found the use of space can communicate a sense of social power, which can promote engagement or disengagement. They report the case of a teacher who moved from student to student, checking work while on a swivel chair with casters. In this manner the teacher was able to elicit more spontaneous and relaxed student responses, resulting in greater student involvement and compliance with classroom rules. This was especially so among students who, by virtue of their language, culture, or ethnicity, did not wish to be spotlighted in the traditional teacher-dominated manner.

Other research has studied the compatibility of various classroom management techniques with the culture and background of the teacher. Researchers (Anderson, 1996; Compton-Lilly, 2000; DeLeon, 1996; Lockwood & Secada, 1999; Schwartz, 1998) present convincing arguments that teachers of different cultures interpret disruptive behaviors of children differently. For example, facial expressions during a reprimand have been found to communicate different messages concerning the importance of the reprimand. And research by D. Dillon (1989) and Putnam (1996) has pointed out that some actions of teachers may unintentionally diminish engagement among minority students and/or build resentment because their actions are culturally incongruent. For example, a teacher who constantly stands over students to monitor them can be seen as threatening. Recall the teacher who moved from student to student on a swivel chair to monitor student work so as to be at the same level as the student. Dillon suggests that teachers examine their own value and belief systems to become more aware how different they may be from their students and use the social organization of the classroom to bridge cultural gaps:

- Establish an open, risk-free classroom climate where students can experience mutual trust and confidence.
- Plan and structure lessons that meet the interests and needs of students.
- Implement lessons that allow all students to be active learners through activities and responsibilities that are congruent with the learners' cultures.

These are important considerations in understanding the culture and ethnicity of your classroom and establishing a culturally sensitive classroom management system.

Another classroom management challenge you are likely to face in keeping your class engaged is the learner who is at risk academically (Kaufman, Alt, & Chapman, 2001). Academically **at-risk learners** can be among those who are most often off-task and disengaged. Students at-risk for their academic performance are those who have difficulty learning at an average rate from the instructional resources, texts, workbooks, and learning materials that are designated for the majority of students in the classroom. These students need special instructional pacing, more feedback, supplemental instruction, and/or modified materials, all administered under conditions sufficiently flexible to keep them actively engaged in the learning process.

Learners who are at-risk for poor academic performance usually are taught in one of two possible instructional arrangements: (1) a class composed mostly of average-performing students or (2) a class that is part of a **track system** in which some sections of math, English, science, social studies, and so on, are allocated for lower-performing students. It is estimated that 80% of secondary schools and 60% of elementary schools use some form of tracking (O'Neil, 1992), which has the most negative effects on minorities in the lower tracks (Davenport, et al., 1998; Mickelson & Heath, 1999).

The desirability and fairness of various tracking systems has been extensively debated (Gamoran, 1992; Good & Brophy, 2003; Lou, Abrami, & Spence, 2000; Mansnerus, 1992; Slavin, 1991a). The argument typically offered in favor of tracking is that it allows schools to differentiate instruction better by giving high achievers the challenge and low achievers the support they need to learn. Opponents argue that (1) tracking is undemocratic in that it separates learners into homogeneous groups unrepresentative of the world outside the classroom, and (2) research has indicated that it fails to increase learner achievement beyond what can be expected to occur in heterogeneous classrooms. Time-limited task and ability grouping within heterogeneous classes has produced superior achievement with at-risk learners compared to tracking (Gamoran, 1992; Good & Brophy, 2003; Skirtic, 1991; Slavin, 1990).

Whether you meet at-risk learners in a regular class or in a tracked class, keeping at-risk learners engaged may require more than the usual variation in presentation methods (e.g., recitation, presentation), classroom climate (e.g., cooperative, competitive), and instructional materials (e.g., practice activities, learning centers).

Some characteristics of these learners that place them at-risk for school failure and/or behavioral problems are their deficiency in basic skills (reading, writing, mathematics), their difficulty in dealing with abstractions, and their sometimes unsystematic or careless work habits, which may require instruction in note taking, listening, and organization skills. When these learning strategies are not provided as part of your instruction, the result can be a performance below the child's potential to learn, beginning a cycle of deficiencies that promotes poor self-concept, misbehavior, and disinterest in school—all of which have contributed to a particularly high dropout rate for the at-risk learner (Child Trends DataBank, 2005; Walker & Sylwester, 1991).

However, it is wise to avoid broad generalizations based on your perceptions of the students who may be classified as "at-risk" or who may be assigned to lower-performing classes. Students' dispositions and actions are often surprising, as has been noted in the recent research on "resiliency" (Benard, 1997; Doll, Zucker, & Brehm, 2004). "Resilient" children are those that seem to defy the odds—becoming productive and happy individuals in spite of backgrounds that would suggest otherwise. Several long-term studies suggest that resilient children are more numerous than might be expected. Werner and Smith (1992) noted that between 50% and 70% of children born into extremely high-risk environments "grow up to be not only successful by societal indicators but 'confident, competent, and caring' persons" (Benard, 1997, p. 2). Further, many researchers and teachers believe that resiliency can be fostered in all youth.

Some instructional strategies that can help you keep at-risk learners engaged in your classroom are:

- *Develop some lessons around students' interests, needs, and experiences.* This will help heighten the attention of at-risk learners and actively engage them in the learning process. Oral or written autobiographies at the beginning of the year or simple inventories in which students indicate their hobbies, jobs, and unusual trips or experiences can provide the basis for lesson plans, projects, and assignments that allow learners to construct their own meanings from direct experience and the interactions they have with others around them.

- *Encourage oral as well as written expression.* For at-risk learners, many writing assignments go unattempted or are begun only halfheartedly because these learners recognize their written product will not meet minimal writing standards. Consider an audio- or videotaped assignment at the beginning of the school year; this has the advantage of avoiding spelling, syntax, and writing errors at a crucial time.

- *Provide study aids.* Study aids alert students to the most important problems, content, or issues. They also eliminate irrelevant details that at-risk learners often study in the belief they are important. Examples of test questions or a list of topics for possible questions can help focus student effort.

- *Teach learning strategies.* Learning strategies are general methods of thinking that improve learning across a variety of subject areas. They accomplish this by enhancing the way information is received, placed in memory, and activated when needed. You can increase the engagement of your at-risk learners by teaching elaboration/organization (e.g., note taking and outlining), comprehension and monitoring (e.g., setting goals, focusing attention, self-reinforcement), and problem-solving strategies (e.g., vocal and subvocal rehearsal). We will have more to say about these and other learning strategies that you can teach your learners in chapter 10.

PLANNING YOUR FIRST DAY

If your first class day is like that of most teachers, it will include some or all of these activities (Wong, 2004):

- Keeping order before the bell
- Introducing yourself
- Taking care of administrative business
- Presenting rules and expectations
- Introducing your subject
- Closing

Because your responses in these areas may set the tone in your classroom for the remainder of the year, let's consider your first-day planning in more detail to see how you can prepare an effective routine.

Before the Bell

As the sole person responsible for your classroom, your responsibility extends not just to when your classes are in session but to whenever school is in session. Consequently, you must be prepared to deal with students before your classes begin in the morning, between classes, and after your last class has ended—or anytime you are in your classroom. Your first class day is particularly critical in this regard, because your students' before-class peek at you will set in motion responses, feelings, and concerns that may affect them long after the bell has rung. Following are a few suggestions that can make these responses, feelings, and concerns positive ones:

1. To provide a sense of with-it-ness (defined earlier in this chapter), stand near the door as students enter your classroom. In this way, you will come in direct contact with each student and be visible to them as they take their seats. Your presence at the doorway, where students must come in close contact with you, will encourage an orderly entrance (and exit) from the classroom. Remember, your class starts when the first student walks through your classroom door.

2. Have approximately four to six rules, divided between conduct and work, clearly visible on the chalkboard, bulletin board, overhead, or in the form of a handout already placed on each student's desk. You may want to prepare rules for the areas shown in the upper half of Figure 5.4 that you feel will be most critical to your classes during the first few days of school. You can formally introduce these rules later, but they should be clearly visible as students enter your class the first day.

3. Prepare a brief outline of your opening day's routine. This outline should list all the activities you plan to perform that day (or class period), in the order in which you will perform them. You can make a cue card for yourself with a simple 4-by-6-inch index card to remind yourself to:

- Greet students and introduce yourself (5 minutes)
- Take roll (5 minutes)
- Fill out forms (10 minutes)
- Assign books (15 minutes)
- Present rules (10 minutes)
- Remind students to bring needed materials (2 minutes)

- Introduce subject matter content (or brief overview of daily schedule for the elementary grades) (0 to 10 minutes)
- Close or transition to normal routine for the elementary grades (3 minutes)

Let's look briefly at several of these activities for your first day.

Introducing Yourself

Introduce yourself by giving your name and something special about yourself, such as an area of interest or expertise. Your personality will, and should, unfold in small degrees during the first few weeks of school. There is no need to rush it. However, a small glimpse of the kind of person you are outside of the classroom often is a nice touch for students, who would like to see you as a friend as well as a teacher. A short comment about your interests, hobbies, or special experiences—even family or home life—often is appreciated by students, who at the end of this first day will be struggling to remember just who you are.

Administrative Business

Your first opportunity to meet your students up close will be while taking the roll. This is when you may want to turn the tables and have your students not only identify themselves but indicate some of their own interests, hobbies, or special experiences, especially as they may relate to some of the things you will be teaching.

Your other administrative duties at this time can be considerable, and in some cases can consume most of the remainder of the class period at the upper grades and a full hour or more in the lower grades. Filling out forms requested by the school and school district, checking course schedules, guiding lost students to their correct rooms, and accepting new students during the middle of the class may all be part of your duties this first class day.

Rules and Expectations

Plan to devote some time to discussing your classroom rules and your overall expectations about both conduct and work. This is the time to remove student uncertainties and let your learners know what to expect. There is no better way to begin this process than by referring to the conduct and work rules that you either have posted for all to see or have handed out.

Introducing Your Subject

Although time may not permit you to present much content on the first day, we offer several tips for presenting content during your first lessons.

1. Begin by talking to the whole class. This is a time when not all of your students will be eager to participate in group work or seatwork or be relaxed enough to contribute meaningfully to inquiry or problem-solving-type activities. These instructional approaches depend on the trust and confidence that students acquire from their experience with you over time. They will be acquiring this trust and confidence during your first days and weeks in the classroom.

2. During your initial days in the classroom, choose content activities that you believe everyone can successfully complete. At this time, you will not yet know the difficulty level most appropriate for your learners, so use this time to gradually try out the types of tasks and activities you eventually will ask your learners to perform, beginning with those from which you expect the most student success.

Closure

Have a definite procedure for closing in mind (for example, a preview of things to come, instructions to follow for tomorrow's class, a reminder of things to bring to class). Begin closing a full 3 minutes before the bell is to ring. End with a note of encouragement that all of your students can do well in your grade or class. Follow these suggestions and you will have a great first day!

 Video Window

Planning Your First Day

In this video, we find a fourth-grade teacher meeting her class on the first day of school. You will see how this teacher introduces some of the topics and activities you will discuss with your students on that first day. Running throughout this teacher's activities, you will feel the warmth and nurturance she conveys to her students, making each child feel he or she is special in the teacher's eyes. You will see how to dispel the anxiety that young children often feel on the first day of school and how this teacher builds with both her words as well as actions toward a cohesive classroom that will endure the rest of the year. As you watch, see if you can identify what this teacher does in each of the following areas to convey expectations for the students' conduct and learning and describe an instance of each.

- Keeping order before and at the beginning of class
- Introducing herself
- Taking care of administrative business
- Introducing her subject
- Closing

 To answer these questions online, go to the Video Windows *module for this chapter on the Companion Website at www.prenhall.com/borich.*

SUMMING UP

This chapter introduced you to motivation and classroom management. Its key terms and main points were:

Earning Trust and Becoming a Leader

1. Five types of social power or leadership that a teacher can strive for are expert power, referent power, legitimate power, reward power, and coercive power.

Stages of Group Development

2. Four stages through which a successful group passes are forming, storming, norming, and performing.

3. Distancing is a type of amiable limit testing in which group members challenge academic expectations and rules to establish under what conditions they do or do not apply.
4. Centering is a second type of amiable limit testing in which learners question how they will personally benefit from being a group member.
5. Two basic processes by which norms develop are diffusion and crystallization. The former occurs when different academic and social expectations held by different members are spread throughout the group. The latter occurs when expectations converge and crystallize into a shared perspective.

Establishing an Effective Classroom Climate

6. Classroom climate refers to the atmosphere or mood in which interactions between you and your students take place. A classroom climate can be created by the social environment, which is related to the patterns of interaction you wish to promote in your classroom, and by the organizational environment, which is related to the physical or visual arrangement of the classroom.

7. The social climate of the classroom can extend from authoritarian (in which you are the primary provider of information, opinions, and instruction) to laissez-faire (in which your students become the primary providers of information, opinions, and instruction).

8. Your role in establishing authority in the classroom and the social climate can vary. You can adopt different roles, including the following:
   * Commander in chief who carefully controls and hones student behavior by organizing and providing all the stimuli needed for learning to occur
   * Translator or summarizer of ideas provided by students
   * Equal partner with students in creating ideas and problem solutions

9. The social climate of your classroom also can vary, depending on how competitive, cooperative, or individualistic you wish the interactions among class members to be. Differences among these include extent of opportunities for students to express opinion, time devoted to student talk, and spontaneity with which your students are allowed to respond.

The Organizational Environment

10. Organizational climate pertains to the physical or visual arrangement of the classroom, determined by the positioning of desks, chairs, tables, and other internal features of a classroom.

11. The degree of competition, cooperation, and individuality in your classroom is a result of the social and organizational climate you create.

Establishing Rules and Procedures

12. Rules can relate to one or more of four distinct areas:
    * Academic work
    * Classroom conduct
    * Information you must communicate your first teaching day
    * Information you can communicate later

13. Rules can be communicated orally, on the board, on a transparency, or in a handout. Rules for the early elementary grades should be presented orally, provided as a handout, and posted for reference. Rules for the elementary grades and junior high school may be recited and copied by students. Rules for high school may be given orally and then posted.

14. The following suggestions will help you develop classroom rules:
    * Make rules consistent with your climate.
    * Don't make rules that cannot be enforced.
    * Specify only necessary rules.
    * State rules generally enough to include different but related behaviors.

15. Your inability to enforce a rule over a reasonable period of time is the best sign you need to change the rule.

Problem Areas in Classroom Management

16. Monitoring students, making transitions, giving assignments, and bringing closure are four particularly troublesome areas of classroom management.

17. With-it-ness is a form of monitoring in which you are able to keep track of many different signs of student engagement at the same time.

18. You can convey assignments positively and motivate learners in the following ways:
    * Use praise and encouragement.
    * Provide explanations.
    * Offer to help.
    * Accept diversity.
    * Emphasize reward, not punishment.

19. Problems during transitions most frequently occur when learners are not ready to perform the next activity and do not know what behavior is appropriate during the transition.

20. Homework assignments should be given immediately following the lesson or activities to which they relate and without negative connotations.

21. Closing statements should gradually bring a lesson to an end by combining or consolidating key points into a single overall conclusion, by summarizing or reviewing key content, or by providing a symbol system so students can easily store and later recall the contents of the lesson.

Learner Diversity and Classroom Management

22. You may use the following methods to bridge cultural gaps in the classroom:
    * Establish an open, risk-free climate.
    * Plan lessons that meet student interests and needs.
    * Allow for activities and responsibilities congruent with learners' cultures.

KEY TERMS

At-risk learners, 181
Centering behavior, 163
Coercive power, 161
Crystallization, 164
Diffusion, 164
Distancing behavior, 163
Expert power, 159
Legitimate power, 160
Monitoring, 175

Norms, 163
Organizational environment, 167
Referent power, 160
Reward power, 160
Rules and procedures, 172
Social environment, 167
Social power, 159
Stages of group development, 161
Track system, 181

DISCUSSION AND PRACTICE QUESTIONS

Questions marked with an asterisk are answered in appendix B. See also the Companion Website for this text at *www.prenhall.com/borich* for more assessment options.

*1. Describe in your own words the two types of social power beginning teachers should most quickly achieve. How would you achieve each?

*2. What is meant by the diffusion and crystallization of norms? In what order can you expect these two basic processes of norm development to occur?

*3. What are three roles that communicate different levels of authority you can assume in your classroom? How will expression of student opinions, proportion of student talk to teacher talk, and spontaneity of response change as a function of each of these three roles?

4. Draw three diagrams of the internal features of a classroom, each illustrating how to promote a classroom climate that is either competitive, cooperative, or individualistic.

5. Identify three academic rules and three conduct rules that you believe will be needed on your first day of class. Write out a rule for each of these six areas, exactly as you might show it to

your students on a handout or transparency on the first day of class.

*6. Identify two rules whose retention might be aided if they were communicated in the context of a circumstance or incident requiring the rule. Describe each circumstance or incident.

*7. State three guidelines for developing effective classroom rules. Identify four rules that, in your opinion, follow these guidelines.

*8. Identify a practical strategy for deciding when you should revise or eliminate a rule. Which type of rule, academic or conduct, do you feel would need to be revised most?

*9. What are four teaching practices that can help avoid misbehavior during a transition? Which do you feel you would use the most?

*10. What are two ways discussed in this chapter that out-of-class assignments can be made more meaningful and accepted by your students? What other ways can you think of?

*11. Identify three ways you can bring a lesson to an end that can help students organize the lesson in retrospect. Which one(s) best fit(s) the grade or subject matter you will be teaching? Why?

FIELD EXPERIENCE ACTIVITIES

*1. Imagine a group of learners similar to the classroom in which you will be teaching. Using specific examples of student behavior, identify the four stages of group development you will help your students through so they can function as a cohesive group.

*2. Using examples of student classroom dialogue, illustrate the group behaviors of distancing and centering.

*3. Provide some example classroom activities that would result in (a) a competitive, (b) a cooperative, and (c) an individualistic classroom climate.

*4. Explain in your own words what *with-it-ness* means. Give an example from your own experience of when you displayed *with-it-ness* and when you did not but should have. What were the personal consequences of each event?

5. What information about yourself would you communicate to students on the first day of class? Include information about your expectations for learners and class rules and routines.

*6. If you were teaching in a culturally diverse or heterogeneous classroom, in what ways would you try to bridge different cultures and social classes to form a productive and cohesive classroom?

DIGITAL PORTFOLIO ACTIVITY

The following digital portfolio activity relates to INTASC principles 3 and 5.

Place your responses to Field Experience Activities 5 and 6 into your digital portfolio in a folder titled *Classroom Management*. These will provide examples of your skill at creating a cohesive and nurturing classroom beginning with your very first day and your skill in actively planning to bridge the gap between different cultures and social classes in a heterogeneous classroom.

CLASSROOM OBSERVATION ACTIVITIES

The following classroom observation activities relate to INTASC principles 5 and 6.

1. Using the classroom sketch provided in the *Classroom Observation* module for this chapter on the Companion Website at *www.prenhall.com/borich*, graphically draw with your computer the following three classroom arrangements. In the first place your classroom furniture, including teacher's desk and student desks, to emphasize the acquisition of knowledge, rules, and concepts. In the second emphasize cooperative learning and group inquiry and problem solving. Then, draw a third indicating a compromise classroom arrangement that would allow some students to work independently at their desks while others work cooperatively in groups. Make each of your classrooms distinctive to your personal tastes and teaching style by adding rugs/pillows, learning centers, computers, and learning resources, where appropriate. During a classroom observation use this template for drawing the classroom you are observing. Place these drawings in your *Classroom Management* digital portfolio for future reference in planning your own classroom arrangement.

2. Return to the *Classroom Observation* module in the Companion Website for this chapter where you will find a recording format for *Observing Rules in Frequently Occurring Areas*. This form includes categories for which classroom rules are frequently written, such as getting out of seat, speaking out, completing assessments, communicating during group work, and so on. Write one rule for each of the rule areas listed. Place your rules in your *Classroom Management* digital portfolio folder for future classroom observations in which you will have the opportunity to record other teachers' classroom rules and some additional ideas for your own list of rules.

CHAPTER CASE HISTORY AND PRAXIS TEST PREPARATION

DIRECTIONS: The following case history pertains to chapter 5 content. After reading the case history, answer the short-answer question that follows and consult appendix D to find different levels of scored student responses and the rubric used to determine the quality of each response. You also have the opportunity to submit your responses online to receive feedback by visiting the *Case History* module for this chapter on the Companion Website, where you will also find additional questions pertaining to Praxis test content.

Case History

Ms. Ford is a first-year teacher. Her third-grade class includes a large number of students who could be termed at-risk according to a variety of standards. Many come from single-parent homes; over two thirds qualify for reduced-priced school lunches; and almost one third speak a language other than English at home.

It is the third week of the semester and many of Ms. Ford's worst fears have failed to materialize. Her students have not created any significant classroom management problems. On the contrary, they have been orderly, well behaved, and quiet. Her three rules are posted neatly and clearly on the bulletin board:

Respect other people and their property.

Raise your hand before speaking.

Listen when others talk.

Even though Ms. Ford has spent a great deal of time coming up with clearly defined consequences for not following these rules, she now feels the time has been largely wasted. The problem is not that they speak out without raising their hands; it's that they seldom speak at all. They listen quietly but it is only to her, because few classmates volunteer oral responses except the most simple one-word answers. They sit in their alphabetically assigned seats; they copy the sentences from the board without a sound; and they spend extra effort in forming letters that are as round and perfect as the handwriting exercise models.

She had been all set to "manage" rambunctious 8-year-olds, but Ms. Ford is at a loss to light the spark of engagement in her shy and passive class.

She spends most of the weekend rethinking her classroom strategies and enters on Tuesday with a new plan. Ms. Ford stands in the doorway as her students enter the classroom, but instead of a stoic nod, she now greets them with a smile and a quiet reference here and there to a "pretty new dress," or "a cool backpack." She allows herself to rub Juan's shortly cropped head and asks him if he is going into the Marines. He smiles shyly up at her.

More surprises are in store for the third graders. Gone are the neat rows of desks and in their place are tables set in small groups to accommodate five or six students each. "Find your name at a table and be seated there."

The organization is not alphabetical, but random, or at least it appears to be. It is not necessary to tell the class that the composition of each grouping has entailed the same attention to detail as for a first-draft football selection. At each table there are at least two students whose primary language is English, as well as one who seems conversant in both English and Spanish, which is the dominant second language.

"All of you at the same table will be part of a team that will be working together on several projects and assignments. But first you will need to get to know each other a little bit better. I thought today we might talk about our favorite animals, since each group will be named after the animal of its choice. Ask yourself this question: If I could be any animal for a single day, what animal would I choose and why?

"I'll start. If I could be any animal I wanted for a day it would be a horse, a wild black stallion in the mountains of Wyoming. I would love to run and feel the wind in my mane, to rear up and paw at the sky, and thunder through the canyons. I think it is its freedom and beauty, its speed and strength that I admire so much.

"Take a few minutes to think and then take turns telling your group which animal you would like to be."

Ms. Ford is amazed that after less than a minute, many are already sharing their animal adventures. And she is in for a few surprises, too. Shy Patricia, whose eyes seem always downcast, is demonstrating, in between giggles, what her life as a monkey would be like. Romero, who knows only a few English words, is completely at home as a pouncing and growling black panther.

It is with a sly smile of satisfaction that Ms. Ford has to gently remind them, near the end of the session, to keep their voices down.

Short-Answer Question

This section presents a sample Praxis short-answer question. In appendix D you will find sample responses along with the standards used in scoring these responses.

DIRECTIONS: The following question requires you to write a short answer. Base your answer on your knowledge of principles of learning and teaching in chapter 5. Be sure to answer all parts of the question.

1. Ms. Ford had a classroom with much learner and cultural diversity. Elaborate on at least two pedagogical changes she made to be more effective in reaching these diverse learners and explain why those changes were effective.

Discrete Multiple-Choice Questions

DIRECTIONS: Each of the following multiple-choice questions is based on Praxis-related pedagogical knowledge in chapter 5. Select the answer that is best in each case and compare your results with those in appendix D. See also the Companion Website for this text at *www.prenhall.com/borich* for more assessment options.

1. Ms. Wilson enjoys interactive discussions with her eighth-grade history class. As they contribute their ideas, she writes them on the board. Recently, however, whenever her back is turned to write down a contribution, spitballs fly through the air. Select the answer that best identifies the problem and proposes a workable solution.
   a. The problem involves distancing, which is an amiable form of limit testing that is a part of normal classroom development. It should be ignored and will stop on its own.
   b. The problem involves norms, shared expectations among group members about how they should feel, think, and behave. Have the students set the norms and decide on how to solve the spitball problem.
   c. The problem involves the failure to use coercive power, the teacher's option to punish students who defy authority. Anyone caught throwing spitballs should receive a consequence, such as extra homework or detention after school.
   d. The problem involves monitoring, the process of observing and redirecting student engagement. Because it is impossible to observe students with her back to them, the best solution is for the teacher to use an overhead projector and thus record student ideas while she is facing the class.

2. Research shows that one difference between effective and ineffective teachers is the manner in which they give assignments, particularly homework. When they give assignments, most effective and ineffective teachers do all of the following *except*

   a. Attach the assignment directly to the end of an in-class activity.
   b. Provide a definite completion date.
   c. Communicate rules by which the assignment is to be completed.
   d. Emphasize accuracy and completion.

3. Mr. Eastman always circulated around the room after giving seatwork to his students. This way he could monitor their progress, answer questions, or offer suggestions. His class this year has many at-risk and culturally diverse students who seem uncomfortable when he stands near their desks, and even stop working when he is near. The most probable reason for this response, as well as a solution to the problem, is that
   a. To some students the social power conveyed by the teacher standing over their work causes disengagement. A possible solution would be for the teacher to create a less formal monitoring posture, perhaps with the use of a swivel chair, thus being close but also on their level.
   b. The discomfort is probably initial shyness and will go away with time. The teacher should continue the practice, maybe offering more assistance to learners.
   c. Probably these students are more independent learners and do not like someone peering over their shoulders. The teacher should consider giving them different assignments of an individualistic nature.
   d. These new students are manifesting the same discomfort that all students feel with a teacher in close proximity. The teacher should stay at his desk while the class begins the assignment and then come to them when they are having problems.

4. Mr. Higgins wants his students to engage in a dialogue about the topic of the day's lesson in a small groups format. His primary duty during the lesson is to
   a. Organize the content that will be discussed.
   b. Evaluate the correctness of responses.

c. Stimulate discussion and summarize student contributions.

d. Assign the work and see that orderly progress is made toward its completion.

5. Research in which some classes of math, English, science, social studies, etc. are allocated for lower-performing students has revealed that tracking

a. Works to improve the skills of lower-performing students in subjects like math and science but not language arts and social studies

b. Can improve the affective but not cognitive skills of lower-performing students

c. Fails to increase learner achievement beyond what can be expected in heterogeneous classrooms

d. Represents the real world outside the classroom where people separate into homogeneous groups to which learners should become accustomed

This chapter will help you answer the following questions and meet the following INTASC principles for effective teaching:

1. What is an effective classroom management plan?
2. What techniques do effective classroom managers use?
3. Which is more effective in changing the behavior of learners: rewards or punishment?
4. How do I plan a parent–teacher conference?
5. What is culturally responsive classroom management?

INTASC 2: The teacher understands how children learn and develop, and can provide learning opportunities that support their intellectual, social, and personal development.

INTASC 5: The teacher uses an understanding of individual and group motivation and behavior to create a learning environment that encourages positive social interaction, active engagement in learning, and self-motivation.

INTASC 9: The teacher is a reflective practitioner who continually evaluates the effects of his or her choices and actions on others (students, parents, and other professionals in the learning community) and who actively seeks out opportunities to grow professionally.

INTASC 10: The teacher fosters relationships with school colleagues, parents, and agencies in the larger community to support students' learning and well-being.

*A*nyone who reads the newspaper, listens to candidates running for public office, attends *school board meetings, or overhears conversations in the teachers' lounge quickly realizes that classroom order and discipline are among education's most frequently discussed topics. Inability to control a class is one of the most commonly cited reasons for dismissing or failing to reemploy a teacher, and beginning teachers consistently rate classroom discipline among their most urgent concerns (Kirsch, 2005; Rose & Gallup, 2002; L. Weiner, 2002).*

In chapter 5, you learned about establishing the climate for a manageable classroom. In this chapter, you will learn specific techniques for preventing disruptive behaviors from occurring or dealing with them efficiently, increasing the time your students are actively engaged in learning.

SYSTEMS OF CLASSROOM MANAGEMENT

Approaches to dealing with classroom management can be grouped into three traditions. One tradition emphasizes the critical role of communication and problem solving between teacher and students. This approach is called the **humanist tradition** of classroom management (Bluestein, 2001; Curwin & Mendler, 1997, 2000; Ginott, Ginott, & Goddard, 2003; Glasser, 1998a, 1998b, 1998c). The second tradition comes from the field of **applied behavior analysis.** This approach to classroom management emphasizes behavior modification techniques and reinforcement theory applied to the classroom (Alberto & Troutman, 2002; Canter, 2001; F. C. Jones, 1987). The third approach is the most recent, emphasizing the teaching skills involved in organizing and managing instructional activities and in presenting content, called the **classroom management tradition** (Cotton, 1996; Emmer et al., 2006; Evertson et al., 2006). This third approach, more so than the humanistic and applied behavior analysis traditions, underscores the critical role of prevention in managing classroom behavior.

In this chapter we briefly summarize the main features of these traditions, point out how they are used in the classroom, and show how the best features of each can be seamlessly combined into a single approach. To begin, let's identify six criteria of an effective classroom management plan:

1. *Establish positive relationships among all classroom participants.* A positive, supportive classroom environment that meets students' needs for building trusting relations is a necessary foundation for managing an orderly classroom. In the previous chapter, we saw some of the ways you can build trusting relations among your learners.

2. *Prevent attention-seeking and work-avoidance behavior.* Time devoted to managing the classroom should be directed to engaging students in the learning process and preventing behaviors that interfere with it. Engagement and prevention include both arrangement of physical space and the teaching of rules for working in this space. In the previous chapter, we saw the importance of classroom climate and provided some guidelines and examples for teaching classroom rules.

3. *Quickly and unobtrusively redirect misbehavior once it occurs.* Most classroom problems take the form of minor off-task and attention-seeking behaviors. Techniques for coping with these events should not cause more disruption than the behavior itself.

4. *Stop persistent and chronic misbehavior with strategies that are simple enough to be used consistently.* Management systems that require responses to every act of positive or negative behavior may not be sufficiently practical to be implemented consistently in today's busy classrooms.

5. *Teach self-control.* Students should be allowed the opportunity to exercise internal control before the teacher imposes external control. When external controls are imposed, they should be implemented with plans for fading them out.

6. *Respect cultural differences.* Verbal and nonverbal techniques for redirecting disruptive behavior do not mean the same thing to all cultural groups. Likewise, systematic strategies involving rewards and consequences can violate important cultural norms.

Now let's learn something about each of our three approaches to classroom management. As you read about them, reflect on how each meets these criteria and shares some characteristics with the others.

THE HUMANIST TRADITION IN CLASSROOM MANAGEMENT

The principles underlying the humanist tradition come from the practice of clinical and counseling psychology. It is called *humanist* because it focuses primarily on the inner thoughts, feelings, psychological needs, and emotions of the individual learner. Humanist approaches emphasize the importance of allowing the student time to develop control over his or her behavior rather than insisting on immediate behavioral change or compliance. Teachers using humanist approaches hope to achieve these ends through interventions stressing the use of communication skills, an understanding of student motives, private conferences, individual and group problem solving, and the exercise of referent and expert power.

Ginott's (1995; Ginott, Ginott, & Goddard, 2003) cooperation through congruent communication (also called the communication skills approach) and Glasser's (1998b, 1998c) cooperation through individual and group problem solving (also called cooperative learning and reality therapy) are examples of the humanist tradition. Each emphasizes a different area of skill that the effective classroom manager should possess, but they essentially represent two sides of the same coin.

Ginott's Congruent Communication

The cardinal principle underlying Ginott's **congruent communication** skills approach is that learners are capable of controlling their own behavior if only teachers would allow them to do so. Teachers foster this self-control by allowing learners to choose how they wish to change their own behavior and how the class will be run. In addition, they help their students deal with their inner thoughts and feelings through the use of effective communication skills.

The use of communication skills is the primary vehicle for influencing learners' self-esteem, which, in turn, is the primary force underlying acceptable behavior. Therefore, this tradition tries first and foremost to influence student behavior by enhancing student self-esteem. According to the proponents of this approach, congruent communication is the vehicle for promoting self-esteem.

Teachers have many opportunities during the school day to engage their students in congruent communication, usually during private conferences with students who misbehave. However, such communication also can go on during problem solving with the whole class. At such times, teachers communicate congruently when they do the following:

1. *Express "sane" messages.* Sane messages communicate to students their behavior is unacceptable, but they do so in a manner that does not blame, scold, preach, accuse, demand, threaten, or humiliate. Sane messages describe what should be done rather than scold what was done. "Rosalyn, we are all supposed to be in our seats before the bell rings," in contrast to, "Rosalyn, you're always gossiping at the doorway and coming late to class."

2. *Accept rather than deny feelings.* Teachers should accept the feelings of students about their individual circumstances rather than argue about them. If a student complains, "I have no friends," the teacher should accept the student's feeling of isolation and identify with the student, such as by saying, "So you're feeling you don't belong to any group," rather than by trying to convince the student that he or she has misperceived the social situation.

3. *Avoid the use of labels.* When talking to students about what they do well or poorly, teachers should avoid terms such as *lazy, sloppy,* and *bad attitude,* as well as *dedicated, intelligent,* or *perfectionist.* Instead, teachers should describe, in purely behavioral terms, what they like or don't like about students. "You have a lot of erasures and white-outs on your homework" versus "Your homework is sloppy." "You form your letters correctly" versus "You are a good writer."

4. *Use praise with caution.* Ginott believes many teachers use praise excessively and manipulatively to control student behavior rather than to acknowledge exceptional performance. They use praise judgmentally ("Horace, you are a good student"), confuse correctness with goodness (referring to a student who completes work with a minimum of mistakes as a "good child"), praise students performing minimally acceptable behavior as a way of influencing other students ("I like the way Joan is sitting in her seat"), and praise so often that the statements lose all significance and are not even heard by the students. Ginott urges teachers to use praise only to acknowledge exceptional performance and in terms that separate the deed from the doer, for example, "That essay showed a great deal of original thought and research."

5. *Elicit cooperation.* Once a teacher and student have identified behavioral concerns, Ginott encourages teachers to offer them alternatives to solving the problem rather than using coercive power to tell them what to do. "Cooperate, don't legislate," is a convenient maxim to remember this point.

6. *Communicate anger.* Teachers are people, too. They get frustrated and angry just like anyone else. Ginott believes teachers should express their feelings through the use of "I messages" instead of "you messages." The former focuses on your feelings about the behavior or situation that angered you ("You talked when the guest speaker was presenting, and I feel very unhappy and embarrassed by that"). The latter puts the focus on the students and typically accuses and blames ("You were rude to the guest speaker"). "I messages" should be used when you own the problem, that is, when you are the one who is angry or upset.

If you were to resolve a classroom management problem using the humanist tradition, you might have an open discussion with your students to draw their attention to the problem. Then you would invite their cooperation in developing mutually agreed rules and consequences. Finally, as problems arise, you would have individual conferences with your students during which you would use the preceding steps 1 through 6 to engage them in congruent communication.

Glasser's Cooperative Learning

Glasser (1998b, 1998c) points out that effective classroom managers create a learning environment where students want to be, develop mutually agreed standards of behavior that students must follow to remain in this environment, and conduct problem-solving conferences with those who violate the standards. Glasser advocates **cooperative learning** as a way to make the classroom a place learners want to be. Glasser believes classrooms emphasizing cooperative learning motivate all children to engage in learning activities. He believes whole-group instruction, in which students compete with one another for limited rewards, inevitably causes 50% of the students to be bored, frustrated, inattentive, or disruptive.

For Glasser, dealing with disruptive students is straightforward, given a classroom where students experience belonging, power, and freedom—in other words, a classroom the learner would regret leaving. Faced with a student who persists in violating classroom rules the group believes are essential, Glasser states that the teacher should hold a brief private conference with the student during which the student recalls the rules, and the teacher describes the disruptive behavior, asserts the need for following such rules, and makes clear the consequence for not obeying the rules, for example, removal from the room until the learner chooses to follow the rules. Glasser cautions teachers not to accept excuses from students for why they cannot control their own behavior. He disagrees with teachers who use socioeconomic or sociocultural conditions as scapegoats or excuses for learners not making the right choices. For Glasser, there can be no excuse for disrupting an environment designed to meet learners' needs. Furthermore, when faced with removal from such an environment, Glasser believes students will choose, and will not need to be forced, to behave.

Glasser has a clear directive for you as you begin to manage your classroom: Begin building a more friendly workplace based on principles of cooperative learning. He has specific recommendations:

- Develop with your students rules for the workplace.
- Get support from school administrators for having an area to which disruptive students can be removed.
- Have private conferences with disruptive students during which you stress the importance of right choices and accept no excuses for wrong ones.
- Follow through when students must be removed, but always allow them the opportunity to return when they choose to follow class rules.

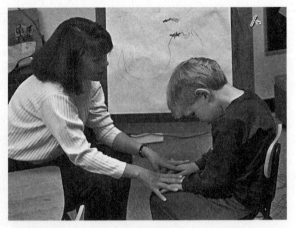

According to Glasser (1990) one response to disruptive behavior is discussing the problem with the student. During that time, you stress the importance of right choices and accept no excuses for wrong ones.

THE APPLIED BEHAVIOR ANALYSIS TRADITION IN CLASSROOM MANAGEMENT

The tradition of applied behavior analysis in classroom management is closely linked with Skinner's (1953) theory of learning called *behaviorism,* or *operant conditioning.* The techniques underlying the practice of behavior modification derive from this theory. Applications of behavior modification to changing socially important behaviors in the fields of education, business, and the social sciences has been called *applied behavior analysis.* To introduce both the strengths and weaknesses of this tradition, we first review the components of behavior modification that have resulted from this approach.

Behavior Modification

Behavior modification, as its name implies, focuses on changing or modifying behavior. Behavior is something a person does that is seen, heard, counted, or captured, say, in a snapshot or a home video.

Figure 6.1 summarizes some of the most important concepts of behavior modification. As Figure 6.1 indicates, when you want to teach a new behavior or make an existing behavior occur more frequently (for example, spell more words correctly), you must follow the behavior with some type of reinforcement. Reinforcement can be both positive and negative. **Positive reinforcement** occurs when a desired stimuli or reward you provide after a behavior increases in frequency of occurrence. **Negative reinforcement** occurs when the frequency of a behavior is increased by ending or terminating some painful, uncomfortable, or aversive state. In other words, the actions you take to turn off an annoying sound (shut the radio off), or relieve a headache (aspirin), or end a frustrating experience (walk away) will likely be repeated again (learned) the next time you experience a similar source of annoyance, discomfort, or frustration.

Negative reinforcement refers to escape or avoidance learning to strengthen the behavior, not simply to the application of discomfort or punishment. Thorndike (1913), for example, used negative reinforcement to teach cats how to escape a puzzle box. To get out of the box, the cat had to pull a cord hanging from the top of the box. As soon as the cat succeeded, the door opened and it escaped. The next time the cat was placed in the same box, the cat pulled the cord because it had learned how to escape to avoid the uncomfortable condition.

The reason negative reinforcement is important in the classroom is that learners often experience events they want to avoid: boring or difficult work, a scolding, requests to do something they do not want to do, or to stop doing something they want to continue. For example, when a shy student learns that when she does not look at the teacher the teacher stops calling on her, then the not-looking-at-the-teacher behavior becomes negatively reinforced by the teacher. The student repeats the behavior to achieve a more desirable state. Or

Figure 6.1 The process of behavior modification.

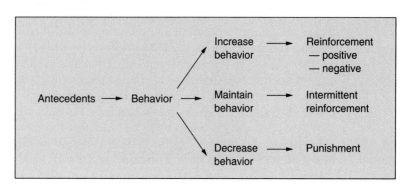

when a learner makes distracting sounds during a lesson to get the teacher to send him out of the room, the teacher negatively reinforces the making-of-annoying-sounds behavior. Or when some learners do not pay attention to get the teacher to stop the lesson, their not-paying-attention behavior becomes negatively reinforced. In other words, the teacher has taught (negatively reinforced) these learners to pursue certain behaviors to escape or avoid an unpleasant condition.

As these examples illustrate, a teacher may inadvertently fall into the trap of "negative reinforcement" that learners unconsciously set. In fact, some psychologists believe more inappropriate behavior is learned through negative than positive reinforcement, that is, by learning what it takes to avoid or escape something undesirable than by being rewarded for doing something appropriate (positive reinforcement) (Iwata, 1987).

When you are satisfied with a particular behavior and how frequently it occurs, intermittent reinforcement can be applied to maintain the behavior at its present level. For example, consider a student who at the start of the school year was consistently late and unprepared for class, but now is beginning to arrive on time. You can maintain this behavior by reinforcing the student on a random or intermittent schedule, for example, every second day, every fourth day, or on randomly selected days. This procedure is called **intermittent reinforcement.** An example of intermittent reinforcement is putting tokens into a slot machine long after your last win or fishing in the same spot long after your last nibble.

Behavioral antecedents are events (or stimuli) that are present when you perform a behavior that elicits or sets off the behavior. Antecedents can be sounds (for example, a noisy room influences students to become more noisy, an insult from a peer influences you to give an insult back, or the tone of voice in a teacher's demand influences a child to argue back), sights (the teacher raises finger to lips to indicate silence or flips the light switch on and off), people (the principal walks in, and everyone gets quiet), materials (math worksheets elicit a groan), or places (the auditorium elicits different behaviors from the principal's office). Behaviorists believe that much of our behavior has come under the control of antecedents (called *antecedent control*) because of the repeated pairing of reinforcers or punishers following the behavior with environmental stimuli (sounds, sights, people, and materials).

Applications of these principles to schools have produced a variety of systems or procedures for changing a student's behavior. Some of these procedures involve ignoring disruptive behavior and immediately reinforcing positive behavior. The assumption underlying these procedures is that disruptive students may have learned misguided ways of satisfying their needs for recognition. These disruptive behaviors will become less frequent when they learn they will only gain recognition and rewards (receive positive reinforcement) when they behave well.

Other systems are built on the assumption that children learn desired behavior most efficiently when adults immediately punish inappropriate behavior and immediately reward appropriate behavior. The authors of these systems believe behavior will improve more rapidly when adults use both timely punishment and timely reward rather than either punishment or reinforcement alone. These systems routinely involve such punishment procedures as *time-out*, where the teacher immediately removes the student to an area where he or she can experience no reinforcement of any kind following a disruptive act; *response cost*, where the teacher removes a student's privilege or reinforcer, contingent on disruptive behavior (also called fines); or *overcorrection*, where students not only make amends for what they did wrong but also go beyond it by contributing something positive. For example, a student who defaces a desk not only must clean the desk he wrote on but must clean every other desk in the room as well. Or a student who insults another student apologizes both to that student and to the whole class.

Although specific approaches may vary, if you were to invite an applied behavior analyst to help you with a behavior problem, he or she would likely suggest the following steps for improving a learner's behavior:

- Identify both the inappropriate behavior you wish to change and the appropriate behavior you want to take its place.
- Identify the antecedents to both the inappropriate and appropriate behavior (for example, influential peer), and make necessary changes in the classroom environment (for example, change seating arrangement) to prevent the former from occurring and to increase the likelihood of the latter.
- Identify the student's goal or purpose behind the inappropriate behavior (for example, attention seeking), and discontinue actions on your part (or those of peers) that satisfy this purpose.
- Establish procedures for reinforcing the appropriate behavior that you want to replace the inappropriate behavior.
- Use punishment only as a last resort.

THE CLASSROOM MANAGEMENT TRADITION

Throughout much of the latter half of the 20th century, classroom discipline was focused on the question of how best to respond to student misbehavior. The humanist and the applied behavior analysis approaches to classroom management shared the spotlight about equally during this period. As shown in the previous sections, both of these traditions are primarily reactive rather than preventive systems of classroom management. That is, they tend to emphasize solutions to misbehavior after rather than before it occurs. More recent writings, however, have provided another approach to classroom management that framed the question of classroom order and discipline, not in terms of reaction, but in terms of prevention. This approach was based on classroom research that examined what effective teachers do to prevent misconduct and what less effective teachers do to create it.

Some of this research involved observation and analysis of both experienced and inexperienced teachers while they taught. The major conclusion of this research was that more effective and less effective classroom managers can be distinguished more by what they do to prevent misbehavior than how they respond to misbehavior. In this section we explain how the researchers came to this conclusion and the characteristics of effective classroom managers they found. But first, let's look at one study of classroom management and how it was conducted.

Emmer, Evertson, and Anderson (1980) recruited 27 third-grade teachers in eight elementary schools into a year-long observation study. During the first 3 weeks of school, observers gathered several types of information on each of the teachers, including room arrangement, classroom rules, consequences of misbehavior, response to inappropriate behavior, consistency of teacher responses, monitoring, and reward systems. In addition, observers counted the number of students who were on-task or off-task at 15-minute intervals to determine the extent to which students were attending to the teacher. From these data the researchers classified the teachers into two groups, one consisting of the more effective managers and the other consisting of the less effective managers, for more in-depth observation the rest of the year.

Those teachers who were categorized as more effective classroom managers had significantly higher student engagement rates (more students actively engaged in the goals of the lesson) and significantly lower student off-task behavior (fewer reprimands and warnings) throughout the school year.

The more effective managers established themselves as instructional leaders early in the school year. They worked on rules and procedures until students learned them. Instructional content was important for these teachers, but they also stressed group cohesiveness and socialization, achieving a common set of classroom norms. By the end of the first 3 weeks, these classes were ready for the rest of the year.

In contrast to the more effective managers, the less effective managers did not have procedures well worked out in advance. This was most evident among the first-year teachers being observed. For example, the researchers described one new teacher who had no procedures for using the bathroom, pencil sharpener, or water fountain, and as a result, the children seemed to come and go, complicating the teacher's instructional tasks.

The poorer managers, like the better managers, had rules, but there was a difference in the way the rules were presented and followed up. In some cases, the rules were vague: "Be in the right place at the right time." In other cases, they were introduced casually without discussion, leaving it unclear to most children when and where a rule applied.

The poorer managers were also ineffective monitors of their classes. This was caused, in part, by the lack of efficient routines for pupil activities. In other cases this was the result of teachers removing themselves from the active surveillance of the whole class to work at length with a single child. A major result of the combination of vague and untaught rules and poor procedures for monitoring and establishing routines was that students were frequently left without sufficient guidance to direct their own activities.

One further characteristic of the less effective managers was that the consequences of good behavior and inappropriate behavior were either not in evidence in those classrooms or were not delivered in a timely manner. For example, sometimes teachers issued general criticisms that failed to identify a specific offender or a particular event. Some of these teachers would frequently threaten or warn children but not follow through, even after several warnings. This tended to allow children to push the teacher to the limits, causing more problems. Others issued vague disciplinary messages ("You're being too noisy") that were not adequately focused to capture the attention of any one child or subgroup of children to whom they were intended. It was easy to see how deficiencies in the areas of rules, establishment of routines, monitoring, and praise and reward structure negatively affected the overall management and organization of the classroom. Most of the time these deficiencies became windows of opportunity that prompted a wider range of pupil misconduct, off-task behavior, and disengagement from the goals of the classroom. After only a few weeks had elapsed in the less effective managers' classrooms, undesirable patterns of behavior and low teacher credibility tended to become established that persisted throughout the school year.

From this and related studies of classroom management (Emmer et al., 2006; Evertson, 1995; Tauber, 1990), we learn that effective classroom managers possess three broad classes of effective teaching behaviors:

- They devote extensive time before and during the first few weeks of school to planning and organizing their classroom to minimize disruption and enhance work engagement.
- They approach the teaching of rules and routines as methodically as they approach teaching their subject area. They provide their students with clear instructions about acceptable behavior and monitor student compliance with these instructions carefully during the first few weeks of school.
- They inform students about the consequences for breaking rules and enforce these consequences consistently.

As you can see, the classroom management tradition is essentially a preventive approach. It has a lot to say about how to ensure that behavior problems do not occur. But it offers few immediate solutions after the problem has occurred, because it emphasizes planning in anticipation of problems, not their resolution afterward. You will need a comprehensive plan incorporating elements of all three traditions to make your classroom a positive environment for learning.

AN INTEGRATED APPROACH TO CLASSROOM MANAGEMENT

All three approaches to classroom management have their advantages and limitations. Although each has made a significant contribution to our understanding of an effective classroom manager, teachers do not need to select one tradition over another. In fact, the research conducted by Emmer et al. (1980), Evertson et al., 2006; Evertson and Emmer (1982), and Doyle (1986) has shown that effective classroom managers are able to blend together the best parts of different approaches. Let's look at some of the ways effective teachers have been able to accomplish this.

Low-Profile Classroom Management

Rinne (1997) and Leriche (1992) have used the concept of **low-profile classroom management** to refer to coping strategies used by effective teachers to stop misbehavior without disrupting the flow of a lesson. These techniques are effective for "surface behaviors" (J. Levin & Nolan, 2003), which represent the majority of disruptive classroom actions. Examples of surface behaviors are laughing, talking out of turn, passing notes, daydreaming, not following directions, combing hair, doodling, humming, tapping, and so on. They are labeled **surface behaviors** because they are the normal developmental behaviors that children find themselves doing when confined to a small space with large numbers of other children. They do not indicate some underlying emotional disorder or personality problem. However, they can disrupt the flow of a lesson and the work engagement of others if left unchecked.

Figure 6.2 depicts the components of low-profile classroom management. Low-profile management for dealing with surface misbehavior is actually a set of techniques that requires *anticipation* by the teacher to prevent problems before they occur; *deflection* to redirect disruptive behavior that is about to occur; and *reaction* to unobtrusively stop disruptions immediately after they occur. Let's look at each of these.

Anticipation. Alert teachers have their antennas up to sense changes in student motivation, attentiveness, arousal level, or excitability as these changes are or are about to happen.

Figure 6.2
Characteristics of low-profile classroom management.

Anticipation	Deflection	Reaction
Lower Profile ←————————→		Higher Profile
• Scanning	• Proximity	• Warning
• Pick up the pace	• Eye contact	• Loss of privileges
• Remove temptation	• Prompting	• "Time-out"
• Boost interest	• Name dropping	• Removal
• Change seating arrangements	• Peer recognition	• Detention

They are aware that, at certain times of the year (before and after holidays), or week (just before a major social event), or day (right after an assembly or physical education class), the readiness of the class for doing work will be different from what usually can be expected. Skilled classroom managers are alert not only to changes in the groups' motivational or attention level but also to changes in specific individuals, which may be noticed as soon as they enter class.

At these times anticipation involves scanning back and forth with active eyes to quickly size up the seriousness of a potential problem and head it off before it emerges or becomes a bigger problem. For example, you may decide to pick up the pace of the class to counter some perceived lethargy in the class after a 3-day weekend or remove magazines or other objects that may distract attention from the individual or group before a long holiday. Some teachers maintain a reserve of activities likely to boost the interest of their students during times when it is difficult to stay focused on normal day-to-day activities. Others boost interest by forcing themselves to be more positive or eager in the face of waning student enthusiasm, for example, by raising and lowering the pitch of their voice and moving to different parts of the room more frequently. At other times it may be necessary to quickly change seating arrangements to minimize antagonisms when arguments between students occur. Anticipation involves not only knowing what to look for but also where and when to look for it. It also involves having a technique ready, no matter how small, for changing the environment quickly and without notice to your students to prevent the problem from occurring or escalating.

Deflection.   As noted, good classroom managers sense when disruption is about to occur. They are attuned to verbal and nonverbal cues that in the past have preceded disruptive behavior. The applied behavior analysts would call these behavioral cues *antecedents* or *precursors*. They take the form of a glance, an abruptly closed textbook, sitting and doing nothing, squirming, asking to be excused, ignoring a request, a sigh of frustration, or a facial expression of annoyance or anger. Although not disruptive by themselves, these behaviors may signal that more disruptive behavior is about to follow.

Some teachers can detect the significance of these antecedents and deflect them by simply moving nearer to the student who may be about to misbehave, thus preventing a more disruptive episode from occurring. Other teachers may make eye contact with the learner combined with certain facial expressions, for example, raising of eyebrows or slight tilt of the head, to communicate a warning. Both these techniques effectively use nonverbal signals to deflect a potential problem. But verbal signals are also effective. Verbal deflection techniques include *prompting*, where the teacher reminds the class of the rule or says, "We are all supposed to be doing math, now"; *name dropping*, when the target student's name is inserted into the teacher's explanation or presentation, as in, "Now if Angela were living in Boston at the time of the Boston Tea Party, she might have . . . "; and *peer recognition*, in which the teacher notices a peer engaged in appropriate behavior and acknowledges this to the class. As potential for the problem to escalate increases, the effective manager shifts from nonverbal to verbal techniques to keep pace with the seriousness of the misbehavior that is about to occur.

Reaction.   Anticipation and deflection can efficiently and unobtrusively prevent actions from disrupting the flow of a lesson. They allow students the opportunity to correct themselves, thus fostering the development of self-control. However, the classroom is a busy place, and you will have many demands on your attention, which may make a behavior difficult to anticipate or to deflect.

When disruptive behavior occurs that you cannot anticipate or unobtrusively redirect, your primary goal should be to end the disruptive episode as quickly as possible. Effective

Video Window

Low-Profile Classroom Management

In this video you will see two teachers, one in the elementary and another at the middle school, applying low-profile classroom management. You will see examples of anticipation, deflection, and reaction in response to student misbehavior in an effort to dispense with a problem quickly and not to disrupt the flow of the lesson. See if you can identify an instance of each of these three low-profile techniques and comment on their effectiveness in modifying the behavior of each student. Using the words in Figure 6.2 as your guide, describe what each teacher does to anticipate, deflect, and react in response to a student's behavior.

 To answer these questions online, go to the Video Windows *module for this chapter on the* Companion Website at www.prenhall.com/borich.

classroom managers, therefore, must at times react to a behavior by providing a warning or an incentive to promote positive self-control. Your reaction requires first that you have included among your class rules a rule that corresponds with the behavior in question and the consequences for violating the rule. Glasser (1998a) points out that an effective consequence for breaking a rule is temporary removal from the classroom—provided your classroom is a place where that student wants to be—or loss of privileges, school detention, loss of recess, or other activity the learner would miss.

When disruptive behavior occurs, your anticipation-deflection-reaction would be similar to the following:

1. As soon as a student disrupts the class, acknowledge a nearby classmate who is performing the expected behavior: "Carrie, I appreciate how hard you are working on the spelling words." Then wait 15 seconds for the disruptive student to change his or her behavior.
2. If the disruption continues say, "Carlos, this is a warning. Complete the spelling assignment and leave Carrie alone." Wait 15 seconds.
3. If the student doesn't follow the request after this warning, say, "Carlos, you were given a warning. You must now leave the room for 5 minutes (or you must stay inside during lunch or you cannot go to the resource center today). I'll talk to you about this during my free period."

Dealing with Persistent Disruptive Behavior

The low-profile techniques of anticipation, deflection, and reaction when used skillfully should promote lesson flow. Occasionally, when these techniques do not work for a particular student or group of students, it may be a signal that the needs of the student are not being met. When disruptive behavior persists and you have assured yourself you have taken low-profile steps to deal with it, you may need to increase the intensity of your involvement in responding to the problem.

Responses to Misbehavior

There are many responses at your disposal for dealing with misbehavior. You may choose to ignore an infraction if it is momentary and not likely to recur (for example, when students jump out of and back into their seats to stretch their legs after a long assignment). At the other extreme, you may call an administrator to help resolve the problem. Between these extremes are many alternatives, listed here in order of increasing severity:

- Look at the student sternly.
- Move closer to the student.
- Call on the student to provide the next response.
- Ask the student to stop.
- Discuss the problem with the student.
- Assign the student to another seat.
- Assign punishment, such as a writing assignment.
- Assign the student to detention.
- Write a note to the student's parents.
- Call the student's parents.

These alternatives vary in severity from simply giving the student a look of dissatisfaction to involving parents in resolving the problem. More important than the variety these alternatives offer, however, is your ability to match the correct response to the type of misbehavior that has occurred. One of the most difficult problems you will encounter in effectively maintaining classroom discipline will be deciding on a response that is neither too mild nor too severe (Emmer et al., 2006; Evertson et al., 2006; Sugai, 1996).

Although all rule violations consistently must receive some response, the severity of the consequence can and should vary according to the nature of the violation and the frequency with which such a violation has occurred in the past. If you respond too mildly to a student who has violated a major rule many times before, nothing is likely to change. If you respond too severely to a student who commits a minor violation for the first time, you will be unfair. Flexibility is important in the resolution of different discipline problems and must take into account both the context in which the violation occurs and the type of misbehavior that has occurred.

Here is some general advice for dealing with mild, moderate, and severe misbehavior:

- Mild misbehaviors like talking out, acting out, getting out of seat, disrupting others, and similar misbehaviors deserve a mild response, at first. But if they occur repeatedly, a moderate response may be appropriate. In unusual cases, such as continual talking that disrupts the class, a severe response may be warranted.
- Moderate misbehaviors like cutting class, abusive conduct toward others, fighting, and use of profanity deserve a moderate response, at first. But if these behaviors become frequent, a severe response may be warranted.
- Severe misbehaviors like theft, vandalism, incorrigible conduct, and substance abuse deserve a severe response. But do not try to handle incidents of these behaviors in your classroom. Immediately bring them to the attention of school administrators.

Table 6.1 presents some responses you can make to mild, moderate, and severe misbehavior.

Reinforcement Theory Applied in the Classroom

There are multiple ways to use your authority in managing discipline problems (you alone decide the consequence; you have students share in the responsibility; you choose the consequence from alternatives provided by the student) and multiple levels of response severity (from a stern glance to calling parents). But still more options exist. In this section you will learn how learners respond to reward and to punishment, why they respond to them differently, and how you can use them effectively in your classroom.

Table 6.1 Examples of mild, moderate, and severe misbehaviors and some alternative responses.

Misbehaviors	Alternative Responses
Mild misbehaviors	**Mild responses**
Minor defacing of school property or property of others	Warning
Acting out (horseplaying or scuffling)	Feedback to student
Talking back	Time-out
Talking without raising hand	Change of seat assignment
Getting out of seat	Withdrawal of privileges
Disrupting others	After-school detention
Sleeping in class	Telephone/note to parents
Tardiness	
Throwing objects	
Exhibiting inappropriate familiarity (kissing, hugging)	
Gambling	
Eating in class	
Moderate misbehaviors	**Moderate responses**
Unauthorized leaving of class	Detention
Abusive conduct toward others	Behavior contract
Noncompliant	Withdrawal of privileges
Smoking or using tobacco in class	Telephone/note to parents
Cutting class	Parent conference
Cheating, plagiarizing, or lying	In-school suspension
Using profanity, vulgar language, or obscene gestures	Restitution of damages
Fighting	Alternative school service (e.g., clean up, tutoring)
Severe misbehaviors	**Severe responses**
Defacing or damaging school property or property of others	Detention
Theft, possession, or sale of another's property	Telephone/note to parents
Truancy	Parent conference
Being under the influence of alcohol or narcotics	In-school suspension
Selling, giving, or delivering to another person alcohol, narcotics, or weapons	Removal from school or alternative school placement
Teacher assault or verbal abuse	
Incorrigible conduct, noncompliance	

Reinforcement theory states that behavior can be controlled by the consequences that immediately follow it. The word *controlled* means the consequences of a particular behavior can change the likelihood that the behavior will recur. Consider the following:

Event	Consequence	Future Event
You start going to the library to study.	Your test grades go up.	You begin going to the library more often.
You go to a new restaurant.	You get lousy service.	You never go there again.
You give your boyfriend or girlfriend a word of encouragement before a big test.	He or she gives you a kiss and a hug.	You give a word of encouragement before every big test.

When the consequence following a behavior changes the probability of that behavior's occurrence (test grades go up; you do not go there again; you get more kisses and hugs), reinforcement has occurred.

In your classroom, many events and their consequences will demonstrate the effects of reinforcement—whether you intend it or not. You may be surprised to learn you are unintentionally increasing the frequency of some misbehaviors in your classroom through reinforcement. How can this happen? Consider another sequence of behaviors that, unknown to you, may occur in your classroom:

Event	Consequence	Future Event
Shane cheats on a test.	He gets a good grade.	Shane plans to cheat again.
Carla passes a note to her boyfriend.	Her boyfriend is able to pass the note back.	Carla buys a special pad of perfumed paper for writing her notes.
Bobby skips school.	He earns $5 helping a friend work on a car.	Bobby plans to skip again the next time his friend needs help.

In each instance an undesirable behavior was reinforced (with a good grade, a returned note, $5). In each case the probability of recurrence increased because the consequence was desirable. In these examples, there is nothing you could have done, because your vigilance cannot be perfect: You didn't know about the cheating, the note, or that school was missed for the wrong reason. But here are some ways you may unwittingly reinforce undesirable behaviors, which you can do something about:

- A student complains incessantly that her essay was graded too harshly. To quiet her, you add a point to her score. Reinforced, she complains after every essay for the rest of the year.
- Parents complain to you about their child's poor class participation grade. You start calling on the student more often, probing and personally eliciting responses. Reinforced, the student believes she no longer needs to volunteer or raise her hand.
- A student talks back every time you call on him, so you stop calling on him. Reinforced, he does the same in his other classes, to be left alone.

In each of these cases, the link connecting the behavior, the consequence, and the students' perception of the consequence might not be immediately apparent to you. Nevertheless, reinforcement of an undesirable behavior occurred.

The problem in each instance was that you chose to remove the misbehavior in a way that rewarded the student, thereby actually reinforcing the misbehavior. Notice that in each case you considered the consequence of your actions *only from your own point of view* (for example, quieting an annoying student, preventing a parent from calling back, avoiding an ill-mannered student), without realizing your actions reinforced the very behavior you wished to discourage.

Now that you see how reinforcement theory works, here are some guidelines for making it work not against you but for you.

Rewards and Reinforcement. Many types of rewards and reinforcement are available to increase the probability of a desirable response. A reward or reinforcement can be external, delivered by some other person, or internal, provided by the learner himself or herself. Here are some familiar external rewards commonly found in the classroom:

- Verbal or written praise
- Smile, a head nod
- Special privileges (for example, visit to the learning center, library, etc.)
- Time-out of regular work to pursue a special project (e.g., science exhibit)
- Permission to choose a topic or assignment
- Getting to work in a group
- Extra points toward grade
- "Smiley face" stickers on assignments
- Note to parents on top of a test or paper
- Posting a good exam or homework for others to see
- Special recognitions and certificates (for example, "most improved," "good conduct award," "neatest," "hardest worker," etc.)

Not all of these external rewards may be equally reinforcing, however. Some learners may disdain verbal praise; others will have no desire to visit the library or learning center. Some students like to be called on; others may be too shy and dislike the added attention. A reinforcement for one student may be completely irrelevant to another.

Educators have sometimes been criticized for creating a generation of learners who are hooked on artificial or extrinsic rewards in order to learn and behave in classrooms. This has led to an increased interest in the use of internal rewards, also called **natural reinforcers.** An internal (natural) reward or reinforcer is one that is naturally present in the setting where the behavior occurs.

Some learners are naturally reinforced by learning to write, read, color, answer questions, play sports, solve equations, answer textbook questions, and write essays. But some are not.

Many learners may require external reinforcers to begin to engage in certain classroom activities they do not find naturally reinforcing. For such children, external reinforcers have an important role to play: They (1) allow you to shape and improve the behaviors you desire through the use of positive reinforcement and (2) enable you to transfer their control over the learner's behavior to natural reinforcers. This transfer from external to internal control is called **operant conditioning** (Horcones, 1992). Over the past decade, researchers have developed strategies for transferring the control of extrinsic reinforcers to that of natural reinforcers. Here are some steps they recommend:

Rewards consistent with the goals of your classroom and matched to student interests keep learners engaged in the learning process and responding at high rates of success.

Step 1. Select the target behavior. This could be forming letters correctly, solving multiplication problems, drawing geometric figures, bisecting angles, writing compositions, or whatever is appropriate.

Step 2. Identify the natural consequences of the selected behavior. For example, writing on a piece of paper produces many natural consequences: a scratching sound, the formation of letters, the filling up of a page, the gradual wearing away of a pencil point. Writing an essay has similar natural consequences but, in addition, produces sentences that express thoughts, ideas, images, and so on.

Step 3. Choose intrinsic consequences. From your list of natural consequences, select those likely to be reinforcing to the person and relevant to the purpose of the activity. For example, the formation of the letters is a more appropriate consequence to focus on than the scratching sound on the paper or the filling up of the page.

Step 4. Identify those consequences the learner may more easily notice. The more conspicuous the consequence to the learner, the easier it will be to condition this as a natural reinforcer. For example, the shape of a printed word is a conspicuous consequence of correct handwriting and may serve as a natural reinforcer. Likewise, writing a complete thought, coming up with an answer that matches that in the back of the textbook, or the feeling you get when something is finished can all serve as natural reinforcers.

Step 5. Design your lessons in such a way that you make conspicuous the occurrence of natural consequences. Rather than focusing only on the right answer to a problem, point out and describe for the learner the sequence involved. In general, focus on how something was done, not just on the end result. Some learners may not notice or direct their attention to the natural consequences of their work. By setting up instructional conditions to do this, you allow for natural reinforcers to acquire power over behavior.

Step 6. Select appropriate backup reinforcers. To transfer the power an extrinsic reinforcer has over behavior to a natural consequence, you must select extrinsic or backup reinforcers. These reinforcers should have educational value, be available in your classroom, and, ideally, involve you in the reinforcing activity (Horcones, 1991).

Step 7. Condition the natural reinforcer. Have your learners engage in the behavior. As soon as possible, give informational feedback, pointing out the natural consequences that you hope will become natural reinforcers. Immediately, give the backup reinforcers. Gradually, remove these reinforcers from the learning setting but continue to point out and illustrate the natural consequences of what the learner did. Gradually, point out the natural consequences less and less. Deliver and intermittently pair the backup reinforcers with the natural reinforcers.

Punishment

Punishment is used to decrease the probability or likelihood that a behavior will occur. For example, you can try to keep Daniel in his seat either (1) by giving him an extra assignment every time he is out of his seat or (2) by giving him a trip to the reading center for every 30 minutes he stays in his seat. In the first instance, you are giving Daniel a punishment to encourage him to do what is expected, and in the second you are giving him a reward to achieve this same end. Punishment creates an avoidance response to an undesirable behavior. In contrast, a reward encourages a desirable behavior to recur by dispensing something pleasant or rewarding immediately after the desirable behavior.

But rewards and punishments generally are not equally effective in promoting a desired behavior. Given two choices to keep Daniel in his seat—the punishment of extra homework or reward of something interesting to work on—the reward usually will be more successful. Here are several reasons:

Punishment does not guarantee the desired response will occur. The extra homework may indeed keep Daniel in his seat the next time he thinks of moving about, but it by no means ensures he will pursue the truly desired behavior, which is to perform some meaningful instructional activity while he is there. Instead, he can daydream, write notes to friends, or even pull Rebecca's hair. All succeed in keeping him from being punished again for getting out of his seat. Punishment in the absence of rewards can create other undesired behaviors.

The effects of punishment usually are specific to a particular context and behavior. This means extra homework is not likely to keep Daniel in his seat when a substitute teacher arrives, because it was not that teacher who assigned the punishment. Also, that punishment is not likely to deter Daniel from pulling Rebecca's hair, because the punishment was associated only with keeping him in his seat. Punishment rarely keeps one from misbehaving beyond the specific context and behavior to which it was most closely associated.

The effects of punishment can have undesirable side effects. If extra homework is truly an aversive for Daniel—if it is a highly undesirable and painful consequence in his eyes—he may decide never to risk leaving his seat again, even to ask for your assistance or to use the restroom. Daniel may decide to take no chances about leaving his seat and not even to trust his own judgment about when an exception to the rule may be appropriate.

Punishment sometimes elicits hostile and aggressive responses. Although any single punishment is unlikely to provoke an emotional response, students receive punishment in various forms all day long, both at school and at home. If your punishment is the "straw that breaks the camel's back," do not be surprised to observe an emotional outburst that is inconsistent with the amount of punishment rendered. When punishment is used, it should be used sparingly and in association with rewards.

The punishment can become associated with the punisher. If you use punishment consistently as a tool for increasing the likelihood a desirable behavior will occur, you may lose the cooperation you must have for managing your classroom effectively. With this cooperation gone, you will find the vital link for making management techniques work is gone. Plan not to solve every discipline problem by using punishment; otherwise, the punishment could become more strongly associated with you than the desired behavior you wish to encourage.

Punishment that is rendered to stop an undesired behavior, but is not immediately associated with the desired behavior, seldom has a lasting effect. If the desired behavior is not clear to your students at the time you administer punishment, they will see the punishment only as an attempt to hurt and not as an attempt to encourage the desired behavior.

Warnings.   Warnings can prevent minor problems from intensifying to where punishment is the only recourse. For the misbehaviors listed as mild in Table 6.1, it is not unusual to provide several warnings before dispensing some kind of consequence. However, after two or three warnings, you should assign some type of consequence, because waiting longer reinforces the student's belief that you are not serious about the misbehavior. This undermines the integrity of the rule being violated and your credibility.

Corporal Punishment.   Absent from the common responses to misbehavor listed in Table 6.1 is any form of corporal punishment, such as paddling a student. Such punishment, although permissible in some school districts when administered by a specifically designated school authority, generally has not proven effective in deterring misbehavior.

A reason is that the heightened emotion and anxiety on the part of the student (and the administrator) at the time of the punishment often prevent rational discussion of the appropriate behavior the punishment is supposed to encourage. In addition, corporal punishment easily can provoke aggression and cause hostility in both students and parents. This can outweigh any immediate benefit that might accrue from the punishment.

Generally, you should avoid physical contact with a student, because such contacts are easily misunderstood. This applies whether the contact is to administer punishment or, in the case of older students, is a reward (patting a student for doing a good job) or assistance (placing your arm around a student in times of high anxiety). Although your own judgment, the situation, and the age of the student will be your best guides, the only clear exception is a situation requiring your immediate assistance. Examples of such situations are breaking up a fight to prevent physical injury, curtailing the movement of a student who is hurting another, or restraining a student from self-injury. At such times, call an administrator as quickly as possible.

THE PARENT–TEACHER CONFERENCE

When a major infraction of a school or classroom rule has occurred or the motivation to learn is seriously lacking, more effective than any other form of response is the parent–teacher conference. This is your opportunity to inform one or both parents of the severity of the problem and for eliciting their active help in preventing it. Without the support of the student's family in providing the appropriate response at home, there is little chance that interventions at school will have a lasting effect in correcting the problem and deterring its occurrence at another time (Lawrence-Lightfoot, 2003; Rotter, Robinson, & Fey, 1987).

Being grounded for the week, having to be in at a certain time, completing extra study time in the quiet of one's bedroom, or performing extra chores around the house always will have more impact than any aversive that can be administered during the school day, as long as they are administered with a clear understanding of the desired classroom behavior (Rich, 1987).

Notifying parents that a conference is desired usually is your responsibility, if the request for a conference is the result of a specific problem in your classroom. This notification should consist of a call or letter expressing to the parent(s) or guardian the following:

1. Purpose of the conference, including a statement of the joint goal of supporting the student's success in school
2. Statement or comment pointing out the integral role of the parent(s) or guardian in the discipline management process (this may include a citation from state or school policy regarding such matters)
3. Possible dates, times, and location of conference
4. A contact person and phone number, if a parent is unable to reach you directly

If you request a conference with the student's parents by phone, be sure to ask the parent to record the date, time, location, and contact person for the conference at the time of the call. During the conference, do the following:

- Try to gain the parents' acknowledgment of the problem and their participation in the discipline management process.
- Present a plan of action for addressing the problem at home and at school.
- Identify follow-up activities (for example, note home each week indicating progress, immediate phone call if problem should recur, a review of the situation at the next parent–teacher night).
- Document what took place at the conference for future reference, including the agreements and disagreements.

Conducting the Parent Conference

In addition to these general guidelines, during the parent conference, you will be expected to talk plainly, listen, and use "I messages" (Swap, 1987).

Plain Talk. New teachers—particularly when they first meet parents or address them at group meetings—rely on familiar jargon, terms such as *norms, developmental needs, heterogeneous grouping, cognitive skills, higher-order thinking*, which may mean little to some parents. Jargon, however familiar to you, will diminish rather than increase your credibility with parents.

Listen. Listening is your most important communication skill. Parents, particularly when they are upset, want to be heard. One of the most frequent complaints leveled by parents against teachers is that they do not listen. The Appalachian Educational Laboratory (Shalaway, 1999) offers the following list of hints for you to become a good listener:

1. Maintain eye contact: Face the parent and lean forward slightly.
2. Nod or give other noninterrupting acknowledgments. The parent will want to know you are listening.
3. When the parent pauses, allow him or her to continue without interrupting. Wait to add your comments until the speaker is finished.
4. Ignore distractions, such as others seeking your attention during the conference.
5. Check your understanding by summarizing the essential aspects of what the parent tried to say or the feeling he or she tried to convey.
6. Ask for clarification when necessary.

This last skill requires active listening. It is particularly valuable during reactive parent conferences—or conferences requested by parents who are upset over something they perceive you said or did. Such conferences can be emotionally charged. Teachers typically take a defensive or aggressive posture when confronted by an angry parent. Rather than listen to what the parents have to say—regardless of how inaccurate it may seem—the teacher follows the parents' statement with a denial, or a defensive statement, or a refusal to talk further.

Active listening is when the listener provides feedback to the speaker on the message heard and the emotion conveyed and opens doors to further communication by letting the speaker know she or he was being understood and respected. Active listening is an essential communication skill to be used with the parents of learners and the learners themselves. It requires the ability to concentrate on what someone is saying even when you strongly object to what is being said. Like any skill, it must be practiced before you can use it naturally and automatically.

Use "I Messages" to Express Your Feelings. Particularly when you are upset about the actions of a learner or the words and actions of a parent, it is important to clearly communicate your feelings. However, the way to do this is not by criticizing or blaming (with a "you message") but rather by describing (1) what you find offensive, (2) the feeling or emotion you experience when the offensive condition occurs, and (3) a statement of the reason for the feeling. For example, "When Amanda talks back to me, her behavior is disruptive to the entire class, and that makes me angry because I have to take time away from all the other students in the class to deal with her." This message is right on target—it focuses on your reaction to the problem rather than on what the child said or did. It opens up positive avenues to further communication.

Evaluating the Parent Conference

Following the conference, summarize what was said and agreed on, and make a list of any actions to be taken by you or the parent. Make follow-up calls, send notes, and follow through on whatever you committed yourself to. Finally, take a moment to reflect on how well you communicated with the parents and achieved your goals and what you might change or do differently the next time you have a parent conference. This moment of reflection will be one of the most important aids to sharpening your parent conferencing skills. See In Practice: Getting Parents Involved.

IN PRACTICE

Focus on Getting Parents Involved

Adapted from Increasing Student Engagement and Motivation: From Time-on-Task to Homework, *by Cori Brewster & Jennifer Fager, October 2000, Northwest Regional Educational Laboratory. www.nwrel.org/request/oct00/textonly.html.*

Active parent involvement has been associated with numerous benefits for students, including increasing student motivation and engagement in school. When it comes to homework, though, parent involvement can take many different shapes, not all of which have a positive impact on learning. When working to increase student engagement and motivation, it is important to include parents and discuss ways they can support their children's learning both at school and at home (Patton, 1994; Paulu, 1998).

First, it is important that parents understand what role teachers expect them to play, especially in terms of homework (Gaillard, 1994; Paulu, 1998). What one parent views as helping out, a teacher might perceive as interference or cheating. And what a teacher might take for granted that parents can do—such as signing off on homework or checking spelling words—a parent may not have the skills or the time to follow through on. Clearly, it is important to communicate with parents about how to best help children learn. It is also necessary for educators to be sure their expectations are realistic, given parents' skills and schedules (Paulu, 1998).

It is equally important to be clear with parents about what kinds of involvement are actually beneficial to students. Studies have shown that parents who offer rewards for grades, or who punish students for poor performance, may actually decrease students' motivation to do well (Dev, 1997; Patton, 1994). Fear of punishment, anxiety about meeting parents' expectations, and worrying about being compared to siblings not only cause stress for students, but can also detract from their intrinsic motivation and interest in learning (Dev, 1997). This is not to say that parents shouldn't be invested in how their children are doing in school. Rather, it suggests that there are more productive ways for them to be involved and show their interest in students' progress.

To help children be successful with work at home and at school, parents can:

- *Create a place at home that is conducive to studying (Patton, 1994; Paulu, 1998).* Good study environments are well lit and quiet. Although every child's learning style is different, most educators agree that students do best when the television is off and the student is free from distractions (Gaillard, 1994; Paulu, 1998).
- *Set aside a specific time for homework each day (Paulu, 1998).* This might involve limiting television-watching or phone calls until homework is finished (Gaillard, 1994). Parents should be careful, though, not to pit homework against activities students enjoy, or to create situations in which students rush through their work in order to get back to other activities (Black, 1996). Paulu (1998) notes that family routines—which include set homework times—have been linked to higher student achievement.
- *Make sure students have all the supplies they need (Paulu, 1998).* Parents should check in with students ahead of time about the kinds of projects they will be doing: It might be tough to find a calculator or a report cover at 9:00 the night before an assignment is due.
- *Be available if students have questions.* Parents can support their children by looking over homework and giving suggestions, but should not do the homework for them (Paulu, 1998).
- *Make an effort to communicate regularly with teachers (Corno, 1996).* If necessary, parents should ask teachers to clarify their expectations. It is also a good idea to find out ahead of time what kinds of resources—such as tutors or services for second language students—are available to students if they need help.

- *Avoid linking rewards or punishment to school performance (Dev, 1997).* While it is important for parents to recognize students' achievements, they should avoid external motivators for performance. Instead, parents should emphasize the value of learning and show they appreciate their child's hard work (Patton, 1994).

These expectations can be sent home to parents at the beginning of school and made available at Parent-Teacher night.

Related Link:

For more about parent involvement see *Parent Partners: Using Parents to Enhance Education* at *www.nwrel.org/request/march99/index.html.*

THE INFLUENCE OF HOME AND FAMILY ON CLASSROOM BEHAVIOR PROBLEMS

Finally, it is important to note that some of the discipline problems you will face in your classroom have their origin at home. Living in a fast-paced, upwardly mobile society has created family stresses and strains that our grandparents could not have imagined. Their lives while growing up were not necessarily any easier than yours or your students' lives, but they were most assuredly different, particularly in the intensity and rapidity with which children today experience developmental stages and life cycle changes.

For example, by some estimates, boys and girls are maturing earlier than they did 50 years ago. This means they come under the influence of the intense emotions of sex, aggression, love, affiliation, jealousy, and competitiveness far earlier than our own parents may have. Teachers in the elementary grades are no longer surprised by the depth of understanding and ability of young students to emulate the media's attractively packaged images of adult behavior and lifestyles, especially as they relate to clothes, relationships, and dominance.

Although not often recognized, these generational differences sometimes are even more difficult for parents to accept than for you, the teacher. This often leads to major conflicts at home that surface in your classroom as seemingly minor but persistent misbehaviors. You can have little influence over home conflicts, except to understand they originate in the home and not in your classroom. In other words, there may be times when no amount of reward will seem to work, because the source of the problem is within the home and may be far more serious than you suppose—including marital discord, verbal or physical abuse, competition among siblings, financial distress, and divorce. One or more of these family disturbances could be occurring in the families of some of your students.

These are not trivial burdens for students, especially when combined with the social and academic demands of school, the uncertainties of a future job or education, and the developmental "crises" that school-age children feel between youth and adulthood (Erikson, 1968). If a problem persists and your efforts to resolve it are to no avail, consider the possibility that such a family problem may be occurring. Although there is no easy way to know what is happening in the lives of your students at home, many students welcome the opportunity to reveal the nature of these problems, when they are asked. For some it will be just the opportunity they have sought to shed some of the emotional burden these events are creating in their lives.

It is not your role to resolve such problems, but knowing the reason they are occurring may explain why your solutions to a behavioral problem may not be working. Knowing the

Video Window

The Parent–Teacher Conference

In this video, you will listen in on two parent–teacher conferences in which the parents are confronted with a problem with their child. You will watch how two teachers deal with both cooperative and uncooperative parents and how with the proper approach they turn these parents in a constructive and cooperative direction for resolving their child's problem. Specifically, you will see how to listen to parents so you can hear their concerns, cite specific instances of the problem their child is having, avoid jargon and technical language that can confuse and distance parents, remain nonjudgmental, and, finally, seek to empower parents to become active participants working with you. See if you can identify and describe instances of how these teachers:

- Gain the parents' acknowledgment of the problem and their participation in the management process.
- Present a plan of action for addressing the problem at home and at school.
- Identify follow-up activities for remediating the problem.
- Document what takes place at the conference, including agreements and disagreements.

 To answer these questions online, go to the Video Windows *module for this chapter on the* Companion Website *at www.prenhall.com/borich.*

reason also can help you decide whether to refer the problem to other professionals who are in a position to help, such as a social worker, school nurse, or school psychologist.

CULTURALLY RESPONSIVE CLASSROOM MANAGEMENT

One of the most encouraging advances in the understanding of classroom management is the emerging field of **culturally responsive teaching.** As we saw in previous chapters, the writings and research of Bowers and Flinders (1991), Gay (2000), Tharp (1997), and Tharp and Gallimore (1989) present convincing arguments that different cultures react differently to nonverbal and verbal behavior management techniques, including proximity control, eye contact, warnings, and classroom arrangement. Furthermore, they cite numerous examples of how teachers of one culture interpret disruptive behaviors of children differently from those of another culture. Therefore, be aware that many of the behavioral management techniques presented in this and chapter 5 may be culturally sensitive and that the effective classroom manager matches not only the technique he or she uses with the situation but also with the cultural history of the learner.

If the research supporting culturally responsive teaching has yet to provide explicit prescriptions for teaching culturally different learners, what does it tell us about better understanding students in multicultural classrooms?

The traditional method of conducting classroom research is to study large groups of teachers, classify their teaching methods, give learners achievement tests, and try to find relationships between achievement test scores and particular teaching practices. D. Dillon (1989), however, used a different approach. She studied one teacher, Mr. Appleby, and his class for a year using a research method called *microethnography*. Her study provided valuable insights into what a teacher can do to create a classroom where culturally different learners experience academic and personal success.

Dillon concludes that Appleby's effectiveness as a classroom teacher was due to his ability to assume the role of "translator and intercultural broker" between the middle-class white culture of the school and the lower-class African American culture of his students. As a cultural broker and translator, Appleby was thoroughly knowledgeable about the backgrounds of his learners and, as a result, he was able to bridge the differences between school and community/home cultures. He had acquired a high degree of what Lustig and Koester (1998) call **intercultural competence** (DeMeulenaere, 2001). With this cultural knowledge, Appleby created a classroom with three significant attributes:

1. He created a social organization in which teacher and learners knew one another, trusted one another, and felt free to express their opinions and feelings.
2. He taught lessons built around the prior knowledge and experiences of his learners. Because of his knowledge of his learners' background, he was familiar with their knowledge, skills, and attitudes toward the content. This knowledge allowed him to represent the subject matter in ways that encouraged his students to link it with what they already knew and felt.
3. He used instructional methods that allowed learners to actively participate in lessons, to use the language and sociolinguistic patterns of their culture, and to use the language and social interaction patterns both he and his learners were familiar with.

Antón-Oldenburg (2000), H. M. Miller (2000), and Lustig and Koester (1998) conclude that what teachers need to know in order to teach successfully in multicultural classrooms has more to do with knowing the values, socialization practices, interests, and concerns of their learners than with knowing about presumed learning style preferences and cognitive styles and the do's and don'ts of teaching learners with these traits. Rather, researchers believe the cultural knowledge teachers such as Appleby have about their learners allows them to represent subject-matter content in ways that are meaningful to students, to develop lessons that gain their active participation, and to create social organizations in the classroom within which learners feel free to be themselves.

SUMMING UP

This chapter introduced you to some classroom management concepts and techniques for promoting student engagement. Its key terms and main points were:

The Humanist Tradition in Classroom Management

1. Most classroom discipline problems are low intensity, continuous, and unconnected with any larger, more serious event.
2. The humanist tradition of classroom management focuses on the inner thoughts, feelings, psychological needs, and emotions of the individual learner. Humanist approaches emphasize the importance of allowing the student time to control his or her own behavior.
3. Ginott's "sane messages" communicate to students that their behavior is unacceptable but in a manner that does not blame, scold, or humiliate.
4. Glasser's cooperative learning emphasizes building a more friendly workplace that the learner would regret leaving because of misbehavior, if told to do so.
5. The humanist tradition focuses on developing rules, getting support from school administrators, holding private conferences with students, and following through when students must be removed from the classroom.

The Applied Behavior Analysis Tradition in Classroom Management

6. The applied behavior analysis tradition of classroom management applies the techniques of

operant conditioning to change socially important behaviors.

7. Behavior modification focuses on changing or modifying behavior by following a behavior with some type of reinforcement.

8. Positive reinforcement occurs when a desired stimuli or reward is provided after a desired behavior to increase its frequency.

9. Negative reinforcement occurs when a painful, uncomfortable, or aversive state is avoided to achieve a more desirable state.

10. Antecedents are events or stimuli present when you perform a behavior that elicits or sets off the behavior, such as sounds, sights, or people.

11. The applied behavior analysis tradition focuses on identifying the appropriate and inappropriate behavior, identifying antecedents that could trigger these behaviors, the student's goal for the misbehavior, and procedures for reinforcing the appropriate behavior.

The Classroom Management Tradition

12. The classroom management tradition frames the question of classroom order and discipline, not in terms of reaction, but in terms of prevention.

13. The classroom management tradition focuses on planning and organizing the classroom, teaching rules and routines, and informing students of the consequences of breaking the rules.

An Integrated Approach to Classroom Management

14. Low-profile classroom control refers to coping strategies used by effective teachers to stop misbehavior without disrupting the flow of a lesson.

Dealing with Persistent Disruptive Behavior

15. Three ways to apply your authority in dealing with misbehavior are as follows:
    - You alone judge what occurred and what the punishment should be.
    - You provide some alternative forms of punishment from which the student must choose.
    - You select a punishment from alternatives that the students provide.

16. The level of severity with which you respond to a misbehavior should match the misbehavior that has occurred.

Reinforcement Theory Applied in the Classroom

17. The idea behind reinforcement theory is that any behavior can be controlled by the consequences that immediately follow it. When the consequences that follow a behavior change the probability of the behavior's recurrence, reinforcement has occurred.

18. Some misbehaviors that occur in classrooms are unintentionally increased through reinforcement, in which case the probability of the misbehavior increases because a consequence that follows the misbehavior is perceived as desirable by the student.

19. Both rewards and punishment can increase the probability of a behavior, although punishment without reward is rarely effective.

20. Punishment in the absence of rewards tends to be less effective in increasing the probability of a desired behavior for the following reasons:
    - Punishment does not guarantee the desirable response will occur.
    - The effects of punishment are specific to a particular context.
    - The effects of punishment can spread to undesirable behavior.
    - Punishment can create hostile and aggressive responses.
    - Punishment can become associated with the punisher.

21. After two or three warnings, a punishment should be assigned.

22. Corporal punishment is rarely effective in deterring misbehavior.

The Parent-Teacher Conference

23. One feature of the parent–teacher conference that accounts for its effectiveness is the involvement of the parent in eliminating the misbehavior.

24. During the parent conference, you are expected to talk plainly, listen and use "I messages."

Culturally Responsive Classroom Management

25. Culturally responsive teaching represents the teacher's ability to react to different cultures with different verbal and nonverbal classroom management techniques.

26. Intercultural competence refers to the teacher's ability to act as a translator and intercultural broker between students of different cultures, ethnicities, and social classes.

KEY TERMS

Active listening,   211
Applied behavior analysis,   193
Behavior modification,   197
Behavioral antecedents,   198
Classroom management tradition,   193
Congruent communication,   194
Cooperative learning,   196
Culturally responsive teaching,   214
Humanist tradition,   193

Intercultural competence,   215
Intermittent reinforcement,   198
Low-profile classroom management,   201
Natural reinforcers,   207
Negative reinforcement,   197
Operant conditioning,   207
Positive reinforcement,   197
Surface behaviors,   201

DISCUSSION AND PRACTICE QUESTIONS

Questions marked with an asterisk are answered in appendix B. See also the Companion Website for this text at *www.prenhall.com/borich* for more assessment options.

*1. What are six criteria for developing an effective classroom management plan? Which, in your opinion, will be the easiest to achieve in your classroom, and which will be the most difficult?

*2. What are several specific recommendations Glasser would have you do as you begin to manage your classroom? Which do you feel is (are) the most important?

*3. How might you use both positive and negative reinforcement to stop a student from repeatedly talking? Use an example of each to make your point.

*4. Describe time-out and response cost. What would be a classroom situation in which you would use each of these?

*5. According to research studies of classroom management, what are three broad classes of preventive classroom management techniques? List the three in order of least to most difficult to implement at your grade level.

*6. In what ways can you use your authority to assign consequences to a student for misbehaving? Which would you feel most comfortable using?

7. For the following misbehaviors, identify a consequence that reflects the severity of the offense. Do not use the same response more than once.

• Talking back
• Cutting class
• Eating in class
• Jumping out of seat
• Sleeping in class
• Acting out
• Obscene gesturing
• Selling or using drugs
• Fighting

8. What reward would you give to get a student to do each of the following?
• Homework
• Stop talking
• Stop talking back
• Turn in assignments on time
• Be on time for class
• Remember to bring pen and pencil
• Not talk without raising hand

*9. What steps would you follow to transfer the control from an extrinsic reinforcer to that of a natural reinforcer? Identify a reinforcer at your grade in which you might follow these steps.

*10. Identify five reasons why punishment is rarely effective in the absence of rewards. Looking back at your own school days, which seems the most true for you?

*11. What are the two objectives for having a parent–teacher conference discussed in this chapter? What might be some others?

FIELD EXPERIENCE ACTIVITIES

*1. Describe what Ginott calls "sane messages," and compose an example at your grade level using teacher dialogue.

*2. Using an example of teacher dialogue, provide an example of an "I message" to communicate your disappointment to a student.

3. Create a brief teacher–student dialogue that describes a low-profile anticipation-deflection-reaction sequence directed to a child who leaves a seat without permission.

*4. Using a specific example in the classroom, under what two conditions is the use of punishment most effective?

5. In your own words, what is meant by culturally responsive classroom management? Provide a scenario of how you would respond in a culturally responsive manner to a student who failed to complete a homework assignment. What might a culturally unresponsive reply be in this situation?

DIGITAL PORTFOLIO ACTIVITIES

The following digital portfolio activities relate to INTASC principles 9 and 10.

1. Imagine having to conduct a teacher–parent conference concerning a student's failure to complete assignments on time. Prepare some "talking points" in an outline format that you want to be sure to bring up during the conference. Your talking points should include:
   - What you would do to gain the parents' acknowledgment of the problem
   - A plan of action for addressing the problem at home and at school
   - Follow-up activities that would monitor that progress is being made
   - A summary or restatement of the agreements made between you and the parent

   Place your talking points in the *Classroom Management* folder of your digital portfolio as a reminder of key issues to discuss during a parent–teacher conference.

2. In Field Experience Activity 5 you provided a scenario of how you would respond in a culturally responsive manner to a student who failed to complete a homework assignment. Place this scenario in the *Classroom Management* folder of your digital portfolio as a reminder of a reply that would be culturally responsive.

CLASSROOM OBSERVATION ACTIVITIES

The following classroom observation activities relate to INTASC principle 5.

1. Use the record for *Observing Low-Profile Classroom Control* provided on the Companion Website at *www.prenhall.com/borich* for this chapter to record each occurrence you observe of anticipation, nonverbal deflection, verbal deflection, and reaction techniques in a classroom or from a classroom video. Write down any other responses that you believe represent low-profile classroom control. Add up how many times you observed each example of low-profile classroom control. Which was used most often? Which were used least often or not at all? Place the low-profile classroom control record into the *Classroom Management* folder of your digital portfolio for use in future observations.

2. Use the *Checklist for Observing Dimensions of Classroom Management* to record whether a classroom arrangement matches the instructional goals of the teacher, has preestablished classroom rules, exhibits use of instructional routines, uses incentives to promote appropriate behavior, and uses low-profile

classroom management. At the end of your observation, add a brief description to each box, highlighting at least one specific reason why you placed each of your checkmarks as you did. Place the checklist into the *Classroom Management* folder of your digital portfolio for future use in observing classroom management.

CHAPTER CASE HISTORY AND PRAXIS TEST PREPARATION

DIRECTIONS: The following case history pertains to chapter 6 content. After reading the case history, answer the short-answer question that follows and consult appendix D to find different levels of scored student responses and the rubric used to determine the quality of each response. You also have the opportunity to submit your responses online to receive feedback by visiting the *Case History* module for this chapter on the Companion Website, where you will also find additional questions pertaining to Praxis test content.

Case History

Mr. Scott's tenth-grade English class has just finished a unit on Shakespeare's *Julius Caesar*. Today he wants to have a discussion that will crystallize some of the key concepts from the play. He also hopes a fruitful discussion will help prepare the class for the upcoming test over this material. However, in the past, discussions have been marred by many disruptions, such as talking out of turn, interrupting others, and a flurry of requests for hall passes to the bathroom because "we're not doing anything for a grade right now."

Today, Mr. Scott introduces the concept of a graded discussion. So he can keep the discussion focused, he has selected Susan to record the student contributions. Susan is an "A" student, but she tends to dominate classroom exchanges, and students sometimes wait for her ideas rather than volunteering their own. Some even get resentful and refuse to answer at all. Susan will be guaranteed a 110, the highest grade, for her task of recording student contributions, but she will not be able to contribute to the discussion. The next recorder will be selected from those who get the maximum score in today's discussion.

Susan will sit in the front of the classroom with a copy of the seating chart and will put a check down for every comment a student makes. For the comment to be counted, the student must raise his or her hand and be acknowledged by Mr. Scott before talking. For certain responses, such as ideas that build on the comments of other students or for answers to particularly hard questions, the student may receive two checks. Every check counts as 5 points.

Every student who arrives in class promptly will begin with a base score of 70. Those who are late will begin with a 10-point deduction from that base score. The maximum score is 110 and will count as one section of the unit test.

Mr. Scott tosses out the initial question. "Many scholars accept that the protagonist of the play is the title character, Julius Caesar, but others suggest it is really Brutus who dominates and wrestles with the moral dilemmas that charge the action. What do you think? Be sure to give reasons for your opinions."

Everyone looks to Susan, whose opinion must be the right one, and she squirms in her seat with obvious frustration. After a short pause wherein all realize they cannot depend on her, Jeremy raises his hand. "Now that I think of it, I think the second guys are right. It's really Brutus who we care about. When Caesar was killed, I didn't feel that bad. He almost deserved it the way he was acting, like he was high and mighty, but I really felt bad when Brutus killed himself." Mr. Scott checks to see that Susan has recorded a check for Jeremy and points to Juanita.

"I don't know if you have to feel bad when someone dies for them to be the main character in a play, but you said something that got me thinking, Jeremy. Caesar dies in the third act. We have almost half the play without him, but Brutus sticks in there until the end."

"Juanita, you were really a good listener and built on Jeremy's idea. Make sure she gets two checks for her comments, Susan."

Mack, who has been hurriedly arranging his notebook and books after his late arrival to class, raises his hand. "Sure, he dies in the third act, but don't forget his ghost in Act IV. And Brutus even mentions Caesar's name when he kills himself—'I killed not thee with half so good a will' or something like that. So I think he's there in spirit throughout the whole play."

"Well, Mack, your responses not only built on Juanita's idea, but you even paraphrased an actual quote from the play. You have now recovered from the 10-point deduction for being late."

Andrea bursts in with, "What about Antony, Mr. Scott?"

Before she can continue, Mr. Scott puts his hands up to his ear, pretending not to hear. "I can't hear anyone who doesn't raise their hand."

Andrea raises her hand and waits for Mr. Scott to nod before she continues.

"'Friends, Romans, Countrymen, I come to bury Caesar, not to praise him . . .' I mean, that is the coolest speech ever. He had the whole audience in the palm of his hand. That was really a climactic moment in the whole play."

"So now we have three candidates for protagonist: Caesar, Brutus, and Antony. Any opinions on that newest idea?" A wave of hands goes up. No one is waiting for cues from Susan now.

Short-Answer Question

This section presents a sample Praxis short-answer question. In appendix D you will find sample responses along with the standards used in scoring these responses.

DIRECTIONS: The following question requires you to write a short answer. Base your answer on your knowledge of principles of learning and teaching from chapter 6. Be sure to answer all parts of the question.

1. A time-honored consequence for classroom tardiness is after-school detention or some other mild punishment. In today's lesson, Mr. Scott incorporates tardiness into his grading scheme by taking away 10 points from the discussion grade for those late to class. However, students can regain these lost points by making positive contributions to the commentary. Discuss some positive and some negative aspects of Mr. Scott's way of dealing with tardiness in the preceding case history.

Discrete Multiple-Choice Questions

DIRECTIONS: Each of the multiple-choice questions that follow is based on Praxis-related pedagogical knowledge in chapter 6. Select the answer that is best in each case and compare your results with those in appendix D. See also the Companion Website for this text at *www.prenhall.com/borich* for more assessment options.

1. Tina was a strong student who did all her assignments with accuracy and in a timely manner. She could be counted on to make valuable contributions to classroom discussions as well. But she always put up her books several minutes before the bell, and Mrs. Brooks made her stay one minute after class each time she did so. After a few times Tina stopped putting things away early, but she also stopped contributing to class discussions. Which statement about the effects of punishment best explains Tina's actions?
    a. Punishment does not guarantee that the desired responses will occur.
    b. The effects of punishment usually are specific to a particular context and behavior.
    c. The effects of punishment can have undesirable side effects.
    d. Punishment sometimes elicits hostile and aggressive responses.

2. Which of the four approaches to classroom order and discipline focuses almost exclusively on prevention of rather than reaction to behavior problems?
    a. The humanistic tradition
    b. The applied behavior analysis tradition
    c. The classroom management tradition
    d. The integrated approach to classroom management

3. Which of the following is of foremost importance in developing a culturally responsive classroom?
    a. Lessons are built around the prior knowledge and experience of learners.
    b. Lessons are built around learning style preferences and cognitive styles.
    c. Lessons are built around a set of rules and consistent enforcement of them.
    d. Lessons involve direct instruction followed by drill and practice.

4. Which of the following responses by the teacher would be an example of low-profile classroom management when Amanda is talking to Rhona, who is trying to work on her math assignment?
    a. "Rhona, tell the class what our rules are about talking in class."
    b. "Rhona, I can see how hard you are trying to work on the math assignment."
    c. "Amanda and Rhona, if you continue to talk I will ask you to leave the classroom."
    d. "Amanda, why not tell us what you are talking to Rhona about."

Chapter 7

Teaching Strategies for Direct Instruction

This chapter will help you answer the following questions and meet the following INTASC principles for effective teaching:

1. What is the direct instruction model?
2. How do I organize lesson content for direct instruction?
3. How can I encourage my learners to actively respond during direct instruction?
4. What are some ways of promoting the goals of direct instruction in a culturally diverse classroom?

INTASC 1: The teacher understands the central concepts, tools of inquiry, and structures of the discipline(s) he or she teaches and can create learning experiences that make these aspects of subject matter meaningful for students.

INTASC 2: The teacher understands how children learn and develop and can provide learning opportunities that support their intellectual, social, and personal development.

INTASC 4: The teacher understands and uses a variety of instructional strategies to encourage students' development of critical thinking, problem solving, and performance skills.

INTASC 5: The teacher uses an understanding of individual and group motivation and behavior to create a learning environment that encourages positive social interaction, active engagement in learning, and self-motivation.

*O*ur chapter on lesson planning presented seven instructional events that form the structure of a lesson plan:

1. *Gaining attention*
2. *Informing the learner of the objective*
3. *Stimulating recall of prerequisite learning*
4. *Presenting the stimulus material*
5. *Eliciting the desired behavior*
6. *Providing feedback*
7. *Assessing the behavior*

To add flesh to this structure, this and subsequent chapters present different instructional strategies by which these seven events can be implemented. This chapter presents strategies for direct teaching that include explanations, examples, review, practice, and feedback in the context of a presentation and recitation format.

Have you ever wondered why some teachers are more liked than others? Students cannot wait to attend the classes of some teachers but dread attending the classes of others. Teachers who are more "liked" often are described with phrases such as "is more organized," "has a better personality," and "is warmer and friendlier." Although these qualities may be present in teachers judged to be among the most liked, they are not the only reasons that some teachers are more interesting than others to their learners.

One of the most important factors in how interesting teachers are to their students is their use of the key behavior, instructional variety. In a study of experienced and inexperienced teachers (Emmer et al., 1980; Emmer et al., 2006; Evertson et al., 2006), experienced teachers who showed flexibility and variety in their instructional strategies were found to be more interesting than inexperienced teachers who had no knowledge of alternative teaching strategies.

Knowledge of a variety of instructional strategies and the flexibility to change them both within and among lessons are two of the greatest assets a teacher can have. Without variety and flexibility to capture the interest and attention of your students, it is unlikely that any other key behavior, however well executed, will have the desired effect. This chapter provides a variety of teaching strategies you can use to compose lesson plans and to create and maintain an atmosphere of interest and variety in your classroom using a direct instruction format.

CATEGORIES OF TEACHING AND LEARNING

Just as the carpenter, electrician, and plumber must select the proper tool for a specific task, you must select the proper instructional strategy for a learning outcome. To help determine your choice of strategies, here are two broad classifications of learning outcomes:

Type 1: Facts, rules, and action sequences
Type 2: Concepts, patterns, and abstractions

Type 1 outcomes often represent behaviors at lower levels of complexity in the cognitive, affective, and psychomotor domains. These include the knowledge, comprehension, and application levels of the cognitive domain; the awareness, responding, and valuing levels of the affective domain; and the imitation, manipulation, and precision levels of the psychomotor domain.

Type 2 outcomes represent behaviors at the higher levels of complexity in these domains. They include outcomes at the analysis, synthesis, and evaluation levels of the cognitive domain; the organization and characterization levels of the affective domain; and the articulation and naturalization levels of the psychomotor domain. Examples of Type 1 and Type 2 outcomes are shown in Tables 7.1 and 7.2.

Some important differences between instructional goals requiring these two types of learning are shown in Table 7.3.

Notice across the left and right columns of Table 7.3 that these two types of learning are being required. In the left column, Type 1 tasks require combining facts and rules at the

Table 7.1 Example of Type 1 outcomes: Facts, rules, and action sequences.

Facts	Rules	Action Sequences
1. Recognize multiplication with two-digit numbers	Carrying with two-digit numbers	Multiplying to "1,000"
2. Identify apostrophe "s"	Finding words with apostrophe "s"	Using apostrophe "s" in a sentence
3. Select multisyllable words from list	Pronouncing multisyllable words	Reading stories with multisyllable words
4. State chemical composition of water	Combining 2 parts hydrogen with 1 part oxygen	Writing the expression for water

Table 7.2 Example of Type 2 outcomes: Concepts, patterns, and abstractions.

Concepts	Patterns	Abstractions
1. Positive and negative numbers	$-3 \, (-4) \, 11 =$ $10 \times (-6) =$	Signed numbers
2. Possessive form	Police officer's daughter Mrs. Burns's paper	Ownership
3. Vowels (v) and consonants (c)	cv order cvc order	Vowel/consonant blends
4. Element, atomic weight, and valence	H_2O	Molecular structure

Table 7.3 Instructional objectives requiring Type 1 and Type 2 outcomes.

Type 1: Objectives Requiring Facts, Rules, and Sequences	Type 2: Objectives Requiring Concepts, Patterns, and Abstractions
1. IF Objective is to *recognize* multiplication to "1,000" THEN TEACH the multiplication tables, and then have student *find examples*	BUT IF Objective is to *understand* multiplication of signed numbers THEN TEACH the concept of negative and positive numbers and *show how they are multiplied*
2. IF Objective is to *identify* the apostrophe "s" THEN TEACH words using the apostrophe "s", and then have student *find words denoting possession*	BUT IF Objective is to *express* ownership THEN TEACH the concept of the possessive form, and then have student *practice writing paragraphs* showing forms of possession
3. IF Objective is to *select* multisyllable words THEN TEACH how to *find each of the words* on a list, and then have student write words	BUT IF Objective is to *pronounce* vowel/consonant blends THEN TEACH vowels and consonants, and then have student *read story aloud*
4. IF Objective is to *state* the chemical composition of water THEN TEACH the symbol for 2 parts hydrogen and 1 part oxygen, and then have student *write the chemical composition of water*	BUT IF Objective is to *determine* the molecular structure of chemical substances THEN TEACH the concept of element, atomic weight, and valence, and then have student *practice balancing the atomic weights of chemical substances*

knowledge and comprehension levels into a sequence of actions that could be learned by observation, rote repetition, and practice. Students can learn the right answers by memorizing and practicing behaviors you model.

In the right column, a quite different learning type is called for. The right answers are not so closely connected to facts, rules, or action sequences that can be memorized and practiced in some limited context. Something more is needed to help the learner go beyond the facts, rules, or sequences to create, synthesize, and ultimately identify and recognize an answer that cannot be easily modeled or memorized. The missing link involves learning a concept, pattern, or abstraction.

For example, to learn the concept of a frog involves learning the essential characteristics that make an organism a frog, as distinguished from closely similar animals (green chameleons). In other words, the learner needs to know not only the characteristics that all frogs have but also what characteristics distinguish frogs from other animals. If we classified frogs only on the characteristics of being green, having four legs, eating insects, and being amphibious, some turtles could be misidentified as frogs. Another category of knowledge must be learned that contains characteristics that separate frogs from similar animals (e.g., frogs have soft bodies, moist skin, strong hind limbs, and do not change color).

Figure 7.1 Learning the concept of *frog*.

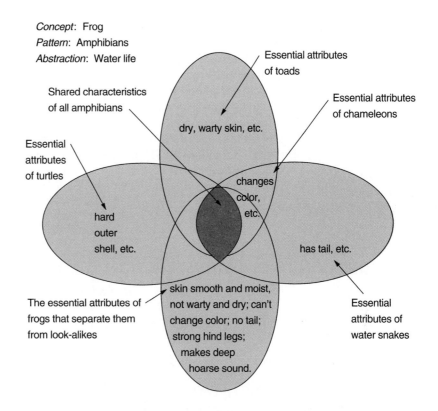

Concept: Frog
Pattern: Amphibians
Abstraction: Water life

Essential attributes of toads

Essential attributes of chameleons

Shared characteristics of all amphibians

Essential attributes of turtles

dry, warty skin, etc.

changes color, etc.

hard outer shell, etc.

has tail, etc.

The essential attributes of frogs that separate them from look-alikes

skin smooth and moist, not warty and dry; can't change color; no tail; strong hind legs; makes deep hoarse sound.

Essential attributes of water snakes

Figure 7.1 presents an advance organizer showing the abundance of information involved in learning the concept of *frog*. Notice that to properly classify a frog among other animals that may look like one, both nonessential and essential frog attributes need to be learned. The nonessential attributes can be learned only by studying nonexamples, thus allowing learners to eliminate characteristics that are not unique to frogs. Finally, as the learner gains more practice with both examples and nonexamples, the concept of a frog emerges as a tightly woven combination of characteristics. Now the learner is able to disregard superficial characteristics such as color and to focus on characteristics unique to frogs. Given pictures of various toads, chameleons, turtles, snakes, and so on, the student learns to identify correctly those that are frogs.

At this point the learner has discovered at least some of the essential attributes of a frog and has formed an initial concept. Notice how different this teaching/learning process is from simply having your learners repeat some recently memorized facts about frogs: "Frogs are green, have four legs, eat insects, and can swim." This response does not tell you whether they have acquired the *concept* of a frog, or a *pattern* of which frogs are a part (e.g., amphibian), or even the most general and *abstract* frog characteristics (e.g., water life). Even if they learn the considerably more complex task of how to care for frogs, they still have not learned the concept of a frog. They have only learned how to arrange a constellation of facts into the action sequence of caring for frogs.

The preceding demonstrates how the processes used to learn facts, rules, and action sequences are different from those used to learn concepts, patterns, and abstractions. And, just as different cognitive processes are involved in learning these different outcomes, so are different instructional strategies needed to teach them.

Facts, rules, and action sequences are most commonly taught using instructional strategies that emphasize knowledge acquisition. Concepts, patterns, and abstractions are most commonly taught using strategies that emphasize inquiry or problem solving. These follow distinctions by cognitive psychologists such as J. R. Anderson (1990), E. Gagné, Yekovich, and Yekovich (1993), Huffman (2004), and Mayer (2002), whose writings have highlighted the different instructional strategies required by these two types of learning.

Knowledge acquisition and inquiry are different types of learning outcomes, so each of them must be linked with the specific strategies most likely to produce the desired outcome. This chapter presents a group of strategies for teaching knowledge acquisition involving facts, rules, and action sequences, called **direct instruction.** The next chapter presents strategies for teaching inquiry and problem solving involving concepts, patterns, and abstractions, called **indirect instruction.** In subsequent chapters, both types of learning are combined to show how, together, they can provide a menu of teaching strategies that help your learners solve problems, think critically, and work cooperatively.

INTRODUCTION TO DIRECT INSTRUCTION STRATEGIES

As we have seen the teaching of facts, rules, and action sequences is most efficiently achieved through a process called the *direct instruction model.* Direct instruction is a teacher-centered strategy in which you are the major information provider. In the direct instruction model, your role is to pass facts, rules, or action sequences on to students in the most direct way possible. This usually takes a presentation and recitation format with explanations, examples, and opportunities for practice and feedback. The direct instruction presentation and recitation format not only requires verbal explanations from you but also teacher–student interactions involving questions and answers, review and practice, and the correction of student errors.

In the direct instruction model, the concept of a presentation in the elementary and secondary classroom differs considerably from the concept of a lecture in a college classroom. The typical college lecture rarely will be suitable for your classroom, because your learners' attention spans, interest levels, and motivation will not be the same as those of a college student. Therefore, the "lecture" as presented here is neither a lengthy monologue nor an open, free-wheeling discussion. Instead, it is a quickly paced, highly organized set of interchanges that you control, focusing exclusively on acquiring a limited set of predetermined facts, rules, or action sequences.

Rosenshine and Stevens (1986) have equated this type of instruction with that of an effective demonstration in which the following occurs:

1. You clearly present goals and main points.
   a. State goals or objectives of the presentation beforehand.
   b. Focus on one thought (point, direction) at a time.
   c. Avoid digressions.
   d. Avoid ambiguous phrases and pronouns.
2. You present content sequentially.
   a. Present material in small steps.
   b. Organize and present material so learners master one point before you go to the next point.
   c. Give explicit, step-by-step directions.
   d. Present an outline when the material is complex.
3. You are specific and concrete.
   a. Model the skill or process (when appropriate).
   b. Give detailed and redundant explanations for difficult points.
   c. Provide students with concrete and varied examples.

4. You check for students' understanding.
   a. Make sure that students understand one point before you proceed to the next.
   b. Ask students questions to monitor their comprehension of what has been presented.
   c. Have students summarize the main points in their own words.
   d. Reteach the parts that students have difficulty comprehending—either through further teaching or explanation or by students tutoring each other.

Table 7.4 provides examples of some of the action verbs that correspond to the objectives most suited for direct instruction. These outcomes are learned through application of facts, rules, and action sequences that usually can be taught in a single lesson. You can most easily and directly test them with multiple-choice, listing, matching, fill-in, and short-answer questions. Test items would call for the listing of memorized names, dates, and other facts; summarizing or paraphrasing of learned facts, rules, or sequences; or connecting together and applying learned facts, rules, and sequences in a context slightly different from the one in which they were learned.

Both Rosenshine (1986, 1971) and Good (1979) refer to direct instruction as "active teaching," which is characterized by:

- Full-class instruction (as opposed to small-group instruction)
- Organization of learning around questions you pose
- Provision of detailed and redundant practice
- Presenting material so learners master one new fact, rule, or sequence before the teacher presents the next
- Formal arrangement of the classroom to maximize recitation and practice

Figure 7.2 presents the teaching strategies most commonly associated with the direct instruction model. You can see that a large share of teaching time is likely to be devoted to direct instruction, that is, to providing information directly to students interspersed with explanations, examples, practice, and feedback.

Whether explaining, pointing out relationships, giving examples, or correcting errors, there are many advantages to using strategies that follow the direct instruction model. Research indicates that direct instruction strategies are among those that correlate highest with student achievement as measured by standardized tests, which tend to emphasize facts, rules, and sequences (L. Anderson, Evertson, & Brophy, 1982; Rosenshine, 1986, 1995; Walberg, 1991).

Table 7.4 Action verbs that correspond to the objectives most suited for direct instruction.

Cognitive Objectives	Affective Objectives	Psychomotor Objectives
Recall	Listen	Repeat
Describe	Attend	Follow
List	Be aware	Place
Summarize	Comply	Perform accurately
Paraphrase	Follow	Perform independently
Distinguish	Obey	Perform proficiently
Use	Display	Perform with speed
Organize	Express	Perform with coordination
Demonstrate	Prefer	Perform with timing

Figure 7.2 Some direct instruction strategies.

1. Daily review, checking previous day's work, and reteaching (if necessary):
   Checking homework
   Reteaching areas where there were student errors
2. Presenting and structuring new content:
   Provide overview
   Proceed in small steps (if necessary), but at a rapid pace
   If necessary, give detailed or redundant instructions and explanations
   New skills are phased in while old skills are being measured
3. Guided student practice:
   High frequency of questions and overt student practice (from teacher and
      materials)
   Prompts are provided during initial learning (when appropriate)
   All students have a chance to respond and receive feedback
   Teacher *checks for understanding* by evaluating student responses
   Continue practice until student responses are firm
   Success rate of 80% or higher during initial learning
4. Feedback and correctives (and recycling of instruction, if necessary):
   Feedback to students, particularly when they are correct but hesitant
   Student errors provide feedback to the teacher that corrections and/or
      reteaching is necessary
   Corrections by simplifying question, giving clues, explaining or reviewing
      steps, or reteaching last steps
   When necessary, reteach using smaller steps
5. Independent practice so that student responses are firm and automatic:
   Seatwork
   Unitization and automaticity (practice to overlearning)
   Need for procedure to ensure student engagement during seatwork (i.e.,
      teacher or aide monitoring)
   95% correct or higher
6. Weekly and monthly reviews:
   Reteaching, if necessary

Source: From "Teaching Functions in Instructional Programs," by B. Rosenshine, 1983, *Elementary School Journal,* 83, p. 338. Reprinted by permission of the University of Chicago. Copyright © 1986 by the University of Chicago. All rights reserved.

WHEN IS DIRECT INSTRUCTION APPROPRIATE?

When direct instruction strategies are used for the proper purpose, with the appropriate content, and at the right time, they will be important adjuncts to your teaching strategy menu. Most direct instruction strategies are at their best when your purpose is to disseminate information not readily available from texts or workbooks in appropriately sized pieces. If such information were available, your students might well learn the material from these sources independently, with only introductory or structuring comments provided by you. However, when you must partition, subdivide, and translate textbook and workbook material into a more digestible form before it can be understood by your students, direct instruction is appropriate.

Another time for direct instruction strategies is when you wish to arouse or heighten student interest. Students often fail to complete text and workbook readings and exercises in the mistaken belief that the material is boring, not worth their effort, or presents material already learned. Your active participation in the presentation of content can change these misperceptions by mixing interesting supplemental or introductory information with the dry facts, by showing their application to future schoolwork or world events, and by illustrating with questions and answers that the material is neither easy nor previously mastered. Your direct involvement in presenting content provides the human element that may be necessary for learning to occur in many of your students.

Finally, direct instruction strategies are indispensable for achieving content mastery and overlearning of fundamental facts, rules, and action sequences that may be essential to subsequent learning and remembering what was learned long afterwards (Gentile & Lalley, 2003; Lindsley, 1992). The degree of **mastery learning** that occurs is directly related to the time a student is actively engaged in the learning process. The more time spent reviewing and practicing, the greater the retention and ability to put that learning into practice at a later time. Therefore, review and active student practice are important ingredients of mastery learning.

The goals of mastery learning are best achieved by the instructional sequence of review, presenting new content, practice, feedback, and reteaching, as shown in Figure 7.3. These progressive cycles may compose nearly all of the time scheduled for a direct instruction lesson. Many examples in this chapter illustrate this type of instructional sequence. When the content to be taught represents task-relevant prior knowledge for subsequent learning, a direct instruction format is the best insurance that this knowledge will be remembered and available for later use.

There also are times when direct instruction strategies are inappropriate. When objectives other than learning facts, rules, and action sequences are desired, direct instruction strategies become less efficient and often far less effective than the inquiry and problem-solving strategies to be discussed in subsequent chapters. Teaching situations that need strategies other than direct instruction include (1) presenting complex material having objectives at the analysis, synthesis, and evaluation levels of the cognitive domain, and (2) presenting content that must be learned gradually over a long period. Such material requires learner participation to heighten a commitment to the learning process (for example, portfolios, projects, and oral performances) to create the intellectual framework necessary for learning concepts and recognizing patterns. You must also attain this learner participation through carefully crafted classroom dialogue that will be illustrated in chapters 8 and 9. See In Practice: Focus on Mastery Learning.

Figure 7.3 The direct instructional sequence for mastery learning.

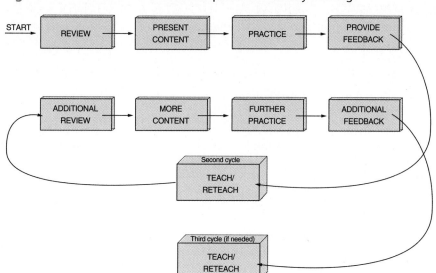

IN PRACTICE

Focus on Mastery Learning

John B. Carroll inaugurated a fundamental change in thinking about the characteristics of instruction in 1963 when he argued for the idea that student aptitudes are reflective of an individual's learning rate and, therefore, some students may need more time to learn than others. In this new paradigm, Carroll suggested that instruction should focus more on the time required for different students to learn the same material. This was in contrast with the classic model in which all students are given the same amount of time to learn and the focus is on differences in ability.

Carroll's new theory was based on the idea that all learners can have the potential to learn any content provided by the teacher, but take different amounts of time to do so. Carroll identified two factors that affected the learning rate of a student: perseverance of the student and the opportunity to learn. The first is controlled by the student, that is, how much time he or she spends on learning; the latter is the time allotted to learn by the teacher.

However, it was Bloom in 1968 who fully developed the concepts now known as *mastery learning*. In the 1960s, Benjamin Bloom was involved in research on the role of individual differences in learning. Impressed with Carroll's ideas, he took them further by concluding that if aptitude could predict the rate at which one learns, the instructional variables under an instructor's control, such as the opportunity to learn and instructional materials and resources, should be able to ensure that all learners can attain mastery of any unit or lesson objective. Bloom concluded that given sufficient time and quality of instruction, nearly all students could learn. Bloom's mastery learning model also became instrumental in the "nature" versus "nurture" controversy sparked by Jensen (1969) by illuminating a model in which the learning environment provided by the teacher and not heredity could account for most of a student's learning.

The theories of mastery learning resulted in a radical shift in responsibility for teachers; the blame for a student's failure rests with the instruction, not the student's lack of ability. In this type of learning environment, the challenge becomes providing enough time and employing effective instructional strategies so that all students achieve the same level of learning (Bloom, 1981; Levine, 1985).

How to instruct for mastery:

1. Clearly state the objective of the unit.
2. Divide the unit objective into lessons, each with its own objectives and assessment.
3. Identify the most effective combination of learning materials and instructional strategies for each lesson, such as presentation, recitation, modeling, questioning, discussion, and so forth.
4. Each unit or lesson starts with a brief diagnostic test or formative assessment of what students know and don't know about the topic.
5. The results of the diagnostic tests are used to provide instruction and corrective activities in a review, present content, practice, feedback order.
6. This cycle is used first with the whole class and repeated, as needed, with the whole class or individuals. No student proceeds to new material until basic material is mastered.

In summary, mastery learning is an instructional strategy based on the principle that all students can attain lesson and unit objectives with the appropriate instruction and sufficient time to learn. Mastery learning puts the techniques of tutoring and individualized instruction into a group learning format and brings the learning strategies of successful students to nearly all the students of a given group. In its full form it includes a philosophy, curriculum structure, instructional model, the alignment of student assessment, and a teaching approach.

AN EXAMPLE OF DIRECT INSTRUCTION

To see what direct instruction looks like in the classroom, consider the following dialogue, in which the teacher begins a direct instruction sequence to teach the acquisition of facts, rules, and action sequences for forming and punctuating possessives. She begins by informing her students of the lesson's objective. As you read, note the direct instruction strategies in bold from Figure 7.2.

◆　　◆　　◆

Teacher:	Today we will learn how to avoid embarrassing errors such as this when forming and punctuating possessives (circles an incorrectly punctuated possessive in a newspaper headline). At the end of the period, I will give each of you several additional examples of errors taken from my collection of mistakes found in other newspapers and magazines. I'll ask you to make the proper corrections and report your changes to the class. Who knows what a possessive is? (***Review and checking***)
Richard:	It means you own something.
Teacher:	Yes, a possessive is a way of indicating ownership. It comes from the word *possession*, which means something owned or something possessed.
	Forming possessives and punctuating them correctly can be difficult, as this newspaper example shows (points to paper again). Today I will give you two simple rules that will help you form possessives correctly. But first, to show ownership or possession, we must know who or what is doing the possessing.
	Lucila, can you recall the parts of speech from last week's lesson? (Lucila hesitates, then nods.) What part of speech is most likely to own or possess something? (***Review and checking***)
Lucila:	Well, umm . . . I think . . . I think a noun can own something.
Teacher:	Yes. A noun can own something. What is an example of a noun that owns something? Brian.
Brian:	I don't know.
Teacher:	Allison.
Allison:	Not sure.
Teacher:	Yungwei.
Yungwei:	A student can own a pencil. The word *student* is a noun.
Teacher:	Good. And who can remember our definition for a noun? (***Review and checking***)
Damian:	It's a person, place, or thing.
Teacher:	Good. Our first rule is: Use the possessive form whenever an *of* phrase can be substituted for a noun (teacher points to this rule written on board). (***Presenting and structuring***) Let's look at some phrases on the board to see when to apply this rule. Jason, what does the first one say? (***Guided student practice***)
Jason:	The daughter of the police officer.
Teacher:	How else could we express the same idea of ownership?
Trena:	We could say "the police officer's daughter."
Teacher:	And we could say "the police officer's daughter" because I can substitute a phrase starting with *of* and ending with *police officer* for the noun *police officer*. Notice how easily I could switch the placement of *police officer* and *daughter* by using the connecting word *of*. Whenever this can be done, you can form a possessive by adding an *apostrophe s* to the noun following *of*. (***Presenting and structuring***)

Now we have the phrase (writes on board) *police officer's daughter* (points to the apostrophe). Erica, what about our next example, *holiday of three days* (pointing to board)? ***(Guided student practice)***

Erica: We could say "three days' holiday."

Teacher: Come up and write that on the board just the way it should be printed in the school paper. (Erica writes *three day's holiday*.)

Would anyone want to change anything?

Desiree: I'm not sure, but I think I would put the apostrophe after the *s* in *days*.

Teacher: You're right ***(Feedback),*** which leads to our second rule: If the word for which we are denoting ownership is a plural ending with *s*, place an apostrophe after the *s*. But if the word is a name—called a *proper noun*—ending with *s*, place an apostrophe and an *s* after the *s*. This is an important rule to remember, because it accounts for many of the mistakes that are made in forming possessives. As I write this rule on the board, copy down these two rules for use later. ***(Presenting and structuring)*** (Finishes writing second rule on board.) Now let's take a moment to convert each of the phrases on the overhead to the possessive form. Write down your answer to the first one. When I see all heads up again, I will write the correct answer. ***(Guided student practice)*** (All heads are up.) Good. Now watch how I change this first one to the possessive form; pay particular attention to where I place the apostrophe, then check your answer with mine. (Converts *delay of a month* to *month's delay*.) Any problems? ***(Checking)*** (Pauses for any response.) OK, do the next one.

(After all heads are up, teacher converts *home of Jenkins* to *Jenkins's home*.) Any problems? (Jason looks distressed.) ***(Checking)***

Teacher: Jason, what did you write?

Jason: *J-E-N-K-I-N apostrophe S.*

Teacher: What is the man's name, Jason?

Jason: Jenkins.

Teacher: Look at what you wrote for the second rule. What does it say? ***(Feedback and corrective)***

Jason: Add an apostrophe and an *s* after the *s* when the word is a name that already ends in an *s*. Oh, I get it. His name already has the *s*, so it would be *s apostrophe s*. That's the mistake you showed us in the headline, isn't it?

Teacher: Now you've got it. Let's continue. (Proceeds with the following in the same manner: *speech of the president* to *president's speech, the television set of Mr. Burns* to *Mr. Burns's television set, pastimes of boys* to *boys' pastimes*.) Now open your workbooks to the exercise on page 87.

Starting with the first row, let's go around the room and hear your possessives for each of the sentences listed. Spell aloud the word indicating ownership, so we can tell if you've placed the apostrophe in the right place. Allison . . . (looking at "wings of geese") ***(Guided student practice)***

Allison: geeses wings . . . spelled *W-I-N-G-S apostrophe.*

Teacher: That's not correct. What word is doing the possessing? ***(Feedback and corrective)***

Allison: The geese, so it must be *G-E-E-S-E apostrophe S.*

Teacher: Good. ***(Feedback)*** Next.

◆   ◆   ◆

Now let's look at our six direct instruction strategies in Figure 7.2 as they relate to the preceding dialogue.

DAILY REVIEW AND CHECKING THE PREVIOUS DAY'S WORK

The first strategy in direct instruction from Figure 7.2 is **daily review and checking.** This function emphasizes the relationship between lessons so students remember previous knowledge and see new knowledge as a logical extension of content already mastered. Notice that early in the example lesson the definition of a noun was brought into the presentation. This provided review of task-relevant prior knowledge needed for the day's lesson.

It also provided students with a sense of wholeness and continuity, assuring them that what was to follow was not isolated knowledge unrelated to past lessons. This is particularly important for securing the engagement of students who do not have appropriate levels of task-relevant prior knowledge or who may be overly anxious about having to master yet another piece of unfamiliar content.

Review and checking at the beginning of a lesson also are the most efficient and timely ways of finding out if your students have mastered task-relevant prior knowledge sufficiently to begin a new lesson; if not, you may reteach the missing content, as shown in Figure 7.2.

You might think that beginning a lesson by checking previously learned task-relevant knowledge needed for the day's lesson is a common practice. Yet many teachers fail to begin a lesson by checking for this knowledge. Daily review and checking at the beginning of a lesson can be easily accomplished in one of several ways:

1. Having students correct each other's homework at the beginning of class
2. Having students identify especially difficult homework problems in a question-and-answer format
3. Sampling the understanding of a few students who are good indicators of the range of knowledge possessed by the entire class
4. Explicitly reviewing the task-relevant information that is necessary for the day's lesson

Dahllof and Lundgren (1970) proposed the use of a steering group of lower- to average-performing students as a particularly effective way of determining the extent to which review and reteaching may be needed. An expanded notion of the steering group is a small number of low, average, and high performers who can be queried at the start of class on the task-relevant prior knowledge needed for the day's lesson. When high performers miss a large

A major purpose of daily review and checking is to emphasize the relationships between lessons and to provide students with a sense of wholeness and continuity, assuring them that what is to follow is a logical extension of content already mastered.

proportion of answers, this warns you that extensive reteaching for the entire class may be necessary. When high performers answer questions correctly but average performers do not, some reteaching should be undertaken before the start of the lesson. And, finally, if most of the high and average performers answer the questions correctly but most of the low performers do not, you may need to consider individualized materials, practice exercises, summary and review sheets, or tutorial arrangements and supplementary instructional software. This ensures that large amounts of class time are not devoted to review and reteaching that may benefit only a small number of students.

The strategy of daily review and checking, especially when used with a carefully selected steering group, is indispensable for warning you that previous instruction was over the heads of some or most of your students and, therefore, that additional review and reteaching are necessary.

PRESENTING AND STRUCTURING

The second strategy in the direct instruction model consists of **presenting and structuring** new content. One of the primary ingredients of the direct instruction model is presenting material in small steps. Lessons must be served up in small portions that are consistent with the previous knowledge, ability level, and experience of your students. Likewise, the content within the lessons must be partitioned and subdivided to organize it into small bits. No portion can be too large, or you will lose your students' attention.

The key is to focus the material on one idea at a time and to present it so learners master one point before the teacher introduces the next point. This is most easily accomplished by dividing a lesson into easily recognizable subparts, rules, or categories. It is no coincidence that the strategy of divide and conquer is as appropriate in the classroom as in military battles. Just like any great warrior, you can derive much benefit from it.

Remember that the subdivisions you use can be your own; they need not always follow those provided by the text, workbook, or curriculum guide. There is an important difference between content divisions used in books and content divisions needed in teaching: Content divisions in texts, workbooks, and curriculum guides generally are created for the purpose of communicating content intended to be read, not for the purpose of presenting content that must be explained orally to learners within the time frame of a specific lesson. Consequently, published divisions like chapter titles, subheadings, or Roman numerals in outlines and texts sometimes are too broad to form bite-sized pieces that students can easily digest within a lesson.

Unfortunately, many beginning teachers stick tenaciously to these formal headings without realizing either the volume of content that falls within them or the time it takes to orally explain, illustrate, and practice this content. The truth is that you are not discarding content if you create new, more manageable, organizational divisions; you only are breaking content into smaller steps suitable for presentation in a single period. You can create your own subdivisions consisting of rules ("Here are some rules to follow"), steps ("We will do this, then that"), or practices ("Here is the first of five things we will cover"). These subdivisions pre-organize your instruction into bite-sized pieces and, most importantly, communicate this organization to your students.

In chapter 2 (Figures 2.2 and 2.3) we illustrated the importance of structuring content in ways that are meaningful to students (e.g., general to detailed, simple to complex, etc.). Following are some additional ways of structuring content that are particularly relevant to direct instruction. These are the part–whole, sequential, combinations, and comparative methods of structuring content.

Figure 7.4 Structuring a lesson by identifying part–whole relationships.

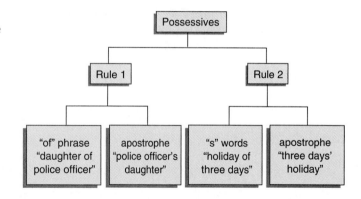

Part–Whole Relationships

A part–whole organizational format introduces the topic in its most general form ("What is a possessive?") and then divides the topic into easy-to-distinguish subdivisions (Rule 1, Rule 2). This creates subdivisions that are easily digested and presents them in ways that always relate back to the whole. Students should always be aware of the part being covered at any particular time ("This is Rule 2") and its relationship to the whole ("This leads to our second rule for denoting ownership"). Use verbal markers to alert students that a transition is under way ("This is Rule 1," "Here is the first part," "This is the last example of this type; now let's move to the next type").

This type of organization creates bite-sized chunks; it helps students organize and see what is being taught and informs them of what portion they are studying. A part–whole organization is illustrated in Figure 7.4.

Sequential Relationships

Another way of structuring content is by sequential ordering; you teach the content according to the way in which the facts, rules, or sequences to be learned occur in the real world. Students may already have a feel for sequential ordering from practical experience.

In algebra, for example, equations are solved by first multiplying, then dividing, then adding, and finally subtracting. This order of operations must occur for a solution to be correct. A sequentially structured lesson, therefore, might introduce the manipulation of signed numbers in the order multiplication-division-addition-subtraction, which reinforces the way equations must actually be solved, making the skill and behavior you are teaching more authentic. In other words, you would complete all examples used in teaching signed-number multiplication before introducing any examples about division, thereby teaching the correct sequence as well as the intended content. Sequential ordering is illustrated in Figure 7.5.

Combinations of Relationships

A third way you can structure lesson content is to bring together in a single format various elements or dimensions that influence the use of facts, rules, and sequences. This allows an overall framework to direct the order of content by showing the logic of some combinations of facts, rules, and sequences and the illogic of other combinations.

For example, in teaching a direct instruction lesson in geography, you might develop a scheme to reveal the relationship between marketable products and the various means of transporting them to market. You could draw an organizational chart (Figure 7.6) to structure the content. You could show the chart to your students and then teach all the relevant facts

Figure 7.5 Structuring a lesson by identifying sequential relationships.

$$y = a - b + \frac{cd}{e}$$

1. First, let's determine cd when

$c = -1, d = 2$

$c = 0, d = -4$

$c = 2, d = -3$

2. Next, let's determine $\frac{cd}{e}$ when

$cd = -2, e = -2$

$cd = 0, e = 1$

$cd = -6, e = 4$

3. Now, let's determine $b + \frac{cd}{e}$ when

$b = 1, \frac{cd}{e} = 1$

$b = -2, \frac{cd}{e} = 0$

$b = 2, \frac{cd}{e} = -1.5$

4. Finally, let's determine $a - b + \frac{cd}{e}$ when

$a = 10, b + \frac{cd}{e} = 2$

$a = 7, b + \frac{cd}{e} = -3$

$a = 5, b + \frac{cd}{e} = .5$

Figure 7.6 Structuring a lesson by identifying combinations of relationships.

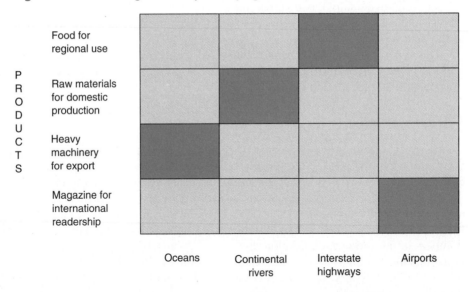

PRODUCTS

Food for regional use

Raw materials for domestic production

Heavy machinery for export

Magazine for international readership

Oceans | Continental rivers | Interstate highways | Airports

TRANSPORTATION SYSTEMS

(e.g., relative weights of products), rules (the heavier the product, the more efficient the transportation system must be), and action sequences (first analyze the product's size and weight, then choose the best location). The shaded cells in Figure 7.6 identify the combinations, or dimensions of content, that are most relevant to the lesson objectives.

Comparative Relationships

With this method of structuring content, you place different categories of content or topics side by side so that learners can compare and contrast them. Placing facts, rules, and sequences side by side across two or more categories enables students to observe their similarities and differences. For example, you might want to compare and contrast

Figure 7.7 Structuring a relationship by identifying comparative relationships.

Points of Comparison	United States	England
Economics	Capitalism	Capitalism
Politics	Representative democracy	Parliamentary democracy
Source of laws	U.S. Constitution	English legal codes
Representative body	Congress	Parliament

governmental aspects of the United States and England. You could order the instruction according to the format shown in Figure 7.7. Then you could teach the relevant facts (economic systems), politics (type of government), and source of laws (U.S. Constitution vs. legal codes) by moving first across the chart and then down. The chart structures content in advance, and students can easily see the structure and content to be covered as it is being taught.

Using the Methods

Whether you use one structuring method or a combination to organize a lesson, remember to divide the content into bite-sized pieces. To the extent these structuring techniques divide larger units of content into smaller and more meaningful units, they will have served an important purpose.

Finally, note how the teacher in our classroom dialogue combined rules and examples in organizing and presenting the content. She always presented the rule first and then followed with one or more examples. Note also that after some examples illustrating the rule, she repeated it—either by having students write the rule after seeing it on the board or by having a student repeat it to the class. Giving a rule, then an example of the rule, followed by repetition of the rule is called the **rule-example-rule order.** It generally is more effective than simply giving the rule and then an example (rule-example order) or giving an example followed by the rule. Also, learning a rule in one sensory modality (e.g., seeing it on the board) and then recreating it in a different sensory modality (e.g., writing or speaking it) will promote greater learning and retention than seeing the rule only once or reproducing it in the same modality in which it was learned.

GUIDED STUDENT PRACTICE

The third step in the direct instruction model is **guided student practice.** Recall from the structure of a lesson plan that presentation of stimulus material is followed by eliciting practice with the desired behavior. This section presents several ways of accomplishing this in the context of the direct instruction model. These elicitations are teacher guided, providing students with guided practice that you organize and direct.

Recall the important ingredients for eliciting a student response. One is to elicit the response in as nonevaluative an atmosphere as possible; this frees students to risk creating responses about which they may be unsure but from which they can begin to build a correct response. Any response, however crude or incorrect, can be the basis for learning if it is followed by nonevaluative feedback and correctives.

A second ingredient for eliciting a student response is the use of covert responses. This not only ensures a nonthreatening environment but also encourages student engagement in the learning task with the least expenditure of your time and effort. In the preceding example dialogue, by having students privately write their responses before seeing the correct answers on the overhead, the teacher guided each student to formulate a response; it was not necessary to call on each of them. She guided the students into responding by encouraging, and later rewarding, their covert responses.

An equally important aspect of eliciting a desired response is to check for student understanding. When necessary, prompt to convert wrong answers to right ones. In the example dialogue, the teacher stopped after every item to see if there were problems and prompted students to create correct answers when necessary. Prompting is an important part of eliciting the desired behavior, because it strengthens and builds the learners' confidence by encouraging them to use some aspects of the answer that have already been given in formulating the correct response (E. Gagné et al., 1993). In the example dialogue, Jason was encouraged to *rethink* his response, to *focus* consciously on the specific part of the problem causing the error, and to *remember* the rule that will prevent such errors in the future.

Prompting

One guided student practice during direct instruction is providing prompts, hints, and other types of supplementary instructional stimuli to help learners make the correct response. You can use three categories of prompts to shape the correct performance of your learners: verbal prompts, gestural prompts, and physical prompts.

Verbal Prompts.　**Verbal prompts** can be cues, reminders, or instructions to learners that help them perform correctly the skill you are teaching. For example, saying to a first-grade learner as he is writing, "Leave a space between words," reminds him what you previously said about neat handwriting. Or saying, "First adjust the object lens," to a learner while she is looking at a microscope slide prompts her as she is learning how to use a microscope. Verbal prompts help guide the learner to connect performances and prevent mistakes and frustration.

Gestural Prompts.　**Gestural prompts** model or demonstrate for learners a particular skill you want them to perform. For example, if you were to point to the fine adjustment knob on the microscope and make a turning gesture with your hand, you would be prompting, or reminding, the student to perform this step of the process. Gestural prompts are particularly helpful when you anticipate that the learner may make a mistake. You can use gestural prompts routinely to remind learners how to fold a piece of paper, how to grasp a pair of scissors, how to raise their hand before asking a question, or how to hold a pen properly when writing.

Physical Prompts.　Some learners may lack the fine muscle control to follow a demonstration and imitate the action being modeled. For example, you might verbally describe how to form the letter *a* and demonstrate this for the learner, and the learner may still be unable to write *a* correctly. In such a case, you might use your hand to guide the learner's hand as he writes. This is called a **physical prompt.** With a physical prompt, you use hand-over-hand assistance to guide the learner to the correct performance. You can routinely use physical prompts to assist learners with handwriting, cutting out shapes, tying shoelaces, correctly holding a dissecting tool, or performing a complex dance routine.

Least-to-Most Intrusive Prompting. Many educators recommend that you use the least intrusive prompt first when guiding a learner's performance. Verbal prompts are the least intrusive; physical prompts are the most intrusive (Cooper, Heron, & Heward, 1987). Thus it would be more appropriate, first, to say, "Don't forget the fine adjustment!" when guiding a learner in the use of a microscope than to take the learner's hand and physically assist her. The reasoning behind using a least-to-most intrusive order is that verbal prompts are easier to remove or fade than are physical prompts. Learners who are dependent on physical prompts to perform correctly will find it more difficult to demonstrate a skill independently of the teacher and to acquire authentic behavior.

Full-Class Prompting. You can also check for understanding and prompt for correct responses using the full class. The example dialogue showed one approach: The teacher asked all the students to respond privately at the same time and then encouraged them to ask for individual help ("Any problems?").

Another approach is to call on students whether or not their hands are raised, thereby seeking opportunities to prompt and correct wrong answers. One version of this is called **ordered turns,** in which you systematically go through the class and expect students to respond when their turn arrives. When groups are small, this approach can be more effective in producing student achievement gains than randomly calling on students, because everyone is likely to get one or more repeated turns. But, generally, the ordered turns method is less efficient when selecting students to respond during full-class instruction because students can easily gauge the time they will have to be disengaged until their turn arrives.

Yet another approach is to have students write out answers to be checked and perhaps corrected by a classmate. Finally, you can develop questions beforehand to test for the most common errors. Check student responses for accuracy and prompt when necessary. This approach has the advantage of assuming that not everyone understands or has the correct answer when no responses are received. Researchers have found this approach to be particularly effective in increasing student achievement (Rosenshine, 1995; Rosenshine & Stevens, 1986; Singer & Donlon, 1982).

Modeling

Another guided student practice is modeling. Modeling is a teaching activity that involves demonstrating to learners what you want them to do or think. When used correctly, modeling can assist learners to acquire a variety of intellectual and social skills more effortlessly and efficiently than with verbal, gestural, or physical prompts alone. Modeling is particularly effective for younger learners who may not be able to follow complex verbal explanations, for visually dominant learners who may need to see how something is done before they can actually do it, and for communicating mental strategies for problem solving to all ages of learners.

Bandura and his colleagues have studied how and why we learn from models (Bandura, 1997; Zimmerman, 1989). Their research on modeling is referred to as **social learning theory,** and it attempts to explain how people learn from observing other people. From their work we know that children not only can learn attitudes, values, and standards of behavior from observing adults and peers but may also learn physical and intellectual skills.

Some of this learning takes place by directly imitating what a teacher is doing; other learning takes place by inferring why the model is acting a certain way or what type of person the model is. For example, learners acquire certain values about the importance of learning, caring for others, doing work neatly, or respect for other cultures by observing how their parents, friends, and teachers actually behave in the real world, and then inferring from their observations how they, too, should behave. Although teachers model all the time, we know that some forms of modeling are better than others. Zimmerman (1989) found that teachers who were taught the practice of modeling were far more effective at helping young children to learn than teachers who were not.

Modeling is a direct teaching activity that allows students to imitate from demonstration or infer from observation the behavior to be learned. Four psychological processes need to occur for your learners to benefit from modeling:

1. Attention
2. Retention
3. Production
4. Motivation

Let's take a closer look at these to discover how students learn from what they see.

Attention.   Demonstrations are only of value if learners are looking and/or listening to them. In other words, without attention there can be no imitation or observational learning. The previous section highlighted the importance of gaining a learner's attention. Modeling requires that you not only gain your learners' attention but that you retain it throughout the lesson. Bandura (1986) found that learners hold their attention better under the following conditions:

1. The model is someone who is respected as an expert in his or her field.
2. The model is demonstrating something that has functional value to the learner. Learners pay little attention to those things for which they see no immediate relevance.
3. The demonstration is simplified by subdividing it into component parts and presented in a clearly discernible step-by-step fashion.

Retention.   Teachers model because they want their learners to be able to repeat their same actions when they are no longer present. For example, teachers typically model when they demonstrate how to add a column of numbers, sound out a word, or evaluate a short essay. But the transfer of these demonstrated actions will only occur if learners remember what they saw or heard. Demonstrations from which imitation is to occur must be planned with the goal of retention in mind.

Learners are more likely to remember the following types of demonstrations:

1. Demonstrations linked to previous skills or ideas they have already learned. The more meaningful the demonstration, the more likely it will be retained. ("Remember how yesterday we added one-digit numbers in a column? Well, today we will use the same procedure on numbers that have two or more digits.")
2. Demonstrations that include concise labels, vivid images, code words, or visual mnemonics (discussed in chapter 10), which help learners hold new learning in memory. ("Look at how I hold my lips when I pronounce this next word.")
3. Demonstrations that are immediately rehearsed. This rehearsal can be overt, as when the teacher asks learners to say or do something immediately following the demonstration, or covert. Covert rehearsal occurs when the learner visualizes or mentally creates an image of what the teacher demonstrated. ("Now, everyone read the next passage to themselves, repeating silently the sequence of steps I just demonstrated.")

Production.　The third component of the modeling process occurs when learners actually do what the teacher demonstrated. In this stage of the process, the mental images or verbal codes learners retained in memory direct their actual performance. Learners recall these images or codes by the practice situation the teacher creates and by the verbal cues given. Having been evoked, these images guide the actual performance of what was learned during the demonstration.

Learners are more likely to produce what they saw under the following conditions:

1. Production closely follows the retention phase. ("OK, now that you've practiced remembering the correct sequence of steps I demonstrated, let's use them to interpret the meaning of the following passage.")
2. The practice situation contains cues or stimuli that evoke the retained mental images or verbal codes. ("This next word requires you to position your lips exactly as you saw me do in the last example.")
3. The performance immediately follows mental rehearsal. ("Let's switch to several new examples that you haven't seen before.")

The production phase increases the likelihood that images of the demonstration learners have remembered will guide the production of newly acquired behavior. In addition, this phase allows the teacher to observe learners and give feedback on how well they have mastered the behavior. Giving learners information about the correctness of their actions—without expressing negativity or dissatisfaction—has been shown to increase the likelihood of a correct performance (Borich & Tombari, 1997, pp. 341–342).

Motivation.　The final stage of the process of learning through modeling occurs when learners experience desirable outcomes following their performance. Desirable outcomes usually take the form of some type of teacher praise, which motivates learners to want to imitate at some future time what they have seen. Learners are less likely to repeat the actions of a model if they have experienced punishing or unsatisfying consequences following their initial attempts to imitate the model.

Learners are more likely to repeat the actions of a model both immediately and to transfer it to new situations over time when the following occur:

1. Praise and encouragement rather than criticism immediately follow performance. ("Your answer is partly correct; think some more about what we've just discussed," as opposed to, "Your answer is wrong. You're not listening again.")
2. The praise is directed at specific aspects of the performance. ("I like how you left enough space between your words," as opposed to, "That's neat.")
3. Directions rather than corrections follow incorrect performance. ("Remember, the first step is to generate a hypothesis," as opposed to, "You don't describe the research conclusions before you state the hypothesis!")

FEEDBACK AND CORRECTIVES

Our next strategy in the direct instruction model is provision of **feedback and correctives.** You need strategies for handling right and wrong answers. Based on several studies, Rosenshine (1983) and Rosenshine and Stevens (1986) identified four broad categories of student response: (1) correct, quick, and firm; (2) correct but hesitant; (3) incorrect due to carelessness; and (4) incorrect due to lack of knowledge. These are described next, with some direct instruction strategies for handling them.

Correct, Quick, and Firm

The student response that teachers strive most to inspire is correct, quick, and firm. Such a response most frequently occurs during the latter stages of a lesson or unit, but it can occur almost anytime during a lesson or unit if you have divided the content into bite-sized portions. A moderate-to-high percentage of correct, quick, and firm responses is important if students are to become actively engaged in the learning process. Not every response from every student must be a correct one, but for most learning that involves knowledge acquisition, make the steps between successive portions of your lesson small enough to produce approximately 60% to 80% correct answers in a practice and feedback session (Bennett, Desforges, Cockburn, & Wilkinson, 1981; Brophy & Evertson, 1976b; Lindsley, 1991). Once 60% to 80% right answers are produced, you will have created a rhythm and momentum that heighten student attention and engagement and provide for a high level of task orientation. The brisk pace of right answers also will help minimize irrelevant student responses and classroom distractions.

Correct but Hesitant

The second type of student response is correct but hesitant. This type frequently occurs in a practice and feedback session at the beginning or middle of a lesson. Positive feedback to the student who supplies a correct but hesitant response is essential. The first feedback to provide in this instance is a positive, reinforcing statement, such as "good," or "that's correct," because the correct but hesitant response is more likely to be remembered when linked to a warm reply. The second feedback to provide is to restate the answer, assuring the student that it is correct. This will not only aid the student who is giving the correct but hesitant response, but also help reduce hesitant responses among other students who hear the restatement.

Incorrect Because of Carelessness

The third type of student response is incorrect because of carelessness. As many as 20% of student responses fall into this category, depending on the time of day and the students' level of fatigue and inattentiveness. When this occurs, and you feel they really know the correct response, you may be tempted to scold, admonish, or even verbally punish students for responding thoughtlessly (e.g., "I'm ashamed of you," "That's a dumb mistake," "I thought you were brighter than that"). However, resist this temptation, no matter how justified it seems. Nothing is more frustrating than to repress genuine emotions, but researchers and experienced teachers agree that you do more harm than good if you react emotionally to this type of response. Verbal punishment rarely teaches students to avoid careless mistakes. The best response is to acknowledge that the answer is wrong and to move immediately to the next student for the correct response. By doing so, you will make a point to the careless student that he or she lost the opportunity for a correct response and the praise that goes with it.

Incorrect Because of Lack of Knowledge

The fourth type of student response is incorrect because of a lack of knowledge. These errors typically occur, sometimes in large numbers, during the initial stages of a lesson or unit. It is better to provide hints, probe, or change the question or stimulus to a simpler one that engages the student in finding the correct response than to simply give the student the correct response. Your most important goal at this stage of the lesson or unit is to engage the learner in the process by which the right answer can be found.

In the example lesson, the teacher tried to focus Jason on the *apostrophe s* he had missed at the end of the proper noun *Jenkins* and to restate the rule concerning formation of possessives in words ending in *s*. Likewise, the teacher probed Allison after her wrong answer by asking, "What word is doing the possessing?" Each of these instances led to the right answer without actually telling the student the right answer. When your strategy channels a student's thoughts to produce the right answer without your actually giving it, you provide a framework for producing a correct response to all similar problems.

Strategies for Incorrect Responses

The most common strategies for incorrect responses are the following:

1. Review key facts or rules needed for a correct solution.
2. Explain the steps used to reach a correct solution.
3. Prompt with clues or hints representing a partially correct answer.
4. Take a different but similar problem and guide the student to the correct answer.

Reviewing, reexplaining, and prompting are effective until approximately 80% of the students respond correctly. After that point, make the correctives briefer, eventually guiding students who are making incorrect responses to helpful exercises in the text or to remedial exercises (N. Bennett & Desforges, 1988).

Lindsley (1992) makes a useful distinction between active and passive responding, which is related to the accuracy of your learners' responses. **Active responding** includes orally responding to a question, writing out the correct answer, calculating an answer, or physically making a response (e.g., focusing a microscope). **Passive responding** includes listening to the teacher's answer, reading about the correct answer, or listening to classmates recite the right answer.

Greenwood, Delguardi, and Hall (1984) and Huffman (2004) report a strong and positive relationship between learner achievement and active responding. They also report that nearly half of a typical learner's day may be involved in passive responding. These researchers urge you to plan your lessons so learners spend about 75% of their time engaged in active responding. They also recommend that you design your practice activities to elicit correct responses about 60% to 80% of the time. Learners acquire basic facts and skills faster when their opportunities for practice result in high rates of success (Lindsley, 1991).

In summary, when providing feedback and corrections:

- Give directions that focus on the response you want learners to make.
- Design instructional materials both for initial learning and practice so learners can produce correct answers 60% to 80% of the time.
- Select activities to engage your learners in active responding about 75% of the time.

INDEPENDENT PRACTICE

The fifth strategy for direct instruction is the opportunity for **independent practice.** Once you have successfully elicited the behavior, provided feedback, and administered correctives, students need the opportunity to practice the behavior independently. Often this is the time when facts and rules come together to form action sequences. For example, learning to drive a car requires a knowledge of terminology and rules. But until the knowledge and rules are put together in an action sequence, meaningful learning has not occurred.

During independent practice, the teacher circulates around the classroom, scanning written responses, prompting for alternative answers, and reminding students of necessary facts or rules, being careful to keep interchanges short so that the work of as many students as possible can be checked.

Independent practice provides the opportunity in a carefully controlled and organized environment to make a meaningful whole out of the bits and pieces. Facts and rules must come together under your guidance and example in ways that (1) force simultaneous consideration of all the individual units of a problem, and (2) connect the units into a single harmonious sequence of action. Learning theorists call these two processes *unitization* and *automaticity*.

Notice the manner in which these two processes were required in the example lesson. The individual units were the definition of a possessive (a fact) and two statements about forming possessives (Rules 1 and 2). The lesson connected these units into a single harmonious sequence of action in two ways. First was the exercise with which the example ends, in which the teacher directed students to a workbook to provide independent practice opportunity. The workbook sentences should contain possessives similar to those found in any newspaper, magazine, or school essay. Second was the teacher's intention to provide examples of real mistakes occurring in newspapers and magazines for additional practice at the end of the lesson. Figure 7.8 traces the steps a student might take in combining the facts and rules into an action sequence for one sentence in the workbook.

Figure 7.8   Steps involved in translating the following sentence into correct possessive form: "In Mrs. Jones paper, there was an article about a friend of Robert."

Step 1   Is ownership indicated in this sentence?
Step 2   If yes, where?
          the paper belongs to Mrs. Jones
          the friend belongs to Robert
Step 3   Has an *of* phrase been substituted for a noun (Rule 1)?
          If yes, where?
          friend of Robert has been substituted for Robert's friend
Step 4   Does any word denoting ownership end in *s*? (Rule 2)
          If yes, where?
          Jones paper should be written *Jones's* paper
Step 5   Therefore, the correct possessive form of this sentence is "In Mrs. Jones's paper there was an article about Robert's friend."

In the preceding dialogue, the teacher's examples of errors from newspapers and magazines provided students an opportunity to form action sequences from the facts and rules they learned. These real-life examples further increased the authenticity of their learning. In your own classroom, make opportunities for practice increasingly resemble applications in the real world until the examples you provide are indistinguishable from those outside the classroom. Using clippings from actual newspapers and magazines was this teacher's way of doing so.

The purpose of providing opportunities for all types of independent practice is to develop automatic responses in students, so they no longer need to recall each individual unit of content but can use all the units simultaneously. Thus the goal of the example lesson was "to write a sentence using possessives correctly" and not "to recite Rule 1 and Rule 2." Automaticity is reached through mastery of the units that make up a complete response and sufficient practice in composing these pieces into a complete action sequence. Your goal is to plan sufficient opportunities for independent practice to allow students' individual responses to become composed and automatic.

Regardless of the type of practice activity used, keep in mind several guidelines for promoting effective practice:

- *Students should understand the reason for practice.* Practice often turns into busywork, which can create boredom, frustration, and noncompliance. Learners should approach classroom practice with the same enthusiasm with which an Olympic athlete pursues laps in the pool or on the track. This is more likely to occur if (1) you make known to learners the purpose of the practice ("We will need to be proficient at solving these problems in order to go on to our next activity"), and (2) practice occurs during as well as after new learning ("Let's stop right here, so you can try some of these problems yourselves").

- *Effective practice is delivered in a manner that is brief, nonevaluative, and supportive.* Practice involves more than simply saying, "OK. Take out your books, turn to page 78, and answer questions 1, 3, 7, and 9. You have 20 minutes." Rather, your introduction to a practice activity should accomplish three objectives: (1) Inform the learners that they are going to practice something they are capable of succeeding at ("You've done part of this before, so this shouldn't be much different"); (2) dispel anxiety about doing the task through the use of nonevaluative and nonthreatening language ("You've got part of it right, Anita. Now, think some more and you'll have it"); and (3) let the learners know that you will be around to monitor their work and support their efforts ("I will be around to help, so let me know if you have a problem").

- *Practice should be designed to ensure success.* Practice makes perfect only when those practicing are doing so correctly. If your learners are making many math, punctuation, or problem-solving mistakes, practice is making imperfect. Design your practice to produce as few errors as possible. For example, develop worksheets to ensure that most learners complete correctly at least 60% to 80% of the problems.

- *Practice should be arranged to allow students to receive feedback.* As we learned earlier in our discussion of modeling, feedback exerts a powerful effect on learning. Develop procedures and routines for rapid checking of work so learners know as soon as possible how well they are performing. Using peers to correct one another's practice is an efficient way to give feedback. Also, having answer sheets handy so learners can check their own work can be a simple and effective means of providing feedback.

- *Practice should have the qualities of progress, challenge, and variety.* Some have found that the key to preventing learners from becoming bored is to design practice opportunities so learners actually see that they are making progress. ("Don't forget to check your answers with the key on the board.") In addition, introduce practice in a challenging and enthusiastic manner. ("This will really test your understanding with some new and interesting kinds of problems.") Finally, practice exercises should include a variety of examples and situations.

Perform the following activities to ensure that students become actively engaged in the practice you provide:

1. *Direct* the class through the first independent practice item by talking through it aloud. This gives the scheduled seatwork a definite beginning, and students who are unclear about the assignment can ask questions without distracting others. This also provides a mental model for attaining a correct answer, which students can use in subsequent problems.

2. *Schedule* seatwork as soon as possible after the eliciting and feedback exercises. This helps students understand that independent practice is relevant to the guided practice provided earlier. If you do not provide opportunities for independent practice immediately but provide them on a later day, students likely will make a high number of requests for information; this will lead you inefficiently to repeat key portions of the previous day's lesson. As with all forms of learning, practice should follow the time of learning as soon as possible for maximum recall and understanding.

3. *Circulate* around the classroom while students are engaged in independent practice to provide feedback, ask questions, and give brief explanations (Emmer et al., 2006). Spend circulation time equally across most of your students—don't concentrate on a small number of students. Try to average 30 seconds or less per student. Minimize your scanning of written responses, prompting for alternative answers, or reminding students of facts and rules so as not to reduce your time available for monitoring the work of other students. Monitoring student responses during independent seatwork can be an important direct instruction function if you keep contacts short and focused on specific issues for which a brief explanation is adequate.

WEEKLY AND MONTHLY REVIEWS

The sixth and final direct instruction strategy involves conducting **weekly and monthly reviews.** Periodic review ensures that you have taught all task-relevant information needed for future lessons and you have identified areas that require the reteaching of key facts, rules, and sequences. Without periodic review, you have no way of knowing whether direct instruction has been successful in teaching the required facts, rules, and sequences.

Periodic review has long been a part of almost every instructional strategy. In the context of direct instruction, however, periodic review and the recycling of instruction take on added importance because of the brisk pace at which direct instruction is conducted. You can establish the proper pace by noting the approximate percentage of errors occurring during guided practice and feedback; 60% to 80% correct responses indicate a satisfactory pace.

Weekly and monthly reviews also help determine whether the pace is right or whether to adjust it before covering too much content. When student responses in weekly and monthly reviews are correct, quick, and firm about 95% of the time, the pace is adequate. Independent practice and homework should raise the percentage of correct responses from approximately 60% to 80% during guided practice and feedback to approximately 95% on weekly and monthly reviews. If results are below these levels—and especially if they are

Figure 7.9   Cycles of rising and falling action.*

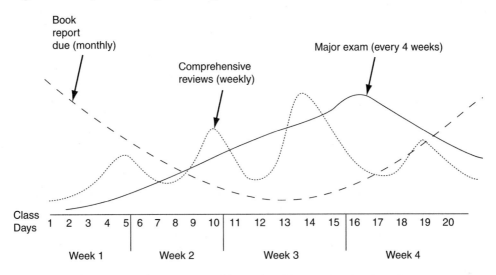

*Height of cycles indicates relative amounts of instructional focus and student intensity.

substantially below—your pace is too fast and some reteaching of facts, rules, and sequences may be necessary, especially if they are prerequisite to later learning.

Another obvious advantage of weekly and monthly reviews is that they strengthen correct but hesitant responses. Reviewing facts, rules, and sequences that are the basis of task-relevant prior understandings for later lessons will give some learners a second chance to grasp material that they missed or only partially learned the first time around. Students often welcome these reviews; it is a chance to go over material they may have missed, was difficult to learn the first time through, and may be covered on unit tests.

Finally, a regular weekly review (not a review "every so often") is the key to performing this direct instruction strategy. The weekly review is intended to build momentum. Momentum results from gradually increasing the coverage and depth of each weekly review until it is time for a comprehensive monthly review or exam (Posner, 1987). The objective is to create a review cycle that rises and falls in about a month, as shown in Figure 7.9. The low point of this cycle occurs at the start of a direct instruction unit, when only a week's material need be reviewed. The weekly reviews then become increasingly comprehensive until a major monthly exam checks for understanding of all the previous month's learning. Momentum is built by targeting greater and greater amounts of instruction for review, while other assignments, for example, a book review, are purposefully scheduled at the low points of the review cycle when students are not responsible for assimilating large amounts of accumulative review material. The comprehensiveness of a review should build gradually so that students are not overwhelmed with lots of unfamiliar review content and always know what will be covered in the next review.

Following is a lesson plan for our direct instruction dialog following the written format provided in chapter 4.

OTHER FORMS OF DIRECT INSTRUCTION

So far, direct instruction has been discussed as though it occurs only in a presentation-recitation format. This is perhaps the most popular format for direct instruction but is by no means the only one. Other ways of executing the direct instruction model (either independent of the presentation-recitation format or in association with it) include computer-assisted instruction,

EXAMPLE DIRECT INSTRUCTION LESSON PLAN: *Grammar*

Unit Title: Punctuation

Lesson Title: Forming and Punctuating Possessives

1 **Gaining attention** Display October school newspaper with punctuation error in headline. Point to error.

2 **Informing the learner of the objective** At the end of the period, students will be able to find mistakes in the newspapers (in my file under "Punctuation") and make the necessary changes.

3 **Stimulating recall of prerequisite learning** Review the part of speech most likely to own or possess something by asking for the definition of a noun.

4 **Presenting the stimulus material** Present two rules of possession: Rule 1. Use the possessive form whenever an *of* phrase can be substituted for a noun. Rule 2. For words that are plurals ending in *s*, place an apostrophe after the *s*. But for proper nouns ending in *s*, place an *apostrophe s* after the *s*. Write rules on board.

5 **Eliciting the desired behavior** Display the following examples on a transparency and ask students to convert them to the possessive form one at a time. See text pp. 101–103 for other examples.

Delay of a month	Speech of the president
Home of Jenkins	The television set of Mr. Burns

6 **Providing feedback** Write the correct possessive form on the transparency as students finish each example. Wait for students to finish (all heads up) before providing the answer for the next example. Probe for complete understanding by asking for the rule.

7 **Assessing the behavior** Use the exercise on page 87 of the workbook to assess student understanding and to provide additional practice. Use ordered recitation until about 90% correct responses are attained. Place 10 possessives on the unit test requiring the application of Rule 1 and Rule 2. Use examples in text, pp. 101–103.

peer and cross-age tutoring, various kinds of audiolingual and communication tools (e.g., recorded lessons for learning to read in the early grades), and the use of the computer and CD-ROM as an information and practice provider.

Some of these approaches have been creatively programmed to include all, or almost all, of the six direct instruction functions (checking, presenting and structuring, guided student practice, feedback and correctives, independent practice, and periodic review). Some of these alternatives to the presentation-recitation format have succeeded with certain types of content and students. However, because these alternative approaches are much less under your control than is the presentation-recitation format you create, you should carefully consider their applicability to your specific instructional goals and students. Although programmed instruction and computer software, and various drill and practice media, such as described in chapter 4, often are associated with the direct instruction model, their treatment of the intended content may be far from direct. Therefore, whenever using these formats and

Video Window

The Direct Instruction Model

In this video, you will see Bob using the direct instruction model to teach a lesson on the Vietnam War in a high school history class. As you watch this lesson unfold, ask yourself whether this teacher's lesson goal is to teach facts, rules, and sequences or to teach concepts, patterns, and abstractions. Taking your answer into account, indicate how well Bob achieved his goal by implementing the following five criteria suggested by Rosenshine and Stevens (1986) for an effective direct instruction lesson. Which criteria were met and which were not?

- Clearly presents goals and main points
- Presents content sequentially
- Is specific and concrete
- Checks for students understanding
- Reteaches what students have difficulty understanding

 To answer these questions online, go to the Video Windows *module for this chapter on the Companion Website at www.prenhall.com/borich.*

associated courseware, be sure to preview both their method and content for adherence to the six strategies of the direct instruction model.

Finally, programmed instruction and computer software, specialized media, and information and communication technologies follow a direct instruction model most closely when they are programmed for basic academic skills. This is where the direct instruction format can be of most benefit in increasing student achievement (Lindsley, 1991, 1992). At the same time, it can relieve you of the sometimes arduous chore of providing individualized remedial instruction to a small number of students. Building a library of individualized courseware that covers the basic skills most frequently needed in your grade level and content area will be an important goal for your classroom.

PROMOTING THE GOALS OF DIRECT INSTRUCTION IN THE CULTURALLY DIVERSE CLASSROOM

We have seen that a task-oriented teacher maximizes content coverage and gives students the greatest opportunity to learn. Likewise, students who are involved in, acting on, and otherwise thinking about the material being presented have the greatest opportunity to learn. The key to bringing these two important dimensions of effective teaching together—task orientation and student engagement—rests with how you interact with your students to invoke a willingness to respond and apply what they have been learning. In classrooms where the range of individual and cultural differences is great, student engagement in the learning process during direct instruction can be a major challenge to achieving performance outcomes.

One facet of research dealing with cultural diversity and student engagement that can help bridge the gap has focused on differences in fluency and oral expression among learners during presentation-recitation. For example, student fluency or quickness to respond can be influenced by nurturing and expressive qualities of the teacher (Lustig & Koester, 2005).

The implication is that student hesitancy in responding and becoming engaged in the learning process may, for some cultural groups, be more a function of the attitude and cultural style of the teacher than of student ability. Also, body posture, language, and eye contact form a pattern of **metacommunication** that is recognized by the learner—and acted on according to the message being conveyed, intentionally or not (Chen & Starasta, 2005). For example, a formal body posture and questions posed in an expressionless voice, without eye contact, may not invoke a commitment to respond. In other words, teachers must convey a sense of caring about the learner before engagement can take place. Engagement techniques alone (e.g., presenting and structuring, guiding student practice, and providing feedback and corrections) will not be sufficient to actively engage students in the learning process unless these techniques are accompanied by the appropriate metacommunication expressing nurturance and caring. Bowers and Flinders (1991) suggest some of the ways teachers can promote student engagement by conveying a sense of nurturance and caring:

- Use appropriate examples to clarify concepts and model performance. "Let me give you an example that will help you see the relationship."
- Accept the student's way of understanding new concepts. "That's an interesting answer. Would you like to tell us how you arrived at it?"
- Reduce feelings of competitiveness. "Today, those who wish can work with a partner on the practice exercise."
- Increase opportunities for social reinforcement. "If you like, you can ask someone sitting nearby how they worked the problem."
- Facilitate group achievement. "When you're finished with your work, you can join another group to help them solve the problem."
- Use and expect culturally appropriate eye contact with students. "Amanda, I'm going to sit down next to you and watch you work the first problem."
- Recognize longer pauses and slower tempo. "Take your time. I'll wait for you to think of an answer."
- Respond to unique or different questions during a response. "You're asking about something else. Let me give you that answer, then we'll go back to the first question."
- Balance compliments and reinforcement equally. "Let's not forget, both Angel and Damon got the right answer but in different ways."

Although much still needs to be known about cultural diversity and student engagement during direct instruction, one thing is clear: Students of any culture are more likely to engage expressively in the learning process in an atmosphere that (1) emphasizes the importance of unique learner responses, (2) reduces feelings of individual competitiveness, (3) promotes a multisensory (e.g., telling as well as performing) learning environment, (4) encourages social reinforcement and peer interaction, and (5) conveys a sense of nurturance and caring.

SUMMING UP

This chapter introduced you to direct instruction strategies. Its key terms and main points were:

Categories of Teaching and Learning

1. Two broad classifications of learning are facts, rules, and action sequences (Type 1) and concepts, patterns, and abstractions (Type 2).

2. Type 1 outcomes generally represent behaviors at the lower levels of complexity in the cognitive, affective, and psychomotor domains; Type 2 outcomes frequently represent behaviors at the higher levels of complexity in these domains.

3. Type 1 teaching activities require combining facts and rules at the knowledge and comprehension

level into a sequence of actions that can be learned through observation, rote repetition, and practice. Type 1 outcomes have "right answers" that can be learned by memorization and practice.

4. Type 2 teaching activities go beyond facts, rules, and sequences to help the learner create, synthesize, identify, and recognize an answer that cannot be easily modeled or memorized. Type 2 outcomes may have many "right answers."

5. The learning of facts, rules, and action sequences is most commonly taught with teaching strategies that emphasize knowledge acquisition; the learning of concepts, patterns, and abstractions is most commonly taught with teaching strategies that emphasize concept learning, inquiry and problem solving.

6. The acquisition of facts, rules, and action sequences is most efficiently achieved through a process known as the direct instruction model. This model is primarily teacher centered; facts, rules, and action sequences are passed on to students in a presentation-recitation format involving large amounts of teacher talk, questions and answers, review and practice, and the immediate correction of student errors.

Introduction to Direct Instruction Strategies

7. The direct instruction model is characterized by full-class (as opposed to small-group) instruction; by the organization of learning based on questions posed by you; by the provision of detailed and redundant practice; by the presentation of material so learners master one new fact, rule, or sequence before the teacher presents the next; and by the formal arrangement of the classroom to maximize drill and practice.

8. Direct instruction is most appropriate when content in texts and workbooks does not appear in appropriately sized pieces, when your active involvement in the teaching process is necessary to arouse or heighten student interest, and when the content to be taught represents task-relevant prior knowledge for subsequent learning.

Daily Review and Checking the Previous Day's Work

9. Techniques for daily review and checking include the following:
   - Have students identify difficult homework problems in a question-and-answer format.
   - Sample the understanding of a few students who are likely to represent the class.
   - Explicitly review task-relevant prior learning required for the day's lesson.

Presenting and Structuring

10. Techniques for presenting and structuring new content include the following:
    - Establish part–whole relationships.
    - Identify sequential relationships.
    - Find combinations of relationships.
    - Draw comparative relationships.

Guiding Student Practice

11. Techniques for guiding student practice include the following:
    - Ask students to respond privately and then be singled out for help.
    - Call on students to respond whether or not their hands are raised.
    - Prepare questions beforehand and randomly ask students to respond.

Feedback and Correctives

12. Providing appropriate feedback and correctives involves knowing how to respond to answers that are (1) correct, quick, and firm; (2) correct but hesitant; (3) incorrect but careless; and (4) incorrect due to lack of knowledge.

13. For a correct, quick, and firm response, acknowledge the correct response and either ask another question of the same student or quickly move on to another student.

14. For a correct but hesitant response, provide a reinforcing statement and quickly restate the facts, rules, or steps needed for the right answer.

15. For a correct but careless response, indicate that the response is incorrect and quickly move to the next student without further comment.

16. For an incorrect response that is not due to carelessness but to a lack of knowledge, engage the student in finding the correct response with hints, probes, or a related but simpler question.

17. For most learning involving knowledge acquisition, the steps between successive portions of your lesson should be made small enough to produce approximately 60% to 80% correct answers in a practice and feedback session.

18. Reviewing, reexplaining, and prompting are effective until approximately 80% of your students respond correctly, after which correctives should be made briefer or students should be guided to individualized learning materials.

Independent Practice

19. Design independent practice so the learner puts together facts and rules to form action sequences that increasingly resemble applications in the real world. Make opportunities for independent practice as soon after the time of learning as possible.

Weekly and Monthly Reviews

20. Pace instruction so student responses to questions posed in weekly and monthly reviews are correct, quick, and firm about 95% of the time.

21. Use independent practice and homework to raise the percentage of correct responses from approximately 60% to 80% during guided practice and feedback to approximately 95% on weekly and monthly reviews.

Promoting the Goals of Direct Instruction in the Culturally Diverse Classroom

22. Student engagement in the culturally diverse classroom is promoted by accepting unique learner responses, reducing competitiveness, promoting peer interaction, and conveying a sense of nurturance and caring.

KEY TERMS

Active responding, 243
Daily review and checking, 233
Direct instruction, 226
Feedback and correctives, 241
Gestural prompts, 238
Guided student practice, 237
Independent practice, 243
Indirect instruction, 226
Mastery learning, 229

Metacommunication, 250
Ordered turns, 239
Passive responding, 243
Physical prompts, 238
Presenting and structuring, 234
Rule-example-rule order, 237
Social learning theory, 239
Verbal prompts, 238
Weekly and monthly reviews, 246

DISCUSSION AND PRACTICE QUESTIONS

Questions marked with an asterisk are answered in appendix B. See also the Companion Website for this text at *www.prenhall.com/borich* for more assessment options.

*1. Identify the learning outcomes associated with Type 1 and Type 2 teaching strategies. To what levels of behavior in the cognitive domain does each type of learning apply?

*2. What type of learning outcomes are elicited by instructional strategies that emphasize knowledge acquisition? What type of learning outcomes are elicited by instructional strategies that emphasize inquiry or problem solving?

*3. If you were to describe the direct instruction model, what instructional characteristics would you associate with it?

*4. Provide some examples of action verbs in the cognitive, affective, and psychomotor domains that describe the type of outcomes expected from the direct instructional model. Which outcomes do you think would be hardest to achieve?

*5. For what instructional goals is the direct instruction model most appropriate? Can you think of any others not cited in the chapter?

*6. Explain why providing guided student practice in a nonevaluative atmosphere is important for learning to occur. What would you do to encourage a reluctant student to make a first crude response?

7. The following second-grade student responses were received by a teacher after asking the question, "What does 5 plus 3 equal?"

◆   ◆   ◆

Brooke: It could be 8.
Juan: 9.
Jason: 53.
Ashley: 8.

◆   ◆   ◆

Provide an appropriate teacher prompt that moves each student closer to the right or more confident answer.

8. The following tenth-grade student responses were received by a teacher who asked, "What was one of the underlying reasons for the Civil War?"

◆   ◆   ◆

Tahnee: The South wanted the land owned by the North.
Akim: I read somewhere it was religious persecution.
Ken: Well, let me think . . . it had something to do with slavery.
Tracy: The economics of the South.

◆   ◆   ◆

Provide an appropriate teacher prompt that moves each student closer to the right or more confident answer.

*9. What approximate percentage of correct answers should you work toward in a practice and feedback session? How would you change your instructional approach if only 30% of your student responses were correct in a practice and feedback session?

*10. What is the primary purpose of independent practice in direct instruction? Choose a lesson in your teaching area and show how you would use independent practice to fulfill this purpose. How would you vary the independent practice if

more time and opportunity for practice became available?

*11. When circulating around the room to monitor independent practice, what would be some of the ways you could make your monitoring time more efficient?

*12. Approximately what percentage of student responses during weekly and monthly review sessions should be correct, quick, and firm? What percentage would prompt you to reconsider your teaching approach to this content?

FIELD EXPERIENCE ACTIVITIES

*1. During direct instruction, what would be some of the ways you might review and check the previous day's work? Which do you feel would be the most appropriate for your classroom?

*2. After identifying the four techniques for structuring content, provide an example of each in a subject you will be teaching. Which do you think most naturally fits the way your subject matter is organized?

*3. Identify the order in which rules and examples of the rules should be given to promote the greatest amount of comprehension and retention of content. Illustrate a rule–example sequence with content from your major teaching area.

*4. During direct instruction, how is prompting used to help a student achieve the correct response? Choose a topic and create an example of a prompt you would give a student after a wrong or partially wrong response. Indicate both the student's incorrect answer and your response.

*5. What are four different degrees at which a student response may vary in its correctness? Create a teacher response that you think is appropriate to each of the four degrees.

*6. What are four strategies cited in this chapter for responding to an incorrect response? Think of at least one more strategy and give an example of how you would use it in your classroom.

*7. For a subject you will teach, describe a cycle of weekly and monthly reviews (for example, daily checks for understanding, weekly reviews, and comprehensive reviews monthly) that you would like to implement in your classroom to increase the percentage of your students responding correctly, quickly and firmly. Indicate your sequence of review activities and how they would engage students in the learning process by heightening student interest and increasing achievement of your lesson and unit outcomes.

8. What metacommunication techniques might be used in a culturally diverse classroom to promote engagement during instruction? With examples, illustrate how some might be more culturally appropriate than others.

DIGITAL PORTFOLIO ACTIVITIES

The following digital portfolio activities relate to INTASC principles 1, 3, and 4.

1. For Field Experience Activity 7 you were asked to describe a cycle of weekly and monthly reviews for raising the percentage of your students' responses that are correct, quick and firm during direct instruction. Now add to your response what other instructional strategies, for example, independent practice and homework, you might use to raise the percentage of correct responses from approximately 60% to 80% during daily guided practice and feedback to approximately 95% of

responses that are correct, quick, and firm on weekly and monthly reviews. Place your description in a folder titled *Direct Instruction* and place it in your digital portfolio. This will remind you during unit planning how you can increase student engagement in your lessons and build momentum that keeps your students focused on achieving unit outcomes.

2. For Field Experience Activity 8 you were asked to demonstrate with examples some of the metacommunication techniques that could be used in a culturally diverse classroom to promote student engagement during direct instruction. Place your response to this question in your *Teaching Diverse Learners* digital portfolio folder as a reminder during your student teaching and beyond of some ways you can heighten the engagement of learners from different cultures, socioeconomic backgrounds, and learning styles in a heterogeneous classroom.

CLASSROOM OBSERVATION ACTIVITIES

The following classroom observation activities relate to INTASC principles 1 and 4.

1. You learned in this chapter that reviewing or summarizing means more than just calling attention to the end of a lesson. Reviews and summaries can, and many times do, go beyond a simple regurgitation of the facts as they were presented. If you can identify key points, a code or symbol system for helping learners retain the content, and/or a generalization that integrates different parts of the lesson, you have observed an effective review. For this observation activity go to the Companion Website for this chapter at *www.prenhall.com/borich* and you will find an observation record titled *Observing Lesson Reviews*. Use this form to observe a lesson to note whether:

   (1) Key points were included in a review in which the teacher reiterated the most important content that was presented.

   (2) The teacher reorganized the content, indicating how it should be stored and remembered, sometimes providing students a memory-aiding code or symbol system by which the contents of the lesson could be more easily stored and recalled for later use.

   (3) The teacher consolidated content by summarizing or touching on only the most general elements of the lesson, providing students with an opportunity to fill in any missing gaps about the main features of the lesson.

2. On the Companion Website for this chapter you will find a *Checklist for Observing Direct Instruction* that lists some of the most important dimensions of direction instruction. Place this scale in your *Direct Instruction* digital portfolio folder to use when you have the opportunity to observe and assess a direct instruction lesson.

CHAPTER CASE HISTORY AND PRAXIS TEST PREPARATION

DIRECTIONS: The following case history pertains to chapter 7 content. After reading the case history, answer the short-answer question that follows and consult appendix D to find different levels of scored student responses and the rubric used to determine the quality of each response. You also have the opportunity to submit your responses online to receive feedback by visiting the *Case History* module for this chapter on the Companion Website, where you will also find additional questions pertaining to Praxis test content.

Case History

Mrs. Martinez teaches fifth grade to a class of 28 students. Recent standardized test scores at the school have been low, particularly in language and reading. Over one half of the class ranked in the lowest third of national norms in last year's test in either the reading or language portion. The school is making a strong effort to upgrade these skills.

Mrs. Martinez is in the midst of a lesson on teaching the appropriate use of *there*, *they're*, and *their*. The three words are written on the board in the following way:

There	**They're**	**Their**
a place	short for "they are"	shows ownership

She points to the first word and spells it. "T-H-E-R-E. I mean a place when I say this word. I might say, 'Put the book over there.' T-H-E-R-E. I mean a specific place.

"Also, take away the *t*" (Mrs. Martinez covers the letter *t* of *there*), "and you have *here*. That's another clue, here and there. Here and there," she repeats, this time pointing to her desk for *here* and to a desk in the middle of the room for *there*.

"Juan, give me another sentence that uses *there* to mean a place."

◆   ◆   ◆

Juan:	I want to go out there. (He looks out the window toward the baseball diamond.)
Mrs. Martinez:	Spell your word correctly.
Juan:	T-H-E-R-E.
Mrs. Martinez:	Well done. Susan, what is the little word inside that is our clue?
	(Susan doesn't answer and looks confused. Mrs. Martinez goes to the board and covers the *t* of *there* to expose *here*.)
Susan:	Here, H-E-R-E. (Mrs. Martinez points to her desk and then to a more distant desk. At first Susan says nothing. Mrs. Martinez gestures again.) Oh, here and there, here and there.
Mrs. Martinez:	You're good at getting clues, Susan. I bet you'd be a good detective. Now, let's look at the next word. They're—T-H-E-Y-'-R-E. It sounds the same as our first word, but it means something very different. T-H-E-Y-'-R-E is not a place; it's a short way to combine two words, *they* and *are*. The apostrophe (here she points appropriately to the board) stands for the letter *a* that we have taken out. "They are my friends." Say it fast and it becomes, "They're my friends." Matt, give us a sentence using our second word, T-H-E-Y-'-R-E.
Matt:	(Matt is a high-performing student whose attention has been on a baseball game going on outside.)
	Their team can't even hit the ball.
Mrs. Martinez:	Is Matt using our second word, T-H-E-Y-'-R-E, the one that is short for *they are*? What do you think, Parish?
Parish:	No, he should have said, "They're not able to hit the ball." T-H-E-Y-'-R-E, short for *they are*.
Mrs. Martinez:	Good, Parish. You even managed to keep the meaning of the sentence Matt used. (She pauses and walks slowly to the window.) Is Mr. Heath's class really that bad? Then I know we can beat them in next week's homeroom challenge.

◆   ◆   ◆

Short-Answer Question

This section presents a sample Praxis short-answer question. In appendix D you will find sample responses along with the standards used in scoring these responses.

DIRECTIONS: The following question requires you to write a short answer. Base your answer on your knowledge of principles of learning and teaching from chapter 7. Be sure to answer all parts of the question.

1. Direct instruction provides information directly to students interspersed with explanation, examples, practice, and feedback. Using your knowledge of research on teaching practices, give three reasons that this teacher-centered strategy is appropriate for Mrs. Martinez's lesson.

Discrete Multiple-Choice Questions

DIRECTIONS: Each of the multiple-choice questions that follow is based on Praxis-related pedagogical knowledge in chapter 7. Select the answer that is best in each case and compare your results with those in appendix D. See also the Companion Website for this text at *www.prenhall.com/borich* for more assessment options.

1. The interactive process between student and teacher that is influenced by the teacher's body posture, language, and eye contact forms a pattern called
   a. Engagement
   b. Metacommunication
   c. Corrective feedback
   d. Essential attributes

2. One way to help students remember behavior modeled by the instructor is to ask learners to visualize or create a mental image of what the teacher has just demonstrated. The student response is called
   a. Mastery learning
   b. Overt rehearsal
   c. Covert rehearsal
   d. Structuring

3. Teacher-led guided practice material should be designed to elicit which approximate percentage of correct answers in practice and feedback sessions?
   a. 50%–70%
   b. 60%–80%
   c. 70%–90%
   d. 80%–100%

4. Which of the following is *not* a characteristic of the direct model of instruction?
   a. Provide student opportunities for guided practice
   b. Review daily and reteach when necessary
   c. Encourage students to relate content to their own experience
   d. After guided practice, allow students opportunities for independent practice

5. During direct instruction the effective teacher often provides prompts, hints, and other types of supplementary instructional stimuli to help learners make the correct response. Which of the following categories of prompts would be the least intrusive, leaving the learner less dependent on the prompt for performing the behavior the next time?
   a. Gestural prompts
   b. Physical prompts
   c. Verbal prompts
   d. Physical and verbal prompts

Chapter 8

Teaching Strategies for Indirect Instruction

This chapter will help you answer the following questions and meet the following INTASC principles for effective teaching:

1. What is concept learning?
2. What is inquiry learning?
3. What is problem-based learning?
4. What are constructivist strategies for teaching?
5. What are some ways of promoting the goals of concept learning, inquiry, and problem solving in a culturally diverse classroom?

INTASC 1: The teacher understands the central concepts, tools of inquiry, and structures of the discipline(s) he or she teaches and can create learning experiences that make these aspects of subject matter meaningful for students.

INTASC 2: The teacher understands how children learn and develop, and can provide learning opportunities that support their intellectual, social, and personal development.

INTASC 3: The teacher understands how students differ in their approaches to learning and creates instructional opportunities that are adapted to diverse learners.

INTASC 4: The teacher understands and uses a variety of instructional strategies to encourage students' development of critical thinking, problem solving, and performance skills.

INTASC 6: The teacher uses knowledge of effective verbal, nonverbal, and media communication techniques to foster active inquiry, collaboration, and supportive interaction in the classroom.

*C*hapter 7 introduced you to direct instruction for teaching facts, rules, and action sequences. Now we consider indirect instruction for teaching concepts, inquiry, and problem solving.

An old adage says: "Tell me and I forget, show me and I remember, involve me and I understand." The teaching of concepts, inquiry, and problem solving are different forms of indirect instruction that actively involve your learners in seeking resolutions to questions and issues while they construct new knowledge. Indirect instruction is an approach to teaching and learning in which (1) the process is inquiry, (2) the content involves concepts, and (3) the context is a problem.

These three ideas are brought together in special ways in the indirect instruction model. This chapter presents teaching strategies you can use to compose your own indirect teaching approach that asks your learners to share the excitement of becoming actively involved in their own learning and contributing new knowledge to solve real-world problems. We begin by looking into two classrooms, one in which Tim Robbins is teaching a lesson with the direct instruction model and the other in which Kay Greer is teaching the same lesson with the indirect instruction model.

It is the third 6 weeks of the fall semester, and Tim Robbins is teaching a unit on fractions to his fourth-grade class. During the first 12 weeks of the year, all fourth graders learned about numbers and number theory. They covered such topics as odd, even, positive, and negative numbers. The fourth graders are also familiar with such numerical concepts as multiples, factors, and the base 10 system for writing numbers.

On this day we observe Mr. Robbins. He is teaching a lesson on equivalent fractions as a way of representing the same amount. During the preceding four lessons, his learners have studied about fractions as quantities and learned how fractions that look different (e.g., $\frac{1}{2}$, $\frac{2}{4}$) actually represent the same amount. The present lesson is intended to reinforce this idea.

Mr. Robbins begins the lesson with a quick review of the previous lesson. On the overhead projector, he shows pictures of objects such as pies and loaves of bread divided to represent different fractions of the whole. In rapid-fire fashion, his learners call out the fractions. He then projects a chart with undivided whole objects and has learners come up and divide them into halves, thirds, fourths, and so on, while other learners do the same on worksheets. Each learner gets immediate feedback on his or her answers.

Next, he signals the class to clear their desks except for a pencil and draws their attention to a large, brightly colored chart hanging from the front blackboard. (The chart is shown in Figure 8.1.)

He passes out a similar dittoed chart to the students. Mr. Robbins explains that for each row the students are to complete the fraction with a denominator of 100 that equals the fraction in the row. Then they are to fill in the third square with the decimal equivalent of that fraction.

Mr. Robbins first models how to do this. He demonstrates (pointing out that they have already learned this) how to make an equivalent fraction by multiplying the original fraction by a fraction that equals 1. He works several examples to be sure his students have the concept and has them copy the examples onto their chart.

He then calls on several students to come to the front of the room and demonstrate several more examples for the class. Mr. Robbins has the students state as they work, for the class to hear, how they are solving the problems. He checks that the rest of the class correctly fills in the chart at their desks.

Finally, he breaks the class into small groups and directs them to fill out the remainder of the chart. He provides each group with a key to immediately check their responses when finished. As the learners busily engage in their seatwork, Mr. Robbins moves from group to

Figure 8.1 Mr. Robbins's chart for teaching fractions.

$\frac{1}{4} \times \frac{25}{25}$	$\frac{25}{100}$	.25
$\frac{1}{2} \times \frac{}{50}$	$\frac{}{100}$	.
$\frac{1}{5} \times$	$\frac{}{100}$	.
$\frac{2}{5}$	$\frac{}{100}$	.
$\frac{3}{4}$	$\frac{}{100}$	.
$\frac{5}{4}$	$\frac{}{100}$	.
$\frac{3}{2}$	$\frac{}{100}$	.

group, checking, giving feedback, correcting, or praising as needed. Mr. Robbins has designed this lesson to show that fractions that look different can be equal in order to point out the relationship of decimals and fractions and to use this as a foundation for teaching the relationships between dollars, decimals, and fractions in a subsequent lesson.

In the classroom next door to Mr. Robbins, Kay Greer also is teaching a unit on fractional equivalents.* As the lesson begins, Mrs. Greer asks Denisha to tell the class what she said yesterday about fractions. "A fraction like $\frac{1}{2}$ isn't a number," she asserts, "because it isn't on the number line." Denisha points to the number line running along the top of the front blackboard. "See! There's no $\frac{1}{2}$. Just 1, 2, 3, 4, . . . like that!"

"Well, class, let's think about what Denisha says. Let me give you a problem, and we'll study it and, then, maybe come to some conclusion about if a fraction is a number." She turns on the overhead and projects the following for all to see:

> *A boy has four loaves of bread that he bought at the local supermarket. He has eight friends, and he wants each friend to get an equal part of the bread. How much bread should he give each of his friends?*

Mrs. Greer draws the four loaves on the overhead and watches as the children, arranged in six groups of five, copy the drawings into their notebook. She walks around the classroom, occasionally prompting groups with the question, "How much bread is each one going to get?"

The children argue among themselves: "You can't do it!" "There isn't enough bread!" "How many slices are in each loaf?" After about 10 minutes Mrs. Greer asks, "Does anyone need more time to work on this? How many are ready to discuss?"

A few raise their hands. The rest are busy drawing and redrawing loaves of bread, sketching lines across them. Several minutes go by, and Mrs. Greer says, "OK, would someone like to show their solution?"

Frank raises his hand, walks to the overhead, and draws his solution. "I'm not sure it's right," he hedges. Frank draws four loaves of bread and divides each loaf into eight slices. (Frank's drawing appears in Figure 8.2a.)

He looks up and announces to the class, "Each friend gets four slices!"

"That's wrong!" challenges Rosa. "Each friend gets two slices, see?" She walks to the overhead, draws four loaves of bread, and divides each loaf into four slices. (Rosa's drawing appears in Figure 8.2b.) "Each friend gets two slices," she asserts, pointing to the equal portions.

"Why not just give each friend half a loaf?" asks Albert.

"Come up here and draw your solution," says Mrs. Greer. Albert walks up to the overhead and sketches his proposal to the class. "Can you write the number that each gets?" she asks. Albert writes the number $\frac{1}{2}$ on the board.

"Well, Albert's and Rosa's slices are bigger than mine," protests Frank.

"Frank," asks Mrs. Greer, "why not write the number that shows how much of the bread your eight friends get? Albert's number is $\frac{1}{2}$. How much is one slice as Albert sees it?" she asks the class.

"One eighth," proposes Cal.

"Can you write that?" inquires Mrs. Greer. Cal comes up to the overhead and writes $\frac{1}{8}$ next to Frank's drawing.

---

*Information from D. L. Ball (1991), "Teaching Mathematics for Understanding: What Do Teachers Need to Know About Subject Matter?" in M. L. Kennedy (Ed.), *Teaching Academic Subjects to Diverse Learners* (pp. 67–69). New York: Teachers College Press.

Figure 8.2a Frank's drawing.

Loaves of bread

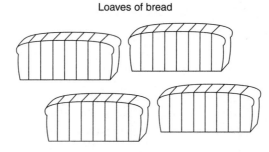

Figure 8.2b Rosa's drawing.

Loaves of bread

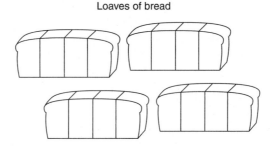

As children write different numbers for their solutions, Mrs. Greer asks, "Well, how can we have three different numbers for each of these solutions? We have one half, two fourths, four eighths," pointing to the different quantities and fractions on the overhead.

After several moments of silence, several hands shoot up, and one by one the children give explanations for the seeming discrepancy.

The lesson continues in this vein until 5 minutes before the bell. Mrs. Greer reviews what was concluded and sets the goal for the next lesson on fractions.

Now let's compare the lessons of Mrs. Greer and Mr. Robbins. Both lessons had the same goal: to help learners understand the concepts of quantity and equivalence pertaining to fractions. But they have designed two very different lessons to achieve this same end!

You may have noticed that the direct instruction approach has heavily influenced Mr. Robbins's lesson. He designed his lesson to elicit a minimum of mistakes. His activities elicit practice of correct responses followed by immediate feedback. For Mr. Robbins, learning involves correct responding, which is best accomplished by a teacher-directed or teacher-centered lesson.

Mrs. Greer, in contrast, has a less direct approach to learning. She is less focused on correct, rapid responses than on thought processes involving concepts, inquiry, and problem solving. Her lesson takes into consideration that her learners already have information and beliefs about fractions that may or may not be correct.

She wants to expose misconceptions and challenge learners to acquire new, more accurate perceptions through their own powers of reasoning. She carefully avoids providing answers. Her objective is to help learners understand fractions by influencing the cognitive processes by which they can elicit correct responses. Let's look at some of the cognitive processes around which she planned her lesson.

THE COGNITIVE PROCESSES OF LEARNING

Cognitive psychologists have identified three essential conditions for meaningful learning (R. E. Mayer, 1987): reception, availability, and activation. The reception and availability conditions are met when teachers focus their learners' attention on a problem and provide a framework or structure that organizes the content into meaningful parts, called an *anticipatory set* (Hunter, 1982) or **advance organizer** (Ausubell, 1968). Teachers fulfill the activation condition by modeling the inquiry process and by skilled questioning techniques. As learners develop greater skill at inquiry and problem solving, the teacher gradually fades assistance and allows learners to assume more and more responsibility for their own learning.

As you may recall, supporting this approach to learning and instruction is a movement called **constructivism.** Constructivist lessons are designed and sequenced to encourage learners to use their own experiences to actively construct meaning that makes sense to them rather than to acquire understanding through exposure to a format exclusively organized by the teacher (Fosnot, 2005; Llewellyn, 2002; Richardson, 1997). By reflecting on their own experiences students may change what they believe, discard old information for new information, and question, explore, and assess what they know.

For example, groups of students in a social studies class are discussing problems of pollution and what needs to be done about them. The teacher focuses on helping students to refocus their questions in ways that could lead to practical solutions. She encourages each student to reflect on his or her current experiences with pollution. When one of her students comes up with a concept that links various forms of pollution together and points to a single source, she seizes upon it to alert the class to this important contribution that would be a promising direction to explore. She encourages the students to consult the Web and other sources to substantiate their hypotheses and the credibility of their proposed solutions. Afterward, the class talks about what they have learned and how their observations and documentation helped them to understand the concept of pollution.

From examples like these, constructivists believe that knowledge results from the individual constructing reality from her or his own experiences. Learning occurs when learners create new rules and hypotheses on their own to explain what is being observed. The need to create new rules and formulate hypotheses is stimulated by classroom dialogue, problem-solving exercises, and individual projects and assignments that create discrepancies—or an imbalance—between old knowledge and new observations. Teachers use direct experience (Piaget, 1977; Stepien & Gallagher, 1993), problem- and project-based learning (Blumenfeld et al., 1991; Markham, Mergendoller, Larmer, & Ravitz, 2003), and social interaction (Vygotsky, 1962) to restore the balance while deemphasizing the role of lecturing and telling. Table 8.1 identifies some of the ways a constructivist classroom differs from a traditional classroom.

Many changes in how reading, writing, mathematics and science, and social studies are taught have followed constructivist thinking and the indirect instructional strategies that support it (T. Duffy & Jonassen, 1992; Fosnot, 2005; Richardson, 1997; Steffe & Gale, 1995). Let's look at some instructional strategies in these areas that have followed constructivist thinking.

Reading

For most of the 20th century, reading curricula have taught the skills of decoding, blending, sequencing, finding main ideas, and so on, outside the context of reading itself. These skills were usually practiced with contrived stories written in basal readers. Constructivist-influenced reading curricula now teach basic reading skills with a balanced approach, such as through the reading of literature while engaged in a search for meaning. Learners often work in small

Table 8.1   A constructivist classroom compared to a traditional classroom.

Traditional Classroom	Constructivist Classroom
Curriculum begins with the parts of the whole. Emphasizes basic skills.	Curriculum emphasizes big concepts, beginning with the whole and expanding to include the parts.
Strict adherence to fixed curriculum is highly valued.	Pursuit of student questions and interests is valued.
Materials are primarily textbooks and workbooks.	Materials include primary sources of material and manipulative materials.
Learning is based on repetition.	Learning is interactive, building on what the student already knows.
Teachers disseminate information to students; students are recipients of knowledge.	Teachers have a dialogue with students, helping students construct their own knowledge.
Teacher's role is directive, rooted in authority.	Teacher's role is interactive, rooted in negotiation.
Assessment is through testing, correct answers.	Assessment includes student works, observations, and points of view, as well as tests. Process is as important as product.
Knowledge is seen as inert.	Knowledge is seen as dynamic, ever changing with our experiences.
Students work primarily alone.	Students work primarily in groups.

Source: Concept to Classroom: A Series of Workshops. 2004 Educational Broadcasting Corporation. Available online at *www.thirteen.org/edonline/concept2class/constructivism/index.html.*

groups, cooperatively reading to one another and asking and answering questions based on extended reading assignments. Fact-oriented worksheets are deemphasized.

Writing

Constructivist-oriented approaches to writing instruction provide a problem-solving context by focusing learners' attention on the importance of communication. They practice writing skills not in isolation but while working on writing activities that require learners to communicate ideas meaningfully to real audiences. From their very earliest attempts at writing, learners realize that someone will read what they write. Thus what they write must be understandable. Writing instruction, then, involves a process of developing initial drafts, revising, and polishing, under the conditions that would prevail in the real world (e.g., extended timelines, access to resources, feedback from peer readers).

Mathematics and Science

Authentic problems, such as the one presented in the dialogue with Mrs. Greer at the beginning of this chapter, are the focus of constructivist approaches to math and science instruction. In such approaches little time is spent on the rote drill and practice of individual math or science facts. Rather, students are taught within a problem-solving or application context from the very beginning. The teacher attempts to have learners become actively involved in exploring, predicting, reasoning, and conjecturing, so that facts become integrated into mathematical skills and strategies that can be applied to authentic real-world problems. Many authentic math and science problems for grades 6 through 12 are becoming available on the Internet. They provide learners the opportunity for real-time problem solving, interactivity, and connectivity with other resources. For examples of online K–12 constructivist math and science curricula visit *www.internet4classrooms.com/math_gen.htm* and *www.goENC.com.*

Social Studies

Constructivist approaches to social studies have the goal of helping learners acquire a rich network of understandings around a limited number of topics. Parker (1991) advocates that the K–12 social studies curriculum should focus on five essential learnings: the democratic process, cultural diversity, economic development, global perspectives, and participatory citizenship. The blending of these critical elements within a single curriculum requires a constructivist view of teaching and learning that promotes the following:

1. *In-depth study*—the sustained examination of a limited number of important topics
2. *Higher-order challenge*—the design of curriculum and instruction that requires students to gather and use information in nonroutine applications
3. *Authentic assessment*—pointing students' schoolwork toward performance-oriented exhibitions of learning

These subject-matter advances assume that students construct their own understanding of skills and knowledge rather than having it told or given to them by the teacher. Therefore, constructivist lesson plans:

- Present instructional activities in the form of problems for students to solve.
- Develop and refine students' answers to problems from the point of view and experience of the student.
- Acknowledge the social nature of learning by encouraging the interaction of teacher with students and students with one another.

Another goal of constructivist teaching is to present **integrated bodies of knowledge.** Integrated units and lessons stress the connections between ideas and the logical coherence of interrelated topics, usually in the form of interdisciplinary or thematic units of instruction (Roberts & Kellough, 2003; Wiggins & McTighe, 1998), as shown in Figure 8.3 for a social studies curriculum suggested by Parker (1991). The role of the constructivist approach is to present authentic problems using the interaction and naturally occurring dialogue of the classroom to foster integrated bodies of knowledge. Let's see how this is done using the indirect model of instruction.

COMPARING DIRECT AND INDIRECT INSTRUCTION

Because direct instruction strategies are best suited for the teaching of facts, rules, and action sequences, it should be no surprise to learn that indirect instruction strategies are best suited for teaching concepts, inquiry, and problem solving.

When you present instructional stimuli to your learners in the form of content, materials, objects, and events and ask them to go beyond the information given to make conclusions and generalizations or find a pattern of relationships, you are using the indirect model of instruction. *Indirect* means the learner acquires a behavior indirectly by

Figure 8.3 Five essential learnings spiral upward through each grade to form an integrated body of knowledge.

Source: From *Renewing the Social Studies Curriculum* (p. 2), by W. Parker, 1991. Alexandria, VA: Association for Supervision and Curriculum Development. Copyright 1991 by Association for Supervision and Curriculum Development. Reprinted with permission.

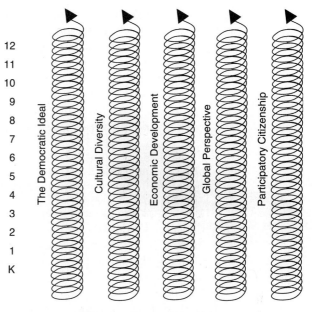

transforming—or constructing—the stimulus material into a meaningful response that differs from both (1) the content used to present the learning, and (2) any previous response given by the student. Because the learner can add to the content and rearrange it to be more meaningful to his or her experience, the elicited response can take many different forms. In contrast to direct instruction outcomes, there is rarely a single best answer when using the indirect model of instruction. Instead, the learner is guided to an answer that goes beyond the specific problem or content presented.

You might have wondered why, if direct instruction is so effective teaching facts, rules, or action sequences, it is not used for teaching concepts, inquiry, and problem solving. The answer is that not all desired outcomes call for responses that are identical to the content taught. Direct instruction is limited to (1) learning units of the content taught so they can be remembered, and (2) composing parts of the content learned into a whole, so a rapid and automatic response can occur.

Learning at the lower levels of the cognitive, affective, and psychomotor domains places heavy reliance on these two processes. Both can be placed into action by content that closely resembles the desired response (e.g., "Look at this word and then say it," "Watch me form a possessive and then you do the next one," "Read the instructions, then focus the microscope."). The desired response need not go much beyond what is provided. The task for the learner is simply to produce a response that mirrors the form and content of the stimulus. A great deal of instruction involves these simple processes. For this, the direct instruction model is most efficient and effective.

Real-world activities, however, often involve analysis, synthesis, and decision-making behaviors in the cognitive domain, organization and characterization behaviors in the affective domain, and articulation and naturalization behaviors in the psychomotor domain. This complicates instruction, because these behaviors are not learned by memorizing the parts and reassembling them into a whole rapidly and automatically, as are behaviors at lower levels of complexity. Instead, they must be constructed by the learner's own attempts to use personal experiences and past learnings to bring meaning to—and make sense out of—the content provided. Lower-level behaviors are required to attain more complex behaviors, but much more is needed by both teacher and learners before higher-order outcomes can be achieved. As you will see in this chapter, teaching for higher-order outcomes requires a different set of instructional strategies that represent the indirect instruction model.

TEACHING STRATEGIES FOR INDIRECT INSTRUCTION

Before describing the strategies that allow your learners to achieve higher-order outcomes, let's consider some topics that require higher-order outcomes.

Suppose you want your students to learn the:

- Meaning of a number line (arithmetic)
- Concept of a quadratic equation (algebra)
- Process of acculturation (social studies)
- Meaning of contact sports (physical education)
- Workings of a democracy (government)
- Playing of a concerto (music)
- Demonstration of photosynthesis (biology)
- Application of the law of conservation of energy (general science)

Learning these topics requires not just facts, rules, and action sequences but much more. If you teach just the facts, rules, and action sequences about the number line—"Here is the definition," "Here is how it is used," or "Follow this sequence of steps"—your students may never learn the concept that binds together problems that require an understanding of the number line or how to use it in new or novel situations. Instead, your students must learn to add to, rearrange, and elaborate on the content you present, using more complex cognitive processes. Let's consider how this is done.

Recall from chapter 7 (Table 7.3) the distinction between Type 1 and Type 2 behaviors. Type 1 behaviors become Type 2 behaviors by using facts, rules, and sequences to form concepts, patterns, and abstractions. As we will see in this chapter, concepts, patterns, and abstractions are most effectively taught in the context of strategies that emphasize concept learning, inquiry, and problem solving. Notice what would be required, for example, if students tried to learn the concept of a frog in the same way they acquired facts, rules, and action sequences about a frog.

First, students would have to commit to memory all possible instances of frogs (of which there may be hundreds). Trying to retain hundreds of frog images in the same form they were presented would quickly overburden your students' memories. Second, even after committing many types of frogs to memory, learners could confuse frogs with similar animals. This is because the memorization process does not include the characteristics that *exclude* other animals from being frogs (e.g., has hard shell, dry skin, color changes, tail).

The process of generalization and discrimination, if planned for in the presentation of your lesson, can help students overcome both of these problems. **Generalization** helps them respond in a similar manner to stimuli that differ but are bound together by a central concept, thereby increasing the range of instances to which particular facts, rules, and sequences apply (e.g., to all types of frogs). In addition, **discrimination** selectively restricts this range by eliminating things that appear to match the student's concept of a frog (e.g., a chameleon) but that differ from it in critical dimensions (e.g., has a tail).

Generalization and discrimination help students classify visually different stimuli into the same category based on critical attributes that act as magnets, drawing together all instances

Figure 8.4 A hierarchy of abstraction representing possible units of instruction in a science curriculum.

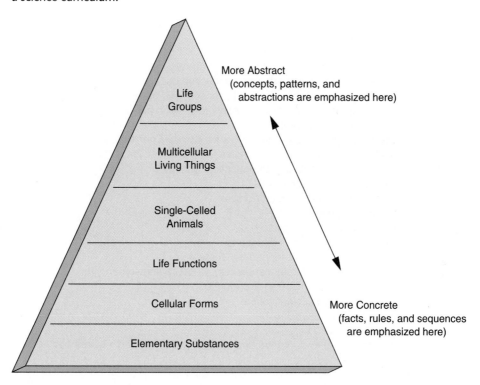

of the same type without requiring the learner to memorize all possible instances. The concept of a frog, then, becomes combined with other concepts to form larger patterns (e.g., amphibians) of increasing complexity. Figure 8.4 shows how concrete facts, rules, and sequences in a science curriculum (e.g., knowledge of elementary substances) must be combined with increasingly more abstract concepts and patterns (e.g., cellular forms, life functions, single-celled animals) to achieve higher-order outcomes (e.g., understanding of multicellular living things and life groups). As lesson and unit goals move up the hierarchy, the teacher must move from a direct to indirect model of instruction.

It is apparent that your role as teacher and your organization of content need to be different for the learning of concepts, patterns, and abstractions than for facts, rules and sequences. Since the stimulus material presented to achieve higher-order outcomes cannot efficiently contain all possible instances of the concept to be taught, it must provide its most critical dimensions.

The indirect instruction model uses instructional strategies that encourage the cognitive processes required both to form concepts and to combine concepts into larger patterns and abstractions that promote inquiry and problem-solving skills. Figure 8.5 shows some of the *indirect instruction strategies* performed by a teacher using this model.

You can see from Figure 8.5 that indirect instruction is more complex than direct instruction. Classroom activities are less teacher centered. This brings student ideas and experiences into the lesson and lets students begin evaluating their own responses. Because the outcomes are more complex, so too are your teaching strategies. To build toward these outcomes, extended forms of reasoning and questioning may be required. The indirect instruction strategies in Figure 8.5 were among those having the highest correlation with positive

Figure 8.5 Some indirect instruction strategies.

1. *Content Organization:* Providing advance organizers that serve as "pegs" on which students
   - Hang key points
   - Focus learning in most productive areas
2. *Conceptual movement:* Induction and deduction using
   - Selected events to establish general concepts and patterns (induction)
   - Principles and generalizations that apply to specific events (deduction)
3. *Examples and nonexamples*
   - Introducing critical attributes that promote accurate generalizations
   - Gradually expanding a set of examples
   - Heightening discrimination with noncritical attributes
4. *Questions:* Raising questions that
   - Guide the search and discovery process
   - Present contradictions
   - Probe for deeper understanding
   - Point the discussion in new directions
   - Pass responsibility for learning to the student
5. *Learner experience* (Using student ideas): Encouraging students to
   - Use references from their own experience
   - Use examples to seek clarification
   - Draw parallels and associations
6. *Student self-evaluation*
   - Asking students to evaluate the appropriateness of their own responses
   - Providing cues, questions, and hints that call attention to inappropriate responses
7. *Discussion:* Promoting classroom dialogue that encourages students to
   - Examine alternatives
   - Judge solutions
   - Make predictions
   - Discover generalizations that encourage critical thinking

student attitudes toward learning in a study by Fielding, Kameenui, and Gerstein (1983). These also are the teaching strategies thought to be most useful in providing behaviors that students will use in subsequent grades, outside of school, and in their adult lives (Borich & Tombari, 2004; Mitchell, 1992; Tombari & Borich, 1999).

AN EXAMPLE OF INDIRECT INSTRUCTION

Now let's peek in on a classroom lesson in which the teacher is using indirect instructional strategies. This dialogue reflects some facts, rules, and sequences that were taught previously, but the ultimate goal is the learning of concepts and the teaching of inquiry and problem solving. As you read, note the italicized indirect instruction strategies from Figure 8.5.

This dialogue is a glimpse into a government class where a lesson on different economic systems is in progress. The teacher gets the students' attention by asking if anyone knows what system of government in the world is undergoing the most change. Marty raises his hand.

◆　　◆　　◆

Teacher:	Marty.
Marty:	I think it's communism, because the Soviet Union broke up, and Russia instituted democratic reforms.
Teacher:	That's right, not unlike some countries in the Middle East that are also undergoing change. And because these changes will probably continue to affect all our lives in the years ahead, it may be a good idea to know what some different forms of government are and why some choose to live or not live under them. To get us started, let me ask if anyone knows where the phrase "government of the people, by the people, for the people" comes from. (Rena raises her hand.) Rena?
Rena:	From Lincoln's Gettysburg Address . . . I think near the end.
Teacher:	That's right. Most nations have similar statements that express the basic principles on which their laws, customs, and economics are based. Today, we will study three systems by which nations can guide and operate their economies. The three systems we will study are capitalism, socialism, and communism. They often are confused with the political systems that tend to be associated with them. A political system not only influences the economic system of a country but also guides individual behavior in many other areas, such as what is taught in schools, the relationship between church and state, how people are chosen for or elected to political office, and what newspapers can print. ***(Content organization)***
	For example, in the United States, we have an economic system that is based on the principles of capitalism—or private ownership of capital—and a political system that is based on the principle of democracy—or rule by the people. These two sets of principles are not the same, and in the next few days, you will see how they sometimes work in harmony and sometimes create contradictions that require changes in an economic or political system, like those occurring today in some countries around the world. ***(Content organization)***
	Today we will cover only systems dealing with the ownership of goods and services in different countries—that is, just the economic systems. Later I will ask you to distinguish these from political systems. Who would like to start by telling us what the word *capitalism* means? ***(Questions)***
Robert:	It means making money.
Teacher:	What else, Robert?
Robert:	Owning land . . . I think.
Teacher:	Not only land, but . . . ***(Probes for deeper understanding)***
Robert:	Owning anything.
Teacher:	The word *capital* means tangible goods or possessions. Is a house tangible? ***(Concept learning: deduction)***
Che-lim:	Yes.
Teacher:	Is a friendship tangible?
Che-lim:	Yes.
Teacher:	What about that, Mark? ***(Asks student to self-evaluate)***
Mark:	I don't think so.
Teacher:	Why?
Mark:	You can't touch it.
Teacher:	Right. You can touch a person who is a friend but not the friendship. Besides, you can't own or possess a person. . . . So what would be a good definition of *tangible goods*?
Che-lim:	Something you own and can touch or see.

| Teacher: | Not bad. Let me list some things on the board, and you tell me whether they could be called *capital*. (Writes the list) ***(Examples and nonexamples)*** |

> car
> stocks and bonds
> religion
> information
> clothes
> vacation

	OK. Who would like to say which of these are *capital?* (Ricky raises his hand.) ***(Concept learning: deduction)***
Ricky:	Car and clothes are the only two I see.
Vanessa:	I'd add stocks and bonds. They say you own a piece of something, although maybe not the whole thing.
Teacher:	Could you see or touch it? ***(Questions)***
Vanessa:	Yes, if you went to see the place or thing you owned a part of.
Teacher:	Good. What about a vacation? Did that give anyone trouble?
Mickey:	Well, you can own it . . . I mean you pay for it, and you can see yourself having a good time. (The class laughs.)
Teacher:	That may be true, so let's add one last condition to our definition of *capital*. You must be able to own it, see or touch it, and it must be durable—or last for a reasonable period of time. So now, how would you define *capitalism?* ***(Concept learning: induction)***
Carey:	An economic system that allows you to have capital—or to own tangible goods that last for a reasonable period of time. And, I suppose, sell the goods, if you wanted.
Teacher:	Very good. Many different countries across the world have this form of economic system. Just to see if you've got the idea, who can name three countries, besides our own, that allow the ownership of tangible goods? ***(Learner experience)***
Anton:	Canada, Japan, Germany.
Teacher:	Good. In all these countries, capital, in the form of tangible goods, can be owned by individuals.

◆ ◆ ◆

This dialogue illustrates one variation of the indirect model of instruction. Notice that this lesson used the naturally occurring dialogue of the classroom to encourage learners to bring their own experiences and past learning to the topic rather than to acquire an understanding by having it presented to them in an already organized form. This lesson required learners to build an understanding of the topic collectively under the guidance of the teacher using one another's predictions, hypotheses, and experiences. Look at Figure 8.5 again to recall the teaching strategies used in indirect instruction. Now, let's consider the extent to which this example lesson contains these key aspects of indirect instruction.

CONTENT ORGANIZATION

Comparing the dialogues for direct and indirect instruction, what differences do you notice? Obviously, they differ in complexity. Teaching for more complex outcomes takes more time and planning. The extensive planning needed for higher-order learning is one of the most overlooked aspects of indirect instruction. With more expansive and complex content, the lesson must be introduced with a framework or structure that organizes the content into meaningful parts. This is the first step in planning for indirect instruction—organizing the content in advance.

One way of providing this framework to your learners is to use advance organizers (Ausubel, 1968; Borich & Tombari, 1997; Woolfolk, 2005). An advance organizer gives learners a conceptual preview of what is to come and helps prepare them to store, label, and package the content for retention and later use. In a sense, an advance organizer is a tree-like structure with main limbs that act as pegs, or place holders, for the branches that are yet to come. Without these pegs on which to hang content, important distinctions can become easily blurred or lost. To reinforce these distinctions, Burnette (1999) recommends concluding lessons or units with the same advance organizer that introduced them, so students better envision where instruction began and ended. Advance organizers have been found especially helpful for students from diverse cultures and English-language learners when the organizer includes links between familiar concepts and the new content to be learned (Lustig & Koester, 2005; Saunders & Goldenberg, 1999; Saunders, O'Brien, Lennon, & McLean, 1999).

For example, recall that our lesson dialogue began with an introduction about coverage of the day's lesson. To set the stage, the teacher introduced two abstractions (economic systems and political systems), each comprising a complex network of concepts (taxes, ownership, goods, services, etc.). At the beginning of the lesson, he alerted students to the reason for drawing such an early distinction between a political and an economic system ("capitalism, socialism, and communism . . . often are confused with the political systems," "Today we will cover only . . . economic systems. Later I will ask you to distinguish these from political systems."). Figure 8.6 represents an advance organizer that this teacher might have used to open the lesson.

Figure 8.6 An advance organizer for a unit on government.

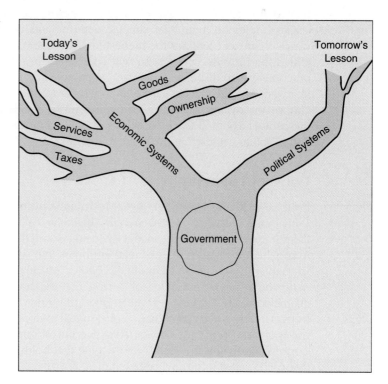

Advance organizers, especially for higher-order outcomes (e.g., application, analysis, synthesis, and evaluation) are rarely single words or phrases that enlighten students when merely uttered. Instead, they are concepts woven into the lesson fabric to provide an overview of the day's work and all topics to which it will subsequently relate. Advance organizers can be presented orally or as charts and diagrams. Here are some examples of advance organizers:

- Showing a chart that illustrates the skeletal evolution of humans before the skeletal relationships among forms of animal life are presented (biology)
- Drawing examples of right, equilateral, and isosceles triangles before introducing the concept of a right triangle (math)
- Discussing the origins of the Civil War before describing its major battles (American history)
- Describing what is meant by a "figure of speech" before introducing the concepts of metaphor and simile (English)
- Listening to examples of both vowels and consonants before teaching the vowel sounds (reading)
- Showing and explaining the origins of rock formations before showing examples of igneous, metamorphic, and sedimentary rocks (science)

Notice that each of these examples presents a general concept into which fits the specific concept that is the subject of the day's lesson. This is not accomplished by reviewing earlier content, which often is confused with the idea of an advance organizer. Instead, it is done by creating a conceptual structure—skeletal evolution, various triangular shapes, Civil War origins, figures of speech, the alphabet, the evolution of rock formations—into which you can place not only the content to be taught but also the content for related lessons.

Therefore, these advance organizers set the groundwork for focusing the lesson topic. They prevent every lesson from being seen as something entirely new. Finally, they integrate related concepts into larger and larger patterns that later become more authentic unit outcomes (evolution, triangular shapes, determinants of Civil War, figures of speech). An advance organizer identifies the highest level outcome resulting from a lesson sequence and to which the present day's lesson will contribute. In our example dialogue, this higher-order outcome was to distinguish between economic and political systems, a distinction organized in advance by the teacher's introductory remarks and graphic representation. But, before you choose an advance organizer, you will want to decide how you will organize and structure the content you will teach. For this you will want to consider the concept learning, inquiry and problem-centered approaches to learning.

Concept Learning

If the goal of your lesson is concept learning your instruction will want to emphasize the essential attributes that bind seemingly dissimilar data, materials, objects, or events together. Here students are taught a concept by seeing examples and nonexamples of an object or event from which they learn the essential attributes that separate seemingly like objects or events. In chapter 7, we saw an example of concept learning and an advance organizer by diagramming the essential attributes of a frog that separates it from look-a-likes (toads, turtles, chameleons, etc.). As the learner is given more practice with examples and nonexamples of frogs, a tightly woven combination of essential attributes emerges (e.g., skin smooth and moist, not warty and dry, can't change color; no tail, strong hind legs; makes deep hoarse sound). Concept learning is the search for the glue that holds similar items together and the attributes that can be used to distinguish examples of a given group or category from nonexamples.

The steps in a concept learning lesson include: identifying the essential and nonessential attributes of the concept that you will present to students, selecting positive and negative examples that distinguish the essential from the nonessential attributes, and, with the participation of your students, developing decision rules that define the essential attributes for defining the concept. Here is an example concept learning lesson: "Math Facts That Equal 10." For this lesson the teacher:

- Makes a list of both positive and negative examples of the concept "10" and places them on flash cards (positive examples, such as $6 + 4$, $12 - 2$, 10×1, etc.; negative examples, such as $7 + 2$, $15 - 4$, 2×4, etc.
- Places the words "Yes" and "No" on the board.
- Presents first flash card, $6 + 4$, and places it in the "Yes" column; presents a second card, $7 + 2$, and places it in the "No" column; and repeats the process with several more positive and negative examples.
- Asks class to look at the examples under each column and determine how they are the same and how they are different.
- Introduces more flash card examples and nonexamples of the concept and asks students to choose under which column to put them. Teacher continues until most students have learned the concept.
- Asks students who have attained the concept to share their essential attributes for the concept "10" with the remainder of the class.
- Asks class to create their own examples and come up and place them in the proper column.

By seeing numbers that do and do not form the concept, learners gradually learn to group all like instances together and arrive at the essential attributes that define the concept. Figure 8.7 shows the advance organizer in the form of an activity sheet that this teacher used to introduce the concept and provide the structure for the lesson.

Inquiry Learning

The higher-order goals of indirect instruction lesson can also include inquiry and problem-based learning. If the goal of your lesson is to promote inquiry you will want your instruction to emphasize how things are organized, how they change, and how they interrelate, within which concept learning may be a part of the larger inquiry process. Here, the emphasis is on "how we come to know something" more than on "what we know" (Borich & Hao, 2006). For example, the teacher conducting our "Math Facts That Equal 10" lesson may find that her lesson can be raised to a higher level by having her students inquire into the use of a number line to show how addition and subtraction and positive and negative numbers can be used to represent the concept "10." The result of this inquiry may be much less definite than the learning of a concept, the end result often being more questions with which to continue the inquiry.

For example, in a physical science lesson on the internal structure of the earth, a teacher promoting facts, rules, and action sequences might give students the names and descriptions of the earth's layers—or "what we know." But another teacher promoting inquiry might direct her students toward "how do we know," for example, "How do we know what the internal structure of the earth is without ever having experienced it?" The former lesson requires the acquisition of facts told by the teacher, but the latter requires exploration and discovery by the students themselves. In this lesson the inquiry process might turn to indirect measures of the internal structure of the earth, and what some of these measures might be. Students might inquire about the methods that could be used to explore beneath the earth's surface,

Figure 8.7 An advance organizer and activity sheet for the concept learning lesson "Math Facts That Equal 10."

What numbers can come together to make the number "10"?

	Yes	No
5 + 5	5 + 5	16 − 5
16 − 5		
11 − 1		
12 − 2		
6 + 6		
6 x 2		
10 x 1		
3 + 4 + 4		
3 + 3		
12 − 4		
9 + 1		
2 + (2 x 3)		
4 x 2		
15 − 1		
3 + 4		
16 − 10		

such as the transmission and reflection of the shockwaves created by earthquakes, seismograph readings from oil exploration, and geological probes driven deep under the earth's surface to see how it has changed over time.

Using examples of shockwaves from around the world, this teacher might ask several questions of her students to organize the inquiry process that:

- *Go beyond immediately available information.* "What do we know from looking at these shockwaves from a recent earthquake?"
- *Interpret the consequences of information or ideas.* "What do the shockwaves from these two different earthquakes tell us about how deep the earth's crust is?"
- *Make predictions as a way of making students use the information they have gained from their inquiry.* "Given the shockwaves from around the world you have seen, where would you predict the next earthquake will be?"

Unlike concept learning, the inquiry approach leads to alternative paths and solutions in the process of exploring and discovering new information about a topic. Figure 8.8 shows the advance organizer that this teacher used to introduce the lesson "Beneath the Earth's Surface" with a framework or structure that organizes its content and promotes the goal of inquiry. See In Practice: Focus on Inquiry-Based Learning.

Figure 8.8 An advance organizer for the inquiry lesson "Beneath the Earth's Surface."

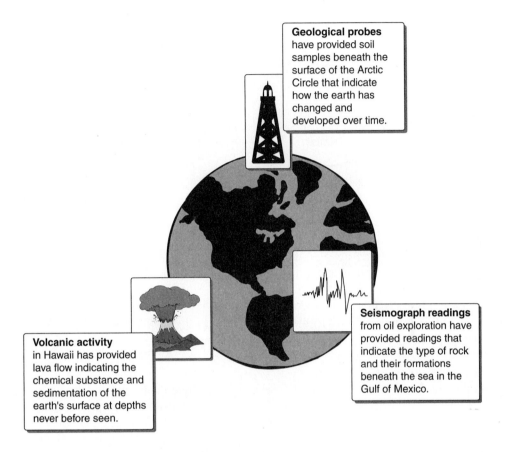

How do we know: What kind of information can these
measures of the Earth beneath the surface give us?

Geological probes have provided soil samples beneath the surface of the Arctic Circle that indicate how the earth has changed and developed over time.

Volcanic activity in Hawaii has provided lava flow indicating the chemical substance and sedimentation of the earth's surface at depths never before seen.

Seismograph readings from oil exploration have provided readings that indicate the type of rock and their formations beneath the sea in the Gulf of Mexico.

IN PRACTICE

Focus on Inquiry-Based Learning

In the process of inquiry, students identify problems, brainstorm solutions, formulate questions, investigate, analyze and interpret results, discuss, reflect, make conclusions, and present results (Bruner, 2004). This cycle of inquiry serves as a general model for teachers planning inquiry-based activities that can guide students through the inquiry process. One version of the inquiry-based learning cycle is the Ask, Investigate, Create, Discuss, and Reflect model illustrated in the accompanying figure. It is a five-step model for implementing an inquiry-based lesson or unit.

Step 1. Ask
To promote the desire to discover, the teacher begins by raising questions and inviting students to plan the inquiry procedures and presentation of findings. The teacher initiates the inquiry process by

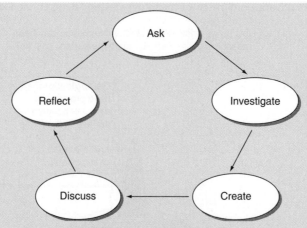

A five-step model for inquiry-based learning.

posing the lesson topic in the form of a question and then probing, prompting, and redirecting student responses to establish the inquiry climate. This is called the *teacher-initiated phase*. When students are comfortable with the process, the teacher encourages students to raise a question of their own, to plan a procedure for answering the question, how the procedure would carry it out, and how the results might be presented. This is called the *student-initiated phase*. Each phase is a vehicle to build student-initiated questions and student-directed procedures that bring students to an independent level of inquiry. A question or a problem is the focus at this stage, which may be redefined later in the inquiry process.

Step 2. Investigate
After a student question is agreed upon, the next step is to investigate it. At this stage of the inquiry students are asked to recall prior knowledge or experiences related to the question and brainstorm possible methods of investigating it by identifying resources and designing and carrying out a plan of action. Students may redefine their question as new information unfolds. This information-gathering stage is a self-motivated process that is owned by the engaged students.

Step 3. Create
When it has been jointly determined by teacher and students that sufficient information has been gathered, students are asked to begin thinking critically about the relationship between information (evidence) and their question; for example, how it may or may not answer the question fully or completely. Here students synthesize the information they have uncovered to create new knowledge, which may be beyond their, and possibly the teacher's, prior experience. They start thinking critically about the appropriateness of their question or hypothesis, redefine their question and/or construct new ones, and decide whether to gather more data. Some interim "product" is expected at this stage, such as a chart synthesizing the information collected, an oral presentation that summarizes progress thus far, or a list of new or redefined questions.

Step 4. Discuss
At this stage, students discuss their findings, new ideas, and experiences with one another. Students share their experiences and investigations in their learning community, which can be a collaborative group or the entire class. When a small group format is used, different groups may use the

inquiry process to answer different questions that may have evolved from steps 2 and 3. The task at this stage may include comparing notes, discussing conclusions, and sharing experiences across groups.

Step 5. Reflect

After discussion, students critique and communicate their results to their learning community (group or class), during which students are expected to reflect on their newly acquired knowledge. Methods for presenting findings are selected in consultation with their teacher. These methods can include traditional written or oral reports or more extensive multimedia presentations, productions, or exhibits (Martinello & Cook, 2000). The tasks include reflecting on the appropriateness of their question, their methods of investigation, and the accuracy of their conclusions. This task encourages students, either in groups or as a class, to evaluate whether a satisfactory solution was found, whether a new question is warranted, and, if so, what the new question might be by taking inventory of what has been done and making new observations. If new questions emerge, the cycle of inquiry can start again with a new lesson.

Problem-Centered Learning

Whereas the inquiry approach leads to alternative paths and solutions in exploring new information, the problem-centered approach to achieving higher-order outcomes identifies and provides for students in advance all the steps required to solve a particular problem. It is, therefore, less "open ended" than the inquiry approach, in which the steps to a task are explored and discovered through student inquiry. For example, you might begin a general science lesson on "The Invisible Forces of Gravity" by demonstrating that liquid cannot be sucked through a straw from a tightly sealed bottle. The question "Why does this happen?" establishes the problem. You then might give your students a problem-solving sequence like the one shown in Figure 8.9 to guide their investigation of the problem. The chart and its sequence of events becomes an advance organizer for the lesson for the class to follow. Each step provides an organizational branch for a particular part of the lesson. Further content organization is provided by another advance organizer in Figure 8.10. Now the problem has been organized hierarchically to show the internal branching, or decisions, that must be followed to arrive at a conclusion. This form of content organizer can provide a particularly effective attention getter when students are asked to contribute decision points to the organizer as the problem is being solved and trace each decision point (indicated by the solid lines) to answer the question "Why doesn't the liquid flow through the straw?"

A problem-centered organization of a lesson or unit recognizes the need to develop problem-solving skills as well as the knowledge and skills to respond to previously unforeseen circumstances. Problem-centered learning has several distinct characteristics that guide lesson and unit development (Delisle, 1997; Ong & Borich, 2006). When planning a problem-centered lesson or unit remember to:

- Clearly define the problem. Although the solution may not be in sight, the problem should be described in detail and placed within a meaningful context close to your learners' everyday experience.
- Make clear to your learners that they are to make a prediction about what would solve the problem. Predictions should be achievable within a realistic time frame and available resources and can be altered as new information is obtained.

Figure 8.9 Sequential advance organizer for the problem-solving lesson "Invisible Forces of Gravity."

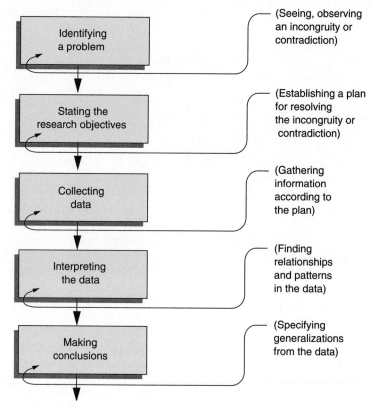

Identifying a problem — (Seeing, observing an incongruity or contradiction)

Stating the research objectives — (Establishing a plan for resolving the incongruity or contradiction)

Collecting data — (Gathering information according to the plan)

Interpreting the data — (Finding relationships and patterns in the data)

Making conclusions — (Specifying generalizations from the data)

Figure 8.10 Hierarchical advance organizer for the problem-solving lesson "Invisible Forces of Gravity."

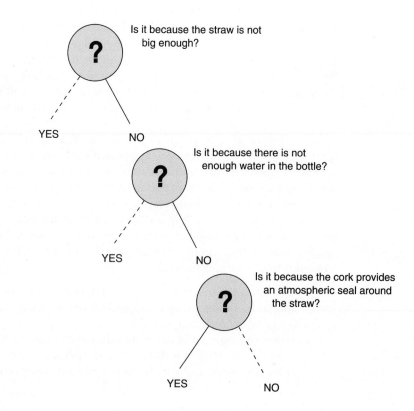

Why doesn't the liquid flow through the straw?

Is it because the straw is not big enough?

YES   NO

Is it because there is not enough water in the bottle?

YES   NO

Is it because the cork provides an atmospheric seal around the straw?

YES   NO

278

- Indicate that learners will be expected to access, evaluate, and utilize data from a variety of sources. They will need to critically examine their sources and reject those that are less credible or are opinion rather than fact.
- Require that solutions must fit the problem and be accompanied by clearly stated reasons as to why a particular solution is best (e.g., can be implemented faster, at less cost, or with superior results).

Concept learning, inquiry, and problem solving, either singly or in combination, are useful tools for organizing your lessons for indirect instruction and providing advance organizers that communicate to your students the key steps, decisions, and relationships that are to be learned. We will have more to say about these and other approaches, including project-based learning, in the chapters ahead.

CONCEPTUAL MOVEMENT: INDUCTION AND DEDUCTION

Our next teaching strategy for indirect instruction is induction and deduction.

Induction is a form of reasoning used to draw a conclusion or make a generalization from specific instances (Tamir, 1995). It is a process in which students observe specific facts and then generalize them to other circumstances. Much of our everyday thinking proceeds in this manner. For example:

1. We notice that rain-slick roads are causing accidents on the way to school, so we reduce speed at all subsequent intersections.
2. We get an unsatisfactory grade on a chemistry exam, so we study 6 extra hours a week for the rest of the semester in all our subjects.
3. We see a close friend suffer from the effects of drug abuse, so we volunteer to disseminate information about substance abuse to all our acquaintances.
4. We experience a math teacher who is cold and unfriendly, so we decide never to enroll in a math course again.

What these instances have in common is that they started with a specific observation of a limited set of data and ended with a generalization to a much broader context. Between the beginning and end of each sequence was an interpretation of observed events and the projection of this interpretation to all similar circumstances.

Deduction is reasoning that proceeds from principles or generalizations to their application in specific instances. Deductive thinking includes testing generalizations to see if they hold in specific cases. Typically, a laboratory experiment in the sciences follows the deductive method. In these fields the experimenter begins with a theory or hypothesis about what should happen and then tests it with an experiment to see if it is confirmed, as was shown by the sequence of steps in Figure 8.9. If it is, the generalization with which the experiment began is true, at least under the conditions of the experiment. The following steps are used in deductive thinking:

1. State a theory or generalization to be tested.
2. Form a hypothesis in the form of a prediction.
3. Observe or collect data to test the hypothesis.
4. Analyze and interpret the data to determine if the prediction is true.
5. Conclude whether the generalization held true in the specific context in which it was tested.

Deductive methods are familiar in everyday life. For example, let's change the four examples of inductive thinking listed previously to examples of deductive thinking. Here are the examples again—this time illustrating deduction:

1. We believe rain-slick roads are the prime contributor to traffic accidents at intersections. We make observations one rainy morning on the way to school and find that, indeed, more accidents have occurred at intersections than usual—our prediction that wet roads cause accidents at intersections was confirmed.

2. We believe that studying more will not substantially raise our grades. We study 6 extra hours for our math test and find that our grade has gone up—our prediction that extra studying won't help our grades turns out to be wrong.

3. We believe that drug abuse can be detrimental to one's physical and emotional well-being. We observe and find physical and emotional effects of drug abuse with acquaintances who have admitted to using them—our prediction that drug abuse and physical and emotional impairment are related has been confirmed.

4. We believe we could never like a math class because they are taught by cold and unfriendly teachers. We are required to take a math class and find we have just such a teacher—our prediction that math classes are taught by cold and unfriendly teachers has been shown to be accurate—at least in this instance.

These examples of deduction have in common the fact that they begin with a general statement of belief—a theory or hypothesis—and end with some conclusion based on an observation that tested the truth of that theory or hypothesis. Of course, since our observation only entailed one instance of that theory or hypothesis, we could be wrong in some other instances (e.g., you might have no problem liking math taught by another instructor or liking sports despite the fact that you once had a cold and unfriendly gym teacher). As you might expect, deductive logic has been most closely associated with the scientific method.

Applying Induction and Deduction

Both induction and deduction are important tools for concept learning, inquiry, and problem solving. Let's see how they were accomplished in our classroom dialogue on economic systems.

Using deduction, the teacher built a definition of tangible goods and tested it with a specific example: "Is a house tangible?" Notice how the examples increased in abstraction to better define what could be considered "tangible" (e.g., stocks and bonds). Also, he provided both examples and nonexamples to fine-tune this concept by showing that tangible goods in a capitalist system could exist at different levels, but some things (e.g., friendships, vacations) could not qualify as tangible goods. Also notice that a brief venture into deduction ended the teacher's introduction to capitalism. By asking students to name three countries that fit the concept of capitalism, he made them find specific instances that fit the general concept. This teacher also skillfully used the inductive process, beginning with specific instances of tangible goods (e.g., owning land) and increasingly broadened these instances to form a generalization (tangible goods are those things that last for a reasonable length of time).

Note that, although the concept of capitalism was understood by most students at the end of the first part of the lesson as an economic system that allows the ownership of tangible goods that last, it was a rather crude interpretation that would fail many subsequent tests. For

Many forms of investigation and laboratory experiments follow the deductive method in which the student begins with a prediction about what should happen in a specific instance and then conducts an investigation to see if the prediction comes true.

example, citizens of most socialist and communist countries own tangible goods that last a reasonable period of time (e.g., a wristwatch, a car, a set of dinnerware). Recall that this crude version of the concept of capitalism emerged even after providing carefully planned examples and nonexamples. This means the teacher's job was not over. Further conceptual movement had to be made to fine-tune this concept, producing more accurate discriminations to be applied to the concept of capitalism.

This occurred in subsequent portions of the lesson, in which the teacher moved students from an initial definition of capitalism as "making money," offered by Robert at the start of the lesson, to a definition that included the following elements:

1. Ownership, of
2. Tangible goods, that are
3. Durable, and
4. Can be sold

The teaching of concepts with the indirect instructional model uses inductive and deductive thinking to process initially crude and overly restrictive concepts into more expansive and accurate understandings. Table 8.2 illustrates the different steps involved in inductive versus deductive teaching.

USING EXAMPLES AND NONEXAMPLES

You may learn the rule "stop at red lights" to perfection, but until you have seen examples of when to modify the rule (e.g., when an emergency vehicle with flashing lights is behind you), you do not have the complete *concept* of a red light—only the *rule*.

To learn concepts, your learners will need to go beyond the acquisition of facts, rules, and sequences to be able to distinguish examples from nonexamples (R. Mayer & Wittrock, 1996). Observing examples and nonexamples—when studying 6 extra hours pays off and when it does not, when disseminating drug abuse literature is likely to help and when it is not, when a cold and unfriendly teacher is likely to adversely affect your performance in a subject and when not—allows you to grasp concepts.

Examples represent the concept being taught by including all of the attributes essential for recognizing that concept as a member of some larger class. **Nonexamples** fail to represent the concept being taught by purposely not including one or more of the attributes essential for recognizing it as a member of some larger class. The use of examples and nonexamples define

Table 8.2 A comparison of steps in inductive versus deductive teaching.

Teaching Inductively	Teaching Deductively
1. Teacher presents specific data from which a generalization is to be drawn.	1. Teacher introduces the generalization to be learned.
2. Each student is allowed uninterrupted time to observe or study the data that illustrates the generalization.	2. Teacher reviews the task-relevant prior facts, rules, and action sequences needed to form the generalization.
3. Students are shown additional examples and then nonexamples containing the generalization.	3. Students raise a question, pose an hypothesis, or make a prediction thought to be contained in the generalization.
4. Student attention is guided first to the critical (relevant) aspects of the data containing the generalization and then to its noncritical (irrelevant) aspects.	4. Data, events, materials, or objects are gathered and observed to test the prediction.
5. A generalization is made that can distinguish the examples from nonexamples.	5. Results of the test are analyzed and a conclusion is made as to whether the prediction is supported by the data, events, materials, or objects that were observed.
	6. The starting generalization is refined or revised in accordance with the observations.

the essential and nonessential attributes of a concept needed to identify the concept and make accurate generalizations.

Recall from our classroom dialogue some of the distinctions between the private ownership of goods and services under socialism compared to capitalism. How would this teacher develop this concept? The teacher would have to make clear that private ownership of goods and services in the context of different economic systems is always a matter of degree. That is, the system determines not only what is owned by the government but how much and, therefore, what is unavailable for private ownership. Accordingly, the teacher might elicit a set of interchanges to bring out these points.

◆   ◆   ◆

Teacher: What types of things could a group of people, say the size of a nation, agree on that would be absolutely essential for everyone's existence?
Ronnie: Food.
Teacher: Good. What else?
Vanessa: Clothes.
Teacher: Very good.
Carey: Cars.
Teacher: What do you think about cars?
Ricky: If they couldn't agree on the importance of cars for everyone, then they would have to agree on some form of public transportation, like buses and trains.

Teacher: Yes, they would, wouldn't they? The examples show that private ownership within different economic systems is a matter of degree that depends on what (a) everyone values equally and (b) everyone needs for everyday existence.

◆ ◆ ◆

The teacher began the discussion by having students think about things that "a group of people, say the size of a nation, could agree on that would be absolutely essential for everyone's existence"—thereby encouraging students to broaden their earlier and perhaps more narrow concepts of capitalism and socialism. The question first generated some nonexamples (e.g., food and clothes) that could not discriminate private ownership among economic systems since everyone in different economic systems equally could be expected to value them. Then Ricky suggests something that may be more valued by the majority in a capitalistic system (privately owned cars), whereas some other method of transportation might be more valued by the majority in a socialistic system (an efficient public transportation system). The class is helped to one of the more subtle distinctions between capitalism and socialism through examples and nonexamples. Notice also how this teacher used examples and nonexamples to sharpen distinctions and deepen understanding by:

1. Using examples that vary in ways that are important to the concept being defined (e.g., a house is tangible, stocks and bonds are abstract, but both are instances of the concept of tangible goods)
2. Including nonexamples of the concept that nonetheless possess important dimensions of the concept (e.g., a vacation can be bought but is not durable and therefore not an instance of the concept of tangible goods)
3. Explaining why nonexamples *are* nonexamples, even though they may share some of the same characteristics (e.g., food and clothes may be equally valued among economic systems but cars versus a public transportation system could not discriminate private ownership among economic systems)

THE USE OF QUESTIONS

Guiding the concept learning, inquiry, and problem-solving process with questions is the fourth indirect instruction strategy. One difference you may have noticed between the direct and indirect instruction dialogues is the way in which the teacher asks questions. In the direct instruction dialogue, the questions were specific and to the point, aimed at eliciting a single right answer. But in the indirect instruction dialogue, questions steered the students to seek and discover the answer with minimum assistance from the teacher. In direct instruction, answering questions is how students show what they know so you may provide clues, hints, and probes. In indirect instruction, your questions guide students into discovering new dimensions of a problem or ways of resolving a dilemma.

The indirect instruction dialogue included several questions that guided the inquiry process. The purpose of this teacher's questions was to focus students' attention and to promote the widest possible discussion of the topic from the students' point of view. In this manner the class begins with everyone being able to participate, regardless of their task-relevant prior knowledge. By accepting almost any answer at the beginning, this teacher used student responses to formulate subsequent questions and begin the inquiry process to shape more accurate responses.

The point of using questioning strategies in indirect instruction, then, is not to arrive at the correct answer in the quickest and most efficient manner. The point is to begin an inquiry process that not only forms successively more correct answers but also forms those answers using a personal search-and-discovery process chosen by the learner and guided by the teacher. For example, the teacher followed up Robert's response that capitalism means "making money" with the phrase, "what else?" and followed Robert's next response ("owning land") with a leading response ("not only land but . . ."), encouraging Robert to broaden his answer.

By beginning with a broad question such as "What does the word *capitalism* mean to you?" this teacher could have been confronted just as easily with the task of narrowing, not broadening, Robert's first response. In the next interchange, this problem actually occurs, because Robert replies that capitalism means "owning anything." Now the job is to narrow or limit his response, which is accomplished by presenting the first essential attribute of the concept of capitalism, tangible goods.

You can see that a single guided question in the context of indirect instruction is seldom useful in itself. Questions must dovetail into other questions that continually refocus the response (e.g., broaden, then narrow, then broaden slightly again) to keep the search going. The process is much like focusing a camera, because rarely is the camera initially set at the right focus for the subject. Similarly, we could not expect Robert's first response to represent perfectly the concept of capitalism. Just as one begins focusing the camera in the appropriate direction, often passing the point at which the subject is in focus, so also the teacher's follow-up probe led Robert to overshoot the mark and respond with too broad a response (e.g., owning anything). The teacher acknowledged the error and slightly narrowed Robert's response by noting, "The word *capitalism* means tangible goods or possessions."

In addition to the questions we saw earlier that can guide the inquiry process, there are others that can:

- *Present contradictions to be resolved*—"Who owns the highways under capitalism?"
- *Probe for deeper, more thorough responses*—"So, what would be a good definition of tangible goods?"
- *Extend the discussion to new areas*—"What things could a group of people, say the size of a nation, agree are absolutely essential for everyone's existence?"
- *Pass responsibility back to the class*—"Good question. Who knows the answer to who pays for services provided under a socialist system?"

Questions like these guide the inquiry process to increasingly better responses. This process is one of the most useful for achieving higher-order outcomes, where the back and forth (first wider, then narrower) focusing of student responses often is required to attain the appropriate level of generalization. We will have more to say about questioning strategies in the next chapter.

LEARNER EXPERIENCE AND USE OF STUDENT IDEAS

The Changing View

Until recently, the use of student ideas was considered the centerpiece of indirect instruction. Using student ideas meant incorporating student experiences, points of view, feelings, and problems into the lesson by making the student the primary point of reference. A completely student-oriented lesson might be initiated by asking students what problems they were having with the content; these problems then would become the focus of the lesson. This approach was intended to heighten student interest, to organize subject content around student problems, to tailor feedback to individual students, and to encourage positive attitudes and feelings toward the subject.

Although a laudable instructional strategy, the goals of incorporating student ideas into the lesson in this format often became the end itself, rather than the means by which learning could be accomplished. Unfortunately, many forms of problem solving, inquiry, and

Small-group discussions often require the teacher to become a moderator, visiting each group periodically to answer questions, review and summarize, redirect group work, provide new or more accurate information, and achieve consensus.

concept learning were thought to be synonymous with open, freewheeling discussions that began and ended with student-determined ideas and content.

Although heightening student interest, selecting content based on student problems, and increasing affect are important goals, they are best achieved in a carefully crafted teacher–student dialogue that promotes higher-order thinking. These goals can and should be achieved in the context of classroom dialogue that encourages students to make reference to, use examples from, and draw parallels and associations with their own experiences in order to achieve specific instructional goals. Therefore, in the indirect instruction model, use of student ideas is the means of promoting inquiry, attaining essential concepts, and solving problems as a springboard to higher-order thinking.

Productively Using Student Ideas

So how can teachers productively use student ideas in the context of indirect instruction? In this context, you can use student ideas in the following ways:

- Encourage students to use *examples* and *references* from their own experience, from which they can construct their own meanings from text.
- Share *mental strategies* by which the students can learn more easily and efficiently by seeing and hearing how you think through a question or problem.
- Ask students to seek clarification of and to draw *parallels* to and *associations* from things they already know.
- Encourage understanding and retention of ideas by relating them to the students' own sphere of *interests, concerns,* and *problems.*

For examples of these uses, recall again the dialogue about economic systems. By asking students to name three other countries that follow a capitalistic economic system, the teacher elicited examples and references from the learners' experience.

Perhaps more important than the questions themselves was the way in which the teacher incorporated student responses into the lesson. By asking what the word *capitalism* "means to you," this teacher was asking students to express themselves by using parallels and associations they already understood—perhaps by having a job, or recalling a conversation with their parents about occupations, or by remembering television images of life in another country. Parallels and associations such as these are likely to be vastly different among students. This is desirable, both for heightening student interest and involvement and for exposing students to a variety of responses, many of which may be appropriate instances of the concept to be learned.

A third way to incorporate student ideas into your lesson is to allow students to respond using their own interests, concerns, and problems. Student interests—and especially individual choices affecting future assignments—can be important motivators for ensuring active student involvement in subsequent assignments that may be lengthy and time consuming.

Finally, notice within the context of our dialogue that student ideas remained content centered. The instruction allowed students to participate in determining the form in which learning occurred but not the substance of what was learned. This substance will usually be determined by your curriculum guide and textbook. Our example dialogue, therefore, contrasts with what is called **student-centered learning,** which allows students to select both the form and substance. This is sometimes associated with **unguided discovery learning,** wherein the goal is to maintain high levels of student interest, accomplished largely by selecting content based on student problems or interests and by providing individually tailored feedback.

Sometimes unguided discovery learning is promoted in the context of independently conducted experiments, projects, portfolios, research papers, and demonstrations, where the topic and form of inquiry may be selected by the student. However, even when unguided discovery learning is desired, the content still must fit within the confines of the curriculum. Therefore, whether your approach is the guided use of student ideas (as in this example) or unguided (as in research assignments), some preorganization and planning always will be necessary before you solicit and use student ideas.

 Video Window

The Indirect Instruction Model

In this video you will see Sue teaching a lesson on graphing to her second-grade learners. As you watch Sue's classroom, notice how she incorporates one of the central principles of the indirect instruction model—the use of questions to guide the search-and-discovery process. Using jellybeans to create an authentic problem requiring her learners to count and organize data, she gets them to actively engage in doing math and graphing with a real-world problem. Notice how, in the spirit of the indirect model of instruction, Sue lets her students discover knowledge and understanding, sometimes through their mistakes—not just by telling them what she wants them to learn. As you look into Sue's classroom, describe specific instances of how Sue's questions aided her learners' search for and discovery of meaning by:

- Resolving problems and contradictions
- Probing deeper for more thorough responses
- Extending the discussion to new areas
- Passing responsibility back to the learner

 To answer these questions online, go to the Video Windows *module of this chapter of the* Companion Website *at www.prenhall.com/borich.*

STUDENT SELF-EVALUATION

The sixth strategy for indirect instruction is to engage students in evaluating their own responses and thereby take responsibility for their own learning. Because there may be many right answers when teaching with the indirect instruction model, it will be virtually impossible for you to judge them all. In direct instruction, nearly all instances of the learned facts, rules, or action sequences likely to be encountered can be learned during guided and independent practice. But because specifying all possible instances of a concept is neither possible nor efficient, you must teach students to look critically at their own responses.

You can encourage self-evaluation by gradually giving control of the evaluation function to students and by letting them provide reasons for their answers so you and other students can suggest needed changes. Recall that early in the dialogue, the teacher let the students know that some of the responsibility for determining appropriate answers would fall on them. After writing a list on the board, he said, "OK. Who would like to say which of these are capital?" The message is received when Ricky responds and Vanessa modifies Ricky's response:

◆   ◆   ◆

Ricky: Car and clothes are the only two I see.
Vanessa: I'd add stocks and bonds. They say you own a piece of something, although maybe not the whole thing.

◆   ◆   ◆

Even after Vanessa's efforts to correct Ricky's response, the teacher still does not supply an answer but instead keeps the evaluation of the previous responses going by responding with, "Could you see or touch it?"

The goal here was to create a student dialogue focused on the appropriateness of previous answers. The success of this self-evaluation strategy is most readily seen in the dialogue that occurs between students and teacher. This strategy promotes a student-to-student-back-to-teacher interchange, as opposed to the more familiar teacher-to-student-back-to-teacher interchange. The teacher's role is to maintain the momentum by offering hints or focusing statements that students can use to evaluate their previous responses. Classes of students who have knowledge of the content can sustain three, four, or even five successive exchanges among students before control returns to the teacher and some redirection becomes necessary.

In the process of these exchanges, students learn the reasons for their answers in slow, measured steps, often from other students. And, by allowing partially correct answers to become the bases for more accurate ones, the teacher can model for the class how to make incorrect and partially correct answers into better ones. Especially during problem solving, inquiry, and concept learning, these layers of refinement, gradually built up by student interchange, help students evaluate and refine their own responses.

USE OF GROUP DISCUSSION

When student-to-student-to-teacher exchanges grow into protracted interactions among large numbers of students, a **full-group discussion** has begun (Burbules & Bruce, 2001). In these discussions, you may intervene only occasionally to review and summarize main points, or you may schedule periodic "time-outs" to evaluate the group's progress and to redirect if necessary.

Group discussions can be useful for encouraging critical thinking, for engaging learners in the learning process, and for promoting the "reasoning together" that is necessary in a democratic society (Brookfield & Presskill, 2005; J. Dillon, 1995; Gall & Gall, 1990; Krabbe & Polivka,

1990). Because group discussion helps students think critically—examine alternatives, judge solutions, make predictions, and discover generalizations—it is yet another approach to teaching concepts, inquiry, and problem solving. It is our seventh and last indirect instruction strategy.

When your objective is to teach content that is well structured in the text or workbook, a presentation-recitation format may be more efficient and effective than a discussion. This might be the case with topics requiring little personal opinion and judgment, in which agreement about the topic may be so high as to preclude the controversy needed to promote alternative viewpoints and solutions.

But sometimes concept learning, inquiry, and problem solving can take on a less formal structure. At these times you may prefer a group discussion to a presentation-recitation format. Here the lack of consensus can make a discussion rewarding. Some examples of discussion-oriented questions within which concept learning, inquiry, and problem solving can occur might be:

- In what ways do you believe our cities of tomorrow accommodate our growing population?
- In what ways in time of crisis or war can the legislative branch of government be influenced by the executive branch?
- Do you think "Little Red Riding Hood" is fact or fiction? In what ways might it have been "real" in the mind of its author?
- Technology, such as computers, automobiles, and television, makes our lives more comfortable and pleasant, but it has also allowed us to become couch potatoes. In what ways can technology be used to help us become more fit?
- We once thought antibiotics were the magic bullet that removed the threat of infectious diseases. Now we know that this has helped create new dangerous and resistant strains of bacteria. What are some other "scientific advancements" that have solved one problem but created another?
- Cinderella was poor and unloved but had a fairy godmother to help her out. Wilbur from *Charlotte's Web* was the runt of a litter saved from death first by Fern and then Charlotte. But most of us who are poor, little, or unloved do not have such magical or determined protectors. What are some ways to overcome these problems by yourself? Can you name people from stories, movies, or real life who tapped the magic in themselves to make their dreams come true?
- With changes in technology and economics, many jobs have been eliminated. We no longer have elevator operators or gas station attendants. Even travel agents are in danger of losing their customers to the Internet. What are some other jobs that may fade away and some that may come into existence with new technological advancements?

Topics such as these that are not formally structured by the text and for which a high degree of consensus does not yet exist make good candidates for discussion sessions for solving problems, promoting inquiry, and learning essential concepts. During these discussions, you are the moderator and your **moderating tasks** are:

1. *Orienting the students to the objective of the discussion.* "Today we will discuss when a nation should decide to go to war. Specifically, we will discuss the meaning of the concept of aggression as it has occurred in history. In the context of wars between nations, your job at the end of the discussion will be to arrive at a concept that could help a president decide if sufficient aggression has occurred to warrant going to war."

2. *Providing new or more accurate information where needed.* "It is not correct to assume that World War II started with the bombing of Pearl Harbor. Many events occurred earlier on the European continent that some nations considered to be aggression."

3. *Reviewing, summarizing, or putting together opinions and facts into a meaningful relationship.* "Jin, Laura, and William, you seem to be arguing that the forcible entry of one nation into the territory of another nation constitutes aggression, and the rest of the class seems to be saying that undermining the economy of another nation also can constitute aggression."

4. *Adjust the flow of information and ideas to be most productive to the goals of the lesson.* "Mark, you seem to have extended our concept of aggression to include criticizing the government of another nation through political means, such as media broadcasts, speeches at the United Nations, and so forth. But that fits better the idea of a cold war, and we are trying to study some of the instances of aggression that might have started World War II."

5. *Combine ideas and promote compromise to arrive at an appropriate consensus.* "We seem to have two concepts of aggression—one dealing with the forcible entry of one nation into the territory of another and another that has to do with undermining a nation's economy. Could we combine these two ideas by saying that anything that threatens either a nation's people or its prosperity, or both, could be considered aggression?"

The moderating functions listed above will help you guide and redirect a large-group discussion without overly restricting the flow of ideas. During a large-group discussion, you should frequently perform one or more of these moderating functions to keep the groups on task and moving toward a final oral report or group product. The more familiar the topic and the greater the consensus, the more you can relinquish authority to the group.

Small-group discussions of about 4 to 6 students per group may also be used during indirect instruction (Cohen, 1994; Marriott & Kupperstein, 1997). When multiple topics must be discussed within the same lesson and time does not permit full-class discussion of the topics in sequential order, try using three, four, or five small groups simultaneously. You have three tasks in forming and guiding the groups: (1) to form groups whose members can work together, (2) to distribute students with diverse learning needs across groups, and (3) to move among the groups to periodically focus the discussion and resolve problems. Stopping the groups periodically, either to inform the entire class of important insights discovered by a group or to apply moderating functions, will help keep the groups close together and maintain your direction and authority (Cragan & Wright, 1999).

Another group format for indirect instruction is to have students work in pairs or teams. This can be an effective format when the discussion entails writing (e.g., a summary report), looking up information (in the text, encyclopedia, etc.), or preparing materials (chart, diagram, graph, etc.) (Johnson & Johnson, 1999; Slavin, 1993; Vermette, 1997). In the **pair or team discussions** arrangement, your role as moderator increases in proportion to the number of pairs or teams, so only brief interchanges with each may be possible.

The pair or team approach works best when the task is highly structured, when some consensus about the topic already exists, and when the orienting instructions fully define each member's role (e.g., student A searches for the information, student B writes a summary description of what is found, and both students read the summary for final agreement). Pairs or teams frequently become highly task oriented, so pairing or teaming tends to be most productive when discussion objectives go beyond just an oral report to include a product to be delivered to the class.

Gunter, Estes, & Schwab, (1999, p. 279–280) describe a pair arrangement based on the work of Lyman (1981). **Think, pair, share** is a simple technique in which students learn from one another and get to try out their ideas in a non-threatening context before presenting their ideas to the class. The benefits for the teacher include increased time-on-task in the classroom and greater quality of students' contributions to class discussions. There are four steps to think, pair, share, with a time limit on each step signaled by the teacher.

Step One—Teacher poses a question. The process of think, pair, share begins when the teacher poses a thought-provoking question for the entire class. Single right answer questions are avoided. Questions must pose problems or dilemmas that students will be willing and able to think about.

Step Two — Students think individually. At a signal from the teacher, students are given a limited amount of time to think of their own answer to the problematic question. The time should be decided by the teacher on the basis of knowledge of the students, the nature of the question, and the demands of the schedule.

Step Three — Each student discusses his or her answer with a fellow student. The end of the think step signals to the students it is time to begin working with one other student to reach consensus on an answer to the question. Each student now has a chance to try out possibilities. Together, each pair of students can reformulate a common answer based on their collective insights to possible solutions to the problem.

Step Four — Students share their answers with the whole class. In this final step, individuals present solutions individually or cooperatively to the class as a whole group. Where pairs of students have constructed displays of their answers, as in a chart or diagram, each member of the pair can take credit for their specific contribution.

The success and quality of the think, pair, share activity will depend on the quality of the question posed in step one. If the question promotes genuine thought for students, genuine discussion and sharing will emerge from the successive steps.

Here is a lesson plan for our indirect instruction dialogue, following the written format provided in chapter 4.

EXAMPLE INDIRECT INSTRUCTION LESSON PLAN: *Social Studies*

Unit Title: Economic Systems

Lesson Title: Comparisons and Contrasts Among Capitalist, Socialist, and Communist Economies

1 **Gaining attention**   Ask if anyone knows where the phrase "government of the people, by the people, for the people" comes from, to establish the idea that the principles and rules by which a country is governed also influence its economic system.

2 **Informing the learner of the objective**   This session: To relate economic systems to the ownership of goods and services in different countries. Next session: To be able to distinguish economic systems from political systems and to show why some economic systems are changing.

3 **Stimulating recall of prerequisite learning**   Ask for a definition of capitalism, and then refine with questioning and probing of the definition given. Continue probing until students arrive at a definition of capitalism as "an economic system that allows the ownership of tangible goods that last for a reasonable period of time." Check understanding by asking for three countries (other than ours) that have capitalist economies.

4 **Presenting the stimulus material**
A: Ask what the word *socialism* means. Refine the definition by questioning and probing until a definition is arrived at that defines socialism as "an economic system that allows the government to control and make available to everyone as many things as possible that (1) everyone values equally and that (2) are seen as essential for everyday existence." Have students compare capitalism and socialism by degree of ownership of public services and degree of taxes paid under each system.

B: Ask what the word *communism* means, and establish its relationship to the idea of community. Refine the definition, using the concept of degree of ownership by questioning and probing until the students arrive at still more examples of things owned and controlled by the government under communism.

5 **Eliciting the desired behavior**
A: Use questions to encourage the identification of public services most commonly owned under socialism, for example, hospitals, trains, and communication systems. Some types of farms and industries will also be accepted when their relation to the public good is understood.

B: Use questions to encourage the identification of those public services most commonly owned under communism, for example, food supply, housing, and industries. Emphasize those services and goods that are different from those identified under socialism.

C: Use questions to identify the amount and types of things owned by the government across the three systems, to establish the concept that differences among the systems are a matter of degree of ownership and degree of taxation.

6 **Providing feedback**   Pose questions in a manner that encourages the student to evaluate his or her own response and those of other students. Probe until student responses approximate an acceptable answer. On the blackboard, place side by side those goods and services the students have identified as likely to be owned by the government in all three systems and those likely to be owned uniquely by any one or combination of systems. Make a distinction between these goods and services and the personal items that students may have mentioned, such as clothes or household goods, which cannot be used to distinguish economic systems.

7 **Assessing the behavior**   After completion of an essay describing three countries of the students' own choosing, each of which represents a different economic system, grade students on their comprehension of the concepts of (1) degree of ownership and (2) degree of taxation as cited in our text.

COMPARISON OF DIRECT AND INDIRECT INSTRUCTION

The direct and indirect instruction models were presented in separate chapters because each includes distinctive teaching strategies. But neither model need be used to the exclusion of the other. Many times the two models can be effectively interwoven in a single lesson, as when a small number of facts, rules, or action sequences must be acquired before introducing a concept to be learned or problem to be solved. As you have seen, the models have two different purposes:

- The direct instruction model is best suited to the teaching of facts, rules, and action sequences and comprises six teaching strategies: daily review and checking, presenting and structuring new content, guided student practice, feedback and correctives, independent practice, and weekly and monthly reviews.
- The indirect instruction model is best suited for problem-centered, inquiry-centered, and concept-centered lessons and comprises seven teaching strategies: advance organization of content, induction and deduction, use of examples and nonexamples, use of questions to guide search and discovery, use of student ideas, student self-evaluation, and group discussion.

Table 8.3 places the direct and indirect models of instruction side by side for comparison and presents some teaching events that distinguish these models.

Table 8.3 Some examples of events under the direct and indirect models of instruction.

Direct Instruction	Indirect Instruction
Objective: To teach facts, rules, and action sequences	Objective: To teach concepts, patterns, and abstractions
Teacher begins the lesson with a review of the previous day's work.	Teacher begins the lesson with advance organizers that provide an overall picture and allow for concept expansion.
Teacher presents new content in small steps with explanations and examples.	Teacher focuses student responses using induction and/or deduction to refine and focus generalizations.
Teacher provides an opportunity for guided practice on a small number of sample problems. Prompts and models when necessary to attain 60%–80% accuracy.	Teacher presents examples and nonexamples of the generalization, identifying critical and noncritical attributes.
Teacher provides feedback and corrections according to whether the answer was correct, quick, and firm; correct, but hesitant; careless; or incorrect.	Teacher draws additional examples from students' own experiences, interests, and problems.
Teacher provides an opportunity for independent practice with seatwork. Strives for automatic responses that are 95% correct or higher.	Teacher uses questions to guide discovery and articulation of the generalization.
Teacher provides weekly and monthly (cumulative) reviews and reteaches unlearned content.	Teacher involves students in evaluating their own responses.
	Teacher promotes and moderates discussion to firm up and extend generalizations when necessary.

Under direct instruction, the objective is rapid attainment of facts, rules, and action sequences. Content is divided into small, easily learned steps through a presentation format involving brief explanations, examples, practice, and feedback. Both guided and independent practice help ensure that students are actively engaged in the learning process at high rates of success. Weekly and monthly reviews reinforce learned content and indicate what may need to be retaught.

Under indirect instruction, the objective is to teach concepts, patterns and abstractions with a problem-, inquiry- or concept-centered lesson. Here the teacher prepares for teaching higher-order outcomes by providing an overall framework or content organization into which the day's lesson is placed, allowing for problem solutions, paths of inquiry, and concepts to be developed. Initially crude and inaccurate responses are gradually refined through induction and deduction, focusing on the generalization of what is learned to some larger context. To accomplish this, both examples and nonexamples, some drawn from student interests and experiences, are used to distinguish essential from nonessential attributes. Throughout, the teacher uses questions to guide students to inquire about and discover concepts and problem solutions and to evaluate their own responses. When the content is relatively unstructured, discussion groups may replace a more teacher-controlled format, and the teacher becomes a moderator.

PROMOTING THE GOALS OF INDIRECT INSTRUCTION IN THE CULTURALLY DIVERSE CLASSROOM

Culturally sensitive teachers consider students' cultures and language skills when planning learning objectives and activities. They also realize that lesson objectives should include more than just delivering content knowledge—diverse students are often motivated by objectives that include the opportunity for affective and personal development as well (Burbules & Bruce, 2001; Burnette, 1999; Lustig & Koester, 2005). Effective teachers thus consider how to include students' backgrounds, perspectives, and experiences in "framing" the knowledge to be gained or the activities to be accomplished.

A concept that can help foster the affective and personal nature of your classroom is **social framing,** the context in which a message, such as a lesson, is received and understood. Tannen (1986) defined a social frame as a taken-for-granted context that delimits the sources from which meaning can be derived. When a teacher announces at the start of class, "Today's lesson will expect you to know the events that led up to the Civil War," the teacher has implicitly set how you are supposed to participate and respond—a social frame. Social frames can be created that can make a lesson more or less understandable to cultural or ethnic groups that may be accustomed to an alternate frame. For example, Michaels and Collins (1984) report an example of an Anglo teacher who framed a story with linear, topic-centered patterns (e.g., "Today I will read you a series of events that happened in the lives of three characters"), whereas her African American students framed the task according to topic-associating patterns (e.g., "She's going to tell us the kinds of things that can happen to people"). While one group primarily looked for a sequential list of events that unfolded from the beginning to the end of the story, the other group made notes about the events and the memories they evoked. Thus frames that are ambiguous or less appropriate to one group than another can alter how and what content is "heard" or "seen."

Bowers and Flinders (1991) and Lustig and Koester (2005) make a case for understanding the context in which different cultures expect information to be transmitted that is particularly relevant during indirect instruction. They recommend that the teacher (1) present content from the frame most dominant to the classroom; (2) make explicit what the frame is through which learners must see and interact with the content (e.g., as facts to be learned, skills to be performed, or concepts to think about); and/or (3) negotiate, when necessary, the frame with students at the start of the lesson. Walqui (2000a) points out that frames in which English-language learners could expect more interactive instructional approaches resulted in deeper language processing and conceptual learning. These frames also provided learners with a greater opportunity for affective and personal development.

Bowers and Flinders (1991) suggest three ways of establishing a frame at the start of a lesson that encourage students to respond in like manner. These approaches involve self-disclosure, humor, and dialogue. Curwin and Mendler (1997) suggest that each is an effective technique for adding an affective and personal dimension to your frame:

- *Self-disclosure* involves being open about your feelings and emotions that lead up to the lesson. "I've been struggling to make this topic meaningful, and here's what I've come up with." This will encourage similar statements of self-disclosure from students, which can be used to frame the lesson.
- *Humor* at the start of a lesson establishes a flexible, spontaneous, expressive mood from which frames can become established. "Here's a funny thing that happened to me that's connected to what we're going to study today" will encourage students to share other personal episodes that can be used to provide a context for the lesson.
- *Dialogue* involves the back-and-forth discussion of lesson content involving random and simultaneous responding. Here every student can expect to be heard, and the

teacher expresses lesson content idiosyncratically in the words of the learners. The teacher uses the responses of students to further structure and elaborate lesson content.

Each of these framing techniques is believed to enhance student engagement during indirect instruction across cultural and ethnic groups, some of whom may be less responsive to the traditional frames of prepackaged lesson plans and textbooks.

A FINAL WORD

This chapter and the preceding one presented a variety of teaching strategies. When used with the appropriate content and purpose, these strategies can significantly improve your teaching effectiveness. Although both the direct and indirect models of instruction are significant contributions to teaching and learning, neither should exclusively dominate your instructional style. It would be unfortunate if your teaching exemplified only the direct model or the indirect model, because the original purpose of introducing these models is to increase the variety of instructional strategies at your disposal.

These models and their strategies provide a variety of instructional tools that you can mix in many combinations to match your particular objectives and students. Just as different entrées have prominent and equal places on a menu, so do the direct and indirect models have prominent and equal places in your classroom.

The underlying point of these two chapters is that you should alternately employ the direct and indirect models to create tantalizing combinations of educational flavors for your students. Your own objectives are the best guide to what combination from the menu you will serve on any given day. In the chapters ahead, we extend this basic menu to provide still greater variety in the teaching methods you will have at your command.

SUMMING UP

This chapter introduced you to indirect instruction strategies. Its key terms and main points were:

Comparing Direct and Indirect Instruction

1. Indirect instruction is an approach to teaching and learning in which concepts, patterns, and abstractions are taught in the context of strategies that emphasize concept learning, inquiry, and problem solving.

2. In indirect instruction, the learner acquires information by transforming stimulus material into a response that requires the learner to rearrange and elaborate on the stimulus material.

Examples of Problem Solving, Inquiry, and Concept Attainment Strategies

3. Generalization is a process by which the learner responds in a similar manner to different stimuli, thereby increasing the range of instances to which particular facts, rules, and sequences apply.

4. Discrimination is a process by which the learner selectively restricts the acceptable range of instances by eliminating things that may look like the concept but differ from it on critical dimensions.

5. The processes of generalization and discrimination together help students classify different-appearing stimuli into the same categories on the basis of essential attributes. Essential attributes act as magnets, drawing together all instances of a concept without the learner having to see or memorize all instances of it.

6. The following are instructional strategies of the indirect model:
   - Use of advance organizers
   - Conceptual movement—inductive and deductive
   - Use of examples and nonexamples
   - Use of questions to guide search and discovery
   - Use of student ideas
   - Student self-evaluation
   - Use of group discussion

Content Organization

7. An advance organizer gives learners a conceptual preview of what is to come and helps them store, label, and package content for retention and later use.

8. Three approaches to organizing content and composing advance organizers are the concept learning, inquiry, and problem-solving approaches.

Conceptual Movement: Induction and Deduction

9. Induction starts with a specific observation of a limited set of data and ends with a generalization about a much broader context.

10. Deduction proceeds from principles or generalizations to their application in specific contexts.

Using Examples and Nonexamples

11. Providing examples and nonexamples helps define the essential and nonessential attributes needed for making accurate generalizations.

12. Using examples and nonexamples includes the following steps:
    • Providing more than a single example
    • Using examples that vary in ways that are irrelevant to the concept being defined
    • Using nonexamples that also include relevant dimensions of the concept
    • Explaining why nonexamples have some of the same characteristics as examples

The Use of Questions to Guide Search and Discovery

13. In indirect instruction, the role of questions is to guide students into discovering new dimensions of a problem or new ways of resolving a dilemma.

14. Some uses of questions during indirect instruction include the following:
    • Refocusing
    • Presenting contradictions to be resolved
    • Probing for deeper, more thorough responses
    • Extending the discussion to new areas
    • Passing responsibility to the class

Learner Experience and Use of Student Ideas

15. Student ideas can be used to heighten student interest, to organize subject content around student problems, to tailor feedback to fit individual students, and to encourage positive attitudes toward the subject. Because these goals should not become ends unto themselves, there should be a plan and structure for using student ideas in the context of strategies to promote problem solving, inquiry, and concept learning.

16. Student-centered learning, sometimes called unguided discovery learning, allows the student to select both the form and substance of the learning experience. This is appropriate in the context of independently conducted experiments, research projects, science fair projects, and demonstrations. However, the preorganization of content is always necessary to ensure that the use of student ideas promotes the goals of the curriculum.

Student Self-Evaluation

17. Self-evaluation of student responses occurs during indirect instruction when you give students the opportunity to reason out their answers so you and other students can suggest needed changes. Students can most easily conduct self-evaluation in the context of student-to-student-to-teacher exchanges, wherein you encourage students to comment on and consider the accuracy of their own and each others' responses.

Use of Group Discussion

18. A group discussion involves student exchanges with successive interactions among large numbers of students. During these exchanges, you may intervene only occasionally to review and summarize, or you may schedule periodic interaction to evaluate each group's progress and to redirect the discussion when necessary.

19. The best topics for discussion include those that are not formally structured by texts and workbooks and for which a high degree of consensus among your students does not yet exist.

20. Your moderating functions during discussion include the following:
    • Orient students to the objective of the discussion.
    • Provide new or more accurate information that may be needed.
    • Review, summarize, and relate opinions and facts.
    • Redirect the flow of information and ideas back to the objective of the discussion.

Final Word

21. Direct and indirect instruction is often used together, even within the same lesson, and you should not adopt one model to the exclusion of the other. Each contains a set of strategies that can compose an efficient and effective method for the teaching of facts, rules, and sequences and to solve problems, inquire, and learn concepts.

KEY TERMS

Advance organizer, 262
Constructivism, 262
Deduction, 279
Discrimination, 266
Examples, 281
Full-group discussion, 287
Generalization, 266
Induction, 279
Integrated bodies of knowledge, 264

Moderating tasks, 288
Nonexamples, 281
Pair or team discussions, 289
Small-group discussions, 289
Social framing, 293
Student-centered learning, 286
Think, pair, share, 289
Unguided discovery learning, 286

DISCUSSION AND PRACTICE QUESTIONS

Questions marked with an asterisk are answered in appendix B. See also the Companion Website for this text at *www.prenhall.com/borich* for more assessment options.

*1. What three ingredients are brought together in the indirect model of instruction? Provide a content example in which all three are present.

*2. What types of behavioral outcomes are the direct and indirect instructional models most effective in achieving?

*3. How would you explain where the word *indirect* comes from in the indirect instruction model? Provide an example to illustrate your point.

*4. Why can't direct instruction be used all the time? Give an example in which it would clearly not be appropriate.

*5. Explain in your own words what is meant by the words *generalization* and *discrimination*. Give an example of a single learning task that requires both these processes.

*6. Identify which of the following learning tasks require only facts, rules, or action sequences (Type 1) and which, in addition, would require the outcomes expected from concept learning, inquiry, or problem solving (Type 2):
   a. Naming the presidents
   b. Selecting the best speech
   c. Shifting the gearshift in a car
   d. Writing an essay
   e. Describing the main theme in George Orwell's *1984*
   f. Hitting a tennis ball
   g. Winning a tennis match
   h. Inventing a new soft drink
   i. Reciting the vowel sounds
   j. Becoming an effective teacher

*7. Describe two problems that would result if a concept had to be learned using only the cognitive processes by which facts, rules, and sequences are acquired.

8. For each of the following, show with specific examples how the concept might best be taught inductively or deductively. Pay particular attention to whether your instruction should begin or end with a generalization.
   • Democracy
   • Freedom
   • Education
   • Effective teaching
   • Parenting

*9. For the concept of effective teaching, identify five essential attributes and examples of five nonessential attributes. Then, using what you have written, write a paragraph explaining what the concept of effective teaching is.

*10. Using what you have learned in this and the previous chapter, distinguish the different purposes for asking questions in the direct and indirect model of instruction.

*11. What type of learning might be represented by discussions that begin and end with student-determined ideas and content? How is this different from the use of student ideas in the context of the indirect instruction model?

*12. For which of the following teaching objectives might you use the direct model of instruction, and for which might you use the indirect model? Teaching your class to do the following:
   a. Sing
   b. Use a microscope properly
   c. Appreciate Milton's *Paradise Lost*
   d. Become aware of the pollutants around us
   e. Solve an equation with two unknowns
   f. Read at grade level
   g. Type at the rate of 25 words per minute
   h. Write an original short story
   i. Build a winning science fair project
   j. Distinguish war from aggression
   Are there any for which you might use both models?

FIELD EXPERIENCE ACTIVITIES

1. Prepare a 2-minute introduction to a lesson of your own choosing that provides your students with an advance organizer.

2. Provide one example each of an advance organizer that reflects a concept learning, inquiry, and problem-solving lesson.

*3. In your own words, define inductive and deductive reasoning. Give an example of each, using content from a grade you will be teaching.

*4. Identify the five steps to deductive reasoning commonly applied in the scientific laboratory. With what teaching content would you consider using these steps?

*5. Identify four ways in which examples and nonexamples can be used in the teaching of concepts. Show how they can be applied with a topic you will be teaching.

*6. What purposes do questions serve in the inquiry process? Choose a lesson topic and provide an example of each of these types of questions.

*7. What are three ways student ideas might be incorporated into an indirect instruction lesson? Show how they would apply to a lesson you are likely to teach.

*8. Why is student self-evaluation more important in the indirect model of instruction than in the direct model of instruction? What is a way you could promote student self-evaluation in your classroom?

*9. What are five moderating responsibilities of the teacher during group discussion? Identify a group discussion topic in your teaching area to which they could be applied.

10. Provide an example of social framing using a topic you are likely to teach. Write a brief class introduction to indicate the words you might use to convey this frame to students at the beginning of class.

DIGITAL PORTFOLIO ACTIVITIES

The following digital portfolio activities relate to INTASC principles 4 and 6.

1. In Field Experience Activity 2 you provided an example of an advance organizer for a concept learning, inquiry, and problem-centered lesson that you are likely to teach. Place these example organizers in a digital portfolio folder labeled *Advance Organizers* and add to them other advance organizers you observe or read about that provide examples in the areas you will teach.

2. In Field Experience Activity 9 you were asked to identify five moderating responsibilities of the teacher during group discussion. Place these in a digital portfolio folder titled *Group Discussions* as a reminder, together with several additional discussion topics in your teaching area to which they could be applied.

CLASSROOM OBSERVATION ACTIVITIES

The following classroom observation activities relate to INTASC principles 4 and 6.

1. Seeing some of the many types of advance organizers and how they are delivered verbally and visually will be helpful to you in planning your own advance organizers. On the Companion Website for this chapter you will find a *Checklist for Observing Advance Organizers* that is divided into verbally delivered organizers and visual organizers (e.g., on board, transparency, or handout) and whether the organizer is used at the beginning, middle, or end of the class or lesson. Use several of your college classes to record the advance organizers that you see, if you cannot make a school visit. Place the checklist in your *Advance Organizer* digital portfolio folder for use when you begin systematic classroom observation.

2. One aspect of a good group discussion is the extent to which the teacher is able to use student ideas to expand the discussion to related concepts and include other students. Several authors have described different ways of using student ideas, some of which are:

Acknowledging—using the student's idea by repeating the logic of the idea expressed by the student

Modifying—using the student's idea by rephrasing it or conceptualizing it in the teacher's own words

Applying—using the student's idea to teach an inference or predict the next step in a logical analysis of a problem

Comparing—using the student's idea by drawing a relationship between it and ideas expressed earlier

Summarizing—using what was said by an individual student or a group of students as a summarization of concepts

On the Companion Website for this chapter you will find a recording format titled *Observing Use of Student Ideas*. This record lists these five strategies for using student ideas and then provides space for checking off the number of times the teacher uses each one. Look for the use of student ideas in a school or college classroom (maybe this very one) using the recording format provided. Place this record in your digital portfolio *Group Discussion* folder for future classroom observations.

CHAPTER CASE HISTORY AND PRAXIS TEST PREPARATION

DIRECTIONS: The following case history pertains to chapter 8 content. After reading the case history, answer the short-answer question that follows and consult appendix D to find different levels of scored student responses and the rubric used to determine the quality of each response. You also have the opportunity to submit your responses online to receive feedback by visiting the *Case History* module for this chapter on the Companion Website, where you will also find additional questions pertaining to Praxis test content.

Case History

Mr. Peterson's eighth-grade social studies class consists of approximately 30 students and is culturally diverse. They are currently studying a unit on economic systems. They have already established the similarities and differences between the "private" and "public" sectors of the economy. Today, Mr. Peterson wants them to consider a factor that influences all economies.

◆ ◆ ◆

Mr. Peterson: Amy, how many blacksmiths do you know?
Amy: Well, none.
Josh: What about the horseshoers who work at the racetrack?
Amy: But they don't heat up the iron like the "village smithy," do they?
Mr. Peterson: You're right, Amy. Most of them just fit ready-made shoes nowadays. (Pause while Mr. Peterson looks dramatically at the wall calendar.) Well, before we know it, it will be summer break, and I'll be needing a summer job to keep me busy. What do you think I should try this summer, Roberto? Maybe I'll be a gas station attendant. I always did like cars.
Roberto: (A bewildered pause) A gas station attendant? You mean those guys that used to wipe your windshield and ask if you wanted regular or premium? Hey, Mr. Peterson, they're not around anymore.
Mr. Peterson: All right. What about being an elevator operator?
Rosalia: You mean like the ones in the old movies who said, "What floor, please," and then opened the door with a lever or something? (She smiles) I think you're trying to have some fun with us, Mr. Peterson. Those jobs just don't exist anymore.
Mr. Peterson: Now, why do you think those jobs—the blacksmith, the gasoline attendant, and the elevator operator—have all but disappeared?
Parish: Well, we drive cars to work today. We don't ride horses except for fun.

Amber:	You can just slide your credit card into the machine at the pump and get your own gas.
Rosalia:	And all you have to do in an elevator is push a button for your floor—and the door opens automatically.
Mr. Peterson:	So what's the common denominator? (A pause with no response.) What has made all these occupations obsolete? What do you think, Monique?
Monique:	Changing times, I guess.
Mr. Peterson:	But what has changed, Monique? Do you mean hairstyles or pop music or the latest shade of nail polish?
Monique:	No. (She smiles as she looks down at her bright turquoise nails.) I guess I mean modern times, you know—machines and things.
Gilbert:	They call it high tech, Monique.
Mr. Peterson:	Machines? High tech? Any other ideas?
Rosalia:	Well, I don't know how high tech cars are. After all, Gilbert, they've been around for a century. Maybe just changing technology.
Mr. Peterson:	A very good term, Rosalia. You used Monique's idea of "changing times" and Gilbert's of "high tech." Gilbert's was too narrow to include the blacksmith example, and I showed Monique that "changing times" included too much, everything from pop music to nail polish. So to summarize, we could say that . . .
Roberto:	Changes in technology influence the job market by eliminating some jobs.
Mr. Peterson:	I couldn't have said it better, Roberto. Now tomorrow, we'll consider the role of technology in creating new jobs.

◆　◆　◆

Short-Answer Question

This section presents a sample Praxis short-answer question. In appendix D you will find sample responses along with the standards used in scoring these responses.

DIRECTIONS: The following question requires you to write a short answer. Base your answer on your knowledge of principles of learning and teaching from chapter 8. Be sure to answer all parts of the question.

1. Research on teaching practices indicates that certain approaches to instruction for diverse classrooms, one of which is called *social framing*, can enhance student engagement during indirect instruction across cultural and ethnic groups. Explain briefly two other techniques Mr. Peterson used to encourage the affective and personal responses of his students to engage them more intently in the lesson.

Discrete Multiple-Choice Questions

DIRECTIONS: Each of the multiple-choice questions that follow is based on Praxis-related pedagogical knowledge in chapter 8. Select the answer that is best in each case and compare your results with those in appendix D. See also the Companion Website for this text at *www.prenhall.com/borich* for more assessment options.

1. A conceptual framework usually presented at the beginning of a lesson that structures the content to be presented is called
   a. Pre-dialogue
   b. Advance organizer
   c. Problem-solving framework
   d. Authentic beginning

2. Questioning during indirect instruction is
   a. Directed at eliciting single right answers
   b. Efficient, specific, and to the point
   c. Intended to promote search and discovery
   d. Designed to elicit the practice of correct responses

3. When the teacher encourages students to comment on and consider the accuracy of their own and one another's responses, they are engaging in
   a. Refocusing
   b. Networking
   c. Problem solving

d. Self-evaluation

4. Which of the following best express the intent of a constructivist lesson?
   a. Instructional activities are presented in the form of problems to solve.
   b. Students refine answers to problems from their point of view and experience.
   c. The social nature of learning is encouraged by the interaction of teacher with students and students with one another.
   d. Students are given the freedom to chart their own course and set their own goals.

5. Which of the following lesson objectives would best represent the goal of (a) a concept learning lesson, (b) an inquiry lesson, and (c) a problem-solving lesson?

   ____ 1. Students will learn the essential attributes required for a representative government.

   ____ 2. Students will be able to investigate on their own why bond and stock prices often move in opposite directions.

   ____ 3. Students will be able to determine two primary sources of industrial pollution and recommend cost-effective remedies.

   ____ 4. Students will be able to distinguish effective from ineffective strategies for identifying learners who are academically at risk.

Chapter 9

Questioning Strategies

This chapter will help you answer the following questions and meet the following INTASC principles for effective teaching:

1. What is an effective question?
2. What are some different types of questions?
3. What is a question-asking sequence?
4. How do I ask questions at different levels of cognitive complexity?
5. How do I ask questions that promote inquiry and problem solving?

INTASC 1: The teacher understands the central concepts, tools of inquiry, and structures of the discipline(s) he or she teaches and can create learning experiences that make these aspects of subject matter meaningful for students.

INTASC 3: The teacher understands how students differ in their approaches to learning and creates instructional opportunities that are adapted to diverse learners.

INTASC 4: The teacher understands and uses a variety of instructional strategies to encourage students' development of critical thinking, problem solving, and performance skills.

INTASC 6: The teacher uses knowledge of effective verbal, nonverbal, and media communication techniques to foster active inquiry, collaboration, and supportive interaction in the classroom.

In the classroom dialogues of previous chapters, you saw the important role of questions in the effective teacher's menu. This is no coincidence, because most exchanges between teachers and students involve questions in some form. This chapter builds upon earlier examples to define an effective question, the varied ways questions can be asked, and the types of questions you should ask more frequently than others.

Also discussed is the closely related topic of probes. Like questions, probes are effective catalysts for performing the five key behaviors of (1) lesson clarity, (2) instructional variety, (3) task orientation, (4) student engagement in the learning process, and (5) student success. Subsequent chapters will show you how to combine these questioning techniques with other teaching strategies.

WHAT IS A QUESTION?

In the context of a lively and fast-paced exchange in a classroom, questions are not always obvious. As observed by Dantonio and Beisenherz (2000) and Brown and Wragg (1993), students routinely report difficulty in distinguishing some types of questions during a classroom dialogue—and even whether a question has been asked. For example, imagine hearing these two questions:

Raise your hand if you know the answer.
Aren't you going to *answer the question*?

The first is expressed in command form (italics), yet it contains an implicit question. The second sounds like a question, yet contains an implicit command. Will your students perceive both of these statements as questions? Will they both evoke the same response?

Voice inflection is another source of confusion; it can indicate a question even when sentence syntax does not. For example, imagine hearing the following two sentences spoken with the emphasis shown:

You *said* the president can have two terms in office?
The president can have *two* terms in office?

The proper voice inflection can turn almost any sentence into a question, whether you intend it or not. In addition, a real question can be perceived as a rhetorical question because of inflection and word choice:

We all have done our homework today, *haven't we?*

Whether this is intended as a question or not, it is certain that all who failed to complete their homework will assume the question to be rhetorical.

Effective questions are ones for which students actively compose a response and thereby become engaged in the learning process (Chuska, 2003; Wilen, 1991). The previous examples show that effective questions depend on more than just words. Their effectiveness also depends on voice inflection, word emphasis, word choice, and the context in which the question is raised. Questions can be raised in many ways, and each way can determine whether the question is perceived by your students, and how.

In this chapter any oral statement or gesture intended to evoke a student response is considered to be a question. And if it evokes a response that actively engages a student in the learning process, it is an effective question. With this distinction in mind, let us now explore many ways of asking questions that actively engage students in the learning process.

What Consumes 80% of Class Time?

In almost any classroom at any time, you can observe a sequence of events in which the teacher structures the content to be discussed, solicits a student response, and then reacts to the response. These activities performed in sequence are the most common behaviors in any classroom. They represent the following chain of events:

1. The teacher provides structure, briefly formulating the topic or issue to be discussed.
2. The teacher solicits a response or asks a question of one or more students.
3. The student responds or answers the question.
4. The teacher reacts to the student's answer.

The teacher behaviors in this chain of events compose the activities of **structuring, soliciting,** and **reacting.** At the heart of this chain is soliciting, or question-asking behavior. Questions are the tool for bridging the gap between your presentation of content and the student's understanding of it. The purpose of using questions must not be lost among the many forms and varieties of questions presented in this chapter. Like all the ingredients of direct and indirect instruction, questions are tools to encourage students to think about and act on the material you have structured.

The centerpiece of this chain—soliciting or questioning—is so prevalent that as many as 100 questions per class hour may be asked in the typical elementary and secondary classroom. Sometimes as much as 80% of all school time can be devoted to questions and answers. This enormous concentration on a single strategy attests both to its convenience and to its perceived effectiveness. But, as noted, not all questions are effective questions. That is, not all questions actively engage students in the learning process.

Are We Asking the Right Questions?

Some research data indeed show that not all questions actively engage students in the learning process. Early studies estimated that 70% to 80% of all questions require the simple recall of facts; only 20% to 30% require the higher-level thought processes of clarifying, expanding, generalizing, and making inferences (Corey, 1940; Haynes, 1935). Evidently little has changed since these early studies. More recent work in the United States and England indicates that, of every five questions asked, about three require data recall, one is managerial, and only one requires higher-level thought processes (Atwood & Wilen, 1991; G. Brown & Wragg, 1993; Wilen, 1991).

This lopsided proportion of recall questions to thought questions is alarming. Behaviors most frequently required in adult life, at work, and in advanced training—those at the higher levels of cognitive complexity involving analysis, synthesis, and evaluation—seem to be the least emphasized behaviors in the classroom (Chuska, 2003; Dantonio & Beisenherz, 2000; Power & Hubbard, 1999).

WHAT ARE THE PURPOSES OF QUESTIONS?

It would be easy to classify all questions as either lower order (requiring the recall of information) or higher order (requiring clarification, expansion, generalization, and inference). But such a broad distinction would ignore the many specific purposes for which questions are used. Most reasons for asking questions can be classified into the following general categories:

1. *Interest getting and attention getting:* "If you could go to the moon, what would be the first thing you would notice?"
2. *Diagnosing and checking:* "Does anyone know the meaning of the Latin word *via?*"
3. *Recalling specific facts or information:* "Who can name each of the main characters in *The Adventures of Huckleberry Finn?*"
4. *Managing:* "Did you ask my permission?"
5. *Encouraging higher-level thought processes:* "Putting together all that we learned, what household products exhibit characteristics associated with the element sodium?"
6. *Structuring and redirecting learning:* "Now that we've covered the narrative form, who can tell me what an expository sentence is?"
7. *Allowing expression of affect:* "What did you like about *Of Mice and Men?*"

Most of the questions in these categories have the purpose of shaping or setting up the learner's response. In this sense, a well-formulated question serves as an advance organizer, providing the framework for the response that is to follow.

WHAT ARE CONVERGENT AND DIVERGENT QUESTIONS?

Questions can be narrow or broad, encouraging either a specific, limited response or a general, expansive one. A question that limits an answer to a single or small number of responses is called a **convergent** (or direct or closed) **question.** For these questions, the learner has previously read or heard the answer and so has only to recall certain facts.

Convergent questions set up the learner to respond in a limited, restrictive manner: "Does anyone know the meaning of the Latin word *via?*" "Who can name the main characters in *The Adventures of Huckleberry Finn?*" The answers to these questions are easily judged right or wrong. Many convergent, or closed, questions are used in direct instruction. As mentioned, up to 80% of all questions may be of this type.

Another type of question encourages a general or open response. This is the **divergent,** or indirect, **question.** It has no single best answer, but it can have wrong answers. This is perhaps the most misunderstood aspect of a divergent question. Not just any answer will be correct, even in the case of divergent questions raised for the purpose of allowing students to express their feelings. If Carlos is asked what he liked about *Of Mice and Men* and says "Nothing," or "The happy ending," then either Carlos has not read the book or he needs help in better understanding the events that took place. A passive or accepting response on your part to answers like these is inappropriate, regardless of your intent to allow an open response.

You can expect far more diverse responses from divergent questions than from convergent questions—which may explain why only 20% of all questions are divergent. It will be easier to determine the right or wrong answer to a convergent question than it will be to sift through the range of acceptable responses to a divergent question. Even so, it is your responsibility to identify inappropriate responses, to follow them up, and to bring them back into the acceptable range. Thus you often will need to follow up divergent questions with more detail, new information, or encouragement. In this sense, divergent questions become a rich source of lively, spontaneous follow-up material that can make your teaching fresh and interesting.

Note that the same question can be convergent under one set of circumstances and divergent under another. Suppose you ask a student to decide or evaluate, according to a set of criteria, which household products exhibit characteristics of the element sodium. If the student only recalls products from a previously memorized list, the question is convergent. But if the student has never seen such a list and must analyze the physical properties of products for the first time, the question is divergent.

Convergent questions also can inadvertently turn into divergent questions. When the answer to a question thought to involve simple recall ("Does anyone know the meaning of the Latin word *via*?") has never been seen before, and the student arrives at the right answer through generalization and inductive reasoning (e.g., by thinking about the meaning of the English word *viaduct* or the phrase "via route 35"), the question is divergent.

A convergent question in one context may be a divergent question in another and vice versa. The question "What do you think of disarmament?" may require the use of evaluation skills by eighth graders but only the recall of facts by twelfth graders who have just finished memorizing the details of the Strategic Arms Limitation Treaty. Also, both of the questions "What do you think about disarmament?" and "What do you think about the Dallas Cowboys?" may require some analysis, synthesis, or decision making, but for most of your students, disarmament will require a higher level of thought than will the Dallas Cowboys. As has been shown, effective questions depend on more than just words—they depend on the context of the discussion in which the question is raised, voice inflection, word emphasis, and word choice.

WHAT DOES THE RESEARCH SAY ABOUT ASKING CONVERGENT AND DIVERGENT QUESTIONS?

Classroom researchers have studied the effects on student achievement of convergent and divergent questions (Cecil, 1995; J. Dillon, 1990; Gall, 1984). Remember that far more convergent questions are raised in classrooms than divergent questions; the ratio is about 4:1. Most rationales for using higher-level, divergent-type questions include promotion of thinking, formation of concepts and abstractions, encouragement of analysis-synthesis-evaluation, and so on (Bransford, Brown, & Cocking, 2000; Chuska, 2003; Richardson, 1997). But interestingly, research has not clearly substantiated that the use of higher-level questions is related to gains in student achievement—at least not as measured by tests of standardized achievement.

Although some studies report modest improvements in achievement scores with the use of divergent questioning strategies, others have not. Some studies even report larger achievement gains with convergent questioning than with divergent questioning strategies. Although these studies found a large imbalance in favor of convergent questions, four important factors must be considered when looking at their results:

1. Tests of achievement—and particularly tests of standardized achievement—employ multiple-choice items that generally test for behaviors at lower levels of cognitive complexity.

Therefore, the achievement measures in these studies may have been unable to detect increases in behaviors at the higher levels of cognitive complexity, increases that might have resulted from the use of divergent questions.

2. The diversity of responses normally expected from divergent questions, and the added time needed to build on and follow up on responses, may prohibit large amounts of class time from being devoted to higher-order questioning. Because less instructional time often is devoted to divergent questioning than to convergent questioning, some study results may simply reflect the imbalance in instructional time, not their relative effectiveness.

3. The content best suited for teaching more complex behavior may constitute only a small amount of the content in existing texts, workbooks, and curriculum guides. Although this is changing as a result of constructivist views on teaching and learning, much of the typical curricula in math, science, English, and even the social sciences emphasize facts and understandings at the knowledge and comprehension level. Until larger portions of curricula are written to encourage or require higher-level thought processes, the time teachers actually devote to these behaviors may not increase.

4. Thinking and problem-solving behaviors most closely associated with divergent questions may take much longer to detect in the behavior of learners than less complex behaviors. Less complex behaviors (learning to form possessives, memorizing Latin roots, knowing multiplication tables) are quickly elicited with convergent questioning strategies and are readily detected with fill-in, matching, or multiple-choice exams at the end of a lesson or unit. But more complex and authentic behaviors (being able to derive meaning and interpretations from reading stories such as *Charlotte's Web*, learning to distinguish economic systems from political systems, learning to analyze household products for their capacity to pollute the air we breathe, recognizing forms of quadratic equations) may take a unit, a grading period, or longer to build to a measurable outcome. This time span is beyond that of most, if not all, of the studies that have compared the effects of convergent and divergent strategies on school achievement.

Thus the seeming imbalance in the use and effectiveness of divergent and convergent questioning strategies may have little to do with the effectiveness of the strategies themselves. Because factual recall always will be required for higher-order thought processes, convergent questions always will be a necessary precondition for achieving higher-level behaviors (Bruning, Schraw, Norby, & Ronning, 2004; Mayer, 2002). Also, because more instructional time is required for higher-order questioning, consistent use of moderate amounts of divergent questions may be more practical and effective than intense but brief episodes of divergent questioning. The most appropriate convergent/divergent question ratio may be about 70:30 in classrooms where lesson content emphasizes lower levels of cognitive complexity, to about 60:40 in classrooms where lesson content emphasizes higher levels.

Many of the same studies that fail to link higher-order questioning with increases in school achievement indicate that higher-order questioning tends to encourage students to use higher thought processes in composing a question response. Research (J. T. Dillon, 1988b) suggests that teachers who ask questions requiring analysis, synthesis, and evaluation tend to elicit these cognitive processes from their students more frequently than teachers who use fewer higher-level questions. Therefore, asking divergent questions seems desirable, regardless of whether their immediate effects show up on tests of standardized achievement. Most researchers would agree that the effects of higher-level questioning on the cognitive processes of learning justifies your including higher-level questions with most of your lessons (Eggen & Kauchack, 2004; Ormrod, 2003).

WHO ARE THE TARGETS OF QUESTIONS?

Research by G. Brown and Wragg (1993) suggests that questions at various levels of cognitive complexity can be directed to individuals, to groups, or to the entire class. Occasionally posing questions over the heads of some learners and under the heads of others will keep all students alert and engaged in the learning process (Stipek, 2003).

In more homogeneously grouped classes, questions can be spread across individuals, groups, and the full class but crafted to fit the cognitive complexity most appropriate for the learners being taught. For example, a general question can be composed requiring more or less cognitive complexity and prerequisite knowledge, as illustrated in the following examples:

Less Complex	More Complex
"Tell me, Lupe, if you sat down to breakfast, what things at the breakfast table would most likely contain the element of sodium?"	"Lupe, what are some forms of the element sodium in our universe?"
"After the death of Lenny in *Of Mice and Men*, what happens to the other main character?"	"What would be an example of dramatic irony in *Of Mice and Men*?"
"After thinking about the words *photo* and *synthesis*, who wants to guess what photosynthesis means?"	"Who can tell me how photosynthesis supports plant life?"
"Ted, if we have the equation $10 = 2/x$, do we find x by multiplying or dividing?"	"Ted, can you solve this problem for x? $10 = 2/x$."

Notice that these examples vary not only in cognitive processes that are being required but also in how they are framed, or phrased. More advance organizers, hints, and clues will be more appropriate for some types of learners than for others (Ngeow, 1998).

One way of framing questions for heterogeneous classes is to design them so different responses at various levels of complexity are being required. You can accept less complex responses as being just as correct as more complex answers, if they match the level of the question being asked. Although a response from some learners may not be as complete, you can evaluate the response in terms of the cognitive complexity required by the question and the student's ability to respond to it. Therefore, the elaboration given and depth of understanding required may be less for one type of learner than for another. Table 9.1 suggests specific questioning strategies.

WHAT SEQUENCES OF QUESTIONS ARE USED?

Questions also can vary according to the sequence in which they are used. Recall that the most basic **question sequence** involves structuring, soliciting, and reacting. However, many variations are possible. Studies by Wilen (1991) note that one of the most popular sequences employs divergent questions that lead to convergent questions. Many teachers begin the structuring-soliciting-reacting process by starting with an open question that leads to further structuring, and then to subsequent questions that involve recall or simple deduction.

Table 9.1   Characteristics of more and less complex questions.

More Complex Questions	Less Complex Questions
Require the student to generalize the content to new problems	Require the student to recall task-relevant prior knowledge
Stymie, mystify, and challenge in ways that do not have predetermined answers	Use specific and concrete examples, settings, and objects with which students are familiar
Are delivered in the context of an investigation or problem that is broader than the question itself	Use a step-by-step approach, where each question is narrower than the preceding one
Ask students to go deeper, clarify, and provide additional justification or reasons for the answers they provide	Rephrase or reiterate the answers to previous questions
Use more abstract concepts by asking students to see how their answers may apply across settings or objects	Suggest one or two probable answers that lead students in the right direction
Are part of a sequence of questions that builds to higher and more complex concepts, patterns, and abstractions	Are placed in the context of a game (e.g., 20 questions) with points and rewards

This general-to-specific approach can take several twists and turns. For example, in the following dialogue, the teacher begins by encouraging speculative responses and then narrows to a question requiring simple deduction:

◆   ◆   ◆

Teacher: What do astronauts wear on the moon?
Students: Spacesuits.
Teacher: So what element in our atmosphere must not be in the atmosphere on the moon?

◆   ◆   ◆

It is the same approach when a teacher poses a problem, asks several simple recall questions, and then reformulates the question to narrow the problem still further:

◆   ◆   ◆

Teacher: If the Alaskan Eskimos originally came from Siberia on the Asian continent, how do you suppose they got to Alaska?
Students: (No response.)
Teacher: We studied the Bering Strait, which separates North America from Asia. How wide is the water between these two continents at their closest point?
Student: About 60 miles. The Little and Big Diomede Islands are in between.
Teacher: If this expanse of water were completely frozen, which some scientists believe it was years ago, how might Asians have come to the North American continent?

◆   ◆   ◆

Teachers frequently employ this type of funneling: adding conditions of increasing specificity to a question. However, no evidence indicates that one sequencing strategy is any more effective in promoting student achievement than any other. The specific sequence you choose should depend on your behavioral objectives, the instructional content being taught, and the ability level of your students.

Other types of questioning sequences that teachers can implement in a cycle of structuring, soliciting, and reacting, suggested by Brown and Edmondson (1984), are illustrated in Table 9.2. These offer useful additions to your questioning strategies menu.

Table 9.2 Some sequences of questions.

Type		Description
Extending	⎯⎯⎯	A string of questions of the same type and on the same topic
Extending and lifting	⌐	Initial questions request examples and instances of the same type, followed by a leap to a different type of question; a common sequence is likely to be recall, simple deduction and descriptions leading to reasons, hypothesis
Funneling	＜	Begins with open questions and proceeds to narrow down to simple deductions and recall or to reasons and problem solving
Sowing and reaping	◇	Problem posed, open questions asked, followed by more specific questions and restatement of initial problem
Step-by-step up	⌐⌐	A sequence of questions moving systematically from recall to problem solving, evaluation or open ended
Step-by-step down	⌐⌐	Begins with evaluation questions and moves systematically through problem solving toward direct recall
Nose-dive	⌐	Begins with evaluation and problem solving and then moves straight to simple recall

Source: From "Asking Questions" by G. Brown and R. Edmondson, in *Classroom Teaching Skills* (pp. 97–119), edited by E. Wragg. Copyright © 1984 by Nichols Publishing Company.

WHAT LEVELS OF QUESTIONS ARE USED?

As we have seen, as an effective teacher, you must be able to formulate divergent and convergent questions, to target questions to specific types of learners, and to arrange questions in meaningful sequences. You also must be able to formulate questions at different levels of cognitive complexity.

One of the best known systems for classifying questions according to cognitive complexity is the taxonomy of objectives in the cognitive domain that was presented in chapter 3. This system has the advantage of going beyond the simple recall-versus-thought dichotomy frequently used in the research cited previously to provide learning outcomes at intermediate levels of cognitive complexity as well. A continuum of question complexity that fills the space between these ends of the scale is a useful addition to the art of asking questions.

Recall that the basic cognitive domain taxonomy contains six levels of cognitive complexity:

- Knowledge
- Comprehension
- Application
- Analysis
- Synthesis
- Evaluation

Table 9-3 A question classification scheme.

Level of Behavioral Complexity	Expected Student Behavior	Instructional Processes	Key Words
Knowledge (remembering)	Student is able to remember or recall information and recognize facts, terminology, and rules.	repetition memorization	define describe identify
Comprehension (understanding)	Student is able to change the form of a communication by translating and rephrasing what has been read or spoken.	explanation illustration	summarize paraphrase rephrase
Application (transferring)	Student is able to apply the information learned to a context different than the one in which it was learned.	practice transfer	apply use employ
Analysis (relating)	Student is able to break a problem down into its component parts and to draw relationships among the parts.	induction deduction	relate distinguish differentiate
Synthesis (creating)	Student is able to combine parts to form a unique or novel solution to a problem.	divergence generalization	formulate compose produce
Evaluation (judging)	Student is able to make decisions about the value or worth of methods, ideas, people, or products according to expressed criteria.	discrimination inference	appraise decide justify

Table 9.3 identifies the types of student outcomes associated with each level. Look at each level to get a feel for the question-asking strategies that go along with it.

Knowledge

Recall from chapter 3 that knowledge objectives require the student to recall, describe, define, or recognize facts that already have been committed to memory. Some action verbs you can use to formulate questions at the knowledge level follow:

define	list
describe	name
identify	recite

Sample questions are

- What is the definition of *capitalism*?
- How many digits are needed to make the number 12?
- Can you recite the first rule for forming possessives?
- What is the definition of a *triangle*?

Notice that each of these questions can be answered correctly simply by recalling previously memorized facts. They do not require understanding of what was memorized or the ability to use the learned facts in a problem-solving context. However, when facts are linked to other forms of knowledge, such as those in subsequent lessons and units, they become stepping-stones for gradually increasing the complexity of teaching outcomes. To avoid the overuse or disconnected use of questions at the knowledge level, ask yourself: Do the facts required by my questions represent task-relevant prior knowledge for subsequent learning? If your answer is no, you might consider assigning text, workbook, or supplemental material that contains the facts, instead of incorporating them into your question-asking behavior. If your answer is yes, then determine in what ways learners will use the facts in subsequent lessons, and raise questions that eventually will help form more complex behaviors.

Your students may not need the ability to recite the names of the presidents, the Declaration of Independence, or the elements in the periodic table, because these facts may not be task-relevant prior knowledge for more higher-order outcomes. However, it is likely your learners will need to recite the multiplication tables, the parts of speech, and the rules for adding, subtracting, multiplying, and dividing signed numbers, for these will be used countless times in completing exercises and solving problems at higher levels of cognitive complexity. Always take time to ask yourself: Are the facts that I am about to teach relevant for attaining the desired outcomes of subsequent lessons? By doing so, you will avoid knowledge questions that may be trivial or irrelevant.

Comprehension

Comprehension questions require some level of understanding of facts the student has committed to memory. Responses to these questions should show that the learner can explain, summarize, or elaborate on the facts that have been learned. Some action verbs you can use in formulating questions at the comprehension level are:

convert	paraphrase
explain	rephrase
extend	summarize

Here are sample questions:

- Can you, in your own words, explain the concept of capitalism?
- How many units are there in the number 12?
- In converting a possessive back to the nonpossessive form, what must be rephrased so the first rule applies?
- What steps are required to draw a triangle?

In responding to each of these questions, the student acts on previously learned material by changing it from the form in which it was first learned. For example, the teacher asks not for the definition of capitalism, but "in your own words, explain the concept of capitalism." This requires translation or conversion of the original definition (the teacher's) into another (the student's).

There is an important step in moving from knowledge-level questions to comprehension-level questions. Knowledge-level questions require no cognitive processing at the time of the response, but comprehension-level questions do. In the former case, the learner actually may think about the material only once, at the time it was originally learned. In the latter case, the learner must actively think about the content twice: once when the facts are memorized and again when they must be composed into a response in a different form. Although fact questions must logically precede comprehension questions, comprehension questions are superior to knowledge questions by encouraging longer-term retention, understanding, and eventual use of the learned material in more authentic contexts.

Application

Application questions extend facts and understanding to the next level of authenticity. They go beyond memorization and translation of facts. Application questions require the student to apply facts to a problem, context, or environment that is different from the one in which the information was learned. Thus the student can rely on neither the original context nor the original content to solve the problem.

Here are some action verbs you can use in formulating questions at the application level:

apply	operate
demonstrate	solve
employ	use

Here are some sample questions:

* What countries from among those listed do you believe have a capitalist economic system?
* Can you show me 12 pencils?
* Consider the first rule for forming possessives; who can apply it to the errors in the following newspaper article?
* Can you draw a triangle for me?

Your job in application questions is to present your learners with a context or problem different from that in which they learned the material. Application questions encourage the transfer of newly learned material to a new and different environment.

Application questions require two related cognitive processes: (1) the simultaneous recall and consideration of all the individual units (facts) pertaining to the question, and (2) the composing of units into a single harmonious sequence wherein the response becomes rapid and automatic. Application questions ask students to compose previously learned responses under conditions approximating some real-world problem. You can see that action sequences require two precedents: learned facts and understandings acquired from knowledge and comprehension questions and the use of previously learned facts and rules in new contexts. The number and quality of your application questions will determine how rapid and automatic your learners' action sequences become.

Like other types of higher-order questions, the number of application questions you ask may be less important than your consistency in asking them. Many beginning teachers inappropriately believe that application questions should be reserved for the end of a unit or even the end of a grading period. But, as you have seen, they are essential whenever a rapid, automatic response involving facts or rules is desired or when an action sequence is the lesson goal.

The quality of your application questions will be determined largely by how much you change the problem, context, or environment in which the students learned the facts or rules. If your change is too small, transfer of learning to an expanded context will not occur, and your "parrots" will recite facts and rules from the earlier context. But, if your change is too great, the new context may require a response beyond the grasp of most of your learners. The key to asking questions that require the transfer of learning to new problems or contexts is to be sure you have taught all the lower-order behaviors relevant for exhibiting the behavior in a new context. The easiest way to accomplish this is to change the context only a bit at first and then gradually shift to more unfamiliar contexts.

Analysis

Questions at the analysis level require the student to break a problem into its component parts and to draw relationships among the parts. Some purposes of questions at the analysis level are to identify logical errors; to differentiate among facts, opinions, and assumptions; to derive conclusions; and to find inferences or generalizations—in short, to discover the reasons behind the information given.

Here are some action verbs you can use in formulating questions at the analysis level:

break down	distinguish	relate
differentiate	point out	support

Here are some sample questions:

- What factors distinguish capitalism from socialism?
- Which of the boxes do not contain 12 things?
- In what ways can you differentiate Rule 1 possessive errors from Rule 2 possessive errors in the following essay?
- In which of the following pictures do you see a triangle?

Analysis questions tend to promote behaviors in the form of concepts, patterns, and abstractions. They generally signal the start of the concept learning, inquiry and problem-solving process, and the beginning of a change from direct to indirect instructional strategies. However, the majority of analysis questions will lack a single best answer common with the teaching of facts, rules, and action sequences. Consequently, you will have to evaluate a much broader range of responses at the analysis level. Even though you may not be able to anticipate all these responses, you can prepare yourself psychologically by shifting to a less regimented, more deliberate, and slower pace to give yourself more time to evaluate a student's answer and to compose a thoughtful response. And you should expect some responses for which a definitive response on your part may not be possible within the confines of your question and answer session.

Synthesis

Questions at the synthesis level ask the student to produce something unique or original—to design a solution, compose a response, or predict an outcome to a problem for which the student has never before seen, read, or heard a response. This level often is associated with directed creativity (Anderson and Krathwohl, 2001) in which not all responses may be equally acceptable. The facts, rules, action sequences, and any analysis questions that have gone before may define the limits and directions of the synthesis requested.

Here are some action verbs you can use in formulating questions at the synthesis level:

compare	formulate	create
predict	devise	produce

Here are some sample questions:

- What would an economic system be like that combines the main features of capitalism and socialism?
- What new numbers can you make by adding by 12s?
- How could you write a paragraph showing possession without using the apostrophe s?
- What are some of the ways you could make a triangle without using a ruler?

Even more diversity in answers can be expected with synthesis questions than with analysis questions. Therefore, your preparation for diversity is critical to how your students receive your synthesis questions. For example, a question asking for ways to identify undiscovered elements other than by using the periodic table of chemistry opens up many possible responses. Some may not be acceptable ("consult an astrologer"), but others may be ("analyze minerals from the moon and other planets"). You will want to accept all reasonable answers, even though your own solutions may be limited to only a few, and to keep in mind that some initially less acceptable responses can be built into more accurate, plausible, or efficient responses with additional questioning. Recall that Table 9.2 showed different types of questioning sequences. These types of question sequences can be used to expand upon or restrict the initial question to better focus a student response and improve its accuracy, plausibility or efficiency, as this dialogue illustrates:

◆ ◆ ◆

Teacher: In what ways other than from the periodic table might we predict the undiscovered elements?

Carlos: We could go to the moon and see if there are some elements there we don't have.

Jessica: We could dig down to the center of the earth and see if we find any of the missing elements.

Daniel: We could study debris from meteorites—if we can find any.

Teacher: Those are all good answers. But what if those excursions to the moon, to the center of the earth, or to find meteorites were too costly and time consuming? How might we use the elements we already have here on earth to find some new ones?

Jessica: Oh! Maybe we could try experimenting with combinations of the elements we do have to see if we can make new ones out of them.

◆ ◆ ◆

This simple exchange illustrates a funneling strategy: Broad, expansive answers are accepted and then are followed up with a narrower question on the next round. In this manner, multiple responses that typically result from synthesis questions can be used to gradually structure and deepen an avenue of inquiry, thereby contributing to still higher order outcomes.

Evaluation

Questions at this highest level of cognitive complexity require the student to form judgments and make decisions using stated criteria. These criteria may be subjective (when a personal set of values is used in making a decision) or objective (when scientific evidence or procedures are used in evaluating something). In both cases, however, it is important that the criteria to be expressed be clearly understood—although not necessarily valued—by others.

Here are some action verbs you can use in formulating questions at the evaluation level:

appraise	defend
assess	judge
decide	justify

Here are some sample questions:

- Citing evidence of your own choosing, do capitalist or socialist countries have a higher standard of living?
- Which of the following numbers contain multiples of 12?
- Using Rules 1 and 2 for forming possessives and assigning one point for each correct usage, what grade would you give the following student essay?
- Given the following fragments of geometric shapes, which can be used to construct a triangle?

Evaluation questions have the distinct quality of confronting the learner with authentic problems much as they appear in the real world, as indicated by the list of higher-order thinking and problem-solving behaviors in appendix C. Because decisions and judgments are prime ingredients of adult life, it is essential that classroom experiences link learners to the world in which they will live, regardless of their age or maturity.

Unfortunately, evaluation questions often are reserved for the end of a unit. Even more misguided is the notion that evaluation questions are more suited to middle and high school than to the elementary grades. Both misconceptions have reduced the impact of evaluation questions on learners. If learners are to cope with real-world problems, they must learn to do so starting at the earliest grades and throughout their schooling. Therefore, your ability to ask evaluation questions that can bring the world to your learners at their own level of knowledge and experience is one of the most valued abilities that you, an effective teacher, can have.

This ability, however, does not come easily. To be sure, many of the characteristics of the previously addressed higher-order questions—application, analysis, and synthesis—are present in evaluation questions. But with an evaluation question criteria must be applied in deciding the appropriateness of a solution. Notice in the preceding examples that the criteria (or their source) are identified: "citing evidence of your own choosing," "which of the following," "using Rules 1 and 2," "given the graphs." The more specific your criteria and the better your learners know them, the more actively engaged they will become in answering the question by using specified criteria from which to make a judgment.

Summary of Question Types

You now know the levels of questions that can be asked of learners and some factors to consider in selecting the appropriate type of question. To summarize:

- *Type 1 behaviors* (those calling for the acquisition of facts, rules, and action sequences) generally are most efficiently taught with convergent questions that have a single best answer (or a small number of easily definable answers). Type 1 behaviors are most effectively learned with a direct instruction model that focuses convergent questions at the knowledge, comprehension, and application levels of cognitive complexity.
- *Type 2 behaviors* (those calling for the acquisition of concepts, patterns, and abstractions) generally are most efficiently taught with divergent questions, for which many different answers may be appropriate. These behaviors are most effectively learned with an indirect instruction model that poses divergent questions at the analysis, synthesis, and evaluation levels of cognitive complexity.

Now that you are acquainted with these broad distinctions among types of questions, we turn to several specific techniques that can help you deliver these questions to your students with ease and perfection.

WHAT IS A PROBE?

A probe is a question that immediately follows a student's response to a question for the purpose of:

- Eliciting clarification of the student's response
- Soliciting new information to extend or build on the student's response
- Redirecting or restructuring the student's response in a more productive direction

Use probes that elicit clarification to have students rephrase or reword a response so you can determine its appropriateness or correctness. **Eliciting probes,** such as "Could you say that in another way?" or "How would that answer apply in the case of _____?" encourage learners to show more of what they know, thereby exposing exactly what they understand (Dann, 1995). The brief and vague responses often given in the context of a fast-paced and lively classroom discussion can mask partially correct answers or answers that are correct but were arrived at with flawed reasoning. When you are unsure how much understanding underlies a correct response, slow the pace with a probe for clarification.

Use **soliciting probes** that ask for new information following a response that is at least partially correct or indicates an acceptable level of understanding. This time you are using the probe to push the learner's response to a more complex level (e.g., "Now that you've decided the laboratory is the best environment for discovering new elements, what kind of experiments would you conduct in this laboratory?" or "Now that you've taken the square root of that number, how could you extend the same idea to find its cube root?").

This type of probe builds higher and higher plateaus of understanding by using the previous response as a stepping-stone to greater expectations and more complete responses. This involves treating incomplete responses as part of the next higher-level response—not as wrong answers. The key to probing for new information is to make your follow-up question only a small extension of your previous question; otherwise, the leap will be too great and the learner will be stymied by what appears to be an entirely new question. This type of probe, therefore, requires much the same process for finding the right answer as does the previously correct question, only this time applied to a different and slightly more complex problem.

 Video Window

Higher-Order Questioning

In this video you will see a high school literature class being taught *The Scarlet Letter*. Instead of just "telling" her learners about the story, this teacher draws out from her students the meaning of its characters with an in-class activity that asks them to feel and think like the main characters in the story. The dialogue of the classroom is lifted to a higher level than simply "telling" or "discussing," setting the stage for her students to acquire the higher-order outcomes of application, analysis, synthesis, and evaluation. Can you find specific instances in which this teacher asks a question at these higher levels? From viewing the reaction of her students, do you think they enjoyed this activity more than listening to a lecture on *The Scarlet Letter*?

 To answer these questions online, go to the Video Windows *module of this chapter of the* Companion Website *at www.prenhall.com/borich.*

Probes follow questions and are used to clarify a student's response, solicit new information, or redirect a response in a more productive direction.

Use **redirecting probes** to channel the flow of ideas instead of using awkward and often punishing responses such as "You're on the wrong track," "That's not relevant," or "You're not getting the idea." Probes for redirecting responses into a more productive area can accomplish the needed shift less abruptly and more positively, to avoid discouraging students from offering another response. A probe that accomplishes this purpose moves the discussion sideways, setting a new condition for a subsequent response that does not negate a previous response.

Probing to redirect or restructure a discussion can be a smooth and effortless way of getting learners back on track. Notice in the following example how the teacher blends the use of all three types of probes in the context of a single discussion:

◆ ◆ ◆

Teacher:	What do we call the grid system by which we can identify the location of any place on the globe? (To begin the questioning.)
Jason:	Latitude and longitude.
Teacher:	Good. What does *longitude* mean? (**To solicit** new information.)
Jason:	It's the grid lines on the globe that . . . go up and down.
Teacher:	What do you mean by *up and down?* (**To elicit** clarification.)
Jason:	They extend north and south at equal intervals.
Teacher:	OK. Now tell me, where do they begin? (**To solicit** new information.)
Jason:	Well, I think they begin wherever it's midnight and end where it's almost midnight again.
Teacher:	Let's think about that for a minute. Wouldn't that mean the point of origin would always be changing according to where it happened to be midnight? (**To redirect**.)
Jason:	I see, so the grids must start at some fixed point.
Teacher:	Anybody know where they begin? (**To solicit** new information.)
La Jonne:	Our book says the first one marked *0* starts at a place called Greenwich, England.
Teacher:	How can a grid that runs continuously north and south around the globe *start* anyplace, La Jonne? (**To elicit** clarification.)
La Jonne:	I meant to say that it *runs through* Greenwich, England.
Teacher:	Good. Now let's return to Jason's point about time. If we have a fixed line of longitude, marked *0*, how might we use it to establish time? (**To solicit** new information.)
Jason:	Now I remember. Midnight at the *0* longitude—or in Greenwich, England—is called *0* hours. Starting from there, there are timelines drawn around the world, so that when it's midnight at the first timeline, it will be one o'clock back at Greenwich, England; and when it's midnight at the next timeline, it will be two o'clock back at Greenwich, England, and so on.
Teacher:	What does that mean? (**To elicit** clarification.)

Jason: Each line equals 1 hour—so . . . so there must be 24 of them!

Teacher: It should be no surprise to learn that time determined in reference to the *0* grid of longitude is called Greenwich Mean Time or Coordinated Universal Time.

◆   ◆   ◆

HOW SHOULD YOU USE WAIT TIME?

An important consideration during questioning and probing is how long to wait before initiating another question. Sometimes your "wait time" can be as effective in contributing to the desired response as the question or probe itself, especially when you give students time to thoughtfully compose their answers. Wait times that are either too short or too long can be detrimental and, when too long, they also waste valuable instructional time. Obviously, wait time will be longer when students are weighing alternative responses (which often occurs during indirect instruction) than it will when their responses must be correct, quick, and firm (which often occurs during direct instruction).

Rowe (1986, 1987) and Tobin (1987) distinguish two different wait times. **Wait-time 1** refers to the amount of time a teacher gives a learner to respond when first asked a question. Classrooms with short wait-time 1s do not give learners much time to think before answering the question. In these classrooms, the teacher is repeating the question or calling on another learner to answer the same question after only a 2- or 3-second period of silence.

Wait-time 2 refers to the interval of time after a learner's first response until the teacher or other students affirm or negate the answer and the teacher then moves on. Teachers with long wait-time 2s wait several seconds before asking a follow-up question, correcting the answer, or otherwise commenting on what the learner said, giving that learner and others time to rethink, extend, or modify a response. Classrooms with short wait-time 2s are characterized by frequent interruptions of learners before they finish answering.

The following dialogue illustrates wait-time 1 and wait-time 2:

◆   ◆   ◆

Teacher: From our discussion yesterday about volcanos, can anyone tell us what a caldera is?

        (Wait-time 1: The teacher gives students time to think about the question and read nonverbal cues indicating the possible need for a probe—especially important for divergent and higher-order questions.)

Nelda: I remember. It's the crater formed by the collapse of the central part of the volcano. I'm not sure, but I think it's used to vent all the steam and gases that spew out. . . .

        (Wait-time 2: The teacher waits for other students or Nelda to think about and affirm or negate what was said—especially important for responses that are hesitant or only partially correct.)

        Yes, that's it, now I remember the picture in the text with all the smoke coming out of it.

Martin: She's right. That's how we drew it on the board. Everyone remember?

Teacher: And what else did the picture on the board show?

◆   ◆   ◆

Wait-time 1 refers to the amount of time a teacher gives a learner to respond to a question. Classrooms with short wait-time 1s do not give learners sufficient time to think before answering the question.

Increasing either wait time has the following effects on learner responses:

- Learners give longer answers to questions.
- Learners volunteer more responses.
- There are fewer unanswered questions.
- Learners are more certain of their answers.
- Learners are more willing to give speculative answers.
- The frequency of learner questions increases.

Generally, you should wait *at least 3 seconds* before asking another question, or repeating the previous question, or calling on another student. During indirect instruction, when divergent questions may require thinking through and weighing alternatives, *up to 15 seconds* of wait time may be appropriate.

These research findings provide impressive testimony to the important effect that wait time can have on your learners' responses. If only one piece of advice were given to beginning teachers concerning wait time, it would be to slow down and pause longer between questions and answers than what at first feels comfortable. See In Practice: Focus on Effective Classroom Questioning.

Finally, remember that questions are a principal means of engaging students in the learning process by getting them to think through and problem-solve with the material you are

In Practice

Focus on Effective Classroom Questioning

In 2001 the Northwest Regional Educational Laboratory conducted an extensive study of the research on teacher questioning in the classroom. Their study included research that had been conducted across the K–12 grades, the majority of which was concerned with the effects on student learning produced by questions at higher and lower cognitive levels. Here are some of their major findings from a report by Kathleen Cotton drawn from 37 research documents and reported in *School Improvement Research Series: Research You Can Use, Close-Up #5*, available at *www.nwrel.org/index.html.*

The Research on Classroom Questioning Findings

Some researchers have conducted general investigations of the role of classroom questioning and have drawn the following conclusions:

General Findings

- Instruction that includes posing questions during lessons is more effective in producing achievement gains than instruction carried out without questioning students.
- Students perform better on test items previously asked as recitation questions than on items they have not been exposed to before.
- Oral questions posed during classroom recitations are more effective in fostering learning than are written questions.
- Questions that focus student attention on salient elements in the lesson result in better comprehension than questions that do not.

Placement and Timing of Questions

- Asking questions frequently during class discussions is positively related to learning facts.
- Posing questions before reading and studying material is effective for students who are older, have higher ability, and/or are known to be interested in the subject matter.
- Very young children and poor readers tend to focus on content better if questions are posed about the content before the lesson is presented.

Cognitive Level of Questions

Should we be asking questions that require literal recall of text content and only very basic reasoning? Or ought we to be posing questions that call for speculative, inferential, and evaluative thinking?

When researchers looked at the cognitive level of teachers' questions in relation to the subject matter, the students, and the teachers' intent, their conclusions indicated:

- On average, during classroom recitations, approximately 60% of the questions asked are lower cognitive questions, 20% are higher cognitive questions, and 20% are procedural.
- Lower cognitive questions are more effective than higher-level questions with young (primary level) children, particularly the disadvantaged.
- Lower cognitive questions are more effective when the teacher's purpose is to impart factual knowledge and assist students in committing this knowledge to memory.
- In settings where a high incidence of lower-level questions is appropriate, greater frequency of questions is positively related to student achievement.
- When predominantly lower-level questions are used, their level of difficulty should be such that most will elicit correct responses.
- In most classes above the primary grades, a combination of higher and lower cognitive questions is superior to exclusive use of one or the other.
- Students whom teachers perceive as slow or poor learners are asked fewer higher cognitive questions than students perceived as more capable learners.
- Increasing the use of higher cognitive questions (to more than 20%) produces superior learning gains for students above the primary grades and particularly for secondary students.

- Teaching students to draw inferences and giving them practice in doing so results in higher cognitive responses and greater learning gains.
- For older students, increases in the use of higher cognitive questions (up to 50% or more) are positively related to increases in class participation, on-task behavior, and length of student responses.

They conclude their report by stating that better preservice training in the art of posing classroom questions, together with inservice training to sharpen teachers' questioning skills, have potential for increasing students' classroom participation and achievement. Increasing wait time (the time the teacher allows the student to respond and the time allowed for the student to complete an answer) and the frequency of higher cognitive questions, in particular, have considerable promise for improving the effectiveness of classroom instruction.

presenting. Following are suggestions for using questions to promote your learners' thinking and problem solving:

- *Plan in advance the type of questions you will ask.* Although talk-show hosts make it appear as if their questions are spontaneous and unrehearsed, this seldom is the case. In reality, ad-libbing and spontaneity can lead to as much dead time on the air as they can in your classroom. The type of questions you select, their level of difficulty, and the sequence in which you ask them should be based on your lesson objectives.
- *Deliver questions in a style that is concise, clear, and to the point.* Effective oral questions are like effective writing; every word should be needed. Pose questions in the same natural conversational language you would use with any close friend.
- *Allow time for students to think: Wait-time 1.* Research on question asking points to the fact that many teachers do not allow learners sufficient time to answer a question before calling on someone else or moving to the next question. Gage and Berliner (1998) report that, on average, teachers wait only about 1 second for learners to respond. These researchers recommend that you increase wait time to 3 to 4 seconds for lower-level questions and as much as 15 seconds for higher-level questions.
- *Keep the students in suspense.* First deliver the question, then mention the student's name. Similarly, randomly select the students you want to answer your questions. You want your learners to anticipate that they can be called on at any time. This both increases accountability and maintains attention and alertness.
- *Give students sufficient time to complete their response before redirecting the question or probing: Wait-time 2.* Wait-time 2 is the time you wait following a student answer before probing for deeper understanding or redirecting the question when the answer is incomplete or wrong. Teachers who are making a deliberate effort to maintain lesson momentum often interrupt before a learner is finished responding. Some cultural and ethnic groups have a different wait-time 2 than others. Tharp and Gallimore (1989) relate that in certain cultures a long wait-time 2 makes the teacher appear disinterested in the lesson; in other cultures, this is a sign of respect for the speaker. This cultural difference is discussed in the next section.

- *Provide immediate feedback to the learner.* Correct answers should be acknowledged and followed by either encouragement, elaborations on the response, further probing, or moving on to another question. The important point is to communicate to the learner that you heard and evaluated the answer. Often learners (unbeknown to the teacher) perceive that their answers have been ignored. Incorrect, incomplete, or inadequate answers should be followed by probes or redirection of the question to another student. Research, which we now examine more closely, suggests that learners of different achievement levels and social class benefit from different redirecting and probing techniques.

ARE QUESTIONING TECHNIQUES CULTURE SPECIFIC?

Sociolinguistics is the study of how cultural groups differ in the courtesies and conventions of language rather than in the grammatical structure of what is said. Sociolinguistics examines the **culture-specific questioning** rules that govern social conversation: with whom to speak, in what manner, when to pause, when to ask and answer questions, how to interrupt a speaker. Sociolinguists study, for example, aspects of communication as revealed by the average length of utterances, time between utterances, speech rhythms, and rules for when, how, and about what people converse with each other.

These researchers point out that classrooms and schools are governed by linguistic, sociocultural, and social interaction codes that can diverge from those found in the home, peers, and community of immigrant children. Delgado-Gaitan and Trueba (1991), for example, point out that pedagogical practices in the schools they studied in California contradicted culturally sanctioned patterns of sharing, leadership, and oral storytelling among Mexican American students. Teachers in mainstreamed classes, rather than change their interaction patterns to accommodate their students, attributed their lower performance to "deficiencies" and insisted on Anglo norms of interaction that were at odds with the students' culture. Among the aspects of communication and interaction most frequently studied are wait time, rhythm, participation structure, and language (Minami & Ovando, 2001).

Wait Time

Tharp (1989) reports that different cultures often have different wait times. Navajo children, for example, are raised in a culture that allows longer responses (wait-time 2) than Anglo culture. Some studies show that Navajo children speak in longer sentences and volunteer more answers when given more time to respond. In contrast, Tharp reports that in Hawaiian culture, interruptions are a sign of interest in the speaker and in what she is saying. Conversely, long wait-time 2s suggest to Hawaiian learners that the speaker is uninterested or bored with the conversation. Other studies of Hispanic and African American learners appear to suggest that optimal wait times are culture and even context specific (Hill, 1989). Although specific prescriptions cannot be made from this research, it does suggest that teachers must determine the way they pose a question and the appropriate wait time between questions and answers within the cultural context and learning history of their learners.

Rhythm

Conversational rhythm pertains to the tempo, inflections, and speed of conversations between two speakers as they converse. Young (1970) and Piestrup (1973) were among the first to observe that African American children and their mothers converse with one another using rapid rhythms and a "contest" style of interaction. Mothers encourage their children to be assertive. Directions for household chores and the children's responses to these directions take on an almost debate-like tone with the mother directing or calling and the children responding. Franklin (1992) suggests that this style of interaction creates a high-energy, fast-paced home environment that contrasts with the low-energy, slow-paced environment of the typical classroom.

Franklin speculates that this contrast between the pace of conversation at home and in school may be one reason why some African American children may be inappropriately referred for behavior problems in the classroom. Similarly, M. G. Anderson (1992) states that many Anglo teachers overreact to the conversational style of African American adolescents, which may explain the disproportionate referral of these children to programs for learners with behavior disorders. Anderson recommends that teachers allow African American learners to use in the classroom the conversational style they bring from home. This would include speaking more rhythmically, with greater variation in intonation, and engaging in more fast-paced verbal interplay.

Participation Structure

The typical classroom conversation occurs in a one-to-one, question-and-answer type participation structure or format. A teacher looks directly at a child, asks him or her a question, and waits for an answer before making a follow-up response. Tharp and Gallimore (1989) observe that such a participation structure results in very little participation by Hawaiian or Navajo children.

For these children both at home and in the community, the typical participation structure when adults are present involves a relatively small group of children together with an encouraging, participating, but nondirective adult in an informal setting. For example, when the classroom participation structures were based on those found in their cultures, both Hawaiian and Navajo children, who rarely participated in classroom discussions or question-and-answer formats, became surprisingly verbal.

Sociolinguists point out that children are more comfortable in classrooms where the sociolinguistic patterns (wait times, rhythms, participation structures, etc.) are compatible with those of their home and community. Some teachers and schools may view African American or Hispanic children as less verbal (Delgado-Gaitan & Trueba, 1991). Yet, when observed in familiar home or neighborhood environments, they use vibrant, expressive, and creative language patterns. Those researchers observe that the sociolinguistic patterns of the typical American classroom make certain minority group learners uncomfortable. This, in turn, causes those students to participate less in class, in ways Anglo American teachers view as deficient or inappropriate, and to achieve less. Supporting this finding, Gibson (1991) concluded that immigrant children's school success can be explained more by a strong home culture and positive sense of ethnic identity (which should be preserved at school) than by assimilation.

Language

Because much questioning is conducted in the formal language of the classroom, you should know your learners' language abilities. Approximately 5 million students—about 10% of the school-age population—have a primary language other than English. For some, English is their dominant language in the receptive mode (listening, reading); for others, English may be their dominant language in the expressive mode (talking, writing).

It is not unusual to find bilingual learners who choose, for example, Spanish as their dominant means of speaking but English as their dominant means of listening (Moran & Hakuta, 2001). This allows you to speak and be understood in English even though at least some of the learners' communications to you might be in Spanish. Knowing your learners' dominant means of expression will provide more opportunities to engage all your students in the learning process. If a learner does not use English as his or her dominant language, either in the expressive or receptive mode, and you do not speak that language, you can

1. Emphasize other forms of communication including the visual, kinesthetic, and tactile modalities to supplement your teaching objectives, thus bringing a multisensory approach to your teaching.

2. Be sensitive to cultural differences. For example, frequent meaningful praise and encouragement can set the stage for learning more efficiently than the repeated recitation of rules and warnings, which may not be fully understood by some of your learners.

3. Evaluate the reading level and format of the materials you use. When selecting or adapting materials, you may find a Spanish version of comparable content and reading level. After a trial period, evaluate the materials again and adjust the reading level accordingly.

4. Don't confuse language proficiency with subject matter achievement or ability. Research by McCown and Roop (1992) and Hakuta, Ferdman, and Diaz (1987) indicate that bilingual children, in comparison to monolingual children, show superior performance on tests of analytical reasoning, concept formation, and cognitive flexibility. Other research shows that learners who are fluent in two or more languages have a better knowledge of language structure and detail, understand that words are arbitrary symbols for other words and actions, and can better detect grammatical errors in written and spoken communication (Galambos & Goldin-Meadow, 1990; Portes & Rumbaut, 1990). It is also important to note that some early researchers suggested that children from economically impoverished areas who speak a nonstandard form of English (e.g., Black English) may suffer impaired cognitive development as a result (Bereiter & Englemann, 1966; Hess & Shipman, 1965). But this hypothesis has been conclusively refuted (Dillard, 1972; Henderson, Swanson, & Zimmerman, 1974; Masahiko & Ovando, 2001). We now know that all languages, including dialects and other forms of nonstandard English, are equally complex and equally capable of being used for learning and problem solving (Jordan, 1988; Oakes & Lipton, 1999). Linguists have demonstrated that languages cannot be ranked in terms of intellectual sophistication. Consequently, intellectual impairment or slow cognitive development cannot result from the primary language a learner speaks, regardless of how nonstandard that language is.

WHAT ARE COMMON PROBLEMS IN USING QUESTIONS?

Based on classroom observations of the question-asking behavior of beginning teachers, here are some of the most frequently observed problems to watch for and suggested remedies.

Do You Use Complex, Ambiguous, or Double Questions?

One of the most common question-asking problems of beginning teachers is the use of the complex, ambiguous, or double question. This is a question so long and complicated that students easily lose track of the main idea by the time it is completed. Sometimes, a teacher unknowingly packs two (or even more) questions within its complicated structure.

Because such questions are delivered orally and are not written, students have no way of rereading the question to gain its full intent. It is unfortunate that these questions sometimes are so complicated that even the teacher cannot repeat the question precisely when requested, thus providing different versions of the same question. Consider the following three examples of needlessly complex questions and their simpler but equally effective revisions.

Example 1

Complex form: "We all know what the three branches of government are, but where did they come from, how were they devised, and in what manner do they relate?"

This question is actually three questions in one and requires too long a response if each point in the question were responded to individually. In addition, the first two questions may be redundant—or are they?—and the third is sufficiently vague to bewilder most students. Finally, what if some students do not know or cannot recall the three branches of government? For those students, everything that follows is irrelevant, opening the door to boredom and off-task behavior.

Simpler form: "Recall that there are three branches of government: the executive, judicial, and legislative. What governmental functions are assigned to each branch by the Constitution?"

Example 2

Complex form: "How do single-celled animals propagate themselves and divide up to create similar animal life that looks like themselves?"

If you were to ask this question, you can be sure some of your students would ask you to repeat the question, in which case you might not remember your own complex wording. This question fails to get to the point quickly and appears to ask the same thing three times: how do single-celled animals propagate . . . divide up . . . create similar animal life? This redundancy could easily be mistaken for three separate questions by students struggling to understand single-celled reproduction at an elementary level. State your questions only one way and rephrase later, if need be, when students know it is the same question being rephrased.

Simpler form: "By what process do single-celled animals reproduce?"

Example 3

Complex form: "What do you think about the Civil War, or the Iraq War, or war in general?"

Depending on what part of this question a student wants to hear, you may get noticeably different answers. The intention was to raise a question that would provide enough options to get almost any student involved in composing a response; but, unless you intend only to start a controversy, the range of responses will probably be so broad that moving to the next substantive point may be impossible. This question may leave students arguing feverishly for the entire period without being able to focus on the real purpose for raising the question in the first place (e.g., as an introduction to the Civil War, or to unpopular wars, or to the concept of war). This question is too broad, too open, and too divergent to be of practical value for framing a day's lesson.

Simpler form: "What are the factors that you believe would justify a war among groups within the same nation?"

Here are basic rules for avoiding complex, ambiguous, or double questions:

- Focus each question on only one idea.
- State the main idea only once.
- Use concrete language.
- State the question in as few words as possible.

Do You Accept Only the Answers You Expect?

Another common mistake of beginning teachers is to rely almost exclusively on the answer they expect. Recall the discussion in chapter 2 regarding the bias that teachers sometimes have about whom they call on and interact with in classroom exchanges. Biases can extend to favorite answers as well as to favorite students. When teaching new content, which frequently is the case during your first year, you naturally strive to become more secure and confident by limiting answers to those with which you are most familiar. Your first reaction will be to discourage responses at the edge of what you consider to be the appropriate range. This range is directly related to the openness of your questions. Open questions encourage diversity, and it is this diversity that often catches the beginning teacher off guard and forces an expansive question into a limited one. Note in the following dialogue how this teacher's posture is changed by the nature of the response:

◆ ◆ ◆

Teacher:	OK, today we will study the European settlers who came to America, and why they came here. Why did they come to America?
Student 1:	To farm.
Teacher:	No, not to farm.
Student 2:	To build houses and churches.
Teacher:	No, that's not right either.

◆ ◆ ◆

If this exchange were to continue for very long, it no doubt would turn off many students, if only because they know these responses cannot be entirely wrong even if they are not what the teacher wants. What does the teacher want? Probably, the desired answer is that the early Americans came because of religious persecution in their European communities. The last student's response, "to build houses and churches," was a perfect opportunity for a probe that simply asked "Why churches?" Unfortunately, this teacher missed that opportunity in favor of waiting for the exact response, because this teacher was unable or unwilling to build on existing responses. This teacher may have a long wait, in which case valuable instructional time will be lost by calling on student after student in the hope that the only acceptable answer will eventually emerge.

Answers that are just what you are looking for are always desirable, but remember that partially correct answers and even unusual and unexpected ones can become effective additions to the discussion through the use of probes. The solution to this problem is to use probes that build gradually toward your targeted responses.

Why Are You Asking This Question?

Perhaps the most serious fault of all in question asking is not being certain of why you are asking a question. Remember, questions are tools that support the teaching and learning processes. Your first decision in composing questions is to determine whether your lesson is teaching facts, rules, and action sequences or concepts, patterns, and abstractions. If the former is your goal, convergent questions at the knowledge, comprehension, or application levels probably are the ones to ask. If the latter is your goal, then divergent questions at the analysis, synthesis, or evaluation levels usually are the questions to ask. This decision strategy is summarized in Figure 9.1.

If you have not determined where you are on Figure 9.1, you are likely to ask the wrong type of question, and your questions will lack logical sequence. They may jump from

Figure 9.1 A decision tree for deciding on the types of questions to ask.

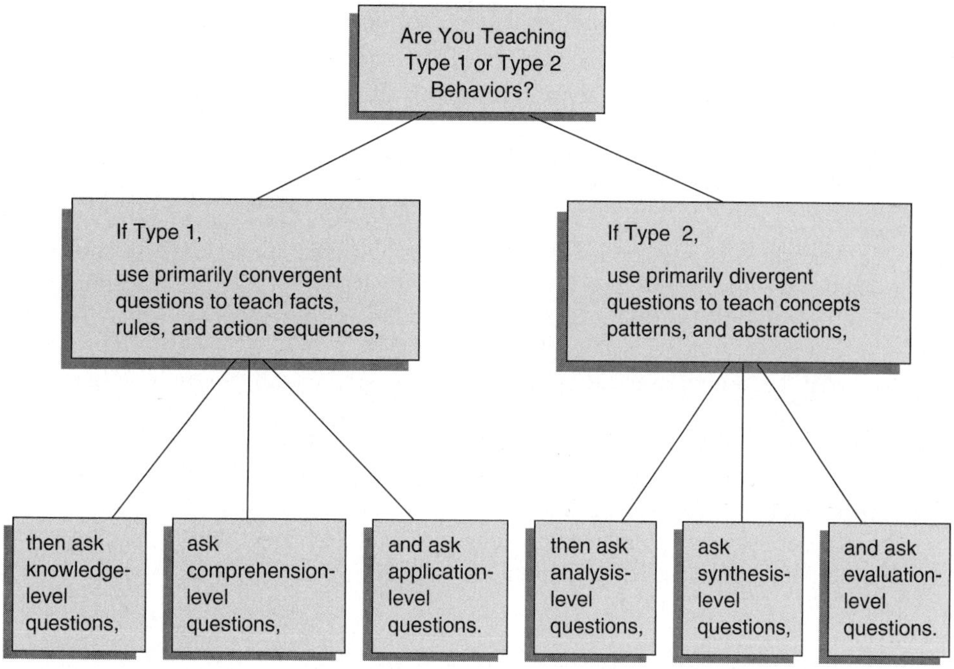

convergent to divergent and move back and forth from simple recall of facts to the acquisition of concepts and patterns. Your students will find your questions disconcerting, because your ideas will not be linked by any common thread (at least, not by one they can follow), and you will be seen as vague or lacking the ability to connect content in meaningful ways. Therefore, it is important that you decide in advance where your questioning strategy is going and then move toward this goal by choosing appropriate questions and levels of cognitive complexity.

Finally, it is important to note that just because your goal may be Type 1 or Type 2 behaviors, this does not mean you cannot vary your questioning strategy across the levels shown on Figure 9.1. Questions should vary across types of learning (e.g., from knowledge to application or from analysis to synthesis). Keep in mind your ultimate goal for the lesson and choose the best combination of questions to reach that goal.

Do You Answer the Question Yourself?

Another common problem is posing a question and then answering it yourself. Sometimes a student begins a response but is cut off, only to hear the remainder of the response supplied by the teacher:

◆ ◆ ◆

Teacher: So who was the president who freed the slaves?
Student: Abraham—
Teacher: Lincoln! Yes, that's right.

◆ ◆ ◆

Sometimes the reverse occurs: A student begins a response that the teacher knows is wrong and then is cut off by the teacher, who gives the correct response:

◆　◆　◆

Teacher:	So who was the president who freed the slaves?
Student:	George—
Teacher:	No, no! It was Abraham Lincoln.

◆　◆　◆

Needless to say, both outcomes demoralize the student, who either is deprived of the chance to completely give a right answer or is shown to have a response so incorrect it is not even worth hearing in its entirety. Neither of these outcomes may be intended, but this is how your students will see it.

Your job is to use student responses to build to other more complex outcomes. Probes to elicit new information, to go beyond an already-correct answer, or to provide hints and clues after a wrong answer are particularly useful, because they extend to your students the right to give a full and deliberate response, right or wrong. Teachers who frequently interrupt student responses because of a desire for perfect answers, a dominant personality, or talkativeness may ultimately produce frustrated learners who never learn to give full and thoughtful responses or to participate voluntarily.

Do You Use Questions as Punishment?

Our final problem, and perhaps the most difficult, is the use—or rather, abuse—of questions to punish or to put a student on the defensive. Being asked a question can be a punishment as well as a reward. For example, questions can be used as punishment in the following ways:

1. A student who forgot to do the homework is deliberately asked a question from that homework.
2. A student who never volunteers is always asked a question.
3. A student gives a wrong response and then is asked an even harder question.
4. A student who disrupts the class is asked a question for which the answer cannot possibly be known.
5. A student who gives a careless response is asked four questions in a row.

Nearly every teacher has, at one time or another, used questions in one or more of these ways. Interestingly, some teachers do not always see these uses as punishment. Regardless of intent, however, such questions are punishment in that they (1) are unlikely to engage the student actively in meaningful learning, and (2) leave the student with a poorer self-image, less confidence, and more anxiety (perhaps anger) than before the question. These are behaviors that can only impede the learning process and that, therefore, have no place in your repertoire of questioning strategies. Each of the student-centered problems reflected in the preceding examples could have been handled more effectively by:

1. Making a list of students who don't do homework
2. Providing example questions beforehand to students who never volunteer
3. Giving another try and providing hints and clues to students who give wrong responses until they give partially correct answers
4. Assigning disciplinary warnings or reprimands to students who disrupt class
5. Passing quickly to another student after receiving a careless answer

Ample means are available for dealing with misbehavior, and such means are far more effective than using questions. Questions are instructional tools that should be prized and protected for their chosen purpose. To misuse them or to use them for any other purpose may affect how your students will perceive your questions ("Did I get the hard question because she thinks I'm smart or because I'm being punished?"). Such conflicts can drain students of the energy and concentration needed to answer your questions and may forever cast doubts on your motives.

The other side of questions is that they can be implicit rewards when used correctly. The opportunity to shine, to know and display the correct answer in front of others, and to be tested and get an approving grade are rewarding experiences for any learner. Consequently, every learner, regardless of ability level or knowledge of a correct response, should periodically experience these emotions.

Don't ignore students who have difficulty responding, and don't accept wrong answers. Instead, occasionally try a broader criterion than correct/incorrect to help all students share in the emotional and intellectual rewards of answering questions. For example, try rewarding the most novel, most futuristic, most practical, and most thought-provoking answers along with the most accurate response. This will let every learner share in the challenge and excitement of questions. Questions are another tool to add to your teaching menu. Because of their almost endless variety, they may well be the most flexible tool on your menu.

SUMMING UP

This chapter introduced you to questioning strategies. Its key terms and main points were:

What Is a Question?

1. An effective question is one for which students actively compose a response and thereby become engaged in the learning process.
2. An effective question depends on voice inflection, word emphasis, word choice, and the context in which it is raised.
3. The three most commonly observed teacher behaviors in the classroom are structuring, soliciting, and reacting.
4. Soliciting—or question-asking behavior—encourages students to act on and think about the structured material as quickly as possible after it has been presented.
5. It has been estimated that 70% to 80% of all questions require the simple recall of facts, but only 20% to 30% require clarifying, expanding, generalizing, and making inferences. In other words, as few as one of every five questions may require higher-level thought processes, even though behaviors at the higher levels of cognitive complexity are among those most frequently required in adult life, at work, and in advanced training.

What Are the Purposes of Questions?

6. Common purposes for asking questions include the following:

   - Getting interest and attention
   - Diagnosing and checking
   - Recalling specific facts or information
   - Managing
   - Encouraging higher-level thought processes
   - Structuring and redirecting learning
   - Allowing expression of affect

What Are Convergent and Divergent Questions?

7. A question that limits possible responses to one or a small number is called a *convergent, direct,* or *closed question.* This type of question teaches the learner to respond in a limited, restrictive manner.
8. A question that has many right answers or a broad range of acceptable responses is called a *divergent question.* Divergent questions, however, can have wrong answers.
9. The same question can be convergent under one set of circumstances and divergent under another, as when so-called creative answers to a divergent question have been memorized from a list.

What Does the Research Say About Asking Convergent and Divergent Questions?

10. Research has not established that the use of higher-order questions is related to improved performance on standardized achievement tests. However, higher-order questions have been found to elicit analysis, synthesis, and evaluation skills, which are among the skills most sought in adult life.

Who Are the Targets of Questions?

11. Questions can be specifically worded for cognitive complexity as well as directed to individuals, groups, or the entire class.

What Sequences of Questions Are Used?

12. Questions may be used in the context of many different sequences, such as funneling, where increasingly specific conditions are added to an original question, narrowing it to one requiring simple deduction.

What Levels of Questions Are Used?

13. In addition to being divergent, convergent, and targeted to specific types of learners, questions can be formulated at different levels of cognitive complexity that comprise the knowledge, comprehension, application, analysis, synthesis, and evaluation levels of the cognitive domain.
14. Knowledge questions ask the learner to recall, describe, define, or recognize facts that already have been committed to memory.
15. Comprehension questions ask the learner to explain, summarize, or elaborate on previously learned facts.
16. Application questions ask the learner to go beyond the memorization of facts and their translation and to use previously acquired facts and understandings in a new and different environment.
17. Analysis questions ask the learner to break a problem into its component parts and to draw relationships among the parts.
18. Synthesis questions ask the learner to design or produce a unique or unusual response to an unfamiliar problem.
19. Evaluation questions ask the learner to form judgments and make decisions, using stated criteria for determining the adequacy of the response.

What Is a Probe?

20. A probe is a question that immediately follows a student's response to a question; its purpose is to elicit clarification, to solicit new information, or to redirect or restructure a student's response.
21. The key to probing for new information is to make the follow-up question only a small extension of the previous question.

How Should You Use Wait Time?

22. The time you wait before initiating another question or turning to another student may be as important in actively engaging the learner in the learning process as the question itself. Teachers should observe a wait time of at least 3 seconds before asking another question, repeating the previous question, or calling on another student.
23. Longer wait times have been associated with longer responses, greater numbers of voluntary responses, greater behavioral complexity of the response, greater frequency of student questions, and increased confidence in responding.

Are Questioning Techniques Culture Specific?

24. Researchers point out that classrooms and schools are governed by linguistic, sociocultural, and social interaction patterns that can diverge from those found in the home, peers, and community of immigrant children.
25. Cultural-specific questions are questions that take into account the wait time, rhythm, participation structure, and dominant means of expression predominant among a culture.

What Are Common Problems in Using Questions?

26. Avoid problems commonly observed in the question-asking behavior of beginning teachers:
    - Do not raise overly complex or ambiguous questions that may require several different answers.
    - Be prepared to expect correct but unusual answers, especially when raising divergent questions.
    - Always establish beforehand why you are asking a particular question. Know the complexity of behavior you may expect as a result of the question.
    - Never supply the correct answer to your own questions without first probing. Never prevent a student from completing a response to a question, even if incorrect. Use partially correct or wrong answers as a platform for eliciting clarification, soliciting new information, or redirecting.

- Never use questions as a form of embarrassment or punishment. Such misuse of questions rarely changes misbehavior, and questions are academic tools that should be

prized and protected for their chosen purpose. To misuse them or to use them for any other purpose may affect how your students will perceive your questions.

KEY TERMS

Convergent question, 304
Culture-specific questioning, 322
Divergent question, 304
Effective questions, 303
Eliciting probes, 316
Question sequence, 307
Reacting, 303

Redircting probes, 317
Sociolinguistics, 322
Soliciting, 303
Soliciting probes, 316
Structuring, 303
Wait-time 1, 318
Wait-time 2, 318

DISCUSSION AND PRACTICE QUESTIONS

Questions marked with an asterisk are answered in appendix B. See also the Companion Website for this text at *www.prenhall.com/borich* for more assessment options.

*1. What is the definition of an *effective question* as used in this chapter? Pose a question that you believe represents this definition.

*2. Approximately what percentage of all school time may be devoted to questions and answers? What is your opinion as to why this percentage is so high?

*3. Approximately what percentage of questions asked require simple recall of facts, and approximately what percentage require clarifying, expanding, generalizing, and making inferences? What is your opinion as to why the latter percentage is so low?

*4. In your own words, what is a convergent question and what is a divergent question? How do they differ with respect to right answers? How are they the same with respect to wrong answers?

5. Using the same question content, give an example of both a convergent and a divergent question.

*6. According to research, how does the asking of higher-order questions affect (1) a learner's standardized achievement score, and (2) a learner's use of analysis, synthesis, and evaluation skills in thinking through a problem?

7. Compose a question that is more cognitively complex and another that is less cognitively complex. How do these two questions differ in cues, hints, and advance organizers?

8. Using Table 9.2 as a guide, compose a sequence of related questions that extend and lift student responses.

9. Using the same content as in question 8, prepare one question that elicits the appropriate level of behavioral complexity at each level of the cognitive domain—knowledge, comprehension, application, analysis, synthesis, and evaluation.

*10. What is meant by the phrase *wait time*? Generally speaking, why should beginning teachers work to increase their wait time?

*11. Identify and give an example of the five most troublesome question-asking problems for the beginning teacher. Which fault do you feel most likely to make?

FIELD EXPERIENCE ACTIVITIES

*1. Identify the chain of events that forms the most frequently observed cycle of teacher–student interaction. For a topic you will be teaching, show how this chain of events would unfold using actual teacher and student dialogue.

*2. What are seven specific purposes for asking questions? Give an example of each with content you will be teaching.

3. Write a brief classroom dialogue of teacher questions and student responses illustrating the funneling of student responses.

4. In the context of a brief classroom dialogue, provide one example each of questions that (1) elicit clarification, (2) solicit new information, and (3) redirect or restructure a student's response. In which order did these occur?

5. What is sociolinguistics, and why is this area of study important in a culturally diverse classroom? Can you think of one sociolinguistic finding that will be important to you in your classroom?

DIGITAL PORTFOLIO ACTIVITIES

The following digital portfolio activities relate to INTASC principles 4, 5, and 6.

1. In Field Experience Activity 2 you were asked to identify seven types of questions and apply each to a topic you are likely to teach. Now using examples from the chapter identify for each question the purpose it is intended to serve and place these questions and purposes into your digital portfolio in a folder labeled *Questioning Strategies*. Your example questions will be valuable reminders of the variety of ways in which questions can shape and set up a student's response to more accurately reveal what is known or not known. These will also provide a future reference for you during lesson and unit planning.

2. In Discussion and Practice Question 9, you prepared one question each at the knowledge, comprehension, application, analysis, synthesis, and evaluation levels. Place these questions in the *Questioning Strategies* folder of your digital portfolio as models that elicit increasingly complex learning outcomes.

CLASSROOM OBSERVATION ACTIVITY

The following classroom observation activity relates to INTASC principles 4, 5, and 6.

One of the most popular ways to discriminate among different types of questions is to consider the six levels of student outcome a question can elicit: knowledge (remembering), comprehension (understanding), application (transferring), analysis (relating), synthesis (creating), and evaluation (judging). On the Companion Website for this chapter you will find a form for *Distinguishing Among Six Types of Questions*. You will notice that these six types of questions are also grouped into "lower-order questions," comprising knowledge, comprehension, and application and "higher-order questions," comprising analysis, synthesis, and evaluation. The record also provides the opportunity to record the amount of time a teacher waits ("wait time") between question and student response before the teacher answers the question or moves on to another student. Use this form to record the number and levels of questions in either a school or university classroom and your observed wait times. If you observe in both a school and university classroom compare your results to see if more higher-order questions are used in one more than the other and how their wait times differ. Place this record in your *Questioning Strategies* folder for use in future classroom observations.

Chapter Case History and Praxis Test Preparation

DIRECTIONS: The following case history pertains to chapter 9 content. After reading the case history, answer the short-answer question that follows and consult appendix D to find different levels of scored student responses and the rubric used to determine the quality of each response. You also have the opportunity to submit your responses online to receive feedback by visiting the *Case History* module for this chapter on the Companion Website, where you will also find additional questions pertaining to Praxis test content.

Case History

Mr. Cole's middle school science class is heterogeneous in many ways. There is an ethnic and racial mix of Anglo, Hispanic, and African American students, with a small number of Asian Americans. Several are recent immigrants who understand and read English better than they speak it. Ability levels run from very low to high with a large portion in the middle. Currently the class is studying the effects of invention and discovery on society.

Mr. Cole:	My great-uncle played football in college. But when he was in his twenties, he got pneumonia and died in three days. Could that happen today, Carla?
Carla:	Well, my grandfather died of pneumonia last winter, but I don't think it happened that fast. I guess it could happen.
Mr. Cole:	You're probably right, Carla. People still die from diseases like pneumonia, especially if they are elderly and have another illness. Maybe that was true with your grandfather?
Carla:	(Her eyes wide with surprise) He was sick for a long time.
Mr. Cole:	But what about healthy athletes in their twenties? Do many of them die from pneumonia today? What do you think, Thomas?
Thomas:	No, today we just give them antibiotics and they get well pretty fast. I get your hint, Mr. Cole. Antibiotics are another invention that has really helped society.
Curtis:	I had bronchitis last year and the antibiotics didn't seem to help much at all. They aren't that great, in my opinion.
Ramona:	My baby sister gets ear infections and the medicine used to clear them up right away. But, now, it doesn't help all that much.
Mr. Cole:	So, I see some of you have mixed experiences with antibiotics. Why do you think that is? Millie, you have your hand up. What do you think?
Millie:	I saw this program on TV a couple of weeks ago that said we take antibiotics too much and that they don't work as well now. Some germs have gotten used to them. There're some kinds of infections now that don't go away with antibiotics anymore.
Mr. Cole:	Maybe there can be too much of a good thing, then? Could it be that some inventions seem good at first, but after a while we see that maybe they solve one problem and create another? Antibiotics cure simple pneumonia, but they can also produce what are called "resistive strains," which are even more difficult to kill. Let's think about some other inventions that also created problems as well as solved them. I'll give you some time to think of a good example. (Thirty seconds goes by.) Jason, what have you thought of?
Jason:	Well, what about cars? Sure, we can get around a lot better, but they cause a lot of pollution, too.
Curtis:	Not to mention all the people who die in accidents each year.
Millie:	I say computers. Some people are addicted to the Internet and don't spend time with their family anymore. Plus, they get a lot of junk e-mail they don't want.
Thomas:	It really creeps me out to get a phone call from a computer. I mean, people selling you stuff on the telephone is bad enough, but a computer . . .
Millie:	What about that time the computer here at school gave everybody incompletes by mistake? (The class groans in remembrance.)

Short-Answer Question

This section presents a sample Praxis short-answer question. In appendix D you will find sample responses along with the standards used in scoring these responses.

DIRECTIONS: The following question requires you to write a short answer. Base your answer on your knowledge of principles of learning and teaching from chapter 9. Be sure to answer all parts of the question.

1. Mr. Cole used several types of higher-order questions to encourage his students to think deeply about the topic. Research has not yet shown, however, that the use of higher-order questions is related to gains in student achievement—at least not as measured by tests of standardized achievement. Give two reasons and an example from Mr. Cole's classroom to justify the use of higher-order questioning in the classroom in the absence of research confirming their success in improving standardized achievement scores.

Discrete Multiple-Choice Questions

DIRECTIONS: Each of the multiple-choice questions that follow is based on Praxis-related pedagogical knowledge in chapter 9. Select the answer that is best in each case and compare your results with those in appendix D. See also the Companion Website for this text at *www.prenhall.com/borich* for more assessment options.

1. Which of the following is the most complex thinking behavior from Bloom et al.'s *Taxonomy of Behaviors in the Cognitive Domain*?
   a. Application
   b. Evaluation
   c. Analysis
   d. Synthesis

2. According to research on teacher practices, which outcome is *not* the result of increased wait time between a teacher's question and a student's response?
   a. Learners' responses are more accurate
   b. Learners are more certain of their answer
   c. Learners volunteer more responses
   d. Learners give longer answers to questions

3. What is the approximate ratio of the percentage of teacher convergent to divergent questions in the typical classroom?
   a. 60% convergent to 40% divergent
   b. 70% convergent to 30% divergent
   c. 80% convergent to 20% divergent
   d. 90% convergent to 10% divergent

4. If you had to give advice to a new teacher concerning the amount of time to wait between when you ask a question and the student attempts a response, which of the following would you recommend?
   a. Gage your wait time to the aptitude of the student, higher-performing learners being given less wait time than lower-performing students.
   b. If after 2 or 3 seconds the student has not begun a response, follow up with a probe.
   c. Wait longer than you might at first feel comfortable: at least 3 or more seconds for convergent questions and up to 15 seconds for divergent questions.
   d. If after a few seconds the student has not responded, nurture the student along with warm encouragement, such as, "Come on, you can do it."

5. If a new learner to your classroom does not use English as his or her dominant language in either the expressive or receptive mode, and you do not speak that language, which of the following would be the best alternative to pursue?
   a. Emphasize other forms of communication including the visual, kinesthetic, and tactile modalities to supplement your teaching objectives.
   b. Recommend to the student's parents that he or she receive intensive English language instruction.
   c. Have the student's subject knowledge tested in his or her native language to determine how much language may be a barrier to learning.
   d. Before choosing any other alternative have the school counselor or special educator check for disabilities that could impede language acquisition and learning.

Chapter 10

Self-Directed Learning

This chapter will help you answer the following questions and meet the following INTASC principles for effective teaching:

1. How can I get my learners to unleash their imaginative and intuitive capacities through self-directed learning?
2. How do I get learners to accept responsibility for their own learning?
3. What are some cognitive strategies that can help my learners retain, order, and comprehend new information?
4. How can I engage my learners in project-based learning?
5. How can I promote the goals of self-directed learning in a culturally diverse classroom?

INTASC 1: The teacher understands the central concepts, tools of inquiry, and structures of the discipline(s) he or she teaches and can create learning experiences that make these aspects of subject matter meaningful for students.

INTASC 2: The teacher understands how children learn and develop, and can provide learning opportunities that support their intellectual, social, and personal development.

INTASC 3: The teacher understands how students differ in their approaches to learning and creates instructional opportunities that are adapted to diverse learners.

INTASC 4: The teacher understands and uses a variety of instructional strategies to encourage students' development of critical thinking, problem solving, and performance skills.

INTASC 6: The teacher uses knowledge of effective verbal, nonverbal, and media communication techniques to foster active inquiry, collaboration, and supportive interaction in the classroom.

In this chapter, you will study an important method for engaging your students in the learning process. Here you will learn how to teach learners to go beyond the content given—to think critically, reason, and problem-solve—using a self-directed approach to learning. You will see how to use self-directed strategies to actively engage your students in the learning process and to help them acquire the reasoning, critical thinking, and problem-solving skills required in today's complex society.

SELF-DIRECTED LEARNING

Much of today's classroom learning is focused on activities by which the learner acquires facts, rules, and action sequences. The majority of lessons require outcomes only at the lower levels of cognition: knowledge, comprehension, and application. This may explain why some national studies of the state of education in the United States (National Council for the Social Studies, 1994, 2002; National Council of Teachers of English, 1996; National Council of Teachers of Mathematics, 1995, 2000; National Research Council, 2001) found many students unable to think independently of the teacher or to go beyond the content in their texts and workbooks. These reports suggest that the manner in which most schooling occurs may not be teaching students to become aware of their own learning, to think critically, and to derive their own patterns of thought and meaning from the content presented, as suggested by the cognitive outcomes identified in the *Higher-Order Thinking and Problem-Solving Checklist* in appendix C (Beyer, 1995; Borich & Tombari, 2004; Hester, 1994).

Self-directed learning is an approach to both teaching and learning that actively engages students in the learning process to acquire higher-order thinking skills. Self-directed learning helps students construct their own understanding and meaning and helps them to reason, problem-solve, and think critically about the content (Costa & Kallick, 2003; Kerns, 1998). Self-directed learning requires you to perform several unique teaching functions:

1. Provide information about when and how to use mental strategies for learning.
2. Explicitly illustrate how to use these strategies to think through solutions to real-world problems.

3. Encourage your learners to become actively involved in the subject matter by going beyond the information given, to restructure it in their own way of thinking and prior understanding.

4. Gradually shift the responsibility for learning to your students through practice exercises, question-and-answer dialogues, and/or discussions that engage them in increasingly complex thought patterns.

Consider the following excerpt, which illustrates how some of these teaching functions might be accomplished in a typical lesson:

◆   ◆   ◆

Teacher: (A poem is written on the board; teacher reads it to class:)
Man is but a mortal fool
When it's hot, he wants it cool
When it's cool, he wants it hot
He's always wanting what is not.
    Today I want to illustrate some ways to understand a poem like the one I've just read. This may seem like a simple poem, but its author put a lot of meaning into each one of its words. Now let me give you an approach to studying poems like these and gaining from them the meaning intended by their authors. First, let's identify the key words in this poem. Earl, what do you think are some of the most important ones?

Earl: Well, I'd say the word *man* because it's the first.

Teacher: Any others? (Still looking at Earl.)

Earl: Not that I can see.

Teacher: Anita?

Anita: The words *hot* and *cool* have to be important, because they appear twice and they rhyme with the last words of the first and last lines.

Teacher: Any other key words? Rick?

Rick: Well, I think *a mortal fool* is supposed to be telling us something, but I don't know what.

Teacher: Good. So now we've identified some words we think are especially important for understanding this poem. Why don't we look up in the dictionary the meanings of any of these words we don't know or are unsure of? That will be our *second* step. Ted, look up the word *mortal* for us while we begin work on our third step. The *third* step is to paraphrase what you think this author is saying. Susan, can you paraphrase what he is saying?

Susan: I think he's saying we're always changing our minds, and that's why we look so stupid sometimes.

Teacher: We are all human, so we certainly change our minds a lot, don't we? Rhonda looks like she wants to say something. Rhonda?

Rhonda: Well, I'd say it's not that we're stupid that we change our minds, but that it's just part of who we are—we can't help wanting what we can't have.

Teacher: So you've added a little something to Susan's interpretation. What do you think, Susan? Do you agree?

Susan: Yeah, we're not stupid; we're just mortals.

Teacher: Chris, do you want to add anything?

Chris: I'd say that we're not stupid at all. That to really enjoy something, we must have experienced its opposite—otherwise we wouldn't know how good it is.

Teacher: Now that brings us to our *fourth* and last step. Let's try to relate what Chris just said to our own experience. Anyone ready? Earl?

Earl:	I agree with Chris, because I remember thinking how much I welcomed winter because of how hot it was last summer.
Teacher:	(Marcia is waving her hand.) Marcia, what do you have to say about that?
Marcia:	But now that it's winter, I can't wait for the cold weather to end, so I can go swimming again. (Class nods in agreement.)
Teacher:	It looks as though Chris was right. We sometimes have to see both sides of something—hot/cold, good/bad, light/dark—to fully appreciate it. Now, Ted, what did you find for *mortal* in the dictionary?
Ted:	It says "having caused or being about to cause death," "subject to death," and "marked by vulnerability."
Teacher:	Which of those do you think best fits the use of *mortal fool* in our poem?
Ted:	Well, hmm . . . the last one, because it kind of goes with what we have been saying about how we choose one thing and then another . . . like when we get too cold, dream of summer, and then when summer comes, think it's too hot.
Teacher:	I agree; it fits with what we all have experienced in our lives—and that means we are on the right track to the interpretation the author intended. Now let's go one step further. Putting all of our ideas together, what is this poet saying? (Nodding to Alex.)
Alex:	Well, I'd say life's a kind of circle. We keep going around and around—back to where we've come and then trying to escape to where we've been—maybe that's one kind of vulnerability—like it said in the dictionary.
Teacher:	That's good thinking, Alex. Earl, because we began with you, I'll let you have the final word.
Earl:	I think Alex got it, because now I understand why the author thinks we're all fools. We're like a dog going in circles chasing our tails, always wanting what we don't have. That explains the first and the last line, doesn't it? Because we are human, we are vulnerable to always ". . . wanting what is not." Yes, so we're mortal fools. I get it.
Teacher:	Very good. Now let's think for a moment about the four steps we just went through to understand this poem. I will repeat them slowly while you write them down. They will become your guide for reading the rest of the poems we study.

◆   ◆   ◆

Notice how this teacher contributed something to each of the four components of self-directed learning. First, she provided the learners with a mental strategy for learning—in this case a framework of four easy-to-follow steps for interpreting poetry. These steps were sufficiently familiar and practical enough to be followed by almost any student, regardless of prior knowledge or experience. Notice that they were not just divisions of the task but steps that ultimately force learners to go beyond the content presented to find their own meaning and understanding, based on personal experience and individual thinking. In other words, there were no wrong answers with this strategy—only answers that could be improved to lift the learner onto the next rung of the learning ladder.

Second, the strategy provided was not just routinely given to the learners by listing its steps on the board; the steps were illustrated in the context of a real problem. The application was real world and typical of other examples to which they would be asked to apply the strategy.

Third, the learners were invited to become participants in the learning, not just passive listeners waiting to be told what to do. Because the teacher started a question-and-answer dialogue to provide a structure for the learners' opinions and experiences, students became an active part of the process by which new knowledge was being generated. They were, in a sense, their own teachers without knowing it. This was made possible through the format of an unscripted discussion, which removed any fear of producing a wrong response that might have prevented some learners from participating.

And fourth, note that as the lesson evolved, more and more of the most important conclusions were provided by the students, not the teacher. The highest level of interpretation with which the lesson ended came almost entirely from the summarizing remarks of students. By the end of the lesson, the teacher's role was more that of a monitor and co-inquirer than of an information provider; that role had been assumed by the students themselves as they actively applied each of the steps given earlier in the lesson.

Now let's look more closely at some of the mental strategies that learners can actually use to acquire meaning and understanding from text.

METACOGNITION

One strategy for self-directed learning is **metacognition,** mental processes that assist learners to reflect on their thinking by internalizing, understanding, and recalling the content to be learned. They include invisible thinking skills such as self-interrogation, self-checking, self-monitoring, and analyzing, as well as memory aids (called *mnemonics*) for classifying and recalling content.

Metacognitive strategies are most easily conveyed to learners through a process called *mental modeling* (G. Duffy, Roehler, & Herrman, 1988; Rekrut, 1999). **Mental modeling** helps students internalize, recall, and then generalize problem solutions to different content at a later time. The teacher does not just convey information but demonstrates the decision-making process as it occurs. By contrast, the mechanical memorization of steps rarely helps learners solve similar problems in other contexts or allows content to be recalled when the present topic has lost its immediate importance (no exam in sight or no homework due).

Mental modeling is particularly important when asking students to engage in complex tasks, such as Internet searches—which require higher-order thinking skills to revise a search strategy, evaluate its result, discard inapplicable items, and synthesize findings. Each of these tasks poses challenges for learners that can be addressed through modeling ways for students to organize their thinking (Rekrut, 1999). As you observe in classrooms, you will want to watch for instances of mental modeling and note particularly effective approaches you see and how they help learners increase responsibility for their own learning by implementing and monitoring a previously modeled way of thinking. Mental modeling involves three important stages (G. Duffy & Roehler, 1989):

- Showing students the reasoning involved
- Making students conscious of the reasoning involved
- Focusing students on applying the reasoning

These steps usually are carried out through verbal statements that walk learners through the process of attaining a correct solution. They begin with verbal markers such as the following:

Now, I will show you how to solve this problem by talking out loud as I go through it, identifying exactly what is going on in my mind. Think about each decision I make, where I stop to think, and what alternatives I choose—as though you are making the same decisions in your own mind."

Notice that the teacher is not giving the learner the mechanics of getting a right answer: do step A, then B, then C. More importantly, the teacher is providing an actual live demonstration of the mental procedures that may lie behind the routine completion of a problem.

Research on what makes a good demonstration (Borich & Tombari, 1997, 2004; Good & Brophy, 1995) indicates that skilled demonstrators of mental procedures do the following:

- *Focus the learners' attention.* They begin their demonstration only when their learners' attention is focused on them. Then they direct students' attention to the thinking or reasoning skill they want them to learn.
- *Stress the value of the demonstration.* They briefly and concisely point out why their learners should observe what they are about to demonstrate. They relate the thinking skill to the content to be learned.
- *Talk in conversational language while demonstrating.* They back up to cover unfamiliar concepts and repeat actions when needed, use analogies to bridge content gaps, and use examples to reinforce learning. They then probe for understanding.
- *Make the steps simple and obvious.* They break complex actions into simple steps that can be followed one at a time. They point out what to do next and then describe the action as it is being performed by thinking out loud while acting.
- *Help learners remember the demonstration.* They go slow ("Stop me if I'm going too fast"), exaggerate certain actions ("Now I'll ask myself a question"), highlight distinctive features ("Notice where I pause"), and give simple memory aids to help learners retain what they have seen and heard.

These mental procedures help students internalize, recall, and then generalize problem solutions to different content at a later time. You do not just convey information according to the preceding steps but actually demonstrate the decision-making process as it occurs within your own thoughts. You then monitor the process as it occurs in the learner, provide feedback, and adjust the complexity and flow rate of content as needed. This leads to a second important concept for self-directed learning called *mediation.*

TEACHER MEDIATION

On-the-spot adjustments to content flow and complexity that you make to accommodate idiosyncratic learning needs are called *teacher mediation.* Your role during **teacher-mediated learning** is to adjust the instructional dialogue to help students restructure their learning and move them closer to the intended outcome. In other words, the interactive dialogue you provide helps learners construct their own meanings from the content. This aids retention and the generalization of the reasoning process to other contexts.

The knowledge and skills that learners are to acquire are not given to them in the form of end products. Instead, you provide the cognitive stimulation at just the proper times for them to acquire the end products through their own reasoning. The need for adjustment of flow and content seldom can be anticipated. It requires mediation—your on-the-spot judgment of what new information would bring a learner's response to the next level of refinement of which the learner is capable at that moment. This next level reflects the content difficulty and cognitive complexity from which the student can most benefit at that moment.

The Zone of Maximum Response Opportunity

This level of content difficulty and cognitive complexity is the learner's **zone of maximum response opportunity.*** It is the zone of behavior that, if stimulated by you, will bring a learner's response to the next level of refinement. Thus your response directed at the

---

*The zone of maximum response opportunity is called the "zone of proximal development" by Vygotsky (Kozulin, 1990).

 Video Window

Demonstrating

In this video you will see Scott presenting a science demonstration to his middle school students. Watch how he engages each of his students in the demonstration, giving them a sense of ownership by letting them experience for themselves the scientific principle being studied and thereby heightening their curiosity and motivation to learn more. See if you can find instances in which Scott applied the following criteria for presenting an effective demonstration.

- Focused his learners' attention.
- Stressed the value of the demonstration.
- Talked in conversational language while demonstrating.
- Made the steps simple and obvious.
- Helped learners remember the demonstration.

 To answer these questions online, go to the Video Windows *module of this chapter of the Companion Website at www.prenhall.com/borich.*

---

zone of maximum response opportunity must be at or near the learner's current level of understanding but also designed to lift the learner's following response to the next higher level. Your directed response need not elicit the correct answer, because the learner at that precise moment may be incapable of benefiting from it. It should, however, encourage the learner to refine an initially crude response.

Here are two classroom dialogues in which the first teacher hits the learner's zone of maximum response opportunity, but the second misses it:

◆ ◆ ◆

Teacher:	When you see a proportion or ratio, such as $\frac{4}{5}$ (writes it on board), think of the number on top as "what is" and the number on the bottom as "what could be." Think about a box of cereal that you have for breakfast. If I wrote the proportion of cereal in the box as $\frac{3}{4}$ (writes it on board), I would say to myself, the full box is equal to the number 4—that's the "could be" part. But this morning, after I fixed my breakfast, what's left is only the number 3, which is the "what is" part. That's how I can tell the box is still pretty full, because the number for "what is" is close to the number for "what could be."
	Now Megan, explain to me what it means when it says on a label that the proportion of vitamin C for one 4-ounce glass of orange juice is half the minimum daily requirement.
Megan:	I'm not sure.
Teacher:	OK, what words can we use to describe the number on top?
Megan:	You said it's "what is."
Teacher:	What does that mean?
Megan:	I guess it's how much vitamin C is really in the glass.
Teacher:	And now for the bottom.
Megan:	You said the bottom is "what could be." Does that mean that it's all you need?
Teacher:	Yes, it does—good. Now, think of another example—one of your own—in which something was less than it could have been.
Megan:	Well, I finished Ms. Enro's social studies test before the end of the period.

Teacher:	And how long was the period?
Megan:	Umm, about 40 minutes, I guess.
Teacher:	Using our words, what would you call that part of the problem?
Megan:	"What could be." OK, I get it. Then the time I actually took is what really happened? Yeah, I finished the test in about 20 minutes.
Teacher:	So how would you express that proportion in numbers?
Megan:	It would be 20, for "what is," over 40, for "what could be." The top is half of the bottom, so I guess one glass of orange juice gives you half the vitamin C you need in a day.
Teacher:	OK. Let's retrace the steps you just followed for another problem.

◆　◆　◆

Now let's imagine that Megan relives this episode in another classroom. After the same introductory remarks, Megan is asked the identical question:

◆　◆　◆

Teacher:	Now Megan, explain to me what it means when it says on a label that the proportion of vitamin C for one 4-ounce glass of orange juice is half the minimum daily requirement.
Megan:	I'm not sure.
Teacher:	Look, if the number 1 is on the top and the number 2 is on the bottom, it must mean the top is less than the bottom. Right?
Megan:	Right.
Teacher:	So if the top number represents what is and the bottom number what could be, then "what is" is one half less than "what could be." And that can only mean the glass contains half of the minimum daily requirement of vitamin C. Got it?
Megan:	Yep.

◆　◆　◆

Well, maybe she does and maybe she doesn't. Notice in the first example that, by retracing the mental steps for Megan to recall, the teacher hit Megan's zone of maximum response opportunity because her prior understanding and response were taken into account in moving the dialogue forward, closer to the intended goal of the lesson. It provided a peg with which Megan lifted herself onto the next rung of the learning ladder.

The second teacher simply provided the right answer. This gave Megan no opportunity to construct her own response by using the mental steps provided and thereby derive a process to use for independently arriving at other right answers in similar circumstances. The first teacher focused on developing for the learner a process of reasoning—a line of thinking—that would give the content its own individual meaning and yet be consistent with the intended goal of the lesson.

Through classroom dialogues such as these, you can encourage your learners to construct their own meanings and interpretations, for example, to substitute their own unique constructions for what is and what could be, and to share them with others through discussion and classroom dialogue. Such diversity among self-directed learners activates their unique learning histories, specialized abilities, and personal experiences, thus engaging them in the learning process.

Hitting the Zone of Maximum Response Opportunity

The zone of maximum response opportunity is particularly important in self-directed learning, because you can rarely provide the most appropriate response to each learner at all times. This is the key difference between individualized learning (for example, in programmed and computerized instruction) and self-directed learning. In individualized learning, the content writer anticipates the most probable errors and provides remedial or alternative learning routes (called branching) for all learners, regardless of their zones of maximum response opportunity. Because the instruction assumes that relatively homogeneous groups of individual learners will work through the content, the same types of errors must be anticipated for all learners. In some cases the remedial steps or alternative branching provided may fall within a learner's zone of maximum response opportunity, but in some cases it may not.

Because self-directed learning almost always occurs during a student response–teacher reaction sequence, it affords the opportunity to more accurately aim your spoken or written reaction at the learner's zone of maximum response opportunity. However, a variety of teacher reactions can fall within the learner's zone of maximum response opportunity with equal effect. After all, your target is not a point but a zone that in some instances may be as broad as the outfield in a major league ballpark.

In this broad field, a hit is a hit, whether it falls in left field, center field, or right field, as long as it is within the appointed zone. This is an important point, because aiming your reaction to a student response too sharply—to a fixed point like lower center field—may so restrict your response that it will exclude the learning history, specialized abilities, and personal experiences of the learner. And it may not consider your own content knowledge, specialized abilities, and instructional style. Figure 10.1 illustrates the zone of maximum response opportunity for a lesson in reading.

Thus the concept of a zone affords both you and your students some latitude within which to construct and to create meanings and understandings that consider the unique needs of both. In this manner, self-directed learning promotes a gentle interplay between the minds of learner and teacher, pulling and pushing each other in a student response–teacher reaction sequence designed to help the learner climb to the next rung of the learning ladder.

Diversity among self-directed learners can be activated by teacher interaction and the gentle interplay that taps the learner's zone of maximum response opportunity and provides appropriate stepping-stones to higher levels of learning.

Figure 10.1 The zone of maximum response opportunity for a reading lesson.

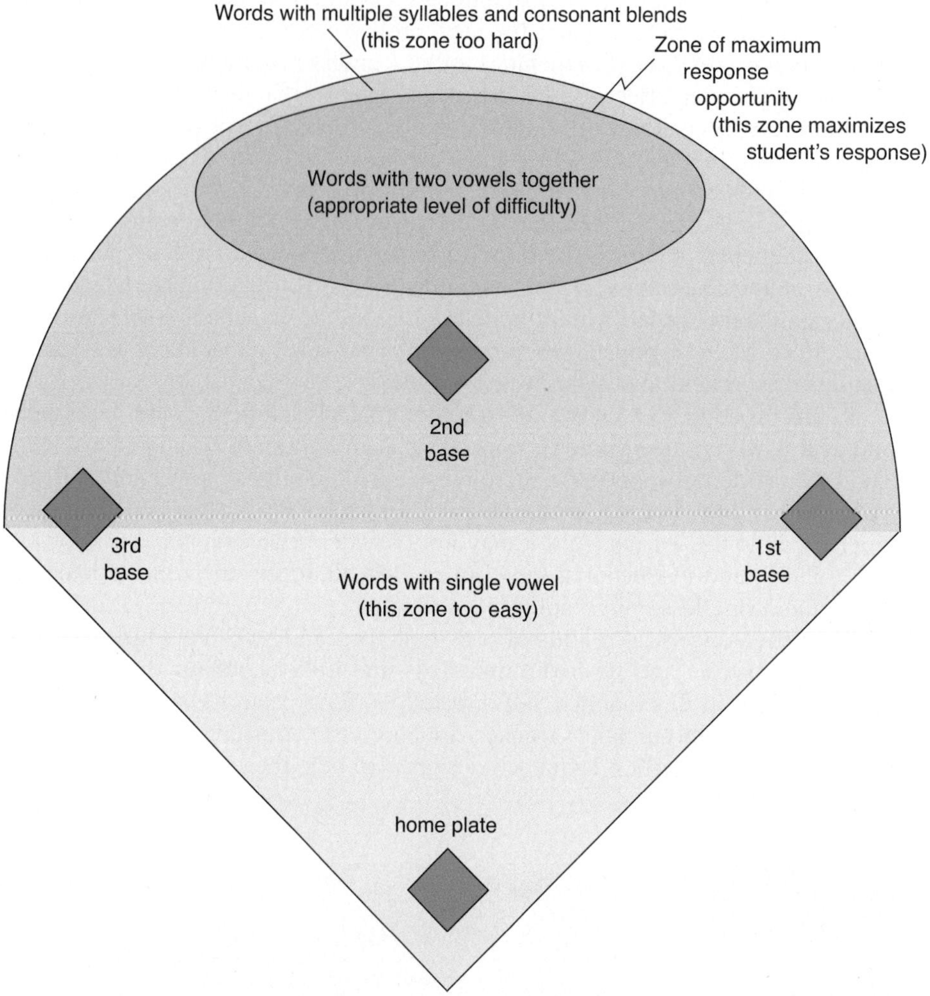

Words with multiple syllables and consonant blends
(this zone too hard)

Zone of maximum
response
opportunity
(this zone maximizes
student's response)

Words with two vowels together
(appropriate level of difficulty)

2nd
base

3rd
base

1st
base

Words with single vowel
(this zone too easy)

home plate

FUNCTIONAL ERRORS

Another concept important to self-directed learning is **functional errors.** Student errors play an important role in the gentle interplay between learner and teacher (Stipek, 1996). If your reaction promotes an inaccurate and meaningless response, the interplay may not be so gentle, at least not in the learner's mind. But if your reaction creates (or even intentionally promotes) a student response that is inaccurate but *meaningful,* interplay returns to a gentler state.

The latter condition describes a class of student errors called *functional errors.* Whether these errors are unexpected or planned for, they enhance the learner's understanding of content. Functional errors provide a logical stepping-stone for climbing to the next rung of the ladder, which may eliminate an erroneous thought process from ever occurring again in the learner's mind. For example, such an error may be necessary so the student will not arrive at the right answer for the wrong reason, thereby compounding the mistake in other contexts.

Consider the following dialogue in which a student error becomes a functional stepping-stone to the next level of understanding:

◆ ◆ ◆

Teacher: As you recall from yesterday, we were studying the reasons behind the Civil War. Does anyone recall under what president of the United States the Civil War began?

Alexis: Our book says Jefferson Davis.

Teacher: Well, it so happens Jefferson Davis was a president at the time. But that's not the right answer. Now how do you think Jefferson Davis could be a president, but not the president of the United States at the time of the Civil War?

Alexis: Well, maybe at the start of the war there were two presidents, Jefferson Davis and someone else.

Teacher: As a matter of fact, there were two presidents, but only one could be president of the United States.

Alexis: Well, if he wasn't president of the United States he must have been president of the other side.

Teacher: But do you recall the name of the government that represented the other side?

Alexis: Yeah, now I remember. It was the Confederacy. It was Lincoln who was the president of the North—which must have been called the United States—and Jefferson Davis, who must have been the president of the South, called the Confederacy. I guess I got confused with all the different names.

◆ ◆ ◆

Even though the student response was incorrect, this teacher's reaction fell within the student's zone of maximum response opportunity, because from it directly followed a more correct response. Notice also how the teacher encouraged the learner to supply the answer, using her previous mistake as an aid to obtaining the correct answer. This strategy actually led to information that went beyond the question itself—to putting Jefferson Davis in geographic perspective and in correctly naming the governments representing both North and South.

But what if this teacher had made a less thoughtful reaction, encouraging not only another inaccurate response but, worse, a blind alley not useful for refining or extending the student's initial response? What might such a reaction look like?

◆ ◆ ◆

Teacher: Does anyone recall under what president of the United States the Civil War began?

Alexis: Our book says Jefferson Davis.

Teacher: I said president of the United States, not president of the Confederate States of America. See the difference?

Alexis: I guess so.

Teacher: Well, OK. Then let's go on to Mark.

◆ ◆ ◆

The interplay here becomes considerably less gentle, as the specter of failure is left hanging over the learner, and the teacher has no easy way out of this awkward ending. This is why self-directed learning requires a flexible teacher response that is always at or slightly above the learner's current level of understanding to promote a student response, correct or incorrect, that is functional for achieving the intended goal of the lesson. This is also why scripted approaches to instruction (like programmed instruction and some computer software) cannot replace the gentle interplay between student response and teacher reaction supported by the classroom dialogue and group discussion methods of self-directed learning.

RECIPROCAL TEACHING

One way you can apply self-directed learning in your classroom is with a strategy called *reciprocal teaching* (Lubliner & Palincsar, 2001; Oczkus, 2003; Palincsar & Brown, 1989; Rosenshine & Meister, 1994). **Reciprocal teaching** provides opportunities to explore the content to be learned via classroom dialogue. At the center of reciprocal teaching are group discussions in which you and your students take turns as leader in discussing the text.

Slavin (1990, 2001) observed that most classroom discussions amount to little more than recitation of facts by students with the aid of question-and-answer sequences in which all or most of the answers are known. This leaves little opportunity for students to construct their own meaning and content interpretation so they can attain higher levels of understanding. In practice, many classroom discussions promote little meaningful dialogue that actually helps students struggle with the adequacy of their ideas and opinions on their way to obtaining acceptable solutions. More often, these discussions are driven by text content, with rapid fire questions that stay close to the facts as presented in the text.

Reciprocal teaching is a strategy that makes a typical discussion into a more productive and self-directed learning experience. It accomplishes this through four activities: predicting, questioning, summarizing, and clarifying. These unfold into the following sequence, described by Palincsar and Brown (1989):

- *Predicting.* Discussion begins by generating predictions about the content to be learned from the text, based on
  a. Its title or subheading in the text
  b. The group's prior knowledge or information pertaining to the topic
  c. Experience with similar kinds of information

Following the group's predictions about what they expect to learn from the text, the group reads and/or listens to a portion of it.

- *Questioning.* The teacher chooses one individual to lead a discussion of each portion of the text that is read. Afterward, the discussion leader asks questions about the information. Students respond to the questions and raise additional questions.
- *Summarizing.* The discussion leader then summarizes the text, and the teacher invites other students to comment or elaborate on the summary.
- *Clarifying.* If points in the text were unclear (e.g., concepts or vocabulary), they are discussed until clarity is achieved. In this case, students may make more predictions and reread portions of the text for greater clarity.

The following dialogue (based on Palincsar & Brown, 1989) illustrates the four activities of predicting, questioning, summarizing, and clarifying that comprise reciprocal teaching.

◆　◆　◆

Teacher:　　(Reading from text.) "The pipefish change their color and movements to blend with their surroundings. For example, pipefish that live among green plants change their color to a shade of green to match the plants."

Claire:　　(Leading the discussion.) One question that I had about this paragraph is: What is special about the way the pipefish looks?

Teacher:　　(Clarifying.) Do you mean the way that it is green?

Andy:	(Elaborating.) It's not just that it's green, it's that it's the same color as the plants around it, all around it.
Claire:	(Continuing.) Yes, that's it. My summary of this part tells how the pipefish looks and that it looks like what is around it. My prediction is that this is about its enemies and how it protects itself and who the enemies are.
Monty:	(Adding to the summary.) They also talked about how the pipefish moves . . .
Keith:	(Rejoining.) It sways back and forth . . .
Andy:	(Adding.) . . . along with the other plants.
Teacher:	(Questioning.) What do we call it when something looks like and acts like something else? The way we saw the insect called a *walking stick* yesterday? We clarified this word when we talked about the walking stick.
Angel:	Mimic.
Teacher:	That's right. We said we would say that the pipefish mimics the . . .
Students:	(Together.) . . . plants.
Teacher:	OK! Let's see if Claire's predictions come true. (Class turns to the text.)

◆   ◆   ◆

Notice in this discussion how the teacher supports student participation in the dialogue. The teacher's aim is to engage as many students as possible in the learning process by providing reactions to student responses that are in their zones of maximum response opportunity. This is accomplished by elaborating on student responses and allowing ample opportunity for students to participate in the dialogue, from their perspective (R. Mayer & Wittrock, 1996). This gives the teacher ample data on which to form a reaction that is within their zone of maximum response opportunity.

As the discussion continues, more responsibility for reading and developing the dialogue is given over to the students until, over time, the teacher becomes more of an adviser—or coach—who refines responses instead of providing them. At that point, more and more of the discussion represents the internalization of the text by the students, who now express it through their unique learning histories, specialized abilities, and experiences.

The ultimate goal of reciprocal teaching is to sufficiently engage students in the learning process so they become conscious of their reasoning process. This occurs through their own and other students' modeling, and the teacher's modeling of that process, and is refined in the context of classroom dialogues. This requires your continuous attention to the ongoing dialogue and to the meanings students are deriving from the text so you can continually adjust the instructional content to meet your learners' current level of understanding.

As students gradually accept the shift in responsibility from teacher to student, you reduce the amount of explaining, explicitness of cues, and prompting that may have marked the earlier part of the lesson. Figure 10.2 indicates some classroom activities that can guide the gradual shift of responsibility from teacher to learner during self-directed learning.

Palincsar and Brown (1989) summarize the teacher's role during reciprocal teaching in the following list:

- The teacher and students share responsibility for acquiring the strategies employed in reciprocal teaching.
- The teacher initially assumes major responsibility for teaching these strategies ("thinks aloud" how to make a prediction, how to ask a question, how to summarize, how to clarify), but gradually transfers responsibility to the students for demonstrating use of the strategies.
- The teacher expects all students to participate in the discussion and gives all students the opportunity to lead it. The teacher encourages participation by supporting students

Figure 10.2 Shifting responsibility from teacher to learners.

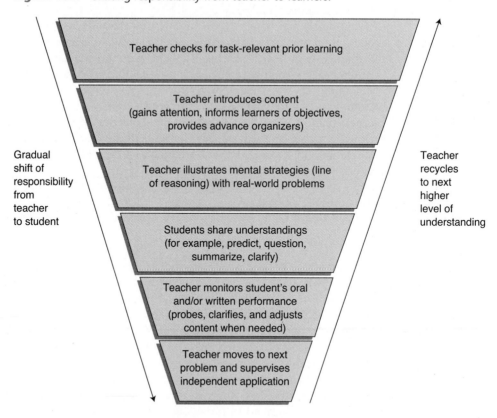

Teacher checks for task-relevant prior learning

Teacher introduces content
(gains attention, informs learners of objectives,
provides advance organizers)

Teacher illustrates mental strategies (line
of reasoning) with real-world problems

Students share understandings
(for example, predict, question,
summarize, clarify)

Teacher monitors student's oral
and/or written performance
(probes, clarifies, and adjusts
content when needed)

Teacher moves to next
problem and supervises
independent application

Gradual
shift of
responsibility
from
teacher
to student

Teacher
recycles
to next
higher
level of
understanding

through prompting, providing additional information, or raising/lowering the demand on students so learners will achieve meaningful responses.
- Throughout each self-directed lesson, the teacher consciously monitors how successfully comprehension is occurring and adjusts the content as needed to the zone of maximum response opportunity.

SOCIAL DIALOGUE VERSUS CLASS DISCUSSION

As the preceding dialogues demonstrated, classroom conversation between teacher and students is central to self-directed learning. Verbal interactions within a classroom are vastly different from those occurring outside of it. In many classrooms, verbalizations are adult dominated, leaving students with little alternative but to respond to teacher requests for facts and information. These traditional teaching settings may offer few opportunities for students to elaborate or comment on the topic at hand.

However, self-directed learning strategies use classroom dialogue differently. Instead of verbalizations intended to confirm the teacher's authority, classroom dialogue is purposefully guided to gradually shift responsibility to the learner. The teacher scaffolds knowledge, building the dialogue layer by layer, each time increasing the challenge to the learner to think independently of earlier constructions provided by the teacher.

Scaffolding must be done carefully to keep the challenge within the learner's zone of maximum response opportunity. This requires that you be aware of the learner's present level of understanding (for example, familiarity with the task) and the level at which the learner can reasonably be expected to perform (for example, from past learning performance).

Attention to these details lets you scaffold the cognitive demands placed on the learner. You do so to increasingly shift the learner from just responding to textual material to *internalizing* its meaning by elaborating, extending, and commenting on it.

As we have seen, the strategy of reciprocal teaching uses group discussion and rotating discussion leaders to achieve this goal. It does so not just by getting students to talk, as do many traditional discussions, but by getting them to elaborate the processes by which they are learning the content. The clear articulation and rehearsal of these mental strategies (1) guide the learner in subsequent performances, and (2) help you adjust the flow and level of prompts, cues, and questions to hit inside the learner's zone of maximum response opportunity.

THE ROLE OF INNER SPEECH

As we have seen, an important aspect of classroom dialogue in self-directed learning is the increasing responsibility it places on the learner for creating original responses in the form of comments, elaborations, and extensions to what is being read or being said. These verbalizations, if properly scaffolded, are believed to create an inner speech within the learner (L. Resnick & Klopfer, 1989; Simmons, 1995; Vygotsky, 1962). This **inner speech** ultimately leads to a private internal dialogue in the mind of the learner that takes the place of the teacher's prompts and questions and self-guides the learner through similar problems.

As the responsibility for unique and original productions beyond the text gradually shifts to the learner, the learner increasingly acquires the ability to "speak" internally, modeling the same line of reasoning and mimicking the same types of questions, prompts, and cues used by the teacher at an earlier stage. In other words, the verbal interactions that the teacher increasingly asks of the learner become internalized in the form of private speech used by the learner in the absence of direct teacher involvement.

The teacher's role now turns to one of monitoring. The teacher prompts and cues only when necessary to keep students on track. Ultimately, by internalizing the scaffold verbalizations of the teacher and recalling them at will in private dialogue, students become their own teachers, mimicking the logic and reasoning process modeled by the teacher. Self-direction can be stimulated by many different techniques in addition to reciprocal teaching, including many forms of cooperative and group learning (Rosenshine, 1997; Rosenshine & Meister, 1992).

The role of inner speech in guiding the behavior of both children and adults is central to self-directed learning strategies.

Outward verbalizations by the learner, if properly scaffolded, can be turned into inner speech that eventually replaces the teacher's prompts and self-guides the learner through similar problems.

SAMPLE DIALOGUES OF SELF-DIRECTED LEARNING

Let's look at three classroom dialogues that exhibit characteristics of self-directed inquiry. In different teaching contexts, these dialogues illustrate the following:

- How a teacher models the process by which meaning and understanding can be derived from textual material.
- How questions, prompts, and cues can be used to scaffold responses, gradually shifting the responsibility for learning to the student.
- How the teacher thereafter can monitor student responses for continued understanding.

First, let's look at a fourth-grade classroom in which Ms. Koker is teaching reading. We'll observe how she models the process by which meaning and understanding can be derived from text. Our discussion begins with Ms. Koker reading an excerpt from a short story to the class from the daily reader:

◆　◆　◆

Ms. Koker:	(Reading.) "Some of the coldest climate on earth occurs in the northern parts of Alaska. In this land, a small but hardy group of Native Americans lives and prospers in small villages where hunting and fishing is a way of life. This small group of villagers . . ."
Debbie:	(Interrupting.) Ms. Koker, I don't know what the word *hardy* means.
Ms. Koker:	What do you think it means, Debbie? (Asking her to make a prediction.)
Debbie:	Well, something that's hard—like, maybe, ice.
Ms. Koker:	Let's see if you are right. Let's think of some other words that might mean almost the same thing as *hard*. (Introducing the idea of synonyms.)
Tim:	Something that's hard is strong.
Mickey:	Yeah, and it also lasts a long time.
Kim Lee:	If you're strong, you can't be hurt.
Ms. Koker:	OK, now let's see if any of these ideas fit with the sentence, "In this land a small but hardy group of Native Americans lives and prospers in small villages where hunting and fishing is a way of life." What do you think, Tim? (Encouraging the idea of fitting synonyms into the text to clarify meaning.)
Tim:	Well, if we took the word *hardy* out and put in the word *strong,* I think it would mean the same thing.
Ms. Koker:	What do you think, Itsuko?
Itsuko:	It makes sense, because when you're strong you can't be hurt—say by all the cold up north—and then you live a long time. (Summarizing.)
Mickey:	But how do we know they live a long time, just because they're strong? (Asking for clarification.)
Ms. Koker:	That's a good point; we really don't know that yet, so what do you think? (Calling for a prediction again.)
Tina:	I think they won't live as long as us because of all the cold weather.
Ms. Koker:	So how do you think they stay warm? Let's read on to see.

◆　◆　◆

Notice that Ms. Koker was modeling a strategy for deriving meaning from text. To accomplish this, she introduced the idea of synonyms, by asking Debbie what she thought the word *hardy* meant and then by asking her students to insert the synonym into the text to check its appropriateness. Thus she was conveying a model—a mental strategy—that students can use time and again, unaided by the teacher, whenever they encounter an unknown word.

Next let's observe Mr. Willis's junior high science class to see how he uses questions, prompts, and cues to encourage self-direction. In the following discussion, Mr. Willis is teaching a fundamental law of physics by providing questions and reactions that are scaffolded to his learners' zones of maximum response opportunity:

◆ ◆ ◆

Mr. Willis:	Here you see a balloon, a punching bag, and a tire pump. Watch carefully as I let the air out of the balloon (lets air out), punch the bag (punches it), and press down on the pump handle (pushes handle). What did you notice about all three actions? Chet?
Chet:	You got tired. (Class laughs.)
Mr. Willis:	You're right about that, especially when I did the punching and pumping. (Reaching to Chet's current level of understanding.) Yes, you saw a reaction in me; I got tired. What other action did you see?
Chet:	The balloon flitted across the room.
Mr. Willis:	And what else?
Chet:	The punching bag moved forward—and, well, the pump handle went down and then a little up.
Mr. Willis:	You saw several reactions, didn't you? What were they?
Chet:	Something happened to the object you were playing with and . . . well . . . I guess something else was going on, too.
Mr. Willis:	Anita, what did you see in all three cases?
Anita:	Movement in two directions, I think.
Mr. Willis:	What were the movements?
Anita:	Well, for the balloon, it went forward, but also it pushed the air backward . . . over your face. And, for the punching bag, it went forward . . . umph (mimics the sound) . . . and stopped. I don't know what other movement there was.
Mr. Willis:	(Pushing to the next higher level of understanding.) Think about what happened both after and before I punched the bag. To help you, write on the top of a piece of paper the words *before* and *after*. Now write down what you saw in each of these three instances—the balloon, the punching bag, and the pump. Let's all take a minute to do this.
Anita:	(After about a minute.) Now I remember. The punching bag came back to hit your hand again. That was the second movement.
Mr. Willis:	(Checking for understanding among the others.) And what about the tire pump? Michael, you have your hand up.
Michael:	When you pushed the pump handle down to inflate the tire, it came back up a little.
Mr. Willis:	You're both right. There were two identifiable movements, which we will call an *action* and a *reaction*. The fundamental law of physics we have been discussing is that "Whenever there is an action, there must be a reaction." Now let's check to see if this is true for some other movements by identifying on your paper the action and reactions associated with the following. I'll say them slowly so you have time to write:

> The space shuttle taking off from Cape Canaveral
>
> An automobile moving down the street
>
> A gunshot
>
> A football being kicked over a goalpost

◆ ◆ ◆

Notice how Mr. Willis used questions targeted to his students' current level of understanding. This allowed them to respond in some meaningful way, which gave him the opportunity to build on an earlier incomplete response to reach the next higher level of understanding. For example, Mr. Willis used Chet's first crude response, aided by the prompt "What other action did you see?" to introduce the concept of action followed by a reaction. Each time the questioning turned to a new student, Mr. Willis targeted his question, prompt, or cue higher but still within that learner's zone of maximum response opportunity.

Also, the idea of thinking through a solution on paper—called *think sheets*—kept students actively engaged in working through their responses. At the same time, it provided a strategy from which they might more easily derive actions and reactions for the new problems presented at the end of the dialogue. Mr. Willis's use of questions, prompts, and cues at various levels of difficulty kept this class moving through the lesson with increasingly more sophisticated responses.

Now let's look in on a third classroom. Mrs. LeFluir is teaching Spanish to a high school class not just by altering the level of questioning, as did Mr. Willis, but by altering the tasks from which learners experience the application of content firsthand. Without realizing it, Mrs. LeFluir's class is experiencing the difference between **declarative knowledge**—facts, concepts, rules, and geneneralizations intended for oral or written regurgitation—and **procedural knowledge**—action sequences or procedures used in a problem-solving or decision-making task.

◆　◆　◆

Mrs. LeFluir:	Today, we will study the gender of nouns. In Spanish all nouns are either masculine or feminine. Nouns ending in *o* are generally masculine, and those ending in *a* are generally feminine. Tisha, can you identify the following nouns as either masculine or feminine? (Writes on board.)

> *libro*
>
> *pluma*
>
> *cuaderno*
>
> *gramática*

Tisha:	(Correctly identifies each.)
Mrs. LeFluir:	Now let's see how you identified each of the words and what each word means.
Tisha:	Well, I followed the rule that if it ends in an *o* it will be masculine but if it ends in an *a* it will be feminine. I think the words are *book, pen, notebook,* and *grammar.*
Mrs. LeFluir:	Good. Now for the next step, you've all used indefinite articles *a* and *an* many times in your speaking and writing. In Spanish the word *un* is used for *a* or *an* before a masculine noun, and *una* is used for *a* or *an* before a feminine noun. In Spanish the article is repeated before each noun. Using the vocabulary words on the board, let's place the correct form of the indefinite article in front of each word. (Shifting the task demand.) Why don't you take the first one, Ted?
Ted:	It would be *un libro.*
Mrs. LeFluir:	Maria.
Maria:	*Una pluma.*
Mrs. LeFluir:	Juan and Marcos, take the next two.
Juan:	*Un cuaderno.*
Marcos:	*Una gramática.*
Mrs. LeFluir:	OK. Now, we are ready to put our knowledge to work. I will give you a sentence in English, and you translate it into Spanish, being sure to include the correct form of the indefinite article. (Shifting the task demand again.) For this you will need to remember your vocabulary from last week. If you need to,

look up the words you don't remember. Mark, let's start with you. Come up to the board and write, "Do you want a book?"

Mark: (Writes on board) *Desea usted un libro?*
Mrs. LeFluir: Good. And how did you decide to use *un* instead of *una?*
Mark: The noun ended in *o.*
Mrs. LeFluir: (Continues with three other examples.)

Do you need grammar?

Do you want to study a language?

Do you need a notebook?

(After the students respond, she shifts the task demand again by moving to the following activity.) Now read each sentence on the transparency and write down the correct form of the indefinite article that goes before the noun. (Shows transparency.)

Yo necesito _____ gramática.

Nosotros estudiamos _____ lengua.

Necesita Tomás _____ libro?

Es _____ pluma?

(After the students respond, she moves to a final activity and yet another task demand.) Now for the following sentences, I will speak in English, and I want you to repeat the same sentence entirely in Spanish. Be sure, once again, to include the correct form of the indefinite article.

◆   ◆   ◆

Notice in this episode the different activities required of the students and how they differ in cognitive complexity. Mrs. LeFluir gradually changed the demands on her learners by shifting the tasks to which they were to respond. Her lesson began by asking only for the simple regurgitation of rules (declarative knowledge) but ended by engaging students in an oral sequence of actions of the kind that might be required in having a conversation in Spanish (procedural knowledge). She gradually shifted her tasks from declarative to procedural in small enough degrees to ensure that all her students, or at least most of them, could follow.

This process also conveyed a language-learning model that will be helpful in subsequent contexts by providing a learning strategy that flows from memorization of rules and vocabulary, through completion and fill-in, to oral delivery. Notice that this sequence was completed even for this elementary lesson. This tells the learners that oral and written delivery, and not the regurgitation of rules, is the end goal to which all previous learning must contribute and toward which they must strive in their own individual learning and practice.

The systematic varying of task demands within a unit comprises an **activity structure.** Activity structures are most effective for self-directed learning when they vary the demands or problems being placed on the learner in ways that gradually require the learner to assume responsibility for learning the content at a higher level of understanding. The following list indicates some of the steps in teaching self-directed inquiry to individual learners.

Steps in Teaching Self-Directed Inquiry to Individual Learners

- Provide a new learning task and observe how the student approaches it (for example, reading a short selection in a history text that will be the basis for an essay exam).
- Ask the student to explain how she or he approaches the task of learning the textual information—for example, in preparation for the exam. (This helps the student analyze her or his own cognitive approach.)

- Describe and model a more effective procedure for organizing and accomplishing the task. For example, explain and demonstrate how to use the study questions at the end of the selection to help focus reading; highlight the main ideas in each paragraph of the selection with a fluorescent marker; write outline notes of key points on a separate sheet or on note cards as a study guide for later review. This gives the student new strategies for cognitively organizing the learning task.
- Provide the student with another, similar learning task for practicing the new cognitive strategies. Observe as the student proceeds with the task, giving reminders and corrective feedback.
- Model self-questioning behavior as you demonstrate analysis of a similar problem. For example, "What are the key questions you will need to answer?" or "What is the main idea in this paragraph?" Write such questions on a small card for the student to use as a reminder.
- Provide another opportunity for the student to practice the skills using self-direction, decreasing your role as monitor.
- Check the result of the learning task by questioning for comprehension and asking the student to recall the specific learning strategies used.

OTHER COGNITIVE STRATEGIES

When you use a mental strategy to help you learn on your own, you have learned what psychologists call a **cognitive learning strategy,** general methods of thinking that improve learning across a variety of subject areas. They accomplish this by helping the learner to retain incoming information (called *reception*), recall task-relevant prior knowledge (called *availability*), and build logical connections among incoming knowledge (called *activation*). These strategies (Goetz, Alexander, & Ash, 1992; Woolfolk, 2003) include

- Mnemonics (memory aids)
- Elaboration/organization (note taking)
- Comprehension-monitoring strategies
- Problem-solving strategies
- Project-based strategies

Let's take a look at each of these.

Mnemonics

Early cognitive psychologists such as Bruner (1966) and Ausubel (1968) advocated that teachers organize their lessons around a limited set of powerful ideas, called *key understandings* and *principles* (Brophy, 1992). Nevertheless, they recognize that all learners will have to learn facts as well in order to grasp the key ideas. Some cognitive strategies for helping to learn facts, dates, rules, classifications, and so on, in order to grasp key understandings and principles are discussed here.

Jingles or Trigger Sentences.   Jingles or trigger sentences can cue sequential letters, patterns, or special historical dates. For example, most music students learn some variation of the sentence, "Every Good Boy Does Fine," to recall the musical notes EGBDF on the lines of a music treble staff. "Spring forward, fall back" helps us remember which way to adjust clocks at the spring and autumn time changes. And many schoolchildren learn that "In fourteen hundred and ninety-two, Columbus sailed the ocean blue." Such devices also can be used for recalling the steps of a mental strategy.

Narrative Chaining.   Narrative chaining is the process of weaving a list of key words you wish to remember into a brief story. For example, if you need to memorize the life cycle of a butterfly in sequence, including the key stages of egg, larva, pupa, and adult, you could invent a narrative such as the following:

> *This morning I cooked an egg for breakfast, but I heated it so long that it looked like molten lava from a volcano. A pupil from a nearby school stopped by, and when he saw my egg-turned-lava, he yelled, "I'm just a pupil! You're the adult! Couldn't you cook an egg better than that?"*

In this case, *lava* and *pupil* sound enough like *larva* and *pupa* to trigger memory of the correct words in the life cycle sequence.

Number Rhyme or Peg Word.   A number-rhyme or peg-word mnemonic system uses words that rhyme with a sequence of numbers as a basis for developing imaginative mental pictures that assist in memorizing a set of other, less related words. Using the life cycle of the butterfly as an example again, you might employ the number-rhyme system this way:

One-Sun Imagine a big fried egg hanging in the sky overhead in place of a brightly shining sun.

Two-Stew Imagine a bubbling stew erupting from a gigantic volcano under the fried egg, drying to form molten lava.

Three-Sea Imagine a tiny screaming pupil afloat on a swirling, angry sea where the hot lava sizzles as it meets the seawater.

Four-Door Imagine a golden door in the side of the volcano that is opened by a gentle, helpful adult who reaches out to pull the pupil from the sea near the lava that was heated by the egglike sun.

Chunking.   Chunking, or grouping bits of information into sets of five to seven discrete pieces, also can assist in memorization. If this is combined by chunking the data into logical categories, the information is then doubly processed in a mental framework for improved recall. A common example is memorizing a grocery list by splitting it into logical categories (dairy products, vegetables, beverages, etc.) of several items each. Teaching students to employ such mental organizers gives them creative alternatives by which to manipulate ideas and information and retain mental strategies for learning, thus internally reinforcing their own learning.

Elaboration/Organization (Note Taking)

Elaboration involves teaching learners how to build internal connections between new knowledge and existing knowledge. Organization entails showing your learners how to order and systematize new information so they can remember it and use it efficiently. The most practical way to help your learners elaborate and organize new knowledge is to teach them how to take notes (Goetz et al., 1992; Turkel & Peterson, 2003).

Note taking can improve information processing in several ways. It enhances reception by prompting learners to attend better to what they are hearing or seeing. Furthermore, note taking assists activation by helping learners make internal connections among information and building a network of external connections with information in memory. You can give your learners several suggestions to help them take notes:

- Read the text before the lesson. This provides advance organizers for the new information.

Figure 10.3 Webbing.

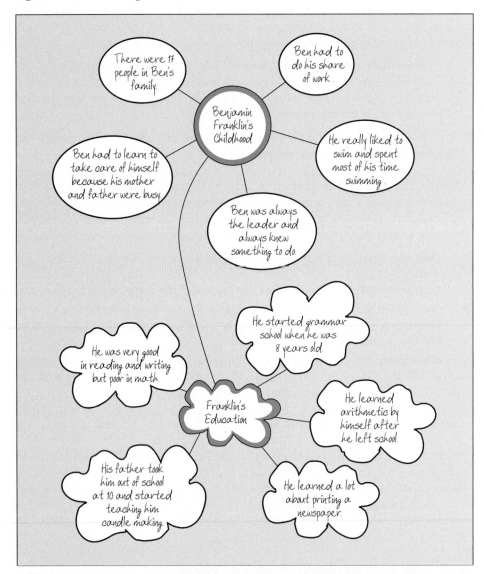

Source: Reprinted from *Learning and study strategies: Issues in assessment, instruction, and education,* C. F. Weinstein, E. T. Goetz, and P. A. Alexander (Eds.), D. F. Dansareau, Cooperative learning strategies, pp. 103–120, Copyright 1988, with permission from Elsevier.

- Watch for signals that indicate important information (gestures, key words, cues to the organization of the information).
- Write down the big ideas, not isolated facts. Try to be selective and not write down everything.
- When needed, use a more free-form outline format, called *webbing* (Buzan, 2002), using pictures, arrows, and code letters. See Figure 10.3 for an example of webbing.
- Write down examples and questions as you listen.
- Leave blanks or some other prompt to indicate what you missed.
- Review your notes as soon as possible.

Comprehension Monitoring

Comprehension monitoring is a strategy in which students learn to evaluate their own understanding by frequently checking their own progress during the course of a lesson (Gagné, Yekovich, & Yekovich, 1993). A. L. Brown (1994) used this strategy based on the reciprocal teaching method described earlier for helping poor as well as good readers. Their teachers modeled for learners the following three skills:

1. Survey the text and make predictions about what it says.
2. Ask questions about the main idea of the text as it is being read.
3. Become aware of unclear passages by monitoring one's own understanding, asking: "Do I understand what I just read?"

Learners who used this strategy increased their reading comprehension from 50% to 80% after only 4 weeks of instruction. Comprehension monitoring strategies have in common the following skills:

- *Setting goals:* "What do I have to do?" "Why am I doing this?"
- *Focusing attention:* "What am I supposed to read?" "What activity must I complete?"
- *Self-reinforcement:* "Great, I understand this. Keep up the good work." "This strategy really works."
- *Coping with problems:* "I don't really understand this. I should go back and read it again." "That's a simple mistake. I can fix that."

Problem-Solving Strategies

Cognitive learning strategists recommend that the school curriculum in most subject areas be organized around real-life problems that learners work on for days or weeks (Viadero, 2003). According to some, we now have curricula isolated by disciplines (algebra, biology, geography, etc.) that identify lists of topics, facts, and skills to be covered by the end of a semester. Such curricula typically place learners in a relatively passive role and encourage rote or nonmeaningful learning.

As an alternative to this approach, growing numbers of educators advocate a type of learning called **problem-based learning** (Delisle, 1997; Verduin, 1996). Problem-based learning organizes the curriculum around loosely structured problems (Goetz et al., 1992) that learners solve by using knowledge and skills from several disciplines. Recall that we introduced this general approach in chapter 4 under the topic of interdisciplinary thematic units and in chapter 8 under the topic of indirect instruction. In both instances we emphasized its importance as a teaching strategy. In this chapter we highlight its importance as a cognitive learning strategy.

To benefit from problem-based learning, however, learners must know how to problemsolve. Because problem solving is a cognitive learning strategy in which few learners receive systematic instruction, teachers increasingly will be called on to teach this skill to their learners.

There are many systems for solving problems that you may teach to learners (Engel, 1998). These methods are generalizable to all curriculum areas and to a variety of problems, whether they are well-defined problems (for example, the word problems typically seen in math curricula) or ill-defined problems with no single answer, with many solution paths, and for which the nature of the problem shifts as learners work on them.

One popular problem-solving system, called IDEAL, involves five stages for teaching problem solving (Bransford & Steen, 1994; Nunn & Kimberly, 2000):

1. *Identify* the problem.   Learners must first know what the problem or problems are before they can solve them. During this stage of problem solving, learners ask themselves if they understand what the problem is and if they have stated it clearly.

2. **D**efine terms. During this stage, learners check that they understand what each word in the problem statement means.
3. **E**xplore strategies. At this point in the IDEAL process, learners compile relevant information and try out strategies to solve the problem. This can involve options such as drawing diagrams, working backward to solve a math or reading comprehension problem, or breaking complex problems into manageable units.
4. **A**ct on the strategy. Once learners have explored a variety of strategy options, they now use one.
5. **L**ook at the effects. During this final stage, learners ask themselves whether they have come up with an acceptable solution.

The following sample dialogue shows how a fifth-grade teacher taught her learners to use IDEAL.

◆   ◆   ◆

Teacher:	Today we're going to think a little more about the greenhouse problem. Remember what we talked about yesterday. The PTA is giving us money to build a greenhouse, but we have a problem about how we can get the flowers and vegetable plants to grow inside a house when they're supposed to grow outside.
Student 1:	First the letter **I.** You identify the problem.
Teacher:	And what do we do when we identify a problem?
Student 2:	We read about the problem and try to figure out what we're supposed to answer or solve.
Teacher:	OK. I'll try to identify one of the problems with the greenhouse and then ask one of you to do the same. One of the problems I see is how the plants will get the food they'll need. Anybody else?
Student 3:	I see a problem: What about when it gets cold?
Teacher:	So what's the problem?
Student 3:	Well, it's how do you make sure they have the right temperature to live?
Teacher:	Good! What was another thing we talked about when you think about problems?
Student 4:	Letter **D?** You define any words you don't understand in the problem.
Teacher:	Why is this important?
Student 4:	Well, you want to make sure you really understand the problem. Sometimes we use words and think we know what they mean, but we really don't. So **D** reminds us to make sure we really know what we mean when we say something.
Teacher:	Good. I'll give you an example, then you give me one. What is a "greenhouse"? Are we all agreed on this?
Student 5:	And "right temperature." What's that mean?
Teacher:	Great. Now what's the third thing we do when we think about solving a problem?

◆   ◆   ◆

Teachers who incorporate cognitive strategies into their lessons have two broad goals: They enhance (1) learner acquisition of knowledge (declarative, procedural, metacognitive), and (2) the cognitive processes (reception, availability, activation) used by their learners. Teachers increase the likelihood of achieving these two goals when they teach cognitive learning strategies (mnemonics, elaboration/organization, comprehension monitoring, and problem solving) to their students.

PROJECT-BASED LEARNING

Phyllis Blumenfeld and others (Blumenfeld et al., 1991; Diffily & Sassman, 2002) propose that teachers who build their instruction around projects provide learners with an environment ideally suited for self-directed inquiry. But they must do this in ways that assure learners that their success depends on factors they control. **Project-based learning** (1) communicates to learners the importance of the learning process and not just the product, (2) helps them set goals, and (3) uses instructional groupings to elicit the cooperation of others in completing the project.

Like problem-based learning, project-based learning makes extensive use of theories of intrinsic motivation to maintain high levels of student engagement and enthusiasm (Affini, 1996; Deci, Vallerand, Pelletier, & Ryan, 1991). However, unlike problem-based learning, project-based learning is targeted toward an achievable end product that is visualized before the process is begun. First, let's examine project-based learning and see how it promotes self-directed inquiry through intrinsic motivation, and then how it guides the inquiry process and the end product.

The Role of Tasks in Project-Based Learning

Project-based learning assigns a critical role in the development of intrinsic motivation to the nature of the classroom learning task. It asks the question, "What kinds of tasks are most likely to induce and support learner interest, effort, and persistence?" Project-based learning advocates the use of projects as the most appropriate vehicles for engaging learners, since they can be structured around student interests. Projects have two essential components: (1) They are built around a central question that serves to organize and energize classroom activities, and (2) they require a product or outcome to answer the question successfully. Project-based learning is different from problem-based learning, however, in that it usually requires the development of a tangible outcome to determine if the end product has been achieved (e.g., a model, poster, demonstration, video, reenactment, or physical construction, such as science exhibit or collaborative school greenhouse or garden), which because of its complexity often involves the participation of others. Both project- and problem-based learning, however, share the same basic inquiry skills of exploration, discovery, and questioning.

Projects may be built around issues of current societal concern or questions of more historical or intellectual interest. Good projects have these critical characteristics:

- They are of extended duration (require several weeks to complete).
- They link several disciplines (e.g., involve math, reading, writing skills).
- The focus is on process as well as product.
- They involve the teacher as coach and often require small-group collaboration to complete.

They should also (1) present a real-world, authentic challenge, (2) allow for some learner choice and control, (3) be doable—capable of being carried out within the time and resource limitations of the student and classroom, (4) require some level of collaboration, and (5) produce a tangible product. Let's look more closely at each of these characteristics.

Present a Challenge. Your projects will meet this important ingredient when they offer learners an authentic, sometimes novel, and always challenging question to investigate, resolve, and report on. This is in contrast to worksheets, exercise books, end-of-chapter question answering, and other routine tasks, which may take up most of learners' academic time.

Allow for Learner Choice and Control.   Effective projects allow learners options regarding modes of investigation (reading, interviewing, observing, controlled experimentation), styles of reporting (written reports, audiotapes or videotapes, visual displays), solutions to problems, or types of products or artifacts to develop.

Be Doable.   Learners will persevere and expend high amounts of effort if they see results. Similarly, they are more likely to believe they can see a project through to a successful conclusion if it is time limited, requires readily available resources, and includes points along the way where they can receive positive feedback, make revisions, and generate further products.

Require Collaboration.   Intrinsic motivation is nurtured in classrooms that allow learners to meet their social needs. This theory points out how learners acquire beliefs about their own capabilities from observing others. Projects that cannot be completed unless a small group of learners adopt different but essential roles are ideal vehicles for incorporating the principles of these motivational theories.

Result in a Concrete Product.   Products that give learners concrete goals to work toward are more likely to sustain intrinsic motivation. Moreover, products and the process involved in producing them allow for performance-based assessment (Borich & Tombari, 2004). This type of assessment allows learners to see the connection between what they do in class and what they have produced. This provides a greater sense of control over their grade, and it better meets their needs for autonomy than grades based on paper and pencil tests alone.

The Role of the Learner in Project-Based Learning

Educators have urged school reforms that engage learners in "hands-on" learning activities as the best way to develop self-directed learning (Viadero, 2003). Project-based learning recognizes that learners will acquire important knowledge and skills from projects only if they (1) attribute their success to effort, (2) believe they can accomplish the goals of the project, and (3) perceive themselves as competent. Project-based learning also recognizes that learners are more likely to perceive themselves as competent if they have the prior knowledge, prerequisite skills, and learning strategies necessary for completing the projects before they begin.

The Role of the Teacher in Project-Based Learning

Students who fail to see the purpose or personal relevance of class activities perform more poorly than those who do see the connections between classwork and their lives. Helping learners take ownership of their learning and allowing them some voice in class activities as well as their evaluation is often suggested as an important part of increasing motivation and thus decreasing apathy. This appears to hold true across cultural and linguistic lines, as well as across academic disciplines (Anderman & Maehr, 1994; Anderman & Midgley, 1998; Ngeow, 1998).

Project-based learning recognizes that the teacher is the last piece in the intrinsic motivational puzzle. The teacher's unique role in project-based learning is that of a supporter of the learner's or group's chosen end product. Consequently, proponents of project-based learning urge teachers to support their learners' interest, effort, and achievement through the following:

- Avoid statements implying innate ability is all that is required to complete a project.
- Focus learners' attention both on the process of completing the project and on the end product.
- Make encouraging statements to learners that promote commitment.

See *In Practice: Focus on Project-Based Learning.*

IN PRACTICE

Focus on Project-Based Learning

Teachers who practice project-based learning, or build their instructional programs around projects, provide learners with an environment ideally suited to the nurturing of motivation (Blumenfeld et al., 1991; Diffily & Sassman, 2002). Cognitive psychologists have proposed three distinct yet overlapping theories of academic motivation: attribution theory, self-efficacy theory, and goal theory. Whether your perspective on motivation leans toward attribution theory, self-efficacy theory, goal theory, or all three, project-based learning offers some solutions to the age-old problem of how to give energy and direction to the classroom behavior of learners.

Attribution Theory

Each of us has succeeded at some endeavors and failed at others. Think about one of your more recent successes or failures. Were you successful or unsuccessful because of the amount of effort that you exerted, your natural ability, luck, or some combination of these? Another way to ask this question is: Do you attribute your success to internal forces, such as effort or ability, or to external forces, such as luck or the difficulty of the task?

Weiner (1986), a leading proponent of attribution theory, believes that people naturally seek to understand why they succeed or fail. Students, for example, when asked to explain why they received a certain grade, typically refer to their hard work or effort, innate ability, an easy or hard test, or luck. These causes originate either within the learner (effort, ability) or outside the learner (luck, task). A cause originating within the learner is said to have an internal locus of causality; one originating outside the learner has an external locus of causality.

Motivational theorists such as Weiner assert that only when learners attribute their success to effort are they likely to exert genuine effort to complete a project or study for a test. If learners attribute their success or failure to ability, luck, or task difficulty—all of which are out of their control—they believe that nothing they can do will improve their situation. Thus, how a student thinks about or interprets success or failure, and not the experience of the outcome itself, determines the energy and direction of her or his efforts.

Self-Efficacy Theory

Self-efficacy theory holds that academic motivation hinges on learners' beliefs that they can succeed at school tasks. Bandura (1986), the originator of self-efficacy theory, has defined self-efficacy as people's judgments of their capabilities to organize and execute courses of actions required to attain desired outcomes. In other words, students are more likely to begin, persist at, and master tasks that they think they are good at. This judgment is what is meant by self-efficacy.

Judgments about self-efficacy differ from attributions. Attributions are perceived causes of success or failure. They influence expectations and behavior. They are one type of information that learners use when making a judgment about self-efficacy. If a learner believes that success in calculus is due to being born with mathematical ability, and believes that she possesses little of such ability, she will have low self-efficacy for calculus.

Bandura has identified several other sources of information that learners use to make judgments about self-efficacy. One is verbal persuasion through which the teacher expresses faith and confidence to learners that they can be successful. Another is seeing peers succeed at a particular task. If a learner sees someone whom he likes and admires receive high marks or praise from a teacher for solving a difficult geometry theorem, he is more likely to believe that he can do likewise.

But the most important piece of information used by learners when making self-efficacy judgments is past experiences of success or failure with a particular task. The learner who has received

(continued)

high marks for her three previous essays will have higher self-efficacy for the next writing project than the learner who consistently earns low grades. Thus, a student weighs a variety of information in addition to attributions when coming to a judgment of self-efficacy for a particular subject. Once made, the judgment directly affects the learner's level of effort and persistence as well as the level of achievement obtained.

Goal Theory

Goal theory, the third and most recent perspective on motivation, focuses on learners' academic goal orientation as a source of motivation. Dweck and Reppucci's (1973) work with fifth-grade math learners showed that uncontrollable failure created in learners' minds a disposition of helplessness that caused them to make no effort to solve easy problems to which they had already given correct answers. In the late 1970s Diener and Dweck (1980) began to investigate whether the goals for learning set by children had a more or less pronounced effect on the development of learned helplessness. They administered psychological tests to groups of children to determine their academic goal orientation. They found that children generally fall into two goal groups with regard to interest in learning. One group, called the *task-focused group,* focused on developing academic competence and improving their skills for purely intrinsic reasons. The other group, called the *ability-focused group,* engaged in learning tasks with the goal of "showing off their ability, outperforming others, and gaining external rewards like praise and good grades." Their study shows that the two categories of goals are distinct and result in dramatically different degrees of academic motivation.

Much of the research on goal theory has shown that, in comparison to ability-oriented learners, students who adopt task-focused or mastery goals are more likely to achieve in school, make more use of cognitive strategies when problem solving, and expend substantial mental effort searching their memories and relating new learning to prior learning. Researchers have documented that as children proceed through the elementary school grades, they increasingly believe that their ability sets a limit on what they can learn (Ames, 1990). And certain classroom activities, such as ability grouping, exacerbate this viewpoint. Thus, goal theory places special emphasis on classroom practices that can enhance a student's personal goal beliefs. These goal beliefs can affect a broad range of student motivational behaviors including persistence, use of learning strategies, choices, and preferences.

Much of the research on goal theory has shown that, in comparison to ability-oriented learners, students who adopt task-focused or mastery goals are more likely to achieve in school, make more use of cognitive strategies when problem solving, and expend substantial mental effort searching their memories and relating new learning to prior learning.

PROMOTING THE GOALS OF SELF-DIRECTED LEARNING IN THE CULTURALLY DIVERSE CLASSROOM

The work of Affini (1996), Bowers and Flinders (1991), Lubliner and Palincsar (2001), and Palincsar and Brown (1989) have underscored two important dimensions of the teacher's role in modifying classroom dialogue to foster the goals of self-directed learning in the culturally diverse classroom. One of these is that of teacher mediation—on-the-spot adjustments made by the teacher to extend or refocus a student response to move the learner to the next rung of the learning ladder. The second dimension is mental modeling—the active demonstration of strategies by which students can better learn and retain the content taught.

These results have been applied to the culturally diverse classroom through various forms of social interaction that encourage students to construct their own meanings and interpretations and revise and extend them under the guidance of the teacher. As we have seen, among the strategies for promoting the concept of teacher mediation are reciprocal teaching (Lubliner & Palincsar, 2001; Rosenshine & Meister, 1994) and problem- and project-based learning (Baden & Mayor, 2004; Blumenfeld et al., 1991). With each of these strategies, the teacher elicits student responses at the student's current level of understanding based on personal experiences with assumptions about, and predictions from, the content to be taught.

Other strategies that can help promote self-directed instruction in a culturally diverse classroom are:

1. Pose challenging problems. Focus the problem so the learner must make key decisions about what is important for a solution. This feeling of responsibility and control over the inquiry is important if the learner is to become engaged and see the learning as truly self-directed.

2. Choose learning activities that allow freedom of choice and include interests. By letting students pursue and investigate some topics of their own, choosing and constructing their own meanings and interpretations, you will be making them participants in the design of their own learning.

3. Plan instruction around group activities during self-directed instruction. This is when learners are the most capable of picking up ideas from others and creating from them new and unusual variations that can be applied during self-directed learning.

4. Include real-life problems that require problem solving. Let learners become actual investigators in solving real-world dilemmas. This will force them to place newly acquired knowledge and understandings in a practical perspective and to increase the problem-solving challenge.

5. In testing, draw out knowledge and understanding using content that is compatible with their culture and culturally familiar to them. Use assessments that make the student go beyond knowing and remembering facts by asking your learners to explain, analyze, compare, contrast, hypothesize, infer, adopt, and justify as a means of indicating they can construct in their own words the meaning of what you are teaching.

With these and similar self-directed approaches to learning, you will be able to support the participation of all your learners in the dialogue of the classroom. Your aim should be to engage as many students as possible in the learning process by providing reactions to student responses that are in their zones of maximum response opportunity. This can be accomplished by the following:

1. Adjust the flow and complexity of content to meet individual learner needs.
2. Offer ample opportunity for all students to participate in the dialogue from their perspective (Stipek, 2002).
3. Provide cognitive strategies with which they can better learn and remember the content taught.

Finally, ask yourself these questions to check on the success of your efforts:

- Has my instruction been focused within my learners' zones of maximum response opportunity? Are learners bored because they have already mastered these skills, or are they frustrated because the skills are beyond what they can be expected to learn?
- Has my instruction been too solitary? Have I met my learners' social learning needs by allowing for sufficient conversation, public reasoning, shared problem solving, and cooperative projects that reproduce the culture in which they spend the most time?
- Have I been expecting learners to acquire knowledge that is incompatible with their cultures? Do I use instructional methods that are culturally unfamiliar, irrelevant, or contradictory?

SUMMING UP

This chapter introduced you to strategies for self-directed learning. Its key terms and main points were:

Self-Directed Learning

1. Self-directed learning is an approach to teaching and learning that actively engages students in the learning process for the purpose of acquiring outcomes at higher levels of cognitive complexity.

2. Self-directed learning involves the following sequence of activities:
   - Provide information about when and how to use mental strategies for learning.
   - Illustrate how the strategies are to be used in the context of real problems.
   - Provide students the opportunity to restructure content in terms of their own ways of thinking and prior understandings.
   - Gradually shift the responsibility for learning to students through activities (exercises, dialogues, discussions) that engage them in increasingly complex patterns of thought.

Metacognition

3. Metacognition is a strategy for self-directed learning that assists learners in internalizing, understanding, and recalling the content to be learned.

4. Metacognitive strategies include self-interrogation, self-checking, self-monitoring, and techniques for classifying and recalling content, called *mnemonics*.

5. Metacognitive strategies are taught through mental modeling in which learners are "walked through" the process of attaining a correct solution. Mental modeling includes:
   - Illustrating for students the reasoning involved
   - Making them conscious of it
   - Focusing learners on the application of the reasoning illustrated

6. Teacher mediation is the teacher's on-the-spot adjustment of content flow rate and complexity to accommodate the individual learning needs of the student.

7. The role of teacher mediation is to adjust the instructional dialogue as needed to help learners restructure what they are learning according to each learner's unique abilities, learning history, and personal experiences.

Zone of Maximum Response Opportunity

8. A zone of maximum response opportunity represents the level of content difficulty and behavioral complexity from which the learner can most benefit at the moment a response is given.

9. The zone of maximum response opportunity is reached through a classroom dialogue in which the teacher provides reactions to student responses that activate the unique learning history, specialized ability, and personal experience of each learner. From these unique characteristics, learners can acquire individual meanings and interpretations of the content.

Functional Errors

10. Functional errors are incorrect or partially correct answers made by the learner that can enhance the meaning and understanding of content and provide a logical stepping-stone for climbing onto the next rung of the learning ladder.

Reciprocal Teaching

11. Reciprocal teaching provides opportunities to explore the content to be learned via group discussion.

12. Reciprocal teaching involves a type of classroom dialogue in which the teacher expects students to make predictions, ask questions, summarize, and clarify when learning from text.

13. Reciprocal teaching involves a sequence of activities that include the following:
    - Generate predictions about the content to be learned from the text in the initial class discussion.
    - Read and/or listen to a portion of the text.
    - Choose a discussion leader who asks other students questions about the text, who then respond with questions of their own.
    - The discussion leader summarizes the text, and the teacher invites other students to comment or elaborate.
    - The teacher clarifies any unresolved questions and rereads portions of text for greater clarity, if needed.

14. The teacher's role during reciprocal teaching is to gradually shift the responsibility for learning to the students by reducing the amount of explaining, explicitness of cues, and prompting that may have marked earlier portions of the lesson.

15. During reciprocal teaching, the teacher's role is to do the following:
    - Jointly share the responsibility for learning with the students.
    - Initially assume responsibility for modeling how to make a prediction, how to ask a question, how to summarize, and how to clarify, but then transfer responsibility to students for demonstrating use of these strategies.

- Encourage all students to participate in the classroom dialogue by prompting, providing additional information, and/or altering the response demand on students.
- Monitor student comprehension and adjust the rate and complexity of information as needed.

Social Dialogue Versus Class Discussion

16. In self-directed learning, the teacher scaffolds—builds the dialogue within a discussion step by step—each time increasing the challenge to the learner to think independently of earlier constructions. Scaffolding must occur to the appropriate degree for each learner response to keep the challenge within the learner's zone of maximum response opportunity.

17. During self-directed learning, inner (private) speech helps the learner elaborate and extend the content in ways unique to the individual. As responsibility for learning beyond the text gradually shifts to the learner, the learner's inner-speech ability increases, modeling the same reasoning and using similar questions, prompts, and cues used by the teacher at an earlier stage.

Sample Dialogues of Self-Directed Learning

18. The following are steps for teaching self-directed inquiry to individual learners:

- Provide a new learning task and observe how the student approaches it.
- Ask the student to explain how he or she would learn the content (e.g., preparing for an exam).
- Describe and model a more effective procedure for organizing and learning the content (e.g., using study questions, notes, or highlighting key features in the text).
- Provide another, similar task on which the student can practice the strategies provided.
- Model self-questioning behavior during the task to ensure the learner follows the strategies

correctly (e.g., "Did I underline the key words?").
- Provide other opportunities for the student to practice, decreasing your role as a monitor.
- Check the result by questioning for comprehension and use of the strategies taught.

Other Cognitive Strategies

19. Other cognitive strategies can be helpful for organizing and remembering new material during self-directed learning:

- Mnemonics
- Elaboration/organization (note taking)
- Comprehension monitoring
- Problem solving

Problem-Based Learning

20. Problem-based learning is an approach to learning that organizes instructional tasks around loosely structured or ill-defined problems that learners solve by using knowledge and skills from several disciplines.

Project-Based Learning

21. Project-based learning is an approach to learning that promotes intrinsic motivation by organizing instruction around tasks most likely to induce and support learner interest, effort, and persistence.

Promoting the Goals of Self-Directed Learning in the Culturally Diverse Classroom

22. Classroom dialogue can be modified to foster the goals of self-directed learning in a culturally diverse classroom by:

- Adjusting the flow and complexity of content
- Offering ample opportunity for all to participate
- Teaching cognitive strategies

KEY TERMS

Activity structure, 353
Cognitive learning strategy, 354
Declarative knowledge, 352
Functional errors, 344
Inner speech, 349
Mental modeling, 339
Metacognition, 339

Problem-based learning, 357
Procedural knowledge, 352
Project-based learning, 359
Reciprocal teaching, 346
Teacher-mediated learning, 340
Zone of maximum response opportunity, 340

DISCUSSION AND PRACTICE QUESTIONS

Questions marked with an asterisk are answered in appendix B. See also the Companion Website for this text at *www.prenhall.com/borich* for more assessment options.

*1. Identify two purposes for engaging your students in self-directed learning. In which content areas that you will be teaching will these purposes most apply?

*2. What are four unique teaching functions associated with self-directed learning? Which order do you think might be most important for their success?

*3. What is metacognition? What can metacognitive strategies accomplish in your classroom?

*4. During a demonstration, what specific outcomes can mental modeling help your students acquire?

*5. What is your role during teacher-mediated learning? How would this role differ from teacher lecture or student recitation?

*6. In your own words, describe the zone of maximum response opportunity. Then, using the natural language of the classroom, write a short teacher–student dialogue that hits the zone of maximum response opportunity.

7. Give an example of a student response–teacher reaction that illustrates the concept of functional failure. Explain how in your example your reaction would promote further learning.

*8. Explain the sequence of activities that would normally occur during reciprocal teaching.

*9. What should be your most important goal in promoting classroom dialogue during self-directed learning?

*10. What is the purpose of inner (private) speech during self-directed learning? Do you recall ever having used inner speech to increase your learning? In what setting?

*11. Describe the difference between declarative knowledge and procedural knowledge. Provide an example of each.

*12. What steps would you follow to teach self-directed learning skills to an individual learner? What student behavior might make you decide to take the extra time to teach these skills?

FIELD EXPERIENCE ACTIVITIES

*1. What are the three stages of mental modeling? Give an example of each stage using subject-matter content that you will be teaching.

2. Provide an example of a verbal marker in your content area that would alert learners that you are about to begin mental modeling.

*3. What is the purpose of reciprocal teaching? With what content or during which instructional activities would you most likely use reciprocal teaching in your classroom?

4. Create a brief excerpt from a classroom dialogue to show what a scaffolded dialogue would look like in your teaching area. Be sure to choose an example that is at your learner's current level of understanding and from which the learner can benefit based on past learning.

5. Think of an example of an activity structure in your subject area or grade level that varies task demand. How would you vary the task for those learners unable to respond to the increase in complexity?

*6. Describe four cognitive strategies for organizing and remembering new material. Considering your subject matter or grade level, which of these do you think you would find most useful?

DIGITAL PORTFOLIO ACTIVITIES

The following digital portfolio activities relate to INTASC principles 2, 4, and 6.

1. In Field Experience Activity 4 you were asked to prepare a brief excerpt from a classroom dialogue that represented what a scaffolded dialogue would be like in your teaching area. Recall that a scaffolded dialogue uses questions, prompts, and hints after each student response to direct the level of discourse to the learner's current level of understanding, called the *zone of maximum response opportunity,* where the student can learn and benefit from his or her own responses. Check to see if your dialogue for Field Experience Activity 4 accomplishes this to your satisfaction. If not, revise it and

place it in your digital portfolio in a folder titled *Self-Directed Learning*. Your dialogue will be an important reminder of the gentle interplay between teacher and student questioning that is required to move student responses up the learning ladder.

2. Field Experience Activity 3 asks you to identify the purpose of reciprocal teaching and the lesson content or topics in your teaching area that might provide a desirable context for reciprocal teaching. Take this knowledge of reciprocal teaching and, following the example in the chapter, prepare a brief classroom dialogue in your subject area that would illustrate your understanding of how to apply reciprocal teaching techniques in your classroom. Place your dialogue in your digital portfolio *Self-Directed Learning* folder as an example of your skill at applying this important concept.

CLASSROOM OBSERVATION ACTIVITIES

The following classroom observation activities relate to INTASC principles 4 and 6.

1. Mental models and strategies help students to use the correct reasoning process to arrive at a solution, make the learner conscious of the steps used, and provide help in applying the steps to independently arrive at answers in similar circumstances. These steps often are accomplished with verbal markers, such as "Now I will show you . . . ," "Think about the steps I'm going through . . . ," or "Listen to how I think through this. . . ." On the Companion Website for this chapter at *www.prenhall.com/borich* you will find a record for *Observing Mental Models and Strategies* and *A Classroom Dialogue of Ms. Brokaw's Literature Class*. Using the record for *Observing Mental Models and Strategies*, which identifies the three steps in applying mental modeling in the classroom, see if you can find the verbal phrases used by Ms. Brokaw during the course of her lesson that represent any or all of these three steps. Place the *Observing Mental Models and Strategies* record in your digital portfolio *Self-Directed Learning* folder for use in future observations.

2. An important aspect of self-directed learning is the teacher's use of examples and illustrations to demonstrate to learners how various cognitive strategies for learning, such as metacognition and mental modeling, can be applied. On the Companion Website for this chapter you will find a record for *Observing Examples and Illustrations for Self-Directed Learning* and *A Classroom Dialogue of Ms. Raskin's Computer Literacy Class*. With it record both the types and numbers of examples and illustrations observed in Ms. Raskin's classroom and note the frequency in which they are visual and orally delivered. Place this record in your digital portfolio *Self-Directed Learning* folder for use in future observations.

CHAPTER CASE HISTORY AND PRAXIS TEST PREPARATION

DIRECTIONS: The following case history pertains to chapter 10 content. After reading the case history, answer the short-answer question that follows and consult appendix D to find different levels of scored student responses and the rubric used to determine the quality of each response. You also have the opportunity to submit your responses online to receive feedback by visiting the *Case History* module for this chapter on the Companion Website, where you will also find additional questions pertaining to Praxis test content.

Case History

Mrs. Henson's culturally diverse fifth-grade class has just read a section in their science books about discoveries that challenged long-held ideas. Two of these long-held ideas were the concept of a flat earth and an earth-centered planetary system. The following is an excerpt from the follow-up discussion:

◆　◆　◆

Mrs. Henson:	Why the big smile, Nate? Was there something in our chapter that tickled your funny bone?
Nate:	Well, it's just pretty weird—thinking of all those tough sailors, making it through storms without a blink, but worrying all the time that they might slip off the edge of the world. I mean, that's pretty dumb, don't you think?

Mrs. Henson:	I don't know. Almost everyone else at the time thought so, too. Did you ever think that centuries from now, some other "Nate" will be sitting in another classroom laughing at us for believing in an idea that everyone else thinks is wrong?
Nate:	I never thought of it that way. You mean, even though we know so much today, we might still have some things completely wrong?
Mrs. Henson:	Let's think about that, class, and make some predictions. How about discussing this topic with the others at your table for a few minutes. What will they be laughing about in classrooms a couple of centuries from now? What beliefs that everyone accepts as truth today do you think will be proved false, and why?
	Mrs. Henson walks around the room as students discuss the possibilities among themselves. She pauses briefly at several tables, sometimes just to listen, sometimes giving encouragement, such as "I never would have thought of that," or "I think you're right on with that one." When she is sure that each table has at least one good suggestion, she reconvenes the full class discussion.
Mrs. Henson:	Loretta, your group had a very interesting idea. Want to share it with us?
Loretta:	Well, you know how everyone is telling us to wash our hands before we eat, or to use this or that detergent or cleaner because it kills germs. Well, we predicted that people in the future will learn that germs are really good for us.
Mrs. Henson:	But what I found most interesting as I listened to your group's conversation was the reasoning behind your prediction. Can you explain a little about that, Freeman?
Freeman:	It's back to the future, I guess. My grandma, she grew up in the country, and her daddy used to say, when her mama fussed at the little ones for putting everything in their mouths, "You got to eat a bushel of dirt in your life, Addie, so don't be too hard on the little ones." According to my grandma, she and her sisters didn't have near the colds that we do now.
Sylvester:	My uncle always says the same thing, too. "A few germs is good for you," he says.
Tiffany:	I don't agree. Maybe the reason your relatives didn't get as sick was 'cause they lived in the country, and they didn't come in contact with as many sick people as we do in the cities now.
Mrs. Henson:	So you think the "germs are good for you" theory fails to consider other changes, or variables as scientists call them.
Sylvester:	No way. My uncle lived in the city, in a small apartment with six brothers and sisters.
Mrs. Henson:	Besides the wisdom of your elders, what other explanations or reasons do you have for this idea?
Loretta:	I guess we figured that it was something like too much of a good thing. Without any germs, we're not used to them, kind of like an only child who never has to share toys. When we meet up with germs after hardly ever having had them before, we're like my cousin when she has to share. She freaks outs and so do our bodies.
Freeman:	And we really had some cool ideas about other things we could do with germs. We domesticated horses. Why not germs? Germs are so small and multiply so rapidly, we could get them to deliver some good things to our bodies, kind of like luggage that just comes along with us. Maybe things that would clear our arteries or protect us from cancer?
Mrs. Henson:	I'm really impressed with your group. Not only did you come up with a prediction and an explanation for it, but you also took it to the next level and created further uses for your idea. Very good work. Now, Carmen, tell us what your group chose.
Carmen:	Old age. It doesn't have to happen.
Mrs. Henson:	Now you have my undivided attention. (Class laughs.)

Short-Answer Question

This section presents a sample Praxis short-answer question. In appendix D you will find sample responses along with the standards used in scoring these responses.

DIRECTIONS: The following question requires you to write a short answer. Base your answer on your knowl-edge of principles of learning and teaching from chapter 10. Be sure to answer all parts of the question.

1. On-the-spot adjustments to content flow and complexity that a teacher makes to accommodate individual learning needs are called *teacher mediation*. In such cases the teacher uses

interactive dialogue to help learners construct their own meanings from the content, which in turn aid in the retention and generalization of the

reasoning process to other contexts. Name and discuss at least two ways in which Mrs. Henson effectively used teacher mediation.

Discrete Multiple-Choice Questions

DIRECTIONS: Each of the multiple-choice questions that follow is based on Praxis-related pedagogical knowledge in chapter 10. Select the answer that is best in each case and compare your results with those in appendix D. See also the Companion Website for this text at: *www.prenhall.com/borich* for more assessment options.

1. The cognitive learning strategy that uses jingles or trigger sentences, narrative chaining, number rhymes or peg words, and chunking is termed
   a. Elaboration
   b. Mnemonics
   c. Comprehension monitoring
   d. Problem solving

DIRECTIONS: Questions 2 and 3 ask you to analyze a teacher's goal and the actions that are intended to lead to the achievement of that goal. Decide whether the teacher's action makes it likely or unlikely that the goal will be achieved. Then select the best reason that the teacher's action is likely or unlikely to lead to the achievement of the goal.

2. *Goal:* To help students acquire reasoning, critical thinking, and problem-solving skills required in today's complex world.

   Action: Teacher instructs the entire class to brainstorm several current controversial issues. She then has small groups draw for a topic, do research to become experts, and debate the pros and cons of their controversial issue. This teacher's action makes the goal:
   a. *Likely,* because the teacher chooses controversial subjects that will arouse and keep the students' interest and motivation. The small-group work also enhances their social skills.
   b. *Likely,* because the teacher is using self-directed learning strategies to attack real-world problems. The teacher has also shifted the responsibility for learning to the students when they debate and agree on the pros and cons of their issue.
   c. *Unlikely,* because dealing with controversial issues usually produces emotional responses in which reasoning and critical thinking can easily be overpowered by feelings.
   d. *Unlikely,* because the teacher needs to assert more control of the content to ensure that

proper thinking patterns are being developed. The goals and content of the subject matter cannot be ignored.

3. *Goal:* To keep students in a culturally diverse classroom intrinsically motivated during a project-based learning activity.

   Action: Each student will work independently on a science project assigned by the teacher. Students must get teacher approval for key elements of design and methods of collecting and displaying data.

   This teacher's action makes the goal:
   a. *Likely,* because working independently allows the student to be in control. He or she does not need to follow a text or compromise with others in the group.
   b. *Likely,* because the teacher's expertise will help the student avoid errors that would lead to frustration and wasted time.
   c. *Unlikely,* because intrinsically motivated project-based learning thrives on student self-direction, collaboration with peers, and freedom of choice involving topics and methods of inquiry.
   d. *Unlikely,* because projects are often completed with the assistance of parents or other students, and the competitive aspects of science projects can cause anxiety that can generalize to other subjects.

4. If your goal were to teach metacognitive skills to assist learners to reflect on their thinking, which of the following student activities would most directly promote your objective?
   a. Self-interrogation
   b. Reviewing previously learned content
   c. Pursuing an inquiry task
   d. Sharing what was learned with other learners

5. To teach self-directed inquiry to individual learners, which of the following would be the *least* effective?
   a. Model the process by which meaning and understanding can be derived.
   b. Use questions, prompts, and cues to shift the responsibility for learning to the student.
   c. Provide the steps to follow to achieve a satisfactory solution.
   d. Monitor student responses for continued understanding.

Chapter
11

Cooperative Learning and the Collaborative Process

This chapter will help you answer the following questions and meet the following INTASC principles for effective teaching:

1. How do I plan a cooperative learning activity?
2. What roles can I assign to group members?
3. What are some of the ways I can reward good group performance?
4. What are some collaborative skills I can teach my learners?
5. How can I promote the goals of cooperative learning in the culturally diverse classroom?

INTASC 1: The teacher understands the central concepts, tools of inquiry, and structures of the discipline(s) he or she teaches and can create learning experiences that make these aspects of subject matter meaningful for students.

INTASC 2: The teacher understands how children learn and develop, and can provide learning opportunities that support their intellectual, social, and personal development.

INTASC 4: The teacher understands and uses a variety of instructional strategies to encourage students' development of critical thinking, problem solving, and performance skills.

INTASC 5: The teacher uses an understanding of individual and group motivation and behavior to create a learning environment that encourages positive social interaction, active engagement in learning, and self-motivation.

INTASC 6: The teacher uses knowledge of effective verbal, nonverbal, and media communication techniques to foster active inquiry, collaboration, and supportive interaction in the classroom.

In chapter 10 you saw how self-directed learning could promote higher forms of thinking with the aid of metacognitive strategies. In this chapter, you will see how these same outcomes can be extended and reinforced through various forms of peer collaboration. You will learn how self-directed and cooperative learning share the complementary objectives of engaging students in the learning process and promoting higher thought processes and more authentic behaviors required in the world of work, family, and community.

OUTCOMES OF COOPERATION

What good are critical thinking, reasoning, and problem-solving skills if your learners cannot apply them in interaction with others? Cooperative learning activities instill in learners important behaviors that prepare them to reason and perform in an adult world (Jacobs, Power, & Loh, 2002; Johnson & Johnson, 1999; Marzano, Pickering, & Pollock, 2001). Let's consider some of these behaviors.

Attitudes and Values

Adult learners form their attitudes and values from social interaction. Although we learn much about the world from books, magazines, newspapers, and audiovisual media, most of our attitudes and values are formed by discussing what we know or think with others. In this manner we exchange our information and knowledge with that of others who have acquired their knowledge in different ways. This exchange shapes our views and perspectives. It turns cold, lifeless facts into feelings, and then to attitudes and values that guide our behavior over longer periods of time.

Our attitudes and values are among the most important outcomes of schooling, because they alone provide the framework for guiding our actions outside the classroom, where there may be no formal sources of knowledge to fall back on. Cooperative learning is important in helping learners acquire from the curriculum the basic cooperative attitudes and values they need to think independently inside and outside of your classroom.

Prosocial Behavior

During close and meaningful encounters among family members, models of **prosocial behavior** are communicated. Children learn right from wrong implicitly through their actions and the actions of others that come to the attention of adult family members. These adults are quick to point out the effects of these actions on family, friends, and the community.

With the decreasing presence of adults in the homes of working parents, the classroom becomes an important vehicle for bolstering home and community values. Cooperative learning brings learners together in adultlike settings which, when carefully planned and executed, can provide appropriate models of social behavior (Stevens & Slavin, 1995). As a teacher, one of your most important roles will be to promote and model positive social interactions and relationships within your classroom (Abruscato, 1994; Kottler & Zehm, 2000).

Alternative Perspectives and Viewpoints

It is no secret that we form our attitudes and values by confronting viewpoints contrary to our own. Our likes and dislikes come from our exposure to alternatives we could not have thought of on our own, given the limitations of our immediate context and experience. These alternatives—some of which we adopt, some we modify, and some we reject—are the raw material from which we form our own attitudes and values.

Confronted with these alternatives, we are forced into an objectivity necessary for thinking critically, reasoning, and problem solving. In other words, we become less self-centered. Depending on the merits of what we see and hear, we grow more open to exchanging our feelings and beliefs with those of others. This active exchange of viewpoints and the tension it sometimes creates within us form the catalyst for our growth. Cooperative learning provides the context or meeting ground where many different viewpoints can be orchestrated, from which we form more articulate attitudes and values of our own.

Integrated Identity

One of the most noticeable outcomes of social interaction is its effect on how we develop our personalities and learn who we are. Social interaction over long periods forces us to see ourselves—our attitudes, values, and abilities—in many different circumstances. The main result is that inconsistencies and contradictions in who we are—or think we are—cannot be hidden, as might be the case in a single interaction or small number of social interactions.

If we say and think one way in one situation, and say and think another way in another situation, we cannot help but notice our own inconsistency and wonder why it exists. We attempt to resolve such contradictions, to clarify what we really believe, and to believe what we really say. Our personality becomes more coherent and integrated and is perceived by others as a more forceful and confident projection of our thoughts and feelings. Over time, repeated social interactions reduce the contradictions until our views become singular and consistent and we achieve an integrated identity. Cooperative learning can be the start of stripping away the irrelevant, overly dramatic, and superficial appendages that mask our deepest thoughts and feelings. Thus we begin to gain an integrated sense of self.

Higher Thought Processes

If all of the preceding benefits of cooperative learning were not enough, the fact that it has been linked to increases in the academic achievement of learners at all ability levels is

Figure 11.1 Outcomes of cooperative learning.

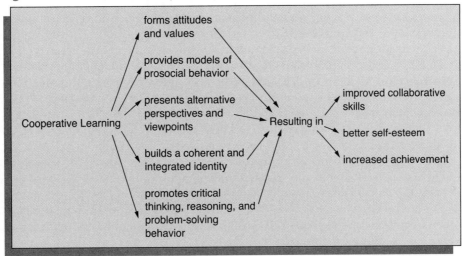

another reason for its use (Stevens & Slavin, 1995). Simply exploring or telling may not be the most effective way of helping students achieve (Bransford et al., 2000). Cooperative learning actively engages the student in the learning process and seeks to improve the critical thinking, reasoning, and problem-solving skills of the learner (Jacobs, Power, & Loh, 2002; Megnin, 1995; Webb, Trooper, & Fall, 1995). Critical thinking cannot occur outside a context of attitudes and values, prosocial behavior, alternative perspectives, and an integrated identity. But, together with these outcomes, cooperative learning can provide the ingredients for higher thought processes and set them to work on realistic and adultlike tasks.

These higher thought processes—required for analyzing, synthesizing, and decision making—are believed to be stimulated more by interaction with others than by books and lectures, which typically are not interactive. Books and lectures may be useful for teaching knowledge, comprehension, and application, but they seldom are sufficient to bring about the private, inner speech required for thinking critically, reasoning, and problem solving in real-life settings. These behaviors require interaction with others as well as oneself to unleash the motivation required for thinking and performing in complex ways. Therefore, it should be no surprise that some of the behaviors in the *Higher-Order Thinking and Problem-Solving Checklist* in appendix C include cooperative behaviors.

The outcomes of cooperative learning we have been discussing are illustrated in Figure 11.1.

COMPONENTS OF A COOPERATIVE LEARNING ACTIVITY

In the rest of this chapter, you will see how to organize your classroom for cooperative learning. In planning a cooperative learning activity, you need to decide on the following:

- The type of interactions you will have with your students
- The type of interactions your students will have with one another
- The task and materials you will select
- Role expectations and responsibilities you will assign

Let's look at each of these more closely.

Teacher–Student Interaction

One purpose of teacher–student interaction during cooperative learning is to promote independent thinking. Much like student response–teacher reaction sequences during self-directed inquiry, exchanges between you and your learners in the cooperative class-room focus on getting learners to think for themselves, independently of the text. To accomplish this goal, you will model and collaborate with learners in much the same way as in the self-directed classroom. The goals of cooperative and self-directed inquiry are complementary.

However, the way you establish teacher–student interaction during cooperative learning is different from self-directed and large group instruction (Burbules & Bruce, 2001). In self-directed inquiry, the interaction usually is one on one, with verbal messages directed to individuals one at a time and adjusted to their zones of maximum response opportunity. In contrast, cooperative learning occurs in groups that share a common purpose and task, so you must broaden interactions to fit the zone of maximum response opportunity that is common to most group members. Your goal is to help the group become more self-reflective and aware of its own performance.

"Think about that some more," "Why not check with the reference at the learning center?" and "Be sure you've followed the guidelines I've given you," are frequent expressions you will address to a group of four or five learners assigned a specific task. Your role is to intervene at critical junctures and then to retreat, allowing the group to grapple with the new perspective or information given. In this manner, you monitor and collaborate with the group during brief but focused interventions, keeping them on course and following a productive line of reasoning.

Student–Student Interaction

Interaction among students in cooperative learning groups is intense and prolonged. Unlike self-directed inquiry, in cooperative learning groups, students gradually take responsibility for each other's learning. The effect may well be the same as in self-directed learning. And this is why cooperative and self-directed learning may be used as complementary learning strategies, with one reinforcing the skills acquired in the other.

During cooperative learning, the feedback, reinforcement, and support come from student peers in the group, as opposed to coming from you. Student–student interaction constitutes the majority of time and activity during cooperative learning, unlike the modest amount of direct student–student interaction that occurs in large group instruction. Groups of four or five, working together in the physical closeness promoted by a common task, encourage collaboration, support, and feedback from the closest, most immediate source—one's peers. An essential ingredient of cooperative learning is each learner's desire to facilitate the task performance of fellow group members.

Task Specialization and Materials

Another component of cooperative learning is the task to be learned and the materials that comprise a cooperative learning activity structure. Cooperative learning tasks are preplanned activities; they are timed, completed in stages, and placed within the context of the work of others. This promotes the sharing of ideas and/or materials and the coordination of efforts among individuals. The choice of task and supporting materials is important to promote meaningful student–student interaction.

Cooperative learning typically uses **task specialization,** or "division of labor," to break a larger task into smaller subparts on which separate groups work. Eventually, these efforts come together to create the whole, to which each member of the class has contributed. Therefore, each group may be asked to specialize, focusing its efforts on a smaller yet meaningful part of some larger end product for which the entire class receives credit. Groups may even compete against one another with the idea of producing a better part or higher-quality product than other groups. However, the purpose is not the competition that produces the final product, but the cooperation within groups that the competition promotes. Cooperative task structures have the goal of dividing and specializing the efforts of small groups of individuals across a larger task whose outcome depends on the sharing, cooperation, and collaboration of individuals within groups.

Role Expectations and Responsibilities

Proper assignment of roles is important to the success of cooperative learning activities. In addition to groups being assigned specialized tasks, individuals often are assigned specialized roles to perform within their groups. Some of the most commonly assigned roles include researcher, runner, recorder, and summarizer, whose specific functions will be defined in the sections ahead.

The success of a cooperative learning activity depends on your communication of role expectations and responsibilities and modeling them when necessary. This is another reason why cooperative learning has little resemblance to loosely formed discussion groups; not only must you divide labor among learners and specialized tasks, but you also must designate the roles that foster the orderly completion of a task.

If someone's duties are unclear, or a group's assignment is ambiguous, cooperative learning quickly degenerates into undisciplined discussion, in which there may be numerous uninvolved and passive participants. Uninvolved and passive participants are individuals who successfully escape sharing anything of themselves. This defeats the purpose of cooperative learning.

If a group produces an outstanding report but only a few students have contributed to it, the group as a whole will have learned no more than if each member had completed the assignment alone. And the critical thinking, reasoning, and problem solving that are so much a part of the shared effort of a cooperative learning activity will not have occurred.

ESTABLISHING A COOPERATIVE TASK STRUCTURE IN YOUR CLASSROOM

Now let us put to work in your classroom the four components of cooperative learning: teacher–student interaction, student–student interaction, task specialization and materials, and role expectations and responsibilities. Establishing a **task structure** for a cooperative learning activity involves five specific steps:

1. Specify the goal of the activity.
2. Structure the task.
3. Teach and evaluate the collaborative process.
4. Monitor group performance.
5. Debrief.

1. Specifying the Goal

The goal of a cooperative learning activity specifies the product and/or behaviors that are expected at the end of the activity. The outcome can take different forms:

- Written group reports, which may include any of the following:
- Higher individual achievement on an end-of-activity test

- Oral performance, articulating the group consensus
- Enumeration and/or resolution of critical issues, decisions, or problems
- Critique of an assigned reading
- Collection of data, physical or bibliographic, for or against an issue

To ensure the desired outcome, your job is to identify the outcome, check for understanding, and set a cooperative tone. Each of these steps is described below.

Identify the Outcome.   As moderator and ultimate leader of the group activity you must clearly articulate the form of the final product or performance expected of your learners in advance. For each of your desired outcomes (for example, from the list above), illustrate the style, format, and length of the product that will constitute acceptable group work. For a written report, you might write on the board the acceptable length and format and display a sample report to guide group efforts. In each case, give your students signs of acceptable progress or milestones to be achieved and, where possible, examples of a successfully completed final product or performance.

Following your clear specification of the goal, place it in the context of past and future learning. Organize the content so students will attach meaning and significance to it and see it in terms of their own experience. Typically, statements like "Remember when we had trouble with . . . " or "Next week we will need these skills to . . . " sufficiently highlight the importance of the impending activity by linking it to past or future activities.

Check for Understanding.   Next, check for understanding of the goal and your directions for achieving it. Using a few average and high performers as a steering group, ask for an oral regurgitation of your goal and directions. The entire class can benefit from hearing them again, and you can correct them if needed. Because groups typically expend so much effort during a cooperative learning activity, misinterpretation of the goal and your directions for attaining it can severely affect classroom morale by needlessly wasting a lot of your learners' time and effort.

In self-directed learning, one individual can be led astray by poorly understood directives. But in cooperative learning, entire groups, not just occasional individuals, can wander off the path, leaving a significant portion of your classroom working toward the wrong goal. Having one member of each group restate the goal and your directions for attaining it is time well spent.

Set a Cooperative Tone.   Your final task in introducing the goal of your cooperative learning activity is to set a tone of cooperation. Students customarily begin cooperative learning activities as they have begun thousands of school activities before—as individuals competing against individuals. This competitive style has been ingrained in us from earliest childhood. It may be difficult for some of your learners to get the competitive spirit out of their blood, because it has become so much a part of their schooling.

Your job at the start of a cooperative learning activity is to set the tone: "Two heads are better than one." Other phrases such as "United we stand, divided we fall" or "Work together or fail together" can remind groups of the cooperative nature of the enterprise. You could ask each group to choose or create a group motto (for example, "All for one and one for all") that provides a distinctive identity and reminds students that collaboration, not competition, is the goal.

Your role also must be one of cooperation, and this too must be communicated at the outset. "I am here to help . . . to answer your questions . . . to be your assistant . . . your consultant . . . your information provider." These reassuring comments can lift your classroom from the realm of competition and into the world of cooperation.

2. Structuring the Task

The structure of the task is what separates just any group activity from a cooperative learning activity. Group discussions have tasks, but they often are so generally defined (discuss the facts, raise issues, form a consensus) that they rarely allow for the division of labor, role responsibilities, collaborative efforts, and end products that promote critical thinking in a cooperative learning activity.

In structuring a cooperative learning task, you must decide several factors in advance:

- How large will the groups be?
- How will group members be selected?
- How much time will be devoted to group work?
- What roles, if any, will you assign to group members?
- What incentives/rewards will you provide for individual and group work?

Let's look at alternatives for each of these factors and how you can choose among them.

Group Size.   How many should be in the group? Group size is one of your most important decisions. Although influenced by the size of your class, the number of individual learners assigned to groups has far-reaching consequences for the:

- Range of abilities within a group
- Time required for a group to reach consensus
- Efficient sharing of materials within a group
- Time needed to complete the end product

Each of these four factors will be altered by the number of members assigned to groups. This is why, when subtasks are comparable, you should make group sizes approximately equal.

The most efficient group size for attaining a goal in the least time is 4 to 6 members (Cohen, 1994; Johnson et al., 1994). Thus, in a class of 25 to 30 students, about five or six groups should be formed. Smaller groups make monitoring of group performance more difficult, because the number of times you can interact with each group is reduced accordingly. But groups of 7 or 8 generally argue more, reach consensus later, have more difficulty sharing limited materials (for example, a reference that must be shared), and take longer to complete the final product.

Thus the rule of thumb is to compose groups of 4 or 5 members for single-period activities and slightly larger groups (of 5 or 6) when the activity stretches over more than a class period, requiring greater task complexity and role specialization.

Division of labor, often overlooked when structuring tasks, is critical to the success of group learning. Allowing students to analyze the task and identify divisions of labor can foster metacognitive growth and higher-order thinking.

Group Composition.   Whom will you select for each group? Unless the task specifically calls for specialized abilities, you will form most groups heterogeneously, with a representative sample of all the learners in a class. Therefore, you will assign to groups a mix of higher/lower performing, more verbal/less verbal, and more task-oriented/less task-oriented learners as well as monitoring gender and ethnicity across groups. This diversity contributes to the collaborative process by creating a natural flow of information from those who have it to those who need it. It also promotes the transmission of alternative perspectives and viewpoints that often sends the flow of information in unexpected and desirable directions (Buehl, 2001; Putnam, 1997).

Groups within a classroom generally should reflect the composition of the community outside it. This composition confronts learners with differences as well as similarities to provide the motivation for dialogue, the need for sharing, and the natural division of interests and abilities needed to get the job done.

It also is important that groups not only represent a diversity of talents, interests, and abilities but that typically nonengaged students be represented across groups. Social scientists long have observed that the pressure from peers working together often pulls in even recalcitrant and passive learners, sweeping them up in the excitement of some larger goal. This is especially true if they are deprived of the support of other passive or inactive participants.

Johnson, Johnson, and Holubec (1994) and Johnson and Johnson (1991) provide additional suggestions for forming groups:

1. Identify isolated students who are not chosen by any other classmates. Then build a group of skillful and supportive students around each isolated learner.

2. Randomly assign students by having them count off; place the ones together, the twos together, and so forth. If groups of 5 are desired in a class of 30, have students count off by 6.

3. To build constructive relationships between majority and minority students, between children with and without disabilities, and between boys and girls, use heterogeneous groups with students from each category.

4. Share with students the process of choosing group members. First you select a member for a group, then that member selects another, and so on, alternating between your choice and students' choices until the group is complete.

One approach to drawing nonengaged learners into the cooperative activity is to structure the task so success depends on the active involvement of all group members. Structuring the task reduces the problems of active and passive uninvolvement. **Active uninvolvement** is when a group member talks about everything but the assigned goal of the group. **Passive uninvolvement** is when a student does not care and becomes a silent member of the group. Here are ways you can structure a cooperative task to increase the likelihood that all group members will be actively involved:

- Request a product that requires a clearly defined division of labor (for example, the division of tasks for a writing project might be looking up new words, writing a topic sentence, preparing a chart, finding examples, etc.). Then assign specific individuals to each activity at the start of the session.
- Within groups, form pairs that are responsible for looking over and actually correcting each other's work/contribution.
- Chart the group's progress on individually assigned tasks and encourage poor or slow performers to work harder to improve the group's overall progress. (A wall chart may be all that is needed.)
- Purposely limit the resources given to a group, so individual members must remain in personal contact to share materials and complete their assigned tasks (for example, one dictionary or hand calculator to share).

- Make one stage of the required product contingent on a previous stage that is the responsibility of another person. This way, encouragement will be given or help provided by group members to those not performing adequately, so they can complete their contribution.

Time on Task. How much time should you allot for group work? This depends on task complexity (for example, single class period or multiple periods), but you must make some more refined estimates as well. You need to determine the time to devote to group work and the time to devote to all groups coming together to share their contributions. This latter time may be used for group reports, a whole-class discussion, debriefing to relate the work experiences of each group to the end product, or some combination.

Group work can easily get out of hand in the excitement, controversy, and natural dialogue that can come from passionate discussions. This requires you to place limits on each stage of the cooperative learning activity, so one stage does not eclipse time from another and leave the task disjointed and incomplete in your learners' minds.

Most time naturally will be devoted to the work of individual groups, where the major portion of the end product is being completed. This normally will consume 60% to 80% of the time devoted to the cooperative learning activity. The remaining time must be divided among individual group presentations and/or whole-class discussion and debriefing that places the group work into the perspective of a single end product.

If you plan both group reports and a whole-class discussion for the same day, be aware that the whole-class discussion probably will get squeezed into a fraction of the time required to make it meaningful. To avoid this, schedule group discussions or debriefings for the following class day, so class members have ample time to reflect on their group reports and to pull together their own thoughts about the collaborative process, which may or may not have occurred as intended. Fifteen or 20 minutes at the beginning of class the next day usually provides students the proper distance to reflect meaningfully on their experiences the day before.

Role Assignment. What roles should you assign to group members? As you saw, division of labor within and across groups is an important dimension of cooperative learning that is not shared by most large group discussion methods. This task specialization, and the division of labor it often requires, promotes the responsibility and idea sharing that marks an effective cooperative learning activity. Teachers can encourage the acceptance of individual responsibility and idea sharing in a cooperative learning experience by role assignments within groups and by task specialization across groups. Teachers use these roles and responsibilities to complement group work and to interconnect the groups.

Some of the more popular **cooperative learning role functions** that teachers can assign within or across groups are suggested by Johnson and Johnson (1996):

1. *Summarizer.* Paraphrases and plays back to the group major conclusions to see if the group agrees and to prepare for (rehearse) the group's contribution before the whole class.
2. *Checker.* Checks controversial or debatable statements and conclusions for authenticity against text, workbook, or references. Ensures that the group will not be using unsubstantiated facts or be challenged by more accurate representations of other groups.
3. *Researcher.* Reads reference documents and acquires background information when more data are needed (e.g., may conduct an interview or seek a resource from the library). The researcher differs from a checker in that the researcher provides critical

information for the group to complete its task, whereas the checker certifies the accuracy of the work in progress and/or after it has been completed.

4. *Runner.* Acquires anything needed to complete the task: materials, equipment, reference works. Far from a subservient role, this requires creativity, shrewdness, and even cunning to find the necessary resources, which may also be diligently sought by other groups.

5. *Recorder.* Commits to writing the major product of the group. The recorder may require individuals to write their own conclusions, in which case the recorder collates, synthesizes, and renders in coherent form the abbreviated work of individual group members.

6. *Supporter.* Chosen for his or her upbeat, positive outlook, the supporter praises members when their individual assignments are completed and consoles them in times of discouragement (for example, if proper references cannot be found). Keeps the group moving forward by recording major milestones achieved on a chart for all the class to see, identifying progress made, and encouraging efforts of individuals, particularly those who may have difficulty participating or completing their tasks.

7. *Observer/Troubleshooter.* Takes notes and records information about the group process that may be useful during whole-class discussion or debriefing. Reports to a class leader or to you when problems appear insurmountable for a group or for individual members.

Typically, any one of the preceding role functions also could serve as a group leader. However, because each of these roles entails some form of leadership, the formal designation of leader may not be necessary. This has the desirable effect of making all role functions more equal and eliminating an authority-based structure that can lead to arguments and disunity among members who may see themselves as more or less powerful than others. Be sure to explain and model the specific duties entailed in each of these roles before assigning them.

In addition to these specific role functions assigned to individual group members, all group members have other responsibilities to perform. You may wish to provide students with the following reminders by writing them on the board or in a handout before a cooperative learning activity:

- Ask other group members to explain their points clearly whenever you do not understand.
- Be sure to check your answers and those of others in your group against references or the text.
- Encourage members of your group to go farther, to expand on their points to surpass previous accomplishments and expectations.
- Let everyone finish what they have to say without interrupting, whether you agree or disagree.
- Don't be bullied into changing your mind, if you really do not want to.
- Criticize ideas, not individuals.

Providing Reinforcement and Rewards.   Besides deciding on group composition, size, time, and the individual responsibilities of group members, establish a system of reinforcement and reward to keep your learners on task and working toward the goal. The following are among the reinforcement strategies that have been used effectively with cooperative learning activities:

- Grades: individual and group
- Bonus points

Figure 11.2 Sample scales for evaluating individual and group effort in a collaborative activity.

1. How active was _____ in helping the group attain its final product?	2. How complete (or accurate, or useful, or original) is this group's final product?
_____ very active	_____ very complete
_____ fairly active	_____ fairly complete
_____ somewhat active	_____ somewhat complete
_____ not too active	_____ not too complete
_____ not active at all	_____ not complete at all

- Social responsibilities
- Tokens or privileges
- Group contingencies

Grades can be used to reinforce and reward the behavior of individuals and groups during cooperative learning. However, use of individual grades in the context of cooperative learning should stress the importance of individual effort in *achieving the group goal*. For this reason, cooperative learning grades usually incorporate both individual performance (quality and/or extensiveness of work toward accomplishing the group goal) and the thoroughness, relevance, and accuracy of the group product. Each individual's grade can be in two separate parts or can be a composite grade that combines his or her own plus the group's effort. Individuals can rate each other on a 5-point scale measuring the active involvement of each teammate in the group process, the average of which could be a score for individual effort. Sample scales for measuring group and individual effort are illustrated in Figure 11.2.

Teachers may also use other types of grades as rewards:

1. Average the individual scores to determine the group grade.
2. Assign all group members the average of the highest (or lowest) half of the members' scores.
3. Average an individual's score with the group score (for example, average an individual score of 4 with a group score of 5: 4 + 5 = 9, divided by 2 = 4.5).
4. Add points to the group score for each active participant within the group (or subtract points from the group score for each nonparticipant).

Another reinforcement technique you can use in partnership with grades is bonus points, earned on the basis of how many group members reach a preestablished level of performance by the end of their group's activity. You might devise a group quiz (or take it from the text or workbook) and then assign an expected score for each individual member, which could vary according to previous performance or difficulty of the task. Those obtaining or exceeding their expected score would earn their group a bonus point.

Another popular form of reinforcement during cooperative learning includes rewarding individual efforts with desirable social responsibilities, such as granting the high performer the first pick of group role next time (observer, supporter, checker, etc.). Also, you can employ tokens or privileges to motivate individuals and group members. You might give the highest performing group independent study time, trips to the learning center, or use of special materials and/or resources. You could accord these same privileges for high-performing individuals within groups.

Finally, teachers frequently have used group contingencies to motivate and reinforce members during cooperative learning. You may choose one of three ways of rewarding the

Video Window

Cooperative Learning

In this video, you will see Jenny teaching a science lesson to her fourth-grade students. She structures part of her lesson around cooperative groups that are given the task of learning to balance a scale by placing the proper amount of weight on either side. Watch how she moves among the groups to reinforce some learners and redirects others toward a correct solution. After watching Jenny's lesson, how would you describe the

- Interactions Jenny had with her students?
- Interactions Jenny's students had with one another?
- Task and materials Jenny selected for her lesson?
- Role expectations and responsibilities she assigned to the groups?

For another scenario of cooperative groups with middle school English students, see the second Video Windows for this chapter on the Companion Website. How would you describe this teacher's cooperative activity using these same four criteria?

 To answer these questions online, go to the Video Windows *module of this chapter of the* Companion Website *at www.prenhall.com/borich.*

group based on the performance of its individuals:

1. *Average-performance contingency,* in which all members are graded or reinforced based on the average performance of all group members
2. *High-performance group contingency,* in which the highest quarter of the group is the basis for grades, reinforcements, or privileges
3. *Low-performance group contingency,* in which the lowest quarter of the group is the basis for individual grades or other forms of reinforcement

3. Teaching and Evaluating the Collaborative Process

Another responsibility you have during cooperative learning is teaching the collaborative process. Most learners lack the collaborative skills needed to benefit from many cooperative learning activities. Therefore, you need to identify collaborative behaviors, place them in proper sequence, and demonstrate them. Just as self-directed learning strategies must be modeled, so must collaborative behaviors.

At the heart of collaborative skills is the ability to exchange thoughts and feelings with others at the same conceptual level. Students need to feel comfortable in communicating their ideas, beliefs, and opinions to others in a timely and efficient manner. Johnson and Johnson (1996) suggest some important cooperative learning skills and some of the ways you can teach them:

1. *Teach how to communicate one's own ideas and feelings.* Encourage use of *I* and *my* to let students know it is their ideas and feelings that make the collaborative process work. Let students know that their personal experiences—events observed, problems encountered, people met—are valued information they can use to justify their own ideas and feelings.
2. *Make messages complete and specific.* Indicate that, along with the message being sent, there should be a frame of reference, perspective, or experience that led to the content of the message. For example, "I got this idea while traveling through a

Pueblo Indian reservation in southern Colorado during our vacation last summer." Or, "I heard the president speak, and his main point reminded me of . . . " or, "I read this newspaper article, and it led me to believe some things about . . . ."

3. *Make verbal and nonverbal messages congruent.* Establish a serious tone in which hidden meanings or snide remarks are not acceptable. Indicate that voice and body language always reinforce the message being conveyed but communicating serious information comically or overdramatizing will confuse both the message and the listener.

4. *Convey an atmosphere of respect and support.* Indicate that all students can contribute information, ideas, feelings, personal experiences, and reactions without fear of ridicule. Make clear that unsupportive behaviors ("You're crazy if you think . . .") are not allowed. Make clear that cooperation rests on sharing both emotional and physical resources, receiving help, dividing responsibility, and looking out for one another's well-being.

5. *Demonstrate how to assess whether the message was properly received.* Instruct your learners in how to ask for interpretive feedback from listeners. Ask them to use phrases such as "What do you think about what I said?" "Does what I said make sense?" "Can you see what I'm trying to say?" The more listeners are asked to paraphrase the message, the more the sender is sure the message has been received as intended.

6. *Teach how to paraphrase another's point of view.* Most learners will want to agree or disagree with the speaker without checking to see if they have the full intent of the message. Make it known that before one can be either critical or supportive of another's viewpoint, it must be paraphrased to the satisfaction of the sender. Teach the following rules of paraphrasing:
   a. Restate the message in your own words, not those of the speaker.
   b. Introduce your paraphrased remarks with phrases such as "It seems to me you're saying . . . " "If I understand you, you believe that . . . " "From what I heard you say, your position is . . . ."
   c. During the paraphrasing, avoid any indication of approval or disapproval. For example, let it be known that responses such as "I disagree with you" or "I think you're right" should not be part of the paraphrased response, for its sole purpose is to determine whether the message has been accurately received.

7. *Demonstrate how to negotiate meanings and understandings.* Often one's understanding of a message must be corrected or fine tuned, because the message was ambiguous, incomplete, or misinterpreted. This means paraphrases often must be recycled to a greater level of understanding, sometimes for the benefit of both sender and receiver. This requires tactful phrases from the sender such as "What I mean to say is . . . " "What I forgot to add was . . . " or "To clarify further . . . ." It also requires tactful phrases from the receiver, such as "What I don't understand is . . . " "Can you say it some other way?" This approach is indispensable for refining the message and ensuring more accurate interpretation. Sender and receiver each must provide a graceful means for the other to correct misperceptions of what was said or heard, without emotional injury to either.

8. *Teach participation and leadership.* Communicate the importance of the following:
   a. Mutual benefit: What benefits the group will benefit the individual.
   b. Common fate: Each individual wins or loses on the basis of the overall performance of group members.
   c. Shared identity: Everyone is a member of a group, emotionally as well as physically.

d. Joint celebration: Receiving satisfaction in the progress of individual group members.

e. Mutual responsibility: Being concerned for underperforming group members.

See *In Practice: Focus on Teaching Cooperative Skills.*

4. Monitoring Group Performance

To establish a cooperative learning structure, you must observe and intervene as needed to assist your learners in acquiring their group's goal. Your most frequent monitoring functions will be telling students where to find needed information, repeating how to complete the task, exhibiting the form of the product to be produced (in whole or part), and/or modeling for a group the process to be used in achieving the group goal. Your role is critical in keeping each group on track. Thus your constant vigilance of group performance is necessary to discover problems and trouble spots before they hamper group progress.

One goal of your monitoring activity should be to identify when a group needs assistance. One common need will be to repeat or remind the group of its goal. Groups easily become disengaged or sidetracked or will invent new and perhaps more interesting goals for themselves. Typically, you will move from group to group at least once at the beginning of a cooperative activity, repeating the task and the goal just to be certain each group understands it.

A second goal of your monitoring activity should be to redirect groups that have discussed themselves into a blind alley. The heat of discussion and debate frequently distracts groups from productive thought, raising issues that may be only marginally relevant to accomplishing the group goal. Key to your monitoring is your ability to recognize when a group is at a difficult juncture. A group might pursue an avenue of fruitless discussion and waste valuable time, when a different avenue could set their course productively toward an attainable goal. Your close vigilance and direction of group work can make the difference between aimless talk and productive discussion.

A third monitoring activity you will perform during cooperative learning is to provide emotional support and encouragement to overwhelmed and frustrated group members. Not all group members will gladly accept their individual assignments, nor will all groups accept their designated goal. Your encouragement and support can instill the confidence some will need to complete a task they may be unsure of and that may not be of their own choosing.

5. Debriefing

Your feedback to the groups on how well they are collaborating is important to their progress in acquiring collaborative skills (Weissglass, 1996). You can accomplish **debriefing** and evaluation at the end of the collaborative activity in the following ways:

- Openly talk about how the groups functioned. Ask students for their opinions. What were the real issues that enhanced or impeded each group (a) in producing the product, and (b) in completing the process?
- Solicit suggestions for improving the process and avoiding problems so higher levels of collaboration can be reached.
- Get viewpoints of predesignated observers. You might assign one or two individuals to record instances of particularly effective and ineffective group collaboration and to report to the full class at the time of the debriefing.

Group members also can rate each other's collaborative skills during debriefing. Individual group members could receive their ratings privately; group averages could be discussed during the debriefing session to pinpoint strengths and deficiencies.

Figure 11.3 Checklist scale for rating collaborative skills of group members.

Collaborative Skills	Names of Group Members				
Provides knowledge and information to help group's progress					
Is open and candid to whole group with personal feelings					
Provides individual assistance and support to group members who need it					
Evaluates contributions of others in a nonjudg-mental, constructive manner					
Shares physical resources—books, handouts, written information—for group to use					
Accurately paraphrases or summarizes what other group members have said					
Gives recognition to other group members when key contributions are made					
Accepts and appreciates cultural, ethnic, and individual differences					

Figure 11.3 is a scale for rating collaborative skills of group members. It can be used (1) by group members to rate each other, (2) by a group member (e.g., an observer) assigned the task of rating group members, or (3) by you, the teacher. Use this scale as a checklist. On it, note the presence or absence of each skill for each group member by placing a checkmark in the appropriate box. Use *NA* (not applicable) for skills that do not apply for a given role or task. If you wish, instead of listing the names of group members, assign each member a number to keep the ratings anonymous. The whole group then could be assigned one point for each check placed on the scale, and the "winning" group could be given a reward or special recognition.

IN PRACTICE

Focus on Teaching Cooperative Skills

Adapted from Johnson, D., Johnson, R., Holubec, E., & Roy, P. (1994). Circles of Learning: Cooperation in the Classroom, *Association for Supervision and Curriculum Development.*

Just as a teacher needs to teach academic skills, social skills also need to be directly addressed. Students who work in teams need "(a) an opportunity to work together cooperatively (where teamwork skills need to be manifested), (b) a motivation to engage in the teamwork skills (a reason to believe that such actions will be beneficial to them), and (c) some proficiency in using teamwork skills" (Johnson et al., 1994). These authors describe four steps used to teach students cooperative skills:

Step 1. Make sure students understand the need for the teamwork skill. To accomplish this, the teacher can do the following:
- Ask students to develop a list of social skills needed to improve group work. From the skills they list, emphasize one or two.
- Present a case to students so they can see it is better to know the skill than not to know it. Compliment the students who use the skills in the classroom.
- Illustrate the need for the skill through a role play that provides a counter-example in which the skill is obviously missing in a group.

Step 2. Make sure the students understand what the cooperative learning skill is, and how and when to use the skill. To accomplish this, the teacher can do the following:
- Define the skill in terms of verbal and nonverbal behaviors and explain thoroughly what students have to do. After the skill is listed (e.g., give directions to the group's work), ask the class: "What would this skill look like?" (nonverbal behaviors) and "What does this skill sound like?" (verbal behaviors).
- Demonstrate and model the skill in front of the students and explain it so students have a concrete idea of what the skill entails in terms of verbal and nonverbal behavior. Showing students within your classroom what these skills look like clarifies exactly what you expect to see from them and what they can expect to see within their groups.
- Have the students practice the skill in their groups before the lesson starts.

Step 3. Set up practice situations to encourage skill mastery. To accomplish this the teacher can do the following:
- Assign a social skill either as a specific role for certain students or as a general responsibility for all members of the group. Skills are introduced gradually, for instance, one new skill every week, and at the same time previously introduced skills are repeated until mastery occurs.
- Observe each group and record who uses the skill, how frequently, and how effectively. You can begin with a very simple observation form that measures only two or three skills. Use student observers as soon as possible.
- Cue the use of skills periodically during a lesson by having a student demonstrate the skill in front of the others.
- Intervene in the cooperative groups to explain the skills and show how to use them.
- Coach students on how to improve the use of the skill.

Step 4. Give students feedback on their use of the skill. Help them reflect on how to engage in the skill more effectively. During cooperative learning have group members report their impressions about their own behavior. The teacher provides feedback to the class as a whole.

Step 5. Make sure students practice the cooperative learning skill until it becomes automatic. There are four stages of skill development:
- Awkward (the beginning stage, when there is awkwardness in engaging in the skill)
- Phony (when students use the skill but feel inauthentic)
- Mechanical (when students use the skill when being observed and reminded)
- Integrated (when the skill occurs naturally)

The following are some verbal phrases and nonverbal expressions with which your students can display social skills during cooperative learning.

Verbal phrases to check for understanding:

Sounds like you're saying . . .

Explain that to me, please.

Can you show me . . .

Tell me (us) how to do it.

How did you get to that conclusion?

Give us some examples, please.

Verbal expressions for contributing ideas:

Looks like . . .

Sounds like . . .

I have a suggestion.

We could . . .

What if . . .

Nonverbal expressions that can complement the verbal phrases include:

Eye contact

Leaning forward while speaking

Gestures

Interested expression

Here is a summary of some obstacles to debriefing and how you can structure your cooperative learning activity to promote evaluation and feedback (based on D. Dishon & O'Leary, 1984):

1. *There is not enough time for debriefing.* For many reasons (announcements, assemblies, ensuing lessons), teachers often believe they do not have the time to evaluate and gather feedback about the cooperative activity. Try the following:
   a. Do a quick debriefing by asking the class to tell how well their groups functioned. You can do this by asking a question, such as "Did each group have enough time?" Then have students indicate agreement or disagreement by answering yes, hand in air; don't know, arms folded; or no, hands down. You can ask and respond to two or three questions in a minute or so.
   b. Do debriefing during the cooperative activity, or have the class complete a questionnaire or checklist at home pertaining to how well their group functioned.
2. *Debriefing stays vague.* When students conclude, "We did OK," "We did a good job," or "Everyone was involved" several times, you know the feedback is not specific enough. Try the following:
   a. Give the group specific written questions to be answered about their group's functioning.
   b. Identify key events or incidents that occurred during the collaborative process for which students must indicate their comfort or satisfaction.
   c. Use student observers so specific events indicating effective and ineffective group functioning are recorded.

3. *Students stay uninvolved in debriefing*. Occasionally there are groups whose members consistently stay uninvolved in the debriefing process. Try the following:
   a. Ask for a written report from the group, reporting the strengths and weaknesses of their group's functioning.
   b. Use questionnaires that require completion by everyone.
   c. Assign a student the job of debriefer for the group.
   d. Have each member sign a statement summarizing how their group functioned.
   e. Give bonus points for good debriefing reports.
4. *Written debriefing reports are incomplete*. Some groups may hand in incomplete debriefing reports. Try the following:
   a. Have group members read and sign each other's debriefing reports to show that each has been checked for accuracy and completeness.
   b. Give bonus points for completeness.
5. *Students use poor collaborative skills during debriefing*. When group members do not listen carefully to each other, when they are afraid to contribute to the debriefing process, or when the discussion becomes divisive, try the following:
   a. Assign specific roles for the debriefing.
   b. Have one group observe the debriefing of another group and discuss the results.

TEAM-ORIENTED COOPERATIVE LEARNING ACTIVITIES

Research indicates that teams of heterogeneous learners can increase the collaborative skills, self-esteem, and achievement of individual learners (Slavin, 2001). Four **team-oriented cooperative learning** techniques have been particularly successful in bringing about these outcomes: Student Teams—Achievement Division, Teams-Games-Tournaments, Jigsaw II, and Team-Assisted Individualization. A brief summary of these follows, based on the work of Slavin (1993).

Student Teams—Achievement Division

In Student Teams—Achievement Division (STAD), the teacher assigns students to 4- or 5-member learning teams. Each team is as heterogeneous as possible to represent the composition of the entire class (boys/girls, higher performing/lower performing, etc.).

Begin the cooperative learning activity by presenting new material via presentation or discussion and providing worksheets of problem sets, vocabulary words, questions, and such, from which students can review the main points of the presentation or discussion. When your presentation, explanation, or introduction is complete, team members study your worksheets, quizzing each other. They work in pairs or in small groups in which team members discuss the worksheet content, clarifying difficult or confusing points among themselves and asking you questions when necessary.

Before team members begin, give one member of each group or pair the answers to all the questions or problems on the worksheet, and assign this member the task of checking the written or oral responses of others. Allow team members sufficient time for everyone to complete the problems or questions on the worksheet (make the worksheet concise to encourage this).

After the teams have had sufficient time to practice with the worksheet and answer key, give individuals a written quiz over the material in which team members may not help one another. Score the quizzes immediately and form individual scores into team scores (for example, by averaging all, top half, or bottom half). Determine the contribution of individual students by how much each student's quiz score exceeds her or his past quiz average or exceeds a preset score based on each student's learning history. This way, the entire group receives a score based on each individual member's performance, and individual learners also receive an improvement score based on the extent to which their individual score exceeds past performance or a preestablished standard that recognizes their learning history.

During STAD, you act as a resource person and monitor group study activities to intervene when necessary to suggest better study techniques ("Why not choose partners now and quiz each other on the questions you've been discussing?").

Research shows that, during STAD, learners gain a sense of camaraderie and helpfulness toward fellow team members, pursue self-directed learning and rehearsal strategies modeled by the teacher, and become self-motivated through having some control over their own learning.

Teams-Games-Tournaments

A cooperative learning activity closely related to STAD is the use of Teams-Games-Tournaments (TGT). TGT uses the same general format as STAD (4- to 5-member groups studying worksheets). However, instead of individually administered quizzes at the end of a study period, students play academic games to show their mastery of the topic studied.

Jigsaw II

In the cooperative learning activity called Jigsaw II, you assign students to 4- to 6-member teams to work on an academic task broken into several subtasks, depending on the number of groups. You assign students to teams and then assign a unique responsibility to each team member. For example, assign each student within each team a section of the text to read. Then give each team member a special task with which to approach the reading. Assign one team member to write down and look up the meanings of any new vocabulary words. Assign another to summarize or outline the main points in the text. Assign another the job of identifying major and minor characters, and so on.

When all team members have their specific assignments, break out from their original group all team members having the same assignment (for example, finding and defining new vocabulary words) to meet as an expert group to discuss their assignment and to share their conclusions and results with one another. Once in an expert group, members may assist each other by comparing notes (for example, definitions) and identifying points overlooked by other group members. When all the expert groups have had the opportunity to share, discuss, and modify their conclusions, return them to their respective home groups. Each member then takes turns teaching their teammates about their respective responsibility.

Jigsaw II heightens interest among group members because the only way other team members can learn about the topics to which they were not assigned is to listen to the teammate who received that assignment. After all the experts make their presentation to the team teaching them what they learned from their expert group, give individual quizzes to assess how much they have learned. As in STAD, you can assign both an overall group score as well as an individual improvement score based on past performance. These scores become the basis for team and individual rewards for the highest scorers.

Team-Assisted Individualization

One of the newest cooperative learning activities is Team-Assisted Individualization (TAI), which combines some of the characteristics of individualized and cooperative learning. Although originally designed for elementary and middle school mathematics classes, TAI can be used with any subject matter and grade level for which some individualized learning materials are available (for example, computer software or self-paced texts). In TAI, you start each student working through the individualized materials at a point designated by a placement test or previous learning history. Thus students may work at different levels depending on the heterogeneity of achievement in the classroom.

Give each student a specified amount of content to work through (for example, pages, problem sets, questions and answers) at his or her own pace. Also, assign each learner to a team selected to represent all achievement levels and, therefore, individuals who enter the individualized materials at different levels of complexity. Heterogeneity within the teams is important, because you then ask each team member to have his or her work checked by another teammate. Checkers are expected to have completed portions of the materials that are more advanced than others. Have as many group members as possible assume the role of checker. When necessary, give the checkers answer sheets.

Have student monitors give quizzes over each unit and score and record the results on a master scorecard. Base team scores on the average number of units completed each week by team members and their scores on the unit quizzes. Reward those teams that complete a preset number of units with a minimum average quiz score (for example, with certificates, independent study time, learning center privileges). Assign one student monitor to each team to manage the routine checking, distribution of the individualized materials, and administering and recording the quizzes.

Because TAI uses individualized materials, it is especially useful for teaching heterogeneous classes that afford you few opportunities for whole-class instruction and little time to instruct numerous small groups who may have diverse learning needs.

Overview of Team-Oriented Cooperative Learning Activities

Similarities and differences among the four cooperative learning methods are summarized in Table 11.1.

Many different forms of cooperative learning have been successfully used in classrooms of all grade levels and subject matter. Some of the most successful cooperative learning activities, however, have come from the ingenuity and creativity of individual teachers who, with little formal preparation, devise a group activity to promote social interaction when the subject they are teaching encourages cooperative outcomes. Although many versions of cooperative learning can be devised from the preceding four, as an effective teacher, you should seize the opportunity to create a cooperative learning experience whenever content goals lend themselves to promoting collaborative skills. This, in turn, can increase your learners' self-esteem, critical thinking, and problem-solving abilities.

PROMOTING THE GOALS OF COOPERATIVE LEARNING IN THE CULTURALLY DIVERSE CLASSROOM

One of the first things you will notice during cooperative learning activities is the variety of learning styles among your students. The variety you will observe in your students' independence, persistence, and flexibility during cooperative learning will be influenced, to some extent, by the predominant cultures and ethnicities in your school and classroom (Banks, 2000; Irvine & York, 2001; Putnam, 1997).

For example, C. Bennett (1990) points out how interactions among students and between students and teacher are influenced by learning styles that are modified by their culture. Cushner, McClelland, and Safford (1992) indicate how being a member of a subculture, minority, or ethnic group can enhance the nature of interpersonal relationships within a classroom by increasing its cohesiveness, informality, interpersonal harmony, and cooperation. Also, Bowers and Flinders (1991) provide examples of how the noise level, use of classroom space, turn taking, and negotiation can vary among social classes and ethnicities to create different but equally productive learning climates when properly managed and matched to cultural expectations.

Table 11.1 Similarities and differences among four cooperative learning activities.

Student Teams-Achievement Division (STAD)	Team-Games-Tournament (TGT)	Jigsaw (II)	Team-Assisted Individualization (TAI)
1. Teacher presents content in lecture or discussion	1. Teacher presents content in lecture or discussion	1. Students read section of text and are assigned unique topic	1. Students are given diagnostic test/exercise by student monitor to determine placement in materials
2. Teams work through problems/questions on worksheets	2. Teams work through problems/questions on worksheets	2. Students within teams with same topic meet in "expert groups"	2. Students work through assigned unit at their own pace
3. Teacher gives quiz over material studied	3. Teams play academic games against each other for points	3. Students return to home group to share knowledge of their topic with teammates	3. Teammate checks text against answers and student monitor gives quiz
4. Teacher determines team average and individual improvement scores	4. Teacher tallies team points over 4-week period to determine best team and best individual scorers	4. Students take quiz over each topic discussed	4. Team quizzes are averaged and number of units completed are counted by monitor to create team scores
		5. Individual quizzes are used to create team scores and individual improvement scores	

During cooperative learning, some learners may benefit more and adapt better to a task orientation that is less structured and more field dependent. Recent findings suggest that some task orientations, such as cooperative learning, may be more appropriate for some groups. Research also suggests that some of today's objectives—such as interdisciplinary thematic units and objectives pertaining to integrated bodies of knowledge—may require cooperative and collaborative activities to achieve their goals.

In chapter 2 we saw that learners could be distinguished on the basis of the cognitive processes they used to learn and whether they were presented a task in a way that allowed them the opportunity to use their preferred learning style. Two of the learning styles that have been frequently studied are field independence and field dependence (Irvine & York, 2001; Wakefield, 1996).

The implications of field independence and field dependence for cooperative learning have been related to students' need for structure. From a review of the literature, Irvine and York (2001) identify characteristics of students who need more or less structure to maximize their opportunity to learn. Some of their characteristics, which have implications for how to plan a cooperative learning activity, follow:

Those needing more structure (field dependent):

- Have shorter attention spans and like to move through material rapidly.
- Are reluctant to try something new and do not like to appear wrong.
- Tend not to ask many questions.
- May need reassurance before starting a task.
- Want to know facts before concepts.
- Usually give only brief answers.

Those needing less structure (field independent):

- Like to discuss and argue.
- Want to solve problems with a minimum of teacher assistance.
- Dislike details or step-by-step formats.
- Are comfortable with abstractions and generalities.
- Emphasize emotions and are open about themselves.
- Tend to make many interpretations and inferences.

Irvine and York also suggest specific ways teachers can orient their cooperative activities to promote particular learning styles. Try these suggestions:

For students who require more structure:

- Have definite and consistent rules.
- Provide specific, step-by-step guides and instructions.
- Make goals and deadlines short and definite.
- Change pace often.
- Assess problems frequently.
- Move gradually from group work to discussion.

For students who require less structure:

- Provide topics to choose from.
- Make assignments longer, with self-imposed deadlines.
- Encourage the use of resources outside the classroom.
- Devote more time to group assignments with teacher serving as a resource.
- Use and encourage interest in the opinions and values of others.
- Provide opportunity for extended follow-up projects and assignments.

Hill (1989) suggests that some cultural and ethnic groups tend to benefit more and adapt better to a task orientation that is less structured and more field dependent. For example, cooperative learning has been shown to increase the school success of Hispanic students (Losey, 1995). These and other authors (Jacobs, 1999) provide alternatives to the notion that the most effective task orientation for the teacher is always to stand in front of the classroom, lecturing or explaining to students seated in neatly arranged rows, who are assumed to have little or no expectations about or experiences with the content being taught.

Cooperative teaching handbooks by Jacobs, Power, and Loh (2002), Stahl (1994, 1995, 1996) and Shlomo (1999) suggest that not only may cooperative learning benefit some cultural and ethnic groups, but cooperative learning may be required for all learners to achieve today's curriculum objectives in social studies, science, mathematics, and the language arts.

SUMMING UP

This chapter introduced you to strategies for cooperative learning. Its key terms and main points were:

Outcomes of Cooperation

1. Critical thinking, reasoning, and problem-solving skills are of little use if they cannot be applied in cooperative interaction with others.

2. Self-directed and cooperative learning share the complementary objectives of engaging students in the learning process and promoting higher (more complex) patterns of behavior.

3. Cooperative learning activities can instill the following in your learners:
   - Attitudes and values that guide the learner's behavior outside of the classroom
   - Acceptable forms of social behavior that may not be modeled in the home
   - Alternative perspectives and viewpoints with which to think objectively
   - An integrated identity that can reduce contradictory thoughts and actions
   - Higher thought processes

Components of a Cooperative Learning Activity

4. Planning for cooperative learning requires decisions pertaining to the following:
   - Teacher–student interaction
   - Student–student interaction
   - Task specialization and materials
   - Role expectations and responsibilities

5. The primary goal of teacher–student interaction during cooperative learning is to promote independent thinking.

6. The primary goal of student–student interaction during cooperative learning is to encourage the active participation and interdependence of all members of the class.

7. The primary goal of task specialization and learning materials during cooperative learning is to create an activity structure whose end product depends on the sharing, cooperation, and collaboration of individuals within groups.

8. The primary goal of assigning roles and responsibilities during cooperative learning is to facilitate the work of the group and to promote communication and sharing among its members.

Establishing a Cooperative Task Structure in Your Classroom

9. Establishing a cooperative task structure involves five steps:
   a. Specify the goal of the activity.
   b. Structure the task.
   c. Teach the collaborative process.
   d. Monitor group performance.
   e. Debrief.

1. Specifying the Goal

10. The goal of a cooperative activity may take different forms, such as the following:
    - Written group reports
    - Higher individual achievement
    - An oral performance
    - An enumeration or listing
    - A critique
    - Bibliographic research

11. You have four responsibilities in specifying the goal of a cooperative activity:
    - Illustrate the style, format, and length of the end product.
    - Place the goal in the context of past and future learning.
    - Check for understanding of the goal and directions given for achieving it.
    - Set a tone of cooperation, as opposed to competition.

2. Structuring the Task

12. Structuring the cooperative learning task involves the following decisions:
    - How large the groups will be
    - How group members will be selected
    - How much time will be devoted to group work
    - What roles group members will be assigned
    - What incentives will be provided for individual and group work

13. Generally, the most efficient size for a group to reach the desired goal in the least amount of time is four to six members.

14. Unless a group task specifically calls for specialized abilities, groups should be formed heterogeneously—or with a representative sample of all learners in the class.

15. Methods for selecting group members include the following:
    a. Ask students to list peers with whom they would like to work.
    b. Randomly assign students to groups.
    c. Choose matched opposites: minority/majority, boy/girl, with/without disabilities, and so on.
    d. Share with students the process of choosing group members (e.g., teacher selects first, then person selected chooses another, etc.).
16. An actively uninvolved group member is one who talks about everything but the assigned goal of the group; a passively uninvolved group member is one who does not care about the work of the group and becomes silent.
17. Methods for discouraging active and passive uninvolvement include the following:
    • Request a product requiring division of labor.
    • Form pairs that oversee each other's work.
    • Chart group progress on individually assigned tasks.
    • Purposefully limit group resources to promote sharing and personal contact.
    • Require a product that is contingent on previous stages that are the work of others.
18. Group work should entail 60% to 80% of the time devoted to a cooperative activity, the remainder being devoted to whole-class discussion and debriefing.
19. Division of labor within a group can be accomplished with role assignments. The following are some of the most popular:
    • Summarizer
    • Checker
    • Researcher
    • Runner
    • Recorder
    • Supporter
    • Observer/troubleshooter
20. The following are among the types of reinforcement strategies that can be used with cooperative learning activities:
    • Individual and group grades
    • Bonus points
    • Social responsibilities
    • Tokens or privileges
    • Group contingencies

3. Teaching and Evaluating the Collaborative Process

21. Teaching the collaborative process involves showing your learners how to do the following:
    • Communicate their own ideas and feelings.
    • Make messages complete and specific.
    • Make verbal and nonverbal messages congruent.
    • Convey respect and support.
    • Assess if the message was properly received.
    • Paraphrase another's point of view.
    • Negotiate meanings and understandings.
    • Actively participate in a group and assume leadership.

4. Monitoring Group Performance

22. During the monitoring of group performance, the teacher's role is to see that each group remains on track, to redirect group efforts when needed, and to provide emotional support and encouragement.

5. Debriefing

23. During debriefing, there are several ways to gather feedback in a whole-class discussion about the collaborative process:
    • Openly talk about how the groups functioned during the cooperative activity.
    • Solicit suggestions for how the process could be improved.
    • Obtain the viewpoints of predesignated observers.

Team-Oriented Cooperative Learning Activities

24. Desirable outcomes have been documented for four popular team-oriented cooperative learning activities:
    • Student Teams—Achievement Division (STAD)
    • Teams-Games-Tournaments (TGT)
    • Jigsaw II
    • Team-Assisted Individualization (TAI)

Promoting the Goals of Cooperative Learning in the Culturally Diverse Classroom

25. The success of a cooperative learning activity has been related to differences in learning styles: field-dependent learners tend to need a more structured cooperative learning activity than field-independent learners.

KEY TERMS

Active uninvolvement, 378
Cooperative learning role functions, 379
Debriefing, 384
Passive uninvolvement, 378

Prosocial behavior, 372
Task specialization, 374
Task structure, 375
Team-oriented cooperative learning, 388

DISCUSSION AND PRACTICE QUESTIONS

Questions marked with an asterisk are answered in appendix B. See also the Companion Website for this text at *www.prenhall.com/borich* for more assessment options.

*1. What two complementary objectives do self-directed and cooperative learning share? Can you think of an instance in which self-directed learning might occur within the context of a cooperative group?

*2. Identify five specific outcomes of a cooperative learning activity. Which will be the most important in your classroom?

*3. What five steps will be required for establishing a cooperative task structure in your classroom? To which step will you devote the most (a) planning time, and (b) classroom time?

*4. What end products or behaviors should you require at the end of a cooperative learning activity? Which product or behavior do you think presents the biggest challenge for evaluation and assessment?

*5. Approximately how large should a cooperative learning group be to reach a specified goal in the least amount of time? Can you think of a situation in which the cooperative learning group could be smaller or larger and still function effectively?

*6. What methods can you use for selecting members of a cooperative group? Can you think of an advantage of using one method over another?

*7. What are three methods for minimizing passive and active uninvolvement in a cooperative learning activity? In your opinion, which method is best for drawing nonengaged learners into the cooperative activity?

*8. Identify the student role functions suggested by D. Johnson and Johnson (1991) that can be assigned to group members. Briefly describe their responsibilities, and add any additional role functions that might be suited to the goals of your classroom.

*9. When combining individual and group work into a single score, what options are available for weighting an individual's work and the work of the group to which the individual belongs?

*10. What are three activities that can be performed during a cooperative learning activity to monitor and, when necessary, improve group performance?

*11. What activities can be used to debrief your class after a cooperative learning activity? Which would you prefer to use in your classroom?

*12. D. Dishon and O'Leary (1984) identify five obstacles to debriefing and several approaches for dealing with each of them. For each obstacle, identify from among the options the one you would first try to improve the debriefing process.

FIELD EXPERIENCE ACTIVITIES

*1. Identify the four most important components of a cooperative learning activity and one critical decision you will have to make pertaining to each.

*2. In what five ways could you reinforce and reward group members for appropriate performance? Create one specific example of each that would be practical for the lesson or unit you have identified.

*3. D. Johnson and Johnson (1991) identify eight communication skills for cooperative learning. In a sentence or two provide an example of how you would teach each of them to your students.

4. Choose one of the team-oriented cooperative learning activities suggested by Slavin that you would be willing to try out in your classroom. Describe how you would implement the technique with respect to the structure of the activity to be performed, the work of the teams, your role as teacher, and procedures for team scoring and recognition.

DIGITAL PORTFOLIO ACTIVITIES

The following digital portfolio activities relate to INTASC principles 2, 4, 5, and 6.

1. In Field Experience Activity 3, you were asked to identify eight communication skills required for cooperative learning and to provide examples of how you would teach them to your students. Since

these are critical skills that are essential for successful cooperative group activities, place them in your digital portfolio in a folder labeled *Cooperative and Collaborative Learning*. Your examples of how you would convey each of the eight skills to your learners will be valuable in forming your first cooperative group activity.

2. In Field Experience Activity 4, you were asked to choose one of the team-oriented cooperative learning activities suggested by Slavin that you would be willing to try out in your classroom and to describe how you would implement it. Read over your response to Field Experience Activity 4 with respect to the specificity with which you described the structure of the activity, the work of the teams, your role as teacher, and procedures for team scoring and recognition to be sure you will know exactly what you have planned at the time of your first cooperative activity. Add any specifics to your descriptions as may be needed and place them in your digital portfolio *Cooperative and Collaborative Learning* folder.

CLASSROOM OBSERVATION ACTIVITY

The following classroom observation activity relates to INTASC principles 2, 4, 5, and 6.

Collaborative and group activities require teacher–student interaction, interaction among students, a specified task and materials, and the assignment of roles. The presence of these four components can determine the effectiveness of a collaborative learning activity. On the Companion Website for this chapter at *www.prenhall.com/borich* you will find a record titled *Group Activity and Task Focus During Collaborative Learning*. This record provides a format to observe and record these four components. Complete this form for Ms. Brokaw's collaborative activity at the end of her lesson, which appears on the Companion Website under chapter 10. Indicate your judgment as to the extent to which all or some of these components were present and place your record into your *Cooperative and Collaborative Learning* digital portfolio folder.

CHAPTER CASE HISTORY AND PRAXIS TEST PREPARATION

DIRECTIONS: The following case history pertains to chapter 11 content. After reading the case history, answer the short-answer question that follows and consult appendix D to find different levels of scored student responses and the rubric used to determine the quality of each response. You also have the opportunity to submit your responses online to receive feedback by visiting the *Case History* module for this chapter on the Companion Website, where you will also find additional questions pertaining to Praxis test content.

Case History

Ms. Choo teaches fourth grade. Test scores for her elementary school have been lower than the state and district average, particularly in math. Her new principal has told the staff that improvement in mathematics is a priority. Students attending the school come from lower socioeconomic and culturally diverse backgrounds. Quite a bit of Ms. Choo's time last year was devoted to trying to manage classroom disruptions, many relating to petty squabbles and rude behavior of the students toward one another.

This year she is going to try to attend to her class's academic and social interaction difficulties by implementing a collaborative task concerning math. Ms. Choo has had her students do "group work" before, but this will be her first attempt to employ collaborative learning in a systematic way. She plans to keep it simple for this time, organizing the class into assignment help line groups. Group members will work together to understand difficult problems. They will make corrections to mistakes by relying on a group member who understands the problems and got the correct answer. The group will also study together before tests with the goal of improving the group test average.

Ms. Choo knows that much of the success of her group rests on its composition, and she has worked hard to ensure that it is heterogeneous in many ways. First of all, she looked at student achievement scores and past grades in math and made sure all levels were represented within each group. She also maintained cultural diversity within the groups as well as male-female balance reflective of the class. She tried to split up cliques or special friends and mix shy with more outgoing students.

Before the groups meet, however, Ms. Choo models and teaches the collaborative process. She tells the class that their group support and social interaction will be as important as the math content of the activity. Each group will have its "life support system" or CPR, which stands for Communication, Participation, and Respect.

To communicate properly, each group member should be able to explain the math steps necessary to reach the solution. Getting the right answer alone is not enough. Participation will be very important. All must play active roles in their group; there will be mutual responsibility and benefit, shared identity, and joint celebration of success. To show respect and support for each other, students must not engage in ridicule or sarcastic comments. Instead, they must try to say constructive things about fellow group members. Instead of "That was really dumb," they might say, "I can understand how you might make that mistake." "Fake it till you can make it," Ms. Choo tells them, meaning that compliments may seem forced at first but will become more natural as time goes on.

To ensure that the collaborative process takes hold, Ms. Choo will give each group a grade based on her CPR model. She will spend some time with each group to see how well they communicate, participate, and show respect. For the first few weeks the collaborative grade will be twice as important as the group average on the weekly test. Students' individual grades on the weekly tests will be recorded as well.

With all this preparation behind her, Ms. Choo ushers in Math Assignment Help Line with high expectations. However, she is somewhat disappointed to see Sally, who has been split up from her best friend, Teresa, sit sullenly and not participate in her group. Ricardo, usually quiet and withdrawn, seems to get along very well with the four members of his group, almost too well. He and Sam seem to talk about their after-school baseball practice as much as they do about the math problems. Troy, a very strong student, stays after class one day to complain about having his high score brought down by the group average. He resents having to explain everything to someone else. He asks if he can work alone because he always gets A's on the tests. The first weeks' tests are averaged and there is no improvement in two of the groups; one group's achievement is up slightly, and three groups have lower scores than before.

Short-Answer Question

This section presents a sample Praxis short-answer question. In appendix D you will find sample responses along with the standards used in scoring these responses.

DIRECTIONS: The following question asks you to write a short answer. Base your answer on your knowledge of principles of learning and teaching from chapter 11. Be sure to answer all parts of the question.

Discrete Multiple-Choice Questions

DIRECTIONS: Each of the multiple-choice questions that follow is based on Praxis-related pedagogical knowledge in chapter 11. Select the answer that is best in each case and compare your results with those in appendix D. See also the Companion Website for this text at *www.prenhall.com/borich* for more assessment options.

1. One of the positive aspects of collaborative learning is the social interaction that over a period of time assists in resolving inconsistencies in our thinking and clarifying what we really believe. This process helps to create
   a. Integrated identity
   b. Task specialization
   c. Role assignment
   d. Student teams

1. Ms. Choo is frustrated by the lack of participation of some students in the cooperative activity. Sally is a passively uninvolved member as indicated by her silence and apparent apathy; Ricardo is actively uninvolved as shown by his off-topic discussion with a fellow group member. Explain briefly two procedures that Ms. Choo might use to structure her task to encourage better group involvement.

2. The teacher's feedback to groups on how well they collaborated is called
   a. Structuring the task
   b. Teaching the collaborative process
   c. Monitoring the group performance
   d. Debriefing

3. During cooperative learning activities the teacher should identify when a group needs assistance, redirect groups toward productive thought, and provide emotional support and encouragement. This instructional activity is called
   a. Direct instruction
   b. Monitoring
   c. Division of labor
   d. Checking for understanding

4. The most convenient size for an effective cooperative group for most classroom objectives is between:
   a. 2 to 3
   b. 4 to 6
   c. 7 to 9
   d. about 10 to 12

5. For the following alternatives, identify which would be most appropriate for a cooperative group whose members may need more structure (MS) and which would be most appropriate for a cooperative group whose members may need less structure (LS).

_____ Have definite and consistent rules

_____ Provide topics to chose from

_____ Change pace often

_____ Provide opportunity for extended follow-up

Chapter 12

Assessing Learners

This chapter will help you answer the following questions and meet the following INTASC principles for effective teaching:

1. What is the difference between a norm-referenced and a criterion-referenced test?
2. What are the advantages and disadvantages of different objective test formats?
3. How can I grade essay tests fairly?
4. How will I know if my tests measure what I say they measure?
5. What is a performance test?
6. How can I use student portfolios to assess my learners?

INTASC 8: The teacher understands and uses formal and informal assessment strategies to evaluate and ensure the continuous intellectual, social, and physical development of the learner.

INTASC 9: The teacher is a reflective practitioner who continually evaluates the effects of his or her choices and actions on others (students, parents, and other professionals in the learning community) and who actively seeks out opportunities to grow professionally.

INTASC 10: The teacher fosters relationships with school colleagues, parents, and agencies in the larger community to support students' learning and well-being (chapters 2, 10).

Some of your strongest childhood and adolescent memories probably include taking tests in school. For that matter, test taking probably is among the most vivid memories of your college experience. If you are like most people who have spent many years in school, you have strong or mixed feelings about tests. In this chapter, we try to dispel some of the discomfort you might feel about tests and show how they can be effective tools in your classroom.

NORM-REFERENCED AND CRITERION-REFERENCED TESTS

To evaluate your learners' progress, what type of information do you need? That depends on your purpose. Testing can provide two types of information:

1. A student's place or rank compared to other students is revealed by a **norm-referenced test (NRT),** so named because it compares a student's performance to that of a norm group (a large, representative sample of learners). Such information is useful when you need to compare a learner's performance to that of others at the same age or grade level.
2. A student's level of proficiency in or mastery of a skill or set of skills is revealed by a **criterion-referenced test (CRT),** so named because it compares student performance with an absolute standard called a *criterion* (such as 75% correct). Such information helps you decide whether a student needs more instruction to acquire a skill or set of skills.

Figure 12.1 illustrates when to use NRTs and CRTs. As the figure indicates, you should identify the type of information needed before selecting a particular test.

Unfortunately, some teachers know little more about a student after testing than they did before. In our technically oriented society, test scores sometimes have become ends in themselves, without the interpretation that is essential for improvement of the learner. In such cases teachers, parents, and others may be quick to denounce a test, often suggesting such abuse of testing proves that test data are useless. In reality, it may only indicate that the teacher who selected the test either failed to identify the specific information needed before administering the test or failed to match the test carefully to this purpose.

Figure 12.1 Relationship of the purpose of testing and information desired to the type of test required.

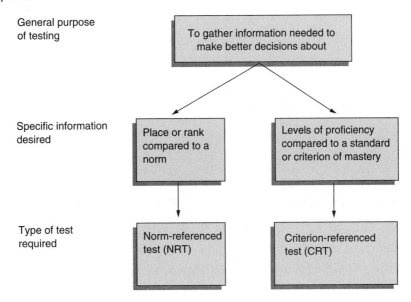

A similar situation can occur when existing test data are inappropriately used or interpreted. An example is the following situation, in which counselor John is checking his records when sixth-grade teacher Mary taps on his door:

◆ ◆ ◆

Mary:	I just stopped by to see you about Danny. He's been in remedial classes for the last 5 years, and now he'll be in my class this year. Mrs. Rodrigues had him last year, and she said you have all the test information on him.
John:	Yeah. In fact, I was just reviewing his folder. Danny's Math Cluster score on the Woodstock-Johnson is at the sixth percentile, and his Reading Cluster is at the first percentile. Good luck with him!
Mary:	Boy, he sure is low. I guess that's why he's been in the remedial classroom for so long.
John:	You've got it!
Mary:	Well, really that's about what I was expecting. What about his skill levels?
John:	What do you mean?
Mary:	You know, his academic skill levels.
John:	Oh, his grade levels! Umm, let's see. . . . His math grade equivalent is 2.6, and his reading grade equivalent is even lower, 1.7.
Mary:	Well . . . that's not really what I need to know. I know he's way below grade level, but I'm wondering about his skills—specific skills, that is. You know, like what words he can read, what phonetic skills he has, if he can subtract two-digit numbers with regrouping . . . things like that.
John:	(Becoming a bit irritated.) Mary, what more do you need than what I've given you? Don't you know how to interpret these scores?
Mary:	(Frustrated.) John, I do know what those scores mean, but they only compare Danny to other students. I'm not interested in that. I want to know

what he can and can't do, so I can begin teaching him at the proper skill level.

John: (Shaking his head.) Look, he's at first-grade level in reading and second-grade level in math. Isn't that enough?

Mary: But what level of mastery has he demonstrated?

John: Mastery? He's years behind! He's mastered very little.

◆ ◆ ◆

It appears there is a communication gap between Mary and John. John has conveyed a lot of test information to Mary, yet she doesn't seem to get much out of it. John is frustrated, Mary is frustrated, and little that will help Danny has been accomplished. What is the problem?

The problem appears to be John's. Mary's questions refer to competencies or mastery of skills. Referring to Figure 12.1, we can conclude that she was interested in information about Danny's *level of proficiency*. But John's answers refer to test performance compared to other students, which means information about Danny's *rank compared to others*. Answers to Mary's questions can come only from a test designed to indicate whether Danny exceeded some standard of performance taken to indicate mastery of some skill.

If a test indicated that Danny could subtract two-digit numbers with regrouping, Mary would say he had mastered this skill if, for example, 80% or more correct was the criterion for mastery. In other words, he would have exceeded the standard of 80% mastery of subtraction of two-digit numbers with regrouping. Recall that a CRT is designed to measure whether a student has mastered a skill, where the definition of mastery depends on an established level or criterion of performance.

But the information John provided was normative or comparative. Danny's grade-equivalent scores allow decisions only involving comparisons between his performance and that of the typical or average performance of learners in a norm group. Danny's grade-equivalent score of 1.7 in reading indicates his reading ability equals that of the average first grader after 7 months in the first grade. It says nothing about which words he knows, nor does it give any information about the process he uses to read new words or how long it takes him to comprehend what he reads or learn the meaning of new words. All this score indicates is that his ability to read is well below that of the average fifth grader and equivalent to that of an average first grader after 7 months of school.

Grade-equivalent scores and other scores obtained from norm-referenced tests thus allow only general, comparative decisions, not decisions about mastery of specific skills.

COMPARING NORM-REFERENCED AND CRITERION-REFERENCED TESTS

As you may have guessed, CRTs must be specific to yield information about individual skills. This is both an advantage and a disadvantage. With a specific test of individual skills, you can be relatively certain your students have either mastered or failed to master the skill in question. However, the major disadvantage is that many CRTs would be necessary to make decisions about the multitude of skills taught in the average classroom.

The NRT, in contrast, tends to be general. It measures a variety of specific and general skills at once but cannot measure them thoroughly. Thus with NRT results, you are not as sure as you would be with CRT results that your students have mastered the individual skills in question. But NRT results give you an estimate of ability in a variety of skills much faster than you could achieve with a large number of CRTs. Because of this trade-off in the uses of criterion-referenced and norm-referenced measures, there are situations in which each is

The appropriateness of a given type of test depends on the purpose of testing. Criterion-referenced tests (CRTs) measure specific skills related to lesson objectives or unit content, while norm-referenced tests (NRTs) measure skills related to general categories of achievement and aptitude.

appropriate. Determining the appropriateness of a given type of test depends on your purpose in testing.

THE TEST BLUEPRINT

In chapter 3 we discussed writing objectives at different levels of cognitive complexity. In this chapter, we introduce the **test blueprint,** which matches test items to your objectives. The test blueprint ensures that you do not overlook details essential to a good test. More specifically, it ensures that a test will sample learning across the range of (1) content areas covered by your instruction and (2) the cognitive and/or affective processes you consider important. It ensures that your test will include a variety of items that tap different levels of cognitive complexity. Figure 12.2 illustrates a test blueprint for a unit on elementary school mathematics.

A test blueprint is constructed according to the following procedure:

1. Classify each instructional objective for the content to be tested according to the behaviors described in chapter 3 (for example, knowledge, comprehension, application, etc.).
2. Record the number of items to be constructed for each objective in the cell corresponding to its behavioral category.
3. Total the items for each instructional objective and record the number in the total row.
4. Total the number of items falling into each behavior and record the number at the bottom of the table.
5. Compute the column and row percentages by dividing each total by the number of items in the test.

Constructing a test blueprint before preparing a test ensures you have adequately sampled the content area and have accurately matched test items to your instructional objectives.

OBJECTIVE TEST ITEMS

Your test blueprint may call for objective test items. Objective test items have one of four formats: true-false, matching, multiple-choice, and completion (short answer). Stiggins (2004) prefers the term *selected response* for these formats to emphasize that it is the system by which these formats are scored that is objective, not the selection of content they measure. In this section we consider characteristics of each format that can make your objective, or selected response, test items more effective.

Figure 12.2 Test blueprint for a unit on subtraction without borrowing.

Content Outline	Knowledge	Comprehension	Application	Total	Percent
1. The student will discriminate the subtraction sign from the addition sign.	1			1	4%
2. The student will discriminate addition problems from subtraction problems.	2			2	8%
3. The student will discriminate correctly solved subtraction problems from incorrectly solved subtraction problems.		4		4	16%
4. The student will solve correctly single-digit subtraction problems.			6	6	24%
5. The student will solve correctly subtraction problems with double-digit numerators and single-digit denominators.			6	6	24%
6. The student will solve correctly double-digit subtraction problems.			6	6	24%
Total	3	4	18	25	
Percent	12%	16%	72%		100%

Your first decision after completing the test blueprint will be to choose a format, or a combination of formats, for your test. The way you wrote the objectives may have predetermined the format, but in many instances you will have a choice among several item formats. For example, consider the following objectives and item formats.

True-False Items

True-false items are popular because they are quick and easy to write, or at least they seem to be. True-false items really do take less time to write than good objective items of any other format, but good true-false items are not so easy to prepare.

As you know from your own experience, every true-false item, regardless of how well or poorly written, gives the student a 50% chance of guessing correctly, even without reading the item. In other words, on a 50-item true-false test, we would expect individuals who were totally unfamiliar with the content being tested to answer about 25 items correctly. Fortunately, ways exist to reduce the effects of guessing:

1. Encourage all students to guess when they do not know the correct answer. Because it is virtually impossible to prevent certain students from guessing, encouraging all students to guess should equalize the effects of guessing. The test scores will then

reflect a more or less equal guessing factor plus the actual level of each student's knowledge. This also will prevent test-wise students from having an unfair advantage over nontest-wise students.

2. Require revision of statements that are false. In this approach, provide space at the end of the item for students to alter false items to make them true. Usually, the student first is asked to underline or circle the false part of the item and then to add the correct wording, as in these examples:

T   F   High IQ children <u>always</u> get high grades in school.

                 <u>tend to</u>

T   F   Panama is <u>north</u> of Cuba.

                 <u>south</u>

T   F   <u>September </u>has an extra day during leap year.

                 <u>February</u>

With this strategy, full credit is awarded only if the revision is correct. The disadvantage of such an approach is that more test time is required for the same number of items, and scoring time is increased.

Suggestions for Writing True-False Items

1. Tell students clearly how to mark *true* or *false* (e.g., circle or underline the T or F) before they begin the test. Write this instruction at the top of the test, too.
2. Construct statements that are definitely true or definitely false, without qualifications. If the item is true or false based on someone's opinion, identify the opinion's source as part of the item. For example, "According to the head of the AFL-CIO, workers' compensation is below desired standards."
3. Keep true and false statements at approximately the same length, and be sure there are approximately equal numbers of true and false items.
4. Avoid using double-negative statements. They take extra time to decipher and are difficult to interpret. For example, avoid statements such as, "It is not true that addition cannot precede subtraction in algebraic operations."
5. Avoid terms denoting indefinite degree (for example, *large, long time, regularly*) or absolutes (*never, only, always*).
6. Avoid placing items in a systematic pattern that some students might detect (for example, True-True-False-False, TFTF, and so on).
7. Don't take statements directly from the text without first making sure you are not taking them out of context.

Matching Items

Like true-false, matching items are a popular and convenient testing format. Just like good true-false items, however, good matching items are not easy to write. Imagine you are back in your ninth-grade American history class, and the following matching item shows up on your test:

Directions: Match A and B.

A	B
1. Lincoln	a. President during the 20th century
2. Nixon	b. Invented the telephone

3. Whitney	c. Delivered the Emancipation Proclamation
4. Ford	d. Only president to resign from office
5. Bell	e. Civil rights leader
6. King	f. Invented the cotton gin
7. Washington	g. Our first president
8. Roosevelt	h. Only president elected for more than two terms

See any problems? Compare the problems you identify with the descriptions of faults that follow.

Homogeneity.   The lists are not homogeneous. Column A contains names of presidents, inventors, and a civil rights leader. Unless specifically taught as a set of related individuals or ideas, this is too wide a variety for a matching exercise.

Order of Lists.   The lists are reversed: Column A should be in place of Column B, and Column B should be in place of Column A. As the exercise is now written, the student reads a name and then has to read through all or many of the more lengthy descriptions to find the answer, a much more time-consuming process. It also is a good idea to introduce some sort of order—chronological, numerical, or alphabetical—to your list of options. This saves the student time.

Easy Guessing.   Notice there are equal numbers of options and descriptions. This increases the chances of guessing correctly through elimination. If there are at least three more options than descriptions, the chance of guessing correctly is reduced to one in four.

Poor Directions.   The instructions are much too brief. Matching directions should specify the basis for matching:

> *Directions:* Column A contains brief descriptions of historical events. Column B contains the names of U.S. presidents. Indicate who was president when the historical event took place by placing the appropriate letter to the left of the number in column A.

Multiple Correct Responses.   The description "president during the 20th century" has three defensible answers: Nixon, Ford, and Roosevelt. And did you mean Henry Ford, inventor of the Model T automobile, or Gerald Ford? Always include first and last names to avoid ambiguities. Here is a corrected version of these matching items:

> *Directions:* Column A describes events associated with U.S. presidents. Indicate which name in Column B matches each event by placing the appropriate letter to the left of the number in Column A. Each name may be used only once.

Column A	Column B
_____ 1. Only president not elected to office	a. Abraham Lincoln
_____ 2. Delivered the Emancipation Proclamation	b. Richard Nixon
	c. Gerald Ford
_____ 3. Only president to resign from office	d. George Washington
_____ 4. Only president elected for more than two terms	e. Franklin Roosevelt
	f. Theodore Roosevelt
_____ 5. Our first president	g. Thomas Jefferson
	h. Woodrow Wilson

Notice that we now have complete directions, more options than descriptions, and homogeneous lists (all items in Column A are about U.S. presidents and all items in Column B are names of presidents), and we have made the alternatives unambiguous.

Suggestions for Writing Matching Items

1. Keep both the descriptions list and the options list short and homogeneous. They should fit together on the same page. Title the lists to ensure homogeneity (for example, Column A, Column B).
2. Make sure all the options are plausible **distracters** (wrong answer choices) for each description to ensure homogeneity of lists.
3. The descriptions list should contain the longer phrases or statements; the options should consist of short phrases, words, or symbols.
4. Number each description (1, 2, 3, etc.), and letter each option (a, b, c, etc.).
5. Include more options than descriptions, or some that match more than one, or both.
6. In the directions, specify the basis for matching and whether options can be used more than once.

Multiple-Choice Items

Another popular item format is the multiple-choice question. Multiple-choice tests are more common in high school and college than in elementary school. Multiple-choice items are unique among objective test items because they enable you to measure some types of higher-level cognitive objectives. When writing multiple-choice items, be careful not to give away answers by inadvertently providing students with clues in the following ways.

Stem Clue. The statement portion of a multiple-choice item is called the **stem,** and the answer choices are called *options* or *response alternatives*. A stem clue occurs when the same word or a close derivative occurs in both the stem and an option, thereby clueing the test taker to the correct answer. For example:

> In the story "Hawaiian Mystery," the name of the volcanic structure Mark and Alisha had to cross to get free was called _____.
> a. volcanic ridge
> b. tectonic plate
> c. caldron
> d. lava

In this item the correct option and the stem both contain the word *volcanic*. Thus the wise test-taker has a good chance of answering the item correctly without mastery of the content being measured.

Grammatical Clue. Consider this item:

> U.S. Grant was an _____.
> a. army general
> b. navy admiral
> c. cavalry commander
> d. senator

Most students would pick up on the easy grammatical clue in the stem. The article *an* eliminates options b, c, and d, because "navy admiral," "cavalry commander," and "senator" are ungrammatical. Option *a* is the only one that forms a grammatical sentence. A way to eliminate the grammatical clue is to replace *an* with *a/an*. Similar examples are *is/are*, *was/were*, *his/her*, and so on. Alternatively, place the article (or verb, or pronoun) in the options list:

> Christopher Columbus came to America in _____.
> a. a car
> b. a boat
> c. an airplane
> d. a balloon

Redundant Words/Unequal Length. Two very common faults in multiple-choice construction are illustrated in this item:

> In the story "Hawaiian Mystery," when Mark and Alisha were held hostage at the top of the volcano,
> a. the police could not see them to free them
> b. the police called for more help
> c. the police attempted to free them by going behind the volcano and risking a rescue
> d. the police asked them to jump to the rock below

The phrase *the police* is included in each option. To save space and time, add it to the stem: "When Mark and Alisha were held hostage at the top of the volcano, the police _____." Second, the length of options could be a giveaway. Multiple-choice item writers have a tendency to include more information in the correct option than in the incorrect options. Test-wise students know that, more often than not, the longer option is the correct one. Avoid making correct answers more than one and a half times the length of incorrect options.

All of the Above/None of the Above. In general, use "none of the above" sparingly. Some item writers use "none of the above" only when no clearly correct option is presented. However, students catch on to this practice and guess that "none of the above" is the correct answer without knowledge of the content being measured. Also, at times it may be justified to use multiple correct answers, such as "both a and c" or "both b and c." Again, use such options sparingly, because inconsistencies can easily exist among alternatives that logically eliminate some from consideration. Avoid using "all of the above," because test items should encourage discrimination, not discourage it.

Higher-Level Multiple-Choice Questions

A good multiple-choice item is the most time-consuming type of objective test item to write. Unfortunately, most multiple-choice items also are written at the knowledge level in the taxonomy of educational objectives. As a new item writer, you will tend to write items at this level, but you need to write some multiple-choice items to measure higher-level cognitive objectives as well.

First, write some of your objectives to measure comprehension, application, analysis, or evaluation. This ensures your items will be at the higher-than-knowledge level. Consult appendix C and chapter 3 for examples of higher-order thinking and problem-solving behavior. Following are some suggestions to make your higher-level multiple-choice questions more authentic.

Use Justification to Assess Reasons Behind an Answer. Questions that follow a multiple-choice item can ask for specifics as to why a particular answer was chosen. For example:

> *Directions:* Choose the most appropriate answer and cite evidence for your selection in the space below.

> The principal value of a balanced diet is that it
> a. increases your intelligence
> b. cures disease
> c. promotes mental health
> d. promotes physical health

Present evidence from the text as to why you chose your answer.

Use Pictorial, Graphical, or Tabular Stimuli. Pictures, drawings, graphs, and tables can require the student to think at least at the application level in the taxonomy of educational objectives and may involve even higher cognitive processes. Also, such stimuli often can generate several higher-level multiple-choice items, as the following questions about Figure 12.3 illustrate.

> *Directions:* Refer to the map [Figure 12.3] to answer these questions.

> Which of the following cities would be the best location for a steel mill?

> a. Li (3A)
> b. Um (3B)
> c. Cot (3D)
> d. Dube (4B)

> Approximately how many miles is it from Dube to Rag?

> a. 100 miles
> b. 150 miles
> c. 200 miles
> d. 250 miles

> In what direction would someone have to travel to get from Wog to Um?

> a. northwest
> b. northeast
> c. southwest
> d. southeast

Use Analogies to Show Relationships Between Terms. To answer analogies correctly, students must not only be familiar with the terms but also be able to understand how the terms relate to each other. For example:

> Physician is to humans as veterinarian is to

> a. fruits
> b. animals
> c. minerals
> d. vegetables

Require Application of Principles or Procedures. To test whether students comprehend the implications of a procedure or principle, have them use the principle or procedure with new information or in a novel way. This requires them to do more than just follow the steps in solving a problem. It asks them to demonstrate an ability to go beyond the context within

Figure 12.3 Use of a pictorial stimulus to measure a higher-level cognitive process.

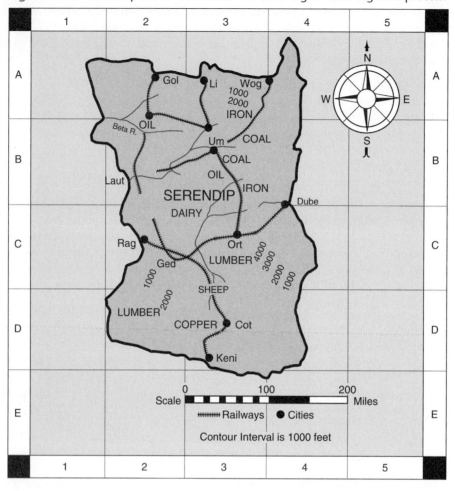

which they originally learned a principle or procedure. Consider this example, from a lesson that taught the computation of ratios and proportions.

You are on vacation and want to drive from Chicago to St. Louis on your way home. The distance between these cities is 300 miles. Your car gets 20 miles per gallon on the highway.

1. How many gallons of gas will it take to make the trip?
   a. 10
   b. 15
   c. 20
   d. 25

2. How many gallons would you have left if you filled up your 23-gallon tank before leaving?
   a. 4
   b. 6
   c. 8
   d. 10

3. If you only got 15 miles per gallon instead of 20 because of some city driving, how many more driving miles would you have left before being empty after leaving St. Louis?
    a. 15
    b. 30
    c. 45
    d. 60

Suggestions for Writing Multiple-Choice Items

1. Be sure there is one and only one correct or clearly best answer.
2. Be sure all wrong-answer choices ("distracters") are plausible. Eliminate unintentional grammatical clues, and keep the length and form of all the answer choices equal. Rotate the position of the correct answer from item to item randomly.
3. Use negative questions or statements only if the knowledge being tested requires it. In most cases it is more important for the student to know what the correct answer is rather than what it is not.
4. Include three to five options (two to four distracters plus one correct answer) to optimize testing for knowledge rather than encouraging guessing. It is not necessary to provide additional distracters for an item simply to maintain the same number of distracters for each item.
5. Use the option "none of the above" sparingly and only when all the answers can be classified unequivocally as wrong.
6. Avoid using "all of the above." It usually is the correct answer and makes the item too easy for students who have only partial information.

Completion Items

Like true-false items, completion items are relatively easy to write. The first tests constructed by classroom teachers and taken by students often are completion tests. Like items of all other formats, there are good and poor completion items.

Suggestions for Writing Completion Items

1. Require a single-word answer or a brief, definite statement. Avoid items so indefinite that they may be logically answered by several terms:

    Poor Item: World War II ended in _____.
    Better Item: World War II ended in the year _____.

2. Be sure the item poses a problem. A direct question often is better than an incomplete statement because it provides more structure for an answer:

    Poor Item: What do you think about a main character in the story "Lilies of the Field"? _____
    Better Item: The main character in the story "Lilies of the Field" was

    _____.

3. Be sure the answer is factually correct. Precisely word the question in relation to the concept or fact being tested. For example, can the answer be found in the text, workbook, or class notes taken by students?

4. Omit only key words; do not eliminate so many elements that the sense of the content is impaired:

    Poor Item: The _____ type of test item usually is graded _____ than the _____ type.

Better Item: The multiple-choice type of test item usually is graded more objectively than the _____ type.

5. Word the statement so the blank is near the end. This prevents awkward sentences.
6. If the problem requires a numerical answer, indicate the units in which it is to be expressed (for example, pounds, ounces, minutes).

Advantages and Disadvantages of Objective-Item Formats

Table 12.1 summarizes the advantages and disadvantages of each of the preceding objective-item formats.

Table 12.1 Advantages and disadvantages of various objective-item formats.

Advantages	Disadvantages
True-False Tests	
Tend to be short, so more materials can be covered than with any other item format; thus, use T-F items when extensive content has been covered.	Tend to emphasize rote memorization of knowledge (although complex questions sometimes can be asked using T-F items).
Faster to construct (but avoid creating an item by taking statements out of context or slightly modifying them).	They assume an unequivocally true or false answer (it is unfair to make students guess at your criteria for evaluating the truth of a statement).
Scoring is easier (tip: provide a "T" and "F" for them to circle, because a student's handwritten "T" or "F" can be hard to decipher).	Allow and may even encourage a high degree of guessing (generally, longer examinations compensate for this).
Matching Items	
Simple to construct and score.	Tend to ask trivial information.
Ideal for measuring associations between facts.	Emphasize memorization.
Can be more efficient than multiple-choice questions because they avoid repetition of options in measuring association.	Most commercial answer sheets can accommodate only five options, thus limiting the size of a matching item.
Reduce the effects of guessing.	
Multiple-Choice Tests	
Versatile in measuring objectives, from the knowledge level to the evaluation level.	Time consuming to write.
Because writing is minimal, considerable course material can be sampled quickly.	If not carefully written, can have more than one defensible correct answer.
Scoring is highly objective, requiring only a count of correct responses.	
Can be written so students must discriminate among options varying in correctness, avoiding the absolute judgments of T-F tests.	
Reduce effects of guessing.	
Amenable to statistical analysis, so you can determine which items are ambiguous or too difficult (see Kubiszyn & Borich, 2007, chapter 10).	

Table 12.1 *Continued*

Completion Tests	
Question construction is relatively easy.	Encourage a low level of response complexity.
Guessing is reduced because the question requires a specific response.	Can be difficult to score (the stem must be general enough to not communicate the answer, leading unintentionally to multiple defensible answers).
Less time is needed to complete than multiple-choice items, so more content can be covered.	Very short answers tend to measure recall of specific facts, names, places, and events instead of more complex behaviors.

ESSAY TEST ITEMS

In this section, we explain what an essay question is, describe the two major types, and provide suggestions for writing them. Essay questions require the learner to supply, rather than select, the correct answer. The student must compose a response to a question for which no single answer can be cited as correct to the exclusion of all others. The accuracy and quality of such a response often can be judged only by a person skilled in the subject area. Essay questions are usually prepared in a written format at the middle school and high school grades but can be administered orally and responded to orally in the early elementary grades, especially when students have yet to acquire sufficient written language competency.

Like objective test items, essay questions may be well constructed or poorly constructed. The well-constructed essay question tests complex cognitive skills by requiring the student to organize, integrate, and synthesize knowledge; to use information to solve novel problems; or to be original and innovative in problem solving. The poorly constructed essay question may require the student to do no more than recall information as it was presented in the textbook or in class. Worse, the poorly constructed essay question may not inform the learner what is required for a satisfactory response. There are two types of essay questions you will want to write: the extended-response essay question and the restricted-response essay question.

Extended-Response Questions

A question that allows the student to determine the length and complexity of a response is called an **extended-response essay** question. This type of question is most useful at the analysis, synthesis, or evaluation levels of cognitive complexity. Because of the length of this type of item and the time required to organize and express the response, the extended-response essay question is sometimes better used as an assignment extended over a number of days or a take-home test. Because of its length and depth, the extended-response question often is of value in assessing communication ability as well as in assessing higher-order thinking skills. For example:

- Compare and contrast the presidential administrations of George W. Bush and Ronald Reagan. Consider economic, social, and military policies. Avoid taking a position in support of either president. Your response will be graded on objectivity, accuracy, organization, and clarity.

- Now that we have studied about the Gold Rush, imagine you are on a wagon train going to California. Write a letter to your relatives back home telling them of some of the hardships you have suffered and the dangers you have experienced.

These questions, while focusing the learner, give the learner considerable latitude in formulating an answer and in determining the length of the response. Now let's look at a restricted-response essay question.

Restricted-Response Questions

A question that poses a specific problem for which the student must recall proper information, organize it in a suitable manner, derive a defensible conclusion, and express it according to specific criteria is called a **restricted-response** question or essay (Borich & Tombari, 2004; Kubiszyn & Borich, 2007). Restricted-response questions can be written or in the early elementary grades posed orally to the learner. They usually require a minute or so of an oral response or a paragraph or two that is written. The statement of the problem given orally by the teacher or as part of the written question specifies the response limitations that guide the student in responding and provides criteria for scoring. For example, the following are examples of restricted-response questions that could be delivered orally or in writing that assess student understanding:

> *In your own words, explain two differences between igneous and sedimentary rock and give one example of each not given in class.*

> *In the story "Ben Franklin's Childhood," give some examples of how he was a born leader and always knew what to do.*

To demonstrate that they know "igneous" and "sedimentary" as concepts and not just simple knowledge, your learners must do two things: They must use their own words to explain the differences and not simply recall what their text said or what they copied from an overhead; and they must give original examples of each rock. If they can do this, you can correctly say they have the concepts.

When Should You Use Essay Questions?

Although each situation must be considered individually, some lend themselves to essay items. For example:

1. The instructional objectives specify high-level cognitive processes; they require supplying information rather than simply recognizing information. These processes often cannot be measured with objective items.
2. Only a few tests or items need to be graded. If you have 30 students and design a test with six extended-response essays, you will spend a great deal of time scoring. Reserve essay questions for objectives that require higher-order thinking and/or use only one or two essay questions in conjunction with objective items.
3. Test security is a consideration. If you are afraid test items will be passed on to future students, it is better to use an essay test. In general, a good essay test takes less time to construct than a good objective test. For orally prepared restricted-response questions for assessent, remember that you will need to prepare individual questions for each student in advance or assign points to other learners who contribute to another's answer.

Following are some learning outcomes and examples for which extended- and restricted-response questions may be used:

- *Analyze relationships*   The colors blue and gray are related to cool temperatures. What are some other colors related to? What effect would these colors have on a picture you might draw?
- *Compare-and-contrast positions*   Compare and contrast two characters from stories you have read to understand how the characters responded differently to conditions in the stories.
- *State necessary assumptions*   When Columbus landed on San Salvador, what did he assume about the land he had discovered? Were his assumptions correct?
- *Identify appropriate conclusions*   What are some of the reasons for and against building a landfill near homes?
- *Explain cause-and-effect relations*   What might have caused early Americans to travel west in the 1800s? Choose one of the pioneers we have studied (like Daniel Boone) and give some of the reasons they traveled west.
- *Make predictions*   What can you predict about a coming storm by observing clouds? Explain what it is about the clouds that helps you predict rain.
- *Organize data to support a viewpoint*   On the board you will find the numbers of new homes built and autos purchased for each month over the past year. Use these data to support the viewpoint that our economy is growing either larger or smaller.
- *Point out strengths and weaknesses*   What is either a strength or a limitation of the following musical instruments for a marching band: oboe, trumpet, tuba, violin?
- *Integrate data from several sources*   Imagine you are celebrating your birthday with nine of your friends. Two pizzas arrive, but each is cut into four pieces. What problem do you have? What method would you choose for seeing that everyone gets a piece of the pizza?
- *Evaluate the quality or worth of an item, product, or action*   What should be considered in choosing a balanced meal from the basic food groups?

Suggestions for Writing Essay Questions

1. Have clearly in mind what mental processes you want the student to use before starting to write the question. Refer to the *Higher-Order Thinking and Problem-solving Checklist* in appendix C and the example verbs in chapter 3 at the various levels in the taxonomy of educational objectives for the cognitive domain (for example, compare and contrast, create alternatives, make choices among).

Poor Item: Criticize the following speech by our president.

Better Item: Consider the following presidential speech. Focus on the section dealing with economic policy and discriminate between factual statements and opinion. List these statements separately, label them, and indicate whether each statement is or is not consistent with the president's overall economic policy.

2. Write the question to define the task clearly and unambiguously to the student. Tasks should be explained (1) in the overall instructions preceding the test items and/or (2) in the test items themselves. Include whether spelling and grammar will be counted and whether organization of the response will be an important scoring element. Also, indicate the level of detail and supporting data required.

Poor Item: Discuss the value of behavioral objectives.

Better Item: Behavioral objectives have enjoyed increased popularity in education over the years. In your text and in class, the advantages and disadvantages of behavioral objectives have been discussed. Take a position for or against the use of behavioral objectives in education and support your position with at least three of the arguments covered in class or in the text.

3. Start essay questions with such words or phrases as *compare, contrast, give reasons for, give original examples of, predict what would happen if,* and so on. Do not begin with such words as *what, who, when,* and *list,* because these words generally lead to tasks that require only recall of information, which is better assessed with objective test items.

Poor Item: List three reasons behind America's withdrawal from Vietnam.

Better Item: After more than 10 years of involvement, the United States withdrew from Vietnam in 1975. Speculate on what would have happened if America had *not* withdrawn at that time and had *not* increased its military presence significantly above 1972 levels.

4. A question dealing with a controversial issue should ask for, and be evaluated in terms of, the presentation of evidence for a position, rather than the position taken. It is not defensible to demand that a student accept a specific conclusion or solution, but it is reasonable to appraise how well he or she has learned to use the evidence on which a specific conclusion is based.

Poor Item: What laws should Congress pass to improve the medical care of all citizens in the United States?

Better Item: Some feel the cost of all medical care should be borne by the federal government. Do you agree or disagree? Support your position with at least three logical arguments.

5. Avoid using optional items. That is, require all students to complete the same items. Allowing students to select 2 of 3, or 3 of 4 decreases the uniformity of the test across all students, which will decrease your basis for comparison among students.

6. Establish reasonable time and/or page limits for each essay item to help the student complete the entire test and to indicate the level of detail you have in mind. Indicate such limits either in the statement of the problem or close to the number of the question.

7. Be sure each question relates to an instructional objective. Check your test blueprint to see if the content of the essay item is represented.

Some Criteria for Scoring Essay Items

Essays can be difficult to score consistently across individuals. That is, the same essay answer may be given an A by one scorer and a B or C by another scorer. Or the same answer may be graded A on one occasion, but B or C on another occasion by the same scorer! Following are several criteria that can help maintain the consistency of your grading across essays.

Content. Although essays are used less to measure factual knowledge than thinking processes, the content should provide material relevant to the facts and adequately cover the question being asked.

Organization.   Beyond the content of a student's response, you may want to include the organization of a response among your grading criteria. For example, does the essay have an introduction, body, and conclusion? Do progressions and sequences follow a logical or chronological development? Also you will want to decide whether spelling and grammar will be included among your grading criteria, and, if so, alert students to this before they take the test.

Process.   If your essay item tests at the application level or above, the most important criteria for scoring will be the extent to which a particular thinking process has been carried out. In addition each thinking process (for example, application, analysis, synthesis, and evaluation) results in a solution, recommendation, or decision. So, your grading criteria should include both the adequacy of the solution, recommendation, or decision and evidence of the thinking process that led to it (for example, have the correct analytical procedures been applied?).

Completeness/Internal Consistency.   Does the essay deal adequately with the problem presented? Is there sufficient detail to support the points being made? And are these points logically related to one another to cover the topic as fully as required?

Originality/Creativity.   You may also want to recognize and encourage original and creative responses. Expect some students to develop new and creative ways of answering your questions, for which you can award credit when appropriate.

Inform your students of any of the preceding criteria you will be using. Typically two or three of the above criteria most relevant to the focus of the exam are chosen and, then, weighted in terms of their importance to the overall grade, for example, 75% on content, 25% on organization, or 33% content, 33% process, 33% organization. Once your students know how you are going to score the test, they can prepare better and more defensible responses. Figure 12.4 illustrates a scale for scoring essays with the preceding criteria.

VALIDITY AND RELIABILITY

Test results are useful only if they are valid and reliable. Although it is unlikely that you will actually determine the reliability or validity of your own classroom tests, you will need to know what these terms mean when evaluating the claims made by published tests which may be purchased by your school or school district, and their applicability to your classroom. These terms are defined as follows:

1. **Validity.** Does the test measure what it is supposed to?
2. **Reliability.** Does the test yield the same or similar scores consistently?

Types of Validity

A test is *valid* if it measures what it says it is measuring. For instance, if it is supposed to be a test of third-grade arithmetic ability, it should measure third-grade arithmetic skills, not fifth-grade arithmetic skills and not reading ability. If it is supposed to be a measure of ability to write behavioral objectives, it should measure that ability, not the ability to recognize poor objectives.

If test results will be used to make any kind of decision and if the test information is to be useful, the test must be valid. There are several ways of deciding whether a test is sufficiently valid to be useful. The three methods most often used are *content validity, concurrent validity*, and *predictive validity*.

Figure 12.4 Example of a scoring scheme for an essay test.

Content

1	2	3	4	5
Very limited investigation. Little or no material related to facts.		Some investigation and attention to the facts are apparent.		Extensive investigation. Good detail and attention to the facts.

Organization

1	2	3	4	5
Very little organization of ideas. Presentation is confusing and hard to follow.		Some organization of ideas, but logical order needs to be improved.		Good organization. Ideas logically connected and built on one another.

Process

1	2	3	4	5
Very little justification or support of ideas. Final solution or decision unsubstantiated.		Some justification and support of ideas. Final solution or decision needs greater substantiation.		Good justification and support of ideas. Final solution or decision well substantiated.

Completeness

1	2	3	4	5
Very little focus on detail. Ideas are superficial and incomplete.		Some attention to detail. Greater focus and attention to detail needed.		Good attention to detail. Ideas are thorough and complete.

Originality

1	2	3	4	5
Response lacks originality. Nothing new or creative.		Some originality. Greater creativity needed.		Response is original and creative. Many novel and unexpected ideas.

Content Validity.   The content validity of a test is established by examining its contents. The teacher inspects test questions to see if they correspond to what should be covered as indicated in the test blueprint (illustrated in Figure 12.2). This is easiest when there is a test blueprint, where it may be fairly easy to specify what to include in a test. But sometimes a test can look valid but measure something different from what is intended, such as guessing ability, reading level, or skills that learners may have acquired before your instruction. Content validity is, therefore, a minimum requirement for a useful test but does not guarantee a valid test.

Concurrent Validity.   To establish concurrent validity, an established test must be administered at the same time as the new test you have designed. Unlike content validity, concurrent validity yields a numerical value in the form of a correlation coefficient, called a *validity coefficient* (see Borich & Tombari, 2004, chapter 4; Kubiszyn & Borich, 2007, chapter 14).

Video Window

Assessing Higher-Order Thinking

In this video, Judy is teaching her ninth-grade social studies class a lesson in how the economy of a region is often related to its geography. Her goal is to help her learners see how differences and similarities in geography across the country allow different products to be made and sold. In this lesson Judy engages her students in a class activity that raises their thinking to a higher level—not just to provide facts but to compare and contrast, to predict, and to think critically in order to arrive at the proper relationships among geography and the economy. Using the suggestions for writing and using essay items in the text as your guide, write an essay item Judy could use to examine her students at the end of this lesson to determine if they understood the concept she was teaching.

 To answer this question online, go to the Video Windows *module of this chapter of the* Companion Website at www.prenhall.com/borich.

The new test and the established test are administered to a group of students and the relationship—the correlation—between the two sets of test scores is determined. If there exists an established test (criterion) with which the new test can be compared and in which people have confidence, concurrent validity provides a good method of determining the validity of a test.

Predictive Validity.   Predictive validity refers to how well the test predicts some future behavior of the examinee that is representative of the test's content. This form of validity is particularly useful for tests that may be used to predict how well the test taker will do in some future setting. Predictive validity also yields a numerical index in the form of a correlation coefficient. This time, however, it is the relationship between the test and some future behavior (for example, on-the-job performance) that is being measured.

All three methods for determining validity—content, concurrent, and predictive—assume that some criterion exists external to the test that can be used to anchor or validate it. In the case of content validity, it is the instructional objectives (for example, in the test blueprint) that provide the anchor or point of reference; in the case of concurrent validity, it is another well-accepted test measuring the same content; and in the case of predictive validity, it is some future behavior or condition we are attempting to predict.

Types of Reliability

The *reliability* of a test refers to the consistency with which it yields the same rank or score for an individual taking the test several times. In other words, a test is reliable if it consistently yields the same, or nearly the same, ranks among all individuals over repeated administrations during which we would not expect the trait being measured to have changed.

There are several ways to estimate the reliability of a test. The three methods most often used are called *test-retest, alternative form,* and *internal consistency.*

Test-Retest.   Test-retest is a method of estimating reliability that is exactly what its name implies. The test is given twice to the same individuals to determine the relationship—or correlation—between the first set of scores and the second set of scores.

Alternate Form.   If two equivalent forms of a test are available, the reliability of the test can be determined by the correlation between them. Both tests are administered to a group of students to determine the relationship (correlation) between the two sets of scores. Large differences in students' scores on two forms of a test that supposedly measures the same behavior would indicate an unreliable test.

Internal Consistency.   If the test measures a single concept (for example, addition), it is reasonable to assume that learners who get one item right will more likely get other, similar items right. In other words, items ought to be related or correlated with each other, and the test ought to be internally consistent. If this is the case, then the reliability of the test can be estimated by the internal-consistency method (Borich & Tombari, 2004; Kubiszyn & Borich, 2007).

Typically, validity coefficients for a test are lower than reliability coefficients. Acceptable validity coefficients for a test generally range between .60 and .80 or higher; acceptable reliability coefficients generally range from .80 to .90 or higher. The maximum coefficient obtainable for either validity or reliability is 1.0. Test accuracy is in part a combined measure of validity and reliability and in part determined by how well the test content matches the prevailing educational curriculum.

MARKS AND MARKING SYSTEMS

After you have administered your test, you will have to score it and assign marks. Often the type of symbol a teacher uses to represent a mark is determined at the school or district level, for example, A–F, Excellent-Good-Satisfactory-Poor-Unsatisfactory, or a numerical marking system. As a classroom teacher you have considerable flexibility in determining how to assign these marks to learners. **Marks and grading systems** are based on comparisons, usually comparisons of students with one or more of the following:

- Other students
- Established standards
- Aptitude
- Actual vs. potential effort
- Actual vs. potential improvement

Comparison with Other Students

The expression "grading on the curve" means your grade or mark depends on how your achievement compares with the achievement of other students in your class. Sometimes districts or schools encourage grading on the curve by specifying the percentages of students who will be assigned various grades. For example, students in the top 10% get an A.

The main advantage of such a system is that it simplifies marking decisions. There is no deliberation or agonizing over what cutoff scores should determine whether students get this grade or that. However, this type of marking system fails to consider differences in the overall knowledge or ability level of the class. Regardless of achievement, in such a system some students always will get A's, and some always will get F's.

Comparison with Established Standards

In the marking system that uses comparison with established standards, it is possible for any student to get an A or F or any grade between. Achievements of individual students are unrelated to other individual students. All that is relevant is whether a student attains a defined standard of achievement or performance. We labeled this approach *criterion-referenced* earlier in this chapter. In such a system, letter grades may be assigned based on the percentage of test items answered correctly, as this distribution illustrates:

Comparisons with other students, established standards, aptitude, effort, and improvement all can be the basis for assigning grades. Ultimately, you must decide the balance of approaches to use that best fits the goals of the classroom and school.

Grade	Percentage of Items Answered Correctly
A	90–100
B	80–89
C	70–79
D	60–69
F	Less than 60

In theory, this system makes it possible for all students to obtain high grades if they put forth sufficient effort (assuming the percentage cutoffs are not unreasonably high). Also, grade assignment is simplified; a student either has correctly answered 90% of the items or has not. As with the comparison with other students method, there is no deliberating or agonizing over assigning grades. Also, teachers who work to improve their teaching effectiveness can observe improvement in grades with the passage of time.

As you might expect, such a system also has its drawbacks. Establishing a standard for each grade attained is no small task, and what is reasonable for an A may vary from school to school and from time to time as a result of ability levels, the content being taught, and curriculum changes.

Comparison with Aptitude

Aptitude is another name for potential or ability. In such systems, students are compared neither to other students nor to established standards. Instead, they are compared to themselves. That is, marks are assigned depending on how closely to their potential they are achieving. Thus students with high aptitude or potential who are achieving at high levels would get high grades, because they would be achieving at their potential. Those with high aptitude and average achievement would get lower grades, because they would be achieving below their potential.

But students with average aptitude and average achievement also would get high grades, because they would be considered to be achieving at their potential. Thus the same grade could mean very different things in terms of absolute achievement.

Comparison of Achievement with Effort

Systems that compare achievement with effort are similar to those that compare achievement with aptitude. Students who get average test scores but have to work hard to get them are given high marks. Students who get average scores but do not have to work hard to get them are given lower grades. The advantage cited for grading on effort is that it motivates slower or turned-off students. However, it also may turn off brighter students, who quickly see such a system as unfair. It may also be difficult to determine if a student has or has not "worked hard."

Comparison of Achievement with Improvement

Such systems compare the amount of improvement between the beginning and end of instruction. Students who show the most progress get the highest grades. An obvious problem occurs for the student who does well on a test at the beginning of the instruction, called the *pretest*, because improvement for this student is likely to be less than for a student who does poorly on the pretest.

Which marking system should you choose? Most now agree that comparisons with established standards (criterion-referenced) would best suit the primary function of marking in the classroom, which is to provide feedback about academic progress. In reality, many schools and districts have adopted multiple marking systems, such as assigning separate grades for achievement and effort or achievement, effort, and improvement. As long as the achievement portion of the grade reflects only achievement, such systems are appropriate.

STANDARDIZED TESTS

So far, we have limited most of our discussion to teacher-constructed tests. However, many teachers also are required at least once a year to administer end-of-year standardized tests, evaluate their results, and interpret them to curious and sometimes concerned parents.

Standardized tests, called *high-stakes* tests, are developed by test construction specialists, usually with the assistance of curriculum experts, teachers, and school administrators, to determine a student's performance level relative to others of similar age and grade. These tests are standardized because they are administered and scored according to specific and uniform (standard) procedures.

When schools use standardized tests, administrators can more easily and confidently compare test results from different students, classes, schools, and districts than is the case with different teacher-made tests. For the most part, schools use standardized tests for comparative purposes. This is quite different from the purposes of teacher-made tests, which are to determine pupil mastery or skill levels, to assign grades, and to provide specific feedback to students and parents. Table 12.2 compares standardized and teacher-made tests on several important dimensions.

The results of standardized tests are reported as percentile ranks. Percentile ranks enable you to determine how a student's performance compares with others of the same grade or age. Keep in mind two points when interpreting percentile ranks:

1. Percentile ranks often are confused with *percentage correct*. In using percentile ranks, be sure you communicate that a percentile rank of, for example, 62 means the individual's

Table 12.2 A comparison of standardized and teacher-made achievement tests.

Dimension	Standardized Achievement Tests	Teacher-Made Achievement Tests
Learning outcomes and content measured	Measures general outcomes and content appropriate to the majority of U.S. schools. These tests of general skills and understanding tend not to reflect specific or unique emphasis of local curricula.	Well adapted to the specific and unique outcomes and content of a local curriculum; adaptable to various sizes of work units, but tend to neglect complex learning outcomes.
Quality of test items	Quality of items generally is high. Items are written by specialists, pretested, and selected on the basis of results from quantitative item analysis.	Quality of item is often unknown. Quality is typically lower than standardized tests due to limited time available to the teacher.
Reliability	Reliability is high, commonly between .80 and .95, and frequently above .90 (highest possible is 1.0).	Reliability is usually unknown, but can be high if items are carefully constructed.
Administration and scoring	Procedures are standardized; specific instructions are provided.	Uniform procedures are possible, but usually are flexible and unwritten.
Interpretation of scores	Scores can be compared to norm groups. Test manual and other guides aid interpretation and use.	Score comparisons and interpretation are limited to local class or school situation. Few if any guidelines are available for interpretation and use.

score was *higher* than 62% of all those who took the test (called the *norming sample*). Or you can say that 62% of those who took the test scored lower than this individual. (Commonly, a score at the 62nd percentile is misinterpreted to mean the student answered only 62% of the items correctly. But a score at the 62nd percentile might be equivalent to a B or a C, whereas a score of 62% likely would be an F.)

2. Equal differences between percentile ranks do not necessarily indicate equal differences in achievement. In a grade of 100 pupils, the difference in achievement between the 2nd percentile and 5th percentile is substantial, whereas the difference between the 47th and 50th percentile is negligible. Interpretation of differences in percentile ranks must take into consideration that percentiles toward the extreme or end points of the percentile distribution tend to be spread out (like a rubber band) and represent much greater changes in achievement than differences in the middle of the scale, where the amount of change between percentiles tends to be small.

Helping Students Prepare for Standardized Tests

Standardized tests are often called "high-stakes" tests because they can be used to determine whether a student receives access to advanced placement and honors courses, is promoted to the next grade, or even graduate from high school. Likewise they are "high stakes" for principals and teachers when they receive recognition or reprimands depending on the test's outcome. Regardless of how you personally may feel about these tests, they are used in all 50 states and are likely to be around for some time to come. So here are some suggestions from Kubiszyn and Borich (2007) that may relieve some of the frustration you may feel about them and can help your students improve their performance on them.

Focus on the Task, Not Your Feelings About It.   Because your students' promotion and your teaching position can be affected by your state's standardized assessment program, it makes sense to focus less on your feelings about the test and more on the demands of the task before you. So it will be critical that you obtain your state's academic standards at your grade level, which are usually available from the Web site for your state education agency. Ensuring that you target your state standards in your classroom is the single most important thing you can do to prepare your students to perform well on these tests. For this you may have to modify your instructional methods some to match the content and processes identified in the state standards.

Inform Students and Parents About the Importance of the Test.   Although some students will already understand the purpose and relevance of the test, there will be some who do not. To get students to try their best, some advocate warning students or issuing rewards. Others say such strategies send the wrong message and only increase the stress and pressure that can impair student performance. Neither of these approaches will be as effective as taking the time to explain to your students the reason the test is being administered, how the results will be used, and how the test is relevant to their learning. In this manner you are more likely to engage and motivate your students to do well and to take the test seriously and carefully. And, instead of presenting a lecture on the pros or cons of tests, keep it simple: Let your students know they have learned what will be necessary to do well on the test, and you expect them to do well.

Teach Test-Taking Skills From the First Day of School as Part of Your Regular Instruction.   Some students seem to perform better on tests than other students. This may seem to be because of luck, aptitude, confidence, or some other factor. However, there also is an element of skill in test taking that affects student performance. If all students in your class are aware of various test-taking skills, their overall performance will increase. For example, you can teach your students to:

1. *Follow directions carefully.*   Some students, especially those who may be impulsive or who have difficulty reading, may neglect to read directions carefully or read them at all. You can address this critical point frequently during your daily classroom routine and remind students about it during your regular classroom tests.

2. *Read test items, passages, and related information carefully.*   Who has not rushed through a test item only to find we missed or misread a word and lost credit as a result? You can reduce the likelihood your pupils will do this by providing practice during in-class and homework assignments and during your regular tests by highlighting key words, rereading items, and double-checking answers. For multiple-choice questions, remind students to read each option before selecting their answer. This may be especially important for pupils who have come from cultures where standardized tests are not used or used as much as they are in the United States.

3. *Manage test-taking time.*   Students must work quickly to complete standardized tests, but they must also work accurately. This skill, too, can be improved with practice in the classroom. Instead of giving students "as much time as they need" to answer questions on a classroom test, impose a time limit for practice. For lengthy tests, have students plan out the number of minutes they will spend on each phase of the test.

4. *Attempt easier items first.*   Many teacher-made tests begin with easy items and then end with the most difficult items. But standardized tests typically have a more random order to their difficulty level. Unprepared students may encounter a difficult question early in the test and spend an inordinate amount of time on a question that even many of the best

students may miss. When you administer your classroom tests, encourage students to answer as many items as they know the answer to before they attempt the more difficult items.

5. *Eliminate options before answering.* Test-wise students know they can increase their chances of answering correctly if they can eliminate one or two multiple-choice or matching options before attempting to choose the correct one. Have your students practice this in class and remind them during your objective tests to follow this strategy.

6. *Teach students to check their answers after completing the test.* Some pupils have such an aversion to tests or take them so lightly that they do not check their answers after they finish a test—even if time remains. You can practice this by reminding your students to use the full testing time to go over their answers when giving your classroom tests.

As the Standardized Test Day Approaches, Respond to Student Questions Openly and Directly. Before a standardized test you can expect that some children will begin to wonder or worry about the test (e.g., What will it look like? Will I be the last one finished? What if I get a bad grade? What can I do if I have a question during the test?). This sense of uncertainty is a common cause of anxiety, too much of which will interfere with your students' test performance. To prevent this before the test day, provide your pupils with as much information about the test's format and administration procedures as you have. This can include basic information such as test days and times and the subjects, format, or style of responding and how their questions may be addressed. You may also want to role-play various scenarios with the class to ensure they are clear on the procedures.

Take Advantage of Whatever Preparation Materials Are Available. In many states your state education agency or school district will provide some helpful practice tests and exercises designed to familiarize students with the style, format, and subject matter of the test. Although these exercises take classroom time, they will help test-taking efficiency and manage your students' stress by minimizing their uncertainties and increasing the time they spend focusing on the test items rather than wondering how they fill in the answer sheets. Take full advantage of the preparation materials provided and supplement them with others of your own, when available.

PERFORMANCE ASSESSMENT

Some skills—particularly those involving independent judgment, critical thinking, and decision making—are best assessed by asking learners to show what they can do. In the field of athletics, diving and gymnastics are examples of performances that show what students can do with what they have learned. Their scores are used to decide, for example, who earns a medal, who wins first, second, third, and so on, or who qualifies for district or regional competition. These are called **performance assessments.** See In Practice: Focus on Performance Assessment.

Teachers use performance assessments to assess complex cognitive processes, as well as attitudes and social skills in academic areas such as science, social studies, or math (National Research Council, 2001). When doing so, they establish situations that allow them directly to observe and to rate learners as they analyze, problem-solve, experiment, make decisions, measure, cooperate with others, present orally, or produce a product. These situations simulate real-world activities, as might be expected in a job, in the community, or in various forms of advanced training.

One of the best ways of getting your learners to exhibit what they can know and can do is through the portfolio. Although some traditional paper and pencil tests strive to measure complex cognitive outcomes, the portfolio is a performance assessment that measures them in more authentic contexts. With the portfolio, the teacher observes and evaluates student abilities to carry out complex activities that are used and valued in as well as outside the classroom.

In Practice

Focus on Performance Assessment

Performance tests can be assessments of processes, products, or both. For example, at the Darwin School in Winnipeg, Manitoba, teachers assess the reading process of each student by noting the percentage of words read accurately during oral reading, the number of sentences read by the learner that are meaningful within the context of the story, and the percentage of story elements that the learner can talk about in his or her own words after reading.

At the West Orient school in Gresham, Oregon, fourth-grade learners assemble portfolios of their writing products. These portfolios include both rough and polished drafts of poetry, essays, biographies, and self-reflections. Several math teachers at Twin Peaks Middle School in Poway, California, require their students to assemble math portfolios, which include the following products of their problem-solving efforts: long-term projects, daily notes, journal entries about troublesome test problems, written explanations of how they solved problems, and the problem solutions themselves.

Social studies learning processes and products are assessed in the Aurora, Colorado, public schools by engaging learners in a variety of projects built around this question: "Based on your study of Colorado history, what current issues in Colorado do you believe are the most important to address, what are your ideas about the resolutions of those issues, and what contributions will you make toward the resolutions?" (Pollock, 1992). Learners answer these questions in a variety of ways involving individual and group writing assignments, oral presentations, and exhibits.

Teachers across the country are using performance tests not only to assess higher-level cognitive skills but also noncognitive outcomes such as self-direction, ability to work with others, and social awareness (Marzano, Pickering, & Pollock, 2001; Redding, 1992). This concern for the affective domain of learning reflects an awareness by educators that the skilled performance of complex tasks involves more than the ability to recall information, form concepts, generalize, and problem-solve. It also involves habits of mind, attitudes, and social skills (Costa & Kallick, 2000a, 2000b).

The Aurora public school system in Colorado has developed a list of learning outcomes and their indicators for learners in kindergarten through 12th grade. These are shown in Figure 12.5.

For each of these 19 indicators, a four-category rating scale serves as a guide for teachers who are unsure of how to define "assumes responsibility" or "demonstrates consideration." While observing learners during performance tests in social studies, science, art, or economics, teachers are alert to recognize and rate those behaviors that suggest learners have acquired the outcomes.

Teachers in the Aurora Public Schools are encouraged to use this list of outcomes when planning their courses. They first ask themselves, What key facts, concepts, and principles should all learners remember? In addition, they try to fuse this subject area content with the five district outcomes by designing special performance tests. For example, a third-grade language arts teacher who is planning a writing unit might choose to focus on indicators 8 and 9 to address district outcomes related to "collaborative worker," indicator 1 for the outcome of "self-directed learner," and 13 for the outcome, "quality producer." She would then design a performance assessment that allows learners to demonstrate learning in these areas. She might select other indicators and outcomes for subsequent units and performance tests.

Figure 12.5 Learning outcomes of Aurora Public Schools.

A Self-Directed Learner

1. Sets priorities and achievable goals.
2. Monitors and evaluates progress.
3. Creates options for self.
4. Assumes responsibility for actions.
5. Creates a positive vision for self and future.

A Collaborative Worker

6. Monitors own behavior as a group member.
7. Assesses and manages group functioning.
8. Demonstrates interactive communication.
9. Demonstrates consideration for individual differences.

A Complex Thinker

10. Uses a wide variety of strategies for managing complex issues.
11. Selects strategies appropriate to the resolution of complex issues and applies the strategies with accuracy and thoroughness.
12. Accesses and uses topic-relevant knowledge.

A Quality Producer

13. Creates products that achieve their purpose.
14. Creates products appropriate to the intended audience.
15. Creates products that reflect craftsmanship.
16. Uses appropriate resources/technology.

A Community Contributor

17. Demonstrates knowledge about his or her diverse communities.
18. Takes action.
19. Reflects on his or her role as a community contributor.

Source: From *Curriculum Report,* Aurora Public Schools, Aurora, Colorado, 1993, p.11.

Likewise, a ninth-grade history teacher, having identified the important content for a unit on civil rights, might develop a performance test to assess district outcomes related to "complex thinker," "collaborative worker," and "community contributor." A performance test (adapted from Redding, 1992, p. 51) might take this form: "A member of a minority in your community has been denied housing, presumably on the basis of race, ethnicity, or religion. What steps do you believe are legally and ethically defensible, and in what order do you believe they should be followed?" This performance test could require extensive research, group collaboration, role-playing, and recommendations for current ways to improve minority rights.

Performance tests represent an addition to objective-type tests. These paper and pencil tests are the most efficient, reliable, and valid instruments available for assessing knowledge, comprehension, and some types of applications. But when it comes to assessing complex thinking skills, attitudes, and social skills, performance tests can, if properly constructed, do a better job. If not properly constructed, however, performance assessments can have some of the same problems with authenticity, scoring efficiency, reliability, and validity as traditional approaches to testing. Borich and Tombari (2004) and Stiggins (2004) emphasize that performance assessments of affect must adhere to the same standards of evaluation and scoring as assessments of achievement, or the results may prove too subjective to be of value. In Borich and Tombari (2004) you will find the step by step procedures that will guide you through a process that will allow you to construct performance assessments in your classroom.

 Video Window

Performance Assessment

In this video you will learn about the many types of assessment activities that are called *performance based* and how they differ from traditional tests and examinations and classroom observations. You will also learn about three topics that are important when planning a performance assessment: constructing a scoring guide—or rubric, determining the role of the student in designing a performance assessment, and the important role of technology in measuring your learners' performance. As you watch this video, see if you can answer the following questions:

- Who can participate in constructing a scoring guide or rubric for a performance assessment?
- What are some criteria you could use in choosing selections for a portfolio?
- What are some examples of the use of technology in constructing a performance assessment?

 To answer these questions online, go to the Video Windows *module for this chapter on the* Companion Website *at www.prenhall.com/borich.*

THE PORTFOLIO

A type of performance assessment that is more than a onetime picture of what a learner has accomplished is called **portfolio assessment.** Its principal purpose is to tell a story of a learner's growth in proficiency, long-term achievement, and significant accomplishments in a given academic area. A portfolio is a planned collection of learner achievement that documents what a student has accomplished and the steps taken to get there. The collection represents a collaborative effort among teacher, learner, and sometimes parent to decide on portfolio purpose, content, and evaluation criteria. The portfolio is a measure of deep understanding that can show growth in competence and understanding across the term or school year (DeFina, 1999; Klenowski, 2002; Kranz, 1998).

Rationale for the Portfolio

As you know from building your own digital portfolio during this course, a portfolio is based on a collection of accomplishments over time. It is one of the best ways your learners can show their final achievement and the effort put into getting there. Portfolios are not new. Painters, fashion designers, artisans, and writers assemble portfolios that embody their best work. Television and radio announcers compile video- and audiotaped excerpts of their best performances that they present when interviewing for a job. A portfolio is their way of showing what they can really do.

Portfolios in the classroom serve a similar purpose. They show off a learner's best writing, artwork, science projects, historical thinking, or mathematical achievement. But they also show the steps the learner took to get there. They compile the learner's best work. But they also include the works-in-progress: the early drafts, test runs, pilot studies, or preliminary trials. Thus they are an ideal way to assess final mastery, effort, reflection, and growth in learning that tell the learner's story of achievement.

There are three types of portfolios: working portfolios, display or "show" portfolios, and assessment portfolios, each of which has its own purpose:

1. *Working portfolios* represent "works in progress." They serve as a depository for student accomplishments on the way to being selected and polished for a more permanent assessment or display portfolio.
2. A student selects his or her best works from a working portfolio for a *display* or *show portfolio*. With the aid of the teacher, the student learns to critically judge the works, focusing on those qualities that make some works stand above others.
3. An *assessment portfolio* may contain all or some of the selections in a display portfolio as well as some of those that began in a working portfolio. Although the purpose of the working portfolio is to develop good products and the display portfolio to show off, some of the contents of these are often used for the purpose of assessment. The teacher, therefore, is the primary audience of the assessment portfolio.

The working, display, and assessment portfolios can be organized and presented digitally or in a binder, accordion file, or box file format. *Digital portfolios* display your student's work with a click of a mouse, utilizing all the multimedia capabilities of the computer, such as audio, video, graphics, and text transformed into computer-readable formats. They have the special advantage of presenting information instantly and interactively instead of linearly to emphasize connections and relationships among entries, which a typical binder presentation can obscure. Commercially available portfolio design software for students (www.aurbach.com), as well as commonly available software such as Microsoft PowerPoint, provide a template for facilitating the development of portfolios. For more information about digital portfolios see Bullock and Hawk (2005).

Many school districts use portfolios and other types of exhibitions to help motivate effort and show achievement and growth in learning. The reliability and validity of a classroom teacher's judgments are always a matter of concern, but they are less so when the teacher has multiple opportunities to interact with learners and numerous occasions to observe their work and confirm judgments about their achievements.

Many believe a portfolio's greatest potential is for showing teachers, parents, and learners a richer array of what students know and can do than paper and pencil tests and other snapshot assessments. If designed properly, portfolios can show a learner's ability to think and problem-solve, to use strategies and procedural-type skills, and to construct knowledge. But in addition, they also tell something about a learner's persistence, effort, willingness to change, skill in monitoring his or her own learning, and ability to be self-reflective or metacognitive (Hebert, 1992). So one purpose for a portfolio is to give a teacher information about a learner that no other measurement tool can provide.

There are other reasons for using portfolios. Portfolios are an ideal way to motivate reluctant learners (Frazier & Paulson, 1992; Gronlund & Engle, 2001). Portfolios also provide a means to communicate to parents and other teachers the level of achievement that a learner has reached. Report card grades give us some idea of this. But portfolios supplement grades by showing the supporting evidence.

Portfolios are not an alternative to paper and pencil tests, essay tests, or performance tests. Each of these tools possesses validity. If you want to assess a learner's factual knowledge base, objective-type tests are appropriate. If you are interested in a snapshot assessment of how well a learner uses a cognitive strategy, there are extended and restricted essays that do not involve the work required for portfolio assessment. But if you want to assess both achievement and growth in an authentic context, a portfolio is the tool you should consider.

Here are five simple steps to building a portfolio for your teaching area.

Step 1: Deciding on the Purposes for a Portfolio

Have your learners think about their purpose in assembling a portfolio. Having learners identify for themselves the purpose of the portfolio is one way to increase the authenticity of the task. However, your learners' purposes (e.g., getting a job with the local news station) will not necessarily coincide with yours (e.g., assessing your learners). So be clear about your purposes at the outset of portfolio design.

Classroom-level purposes that portfolios can achieve include

- Monitoring student progress
- Communicating what has been learned to parents
- Passing on information to subsequent teachers
- Evaluating how well something was taught
- Showing off what has been accomplished
- Assigning a course grade

Step 2: Identifying Cognitive Skills and Dispositions

A portfolio, like any performance assessment, is a measure of deep understanding and genuine achievement. They can measure growth and development of competence in areas like knowledge construction and organization, cognitive strategies (analysis, interpretation, planning, revising), procedural skills (clear communication, editing, drawing, speaking, building), metacognition (self-monitoring, self-reflection), as well as certain dispositions—or habits of mind—such as flexibility, adaptability, acceptance of criticism, persistence, collaboration, and desire for mastery. Throughout this text you have had practice in specifying different types of cognitive outcomes, identifying aspects of these learning types, and planning to assess them. Apply this same practice to specifying what you want to know about your learners from their portfolios. So, as part of your teaching strategy, you will want to decide the types of products, processes, or outcomes you will be expecting of your learners, such as:

- *Products:* Poems, essays, charts, graphs, exhibits, drawings, maps, and so forth
- *Complex cognitive processes:* Skills in acquiring, organizing, and using information
- *Observable performance:* Physical movements, as in dance, gymnastics, or typing; oral presentations; use of specialized procedures, as when dissecting a frog, bisecting an angle, or following a recipe
- *Attitudes and social skills:* Habits of mind, group work, and recognition skills

Step 3: Deciding Who Will Plan the Portfolio

When deciding who will plan the portfolio, consider what is involved in preparing gymnasts or skaters for a major tournament. The parent hires a coach. The coach, pupil, and parent plan together the routines, costumes, practice times, music, and so on. They are a team whose sole purpose is to produce the best performance possible. The gymnast or skater wants to be the best he or she can be. These young athletes also want to please their parents and coach and meet their expectations. The atmosphere is charged with excitement, dedication, and commitment to genuine effort.

This is the atmosphere you are trying to create when using portfolios. You, the learner, and parents are a team for helping the student improve writing, or math reasoning, or scientific thinking and to assemble examples of this growing competence. Learners want to show what they can do and to verify the trust and confidence that you and their family have placed in them. The portfolio is their recital, their tournament, their competition.

The principal stakeholders in the use of the portfolio are you, your learners, and their parents. Therefore, involve parents by sending home an explanation of portfolio assessment and ask that parents and students discuss its goals and content. See Figure 12.6 for an example of a letter one teacher wrote to parents introducing a portfolio project.

Step 4: Deciding Which Products to Put in the Portfolio and How Many Samples of Each Product

When determining what and how much to include in the portfolio, you must make two key decisions: ownership and your portfolio's link with instruction. *Ownership* refers to your learners' perception that the portfolio contains what they want it to. You have considered this issue in step 3. By involving learners and their parents in the planning process, you enhance their sense of ownership. You also do this by giving them a say in what goes into the portfolio. The task is to balance your desire to enhance ownership with your responsibilities to see

Figure 12.6 An example of a teacher letter to parents introducing a portfolio project.

Hello Dear Parent,

I am your child's 8th grade English teacher. I would like your help with an exciting project we are about to begin in our class. The project will be to have each student create during the semester a portfolio of their writing that they can show to you, me and their classmates. The examples of writing that they may choose to put in their portfolio can include letters, essays, writing to persuade someone, criticism, poetry, autobiography, fiction and even dramatic scripts. Your son or daughter can choose from among these combinations of writing they would most like to place in their portfolios.

What I would like to ask of you is your assistance in helping your son or daughter revise and edit their writing so that they are the very best that they can be and in selecting which samples of writing are placed in their portfolio. I have found that one of the best ways to become a good writer is to have someone else read what is written and provide suggestions as to what to edit and revise. Your willingness to read what your child writes and to suggest improvements in spelling, grammar and content would be invaluable in encouraging your child's best work. At the end of the semester we will display everyone's portfolio of writing in the classroom at which time you will be invited to see your and other children's portfolios.

May I ask you to initial each sample of writing that you read to indicate that your son or daughter has sought your assistance in improving their writing sample.

Thank you for your help and I look forward to seeing you at our exhibition of writing skills at the end of the semester.

that the content of the portfolio measures the cognitive skills and dispositions you identified in step 3.

Both learners and their parents need to see that your class instruction focuses on teaching the skills necessary to fashion the portfolio's content. You do not want to require products in math, science, or social studies that you did not prepare learners to create. If it is a writing portfolio, your instructional goals must include teaching skills in writing poems, essays, editorials, or whatever your curriculum specifies. The same holds for science, math, geography, or history portfolios. Thus, in deciding what you would like to see included in your learners' portfolios, you will have to ensure you only require products that your learners were prepared to develop.

The most satisfactory way to satisfy learner needs for ownership and your need to measure what you teach is to require certain categories of products that match your instructional purposes and cognitive outcomes and to allow learners and parents to choose the samples within each category. For example, you may require that an eighth-grade math portfolio contain the following categories of math content (Lane, 1993):

1. Number and operation, in which the learner demonstrates the understanding of the relative magnitude of numbers, the effects of operations on numbers, and the ability to perform those mathematical operations
2. Estimation, in which the learner demonstrates understanding of basic facts, place value, and operations; mental computation; tolerance of error; and flexible use of strategies
3. Predictions, in which learners demonstrate abilities to make predictions based on probabilities; to organize and describe data systematically; to make conjectures based on data analyses; and to construct and interpret graphs, charts, and tables

Learners and their parents would have a choice of which assignments to include in each of the categories listed. For each sample the learner includes a brief statement about what the sample says about his or her development of mathematical thinking skills.

Another example could be a high school writing portfolio. The teacher requires that the following categories of writing be in the portfolio: persuasive editorial, persuasive essay, narrative story, autobiography, and dialogue. Learners choose the samples of writing in each category. For each sample they include a cover letter that explains why they chose this sample and what the sample shows about the learner's development as a writer.

You will also have to decide how many samples of each content category to include in the portfolio. For example, do you require two samples of persuasive writing, one of criticism, three of dialogue? Shavelson, Gao, and Baxter (1991) suggest that as many as eight products or tasks over different topic areas may be needed to obtain a reliable estimate of performance from portfolios. Make this decision after eliciting suggestions from your students.

Step 5: Building the Portfolio Rubrics

In step 2 you identified the major cognitive skills and dispositions that your portfolio will measure. In step 4 you specified the content categories that your portfolio will contain. Now, you must decide what good, average, and poor performance look like for each entry in the portfolio and the portfolio as a whole.

You already have had some experience doing this. For each dimension on which you will rate the content in a portfolio, list the primary traits or characteristics you think are important. For example, for the essay writing portfolio in Figure 12.7, the teacher felt the student's quality of reflection, writing conventions, organization, planning, and quality of

Figure 12.7 Essay portfolio rating form.

___ First Draft
___ Second Draft
___ Final Draft

To Be Completed by Student:

1. Date submitted: _____

2. Briefly explain what this essay says about you. _____

    _____

3. What do you like best about this piece of writing?_____

    _____

4. What do you want to improve on the next draft? _____

    _____

5. If this is your final draft, will you include this in your portfolio and why?_____

    _____

    _____

To Be Completed by Teacher:

Rating	Description

1. Quality of Reflection

5	States very clearly what he or she likes most and least about the essay. Goes into much detail about how to improve the work.
4	States clearly what he or she likes and dislikes about the essay. Gives detail about how to improve the work.
3	States his or her likes and dislikes but could be clearer. Gives some detail about how the work will be improved.
2	Is vague about likes and dislikes. Gives few details about how the essay will be improved.
1	No evidence of any reflection on the work.

2. Writing Conventions

5	The use of writing conventions is very effective. No errors are evident. These conventions are fluid and complex: spelling, punctuation, grammar usage, sentence structure.
4	The use of writing conventions is effective. Only minor errors are evident. These conventions are nearly all effective: punctuation, grammar usage, sentence structure, spelling.
3	The use of writing conventions is somewhat effective. Errors don't interfere with meaning. These conventions are somewhat effective: punctuation, grammar usage, sentence structure, spelling.
2	Errors in the use of writing conventions interfere with meaning. These conventions are limited and uneven: punctuation, grammar usage, sentence structure, spelling.

(continued on next page)

Figure 12.7 *Continued*

Rating	Description
1	Major errors in the use of writing conventions obscures meaning. Lacks understanding of punctuation, grammar usage, sentence structure, spelling.

3. Organization

5	Clearly makes sense.
4	Makes sense.
3	Makes sense for the most part.
2	Attempted but does not make sense.
1	Does not make sense.

4. Planning (1st draft only)

5	Has clear idea of audience. Goals are very clear and explicit. An overall essay plan is evident.
4	Has idea of audience. Goals are clear and explicit. Has a plan for the essay.
3	Somewhat clear about the essay's audience. Goals are stated but somewhat vague. Plan for whole essay somewhat clear.
2	Vague about who the essay is for. Goals are unclear. No clear plan evident.
1	Writing shows no evidence of planning.

5. Quality of Revision (2nd draft only)

5	Follows up on all suggestions for revision. Revisions are a definite improvement.
4	Follows up on most suggestions for revision. Revisions improve on the previous draft.
3	Addresses some but not all suggested revisions. Revisions are a slight improvement over earlier draft.
2	Ignores most suggestions for revision. Revisions made do not improve the earlier draft.
1	Made only a minimal attempt to revise if at all.

Sum of ratings:_____

Average of ratings:_____

Comments: _____

_____

_____

_____

_____

revision were important criteria by which to judge the portfolio entries, Next construct a rating scale that describes the range of student performance that can occur for each of these dimensions, as noted in Figure 12.7. These rating scales, called **rubrics,** express the criteria for assessing the portfolio content. Figure 12.8 shows how this was done for a math problem-solving portfolio for which the teacher wants to assess the cognitive outcomes of reflection, mathematical knowledge, strategic knowledge, and communication.

Figure 12.8 Math problem-solving portfolio rating form.

Content Categories:

_√_ Problem solving	Problem ____ 1
____ Numbers and operations	_√_ 2
____ Estimation	____ 3
____ Predictions	

To Be Completed by Student:

1. Date submitted: _____

2. What does this problem say about you as a problem solver? _____
   _____
   _____

3. What do you like best about how you solved this problem? _____
   _____
   _____

4. How will you improve your problem-solving skill on the next problem?_____
   _____
   _____

To Be Completed by Teacher:

Rating	*Description*

1. Quality of Reflection

5	Has excellent insight into his or her problem-solving abilities and clear ideas of how to get better.
4	Has good insight into his or her problem-solving abilities and some ideas of how to get better.
3	Reflects somewhat on problem-solving strengths and needs. Has some idea of how to improve as a problem solver.
2	Seldom reflects on problem-solving strengths and needs. Has little idea of how to improve as a problem solver.
1	Has no concept of him- or herself as a problem solver.

2. Mathematical Knowledge

5	Shows deep understanding of the problems, math concepts, and principles. Uses appropriate math terms and all calculations are correct.
4	Shows good understanding of math problems, concepts, and principles. Uses appropriate math terms most of the time. Few computational errors.
3	Shows understanding of some of the problems, math concepts, and principles. Uses some terms incorrectly. Contains some computation errors.

(continued on next page)

Figure 12.8 *Continued*

Rating	Description
2	Errors in the use of many problems. Many terms used incorrectly.
1	Major errors in problems. Shows no understanding of math problems, concepts, and principles.

3. Strategic Knowledge

5	Identifies all the important elements of the problem. Reflects an appropriate and systematic strategy for solving the problem; gives clear evidence of a solution process.
4	Identifies most of the important elements of the problem. Reflects an appropriate and systematic strategy for solving the problem and gives clear evidence of a solution process most of the time.
3	Identifies some important elements of the problem. Gives some evidence of a strategy to solve the problem, but the process is incomplete.
2	Identifies few important elements of the problem. Gives little evidence of a strategy to solve the problem, and the process is unknown.
1	Uses irrelevant outside information. Copies parts of the problem; no attempt at solution.

4. Communication

5	Gives a complete response with a clear, unambiguous explanation; includes diagrams and charts when they help clarify explanation; presents strong arguments that are logically developed.
4	Gives good response with fairly clear explanation, which includes some use of diagrams and charts; presents good arguments that are mostly but not always logically developed.
3	Explanations and descriptions of problem solution are somewhat clear but incomplete; makes some use of diagrams and examples to clarify points, but arguments are incomplete.
2	Explanations and descriptions of problem solution are weak; makes little, if any, use of diagrams and examples to clarify points; arguments are seriously flawed.
1	Ineffective communication; diagrams misrepresent the problem; arguments have no sound premise.

Sum of ratings: _____

Average of ratings: _____

Comments: _____

_____

_____

_____

_____

Once you design rubrics for the contents of the portfolio, you may want to design scoring criteria for the portfolio as a whole product. Some traits to consider when developing a scoring mechanism for the entire portfolio are thoroughness, variety, growth or progress,

Figure 12.9   Three examples of different ways to compute and weight grades.

Grading Formula Example #1   ("One, Two, Three Times Plan")

Homework and Classwork: All grades for homework and classwork are totaled and averaged. The average grade will count once.

    Homework and classwork grades followed by the average:
84, 81, 88, 92, 96, 85, 78, 83, 91, 79, 89, 94 = 1040 ÷ 12 = 86.6 = 87 average

Quizzes: All of the quizzes are totaled and averaged. This average grade will count two times.

    Quiz grades followed by the average:
82, 88, 80, 91, 78, 86 = 505 ÷ 6 = 84.2 = 84 average

Tests and Major Projects: All of the tests and major projects are totaled and averaged. This average grade will count three times.

    Test and major project grade followed by the average:
81, 91, 86 = 258 ÷ 3 = 86 average

The six weeks grade is computed as follows:
    87 (one time) + 84 + 84 (two times) + 86 + 86 + 86 (three times) = 513 ÷ 6 = 85.5 = 86 as the grade

Grading Formula Example #2   ("Percentages Plan")

A teacher determines a percentage for each area. For example, homework and classwork count 20% of the grade; quizzes count 40% of the grade; and tests and major projects count 40% of the grade.

Using the same scores as listed above, a student's grade is computed as follows:

    20% of the 86.6 for homework and classwork is 17.3; 40% of the 84.2 for quizzes is 33.7; and 40% of the 86 for tests and major projects is 34.4.

The six weeks grade is: 17.3 + 33.7 + 34.4 = 85.4 = 85. (The average is different because the "weight" put on each area varies in the two examples.)

Grading Formula Example #3   ("Language Arts Plan")

A language arts teacher determines that the publishing, goal meeting, journal, and daily process grades each count one fourth (25%) of the six weeks grade.

A language arts grade is computed as follows:

    The publishing grade is issued only at the end of the six weeks = 88

    The goal meeting grade is issued only at the end of the six weeks = 86

    The journal grades are: 82 + 92 + 94 + 90 + 88 + 86 = 532 ÷ 6 = 88.7 = 89

    The daily process grades are : 78 + 82 + 86 + 94 + 94 + 91 = 525 ÷ 6 = 87.5 = 88

The six weeks grade is: 88 + 86 + 89 + 88 = 351 ÷ 4 = 87.75 = 88

overall quality, self-reflection, flexibility, organization, and appearance. Choose among these traits or include others, and build 5-point rating scales for each characteristic.

Performance and Portfolio Assessment and Report Card Grades

Performance assessments and portfolios require a substantial commitment of teacher time and learner engagement. Consequently, a teacher who decides to use them should ensure that the performance or portfolio grade has substantial weight in the 6-week or final report card grade. One way to accomplish this is to score quizzes, tests, homework assignments, performance tests, and portfolios on the basis of 100 points. Computing the final grade simply involves averaging the grades for each component, multiplying these averages by the weight assigned, and adding these products to determine the total grade. Figure 12.9 provides examples of three formulas for accomplishing this.

Plan a Portfolio Conference

Plan to have a final conference at the end of the year or term with individual learners and, if possible, their parents to discuss the portfolio and what it says about your learners' development and final achievement. Your learners can be responsible for conducting the conference, with a little preparation from you on how to do it. This final event can be a highly motivating force for your learners to produce an exemplary portfolio.

SUMMING UP

This chapter introduced you to some techniques for assessing student learning. Its key terms and main points were:

Norm-Referenced and Criterion-Referenced Tests

1. A test that determines a student's place or rank among other students is called a norm-referenced test (NRT). This type of test conveys information about how a student performed compared to a large sample of pupils at the same age or grade.

2. A test that compares a student's performance to a standard of mastery is called a criterion-referenced test (CRT). This type of test conveys information about whether a student needs additional instruction on some skill or set of skills.

3. The major advantage of an NRT is that it covers many different content areas in a single test; its major disadvantage is that it is too general to be useful in identifying specific strengths and weaknesses tied to individual texts or workbooks.

4. The major advantage of a CRT is that it can yield highly specific information about individual skills or behaviors. Its major disadvantage is that many such tests would be needed to make decisions about the many skills or behaviors typically taught in school.

The Test Blueprint

5. A test blueprint is a table that matches the test items to be written with the content areas and levels of behavioral complexity taught. The test blueprint helps ensure that a test samples learning across (1) the range of content areas covered and (2) the cognitive and/or affective processes considered important.

Objective Test Items

6. Objective test item formats include the following:
   - True-false
   - Matching
   - Multiple choice
   - Completion or short answer

7. Two methods for reducing the effects of guessing in true-false items are (1) to encourage all students to guess when they do not know the answer and (2) to require revision of statements that are false.

8. In constructing matching items:
   - Make lists homogeneous, representing the same kind of events, people, or circumstances.
   - Place the shorter list first and list options in chronological, numbered, or alphabetical order.
   - Provide approximately three more options than descriptions to reduce the chance of guessing correctly.
   - Write directions to identify what the lists contain and specify the basis for matching.
   - Closely check the options for multiple correct answers.

9. Avoid the following flaws when writing multiple-choice items:
   - Stem clues in which the same word or a close derivative appears in both the stem and an option
   - Grammatical clues in which an article, verb, or pronoun eliminates one or more options from being grammatically correct
   - Repeating same words across options that could have been provided only once in the stem
   - Making response options of unequal length, indicating the longer option may be correct

- The use of "all of the above," which discourages response discrimination, or "none of the above," which encourages guessing

10. Suggestions for writing higher-level multiple-choice items include use of the following:
    - Pictorial, graphical, or tabular stimuli
    - Analogies that demonstrate relationships among items
    - Previously learned principles or procedures

11. The following are suggestions for writing completion items:
    - Require a single-word answer.
    - Pose the question or problem in a brief, definite statement.
    - Check to be sure an accurate response can be found in the text, workbook, or class notes.
    - Omit only one or two key words.
    - Word the statement so the blank is near the end.
    - If the question requires a numerical answer, indicate the units in which the answer is to be expressed.

Essay Test Items

12. An extended-response essay item allows the student to determine the length and complexity of a response.

13. A restricted-response essay item poses a specific problem for which the student must recall and organize the proper information, derive a defensible conclusion, and express it within a stated time or length.

14. Essay items are most appropriate when (1) the instructional objectives specify high-level cognitive processes, (2) relatively few test items (students) need to be graded, and (3) test security is a consideration.

15. Suggestions for writing essay items include the following:
    - Identify beforehand the mental processes you want to measure (e.g., application, analysis, decision making).
    - Identify clearly and unambiguously the task to be accomplished by the student.
    - Begin the essay question with key words, such as *compare, give reasons for, predict*.
    - Require presentation of evidence for controversial questions.
    - Avoid optional items.
    - Establish reasonable time and/or page limits.
    - Restrict the use of essay items to those that cannot easily be measured by multiple-choice items.
    - Relate each essay question to an objective on the test blueprint.

16. The following are suggestions for increasing consistency and accuracy when scoring essay items:
    - Specify the response length.
    - Use several restricted-response essay items instead of one extended-response item.
    - Prepare a scoring scheme in which you specify beforehand all ingredients necessary to achieve each of the grades that could be assigned.

Validity and Reliability

17. Validity refers to whether a test measures what it says it measures. Three types of validity are content, concurrent, and predictive.

18. Content validity is established by examining a test's contents. Concurrent validity is established by correlating the scores on a new test with the scores on an established test given to the same set of individuals. Predictive validity is established by correlating the scores on a new test with some future behavior of the examinee that is representative of the test's content.

19. Reliability refers to whether a test yields the same or similar scores consistently. Three types of reliability are test-retest, alternative form, and internal consistency.

20. Test-retest reliability is established by giving the test twice to the same individuals and correlating the first set of scores with the second. Alternative form reliability is established by giving two parallel but different forms of the test to the same individuals and correlating the two sets of scores. Internal consistency reliability is established by determining the extent to which the test measures a single basic concept.

Marks and Marking Systems

21. Marks are based on comparisons, usually comparisons of students with one or more of the following:
    - Other students
    - Established standards
    - Aptitude
    - Actual versus potential effort
    - Actual versus potential improvement

Standardized Tests

22. Standardized tests are developed by test construction specialists to determine a student's performance level relative to others of similar age and grade. They are standardized because they are administered and scored according to specific and uniform procedures.

Performance and Portfolio Assessment

23. A performance assessment asks learners to show what they know by measuring complex cognitive skills with authentic, real-world tasks.

24. A portfolio is a planned collection of learner achievement that documents what a student has accomplished and the steps taken to get there.

KEY TERMS

Criterion-referenced test (CRT), 400
Distracters, 407
Extended-response essay, 413
Marks and grading systems, 420
Norm-referenced test (NRT), 400
Performance assessment, 425
Portfolio assessment, 428

Reliability, 417
Restricted-response, 414
Rubrics, 434
Standardized tests, 422
Stem, 407
Test blueprint, 403
Validity, 417

DISCUSSION AND PRACTICE QUESTIONS

Questions marked with an asterisk are answered in appendix B. See also the Companion Website for this text at *www.prenhall.com/borich* for more assessment options.

*1. Identify the characteristics of a norm-referenced and criterion-referenced test and the purpose for which each is best suited.

*2. What two instructional dimensions are measured by a test blueprint?

*3. Identify four formats for objective test items and give two advantages and two disadvantages of each.

*4. What would be four things to avoid in writing good multiple-choice test items? Which do you feel would be the hardest to avoid?

*5. What three devices may be used to prepare multiple-choice questions at higher levels of cognitive complexity? Prepare an example of a multiple-choice item using one.

*6. Identify the reasons discussed in this chapter for preparing an essay as opposed to an objective test. Can you find any other reasons for using an essay test?

*7. Describe three advantages and three disadvantages of essay items. What, in your opinion, is the biggest advantage and biggest disadvantage?

*8. Identify six possible criteria for scoring higher-level essay items. What percentage weight of 100 would you assign to each?

*9. Describe the concepts of validity and reliability using a recent test you have taken. Were you aware of the reliability and validity of the test? If not, did you know where you might obtain this information?

*10. Provide an approximate range for an acceptable validity and acceptable reliability coefficient. What is the maximum possible size of a validity or reliability coefficient?

*11. What is a standardized test? Name two you have taken most recently.

*12. What does a percentile rank indicate for a given individual? What two points should be kept in mind in interpreting a percentile rank?

13. Describe the procedure you would use to aggregate scores for all the portfolio ratings. By providing hypothetical ratings for the entries on your rating form, indicate with actual numbers and averages how you will (a) calculate weights, (b) take the average score for each entry, (c) add up all the entries to get an overall score, and (d) assign a grade symbol (e.g., A to F) to the average score.

FIELD EXPERIENCE ACTIVITIES

*1. Contrast the characteristics of extended-response and restricted-response essay items. Prepare an example of each in your teaching field.

*2. What is a "scoring rubric" for an essay item? Construct a scoring rubric for each of the essay items you prepared in question 1.

*3. What three methods may be used to determine the validity of a test? Give an example of what information each would provide for a test given in your classroom.

*4. What three methods may be used for determining the reliability of a test? Give an example of what information each would provide for a test given in your classroom.

*5. Identify five procedures for assigning marks and one advantage and one disadvantage of each. Which approach or combination of approaches would you prefer to use in your classroom?

6. Develop a portfolio rating form using Figures 12.7 and 12.8 as a guide. Be sure to include definitions for all the scale alternatives (e.g., 1 to 5) being rated.

DIGITAL PORTFOLIO ACTIVITIES

The following digital portfolio activities relate to INTASC principles 8 and 9.

1. In Field Experience Activities 1 and 2, you were asked to write an example of an extended-response and a restricted-response essay and to prepare scoring rubrics identifying the criteria by which each essay would be assigned a grade. Examine your rubrics for completeness and place each into your digital portfolio in a folder titled *Learner Assessment*.

2. In Field Experience Activity 6 you were asked to develop a portfolio rating form using Figures 12.7 and 12.8 as a guide that would include definitions for all the scale alternatives (e.g., 1 to 5) being rated. These rating forms will serve as a general template from which you can prepare other scales and criteria to match the portfolio products being rated. Place your rating forms in your *Learner Assessment* portfolio folder for future reference when a portfolio project is planned.

CLASSROOM OBSERVATION ACTIVITIES

The following classroom observation activities relate to INTASC principles 8 and 9.

1. Oral performances include a wide range of behavior, from simply answering a teacher's question to giving a speech or report or performing in a classroom skit or play. In any of its varied forms, oral performance is important because of its capacity to translate content learned in one way (e.g., lecture or text) into a new and more complete form (e.g., a report to the class).

For example, most oral performances require the learner to translate, summarize, or paraphrase what has been learned through books or lecture into a more integrated whole, thereby raising the learner's thought process to a higher level; for example, from knowledge of facts to the comprehension and application of these facts in an adultlike task. Since oral performance can be less time-consuming than projects and demonstrations, it can be used more often and in more varied ways. On the Companion Website for this chapter at *www.prenhall.com/borich* you will find a record for *Observing Oral Performance* that provides a format for observing the degree to which various types of oral expression occur in a classroom, such as students responding to questions, reading, discussing an idea or theme, or giving a formal speech, report, or demonstration. Look again at the *Classroom Dialogue of Ms. Brokaw's Literature Class*, which appears in the chapter 10 Companion Website module, and see how many instances of different types of oral performance you can find during her lesson. Place the *Observing Oral Performance* record into your *Learner Assessment* digital portfolio folder for future observations.

2. Performance assessments are authentic assessments in which students are asked to integrate bits of knowledge that may have been learned in isolated contexts into a single, unified product with a

real-world character found outside the classroom. The product should allow the student a degree of flexibility regarding the form in which it is expressed and the resources consulted in producing it. The requirements for grading a portfolio or performance assessment should include both product and process criteria. Product criteria include key observable features of the product or performance, such as technical quality, accuracy, practicality or usability, organization, and application of materials and resources. Process criteria include how the learner went about solving the problem or creating the product, and can include attributes such as creativity, neatness, sharing, articulation, and use of references and resources. Process criteria are often difficult to grade on an all-or-nothing basis, so they often have several degrees of effort assigned to them; for example, 3 = high effort, 2 = average effort, and 1 = low effort.

On the Companion Website for this chapter you will find a record for *Observing a Performance Assessment*. This record asks you to identify how a performance assessment will be rated using both product and process criteria and whether the performance being observed required the learner to display higher-order thinking—that which goes beyond the regurgitation of isolated bits of knowledge. Use this record to evaluate a learner's performance in completing a performance task that produces an observable real-world outcome or product, such as programming a calculator, searching the Internet, using laboratory equipment, typing a business letter, making a map, creating a graph, or telling a story. Place your record into your *Learner Assessment* digital portfolio folder for future observations.

CHAPTER CASE HISTORY AND PRAXIS TEST PREPARATION

DIRECTIONS: The following case history pertains to chapter 12 content. After reading the case history, answer the short-answer question that follows and consult appendix D to find different levels of scored student responses and the rubric used to determine the quality of each response. You also have the opportunity to submit your responses online to receive feedback by visiting the *Case History* module for this chapter on the Companion Website, where you will also find additional questions pertaining to Praxis test content.

Case History

Ms. Velchek had been happy when she was hired for her current teaching job. The middle school was newly built and featured state-of-the-art facilities, including computer, language, and biology labs. When she looked at the standardized test scores of her sixth-grade social studies class, she was pleased. Most of the class was functioning above grade level in the critical areas such as science, vocabulary, reading comprehension, and mathematics, as well as in her own area of social studies. On back-to-school night her classroom had been packed with parents who seemed concerned and supportive.

Now, just 6 weeks into the year, she was discouraged. She was having every bit as much trouble with this "ideal" class as she had had when she taught a crowded inner-city class with at-risk learners. Even though her students excelled on their weekly quizzes and objective tests, she suspected they earned their high grades with only cursory reading of the assignments. Most were earning A's and B's, yet none seemed really interested in class, and she doubted that much of the information they gave back to her on tests was remembered over the long run.

Reading their essays had been exhilarating at first. They wrote well-constructed sentences, their thoughts were fairly well organized, and spelling errors were at a minimum. But now Ms. Velchek wondered if their writing ability was disguising a rather superficial understanding of the concepts she was teaching.

Ms. Velchek thought that by changing her tests and maybe even her grading system she could help promote and test for higher levels of understanding. She decided to eliminate the true/false quizzes in which students could get half of the items correct by guessing. She would continue using multiple-choice items, but write them to elicit her students' skill at applying what they learned, not just memorizing.

The class had just finished a unit on world geography, and her students expected an exam that would emphasize facts about climate and topography. As usual they would come prepared with freshly memorized facts—this time about annual rainfall and the proper names of bodies of water, mountain ranges, and desert regions.

Mark hoped that all the facts and figures he had crammed for while watching TV last night would last until mid-morning. He had given the chapters a quick once-over during breakfast, so he felt as well prepared as always. But his mouth dropped when he saw the first question.

All the memorized figures, the knowledge of rainfall, temperature, and terrain were no help now. What lay before him was an invented country, complete with data on mineral deposits, vegetation, rainfall, temperature, and never seen before rivers, lakes, and mountains.

The question stated: Given your knowledge of geography and its influence on economics and population growth, answer the following questions concerning this hypothetical country. Here are four possible sketches showing population distributions. Using the data given, which of these populations do you believe these data best represent?

Another question asked about economic development, showing four maps with different areas sketched in for livestock ranching, commercial grain, mining, and industry.

Mark swallowed hard and flipped to the last page, the essay question, usually one he could easily answer. Most of the time his paraphrasing of the textbook passages would be sufficient for a high score. He "had a way with words" and made up for forgotten details with well-chosen adjectives. But his narrative ability wouldn't be of much help today. This essay question asked: Write a paragraph explaining in detail the reasoning behind each of your multiple-choice map selections.

It was close to the end of the period, and no one had finished early this time. The puzzled expressions of the students at the beginning of the test had been replaced by looks of determination, and on some faces, subtle satisfaction.

Short-Answer Question

This section presents a sample Praxis short-answer question. In appendix D you will find sample responses along with the standards used in scoring these responses.

DIRECTIONS: The question below requires you to write a short answer. Base your answer on your knowledge of principles of learning and teaching from chapter 12. Be sure to answer all parts of the question.

1. Ms. Velchek made a major change in her test construction and intends to make some modifications in her grading policy as well. To what extent do you think these changes are fair? What might you suggest to make the transition more equitable and comfortable to students?

Discrete Multiple-Choice Questions

DIRECTIONS: Each of the multiple-choice questions that follow is based on Praxis-related pedagogical knowledge in chapter 12. Select the answer that is best in each case and compare your results with those in appendix D. See also the Companion Website for this text at *www.prenhall.com/borich* for more assessment options.

1. Mr. Malone wants to learn to what extent his tenth-grade honors history class understands his unit on complex causes of the Civil War. Which type of assessment would be most likely to give him the information he seeks?
   a. A norm-referenced test
   b. A true-false test
   c. A matching test
   d. An essay test

2. Recent criticism of this type of test has questioned its relevance to day-to-day classroom learning and its usefulness in making instructional decisions. The subject of the preceding criticism is which of the following?
   a. Standardized tests
   b. Criterion-referenced tests
   c. Objective tests
   d. Essay tests

3. Mr. Acuna needs a test he can score quickly and reliably, reduces the effects of guessing, and is capable of measuring higher-level objectives. Which of the objective-item formats is best suited to this purpose?
   a. True-false test
   b. Matching test
   c. Multiple-choice test
   d. Completion test

4. Teachers often use scoring guides that provide preestablished criteria for evaluating student performances. These detailed guides, containing precise definitions by which the quality of a learner's performance is judged against specific criteria, are called
   a. Rubrics
   b. Assessment contexts
   c. Habits of mind
   d. Primary trait scoring

5. Which type of assessment tells the story of a learner's growth, long-term achievement, and significant accomplishments?
   a. Test blueprint
   b. Multimodal assessment
   c. Performance test
   d. Portfolio

Appendix A

Teacher Concerns Checklist

Francis F. Fuller and Gary D. Borich
The University of Texas at Austin

DIRECTIONS: This checklist explores what teachers are concerned about at different stages of their careers. There are no right or wrong answers, because each teacher has his or her own concerns.

Below and on the following page are statements of concerns you might have. Read each statement, and ask yourself: WHEN I THINK ABOUT TEACHING, AM I CONCERNED ABOUT THIS?

- If you are not concerned, or the statement does not apply, write 1 on the line.
- If you are a little concerned, write 2 on the line.
- If you are moderately concerned, write 3 on the line.
- If you are very concerned, write 4 on the line.
- And if you are totally preoccupied with the concern, write 5 on the line.

---

① Not concerned ② A little concerned ③ Moderately concerned
④ Very concerned ⑤ Totally preoccupied

___ 1. Insufficient clerical help for teachers.

___ 2. Whether the students respect me.

___ 3. Too many extra duties and responsibilities.

___ 4. Doing well when I'm observed.

___ 5. Helping students to value learning.

___ 6. Insufficient time for rest and class preparation.

___ 7. Not enough assistance from specialized teachers.

___ 8. Managing my time efficiently.

___ 9. Losing the respect of my peers.

___ 10. Not enough time for grading and testing.

___ 11. The inflexibility of the curriculum.

___ 12. Too many standards and regulations set for teachers.

___ 13. My ability to prepare adequate lesson plans.

___ 14. Having my inadequacies become known to other teachers.

___ 15. Increasing students' feelings of accomplishment.

___ 16. The rigid instructional routine.

___ 17. Diagnosing student learning problems.

___ 18. What the principal may think if there is too much noise in my classroom.

___ 19. Whether each student is reaching his or her potential.

___ 20. Obtaining a favorable evaluation of my teaching.

___ 21. Having too many students in a class.

___ 22. Recognizing the social and emotional needs of students.

___ 23. Challenging unmotivated students.

___ 24. Losing the respect of my students.

___ 25. Lack of public support for schools.

___ 26. My ability to maintain the appropriate degree of class control.

___ 27. Not having sufficient time to plan.

___ 28. Getting students to behave.

___ 29. Understanding why certain students make slow progress.

___ 30. Having an embarrassing incident occur in my classroom for which I might be judged responsible.

___ 31. Not being able to cope with troublemakers in my classes.

___ 32. That my peers may think I'm not doing an adequate job.

___ 33. My ability to work with disruptive students.

___ 34. Understanding ways in which student health and nutrition problems can affect learning.

___ 35. Appearing competent to parents.

___ 36. Meeting the needs of different kinds of students.

___ 37. Seeking alternative ways to ensure that students learn the subject matter.

___ 38. Understanding the psychological and cultural differences that can affect my students' behavior.

___ 39. Adapting myself to the needs of different students.

___ 40. The large number of administrative interruptions.

___ 41. Guiding students toward intellectual and emotional growth.

___ 42. Working with too many students each day.

___ 43. Whether students can apply what they learn.

___ 44. Teaching effectively when another teacher is present.

___ 45. Understanding what factors motivate students to learn.

---

*This instrument was revised with the assistance of John Rogan (Rogan, Borich, & Taylor, 1992).

Appendix B

Answers to Chapter Questions

These are answers to questions marked (*) for the Discussion and Practice and Field Practice Questions of the text chapters.

Chapter 1

Discussion and Practice Questions

1. 1, 2, 1 (or 2), 1 (or 2), 2, 3, 2, 3, 2 (or 1), 3, 2, 3, 3.

Chapter 2

Discussion and Practice Questions

1. a. Match instructional methods to individual learning needs.
   b. Understand the reasons behind the school performance of individual learners.
2. Environmentalists believe that differences in IQ scores among groups can be attributed to social class or environmental differences. Hereditarians believe that heredity rather than the environment is the major factor determining intelligence.
3. By some estimates, social competence may account for about 75% of school learning, leaving only about 25% to the influence of intelligence. If the influence of socioeconomic status on learning could be removed, differences in IQ among learners could be expected to become smaller.
4. Factors that would be more predictive of school learning than general IQ would be specialized abilities such as those suggested by Thurstone and by Gardner and Hatch, which may include verbal intelligence (English), spatial intelligence (art), and interpersonal intelligence (social studies, drama).

7. Front half/back half
   Girls/boys
   More able/less able
   Nonminority/minority
8. Spread interactions across categories of students.
   Select students randomly.
   Pair students.
   Code class notes.

Field Experience Activities

4. Form heterogeneous groups composed of members of different peer groups. Conduct a group discussion of class norms.

Chapter 3

Discussion and Practice Questions

2. (a) Tie general aims and goals to specific classroom strategies that will achieve those aims and goals. (b) Express teaching strategies in a format that allows you to measure their effects on your learners.
3. The behavior is observable, it is measurable, and it occurs in a specifiable period of time.
4. The observable behavior, conditions under which it is to be observed, and level of proficiency at which it is to be displayed.
5. Teachers tended to focus their concerns on self and task, sometimes to the exclusion of their impact on students.
6. Because action verbs truly point toward the goal of achieving the desired behavior and observing its attainment.
7. A, O, A, A, A, O, O, O.
8. The circumstances under which the behavior is to be displayed.

9. By establishing the setting under which the behavior will be tested, which guides them in how and what to study.
10. The extent to which the conditions are similar to those under which the behavior will have to be performed in the real world.
11. The level of proficiency at which the behavior must be displayed.
12. (1) b, (2) a, (3) b, (4) e, (5) f.

Chapter 4

Discussion and Practice Questions

1. Knowledge of aims and goals, knowledge of learners, knowledge of subject-matter content and organization, knowledge of teaching methods, and tacit knowledge.
2. By the way in which individual lessons are sequenced and build on one another to produce a unit.
3. Hierarchy helps us see the relationship between individual lesson outcomes and the unit outcome. It also helps us identify lessons that are not too big or too small, but that are just right. Teachers use task-relevant prior learning to identify the proper sequence of lessons needed to teach the unit outcome. Both help us picture the flow and sequence of a lesson plan.
4. Cognitive: analysis, synthesis, evaluation. Affective: valuing, organization, characterization. Psychomotor: precision, articulation, naturalization.
5. They represent smaller, more detailed portions of content.
6. The former must show hierarchy and sequence; the latter does not.
8. Present the stimulus material.
9. Assess the behavior,
10. Elicit the desired behavior.
11. Provide feedback: immediate and nonevaluative. Assess the behavior: delayed and evaluative.

Field Experience Activities

1. Both help us picture the flow and sequence of a lesson plan.
3. Ability grouping, peer tutoring, learning centers, review, and follow-up materials.
4. Gain attention, inform the learner of the objective, stimulate recall of prerequisite learning, present the stimulus material, elicit the desired behavior, provide feedback, and assess the behavior.

Chapter 5

Discussion and Practice Questions

1. Expert and referent power. By keeping up with developments in your field and giving your students a sense of belonging and acceptance.
2. Diffusion occurs when different academic and social expectations held by different members are spread throughout the group. Crystallization occurs when expectations converge and crystallize into a shared experience. Diffusion precedes crystallization.
3. Sole provider of information (commander in chief), translator or summarizer of student ideas, and equal partner with students in creating ideas and problem solutions; student opinion, student talk, and spontaneity will increase from the former to the latter.
6. Visitor at the door; safety concerning equipment.
7. Make rules consistent with your classroom climate. Make rules that can be enforced. State rules generally enough to include specific behaviors.
8. When the rule cannot be consistently reinforced over a reasonable period of time.
9. a. Allow no talking.
   b. Allow no more time than is absolutely necessary.
   c. Make arrangements according to time to be spent, not exercises to be completed.
   d. Give a 5-minute and a 2-minute warning.
10. Give reasons for the assignment, and give the assignment immediately following the content presentation to which it is related.
11. (a) Restate highest level generalization.
    (b) Summarize key aspects of content taught.
    (c) Provide codes or symbols for remembering the content.

Field Experience Activities

1. Forming, storming, norming, and performing.
3. a. Drill and practice
   b. Group discussion
   c. Seatwork
6. Establish an open risk-free climate. Plan lessons that match student interests and needs. Allow for activities and responsibilities congruent with the learners' cultures.

Chapter 6

Discussion and Practice Questions

1. a. Establish positive relationships.
   b. Prevent attention seeking and work avoidance.

c. Quickly and unobtrusively redirect misbehavior.

d. Stop persistent and chronic misbehavior.

e. Teach self-control.

f. Respect cultural differences.

2. a. Develop classroom rules.

b. Get support from school administrators for an area to which disruptive students can be moved temporarily.

c. Hold private conferences with disruptive students.

d. Follow through by giving students an opportunity to return to the classroom.

3. Positive: Give a reward immediately following a desirable behavior. Negative: End an uncomfortable state when a desirable behavior occurs.

4. Time-out: Remove a student to an area where he or she can receive no reinforcement. Response cost: Remove a reinforcer or privilege contingent on disruptive or inappropriate behavior.

5. (a) They devote extensive time to organizing their classroom to minimize disruption and enhance work engagement. (b) They methodically teach rules and routines and monitor their compliance. (c) They inform students of the consequences for breaking the rules and enforce the consequences.

6. (a) You alone can be the judge of what occurred, what the proper punishment is, and whether the punishment has been met. (b) You provide alternative forms of punishment from which the student must choose. (c) You select a punishment from alternatives provided by the student.

9. a. Select the target behavior.

b. Identify natural consequences of the target behavior.

c. Choose from among the natural consequences those most likely to be reinforcing.

d. Identify from these the natural consequences most easily noticed by the learner.

e. Design lessons that make the natural consequence conspicuous to the learner.

f. Select appropriate backup reinforcers.

g. Condition the natural reinforcer by having learners engage in the behavior.

10. a. Punishment does not guarantee the desirable behavior will occur.

b. The effects of punishment are specific to a particular context and behavior.

c. The effects of punishment can spread to desirable behaviors.

d. Punishment can elicit hostile and aggressive responses.

e. Punishment can become associated with the punisher.

11. (a) Gain support of the parent for assuming some of the responsibility for the discipline management process. (b) Design a plan of action for addressing the problem at home and at school.

Field Experience Activities

1. Sane messages communicate to students that their behavior is unacceptable in a manner that does not blame, scold, or humiliate.

2. "I messages" focus on your feelings about the behavior or situation that angered you.

4. When the desired behavior is made clear at the time of the punishment and when used in conjunction with rewards.

Chapter 7

Discussion and Practice Questions

1. Type 1: facts, rules, action sequences. Type 2: concepts, patterns, abstractions. Type 1 outcomes generally apply to the knowledge, comprehension, and application levels; Type 2 outcomes generally apply to the analysis, synthesis, and evaluation levels.

2. Knowledge acquisition: facts, rules, action sequences. Inquiry or problem solving: concepts, patterns, and abstractions.

3. Full-class instruction; questions posed by the teacher; detailed and redundant practice; one new fact, rule, or sequence mastered before the next is presented; arrangement of classroom to maximize drill and practice.

4. Cognitive: recall, describe, list. Affective: listen, attend, be aware. Psychomotor: repeat, follow, place.

5. (a) Disseminate information that is not readily available from texts or workbooks in appropriately sized pieces. (b) Arouse or heighten student interest. (c) Achieve content mastery.

6. To create a response, however crude, that can become the basis for learning.

9. 60% to 80%. Reduce content coverage, increase opportunities for practice and feedback.

10. To form action sequences. They should increasingly resemble applications in the real world.

11. Keep contacts to a minimum, on the average of 30 seconds; spread contacts across most students, avoiding concentrating on a few students.

12. About 95%.

Field Experience Activities

1. a. Have students correct each other's work.
   b. Have students identify difficult homework problems.
   c. Sample the understanding of a few students who represent the range of students in the class.
   d. Explicitly review the task-relevant information necessary for the day's lesson.
2. Part–whole, sequential, combinations, comparative.
3. Rule-example-rule.
4. It is used to help convert wrong or partially correct answers to right answers by encouraging the student to use some aspects of the answer given in formulating the correct response.
5. a. Correct, quick, and firm: Acknowledge correctness and either ask another question or move on.
   b. Correct but hesitant: Acknowledge correctness and review steps for attaining correct answer.
   c. Incorrect but careless: Acknowledge incorrectness and immediately move on.
   d. Incorrect due to lack of knowledge: Acknowledge incorrectness and then, without actually giving the student the answer, channel student's thoughts in ways that result in a correct answer.
6. Review key facts, explain steps required, prompt with clues or hints, walk student through a similar problem.
7. For example, you might gradually increase the coverage and depth of weekly reviews until time for a comprehensive monthly review arrives.

Chapter 8

Discussion and Practice Questions

1. Inquiry, discovery, and a problem.
2. Type 1: facts, rules, and action sequences. Type 2: concepts, patterns, and abstractions.
3. The learner indirectly acquires a behavior by transforming stimulus material into a response or behavior that differs (a) from the stimulus used to present the learning and (b) from any previous response emitted by the learner.
4. It is not generally efficient or effective for attaining outcomes at the higher levels of complexity involving concepts, patterns, and abstractions.
5. Generalization: classifying apparently different stimuli into the same category on the basis of criterial attributes. Discrimination: distinguishing

examples of a concept from nonexamples. Example: learning the meaning of democracy.

6. a. Type 1
   b. Type 2
   c. Type 1
   d. Type 2
   e. Type 2
   f. Type 1
   g. Type 2
   h. Type 2
   i. Type 1
   j. Type 2
7. Our memories would become overburdened trying to remember all possible instances of the concept; also, instances of the concept could easily be confused with noninstances.
9. Essential: lesson clarity, instructional variety, task orientation, engagement in the learning process, moderate-to-high success rate. Nonessential: number of credit hours attained, degree held, number of in-service workshops attended, college grades, years of teaching experience.
10. Direct instruction: to elicit a single right answer or reveal level of understanding. Indirect instruction: to help the student search for and discover an appropriate answer with a minimum of assistance.
11. Student-centered or unguided discovery learning. In indirect instruction, student ideas are used as a means of accomplishing the goals of the prescribed curriculum.
12. a. direct
    b. direct
    c. indirect
    d. indirect
    e. direct
    f. direct
    g. direct
    h. indirect
    i. indirect
    j. indirect
    Both models might be used for topics c, d, h, and j.

Field Experience Activities

3. Induction: the process of thinking in which a set of specific data is presented or observed and a generalization or unifying pattern is drawn from the data. Deduction: the process of thinking in which the truth or validity of a theory is tested in a specific instance.
4. Stating a theory, forming a hypothesis, observing or collecting data, analyzing and interpreting the data, making a conclusion.

5. a. Provide more than a single example.
   b. Use examples that vary in ways that are unimportant to the concept.
   c. Include nonexamples of the concept that also include important dimensions of the concept.
   d. Explain why nonexamples are nonexamples, even though they have some of the same characteristics as examples.
6. To refocus, present contradictions, probe for deeper responses, extend the discussion, and pass responsibility back to the class.
7. (a) Encourage students to use examples and references from their experience. (b) Ask students to draw parallels and associations from things they already know. (c) Relate ideas to students' interests, concerns, and problems.
8. In direct instruction, nearly all instances of the facts, rules, and sequences are likely to be encountered during instruction. This is not true during indirect instruction, so student self-evaluation is essential.
9. a. Orient students to the objective of the discussion.
   b. Provide new or more accurate information where needed.
   c. Review, summarize, or put together opinions and facts into a meaningful relationship.
   d. Adjust the flow of information and ideas to be most productive to the goals of the lesson.
   e. Combine ideas and promote compromise to arrive at an appropriate consensus.

Chapter 9

Discussion and Practice Questions

1. A question that actively engages a student in the learning process.
2. As much as 80%.
3. Lower-order questions as high as 80%; higher-order questions as low as 20%.
4. A convergent question has only a single or small number of correct responses. A divergent question has no single best answer and generally has multiple answers; however, divergent questions can have wrong answers.
6. Higher-order questions are unlikely to affect standardized achievement but are likely to increase the learner's analysis, synthesis, and evaluation skills.
10. The time the teacher waits for a student to respond to a question. Generally, beginning teachers should work to increase their wait time to encourage a student response that can be

built upon by the teacher and class for further learning.
11. Raising overly complex questions, not being prepared for unusual answers, not knowing the behavioral complexity of the response desired from a question, providing answers to questions before students can respond, using questions as a form of punishment.

Field Experience Activities

1. Structuring, soliciting, reacting.
2. Interest and attention getting, diagnosing and checking, recall of specific facts or information, managerial, encourage higher-level thought processes, structure and redirect learning, allow expression of affect.

Chapter 10

Discussion and Practice Questions

1. (a) To actively engage them in the learning process. (b) To help them acquire reasoning, critical thinking, and problem-solving skills.
2. a. Provide when and how to use mental strategies.
   b. Illustrate how the strategies are to be used.
   c. Encourage learners to go beyond the information given.
   d. Gradually shift the responsibility for learning to the student.
3. Metacognition refers to the mental processes used by the learner to understand the content being taught. Metacognitive strategies are procedures that assist learners in internalizing, understanding, and recalling the content to be learned.
4. Mental modeling can help students internalize, recall, and generalize problem solutions to different content at a later time.
5. During mediation, the teacher helps students restructure what they are learning to move them closer to the intended outcome.
6. The zone of maximum response opportunity is the content difficulty and behavioral complexity from which the student can most benefit at the moment.
8. a. Ask what students think they will learn from the text. Read from the text.
   b. Choose a discussion leader to ask questions regarding the text.
   c. Ask the discussion leader to summarize the text, and invite comments.
   d. Discuss points that remain unclear, invite more predictions, and reread the text if needed.

9. To gradually shift the responsibility for learning to the student through scaffolded discussion.

10. To model the same line of reasoning and the same types of questions, prompts, and cues used by the teacher at an earlier stage.

11. Declarative knowledge is intended only for oral and verbal regurgitation. Procedural knowledge is used in some problem-solving or decision-making task.

12. a. Provide a new learning task.
    b. Ask the student to explain how he or she will complete the task (e.g., learn the content).
    c. Provide another learning task on which the student can try out the new approach.
    d. Model self-questioning behavior for the student as the new material is being learned.
    e. Provide a third opportunity for practice, decreasing your role as monitor.
    f. Check the result by questioning for comprehension.

Field Experience Activities

1. (a) Illustrate the reasoning involved. (b) Make students conscious of it. (c) Focus learners on the application of the reasoning illustrated.

3. Reciprocal teaching provides opportunities to explore the content to be learned via group discussion.

6. a. Jingles or trigger sentences
   b. Narrative chaining
   c. Number rhyme or peg word
   d. Chunking

Chapter 11

Discussion and Practice Questions

1. (a) Engaging students in the learning process. (b) Promoting higher—more complex—patterns of thought.

2. a. Attitudes and values.
   b. Prosocial behavior.
   c. Alternative perspectives and viewpoints.
   d. Integrated identity.
   e. Higher thought processes.

3. a. Specify the goal.
   b. Structure the task.
   c. Teach the collaborative process.
   d. Monitor group performance.
   e. Debrief.

4. Written group reports, assessment of achievement, oral performance, enumeration of issues, critique.

5. 4 or 5 members.

6. a. Ask students to list peers.
   b. Randomly assign students.
   c. Purposefully form groups heterogeneously.
   d. Share with students the selection process.

7. (a) Request a product that requires a clearly defined division of labor. (b) Form pairs within groups that have the responsibility of looking over and correcting each other's work. (c) Visually chart group's progress on individually assigned tasks.

8. a. Summarizer
   b. Checker
   c. Researcher
   d. Runner
   e. Recorder
   f. Supporter
   g. Observer/troubleshooter

9. Forming a ratio, with a score for individual effort on top and a score for the group to which the individual belongs on the bottom.

10. (a) Repeat or remind group of its assigned role. (b) Redirect group's effort to more productive area. (c) Provide emotional support and encouragement.

11. (a) Openly talk about how the groups functioned. (b) Solicit suggestions for how the process could be improved. (c) Get viewpoints of predesignated observers.

12. a. Not enough time for group debriefing.
    b. Debriefing stays vague.
    c. Students stay uninvolved.
    d. Written reports are incomplete or messy.
    e. Students exhibit poor collaborative skills.

Field Experience Activities

1. a. Teacher–student interaction.
   b. Student–student interaction.
   c. Task specialization and materials.
   d. Role expectations and responsibilities.

2. a. Grades—individual and group
   b. Bonus points
   c. Social responsibilities
   d. Tokens or privileges
   e. Group contingencies

3. a. Communicate one's own ideas and feelings.
   b. Make messages complete and specific.
   c. Make verbal and nonverbal messages congruent.
   d. Convey an atmosphere of respect and support.
   e. Assess whether the message was properly received.
   f. Paraphrase another's point of view.
   g. Negotiate meanings and understandings.
   h. Participate and lead.

Chapter 12

Discussion and Practice Questions

1. NRTs compare a student's performance to the performance of a large sample of pupils (called the norm group) representative of those being tested. It is useful when you need to compare a learner's performance to that of others of the same age or grade level. CRTs compare a student's performance to a standard of mastery called a criterion. It is useful when we wish to decide if a student needs more instruction in a certain skill or area of content.

2. (a) Level of cognitive complexity. (b) Area of instructional content.

3. a. True-false
   b. Matching
   c. Multiple choice
   d. Completion or short answer

4. a. Stem clues.
   b. Grammatical clues.
   c. Redundant words/unequal response length.
   d. Use of "all of the above"/"none of the above."

5. (a) Pictorial, graphical, or tabular stimuli. (b) Analogues that demonstrate relationships among terms. (c) Application of previously learned principles or procedures.

6. (a) Higher-level cognitive processes have been taught. (b) Class size is small. (c) Test security is a consideration.

7. Advantages: They require students to use higher-level cognitive processes, some topics and objectives are best suited for them, and they can measure communication skills pertinent to a subject area. Disadvantages: They are tedious to read and score, may be influenced by communication skills of the learner, and may involve some degree of subjectivity on the part of the scorer.

8. a. Content
   b. Organization
   c. Process
   d. Accuracy/reasonableness
   e. Completeness/internal consistency
   f. Originality/creativity

9. Validity: Does the test measure what it is supposed to measure? Reliability: Does the test yield the same or similar scores consistently?

Accuracy: Does the test approximate an individual's true level of knowledge, skill, or ability?

10. Validity: approximately .60 to .80 or higher. Reliability: approximately .80 to .90 or higher. The maximum possible size of a validity or reliability coefficient is 1.0.

11. A test constructed by specialists to determine a student's level of performance relative to other students of similar age and grade.

12. That the student's score associated with the percentile rank was higher than the scores of that percentage of individuals in the norming sample—or that in the norming sample the percentage indicated scored lower than this individual.
    a. It is not the percentage of correct answers.
    b. The extreme or end points of a percentile distribution tend to be spread out, whereas percentiles toward the center tend to be compressed, making comparisons between the same number of points at different portions of the scale difficult.

Field Experience Activities

1. Extended response: Allows student to determine the length and complexity of a response. It is most useful when the problem provides little or no structure and outcomes at the synthesis and evaluation levels are desired. Restricted response: Poses a specific problem for which the student must recall proper information, organize it, derive a defensible conclusion, and express it within the limits of the problem. It is most useful when the problem posed is structured and when outcomes at the application and analysis levels are desired.

2. A guide written in advance, indicating the criteria or components of an acceptable answer.

3. (a) Content, (b) concurrent, (c) predictive.

4. (a) Test-retest, (b) alternate form, (c) internal consistency.

5. Comparisons with
   a. Other students
   b. Established standards
   c. Aptitude
   d. Actual versus potential effort
   e. Actual versus potential improvement

Appendix C

Higher-Order Thinking and Problem-Solving Checklist

Check each column below indicating (a) the extent to which your curriculum *requires* students to achieve the following outcomes and (b) the extent to which *you are teaching* your students to achieve these outcomes.

Assign the number 5 to each checkmark under "Great Extent," a 4 to "Fair Extent," a 3 to "Some Extent," a 2 to "A Little," and a 1 to "Not at All." Subtract your assigned values for the Degree of Implementation column from the Degree of Importance column for each behavior to arrive at your highest priorities.

	Degree of Importance					Degree of Implementation				
	Does your curriculum require students to achieve the following?					Are you teaching your students to achieve the following?				
	(Check one)					(Check one)				
Application of Knowledge	1	2	3	4	5	1	2	3	4	5
1. Search his/her memory for what is already known about a problem.										
2. Draw a picture or diagram that shows what was learned or observed.										
3. Construct and interpret graphs, charts, and tables.										
4. Classify/categorize things into definable attributes.										
5. Communicate the results of what was observed in written and oral format.										
6. Apply given rules to reach a conclusion.										
7. Consult a variety of knowledge sources to gather information.										

	Degree of Importance					Degree of Implementation				
	Does your curriculum require students to achieve the following?					Are you teaching your students to achieve the following?				
	(Check one)					(Check one)				
	1	2	3	4	5	1	2	3	4	5
Analytical Skills										
8. Identify the similarities and differences among various elements.										
9. Compare a problem to problems encountered previously.										
10. Understand the relationship of each component to the whole.										
11. Make reasonable conclusions from observation or analysis of data.										
12. Identify and articulate errors in their own thinking or in that of others.										
13. Explain the reasons for a conclusion.										
14. Predict what will happen given the information you have.										
15. Plan a way to test one's prediction.										
16. Distinguish the most important elements of a problem.										
17. Organize a conclusion about a problem in a logical fashion.										
18. Identify criteria for evaluating a problem solution.										
19. Gather information or evidence to solve a problem.										
20. Find corroborating evidence from among different data sources.										
21. Determine the reliability of the evidence.										
22. Place an interpretation of a problem in the context of prevailing circumstances.										

	Degree of Importance					Degree of Implementation				
	Does your curriculum require students to achieve the following?					Are you teaching your students to achieve the following?				
	(Check one)					(Check one)				
	1	2	3	4	5	1	2	3	4	5
Synthesis/Creativity										
23. Generate new ways of viewing a situation outside the boundaries of standard conventions.										
24. Reformulate a problem to make it more manageable.										
25. Brainstorm new applications of content.										
26. Anticipate potential problems.										
27. Accurately summarize what is read or others have said, orally and in writing.										
Evaluation/Metacognition										
28. Ask yourself what was learned.										
29. Make appropriate revisions on basis of feedback.										
30. Assess risks involved in a solution.										
31. Monitor the outcome and revise a strategy where appropriate.										
32. Judge the credibility of evidence.										
33. Evaluate and revise what is written.										
34. Ask questions to oneself about ideas he/she is unsure of.										
35. Catch fallacies and contradictions.										
Dispositions										
36. Meaningfully praise the performance of others.										
37. Share and take turns.										
38. Help keep others on-task.										

	Degree of Importance					Degree of Implementation				
	Does your curriculum require students to achieve the following?					Are you teaching your students to achieve the following?				
	(Check one)					(Check one)				
	1	2	3	4	5	1	2	3	4	5
39. Provide assistance to others when needed.										
40. Engage in tasks even when answers or solutions are not immediately apparent.										
41. Seek accuracy.										
42. Is flexible to change viewpoint to match the facts.										
43. Demonstrate restraint over impulsive behaviors.										
44. Compose drafts and tryouts in attempts to solve a problem.										
45. Demonstrate persistence in tackling difficult tasks.										
46. Use a constructive tone when responding to others.										
47. Display enthusiasm for learning.										
48. Ask for feedback when needed.										
49. Collaborate with others in team.										
50. Provide assistance to others when asked.										
51. Demonstrate independence in completing a project.										
52. Listen attentively to others.										
53. Ignore distractions that interfere with goal attainment.										
54. Keep record of one's own progress toward important goals.										
55. Realistically evaluate own performance.										
56. Set goals that are achievable within a specific span of time.										

	Degree of Importance					Degree of Implementation				
	Does your curriculum require students to achieve the following?					Are you teaching your students to achieve the following?				
	(Check one)					(Check one)				
	1	2	3	4	5	1	2	3	4	5
Values										
57. Demonstrate awareness of ethical concerns and conflicts.										
58. Adhere to codes of conduct.										
59. Show an ability to resolve ethical dilemmas and conflicts.										
60. Maintain self-discipline in dealing with difficult situations.										
61. Behave in a manner that communicates care and concern for others.										
62. Act responsibly in dealing with tasks and people.										

Answers to Short-Answer and Discrete Multiple-Choice Questions

Scoring Guide for Short-Answer Questions

2 Demonstrates a thorough understanding of the aspects of the case that are relevant to the question.
Responds appropriately to all parts of the question.
If an explanation is required, provides a strong explanation that is well supported by evidence.
Demonstrates a strong knowledge of pedagogical concepts, theories, facts, procedures, or methodologies relevant to the question.

1 Demonstrates some understanding of the aspects of the case that are relevant to the question.
Responds appropriately to a portion of the question.
If an explanation is required, provides a partial explanation that is supported by evidence.
Demonstrates some knowledge of pedagogical concepts, theories, facts, procedures, or methodologies relevant to the question.

0 Demonstrates misunderstanding of the aspects of the case that are relevant to the question.
Fails to respond (blank) or fails to respond to the specific question asked.
If an explanation is required, provides none that is supported by evidence.
Fails to demonstrate any knowledge of pedagogical concepts, theories, facts, procedures, or methodologies relevant to the question.

Chapter 1

Answers to Short-Answer Question

Following are sample responses for the chapter case history and Praxis short-answer question. When you read these sample responses, keep in mind that they are less polished than if they had been developed at home, edited, and carefully presented. Examinees do not know what questions will be asked and must decide, on the spot, how to respond. Readers take these circumstances into account when scoring the responses.

Sample Response That Would Receive a Score of 2

Positive aspects . . . Brady was not reprimanded for reading her novel. After all, she was able to para-phrase the quote quite well, which showed she had mastered the important concept of the warm-up. Her giftedness allowed her to complete the task sooner than other students, and she had found a suitable way to spend the extra time. By ignoring Brady's negative comment about another student and then redirecting her attention to the more productive aspects of her thinking, Mrs. Travis was able to maintain the focus of the discussion.

Negative aspects . . . By allowing Brady to show lack of respect to another classmate and only casually follow the instructional guidelines, Mrs. Travis may be undermining the standards she expects from the other members of the class. Some may claim that she is favoring Brady or letting her get away with things other students would not be allowed to do.

Sample Response That Would Receive a Score of 0

The negative aspect of Mrs. Travis's response to Brady is that she let her say something bad about another classmate. It isn't Jim's fault if he isn't as smart as she is. It was good that Mrs. Travis didn't make fun of the way Brady dressed and that she let her choose her own seat away from everybody else.

Answers to Discrete Multiple-Choice Questions

1. The correct answer is C. Recent teacher research has demonstrated that one of several teacher behaviors that increases student learning and engagement is having assignments that are interesting, worthwhile, and easy enough to be completed without teacher direction.
2. The correct answer is A. Although being a good role model and citizen are admirable qualities expected of teachers, research on teacher practices has concentrated on specific teacher behaviors in the classroom that have direct impact on student achievement.
3. The correct answer is B. Some lower-SES students who already may have poor self-concepts might construe frequent correction of wrong answers as personal criticism. This would be especially likely in the absence of a supporting classroom climate and when the corrections are not made privately.
4. The correct answer is B. Verbal markers emphasize your most important points. Students are being clued that the content being referred to will be needed at a later time.
5. The correct answer is D. A convergent question is a question in which different data sources converge to lead to the same answer. It may have more than a single right answer that requires more than recall and interpretation.

Chapter 2

Answers to Short-Answer Question

Following are sample responses for the chapter case history and Praxis short-answer question. When you read these sample responses, keep in mind that they are less polished than if they had been developed at home, edited, and carefully presented. Examinees do not know what questions will be asked and must decide, on the spot, how to respond. Readers take these circumstances into account when scoring the responses.

Sample Response That Would Receive a Score of 2

The main reason the cooperative learning activity was not successful was the way the groups were selected.

Mrs. Dodge allowed students to form their own groups instead of ensuring that they were heterogeneous in ethnicity as well as math performance levels. One group of high-performing students was allowed to work alone and the interactions of the other groups were mainly social. Anna's group had good intentions, but no one had the skills to assist the others.

Heterogeneous grouping would have solved many of these problems. With different cultural, social, and performance levels dispersed within each group, the more able students could assist the less able ones. Also, because the grouping would not be based on self-selected friendships, there would be fewer opportunities to socialize.

Sample Response That Would Receive a Score of 0

Cooperative learning shouldn't be used for homework. The smart kids do all the work, and the lazy ones get the credit. Use cooperative learning only for things that don't count as a grade or for creative projects.

Answers to Discrete Multiple-Choice Questions

1. The correct answer is A. Intensive English study tries to repair a deficit in language skills. The cultural deficit model from which it derives has drawn much criticism for its emphasis on what is missing in the child. Choices B, C, and D derive from the cultural difference model, which focuses on providing a rich and natural instructional environment to compensate for educational differences.
2. The correct answer is B. Responses A and D are counter to research findings; response C is unsupported. Although some may believe teachers have lower academic expectations for children of single parents, research does not support this.
3. The answer is B. Pairing minority with nonminority learners guards against favoring one group over another and avoids the obvious classification of learners, as long as partners are changed frequently. Alternatives A, C, and D make it appear that minority learners are less able than majority learners or inhibit learning opportunities for nonminority learners.
4. The correct answer is A. Field-dependent learners view the world in terms of large connected patterns that go beyond the details of a subject. B, C, and D are behaviors that would be consistent with a field-independent learner, who would focus more on the specific details of a subject.
5. The correct answer is D. A, B, and C are all relevant sources of information for

understanding the behavior of a learner according to a systems-ecological perspective. INTASC principles, since they are external to the child's world, could not be represented by a systems-ecological perspective.

Chapter 3

Answers to Short-Answer Question

Following are sample responses for the chapter case history and Praxis short-answer question. When you read these sample responses, keep in mind that they are less polished than if they had been developed at home, edited, and carefully presented. Examinees do not know what questions will be asked and must decide, on the spot, how to respond. Readers take these circumstances into account when scoring the responses.

Sample Response That Would Receive a Score of 2

Mr. Goldthorp's leaf unit was more authentic than one merely using texts. When students did field work to collect the leaves, they were behaving more like scientists and practicing behaviors that lots of scientists use in the real world.

The unit also involved many psychomotor skills, many at the precision level. The labeling was being done by hand with the calligraphy pens, or at the computer, where students gained technical experience. This psychomotor or kinesthetic connection can enhance learning with many students.

Also, the unit allowed the students to work independently as well as cooperatively. They had to sustain work on a focused task over a period of time and manage their time independently. Sharing the calligraphy pens, the computers, and the reference material also reinforced social skills necessary in the real world.

Sample Response That Would Receive a Score of 0

1. Mr. Goldthorp's lesson was a lot more fun than just sitting looking at a textbook. Many students would get bored with that task.
2. It is good to get out of the classroom and experience nature.
3. Two weeks is not really that long. Just think how long it took all those trees to grow.

Answers to Discrete Multiple-Choice Questions

1. The correct answer is B. It has an observable outcome; the list of five examples; a set of conditions; the use of current newspaper headlines; and a criterion level of performance, 100% accuracy. Choice A has no criterion level, C involves a learning activity rather than a learning outcome, and D has neither observable outcomes nor a criterion level of performance.
2. The correct answer is D. The action verbs listed correspond to the cognitive level called *analysis.*
3. The correct answer is C. Susan's response shows a strong conviction concerning a single belief. The action verb, *argue*, describes the valuing category of the affective domain.
4. Only the first statement is a learning activity, since it specifies a process and not a behavioral outcome. We do not know the behavioral outcome that will be expected as a result of the practice. "Will know," "will locate," and "will demonstrate" point to outcomes—end products of an instructional lesson or unit.
5. The correct answer is D. All three behaviors represent the Taxonomy of Educational Objectives in the Cognitive Domain— knowledge, analysis, and synthesis, respectively.

Chapter 4

Answers to Short-Answer Question

Following are sample responses for the chapter case history and Praxis short-answer question. When you read these sample responses, keep in mind that they are less polished than if they had been developed at home, edited, and carefully presented. Examinees do not know what questions will be asked and must decide, on the spot, how to respond. Readers take these circumstances into account when scoring the responses.

Sample Response That Would Receive a Score of 2

The lesson was authentic, or related to the real world. It linked the Roman belief that leaders should be physically healthy to the same attitude toward the health of 20th-century American presidents.

The selectivity of the lesson focused students on key points. Mr. Cody used questioning to explore the real reason the Lupercal festivities were important to Julius Caesar. Lupe was correct when she noticed that it showed Caesar's desire to produce an heir and thus demonstrated his ambition.

Another strength of the lesson was Mr. Cody's instructional variety. He began with a student demonstration that was verbal, visual, and tactile. Then he used questioning to focus and elicit higher-level thinking, and finally, he let students write about the topic based on their own opinions and experiences.

Sample Response That Would Receive a Score of 0

The lesson was authentic because it was about Shakespeare. Who's a more real writer than that, not to mention how great he is!

Mr. Cody was selective when he called on different students to answer questions. He was good about not just letting the smart ones answer. There was variety when Mr. Cody allowed the discussion to switch from Julius Caesar to a 20th-century president.

Answers to Discrete Multiple-Choice Questions

1. The correct answer is B. Tacit knowledge, versus formal knowledge gained from academic study, arises through everyday experiences, such as observation, experience in schools, lesson planning, and student teaching.
2. The correct answer is A. Appropriate pacing or tempo, the mode of presentation, the class arrangement, and classroom management are all aspects of teaching methods. Together they form a coherent whole from which teachers present individual lesson objectives.
3. The correct answer is C. Thematic planning, also referred to as interdisciplinary or lateral (across subjects) planning, should be carefully constructed to present learners with the opportunity to discover underlying patterns and relationships that cut across subject matter. Interdisciplinary units often represent themes that can be related to several different content areas at the same time.
4. The correct answer is B, C, and D. A, although necessary, precedes instruction and therefore is not an instructional event that is described in the lesson plan.
5. All of the alternatives are correct and equally valid means of assessing the extent to which the objectives of a lesson or unit have been met.

Chapter 5

Answers to Short-Answer Question

Following are sample responses for the chapter case history and Praxis short-answer question. When you read these sample responses, keep in mind that they are less polished than if they had been developed at home, edited, and carefully presented. Examinees do not know what questions will be asked and must decide, on the spot, how to respond. Readers take these circumstances into account when scoring the responses.

Sample Response That Would Receive a Score of 2

Ms. Ford changed her classroom to make the students feel more confident and comfortable. She met them at the door with warmth and reassurance, complimenting them and using friendly humor. When she shared her fantasy about living one day as a wild black stallion, she became more of a person and less of an authoritarian figure to them.

Her seating plan and group activity allowed the students to interact with each other instead of in front of the whole class. This cooperative system would be especially helpful for the many students not completely at ease with English. The lesson itself, describing an admired animal, was relatively risk free; there could be no wrong answers.

Both the level of comfort and the risk-free nature of the cooperative activity combined to set the stage for all students to be active rather than passive learners.

Sample Response That Would Receive a Score of 0

Ms. Ford decided to focus on fun things, not boring ones like copying sentences or working on handwriting. She knew her students were not up to the usual academic tasks of most third graders and she decided not to push them in that direction.

By letting them work in groups, those that did not know English very well could get the right answers from another member of the group. Ms. Ford made learning easy and fun.

Answers to Discrete Multiple-Choice Questions

1. The correct answer is D. The problem with spitballs arises from the inability of Ms. Wilson to monitor her students with her back to them as she writes on the board. This is an invitation for misbehavior. Use of the overhead would allow her to continue with the discussion centering on student contributions while she is able to face the classroom.
2. The correct answer is A. Much more so than ineffective teachers, effective teachers attached the assignment directly to the end of an in-class activity to emphasize its relevance for present and future learning. This tended to motivate students to complete the assignment and to separate it from any form of punishment.
3. The correct answer is A. Research on teacher practices suggests a relationship between teacher proximity and student engagement and compliance. However, certain students may feel threatened by the social power conveyed by a teacher looming over them monitoring their work. Rather than abandoning close proximity to the learner because of this perceived threat, a better solution would be to lessen the threat with more casual glances, more checks but of

shorter duration—or the teacher's use of a swivel chair that brings the teacher down to the student's level.

4. The correct answer is C. If Mr. Higgins's objective is to engage his students in a discussion about the day's lesson he should focus primarily on encouraging student dialogue by asking stimulating questions and summarizing and refocusing student contributions. Organizing the content, conveying an evaluative tone, and assigning specific work corresponds to a competitive or individualistic classroom climate that would limit the spontaneity and flow of the cooperative discussion which is Mr. Higgins's goal for the lesson.

5. The correct answer is C. Research has not found that the achievement of lower-performing students assigned to tracked classes is any different from that of lower-performing students in heterogeneous classes.

Chapter 6

Answers to Short-Answer Question

Following are sample responses for the chapter case history and Praxis short-answer question. When you read these sample responses, keep in mind that they are less polished than if they had been developed at home, edited, and carefully presented. Examinees do not know what questions will be asked and must decide, on the spot, how to respond. Readers take these circumstances into account when scoring the responses.

Sample Response That Would Receive a Score of 2

The strongest part of Mr. Scott's policy on tardiness on graded discussion days is that it doesn't just punish the bad behavior, but it sets up a positive way of attaining the desired behavior. If the student does very well in the day's task, he or she can regain lost points. Once the ground rules are established, there is no disruption to classroom activity as might be in the assignment of detention involving a student signing up for a date and possibly arguing about its fairness. Nor does the teacher have to be there to monitor and record the detention served.

There are some possible problems with this, however. With just two comments, a student can undo any negative consequences for being tardy, and this might prove to be just too easy. Another problem concerns taking away grade points for a behavior problem. Some might protest that grading concerns be restricted to subject-matter content.

Sample Response That Would Receive a Score of 0

The best part of Mr. Scott's tardy policy is that it gets rid of detention. Most students don't serve the time anyway. They may have football practice, an after-school job, and family responsibilities.

But maybe the student had a perfectly good reason for being late—his locker was jammed or he picked up the wrong book and had to make a second trip. He shouldn't be punished for something that maybe was out of his control.

Answers to Discrete Multiple-Choice Questions

1. The correct answer is C. Although the punishment stopped Tina from putting away her materials too early, it had unintended side effects. Tina stopped participating in class discussions, probably as an emotional response to what she saw as unfair punishment. Thus, although Mrs. Brooks was rid of a minor distraction, she also lost what every teacher wants, an active participant in stimulating dialogue.

2. The correct answer is C. It is the classroom management tradition, with its emphasis on planning, organization, rules, routines, and consequences, that focuses on prevention of problems before they arise.

3. The correct answer is A. Lessons built around the knowledge, experience, and interests of learners allow the culturally responsive teacher to represent subject matter in ways that are meaningful to students. By gaining their interest and engagement, the teacher preempts behavior problems.

4. The correct answer is B. A, C, and D each take additional time away from instruction and could create an even greater distraction: A by having Rhona lecturing the class on rules (which she may not know), C by creating a further distraction by getting both Amanda and Rhona to remove themselves from the classroom, and D by embarrassing Rhona and putting her on the defensive, which could accelerate the problem. B allows the teacher to indirectly get Amanda's attention with the least loss of instructional time.

Chapter 7

Answers to Short-Answer Question

Following are sample responses for the chapter case history and Praxis short-answer question. When you read these sample responses, keep in mind that they are less polished than if they had been developed at home, edited, and carefully presented. Examinees do not know what questions will be asked and must decide, on the spot, how to respond. Readers take these circumstances into account when scoring the responses.

Sample Response That Would Receive a Score of 2

Mrs. Martinez was correct in using direct instruction to teach the proper use of *there*, *they're*, and *their*. This skill involves the learning of facts and rules, which are most efficiently taught with the direct instruction model.

A second reason direct instruction was appropriate would be to arouse and focus interest on content that might be covered in the text, but that might be all too easily overlooked by students or presented with inadequate examples and applications. The presentation, recitation, and redundancy of the lesson helped this content be learned or even overlearned for sustained spontaneous and automatic recall. Overlearning is important in helping students achieve content mastery of fundamentals that are needed for later learning.

Another reason to consider the direct instruction model is that direct instruction corresponds well with the recall of facts, comprehension of information, and application of fundamental skills—the types of student achievement most often measured by standardized tests, which was a weakness this school was trying to address.

Sample Response That Would Receive a Score of 0

Mrs. Martinez was right to use directed instruction. She had to cover the right spelling because students can't find enough of that sort of information in their texts. Such an important and complex concept needs a lot of coverage.

Answers to Discrete Multiple-Choice Questions

1. The correct answer is B. The interaction between teacher and student that is influenced by teacher body posture, language, and eye contact is referred to as metacommunication. Engagement techniques alone will not be sufficient to ensure student attention unless accompanied by metacommunication that expresses nurturance and caring.
2. The correct answer is C. When students visualize what a teacher has just demonstrated (or repeat it subvocally), it is called a *covert rehearsal* because the behavior is not observable. *Overt rehearsal* is behavior readily observable, as when students say or do something audibly in response to a teacher question.
3. The correct answer is B. Guided practice and feedback sessions should aim for a correct response rate of approximately 60% to 80%. Weekly and monthly reviews should increase the rate of correct responses to approximately 95%.
4. The correct answer is C. Although encouraging students to relate content to their own experience is a desirable goal in indirect instruction, it does not foster the goals of direct instruction and could delay the desired outcome of responding correctly, quickly, and firmly.
5. The correct answer is C. The order of intrusiveness is verbal (least intrusive), gestural, and physical (most intrusive). A verbal prompt fades more quickly than the others, leaving the learner less dependent on the prompt for exhibiting the desired behavior the next time.

Chapter 8

Answers to Short-Answer Question

Following are sample responses for the chapter case history and Praxis short-answer question. When you read these sample responses, keep in mind that they are less polished than if they had been developed at home, edited, and carefully presented. Examinees do not know what questions will be asked and must decide, on the spot, how to respond. Readers take these circumstances into account when scoring the responses.

Sample Response That Would Receive a Score of 2

Mr. Peterman used self-disclosure and humor to engage his students. He posed his question about job possibilities in a personal way, saying he would be needing a summer job "to keep him busy," and said that he always did like cars. Students themselves could probably identify with the problem of keeping busy over the summer, and many of them probably were looking for some sort of summer work, too.

His sense of humor was shown in the unlikely choice of jobs he chose to consider and in his interchange with Monique. In order to show Monique that her response, "changing times," was too broad, he asked if she meant to include such objects as "pop music, hairstyles, or the latest shade of nail polish." I think Monique knew he was teasing her with the question that persuaded her to change her response to be more on target.

Sample Response That Would Receive a Score of 0

Mr. Peterson was pretty nice to his class. He let them talk to each other, even when they were showing that another guy's answer might have been dumb, like the one about high tech. They seemed to like him because he listened to their ideas and didn't make fun of them.

Answers to Discrete Multiple-Choice Questions

1. The correct answer is B. The structuring framework used to give learners a conceptual preview of what is to come is called an *advance organizer*, which helps prepare students to store, label, and package content for retention and later use. Advance organizers have been found especially helpful for students from diverse cultures.

2. The correct answer is C. The purpose of questioning during indirect instruction is aimed at the process of search and discovery. It promotes the widest possible discussion of topics from both the student's and teacher's point of view. The teacher begins by accepting almost any answer at the beginning of discussion and then uses student responses to begin to shape more accurate understanding. Direct instruction, by contrast, aims at early demonstration of specific, convergent, and correct answers.

3. The correct answer is D. Self-evaluation is when students begin to take responsibility for their own learning. This essential function of indirect instruction can be encouraged by gradually letting students provide reasons for their answers so the teacher and other students can suggest needed changes.

4. The correct answers are A, B, and C. Constructivist lessons do give students freedom in the manner and spontaneity in which they can respond but always within the context of the goal of the lesson, thereby setting a definite direction to which their point of view and experience and interaction with others can be directed.

5. The correct answers are 1 (a), 2 (b), 3 (c), and 4 (a). Both the first and fourth alternatives represent concept learning tasks that ask students to discriminate and generalize in order to define the essential and nonessential attributes of a concept—representative government and an academically at-risk learner. The second lesson goal is to teach students a means of investigation (for example, by introducing the *Wall Street Journal* online) that they could use on their own to answer a question. The third lesson goal is to arrive at a specific solution within the context of a stated problem.

Chapter 9
Answers to Short-Answer Question

Following are sample responses for the chapter case history and Praxis short-answer question. When you read these sample responses, keep in mind that they are less polished than if they had been developed at home, edited, and carefully presented. Examinees do not know what questions will be asked and must decide, on the spot, how to respond. Readers take these circumstances into account when scoring the responses.

Sample Response That Would Receive a Score of 2

Higher-order questions encourage the kinds of thinking—such as critical thinking, problem solving, decision making—that are most needed outside the classroom, in jobs and in advanced training. Whether one is deciding which person, party, or community proposition to vote for or working as a team member to design new products and marketing strategies, critical thinking, problem solving, and decision making will be required.

Standardized tests are chosen more for their efficient and rapid assessment of fundamental facts and skills than for any proven link to success as an adult. The format is generally multiple choice, which, by its very nature, tests for single correct answers at the knowledge, comprehension, and application levels. Instruction that would only be directed to improving standardized achievement scores would be of limited use outside the classroom and in adult life.

Research has shown that teachers who ask higher-order questions of their students tend to have students that, in turn, raise higher-order questions, preparing them for higher levels of thinking in the real world. Mr. Cole showed this when he asked the class to "think about some other inventions that also created problems as well as solved them" and Jason responded, "Well, what about cars?" which then prompted the class to analyze their pros and cons.

Sample Response That Would Receive a Score of 0

Discussions that make you think are a whole lot more interesting than boring ones that just have all the students reciting answers like a bunch of parrots. Thinking is more important than knowing facts and dates. You can always look up that information on the Internet. Mr. Cole was right to make his students think.

Answers to Discrete Multiple-Choice Questions

1. The correct answer is B. In Bloom et al.'s hierarchy, evaluation questions are at the

highest level of behavioral complexity. They require students to form judgments and make decisions using stated criteria. Because decisions and judgments are prime ingredients of adult life, it is essential that classroom experiences link learners to the world in which they will live.

2. The correct answer is A. Although research has shown increased wait time to generate responses that are longer, more frequent, and more confident, it has not necessarily shown them to be more accurate.

3. The correct answer is C. Approximately 80% of teacher questions in a typical classroom are convergent or direct questions, leaving only 20% for divergent or indirect questions. Divergent questioning takes more time and requires more unexpected and flexible responses from the teacher, which may account for this ratio. However, the value of the higher-order thinking that divergent questions foster suggests that a ratio of 70:30 or 60:40 may be more appropriate.

4. The correct answer is C. Research has shown that classrooms with short wait times do not give students sufficient time to think and thereby learn from the question. Short wait times in which the teacher jumps in to help constrains the thinking process and may intimidate the learner into believing he or she is inadequate or does not know the answer.

5. The correct answer is A. Before other alternatives are chosen, a multisensory approach should be used to soften the transition for the non-English-language learner who is new to your classroom. Over time, if language acquisition does not improve, have the school counselor check for disabilities that could impede language acquisition.

Chapter 10

Answers to Short-Answer Question

Following are sample responses for the chapter case history and Praxis short-answer question. When you read these sample responses, keep in mind that they are less polished than if they had been developed at home, edited, and carefully presented. Examinees do not know what questions will be asked and must decide, on the spot, how to respond. Readers take these circumstances into account when scoring the responses.

Sample Response That Would Receive a Score of 2

Mrs. Henson was very good at using the students' own meaning of the content to structure the class

discussion. She took the facial expression of Nate as a clue to his individual interpretation of the silliness of thinking the earth was flat. She did not ridicule his emotional response but used it as a springboard to create a "what-if" scenario of another Nate in the future.

Another effective use of teacher mediation was how she directed the flow of the discussion. She built on Nate's idea to slow down and refocus the discussion. What scientific misconception would some future Nate be laughing at some time in the future?

Sample Response That Would Receive a Score of 0

Mrs. Henson mediates the discussion by making sure everyone gets a chance to talk. She calls on a lot of different people and doesn't let one person dominate the conversation. Even though Tiffany and Sylvester disagree, she makes sure they don't get into a fight about it.

She tries to use their ideas, too. Especially the one about no more aging. That really gets her attention.

Answers to Discrete Multiple-Choice Questions

1. The correct answer is B. Mnemonics or memory aids enhance cognition by aiding in the mental organization and retention of facts and include the use of jingles or trigger sentences, narrative chaining, number rhymes or peg words, and chunking.

2. The correct answer is B. Self-directed learning, which encourages students to take more responsibility for their own learning by going beyond the information given to attack real-world problems, can be expected to result in higher-level thinking.

3. The correct answer is C. The science project as defined by the teacher fails to allow student self-direction, freedom of choice, or peer collaboration. All of these factors would help provide intrinsic motivation, especially in culturally diverse populations.

4. The correct answer is A. Self-interrogation, self-checking and monitoring of one's own thinking are key skills for metacognition. Answers B, C, and D focus on external means of acquiring content and knowledge (reviewing, inquiry, sharing), not the internal or thinking processes by which content and knowledge can be effectively and efficiently acquired.

5. The correct answer is C. Modeling, questioning, and monitoring are all effective tools for teaching self-directed inquiry. Providing a rigid set of steps to achieve a set end, however, may inhibit self-direction by constraining the original,

intuitive, and imaginative thoughts of the learner, which self-directed learning is intended to promote.

Chapter 11

Answers to Short-Answer Question

Following are sample responses for the chapter case history and Praxis short-answer question. When you read these sample responses, keep in mind that they are less polished than if they had been developed at home, edited, and carefully presented. Examinees do not know what questions will be asked and must decide, on the spot, how to respond. Readers take these circumstances into account when scoring the responses.

Sample Response That Would Receive a Score of 2

Ms. Choo should assign specific roles for all group members, roles that are necessary for them to reach the group goal. Sally could be the checker, for instance, and look up the correct answer or formula in the text. Everyone would be dependent on her for the input needed to complete the task, and so the group would not be as likely to let her drift off.

Another method would be to chart each member's progress on his or her assigned task. Sometimes a chart on display showing each person's participation can act as a motivator. Groups could get bonus points for having everyone participate, thus using peer pressure, again in a positive way.

Sample Response That Would Receive a Score of 0

Ms. Choo should say something to get the attention of Sally or Ricardo. Ask them why they're not helping their group. Maybe they should be given a punishment like extra homework. Or she could call home to let their parents know they are not following the rules.

Another way to deal with this would be to put Sally back with her friend so she is not so angry, and separate Ricardo from his new friend, so they are not always just talking to one another.

Answers to Discrete Multiple-Choice Questions

1. The correct answer is A. The social interactions of collaborative learning help resolve internal conflicts, reveal inconsistencies, and clarify what we really believe to create a coherent personality or integrated identity.
2. The correct answer is D. Debriefing is the final stage of the cooperative process in which the teacher solicits feedback on how well students are collaborating. This self-examination sets the stage for improved group performance.
3. The correct answer is B. Assisting, redirecting, and supporting cooperative learning groups is the role of the teacher in collaborative learning. This important observation and intervention process is called *monitoring group performance.*
4. The correct answer is B. For most classroom objectives, very small groups leave too few options for diversifying the role functions individual members can perform (summarizer, researcher, checker, etc.), and larger groups often promote more off-task behavior and passive, uninvolved learners who can hide behind the work of others.
5. The correct answers are, in order, MS, LS, MS, LS. Having definite and consistent rules and often changing the pace keeps a cooperative group needing more structure more on task and engaged. And providing topics to choose from and opportunities for extended follow-up can promote these same outcomes for cooperative groups who may need less structure.

Chapter 12

Answers to Short-Answer Question

Following are sample responses for the chapter case history and Praxis short-answer question. When you read these sample responses, keep in mind that they are less polished than if they had been developed at home, edited, and carefully presented. Examinees do not know what questions will be asked and must decide, on the spot, how to respond. Readers take these circumstances into account when scoring the responses.

Sample Response That Would Receive a Score of 2

Ms. Velchek's students had been taking shortcuts by memorizing facts and writing superficial essays. However, it was Ms. Velchek who had written tests that emphasized memorization. And it was she who had accepted glib responses to her essays.

She should have prepared the students for the change by mentioning this test would be something different from those in the past, and they should be expected to apply what they learned rather than merely recall and regurgitate it. As for the possible changes in grading, I think Ms. Velchek should discuss the purpose and advantages of any new grading system and elicit input from her students before it is implemented so they know why a particular grading system would be used.

Sample Response That Would Receive a Score of 0

It was fair for Ms. Velchek to make the test and questions harder. She is the teacher and has the right to write a test the way she wants. She doesn't need to tell her class exactly what to expect or else a lot of the class will get high scores. It's better to keep them alert by wondering what type of test they will get.

The grades are different, though. Those kids have been through 5 or 6 years of school with one system that everyone expects. It would be confusing and counterproductive to change at this point in the game.

Answers to Discrete Multiple-Choice Questions

1. The correct answer is D. An essay test is the best option presented for Mr. Malone to assess his students' understanding of the complex causes of the American Civil War. A norm-referenced test would yield information that compares his class to others in the general area of history, but would not be specific enough to tell him if his students have learned what was taught. Both the true-false and the matching tests would tend to emphasize rote memorization of knowledge rather than complex understanding.

2. The correct answer is A. Standardized tests are constructed by test experts to determine a student's performance level relative to others of similar age and grade. Recent criticism has questioned their relevance to classroom learning, their usefulness in making instructional decisions, and their fairness to students of diverse cultural and ethnic backgrounds.

3. The correct answer is C. Of all the objective-item formats, the multiple-choice question is the only one that combines efficiency of construction and grading with versatility in measuring higher levels of cognitive complexity, for example, by using pictorial and tabular aids, using analogies, or requiring the application of procedures and principles. It also reduces the effects of guessing, an inherent weakness in true-false items.

4. The correct answer is A. Rubrics define the precise behaviors by which the quality of a learner's performance can be judged.

5. The correct answer is D. Portfolios tell the story of a learner's growth and long-term accomplishments. Test blueprints, multimodal assessments, and performance tests are snapshots taken at one point in time.

Glossary

A

Active listening The listener provides feedback to the speaker on the message heard and the emotion conveyed, and lets the speaker know he or she is being understood and respected. 211

Active responding Orally responding to a question, writing out the correct answer, calculating an answer, or physically making a response (e.g., focusing a microscope). 243

Active uninvolvement When a group member talks about everything but the assigned goal of the group. 378

Activity structure The systematic varying of task demands within a unit. 353

Adaptive teaching Applying different instructional strategies to different groups of learners so all learners can achieve success. 44

Advance organizer A framework or structure that organizes content into meaningful parts. 262

Affective domain Behaviors that relate to the development of attitudes, beliefs, and values: receiving, responding, valuing, organization, and characterization. 92

Applied behavior analysis Classroom management emphasizing behavior modification techniques and reinforcement theory. 193

At-risk learners Those who are most often off-task and disengaged, and who have difficulty learning at an average rate. 181

Authentic behaviors The types of performances required in the real world. 94

Authentic tests Asking learners to display their skills and behaviors in the way they would be displayed in the real world, outside the classroom. 94

B

Behavioral antecedents Events or stimuli that are present when a behavior is performed that elicit or set off the behavior. 198

Behavioral objective A written statement that identifies specific classroom strategies to achieve desired goals and expresses these strategies in a format that allows their effects on learners to be measured. 85

Behavior modification Changing or modifying a behavior by following the behavior with some type of reinforcement. 197

C

Centering behavior A type of amiable limit testing during which learners question how they will personally benefit from being group members. 163

Classroom management tradition Focuses on planning and organizing the classroom, teaching rules and routines, and informing students of the consequences of breaking the rules. 193

Coercive power Asserting authority by punishing misbehavior. 161

Cognitive domain Behaviors that relate to the development of intellectual abilities and skills: knowledge, comprehension, application, analysis, synthesis, and evaluation. 92

Cognitive learning strategy General methods of thinking that improve learning by helping the learner to retain incoming information (reception), recall task-relevant prior knowledge (availability), and build logical connections among incoming knowledge (activation). 354

Compensatory approach The teacher chooses an instructional method to compensate for learners' lack of information, skills, or ability and alters content presentation to circumvent learners' weaknesses and promote their strengths. 45

Congruent communication Using communication skills to promote learners' self-esteem, which influences them to choose acceptable behavior. 194

Constructivism Designing and sequencing lessons to encourage learners to use their own experiences to actively construct meaning that makes sense to them rather than to acquire understanding through exposure to a format organized by the teacher.   262

Constructivist teaching strategies Instructional tools that emphasize the learner's direct experience and the classroom dialogue while de-emphasizing lecturing and telling.   23

Convergent question One that limits an answer to a single or a small number of responses.   304

Cooperative learning Arrangement in which students work in groups and are rewarded on the basis of the success of the group. And according to Glasser, cooperative learning builds an environment that makes the classroom a place the learner wants to be.   196

Cooperative learning role functions Summarizer, checker, researcher, runner, recorder, supporter, observer/troubleshooter.   379

Criterion level The degree of performance required to achieve a learning objective.   89

Criterion-referenced test (CRT) Compares a student's performance with an absolute standard of mastery, a criterion.   399

Cross-age tutoring One student teaches another; the tutor may be one or more years and grade levels above the learner.   133

Crystallization Learners' expectations converge into a shared perspective of classroom life as they engage in activities together.   164

Cultural deficit model Using genetically or culturally inspired factors to explain differences in such things as aptitude and language between cultural minorities and mainstream learners.   58

Cultural difference model Focusing on solutions that require culturally sensitive links to and responses from the school to improve the performance of students who are socially, economically, and linguistically different from the mainstream.   58

Cultural frame The individual's frame of reference acquired from experience that is the lens through which one interprets and responds to events.   58

Culturally responsive teaching The teacher's ability to react to different cultures with different verbal and nonverbal classroom management techniques.   214

Culture-specific questioning Rules that govern social conversation among different cultural groups used to better target questions to specific populations of learners.   322

Curriculum guides Grade, department, or school district specifications about what content must be covered in what period of time.   115

D

Daily review and checking Direct instruction strategy emphasizing the relationship between lessons so students remember previous knowledge and see new knowledge as a logical extension of content already mastered.   233

Debriefing Gathering feedback about an activity by discussing the activity, soliciting suggestions for improving the activity, and getting observers' viewpoints.   384

Declarative (factual) knowledge Facts, concepts, rules, and generalizations pertaining to a specific area or topic; also, intended to be spoken or written.   352

Deduction Reasoning that proceeds from priniciples or generalizations to their application in specific instances.   279

Diffusion Learners' different academic and social expectations spread through the class as they communicate with one another.   164

Direct instruction A teacher-centered, knowledge-acquisition, presentation-recitation model for teaching facts, rules, and action sequences.   226

Discrimination Selectively restricting a range of instances by eliminating things that appear to match the concept but that differ from it in critical dimensions.   266

Distancing behavior A type of amiable limit testing during which group members challenge academic expectations and rules to establish under what conditions the rules do or do not apply.   163

Distracters Wrong answer choices in a multiple-choice or matching test item.   406

Divergent question One that has many or a broad range of acceptable responses.   304

E

Effective questions Questions for which students actively compose a response, thereby becoming engaged in the learning process.   303

Eliciting probes Seeking clarification of the student's response to determine its appropriateness or correctness.   316

Engaged learning time The amount of time students devote to learning in the classroom.   15

Enviromentalist position The belief that social class and the environment rather than heredity is the major factor in determining intelligence.   46

Examples Representation of the concept by including all the attributes essential for recognizing it as a member of a larger class.   281

Expert power Being seen as competent to explain or do certain things and as knowledgeable about particular topics.   159

Expressive objective A learning objective that may have a variety of correct responses.   90

Extended-response essay An essay question that allows the student to determine the length and complexity of the response.   412

F

Family–school linking mechanisms Opportunities for school and family involvement such as parent–teacher conferences, home visits, teachers participating in community events, newsletters, phone calls, personal notes, parents volunteering as classroom aides, using home-based curriculum materials.   68

Feedback and correctives Direct instruction strategies for handling right and wrong answers.   241

Field dependent Seeing the world in terms of large, connected patterns.   62

Field independent Seeing the world in terms of its specific parts.   62

Full-group discussion Student exchanges with successive interactions among large numbers of students.   287

Functional errors Incorrect or partially correct answers that can enhance the meaning and understanding of content and provide a logical stepping-stone for climbing onto the next rung of the learning ladder.   344

G

Generalization Responding in a similar manner to stimuli that differ but are bound together by a central concept.   266

Gestural prompts Modeling or demonstrating for learners the skill being taught.   238

Goals Derived from standards to more specifically identify what must be accomplished and who must do what in order for the standards to be met.   80

Guided student practice Direct instruction strategy of presenting stimulus material and then eliciting practice, directed by the teacher, of the desired behavior.   237

H

Helping behaviors Behaviors used in combinations to implement the key effective teaching behaviors; among them, using student ideas and contributions, structuring, questioning, probing, and teacher affect (developing the teacher–learner relationship).   10

Hereditarian position The belief that heredity rather than environment is the major factor determining intelligence.   47

Horizontal relationships Successful relationships with peers that meet learners' needs for belonging and allow them to acquire and practice important social skills.   61

Humanist tradition Classroom management focusing on the inner thoughts, feelings, psychological needs, and emotions of individual learners.   193

I

Independent practice Direct instruction strategy in which the teacher brings facts and rules together in ways that force simultaneous consideration of all the individual units of a problem and connect the units into a single harmonious sequence of action.   243

Indirect instruction Teaching strategies that emphasize concept learning, inquiry, and problem solving to teach concepts, patterns, and abstractions.   226

Induction Reasoning used to draw a conclusion or make a generalization from specific instances.   278

Inner speech A learner's private internal dialogue that takes the place of the teacher's prompts and questions and self-guides the learner through similar problems.   349

Instructional variety The teacher's variability or flexibility of delivery during the presentation of a lesson.   11

INTASC standards The 10 principles describing what teachers should know and be able to do, from the Interstate New Teacher Assessment and Support Consortium.   32

Integrated bodies of knowledge Units and lessons that stress the connections between ideas and the logical coherence of interrelated topics.   264

Integrated thematic teaching Relating content and material from various subject areas.   125

Interactive individualized practice activities Lessons on CD-ROMs that use questions and prompts to actively engage learners and give them immediate feedback.   134

Intercultural competence The teacher's ability to act as a translator and intercultural broker between students of different cultures, ethnicities, and social classes.   215

Interdisciplinary unit A laterally planned unit of study in which topics are integrated to focus on a specific theme. 124

Intermittent reinforcement Reinforcing a behavior at random or on an intermittent schedule to maintain the behavior at its present level. 198

K

Key behaviors Five behaviors essential for effective teaching: lesson clarity, instructional variety, teacher task orientation, engagement in the learning process, and student success rate. 10

L

Lateral unit planning Planning units that integrate knowledge across disciplines or content areas to convey relationships, patterns, and abstractions. 119

Learning activities Means of achieving learning outcomes. 87

Learning conditions The specific conditions under which learning will occur. 98

Learning outcome An observable and measurable behavior; the end products of instructional lessons and units. 86

Learning structures The logical progression of ideas with which a lesson is conveyed, identifying what the learner needs to know at each step before new learning can take place. 54

Learning style The instructional and classroom conditions under which an individual prefers to learn. 62

Legitimate power Having influence because of one's title or role rather than one's nature. 160

Lesson clarity The teacher's presentation to the class should make points clear to learners at different levels of understanding and explain concepts in logical, step-by-step order; the oral delivery should be direct, audible to all students, and free of distracting mannerisms. 11

Level of proficiency The minimum degree of performance to achieve a learning objective. 89

Living curriculum Using multimedia, often over the Internet, making a fluid and personalized learning environment. 135

Low-profile classroom management Coping strategies teachers use to stop misbehavior without disrupting the flow of a lesson. 201

M

Marks and grading systems Based on comparison, usually of students with one or more of: other students, established standards, aptitude, actual vs. potential effort, actual vs. potential improvement. 420

Mastery learning An instructional strategy based on the principle that all students can attain lesson and unit objectives with the appropriate instruction and sufficient time to learn. 229

Mental modeling Demonstration of the decision-making process to help students internalize, recall, and generalize problem solutions to different content at a later time. 339

Metacognition Mental processes that assist learners to reflect on their thinking by internalizing, understanding, and recalling the content to be learned. 339

Metacognitive knowledge Thinking about one's thinking to become aware of one's level of knowledge. 93

Metacommunication The pattern of the teacher's body posture, language, and eye contact that is recognized by the learner and acted on according to the message being conveyed, intentionally or not. 250

Moderating tasks The teacher orients students to the objective of the discussion; provides new or more accurate information; reviews, summarizes, and relates opinions and facts; and redirects the flow of information and ideas back to the objective. 288

Monitoring The process of observing, mentally recording, and when necessary, redirecting or correcting students' behaviors. 175

N

Natural reinforcers Internal (natural) rewards or reinforcers that are naturally present in the setting where a behavior occurs. 207

Negative reinforcement Avoiding a painful, uncomfortable, or aversive state to achieve a more desirable state. 197

Nonexamples Failure to represent the concept by purposely not including one or more of the attributes essential for recognizing it as a member of a larger class. 281

Norm-referenced test (NRT) Compares a student's performance to that of a norm group, a large, representative sample of learners. 399

Norms Shared expectations among group members regarding how they should think, feel, and behave. 163

O

Objectives Statements that convey to your learners the specific behaviors to be attained, the conditions under which the behaviors must be demonstrated, and the proficiency at which the behaviors must be demonstrated. 80

Operant conditioning Transferring from external to internal control of behavior. 207

Ordered turns Systematically going through the class and expecting students to respond when their turn comes. 239

Organizational environment The teacher's visual or physical arrangement of the classroom. 167

P

Pair or team discussions Best when the task is highly structured; some consensus about the topic already exists; and the orienting instructions fully define each member's role. 289

Passive responding Listening to the teacher's answer, reading about the correct answer, or listening to classmates recite the right answer. 243

Passive uninvolvement When a group member doesn't care about the goal of the group and falls silent. 378

Peer tutoring One student teaches another at the same grade and age level. 133

Performance assessment Learners show what they know by using complex cognitive skills to perform authentic, real-world tasks; tests that measure a skill or behavior directly, as they are used in the world outside the classroom. 425

Physical prompts Using hand-over-hand assistance to guide the learner to the correct performance. 238

Portfolio assessment Shows a learner's growth in proficiency, long-term achievement, and significant accomplishments in a given academic area. 428

Positive reinforcement Providing a desired stimulus or reward after a behavior increases in frequency. 197

Praxis A series of assessments for entering a teacher training program, becoming licensed, and/or for the first year of teaching. 5

Presenting and structuring new content Direct instruction strategy presenting material in small steps consistent with students' previous knowledge, ability level, and experience, so learners master one point before the teacher introduces the next point. 234

Problem-based learning Organizing instructional tasks around loosely structured or ill-defined problems that learners solve by using knowledge and skills from several disciplines. 357

Procedural knowledge Action sequences or procedures used in a problem-solving or decision-making task; learning action sequences or procedures to follow; knowledge of how to do things. 352

Project-based learning Promoting intrinsic motivation by organizing instruction around tasks most likely to induce and support learner interest, effort, and persistence. 359

Prosocial behavior Appropriate attitudes and values that children learn from close and meaningful encounters among family members and in the classroom. 372

Psychomotor domain Behaviors that relate to the coordination of physical movements and performance: imitation, manipulation, precision, articulation, and naturalization. 92

Q

Question sequence Structuring, soliciting, and reacting, with many possible variations. 307

R

Reacting The teacher's response to students' answers to questions. 303

Reciprocal distancing The effect of teachers from one culture interpreting children's behaviors differently than teachers from another culture. 55

Reciprocal teaching A type of classroom group dialogue in which the teacher expects students to make predictions, ask questions, summarize, and clarify the text. 346

Redirecting probes Restructuring a discussion with follow-up questions to get students back on track. 317

Referent power Being seen as trustworthy, fair, and concerned about students. 160

Reflective practice Teaching that is inspired by the tacit or personal knowledge gained from day-to-day experiences. 114

Reflective teacher A teacher who is thoughtful and self-critical about his or her teaching. 43

Reliability Refers to whether a test consistently yields the same or similar scores. 417

Remediation approach The teacher provides learners with the prerequisite knowledge, skill, or behavior needed to benefit from the planned instruction. 44

Restricted-response essay An essay question that poses a specific problem for which the student must recall proper information, organize it suitably, derive a defensible conclusion, and express it according to specific criteria.   413

Reward power Being able to confer privileges, approval, or tangible compensation.   160

Rubrics Rating scales that express criteria for assessing essay or portfolio content.   434

Rule-example-rule order Giving a rule, then an example of the rule, then a repetition of the rule.   237

Rules and procedures Rules related to academic work, classroom conduct, information the teacher must communicate the first day, and information that can be communicated later.   172

S

Small-group discussions About four to six students per group.   289

Social competence The factors that, in addition to IQ, contribute to learners' success, including motivation, health, social skills, quality of teaching, prior knowledge, emotional well-being, family support.   47

Social environment The interaction patterns the teacher promotes in the classroom.   167

Social framing The context in which a message such as a lesson is received and understood.   293

Social learning theory The study of how people learn from observing others.   239

Social power Being an effective leader; having students' trust and respect.   159

Socioeconomic status (SES) An approximate index of one's income and education level.   28

Sociolinguistics The study of how cultural groups differ in the courtesies and conventions of language rather than in the grammatical structure of what is said.   322

Soliciting Question-asking behavior that encourages students to act on and think about the material.   303

Soliciting probes Asking for new information after a response that is partially correct to push the learner to a more complex level of understanding.   316

Stages of group development A series of stages, called forming, storming, norming, and performing, during which the group has certain tasks to accomplish and concerns to resolve.   161

Standardized tests Administered and scored according to specific and uniform procedures; used to determine a student's performance level relative to others of similar age and grade.   422

Standards General expressions of our values that give us a sense of direction.   80

Stem The statement part of a multiple-choice item.   466

Structuring How the teacher uses questions to direct learning.   303

Student-centered learning Allows the student to select the form and substance of the learning experience.   286

Student success rate The rate at which the students understand and correctly complete exercises and assignments.   16

Surface behaviors Children's normal developmental behaviors that they do when confined to a small space with large numbers of other children.   201

System perspective Planning lessons to be part of the larger system of interrelated learning, the unit.   114

Systems-ecological perspective Viewing the learner as an ecosystem whose major systems include the family, school, and peer group and whose behavior is a product of the learner and the demands and forces operating within the systems of which he or she is a member.   68

T

Tacit knowledge The teacher's reflection on what works in the classroom, discovered over time and through personal experience.   114

Task specialization Breaking a larger task into smaller subparts on which separate groups work.   374

Task structure In cooperative learning, specifying the goal; structuring the task; teaching and evaluating the collaborative process; monitoring group performance; debriefing.   375

Teacher-mediated dialogue The teacher helps learners restructure what is being learned using their own ideas, experiences, and thought patterns.   20

Teacher-mediated learning Adjusting the instructional dialogue to help students restructure their learning and construct their own meanings from the content.   340

Teacher task orientation How much classroom time the teacher devotes to the task of teaching an academic subject.   13

Teaching concerns The stages of concern with which teachers most strongly identify at different periods in their careers.   33

Team-oriented cooperative learning activities Using teams of heterogeneous learners to increase the collaborative skills, self-esteem, and achievement of individual learners.   388

Test blueprint A table that matches the test items to be written with the content areas and levels of behavioral complexity taught.   402

Thematic units A variety of activities and materials focused in several related content areas taught using different instructional strategies.   125

Think, pair, share A technique in which students working in pairs learn from one another and get to try out their ideas in a non-threatening context before presenting their ideas to the class.   289

Thinking curriculum One that focuses on teaching learners how to think critically, reason, and solve problems in authentic, real-world contexts.   83

Track system A system in which some sections of instruction are allocated to lower- and/or higher-performing students.   181

Tutorial and communication technologies Methods that are flexible, allow rapid movement within and across content, provide immediate feedback on accuracy of responses, and gradually shift responsibility for learning from teacher to student.   132

U

Unguided discovery learning To maintain high levels of student interest, selecting content based on student problems or interests and providing individually tailored feedback.   286

V

Validity Refers to whether a test measures what it says it measures.   417

Verbal prompts Cues, reminders, or instructions to learners that help them perform correctly the skill being taught.   238

Vertical relationships Successful relationships with parents and teachers that meet a learner's needs for safety, security, and protection.   61

Vertical unit planning A method of developing units in a discipline by arranging the content to be taught hierarchically or in steps and in an order that ensures that all task-relevant prior knowledge required for subsequent lessons has been taught in previous lessons.   118

W

Wait-time 1 The amount of time a teacher gives a learner to respond when first asked a question.   318

Wait-time 2 The interval of time after a learner's first response until the teacher or other students affirm or negate the answer.   318

Weekly and monthly reviews Direct instruction strategy of conducting periodic reviews to ensure all task-relevant information needed for future lessons has been learned and to see whether reteaching is necessary.   246

Z

Zone of maximum response opportunity The level of content difficulty and behavioral complexity from which the learner can most benefit at the moment a response is given.   340

References

Aaron, K. (2001). *Single parents can raise great children*. New York: Mass Market Paperback.

Abruscato, J. (1994). Boost your students' social skills with this 9 step plan. *Learning, 22(5),* 60–61, 66.

Affini, J. (1996). *150 ways to increase intrinsic motivation in the classroom*. Boston: Allyn & Bacon.

Alberto, P., & Troutman, A. (1986). *Applied behavior analysis for teachers: Influencing student performance* (2nd ed.). Upper Saddle River, NJ: Merrill/Prentice Hall.

Aldrich, C. (2005). *Learning by doing: A comprehensive guide to simulations, computer games, and pedagogy in e-learning and other educational experiences*. Hoboken, NJ: Wiley.

Alexander, P. (Ed.). (1996). The role of knowledge in learning and instruction [Special issue]. *Educational Psychologist, 31(2),* 89–145.

American Association for the Advancement of Sciences. (1993). *Benchmarks for science literacy: Project 2061*. New York: Oxford University Press.

American Association for the Advancement of Science. (1996). *Benchmarks for science literacy*. Cary, NC: Author.

Ames, C. (1990). Motivation: What teachers need to know. *Teachers College Record, 91,* 409–421.

Anderman, E. M., & Maehr, M. L. (1994). Motivation and schooling in the middle grades. *Review of Educational Research, 64(20),* 287–309.

Anderman, L. H., & Midgley, C. (1998). Motivation and middle school students. *ERIC Digest*. Washington, DC: Office of Educational Research and Improvement & U.S. Department of Education. (ERIC Document Reproduction Service No. ED 421 281)

Anderson, J. R. (1990). *Cognitive psychology and its implications* (4th ed.). San Francisco: W. H. Freeman.

Anderson, K. (1996). *Changing woman: A history of racial ethnic women in modern America*. New York: Oxford University Press.

Anderson, L., Evertson, C., & Brophy, J. (1982). *Principles of small group instruction in elementary reading*. East Lansing: Michigan State University, Institute for Research on Teaching.

Anderson, L., & Krathwohl, D. (Ed.). (2001). *Taxonomy for learning, teaching, and assessing: A revision of Bloom's taxonomy of educational objectives*. New York: Longman.

Anderson, L., Stevens, D., Prawat, R., & Nickerson, J. (1988). Classroom task environments and students' risk-related beliefs. *The Elementary School Journal, 88,* 181–296.

Anderson, M. G. (1992). The use of selected theater rehearsal technique activities with African-American adolescents labeled "Behaviorally Disordered." *Exceptional Children, 59,* 132–140.

Antón-Oldenburg, M. (2000, September). Celebrate diversity! *Scholastic Instructor,* pp. 46–48.

Atwood, V., & Wilen, W. (1991). Wait time and effective social studies instruction: What can research in science education tell us? *Social Education, 55,* 179–181.

Ausubel, D. P. (1968). *Educational psychology: A cognitive view*. New York: Holt, Rinehart & Winston.

Baden, M., & Mayor, C. (2004). *Foundations of problem-based learning*. Berkshire, UK: Open University Press.

Ball, L., Lubienski, S., & Mewborn, D. (2001). Research on teaching mathematics: The unsolved problem of teachers' mathematical knowledge. In V. Richardson (Ed.), *Handbook of Research on Teaching* (pp. 433–456). Washington, DC: American Educational Research Association.

Bandura, A. (1986). *Social foundations of thought and action: A social cognitive theory*. Upper Saddle River, NJ: Prentice Hall.

Bandura, A. (1997). *Self-efficacy*. New York: W. H. Freeman.

Banks, J. (1997). *Teaching strategies for ethnic studies* (6th ed.). Needham, MA: Allyn & Bacon.

Banks, J. (2000). *Cultural diversity and education: Foundations, curriculum, and teaching* (4th ed.). Boston: Allyn & Bacon.

Banks, J., & Banks, C. (Eds.). (2001). *Handbook of research on multicultural education*. San Francisco: Jossey-Bass.

Barr, R. (2001). Research on the teaching of reading. In V. Richardson (Ed.), *The Handbook of Research on Teaching* (pp. 360–415). Washington, DC: American Educational Research Association.

Baum, S., Viens, J., & Slatin, B. (2005). *Multiple Intelligences in the elementary classroom: A teacher's toolkit*. New York: Teachers College Press.

Benard, B. (1997). Turning it around for all youth: From risk to resilience. *ERIC/CUE Digest,* Number 126. Washington, DC: ERIC Clearinghouse on Teaching and Teacher Education. (ERIC Document Reproduction Service No. ED 412 309)

Bennett, C. (1990). *Comprehensive multicultural education: Theory and practice* (2nd ed.). Boston: Allyn & Bacon.

Bennett, N., & Desforges, C. (1988). Matching classroom tasks to students' attainments. *The Elementary School Journal, 88,* 221–224.

Bennett, N., Desforges, C., Cockburn, A., & Wilkinson, B. (1981). *The quality of pupil learning experiences: Interim report*. Lancaster, England: University of Lancaster, Centre for Educational Research and Development.

Bereiter, C., & Englemann, S. (1966). *Teaching disadvantaged children in the preschool*. Upper Saddle River, NJ: Prentice Hall.

Berliner, D. (1979). Tempus educare. In P. Peterson & H. Walberg (Eds.), *Research on teaching: Concepts, findings, and implications* (pp. 120–135). Berkeley, CA: McCutchan.

Berliner, D., & Biddle, B. (1995). *The manufactured crisis: Myth, fraud, and the attack on America's public schools*. New York: Addison-Wesley.

Bettencourt, E., Gillett, M., Gall, M., & Hull, R. (1983). Effects of teacher enthusiasm training on student on-task behavior and achievement. *American Educational Research Journal, 20,* 435–450.

Beyer, B. (1995). *Critical thinking*. Bloomington, IN: Phi Delta Kappa Educational Foundation, Fastback No. 385.

Black, S. (1996). The truth about homework. *American School Board Journal, 183*(10), 48–51.

Bloom, B. (1981). *All our children learning*. New York: McGraw-Hill.

Bloom, B., Englehart, M., Hill, W., Furst, E., & Krathwohl, D. (1984). *Taxonomy of educational objectives: The classification of educational goals.* *Handbook I: Cognitive domain*. New York: Longman Green.

Bluestein, J. (2001). *21st century discipline*. Grand Rapids, MI: McGraw-Hill.

Blumenfeld, P. C., Soloway, E., Marx, R. W., Krajcik, J. S., Guzdial, M., & Palincsar, A. (1991). Motivation project-based learning: Sustaining the doing, supporting the learning. *Educational Psychologist, 26,* 369–398.

Borich, G. (1993). *Clearly outstanding: Making each day count in your classroom*. Boston: Allyn & Bacon.

Borich, G. (2003). *Observation skills for effective teaching* (5th ed.). Upper Saddle River, NJ: Merrill/Prentice Hall.

Borich, G. (2004). *Vital impressions: The KPM approach to children*. Austin, TX: The KPM Institute.

Borich, G. (2007). Introduction to thinking. In A. Choo and G. Borich (Eds.), *Teaching strategies to promote thinking skills*. Singapore: McGraw-Hill.

Borich, G. (2007). Introduction to the thinking curriculum. In A. Ong and G. Borich (Eds.), *Teaching strategies that promote thinking*. Singapore: McGraw-Hill.

Borich, G., & Hao, Y. (2007). Inquiry-based learning: A practical example. In A. Ong and G. Borich (Eds.), *Teaching strategies that promote thinking*. Singapore: McGraw-Hill.

Borich, G., & Tombari, M. (2004). *Educational assessment for the elementary and middle school classroom* (2nd ed.). Upper Saddle River, NJ: Merrill/Prentice Hall.

Borich, G., & Tombari, M. (1997). *Educational psychology: A contemporary approach* (2nd ed.). Boston: Allyn & Bacon.

Bowers, C., & Flinders, D. (1991). *Culturally responsive teaching and supervision: A handbook for staff development*. New York: Teachers College Press.

Boyer, E. (1993, March). *Making the connections*. Address presented at the meeting of the Association for Supervision and Curriculum Development, Washington, DC.

Bransford, J., Brown, A., & Cocking, R. (Eds.) (2000). *How people learn: Brain, mind, experiences, and school*. Washington, DC: National Academy Press.

Bransford, J. D., & Steen, B. (1994). *The IDEAL problem solver*. (2nd ed.). New York: Worth.

Bronfenbrenner, V. (1989). Ecological systems theory. In R. Vasta (Ed.), *Annals of child development* (Vol. 6, pp. 187–251). Greenwich, CT: JAI Press.

Brofenbrenner, V. (2005). *The ecology of human development: Experiments by nature and design*. Cambridge, MA: Harvard University Press.

Brookfields, S., & Preskill, S. (2005.). Discussion as a way of teaching: Tools and techniques for democratic classrooms. San Francisco: Jossey-Bass.

Brophy, J. (1981). Teach praise: A functional analysis. *Review of Educational Research, 51,* 5–32.

Brophy, J. (1992). Probing the subtleties of subject-matter teaching. *Educational Leadership, 49(7),* 4–8.

Brophy, J. (1996). *Teaching problem students.* New York: Guilford Press.

Brophy, J. (2002). *Teaching: Educational practices series—1.* United Nations Educational, Social, and Cutural Organization (UNESCO). Geneva, Switzerland: International Bureau of Education. Available from *www.ibe.unesco.org.*

Brophy, J., & Evertson, C. (1976). *Learning from teaching: A developmental perspective.* Boston: Allyn & Bacon.

Brophy, J., & Good, T. (1986). Teacher behavior and student achievement. In M. C. Wittrock (Ed.), *Handbook of research on teaching* (3rd ed., pp. 328–375). Upper Saddle River, NJ: Merrill/Prentice Hall.

Brown, A. L. (1994). The advancement of learning. *Educational Researcher, 23,* 4–12.

Brown, G., & Edmondson, R. (1984). Asking questions. In E. Wragg (Ed.), *Classroom teaching skills* (pp. 97–119). New York: Nichols.

Brown, G., & Wragg, E. (1993). *Questioning.* London: Routledge.

Bruner, J. (2004). *Toward a theory of instruction.* Cambridge, MA: Belknap Press.

Bruner, J. S. (1996). *The culture of education.* Cambridge, MA: Harvard University Press.

Bruning, R., Schraw, G., Norby, M., & Ronning, R. (2004). *Cognitive psychology and instruction* (4th ed.). Upper Saddle River, NJ: Merrill/Prentice Hall.

Buchl, D. (2001). *Classroom strategies for interactive learning.* Newark, DE: International Reading Association.

Bullock, A., & Hawk, P. (2005). *Developing a teaching portfolio.* Upper Saddle River, NJ: Merrill/Prentice Hall.

Burbules, N., & Bruce, B. (2001). Theory and research on teaching as dialogue. In V. Richardson (Ed.), *Handbook of research on teaching* (4th ed.). Washington, D.C.: American Educational Research Association.

Burden, P. (1986). Teacher development: Implications for teacher education. In J. Raths and L. Katz (Eds.), *Advances in teacher education* (Vol. 2). Norwood, NJ: Ablex.

Burnette, J. (1999). *Critical behaviors and strategies for teaching culturally diverse students.* ERIC/OSEP Digest E 584. Reston, VA: ERIC Clearinghouse on Disabilities and Gifted Education. (ERIC Document Reproduction Service No. ED 435 147)

Buzan, T. (2002). *How to mind map.* New York: HarperCollins.

Cabello, B., & Terrell, R. (1994). Making students feel like family: How teachers create warm and caring classroom climates. *Journal of Classroom Interaction, 29,* 17–23.

Campbell, B., Campbell, L., & Dickinson, D. (1996). *Teaching and learning through multiple intelligences.* Boston: Allyn & Bacon.

Canning, C. (1991). What teachers say about reflection. *Educational Leadership, 48(6),* 69–87.

Canter, L. (2001). *Assertive discipline* (3rd ed.). Los Angeles: Canter & Associates.

Cantrell, S. C. (1998/99). Effective teaching and literacy learning: A look inside primary classrooms. *The Reading Teacher, 52(4),* 370–378.

Carlson, C. (1992). Single parenting and stepparenting: Problems, issues and interventions. In M. J. Fine & C. Carlson (Eds.), *The handbook of family-school intervention: A systems perspective* (pp. 188–214). Boston: Allyn & Bacon.

Carpenter, T., Dossey, J., & Koehler, J. (Eds.) (2004). *Classics in mathematics education research.* Reston, VA; National Council of Teachers of Mathematics.

Carroll, J. B. (1963). A model of school learning. *Teachers College Record, 64,* 723–733.

Cassidy, J., & Asher, S. R. (1992). Loneliness and peer relations in young children. *Child Development, 63,* 350–365.

Cecil, N. (1995). *The art of inquiry: Questioning strategies for K–6 classrooms.* Iowa City, IA: Portage & Main Press.

Chen, G., & Starasta, W. (2005). *Foundations of intercultural communication.* Lanham, MD: University Press of America.

Cheng, L. (1996, October). Enhancing communication: Toward optimal language learning for limited English proficient students. *Language, Speech and Hearing Services in Schools, 28(2),* 347–354.

Cheng, L. (1998). *Enhancing the communication skills of newly-arrived Asian American students.* ERIC/CUE Digest, Number 136. New York: ERIC Clearinghouse on Urban Education. (ERIC Document Reproduction Service No. ED 420 726)

Cheng, L., Chen, T., Tsubo, T., Sekandari, N., & Alfafara-Killacky, S. (1997). Challenges of diversity: An Asian Pacific perspective. *Multicultures, 3,* 114–145.

Child Trends DataBank (2005). Retrieved from www.childtrendsdatabank.org/indicators/ 1HighSchoolDropout.cfm.

Christenson, S. L., Rounds, T., & Franklin, M. J. (1992). Home-school collaboration: Effects, issues and opportunities. In S. L. Christenson & J. C. Conoley (Eds.), *Home-school collaboration: Enhancing children's academic and social competence.* Silver Spring, MD: National Association of School Psychologists.

Chuska, K. (2003). *Improving classroom questions: A teacher's guide to increasing student motivation, participation and higher-level thinking* (2nd ed.). Bloomington, IN: Phi Delta Kappa Educational Foundation.

Clark, C., & Peterson, P. (1986). Teachers' thought processes. In M. R. Wittrock (Ed.), *Handbook of research on teaching* (3rd ed., pp. 255–296). Upper Saddle River, NJ: Merrill/Prentice Hall.

Cochran, M., & Dean, C. (1991). Home-school relations and the empowerment process. *Elementary School Journal, 91,* 261–270.

Cohen, E. (1994). Restructuring the classroom: Conditions for productive small groups. *Review of Educational Research, 64(1),* 1–35.

Compton-Lilly, C. (2000). "Staying on children": Challenging stereotypes about urban parents. *Language Arts, 77(5),* 420–427.

Coontz, S., Parson, M., & Raley, G. (Eds.). (1998). *American families: A multicultural reader.* Oxford, UK: Routledge.

Cooper, J. O., Heron, T. E., & Heward, W. L. (1987). *Applied behavior analysis.* Upper Saddle River, NJ: Merrill/Prentice Hall.

Corey, S. (1940). The teachers out-talk the pupils. *School Review, 48,* 745–752.

Corno, L. (1996). Homework is a complicated thing. *Educational Researcher, 25*(8), 27–30.

Corno, L., & Snow, R. (1986). Adapting teaching to individual differences among learners. In M. C. Wittrock (Ed.), *Handbook of research on teaching* (3rd ed., pp. 605–629). Upper Saddle River, NJ: Merrill/Prentice Hall.

Costa, A., & Kallick, B. (Eds.). (2000a). *Activating and engaging habits of mind.* Arlington, VA: Association for Supervision and Curriculum Development.

Costa, A., & Kallick, B. (Eds.). (2000b). *Assessing and reporting on habits of mind.* Arlington, VA: Association for Supervision and Curriculum Development.

Costa, A., & Kallick, B. (2003). *Assessment strategies for self-directed learning.* Thousand Oaks, CA: Corwin Press.

Cotton, K. (1996). Affective and social benefits of small-scale schooling. *ERIC Digest.* Charleston, WV: ERIC/Cooperative Research & Extension Services for Schools.

Council for Basic Education. (1996). *What teachers have to say about teacher education.* New York: Council for Basic Education.

Cragan, J. & Wright, D. (1999). *Communication in small group discussions* (2nd ed). St. Paul, MN: West.

Cronbach, L., & Snow, R. (1981). *Aptitudes and instructional methods.* New York: Irvington/Naiburg.

Cruickshank, D., & Metcalf, K. (1994). Explaining. In T. Husen and T. N. Postlewaite (Eds.), *International Encyclopedia of Education* (2nd ed.). Oxford: Pergamon.

Curwin, R. L., & Mendler, A. N. (1997). *As tough as necessary: Countering violence, aggression, and hostility in our schools.* Alexandria, VA: Association for Supervision and Curriculum Development.

Curwin, R. L., & Mendler, A. N. (2000). *Discipline with dignity.* Upper Saddle River, NJ: Merrill/Prentice Hall.

Cushner, K., McClelland, A., & Safford, P. (1992). *Human diversity in education: An integrative approach.* New York: McGraw-Hill.

Dahllof, U., & Lundgren, U. P. (1970). *Macro- and micro-approaches combined for curriculum process analysis: A Swedish educational field project.* Goteborg, Sweden: University of Goteborg, Institute of Education.

Dann, E. (1995). *Unconsciously learning something: A focus on teaching questioning.* (ERIC Document Reproduction Service No. ED 389 6)

Dantonio, M., & Beisenherz, P. (2000). *Learning to question, questioning to learn: Developing effective teacher questioning practices.* Boston: Allyn & Bacon.

Davenport, E., Davison, M., Kuang, H., Ding, S., Kim, S., & Kwak, N. (1998). High school mathematics course-taking by gender and ethnicity. *American Educational Research Journal, 35,* 497–514.

Deci, E., Vallerand, R., Pelletier, L., & Ryan, R. (1991). Motivation and education: The self-determination perspective. *Educational Psychologist, 26,* 325–346.

DeFina, A. (1999). *Portfolio assessment (Grades K–8).* New York: Scholastic Trade.

DeLeon, B. (1996). Career development of Hispanic adolescent girls. In R. Leadbeater, J. Bonnie, & N. Way (Eds.), *Urban girls: Resisting stereotypes, creating identities* (pp. 380–398). New York: New York University Press.

Delgado-Gaitan, C. (1991). Involving parents in the schools: A process of empowerment. *American Journal of Education, 100(1),* 20–46.

Delgado-Gaitan, C. (1992). School matters in the Mexican-American home: Socializing children to education. *American Educational Research Journal, 29(3),* 495–516.

Delgado-Gaitan, C., & Trueba, H. (1991). *Crossing cultural borders: Education for immigrant families in America.* London: Falmer Press.

Delisle, R. (1997). *How to use problem-based learning in the classroom.* Alexandria, VA: Association for Supervision and Curriculum Development.

DeMeulenaere, E. (2001, April). *Constructing reinventions: Black and Latino students negotiating the transformation of their academic identities and school performance.* Paper presented at the annual meeting of the American Educational Research Association, Seattle, WA.

Dev. P. C. (1997). Intrinsic motivation and academic achievement: What does their relationship imply for the classroom teacher? *Remedial and Special Education, 18(1),* 12–19.

Dewey, J. (1938). *Logic: The theory of inquiry.* New York: Holt.

Diener, C., & Dweck, C. (1980). An analysis of learned helplessness II: The processing of success. *Journal of Personality and Social Psychology, 39,* 940–952.

Diffily, D., & Sassman, C. (2002). *Project-based learning with young children.* Portsmouth, NH: Heineman.

Dillard, J. L. (1972). *Black English: Its history and usage in the United States.* New York: Random House.

Diller, D. (1999). Opening the dialogue: Using culture as a tool in teaching young African American chidren. *The Reading Teacher, 52(8),* 820–828.

Dillon, D. (1989). Showing them that I want them to learn and that I care about who they are: A microethnography of the social organization of a secondary low-track English reading classroom. *American Educational Research Journal, 26,* 227–259.

Dillon, J. (1990). *The practice of questioning.* New York: Routledge.

Dillon, J. (1995). Discussion. In L. W. Anderson (Ed.), *International encyclopedia of teaching and teacher education* (2nd ed., pp. 251–255). Tarrytown, NY: Elsevier Sciences.

Dillon, J. T. (1988b). *Questioning and teaching: A manual of practice.* New York: Teachers College Press.

Dilworth, M., & Brown, C. (2001). Consider the difference: Teaching and learning in culturally rich schools. In V. Richardson (Ed.), *Handbook of research on teaching* (pp. 643–667). Washington, DC: American Educational Research Assocation.

Dishon, D., & O'Leary, P. (1984). *A guidebook for cooperative learning.* Kalamazoo, MI: Learning Publications.

Dishon, T. J., Patterson, G. R., Stoolmiller, M., & Skinner, M. L. (1991). Family, school and behavioral antecedents to early adolescent involvement with antisocial peers. *Developmental Psychology, 27,* 172–180.

Doll, B., Zucker, S., & Brehm, K. (2004). *Resilient classrooms: Creating healthy environments for learning.* New York: Guilford Press.

Doyle, W. (1983). Academic work. *Review of Educational Research, 53,* 159–200.

Doyle, W. (1986). Classroom organization and management. In M. Wittrock (Ed.), *Handbook of research on teaching* (3rd ed., pp. 392–431). Upper Saddle River, NJ: Merrill/Prentice Hall.

Duffy, G., & Roehler, L. (1989). The tension between information-giving and mediation: Perspectives on instructional explanation and teacher change. In J. Brophy (Ed.), *Advances in research on teaching* (Vol. 1, pp. 1–33). Greenwich, CT: JAI Press.

Duffy, G., Roehler, L., & Herrman, B. (1988). Modeling mental processes helps poor readers become strategic readers. *The Reading Teacher, 41(8),* 762–767.

Duffy, T., & Jonassen, D. (1992). *Constructivism and the technology of instruction: A conversation.* Hillsdale, NJ: Erlbaum.

Dunkin, M., & Biddle, B. (1974). *The study of teaching.* New York: Holt, Rinehart & Winston.

Dunn, R., & Griggs, S. (1995). *Multiculturalism and learning styles: Teaching and counseling adolescents.* Westport, CT: Praeger.

Dweck, C., & Reppucci, N. (1973). Learned helplessness and reinforcement responsibility in children. *Journal of Personality and Social Psychology, 25,* 109–116.

Eggen, P., & Kauchak, D. (2004). *Educational psychology: Windows on classrooms* (6th ed.). Upper Saddle River, NJ: Merrill/Prentice Hall.

Eisner, E. (1969). Instructional and expressive educational objectives: Their formulation and use in curriculum. In W. Popham, E. Eisner, H. Sullivan, & L. Tyler (Eds.), *Instructional objectives: AERA monograph series on curriculum evaluation, No. 3* (pp. 1–18). Chicago: Rand McNally.

Eisner, E. (1998). *The enlightened eye: Qualitative inquiry and the enhancement of educational practice.* Upper Saddle River, NJ: Merrill/Prentice Hall.

Emmer, E., Evertson, C., & Anderson, L. (1980). Effective classroom management at the beginning of the school year. *The Elementary School Journal, 80(5),* 219–231.

Emmer, E., Evertson, C., & Worsham, M. (2006). *Classroom management for secondary teachers*. New York: Longman.

Engel, A. (1998). *Problem-solving strategies*. New York: Springer.

English, L. (Ed.) (2002). *Handbook of international research in mathematics education*. Mahwah, NJ: Erlbaum.

Epstein, J. L. (1987). Toward a theory of family-school connections: Teacher practices and parent involvement. In K. Hurrelmann, F. Kauffman, & F. Losel (Eds.), *Social interventions: Potential and constraints* (pp. 121–136). New York: De Gruyter.

Erikson, E. (1968). *Identity, youth and crises*. New York: W. W. Norton.

Evertson, C. (1995). Classroom rules and routines. In L. Anderson (Ed.), *International encyclopedia of teaching and teacher education* (2nd ed., pp. 215–219). Tarrytown, NY: Elsevier Science.

Evertson, C., & Emmer, E. (1982). Effective management at the beginning of the school year in junior high classes. *Journal of Educational Psychology, 74*, 485–498.

Evertson, C., Emmer, E., & Worsham, M. (2006). *Classroom management for secondary teachers*. New York: Longman.

Evertson, C., & Harris, H. (1992). What we know about managing classrooms. *Educational Leadership, 49(7)*, 74–78.

Federal Interagency Forum on Child and Family Statistics (2001). *America's children: Key national indicators of well-being 2001*. Washington, DC: U.S. Government Printing Office.

Fielding, G., Kameenui, E., & Gerstein, R. (1983). A comparison of an inquiry and a direct instruction approach to teaching legal concepts and applications to secondary school students. *Journal of Educational Research, 76*, 243–250.

Flanders, N. (1970). *Analyzing teacher behavior*. Reading, MA: Addison-Wesley.

Fosnot, C. (2005). *Constructivism: Theory perspectives and practice*. New York: Teachers College Press.

Franklin, M. E. (1992). Culturally sensitive instructional practices for African-American learners with disabilities. *Exceptional Children, 59*, 115–122.

Frazier, D. M., & Paulson, F. L. (1992). How portfolios motivate reluctant learners. *Educational Leadership, 49(8)*, 62–65.

French, J., Jr., & Raven, B. (1959). The bases of social power. In D. Cartwright (Ed.), *Studies in social power* (pp. 150–168). Ann Arbor: University of Michigan Press.

Froyen, L. A. (1993). *Classroom management: The reflective teacher-leader* (2nd ed.). Upper Saddle River, NJ: Merrill/Prentice Hall.

Fuller, F. (1969). Concerns of teachers: A developmental conceptualization. *American Educational Research Journal, 6*, 207–226.

Gage, N., & Berliner, D. (1998). *Educational psychology* (6th ed.). Boston: Houghton Mifflin.

Gagné, E., Yekovich, C., & Yekovich, F. (1993). *The cognitive psychology of school learning*. Boston: Little, Brown.

Gagné, R., & Briggs, L. (2005). *Principles of instructional design* (5th ed.). Florence, KY: Wadsworth.

Gaillard, L. (1994, Dec. 14). Hands off homework? *Education Week, 14*(5), 4. Retrieved September 19, 2000, from www.edweek.org/ew/1994/15gaill.h14

Galambos, S. J., & Goldin-Meadow, S. (1990). The effects of learning two languages on levels of metalinguistic awareness. *Cognition, 34*, 1–56.

Gall, J., & Gall, M. (1990). Outcomes of the discussion method. In W. W. Wilen (Ed.), *Teaching and learning through discussion: The theory and practice of the discussion method*. Springfield, IL: C. C. Thomas.

Gall, M. (1984). Synthesis of research on questioning in recitation. *Educational Leadership, 42(3)*, 40–49.

Gamoran, A. (1992). Synthesis of research: Is ability grouping equitable? *Educational Leadership, 50(2)*, 11–13.

Garcia, R. L. (1991). *Teaching in a pluralistic society: Concepts, models, strategies* (2nd ed.). New York: HarperCollins.

Gardner, H. (1999). *Intelligence reframed: Multiple intelligences for the 21st century*. New York: Basic Books.

Gardner, H. (2000). *Intelligence reframed: Multiple intelligence for the 21st century*. New York: Basic Books.

Gardner, H. (2004). *The theory of multiple intelligences revisited*. Invited address presented to the International Conference on Multiple Intelligences, Beijing, China, May 21, 2004.

Gardner, H., & Hatch, T. (1989). Multiple intelligences go to school. *Educational Researcher, 18(8)*, 4–10.

Gay, G. (2000). *Culturally responsive teaching: Theory, research, and practice*. New York: Teachers College Press.

Gentile, J., & Lalley, J. (2003). *Standards and mastery learning*. Thousand Oaks, CA: Corwin Press.

Gibson, M. (1991). Minorities and schooling: Some implications. In M. Gibson & J. Ogbu (Eds.), *Minority status and schooling: A comparative study of immigrant and involuntary minorities* (pp. 357–381). New York: Garland.

Gill, J. (2000). *The tacit mode: Michael Polunya's postmodern philosophy*. Albany, NY: SUNY Press.

Ginott, H. (1995). *Teacher and child: A book for parents and teachers*. New York: Collier.

Ginott, H., Ginott, A., & Goddard, W. (2003). *Between parent and child*. New York: Three Rivers Press.

Glasser, W. (1998a). *Choice theory in the classroom*. New York: HarperPerennial.

Glasser, W. (1998b). *Quality School: Managing students without coercion*. New York: HarperPerennial.

Glasser, W. (1998c). *The Quality School teacher: Specific suggestions for teachers who are trying to implement the lead-management ideas of the Quality School in their classrooms* (rev. ed.). New York: HarperPerennial.

Goetz, E. T., Alexander, P. A., & Ash, M. J. (1992). *Educational psychology: A classroom perspective*. Upper Saddle River, NJ: Merrill/Prentice Hall.

Goldhaber, D., & Anthony, E. (2003). *Indicators of teacher quality*. New York: ERIC Clearinghouse on Urban Education, ED 47808.

Good, T. (1979). Teacher effectiveness in the elementary school. *Journal of Teacher Education, 30*, 52–64.

Good, T., & Brophy, J. (1995). *Contemporary educational psychology* (5th ed.). New York: Longman.

Good, T., & Brophy, J. (2003). *Looking in classrooms* (9th ed.). New York: HarperCollins.

Goodlad, J. (2004). *A place called school*. New York: McGraw-Hill.

Grabe, M., & Grabe, C. (1996). *Integrating technology for meaningful learning*. Boston: Houghton Mifflin.

Grant, C. A. (1991). Culture and teaching: What do teachers need to know? In M. M. Kennedy (Ed.), *Teaching academic subjects to diverse learners* (pp. 237–256). New York: Teachers College Press.

Greenwood, C. R., Delguardi, J. C., & Hall, R. V. (1984). Opportunity to respond and student academic achievement. In W. L. Heward, T. E. Heron, D. S. Hill, & J. Trap-Porter (Eds.), *Focus on behavior analysis in education* (pp. 58–88). Upper Saddle River, NJ: Merrill/Prentice Hall.

Griggs, S., & Dunn, R. (1995). Hispanic-American students and learning style. *Emergency Librarian, 23(2)*, 11–16.

Gronlund, N. (2003). *Writing instructional objectives for teaching and assessment*. Upper Saddle River, NJ: Merrill/Prentice Hall.

Gronlund, G., & Engel, B. (2001). *Focused portfolios: A complete assessment for the young child*. St. Paul, MN: Red Leaf Press.

Grouws, D. A. (Ed.). (1992). *Handbook of research on mathematics teaching and learning*. New York: Macmillan.

Gunter, M. A., Estes, T. H., & Schwab, J. (1999). *Instruction: A models approach* (3rd ed.). Boston: Allyn & Bacon.

Hakuta, K., Ferdman, B. M., & Diaz, R. M. (1987). Bilingualism and cognitive development: Three perspectives. In S. Rosenberg (Ed.), *Advances in applied psycholinguistics: Vol. 2. Reading, writing, and language learning* (pp. 284–319). New York: Cambridge University Press.

Harrow, A. (1972). *A taxonomy of the psychomotor domain: A guide for developing behavioral objectives*. New York: David McKay.

Hartup, W. W. (1989). Social relationships and their developmental significance. *American Psychologist, 44*, 120–126.

Haynes, H. (1935). *The relation of teacher intelligence, teacher experience and type of school to type of questions*. Unpublished doctoral dissertation, George Peabody College for Teachers, Nashville, TN.

Hebert, E. A. (1992). Portfolios invite reflection from students and staff. *Educational Leadership, 49(8)*, 58–61.

Henderson, R. W., Swanson, R. A., & Zimmerman, B. J. (1974). Inquiry response induction in preschool children through televised modeling. *Developmental Psychology, 11(4)*, 523–524.

Herrnstein, R., & Murray, C. (1994). *The bell curve: Intelligence and class structure in America*. New York: Free Press.

Hess, R. D., & Shipman, V. C. (1965). Early experience and the socialization of cognitive modes in children. *Child Development, 36*, 869–886.

Hester, J. (1994). *Teaching for thinking: A program for school improvement through critical thinking across the curriculum*. Durham, NC: Carolina Academic Press.

Hill, H. (1989). *Effective strategies for teaching minority students*. Bloomington, IN: National Educational Service.

Hilliard, A. (1992). The pitfalls and promises of special education practice. *Exceptional Children, 59(2)*, 162–172.

Horcones, J. (1991). Walden Two in real life: Behavior analysis in the design of the culture. In W. Ishag (Ed.), *Human behavior in today's world*. New York: Praeger.

Horcones, J. (1992). Natural reinforcement: A way to improve education. *Journal of Applied Behavior Analysis, 25(1)*, 71–76.

Huffman, K. (2004). *Psychology in action: Active learning edition*. Hoboken, NJ: Wiley.

Hunter, M. (1982). *Mastery teaching*. El Segundo, CA: Instructional Dynamics.

Hyerle, D. (1995–1996). Thinking maps: Seeing is understanding. *Educational Leadership 53(4)*, 85–89.

Irvine, J., & York, D. (2001). Learning styles and culturally diverse students: A literature review. In J. Banks & C. Banks (Eds.), *Handbook of research on multicultural education* (pp. 484–497). San Francisco: Jossey-Bass.

Iwata, B. A. (1987). Negative reinforcement in applied behavior analysis: An emerging technology. *Journal of Applied Behavior Analysis, 20,* 361–387.

Jackson, P. (1968). *Life in classrooms.* New York: Holt, Rinehart & Winston.

Jacobs, E. (1999). *Cooperative learning in context: An educational innovation in everyday classrooms.* Albany: State University of New York Press.

Jacobs, G., Power, M., & Loh, W. (2002). *Teacher's source book for cooperative learning: Practical techniques, basic principles, and frequently asked questions.* Thousand Oaks, CA: Corwin Press.

Jensen, A. (1969). How much can we boost IQ and scholastic achievement? *Harvard Educational Review, 39(1),* 1–123.

Jensen, A. (1998). *The g factor: The science of mental ability.* Westport, CT: Praeger.

Johnson, D., & Johnson, R. (1991). *Learning together and alone* (3rd ed.). Upper Saddle River, NJ: Prentice Hall.

Johnson, D., & Johnson, R. (1996). Cooperative learning and traditional American values: An appreciation. *NASSP Bulletin 80(579),* 63–65.

Johnson, D., & Johnson, R. (1998). *Learning together and alone: Cooperative, competitive, and individualistic learning* (5th ed.). Boston: Allyn & Bacon.

Johnson, D., & Johnson, R. (1999). *Joining together: group theory and group skills* (7th ed.). Upper Saddle River, NJ: Merrill/Prentice Hall.

Johnson, D. W., Johnson, R. T., & Holubec, E. J. (1988). *Cooperation in the classroom.* Edina, MN: Interaction Book Company.

Johnson, D. W., Johnson, R. T., & Holubec, E. J. (1994). *The new circles of learning: Cooperation in the classroom.* Alexandria, VA: ASCD.

Jones, F. C. (1987). *Positive classroom discipline.* New York: McGraw-Hill.

Jones, K. (1995). *Simulations: A handbook for teachers and trainers.* East Brunswick, NJ: Nichols.

Jordan, J. (1988). Nobody mean more to me than you and the future life of Willie Jordan. *Harvard Educational Review, 58,* 363–374.

Kagan, D., & Tippins, D. (1992). The evolution of functional lesson plans among twelve elementary and secondary student teachers. *Elementary School Journal, 92(4),* 477–489.

Karweit, N., & Slavin, R. (1981). Measurement and modeling choices in studies of time and learning. *American Educational Research Journal, 18,* 157–171.

Kaufman, P., Alt, M., & Chapman, C. (2001). *Dropout rates in the United States: 2000.* Washington, DC: National Center for Education Statistics. U.S. Government Printing Office.

Keirns, J. (1998). *Designs for self instruction: Principles, processes, and issues in developing self-directed learning.* Boston: Allyn & Bacon.

Kendall, F. E. (1983). *Diversity in the classroom: A multicultural approach to the education of young children.* New York: Teachers College Press.

Kennedy, M. (Ed.). (1991). *Teaching academic subjects to diverse learners.* New York: Teachers College Press.

Kenny, J. (2004). *Mind-mapping: Cortical clobber.* Times Educational Supplement Online, June, 18, 2004, Issue 4588, p. 29.

Kilpatrick, J., Martin, W. G., & Schifter, D. (2003). *A research companion to principles and standards for school mathematics.* Reston, VA: National Council of Teachers of Mathematics.

Kirsch, T. (2005, April). President's message: Seniority and transfers are under attack. *The PFT Reporter: Official publication of the Philadelphia Federation of Teachers.* Retrieved from www.pft.org/archrept/rep0404/presrep.html.

Klenowski, V. (2002). *Portfolio use and assessment.* New York: Taylor & Francis.

Knapczyk, D., & Rodes, P. (2001). *Teaching social competence.* Verona, VI: Attainment Company.

Knapp, M., & Woolverton, S. (2001). Social class and schooling. In J. Banks & C. Banks (Eds.), *Handbook of research on multicultural education* (pp. 548–569). San Francisco: Jossey-Bass.

Kottler, J., & Zehm, S. (2000). *On being a teacher: The human dimension.* Thousand Oaks, CA: Cowrin Press.

Kounin, J. (1970). *Discipline and group management in the classroom.* New York: Holt, Rinehart & Winston.

Kozulin, A. (1990). *Vygotsky's psychology: A biography of ideas.* Cambridge: Harvard University Press.

Krabbe, M., & Polivka, J. (1990, April). *An analysis of students' perceptions of effective teaching behaviors during discussion activity.* Paper presented at the annual meeting of the American Educational Research Association, Boston.

Kranz, R. (1998). *Portfolio assessment across the curriculum.* Mahwah, NJ: Troll Teacher Idea Book, Troll Association.

Krathwohl, D., Bloom, B., & Masia, B. (1999). *Taxonomy of educational objectives book 2/Affective domain.* Boston: Addison-Wesley.

Kubiszyn, T., & Borich, G. (2007). *Educational testing and measurement: Classroom applications and practice* (8th ed.). Hoboken, NJ: Wiley.

Kuh, G., Kinzie, J., Smith, J., & Whitt, E. (2005). *Assessing conditions to enhance educational effectiveness: The inventory for student engagement and success.* San Francisco: Jossey-Bass.

Lambert, N. (1991). Partnerships of Psychologists, educators, community-based agency personnel, and parents in school redesign. *Educational Psychologist, 26,* 185–198.

Lane, S. (1993, Summer). The conceptual framework for the development of a mathematics performance assessment instrument. *Educational Measurement: Issues and Practice,* pp. 16–23.

Lankes, A. (1995). Electronic portfolios: A new idea in assessment. *ERIC Digest* (EDO-IR-95-9), 95(9), 1–4.

Larson, J., & Irvine, P. D. (1999). "We call him Dr. King": Reciprocal distancing in urban classrooms. *Language Arts, 75(5),* 393–400.

Lavin, J., & Nolan, J. (2003). *Principles of classroom management: Professional decision-making model.* Boston: Allyn & Bacon.

Lawrence-Lightfoot, S. (2003). *The essential conversation: What parents and teachers can learn from each other.* New York: Random House.

Lazear, D. (1992). *Teaching for multiple intelligences. Fastback No. 342.* Bloomington, IN: Phi Delta Kappa Educational Foundation.

Leriche, L. (1992). The sociology of classroom discipline. *The High School Journal, 75(2),* 77–89.

Letts, N. (1999). *Creating a caring classroom (Grades K–6).* New York: Scholastic.

Levin, H. (1986). *Educational reform for disadvantaged students: An emerging crisis.* Washington, DC: National Education Association.

Levin, J., & Nolan, J. F. (1991). *Principles of classroom management: A hierarchical approach.* Upper Saddle River, NJ: Prentice Hall.

Levine, D. (1985). *Improving student achievement through mastery learning programs.* San Francisco: Jossey-Bass.

Levine, D., & Havinghurst, R. (1984). *Society and education* (6th ed.). Boston: Allyn & Bacon.

Levine, D., & Lezotte, L. (2001). Effective schools research. In J. Banks & C. Banks (Eds.), *Handbook of research on multicultural education* (pp. 525–549). San Francisco: Jossey-Bass.

Levis, D. S. (1987). Teachers' personality. In M. J. Dunkin (Ed.), *Encyclopedia of teaching and teacher education* (pp. 585–588). New York: Pergamon.

Lindsley, O. R. (1991). Precision teaching's unique legacy from B. F. Skinner. *Journal of Behavioral Education, 1,* 253–266.

Lindsley, O. R. (1992). Why aren't effective teaching tools widely adopted? *Journal of Applied Behavior Analysis, 25(1),* 21–26.

Linney, J. A., & Vernberg, E. (1983). Changing patterns of parental employment and the family-school relationship. In C. D. Hayes & S. Kamerman (Eds.), *Children of working parents: Experiences and outcomes* (pp. 73–99). Washington, DC: National Academy Press.

Lippitt, R., & Gold, M. (1959). Classroom social structure as a mental health problem. *Journal of Social Issues, 15,* 40–58.

Llewellyn, D. (2002). *Inquire within: Implementing inquiry-based science standards.* Thousand Oaks, CA: Corwin Press.

Lockwood, A. T., & Secada, W. G. (1999, January). Transforming education for Hispanic youth: Exemplary practices, programs, and schools. *NCBE Resource Collection Series, No. 12.* Washington, DC: National Clearinghouse for Bilingual Education.

Losey, K. (1995). Mexican American students and classroom interaction: An overview and critique. *Review of Educational Research, 65(3),* 283–318.

Lou, Y., Abrami, P., & Spence, J. (2000). Effects of within-class grouping on student achievement: An exploratory model. *Journal of Educational Research, 94,* 101–112.

Loucks-Horsley, S., Kapiton, R., Carlson, M. D., Kuerbis, P. J., Clark, P. C., Melle, G. M., et al. (1990). *Elementary school science for the '90s.* Alexandria, VA: Association for Supervision and Curriculum Development.

Lubliner, S., & Palincsar, A. (2001). *A practical guide to reciprocal teaching.* New York: McGraw-Hill.

Lustig, M., & Koester, J. (2005). *Intercultural competence: Interpersonal communication across cultures* (5th ed.). Boston: Addison-Wesley.

Lyman, F. (1981). The responsive classroom discussion. In A. Anderson (Ed.), *Mainstreaming Digest.* College Park, MD: University of Maryland College of Education.

Lysakowski, R., & Walberg H. (1981). Classroom reinforcement and learning: A quantitative synthesis. *Journal of Educational Research, 75,* 69–77.

Mager, R. (1997). *Preparing instructional objectives.* Atlanta: CEP Press.

Mansnerus, L. (1992, November 1). Should tracking be derailed? *Education Life. New York Times Magazine,* pp. 14–16.

Markham, T., Mergendoller, J., Larmer, J., & Ravitz, J. (2003). *Project-based learning handbook.* Novato, CA: Bock Institute for Education.

Marriott, D., & Kupperstein, J. (1997). *What are the other kids doing while you teach small groups?* Reading, CA: Creative Teaching Press.

Martin, P. (1995). Creating lesson blocks: A multi-discipline team effort. *Schools in the Middle, 5(11),* 22–24.

Martinello, M., & Cook, G. (2000). *Interdisciplinary inquiry in teaching and learning* (2nd ed.). Upper Saddle River, NJ: Merrill/Prentice Hall.

Marx, R., & Walsh, J. (1988). Learning from academic tasks. *The Elementary School Journal, 88(3),* 207–219.

Marzano, R., Pickering, J., & Pollock, J. (2001). *Classroom instruction that works: Research-based strategies for increasing student achievement.* Alexandria, VA: Association for Supervision and Curriculum Development.

Masahiko, M., & Ovando, C. (2001). Language issues in multicultural contexts. In J. Banks & C. Banks (Eds.), *Handbook of research on multicultural education* (pp. 427–444). San Francisco: Jossey-Bass.

Mauer, R. E. (1985). *Elementary discipline handbook: Solutions for the K–8 teacher.* West Nyack, NY: The Center for Applied Research in Education.

Mayer, R. (1998). *The promise of educational psychology: Learning in the content areas.* Upper Saddle River, NJ: Merrill/Prentice Hall.

Mayer, R. (2002). *The promise of educational psychology: Vol. II. Teaching for meaningful learning.* Upper Saddle River, NJ: Merrill/Prentice Hall.

Mayer, R., & Wittrock, M. (1996). Problem-solving transfer. In D. Berliner & R. Calfee (Eds.), *Handbook of educational psychology* (pp. 47–62). New York: Macmillan.

Mayer, R. E. (1987). *Educational psychology: A cognitive approach.* Boston: Little, Brown.

McCown, R., & Roop, P. (1992). *Educational psychology and classroom practice: A partnership.* Needham Heights, MA: Allyn & Bacon.

McDonald, J., & Czerniak, C. (1994). Developing interdisciplinary units: Strategies and examples. *School Science and Mathematics, 94(1),* 5–10.

McDonnell, L., & Hill, P. (1993). *Newcomers in American schools: Meeting the needs of immigrant youth.* Santa Monica, CA: Rand Corporation.

Medrich, E. A., Roizen, J. A., Rubin, V., & Burkley, S. (1982). *The serious business of growing up: A study of children's lives outside school.* Berkeley: University of California Press.

Megnin, J. (1995). Combining memory and creativity in teaching math. *Teaching PreK–8, 25(6),* 48–49.

Meichenbaum, D., & Biemiller, A. (1998). *Nurturing independent learners: Helping students take charge of their learning.* Cambridge, MA: Brookline.

Mercado, C. (2001). The learner: "Race," "ethnicity," and linguistic difference. In V. Richardson (Ed.), *Handbook of research on teaching* (pp. 668–694). Washington, DC: American Educational Research Association.

Messick, S. (1995). Cognitive styles and learning. In L. Anderson (Ed.), *International encyclopedia of teaching and teacher education* (2nd ed., pp. 387–390). Tarrytown, NY: Elsevier Science.

Michaels, S., & Collins, J. (1984). Oral discourse styles: Classroom interaction and the acquisition of literacy. In D. Tamen (Ed.), *Coherence in spoken and written discourse.* Norwood, NJ: Ablex.

Mickelson, R., & Heath, D. (1999, April). *The effects of segregation and tracking on African American high school seniors' academic achievement, occupational aspirations, and interracial social networks in Charlotte, North Carolina.* Paper presented at the annual meeting of the American Educational Research Association, Montreal, Canada.

Miller, H. M. (2000). Teaching and learning about cultural diversity: All of us together have a story to tell. *The Reading Teacher, 53(6),* 666–667.

Miller, M. J. (1992). *Model standards for beginning teacher licensing and development: A resource for state dialogue.* [Online]. Available at www.ccsso.org.

Minami, M., & Ovando, C. (2001). Language issues in multicultural contexts. In J. Banks & C. Banks (Eds.), *Handbook of research on multicultural issues* (pp. 427–444). San Francisco: Jossey-Bass.

Mintzes, J., Wandersee, J., & Novak, J. (2000). *Assessing science understanding.* San Diego: Academic Press.

Mislevy, R., Steinberg, L., Almond, R., Haertel, G., & Penuel, W. (2000, February 25–26). *Leverage points for improving educational assessment.* Paper prepared for the Technology Design Workshop, Stanford Research Institute, Menlo Park, CA.

Mitchell, R. (1992). *Testing for learning: How new approaches to evaluation can improve American schools.* New York: Free Press.

Moore, K. (1992). *Classroom teaching skills* (2nd ed.). New York: McGraw-Hill.

Moran, C., & Hakuta, K. (2001). Bilingual education: Broadening research perspectives. In J. Banks & C. Banks (Eds.), *Handbook of research on multicultural education* (pp. 445–462). San Francisco: Jossey-Bass.

National Board for Professional Teaching Standards. (2001). *Five core propositions.* [Online]. Available at www.nbpts.org.

National Council for the Social Studies. (1994). *Expectations of excellence: Curriculum standards for social studies*. Washington, DC: National Council for the Social Studies.

National Council for the Social Studies. (2002). *National standards for social studies teachers*. Silver Springs, MD: Author.

National Council of Teachers of English. (1996). *Standards for the English language arts*. Urbana, IL: National Council of Teachers of English and International Reading Association.

National Council of Teachers of Mathematics. (1995). *Assessment standards for school mathematics*. Reston, VA: National Council of Teachers of Mathematics.

National Council of Teachers of Mathematics. (2000). *Principles and standards for school mathematics*. Reston, VA: Author.

National Mental Health Information Center, U.S. Department of Health and Human Services (2005). *Tips for teachers*. Available at www.mentalhealth.org/cmhs/TraumaticEvents/teachers.asp.

National Research Council. (1996). *National science education standards 1995*. Washington, DC: National Academy Press.

National Research Council. (1999). *Knowing what your students know*. Washington, DC: National Academy Press.

National Research Council. (2001). *Knowing what students know: The science and design of educational assessment*. Washington, DC: National Academy Press.

Neisser, U. (1976). *Cognition and reality*. San Francisco: W.H. Freeman.

Ngeow, K. Y. (1998). Motivation and transfer in language learning. *ERIC Digest*. Bloomington, ERIC Clearinghouse on Reading. (ERIC Document Reproduction Service No. ED 427 318)

Novak, J. (2001). *Learning, creating, and using knowledge: Concept maps as facilitative tools in schools and corporations*. Mahwah, NJ: Lawrence Erlbaum.

Nunn, G., & Kimberly, R. (2000, December). "IDEAL" problem solving using a collaborative effort for special needs and at-risk students. *Education*, 10–16.

Oakes, J., & Lipton, M. (1999). *Teaching to change the world*. Boston: McGraw-Hill.

Oczkus, L. (2003). *Reciprocal teaching at work: Strategies for interpreting reading comprehension*. Newark, DE: International Reading Association.

Ogbu, J. (1995a). Cultural problems in minority education: Their interpretations and consequences—part one: Theoretical background. *The Urban Review, 27(3),* 189–205.

Ogbu, J. (1995b). Cultural problems in minority education: Their interpretations and consequences—part two: Case studies. *The Urban Review, 27(4),* 271–297.

Ogbu, J., & Davis, A. (2003). *Black American students in an affluent suburb: A study of disengagement*. Mahwah, NJ: Lawrence Erlbaum.

Olneck, M. (2001). Immigrants in education. In J. Banks and C. Banks (Eds.), *Handbook of research on multicultural education*. San Francisco: Jossey-Bass.

O'Neil, J. (1992). On tracking and individual differences: A conversation with Jeannie Oakes. *Educational Leadership, 50(2),* 18–21.

Ormrod, J. (2003). *Educational psychology: Developing learners* (4th ed.). Upper Saddle River, NJ: Merrill/Prentice Hall.

Palincsar, A., & Brown, A. (1989). Classroom dialogues to promote self-regulated comprehension. In J. Brophy (Ed.), *Advances in research on teaching* (Vol. 1, pp. 35–71). Greenwich, CT: JAI Press.

Parkay, F., & Hass, G. (2000). *Curriculum planning: A contemporary approach* (7th ed.). Boston: Allyn & Bacon.

Parker, W. C. (1991). *Renewing the social studies curriculum*. Alexandria, VA: Association for Supervision and Curriculum Development.

Patton, J. R. (1994). Practical recommendations for using homework with students with learning disabilities. *Journal of Learning Disabilities, 27(9),* 570–578.

Paul, R. (1990). *Critical thinking*. Rohnert Park, CA: Center for Critical Thinking and Moral Critique, Sonoma State University.

Paulu, N. (1998). *Helping your students with homework: A guide for teachers*. Washington, DC: U.S. Department of Education, Office of Educational Research. Retrieved September 19, 2000, from www.ed.gov/pubs/HelpingStudents/

Phillips, D. (2000). *Constructivism in education*. Chicago: National Society for the Study of Education, The University of Chicago Press.

Piaget, J. (1977). Problems in equilibration. In M. Appel & L. Goldberg (Eds.), *Topics in cognitive development: Vol. 1. Equilibration: Theory, research and application* (pp. 3–13). New York: Plenum.

Piestrup, A. (1973). *Black dialect interference and accommodation of reading instruction in first grade* (Monograph No. 4). Berkeley: University of California, Language Behavior Research Laboratory.

Pintrich, P., & Schunk, D. (2002). *Motivation in education: Theory, research, and applications* (2nd ed.). Upper Saddle River, NJ: Merrill/Prentice Hall.

Polanyi, M. (1958). *Personal knowledge.* Chicago: University of Chicago Press.

Pollock, J. E. (1992). Blueprints for social studies. *Educational Leadership, 49(8),* 52–53.

Porter, A. (1993). School delivery standards. *Educational Researcher, 22,* 24–30.

Portes, A., & Rumbaut, R. (1990). *Immigrant America: A portrait.* Berkeley: University of California Press.

Posner, G. (1987). Pacing and sequencing. In M. J. Dunkin (Ed.), *Encyclopedia of teaching and teacher education* (pp. 266–271). New York: Pergamon.

Power, B., & Hubbard, R. (1999). *Living the questions: A guide for teacher-researchers.* Portland, ME: Stenhouse.

Putnam, J. (1996). *Cooperative learning in diverse classrooms.* Upper Saddle River, NJ: Merrill/Prentice Hall.

Putnam, J., & Burke, J. B. (1992). *Organizing and managing classroom learning communities.* New York: McGraw-Hill.

Raven, B. H. (1974). The comparative analysis of power and power preference. In J. T. Tedeschi (Ed.), *Perspectives on social power* (pp. 172–198). Chicago: Aldine.

Redding, N. (1992). Assessing the big outcomes. *Educational Leadership, 49(8),* 49–53.

Rekrut, M. (1999). Using the Internet in classroom instruction: A primer for teachers. *Journal of Adolescent and Adult Literacy, 42(7),* 546–557.

Resnick, L., & Klopfer, L. (Eds.). (1989). *Toward the thinking curriculum: Current cognitive research.* Arlington, VA: Association for Supervision and Curriculum Development.

Resnick, L. B., & Resnick, D. P. (1991). Assessing the thinking curriculum: New tools for educational reform. In B. R. Gifford & M. C. O'Connor (Eds.), *Future assessments: Changing views of aptitude, achievement and instruction.* Boston: Kluwer.

Rich, D. (1987). *Teachers and parents: An adult-to-adult approach.* Washington, DC: National Education Association.

Richardson, V. (1997). Constructivist teaching and teacher education: Theory and practice. In V. Richardson (Ed.), *Constructivist teacher education: Building new understandings* (pp. 3–14). Washington, DC: Falmer Press.

Richmond, G., & Striley, J. (1994). An integrated approach. *The Science Teacher, 61(7),* 42–45.

Rinne, C. (1997). *Excellent classroom management.* Belmont, CA: Wadsworth.

Ritter, N. (1999). Teaching interdisciplinary thematic units in language arts. *ERIC Digest D142.* Bloomington, IN: ERIC Clearinghouse on Reading, English, and Communication. (ERIC Document Reproduction Service No. ED 436 003)

Roberts, P., & Kellough, R. (2003). *A guide for developing interdisciplinary thematic units* (3rd ed.). Upper Saddle River, NJ: Merrill/Prentice Hall.

Roblyer, M. (2003). *Integrating educational technology into teaching.* Upper Saddle River, NJ: Merrill/Prentice Hall.

Roblyer, M. (2005). *Integrating educational technology into teaching* (4th ed.). Upper Saddle River, NJ: Merrill/Prentice Hall.

Roblyer, M., Edwards, J., & Havriluk, M. (1997). *Integrating educational technology into teaching* (3rd ed.). Upper Saddle River, NJ: Merrill/Prentice Hall.

Rogan, J., Borich, G., & Taylor, H. P. (1992). Validation of the stages of concern questionnaire. *Action in Teacher Education, 14(2),* 43–49.

Rogoff, B. (1990). *Apprenticeship in thinking: Cognitive development in social context.* New York: Oxford University Press.

Rohrkemper, M., & Corno, L. (1988). Success and failure on classroom tasks: Adaptive learning and classroom teaching. *The Elementary School Journal, 83,* 335–351.

Rose, L., & Gallup, A. (2002). The 32nd annual Phi Delta Kappa/Gallup poll of the public's attitudes toward the public schools. *Phi Delta Kappan, 84,* 41–46, 51–56.

Rosenshine, B. (1971). *Teaching behaviors and student achievement.* London: National Foundation for Educational Research in England and Wales.

Rosenshine, B. (1983). Teaching functions in instructional programs. *The Elementary School Journal, 83,* 335–351.

Rosenshine, B. (1986). Synthesis of research on explicit teaching. *Educational Leadership, 43(7),* 60–69.

Rosenshine, B. (1995). Advances in research on instruction. *Journal of Educational Research, 88 (5),* 262–268.

Rosenshine, B. (1997, March). *The case for explicit, teacher-led, cognitive strategy instruction.* Paper presented at the annual meeting of the American Educational Research Association, Chicago.

Rosenshine, B., & Meister, C. (1992). The use of scaffolds for teaching higher-level cognitive strategies. *Educational Leadership, 49(7),* 26–33.

Rosenshine, B., & Meister, C. (1994). Reciprocal teaching: A review of the research. *Review of Educational Research, 64,* 479–530.

Rosenshine, B., & Stevens, R. (1986). Teaching functions. In M. C. Wittrock (Ed.), *Handbook of research on teaching* (3rd ed., pp. 376–391). Upper Saddle River, NJ: Merrill/Prentice Hall.

Rotter, J., Robinson, E., & Fey, M. (1987). *Parent-teacher conferencing*. Washington, DC: National Education Association.

Rowe, M. B. (1986, January-February). Wait time: Slowing down may be a way of speeding up. *Journal of Teacher Education, 23,* 43–49.

Rowe, M. B. (1987). Wait time: Slowing down may be a way of speeding up. *American Educator, 11(1),* 38–43, 47.

Ryan, K. (1992). *The roller coaster year: Essays by and for beginning teachers*. New York: HarperCollins.

Sable, J., & Hoffman, L. (2005). *Characteristics of 100 largest public elementary school districts in the United States: 2002–2003*. Washington, DC: National Center for Educational Statistics, U.S. Department of Education.

Sacks, S. R., & Harrington, C. N. (1982, March). *Student to teacher: The process of role transition*. Paper presented at the meeting of the American Educational Research Association, New York.

Saito, L. T. (1999). *Socio-cultural factors in the educational achievement of Vietnamese American students* (Doctoral dissertation, University of California, Irvine, 1999). Dissertation Abstracts International, 60 (08), 2802A.

Santos, R. M., & Reese, D. (1999). Selecting culturally and linguistically appropriate materials: Suggestions for service providers. *ERIC Digest*. Washington, DC: Office of Educational Research and Improvement & U.S. Department of Education. (ERIC Document Reproduction Service No. ED 431 546)

Saunders, P. (2005). *Characteristics of effective teaching*. Kalamazoo, MI: Western Michigan University, Center for Teaching and Learning.

Saunders, W., & Goldenberg, C. (1999). *The effects of instructional conversations and literature logs on the story comprehension and thematic understanding of English proficient and limited English proficient students*. Washington, DC: Center for Research on Education, Diversity and Excellence.

Saunders, W., O'Brien, G., Lennon, D., & McLean, J. (1999). *Successful transition into mainstream English: Effective strategies for studying literature*. Washington, DC: Center for Research on Education, Diversity and Excellence.

Savage, T. (1991). *Discipline for self-control*. Upper Saddle River, NJ: Prentice Hall.

Savage, T. (1999). *Teaching self-control through management and discipline*. Boston: Allyn & Bacon.

Savery, J. R., & Duffy, T. M. (1995). Problem-based learning: An instructional model and its constructivist framework. *Educational Technology, 35(5),* 31–38.

Scarr, S. (1981). Testing for children: Assessment and the many determinants of intellectual competence. *American Psychologist, 36(10),* 1159–1166.

Schmuck, R., & Schmuck, P. (2001). *Group processes in the classroom* (6th ed.). New York: McGraw-Hill.

Schwartz, W. (1998). The identity development of multiracial youth. *ERIC/CUE Digest,* Number 137. New York: ERIC Clearinghouse on Urban Education.

Shade, B. J. (1982). Afro-American cognitive style: A variable in school success. *Review of Educational Research, 52,* 219–244.

Shalaway, L. (1999). *Learning to teach*. New York: Scholastic.

Shavelson, R. J., & Baxter, G. P. (1992). What we've learned about assessing hands-on science. *Educational Leadership, 49(8),* 20–25.

Shavelson, R. J., Gao, X., & Baxter, G. (1991). *Design theory and psychometrics for complex performance assessment*. Los Angeles: UCLA Center for Research on Evaluation, Standards and Student Testing.

Shlomo, S. (Ed.). (1999). *Handbook of cooperative learning methods*. Westport, CT: Praeger.

Shulman, L. S. (1992). Toward a pedagogy of cases. In J. H. Shulman (Ed.), *Case methods in teacher education* (pp. 72–92). New York: Teachers College Press.

Simmons, P. (1995). Metacognitive strategies: Teaching and assessing. In L. Anderson (Ed.), *International encyclopedia of teaching and teacher education* (2nd ed., pp. 481–485). Tarrytown, NY: Elsevier Science.

Singer, H., & Donlon, D. (1982). Active comprehension problem-solving schema with question generation for comprehension of complex short stories. *Reading Research Quarterly, 17,* 116–186.

Skinner, B. F. (1953). *Science and human behavior*. Upper Saddle River, NJ: Merrill/Prentice Hall.

Skirtic, T. (1991). The special education paradox: Equity as the way to excellence. *Harvard Educational Review, 61(2),* 148–206.

Slavin, R. (1990). Achievement effects of ability grouping in secondary schools: A best evidence synthesis. *Review of Educational Research, 60,* 471–499.

Slavin, R. (1991a). Are cooperative learning and untracking harmful to the gifted? *Educational Leadership, 48,* 68–71.

Slavin, R. (1991b). *Educational psychology: Theory into practice*. Upper Saddle River, NJ: Prentice Hall.

Slavin, R. (1993). *Student team learning: An overview and practical guide*. Washington, DC: National Education Association.

Slavin, R. (2001). Cooperative learning and intergroup relations. In J. Banks & C. Banks (Eds.), *Handbook of research on multicultural education*. San Francisco, CA: Jossey-Bass.

Sleeter, C., & Grant, C. (1991). *Race, class, gender, and disability in current textbooks*. New York: Routledge & Chapman.

Smilansky, M. (1979). *Priorities in education: Preschool, evidence and conclusions*. Washington, DC: World Bank.

Soar, R., & Soar, R. (1983). Context effects in the learning process. In D. C. Smith (Ed.), *Essential knowledge for beginning educators* (pp. 156–192). Washington, DC: American Association of Colleges of Teacher Education.

Stahl, R. (Ed.). (1994). *Cooperative learning in social studies: A handbook for teachers*. Menlo Park, CA: Addison-Wesley.

Stahl, R. (Ed.). (1995). *Cooperative learning in language arts: A handbook for teachers*. Menlo Park, CA: Innovative Learning Publications.

Stahl, R. (Ed.). (1996). *Cooperative learning in science: A handbook for teachers*. Menlo Park, CA: Innovative Learning Publications.

Steffe, L., & Gale, J. (Eds.). (1995). *Constructivism in education*. Hillsdale, NJ: Erlbaum.

Sternberg, R. (1994). *Thinking and problem solving*. San Diego: Academic Press.

Sternberg, R. (1995). *The nature of insight*. Cambridge, MA: MIT Press.

Sternberg, R., (2003). *Wisdom, intelligence, and creativity synthesized*. Cambridge, UK: Cambridge University Press.

Sternberg, R., & Grigorenko, E. (Eds.). (2001). *The evolution of intelligence*. Mahwah, NJ: Erlbaum.

Stevens, R., & Slavin, R. (1995). The cooperative elementary school: Effects on students' achievement, attitudes and social relations. *American Educational Research Journal, 32(2),* 321–351.

Stiggins, R. J. (2004). *Student-centered classroom assessment* (4th ed.). Upper Saddle River, NJ: Merrill/Prentice Hall.

Stipek, D. (1996). Motivation and instruction. In D. C. Berliner & R. C. Calfee (Eds.), *Handbook of educational psychology* (pp. 85–113). New York: Simon & Schuster/Macmillan.

Stipek, D. (2003). *Motivation to learn: Integrating theory and practice* (4th ed.). Boston: Allyn & Bacon.

Sugai, G. (1996, Fall–Winter). UO and public schools design just-in-time learning approaches to find solutions to rising student discipline problems. *Education Matters, 3(1),* 10–11.

Swap, S. (1987). *Enhancing parental involvement in schools*. New York: Teachers College Press.

Tamir, P. (1995). Discovery learning and teaching. In L. Anderson (Ed.), *International encyclopedia of teaching and teacher education* (2nd ed., pp. 149–155). Tarrytown, NY: Elsevier Science.

Tannen, D. (1986). *That's not what I meant!* New York: Morrow.

Tauber, R. (1990). *Classroom management from A to Z*. Chicago: Holt, Rinehart & Winston.

Taylor, B. M., Pearson, P. D., Clark, K. F., & Walpole, S. (1999). Effective schools/accomplished teachers. *The Reading Teacher, 53(2),* 156–159.

Teddlie, C., & Stringfield, S. (1993). *Schools make a difference: Lessons learned from a 10-year study of school effects*. New York: Teachers College Press.

Tharp, R. (1997). *From at-risk to excellence: Research, theory, and principles for practice*. Santa Cruz, CA: Center for Research on Education, Diversity and Excellence.

Tharp, R., & Gallimore, R. (1989). *Rousing minds to life: Teaching, learning and schooling in social context*. New York: Cambridge University Press.

Tharp, R. G. (1989). Psychocultural variables and constants: Effects on teaching and learning in schools. *American Psychologist, 44,* 349–359.

Thorndike, R. L. (1913). *The psychology of learning (Educational psychology II)*. New York: Teachers College Press.

Thurstone, L. (1947). *Primary mental abilities, Form AH*. Chicago: Science Research Associates.

Tobin, K. (1987). The role of wait-time in higher cognitive level learning. *Review of Educational Research, 57,* 69–95.

Tombari, M., & Borich, G. (1999). *Authentic assessment in the classroom: Practice and applications*. Upper Saddle River, NJ: Merrill/Prentice Hall.

Turkel, J., & Peterson, F. (2003). *Note-taking made easy*. Madison, WI: University of Wisconsin Press.

Turnbull, A. P., & Turnbull, H. R. (1986). *Families, professionals and exceptionality*. Upper Saddle River, NJ: Merrill/Prentice Hall.

Tyler, R. W. (1934). *Constructing achievement tests*. Columbus: Ohio State University Press.

Tyler, R. W. (1974). Considerations in selecting objectives. In D. A. Payne (Ed.), *Curriculum evaluation: Commentaries on purpose, process, product*. Lexington, MA: D.C. Heath.

U.S. Department of Education, Office of Educational Research and Development, Education Resources

Information Center. (1998). *Goals 2000: Reforming education to improve student achievement*. Washington, DC: Author.

Valencia, R. (1997). *The evolution of deficit thinking*. London: Falmer Press.

Verduin, J. (1996). *Helping student develop investigative problem solving and thinking skills in a cooperative setting*. Springfield, IL: C. C. Thomas.

Vermette, P. (1997). *Making cooperative learning work: Student teams in K–12 classrooms*. Upper Saddle River, NJ: Prentice Hall.

Viadero, D. (2003). RI district focuses on research-based "common language." *Education Week, 22*(29), 120–121.

Vygotsky, L. (1962). *Thought and language*. Cambridge, MA: MIT Press.

Wakefield, J. (1996). *Educational psychology: Learning to be a problem solver*. Boston: Houghton Mifflin.

Walberg, H. (1986). Syntheses of research on teaching. In M. C. Wittrock (Ed.), *Handbook of research on teaching* (3rd ed., pp. 214–229). Upper Saddle River, NJ: Merrill/Prentice Hall.

Walberg, H. (1991). Productive teaching and instruction: Assessing the knowledge base. In H. Waxman & H. Walbert (Eds.), *Effective teaching: Current research*. Berkeley, CA: McCutchan.

Walker, H., & Sylwester, R. (1991, April). Where is school along the path to prison? *Educational Leadership, 48*, 14–16.

Walqui, A. (2000a). Access and engagement: Program design and instructional approaches for immigrant students in secondary school. In *Topics in immigrant education 4, Language in education: Theory and practice*. 94. Washington, DC.: Center for Applied Linguistics.

Webb, N., Trooper, J., & Fall, R. (1995). Constructive activity and learning in collaborative small groups. *Journal of Educational Psychology, 87*(34), 406–423.

Weinberg, R. (1989). Intelligence and IQ. *American Psychologist, 44*, 98–104.

Weiner, B. (1986). *An attribution theory of motivation and emotion*. New York: Springer-Verlag.

Weiner, L. (2002, April). *Why is classroom management so vexing to urban teachers? New directions in theory and research about classroom management in urban schools*. Paper presented at the annual meeting of the American Educational Research Association, New Orleans, LA.

Weinstein, C., & Mignano, A. (1996). *Elementary classroom management: Lessons from research and practice* (2nd ed.). New York: McGraw-Hill.

Weisner, T., Gallimore, R., & Jordan, C. (1988). Unpackaging cultural effects on classroom learning: Native Hawaiian peer assistance and child-generated activity. *Anthropology and Education Quarterly, 19*, 327–353.

Weiss, E. M., & Weiss, S. G. (1998). New directions in teacher evaluation. *ERIC Digest*. Washington, DC: ERIC Clearinghouse on Teaching and Teacher Education. (ERIC Document Reproduction Service No. ED 429 052)

Weissglass, J. (1996). Transforming schools into caring learning communities. *Journal for a Just and Caring Education, 2(2)*, 175–189.

Werner, E., & Smith, R. (1992). *Overcoming the odds: High-risk children from birth to adulthood*. New York: Cornell University Press.

White, B., & Frederiksen, J. (2000). Metacognitive facilitation: An approach to making science inquiry accessible to all. In J. Minstrell and E. Van Zee (Eds.), *Teaching in the inquiry-based classroom*. Washington, DC: American Association for the Advancement of Science.

Wiggins, G., & McTighe, J. (1998). *Understanding by design*. Alexandria, VA: Association for Supervision and Curriculum Development.

Wilen, W. (1991). *Questioning skills for teachers* (3rd ed.). Washington, DC: National Education Association.

Wong, Harry K. (1998). *The first days of school: How to be an effective teacher*. Mountain View, CA: Harry K. Wong.

Young, V. H. (1970). Family and childhood in a Southern Georgia community. *American Anthropologist, 72*, 269–288.

Zimbardo, P. G. (1992). *Psychology and life*. New York: HarperCollins.

Zimmerman, B. (1989). A social cognitive view of self-regulated academic learning. *Journal of Educational Psychology, 81*, 329–339.

Name Index

Subject Index